Politics and Policy in States and Communities

Eleventh Edition

JOHN J. **HARRIGAN**

Hamline University

DAVID C. **NICE**

Washington State University

PEARSON

Boston   Columbus   Indianapolis   New York   San Francisco   Upper Saddle River
Amsterdam   Cape Town   Dubai   London   Madrid   Milan   Munich   Paris   Montréal   Toronto
Delhi   Mexico City   São Paulo   Sydney   Hong Kong   Seoul   Singapore   Taipei   Tokyo

Editor-in-Chief: Dickson Musslewhite
Senior Acquisitions Editor: Vikram Mukhija
Executive Marketing Manager: Wendy Gordon
Editorial Assistant: Emily Sauerhoff
Pearson In-house PE: Carol O'Rourke
Production Project Manager: Clara Bartunek
Media Editor: Mike Halas
Media Project Manager: Joe Selby
Full Service Vendor: Abinaya Rajendran/Integra Software Services Pvt. Ltd.
Cover Designer: Bruce Kenselaar
Cover Image: © Corbis Nomad/Alamy.com
Printer & Bindery: STP Courier Companies, Westford

Library of Congress Cataloging-in-Publication Data
Harrigan, John J.
   Politics and policy in states and communities/John J. Harrigan,
Hamline University, David C. Nice, Washington State University.—11th ed.
      p. cm.
   ISBN-13: 978-0-205-74549-4 (alk. paper)
   ISBN-10: 0-205-74549-0 (alk. paper)
   1. State governments—United States.   2. Municipal government—
United States.   3. Local government—United States.   I. Nice, David C.,
1952–   II. Title.
   JK2443.H37 2013
   320.973—dc23

                                                              2012030775

1 2 3 4 5 6 7 8 9 10—CRW—16 15 14 13 12

www.pearsonhighered.com   ISBN-13: 978-0-205-74549-4
                          ISBN-10:   0-205-74549-0

BRIEF CONTENTS

DETAILED CONTENTS

CHAPTER 8 State Legislatures and Public Policy 193

CHAPTER 9 Governors and the Challenge of Executive Leadership 221

CHAPTER 10 Administrators and the Implementation of Policy 250

PREFACE

State and local governments directly affect how well we live. Sometimes they give benefits to us, and other times they ask us to pay for services that other people receive. The actions of state and local governments sometimes deeply touch our own personal values about the role of government and about the kind of society in which we want to live. Whether we can influence what these state and local governments do is a direct challenge to our belief in democracy. And whether our governments can cope with the social conflicts of the day will greatly affect the quality of our lives.

For example, one of my students, Derrick Skaug, has had considerable experience in social and political affairs. When he was in high school, he helped lead an organization that raised funds to build schools for displaced children in Uganda. During his university years, he served as a columnist for the student newspaper, held several offices in student government, and volunteered in organizations and programs throughout his community. However, his interest in social and political involvement did not stop there. He began exploring the possibility of joining the Pullman, WA, city council, where he now serves as its youngest appointee.

I have been studying state and local politics and government for roughly 40 years, and I am still fascinated by the many personalities, decisions, and strategies at play in these smaller governing bodies. With roughly 500,000 elective offices and positions in advisory committees, campaign committees, political parties, and interest groups, I wrote this book to help students, like Derrick, become aware of the opportunities that are available for them to impact their communities. However, even if they do not plan on following a path like Derrick's, it is important that every student studying American politics understand the issues that exist at state and local levels and how these decisions impact their daily lives.

NEW TO THIS EDITION

Updated coverage on a number of important developments in state and local politics and government including:

- Education policies, including the Obama administration's Race to the Top reforms and criticisms of excessive reliance on standardized tests for assessing students, teachers, and schools.
- The 2010 midterm elections, the significant shifts in party control within state governments across the country, and the increased political conflict that has emerged in some communities as a result.
- The emergence of the Tea Party as a major force within the Republican Party and its continuing influence in some states.
- The 2010 health care reforms and the state's role in both its creation and the backlash that brought it before the U.S. Supreme Court.

- The Occupy movement in communities throughout the country and the movement's concerns about economic inequality.
- State and local initiatives to address growing environmental concerns that include natural preservation and global warming.

FEATURES

State and local governments make many decisions that affect all of us, and they have changed dramatically over the years. Even though states and localities show great variety, several developments have emerged in a great many places. Four of the developments will be unifying themes in this book. They are:

- The dramatic waves of reform in state and local governments since World War II
- The unprecedented role that state and community governments play today in the political economy and in promoting economic development
- The continuing and escalating ideological conflict over the policy issues that dominate state and community politics
- Social conflicts over ethnicity, gender, sexual preference, and religion

These four themes play important roles in *Politics and Policy in States and Communities*. Examples of the four themes abound. The objective of covering all of these themes: (1) to help the reader better understand his or her own value orientations toward these issues and (2) to provide conceptual tools that the reader can use to evaluate these issues as they arise in the reader's own community.

In order to discuss these important aspects of state and local government in as orderly a way as possible, the first group of chapters examines the constraints or limitations within which state and local governments operate and efforts to influence state and local government actions. Chapter 2 studies the constitutional constraints. Chapter 3 analyzes how federalism has evolved into an elaborate intergovernmental system. State and local governments are part of a complex web of relationships with other governments and with private organizations that also work to help the poor, educate children, protect the environment, and deal with other problems. Each governmental unit is limited by actions of the federal government and by actions of other governments at the state and local levels. Chapter 4 examines political participation, public opinion, and interest group dynamics in state and local politics. Chapter 5 explores elections, political parties, and direct action in state and local political systems.

The next six chapters discuss the policy-making institutions of state and local government. Chapter 6 discusses forms of local government, and Chapter 7 covers the dynamics of community politics. The next four chapters examine the state-level policy-making institutions—the legislatures (Chapter 8), the executives (Chapter 9), the administrative apparatus (Chapter 10), and the courts (Chapter 11). A primary concern of these chapters is to show the impact of the reform movement on the organization and operation of these institutions as well as the nature of the political conflicts that surround and filter into these institutions.

The final group of chapters examines several policy areas—budgeting and taxes (Chapter 12); poverty and welfare (Chapter 13); education (Chapter 14); infrastructure policies regarding housing, community development, and transportation (Chapter 15);

regulatory policies toward the environment, energy, and the economy (Chapter 16); and the politics of economic development (Chapter 17).

In addition, this book contains numerous pedagogical features that aid the instructor in teaching the course and help the student in learning the material:

- **"You Decide."** These are boxed case studies that ask the reader to respond to lively issues that range from deciding welfare eligibility in a complicated case to applying comparable worth to a particular situation.
- **"Where Do I Fit In?"** These boxes suggest ways in which students can become involved in state or local politics or in community life more generally.
- **"The Internet Connection."** This series of exercises introduces students to some major sources of information regarding state and local governments and policies via the Internet.
- **"Highlights."** These are short, boxed case studies that seek to illustrate important points made in the body of the text.
- **Chapter Previews and Summaries.** Chapter previews give the reader a brief outline of the major issues in each chapter. The end-of-chapter summaries seek to wrap up the most important points.
- **Detailed Endnotes.** The reader can use these as a guide to basic literature on research topics.
- **Glossary.** Key terms are defined at the end of the book for ease of reference.

SUPPLEMENTS

Pearson is pleased to offer several resources to qualified adopters of *Politics and Policy in States and Community* and their students that will make teaching and learning from this book even more effective and enjoyable. Several of the supplements for this book are available at the Instructor Resource Center (IRC), an online hub that allows instructors to quickly download book-specific supplements. Please visit the IRC welcome page at **www.pearsonhighered.com/irc** to register for access.

MySearchLab For over 10 years, instructors and students have reported achieving better results and better grades when a Pearson MyLab has been integrated into the course. MySearchLab provides engaging experiences that personalize learning, and comes from a trusted partner with educational expertise and a deep commitment to helping students and instructors achieve their goals. A wide range of writing, grammar, and research tools and access to a variety of academic journals, census data, Associated Press newsfeeds, and discipline-specific readings help you hone your writing and research skills. To order MySearchLab with this text, use ISBN 0-205-92555-3.

Instructor's Manual/Test Bank This resource includes learning objectives, lecture outlines, multiple-choice questions, true/false questions, and essay questions for each chapter. Available exclusively on the IRC.

PowerPoint Presentation Organized around a lecture outline, these multimedia presentations also include figures and tables from each chapter. Available exclusively on the IRC.

Pearson MyTest   This powerful assessment generation program includes multiple-choice questions, true/false questions, and essay questions for each chapter. Questions and tests can be easily created, customized, saved online, and then printed, allowing flexibility to manage assessments anytime and anywhere. Available exclusively on the IRC.

ACKNOWLEDGMENTS

Both authors of this book have a keen interest in state and local politics because it is a topic that is directly involved in people's daily lives, and one that has changed dramatically over the past several decades. We hope that interest is contagious. If it is, we have many people to thank. First, there are the many users of the earlier editions of the book. They will see the approaches they responded to positively in the earlier editions were retained, and will note substantial additions in this edition to accommodate changing events and perspectives. Additionally and more directly, we are greatly indebted to the following reviewers who read part or all of the previous edition(s) and gave their invaluable comments: Shari Garber Bax at Central Missouri State University; Martin Sellers at Campbell University; Mark Griffith at University of West Alabama; James D. Ivers at Southern Illinois University; Richard K. Scher at University of Florida; Martin P. Sutton at Bucks County Community College; Gregory T. Williams at Albany State University; David H. Folz at University of Tennessee; Steven Jones at University of Charleston; Fred Meyer at Ball State University; Allan Saxe at University of Texas–Arlington; Fred Hertrich at Middlesex County College; Arthur Finkle at Kean University; and Dennis Pope at Fairleigh Dickinson University. In addition, Emily Sauerhoff at Pearson was a tremendous help in bringing the new edition to completion.

JOHN J. HARRIGAN
DAVID C. NICE

Introduction to State and Community Politics

CHAPTER PREVIEW

Chapter 1 introduces the central concerns of state and community government today and outlines the plan of this book. In this chapter, we will discuss:

1 How state and local government responsibilities have increased over the years.

2 How state and local governments have reformed and modernized themselves to handle their increased responsibilities.

3 What conflicts arise in states and communities as those governments seek to carry out their responsibilities.

4 How state and local governments have become increasingly concerned with political economy and the politics of economic development.

Introduction

In recent years, state and local governments in the United States have struggled with floods, tornadoes, wildfires, skyrocketing fuel prices, and a faltering economy. Many families fell behind in their home mortgage payments, and a considerable number of families lost their homes. In a number of areas, damage from Hurricane Katrina has yet to be repaired. Many members of National Guard units, which are normally available to help with emergencies within the United States, have been serving in the Middle East. Some have been killed, and others returned with major wounds and without much of their equipment.

Rising fuel prices have created major problems for state and local transportation systems. As we will see later in the book, they were primarily designed and built during an era of cheap, abundant petroleum fuels originating in the United States. With regular-grade gasoline selling for approximately three and a half dollars per gallon and diesel fuel sometimes exceeding four dollars per gallon, many families and businesses are struggling to finance their transportation needs. Sales of American-made automobiles and trucks slumped considerably, a development that has caused great anxiety in communities where American-brand vehicles are made, and eventually led the federal government to provide loans to General Motors and Chrysler to help them survive. Car sales have rebounded somewhat in recent months.

Campaigns for the presidency have been underway for many months, and the nomination contests mobilized millions of new voters. Many of them will eventually vote in state and local elections around the country. A number of states and communities that previously acquired touch-screen computer voting equipment have decided to abandon that equipment due to problems of unreliability and doubts regarding its security. Being prepared for the demands of the general election in November 2012 will be a major challenge, particularly if the bulk of those new voters remain in the electorate.

State and local officials have clashed with the national government and with one another over numerous environmental issues. There have been disputes over global warming, automobile mileage standards, energy development, and water. In addition, state and local officials have criticized the national government's education reforms, health care reforms, and efforts to create nationwide standards for official identification documents. These conflicts are likely to continue for years to come.

State and local politics is rarely dull. People who are involved in it, whether officially or unofficially, face a wide variety of problems. Moreover, there are many arenas of decision making and many groups involved. Political maneuvering to influence elections, policy decisions, and the delivery of services takes place every day. Participants may choose from a wide variety of political tactics and may use several at the same time. The results of that political maneuvering may affect thousands or even millions of people.

ALL LEVELS OF GOVERNMENT ARE IMPORTANT IN THE UNITED STATES

When Americans face a serious problem, they often expect all levels of government to contribute to coping with that problem. One level of government may play a more visible role than the others on a given issue, but all levels are likely to be involved.

On a day-to-day basis, state and local governments often affect our lives more directly than the federal government does. Most of the governmental services we receive are delivered by state or local agencies, not the national government. That includes most of the federal government's domestic programs, such as public housing, Medicaid, highways, and most forms of public welfare. Many people feel, rightly or wrongly, that they can influence what occurs in their city hall or state capitol much more than they can influence what transpires in Washington, DC. Bear in mind, however, that much government activity is not directly visible; some of your neighbors may be receiving Social Security benefits and some of your classmates may be partially financing their education with loans guaranteed by the national government. Moreover, the federal government helps to finance many state and local services.

THE GROWTH OF STATE AND LOCAL GOVERNMENTS

State and community government responsibilities in domestic policy have grown dramatically over the years. This growth is illustrated in Figure 1.1, which shows that growth of state and local government expenditures since 1950 has outpaced both the growth of federal governmental spending (if we exclude war costs and assign federal grants to state and local governments) and

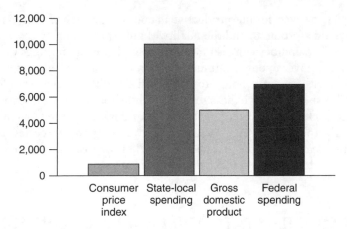

FIGURE 1.1
Governmental and Economic Growth: 1950–2009

Sources: Statistical Abstract, 2011–12 (New York: Skyhorse, 2011), pp. 14, 268, 311, 435, 473; Bureau of the Census, Statistical Abstract, 1971, (Washington, DC. U.S. Government Printing Office), pp. 305, 396; Statistical Abstract, 2011–12 (New York: Skyhorse, 2011), pp. 14, 268, 311, 435, 473; (Washington, DC: U.S. Government Printing Office, 2003), pp. 281, 317, 443; World Almanac 2011 (New York: Infobase Learning, 2011), p. 141; Significant Features of Fiscal Federalism, vol. 2 (Washington, DC: Advisory Commission on Intergovernmental Relations, 1994), pp. 24, 26; Frederick Mosher, The Costs of American Governments (New York: Dodd, Mead, 1964), pp. 154–155. (World Almanac Books, 2008), pp. 39, 40, 56, 124. Federal spending does not include the costs of the Afghan War or the Iraq War and does not include federal grants to state and local governments. State-local spending includes federal grants. The percentages in the body of the table are 2009 values divided by the 1950 values, except the consumer price statistics, which were inverted for ease of comparison.

the growth of the gross domestic product (or GDP, the most common measure of the nation's economic output) and inflation, as measured by change in the Consumer Price Index.

To some extent, state and local government spending has grown because of rising public expectations. Since 1900, the American public has demanded more and better roads and highways, more access to higher education, better health care, more protection for the environment, and a host of other services that cannot be provided without large amounts of money. As we will see later in the chapter, the states, and especially local governments, have not raised all of that money themselves.

The growing role of states and localities in domestic policy also occurred because the federal government since the late 1970s has sometimes been unwilling or unable to tackle some of our most pressing domestic problems, such as air and water pollution, global warming, poverty, and lack of health care coverage to millions of Americans. Even when the national government has taken initiatives in domestic policies, federal officials often prefer to include state and local governments in their efforts. As a result, groups concerned about those policies often turn their attention to state and local governments. States and localities have often served as testing grounds for new programs, and programs that work well (or appear to work well) frequently spread to other states and communities. However, an expert on public policy and administration recently noted that when revenues are tight, as they were in the early 1990s and have been much of the time since 2001, state and local officials are often much less interested in trying any new policies.[1] In addition, some states and localities are much more open to new ideas and approaches than are others.

Especially when officials are not certain how a problem should be handled, the involvement of state and local governments provides many possible advantages. Different governments may try different approaches and assess the success of each. A remedy that is appropriate in one setting may be useless or even counterproductive in another. Experimentation may produce new strategies for attacking a problem, and the quality of governmental services may improve in the process.[2] Sharing responsibilities can also mean sharing blame when things go wrong.

As state and local governments continue to play a major role in almost all domestic issues, they find themselves with difficult choices to make. Which public services should be emphasized? At what levels? Who should receive these services? Who should pay for their cost? Who should provide the services? How should the great burden of coping with environmental, economic, health, educational, and other issues be distributed among the three levels of government (national, state, and local) and/or the private sector? What sorts of values should be incorporated into public policies, and who should make those decisions?

MODERNIZATION OF STATE AND LOCAL GOVERNMENT

The growing responsibilities of state and local governments, as well as changing public expectations, have created pressure for major reforms in many states and localities. For many years, a number of scholars and journalists viewed state and community governments as incompetent at best. State governments were described as "sick,"[3] and state legislatures were caricatured as "horse-and-buggy" institutions.[4] States were sometimes reluctant to tackle major problems.[5] And as states ignored their growing urban problems in the 1950s and 1960s, the federal government picked up much of the slack with a vast expansion of social services and domestic programs. Journalists and social scientists increasingly turned their attention to Washington or to the larger cities, largely ignoring state government as "Dullsville."[6]

Conditions have changed considerably since then. State and community governments have substantially reformed themselves since World War II. In many states there has been a broad upgrading of the professionalism and competence of the governors, legislatures, courts, and especially public bureaucracies. States and localities have embraced new technologies in many fields, including transportation, education, law enforcement, and environmental protection. One of the most dramatic changes involves the growing use of computers and the Internet for a wide range of purposes. The ability of states to cope with domestic problems has been further enhanced by more effective revenue collection systems.[7] According to the Advisory Commission on Intergovernmental Relations, this transformation of state government capability in such a short time "has no parallel in American history."[8]

The pace of reform has varied considerably across the states and across communities, however, and some of the reforms adopted at the local level have had the unfortunate effect of reducing citizen involvement in local politics. Some major reforms of local government have also encountered large-scale obstacles in many communities, and many local governments have been unable to raise enough money to finance major improvements on their own.

By the early 1990s, the predominant buzzword for this reformist impulse was "reinventing government." This term, taken from a book by David Osborne and Ted Gaebler,[9] promotes the idea that governments at all levels should become more flexible, decentralized, entrepreneurial, and consumer oriented in their quest to provide public services. Since then the demands for services by state and local governments have been great, but the financial resources for meeting those demands are scarce. The advocates of reinventing government hope that their entrepreneurial, decentralized approach will rebuild public confidence in government by making governments more effective and possibly less costly. The savings produced by reinvention have not been large enough to enable states and localities to avoid major cuts in some services since the latest recession began in 2007–2008.[10]

Some critics wonder, however, whether reinvention and other recent management reforms may create new problems, such as a loss of accountability and the parochialism that sometimes comes with decentralization. In addition, being more responsive to a program's "consumers" may easily turn into paying too much attention to interest groups, which sometimes are the most vocal consumers of individual programs. New management fads may divert attention from more fundamental needs and concerns.[11] Throughout this book we will examine a variety of reforms and reform proposals and try to assess their effects.

WHAT MATTERS IN STATE AND COMMUNITY POLITICS

The big question about this rejuvenation of government in the past decades is, of course, for what purpose? What is the proper role of government in a democratic society? What problems should government tackle? And in tackling those problems, what should the proper distribution of responsibility be among the federal, state, and local levels of government, as well as the private sector?

These are not easy questions to answer, however, because every major interest group in our society has a different answer. And the clash among these various interests about the purposes of government is at the heart of what state and community politics is about. Because states and communities are heavily involved in all important domestic policies and are sometimes involved in foreign policy as well, conflicts over those issues often erupt in state and local political systems.

Should, for example, teenage girls be permitted to obtain legal abortions without consulting their parents? Should each state be permitted to decide this issue for itself? Or should the will of the federal government prevail on all 50 states? If the federal government tries to impose a uniform policy nationwide, people who dislike that policy will often try to persuade state or local officials to intervene and press for revisions in the policy. Even when the federal government adopts a policy that gives state and/or local officials significant flexibility, opponents of that policy may still try to mobilize opposition from state or local officials, as in the case of the 2010 health care reforms (we will examine that controversy in later chapters).

What we are going to see, as we explore the roles of state and community governments, is that certain facets of our political, social, and economic systems have significant impact on the ability of state and community governments to discharge their responsibilities. Six of these matters are going to gain our attention throughout this book.

Political Economy Matters

One of the things that most affects a state's ability to perform its responsibilities effectively is the **political economy** (the interaction between economic conditions and public policies). Public revenues to provide good schools, for example, will be more plentiful if the state has a dynamic, growing economy. And a state's ability to produce a dynamic, growing economy is in part influenced by policies adopted by the state. However, many forces that affect state and local economies are far beyond the control of state and local officials. They are, consequently, often swept along by economic forces that they cannot influence to any great degree.[12] If they could, every state and community would be prosperous all the time.

A particularly important aspect of the political economy at the local level is the political influence of large companies. Local officials are often reluctant to antagonize the leaders of large businesses because those leaders may decide to close the local firm and move elsewhere (or expand operations somewhere else instead of in the community in question). Losing a major business means a loss of jobs and tax revenues, which in turn undercuts a community's ability to finance public services.

Ideology Matters

More than political economy is involved in state and local politics. Ideology also matters. Citizens and officials in some parts of the country look at poverty and see a natural condition that is the fault of the people who are poor. Other citizens and officials see poverty as a signal for governmental intervention in order to lift people out of poverty. The latter ideological position favors **redistributive policies**. These types of policies try to assist people at the lower end of the income scale, but are financed by revenue collected disproportionately from people at the middle and upper ends of the income scale (depending on the state and locality). When these policies are successful, more people will be able to find decent jobs, and there will be greater equality in the distribution of wealth among the population (although variations will still remain).

Not everybody agrees that public services should be redistributive, and there are ways to ensure that they are not. The first is to minimize government's role and let it provide only very limited services. A second is to provide only the services that disproportionately benefit the middle and upper classes—higher education, public freeways, redevelopment of big-city, central-business districts, and support for the arts. A third is to finance public services through regressive taxes rather than through progressive taxes. (A *regressive tax* takes a bigger percentage of poor people's income than it takes from high-income people. A *progressive tax* does the opposite.) Progressive and regressive taxes are discussed more fully in Chapter 12.

People on the liberal end of the **ideological spectrum** generally support the expansion of government services for low-income people and paying for these services with a progressive tax system. This system redistributes income from the rich to the poor. In contrast, conservatives generally prefer minimal government services and regressive tax systems. This leads to distributive policies; that is, people receive about as much in government services as they pay in taxes. Ideological differences are illustrated in Figure 1.2, which shows that the overwhelming majority of people are middle of the road or lean just slightly away from center. In most years, conservatives significantly outnumber liberals, at least in the abstract.

Redistributive policies usually draw their greatest support from groups representing people low on the socioeconomic scale. These include labor unions (which may want more jobs and higher pay and benefits), welfare rights organizations (which may want higher welfare benefits), minority groups (which may want higher expenditures on health and educational services), the elderly (who may want better transportation services for senior citizens and continuation or expansion of various programs aiding senior citizens), and groups lobbying for other specific categories of people (who may be poor or who may have physical or mental handicaps).

Opposition to redistributive policies usually comes from interest groups representing people who expect to see their taxes rise as a result of higher expenditures—chambers of

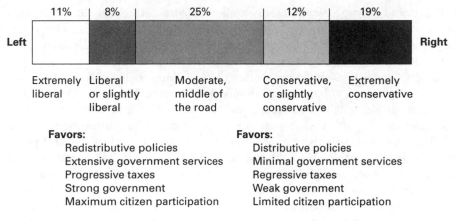

FIGURE 1.2
The Ideological Spectrum

Source: William Flanigan and Nancy Zingale, *Political Behavior of the American Electorate,* 11th ed. (Washington, DC: Congressional Quarterly, 2006), p. 151.

commerce (which may fear potential tax increases), business groups (which may fear that higher taxes will erode the business climate), and ad hoc taxpayers associations (which may resent potential tax increases, welfare expenditures, or higher salaries for public employees).

Redistributive policies also pose problems for the advocates of reinventing government, whom we discussed earlier. At the core of the idea of reinventing government is the desire to make government more efficient and more cost effective. But is cost effectiveness the highest goal of government and, if so, who should define what is cost effective? When it conflicts with other values, which value should prevail?

Remember that public opinion is more complex than just the labels of "liberal," "moderate," or "conservative." Many Americans do not think ideologically, and some who do generally have opinions on individual issues that are not consistent with their overall ideological leanings. In any case, a large body of research finds that the broad climate of opinion varies considerably from state to state and that public sentiments are a strong influence on many state policy decisions and many other aspects of state and local politics.[13]

Citizens Matter: You Matter

If the states are truly laboratories of democracy, as they have sometimes been described, then citizens must have an important role in shaping public policies. And certainly there are ample opportunities to do this. One way is for you to run for and win elective office. There are 7,000 state legislative positions and tens of thousands of other elective offices, the vast majority of them at the local level. In addition, there are large numbers of advisory groups and other appointive positions that may enable people to influence governmental decisions. Thus, many people seriously interested in government and politics can get elected or appointed to *some* office if they do the right things and persist long enough. Not all people have an equal chance, though. Having access to enough funds to run an effective campaign, a prominent, well-respected name, connections with other people who are politically active, and having political skills make gaining access to office a good deal easier.

In addition, citizens can influence policy through interest groups, political parties, and political movements, topics that we will discuss in Chapters 4 and 5. Many of these groups need additional people to help with the groups' activities. With a little luck and a lot of persistence, many citizens *can* affect what their governments do, although some people are likely to be more influential than are others. Note, too, that state and local offices and political organizations provide many of the candidates for national-level office. Many presidents (including five of the six who served from 1977 through 2012), members of Congress, and federal judges began their political careers in state and local politics.

Although state and local political systems are sufficiently open that many energetic citizens can realistically aspire to elective or appointive office, either in government or in a political party or interest group, there is a great danger that less ambitious citizens will be reduced to being passive consumers of public services. Moreover, there have been many efforts to exclude people from the political process over the years and efforts to discourage some types of political involvement. For many years, state and local governments in the South blocked African Americans from voting, conducting public demonstrations, or even meeting with public officials. Much more recently, when student protesters of the Occupy movement, which has criticized the power of big corporations and complained that too much wealth is controlled by too few people, refused to obey a police order to disperse at the University of California-Davis, a number of the demonstrators were attacked with pepper spray. Another demonstrator in the San Francisco Bay area was killed by a projectile apparently fired by the police.[14]

These and other instances raise important questions about whether states and communities are truly laboratories of *democracy*. What role does the average citizen really play in state and community governance? Are these governments really as close to the people as they claim to be in American political mythology? How much do citizens know about state and local governments and politics? And how much citizen participation can take place and still permit effective governance? These are important issues that will surface repeatedly throughout this book. Note, too, that the political arena is not the only place where people can get involved.

Political Culture Matters

State and local politics are affected by **political culture**, the citizens' attitudes, beliefs, and expectations about what governments should do, who should participate, and what rules should govern the political game. Some political cultures may place very strict limits on what a state or local government can do, whereas other political cultures may allow their governments considerable freedom.

Daniel Elazar has described three political cultures—the individualistic, the moralistic, and the traditionalistic.[15] These three cultures differ sharply in the way they view the purpose of government and the role of the average citizen. The **individualistic political culture** believes government exists primarily to distribute favors to government supporters and to regulate the economic marketplace to enable people to pursue their individual goals. It also believes politics exists in part to help politicians make a living and get ahead. The

▶ HIGHLIGHT

But What If I'm Not Comfortable Getting Involved in Politics?

Many Americans believe that the political world is corrupt and/or combative and prefer to stay away from it. Whether you share that view or not, there are still many ways to become involved in community life. In the spring of 2005, many college students spent spring break helping to repair the damage that Hurricane Katrina inflicted on the Gulf Coast. They helped clear away debris and rebuild homes and other buildings. A group of law school students helped people who had problems with their insurance claims or other difficulties. Some students helped tutor children or entertained them, which helped the children cope with the many stresses brought by the hurricane and its aftermath.

Other people become involved by volunteering at nursing homes, libraries, day care centers, or parks. Some people collect trash alongside highways, streets, or streams. Many people recycle cans, bottles, paper, and cardboard and try to buy products with less wasteful packaging. Installing a brighter front porch or yard light or trimming back some shrubs may help to make a dark part of your street safer. Assembling a home emergency kit may help

you to survive a natural disaster or terrorist incident and enable you to help others. Joining a religious organization or a club with which you share an interest is another option. There are literally thousands of ways to become involved.

Bear in mind, however, that politics occurs in all groups. Whenever decisions are made, political maneuvering takes place. In addition, many "nonpolitical" groups work on problems that also concern governments: pollution, crime, poverty, education, and so forth. Sooner or later, many of those groups try to influence governmental decisions. Belonging to any organization makes you part of a social network that helps to distribute information of many types, including political information. You may eventually be drawn into the political arena. ■

Sources: For general information on getting involved, see Hope Egan, *Volunteering* (New York: Barnes and Noble, 2002); Jeffrey Hollender and Linda Catling, *How to Make the World a Better Place* (New York: Norton, 1995); for information on the hurricane volunteers, see Stacey Plaisance, "College Students Spend Spring Break Rebuilding Gulf Coast," *Moscow-Pullman Daily News*, March 18–19, 2006, p. 9A.

individualist culture favors large bureaucracies because they offer opportunity for providing services for voters and patronage jobs for political party workers. But it does not expect the average citizen to participate much beyond voting for candidates selected by career politicians.

The **moralistic political culture**, in contrast, believes government exists to achieve moral goals that are in the public interest. It gives governments a broad role, as long as the governments' actions benefit the public. The moralistic culture places a high value on citizen participation and expects public officials to follow high standards of ethical conduct. The moralistic culture also favors large, professionalized bureaucracies because they are believed to be more competent and to enhance political neutrality in the provision of services. Unlike the individualistic culture, however, the moralistic culture rejects a patronage system of employment (government jobs given to political supporters) and favors a merit system, in which people are hired and promoted on the basis of their qualifications and job performance.

The **traditionalistic political culture** believes government exists to preserve the existing social order. It permits governments to initiate new programs primarily if they serve the interests of the governing elites. It limits political participation to the few appropriate people who know best. Political parties are less important than family or social ties. And bureaucracy is viewed negatively as a force for depersonalizing government. The traditionalistic culture rejects the merit system of employment.

What impact does political culture have on the politics and policies of the different states? Research into this question has produced several conclusions. First, citizen participation in politics is highest in the moralistic cultures and lowest in the traditionalistic cultures.[16] This is due in large measure to the fact that moralistic states facilitate participation by having more lenient requirements for voter registration and voting in elections than do traditionalistic states, and that the institutions of government are more open to citizen input than they are in traditionalistic states.[17]

Second, numerous studies have found that political culture influences the kind of policies adopted by states. Moralistic states tend to pursue more redistributive policies than do the traditionalistic states, but this may be because the moralistic states are also more prosperous.[18] Traditionalistic states also tend to spend less money on government programs than do moralistic or individualistic states.[19] Moralistic states are much more likely to engage in a broad scope of governmental activity, to pursue innovative government programs, and to spend more money on welfare and economic development policies.[20]

A third important impact of political culture on state politics is that moralistic states do indeed have higher ethical standards of public conduct than other states.[21] Public officials in moralistic states are convicted for corrupt behavior much less frequently than are public officials in individualistic and traditionalistic states.[22]

Finally, although Elazar's theory of political culture has been a powerful concept for understanding the variations in politics and policy from one state to another, it is not clear *how* or by what mechanism the political cultures have this impact.[23] Attempts to use public opinion surveys to categorize people into the moralistic, traditionalistic, or individualistic types have been inconclusive.[24]

It also is unlikely that states in the future will continue to fit as neatly into Elazar's three categories as they have in the past. Since Elazar formulated this theory, population migrations have led to a dynamic mixing of cultures that will possibly create new types and combinations of cultures. There has been a heavy migration of people from the individualistic and moralistic regions to the South and Southwest, leading to a very turbulent mixing of cultural values in those regions. The Internet has given people great access to ideas from other parts of the country and the world. It appears the South is becoming somewhat less traditionalistic.[25] And the Southwest is, in a sense, becoming the new melting pot of the nation. It has absorbed substantial immigration of peoples from all three political cultures. It is also absorbing millions of Latin American immigrants who are leaving their imprint on the political culture. And the substantial number of Asian immigrants has influenced local culture, especially on the West Coast. As a consequence of these changes, the three political cultures outlined here will almost certainly evolve into something reflecting the growing diversity of American society.[26] One sign of that development may be the growing value conflicts that are taking place within many states as well as between states.[27]

One sign of the changing dynamics of state political cultures is the Tea Party, which has mobilized in many states to support what their members believe are traditional values, such as lower taxes, reduced federal spending (apparently excepting spending for programs benefiting the members of the Tea Party), and fewer federal regulations. The Tea Party has triggered serious conflicts in Republican Party politics in a number of states, and conflict has erupted within the Tea Party as well.[28]

The Past Matters

When citizens or officials make a decision, they do not begin with a blank slate. Previous commitments, traditions, habits, organizational dynamics, old resentments, and a host of other factors come into play. The past, therefore, is a powerful influence on many aspects of state and local politics. To take an obvious example, consider the number of changes that have occurred in the United States in the last 100 years. In spite of those many changes, however, the boundaries of the states have changed very little (apart from the creation of a few new states), and many county boundaries have changed little more. State policies on civil rights issues in the 1960s bore considerable resemblance to the battle lines of the Civil War a century earlier. The broad contours of budget decisions often show noticeable similarity to decisions a decade or more earlier.

This argument should not be overstated. State and local governments and politics have changed in many ways over the years. Even when changes occur, though, we often find elements of continuity with previous arrangements, and even the most drastic changes are often easier to understand if we know more about the events or conditions that preceded them.

Social Conflict Matters

The United States contains many diverse ethnic, religious, economic, and ideological groups. Most of these groups historically expressed a commitment to the broader whole of American society and eventually grew to tolerate one another, although many people also wanted to preserve aspects of their heritage and sometimes looked down on other groups. Government itself was pledged to a constitutional principle of treating all people equally under the law. No society, of course, has ever treated all people with perfect equality, and in America the principle of equality under the law has been violated in regard to African Americans, Native Americans, Asian Americans, Hispanics, women, and the poor, as well as a variety of other groups.[29] But the existence of the principle of equal treatment under the law at least was a beacon of hope that kept many people striving for greater equality and helped hold the diverse elements of society together. Many people believed in America as a melting pot that would melt all the diverse elements into a new American whole.

Today, this notion of America as a melting pot sounds archaic in the face of social conflicts based on gender, racial differences, ideological differences, religious beliefs, and class discrepancies. The eminent historian Arthur M. Schlesinger, Jr., has written about the *Disuniting of America*.[30] Spokespersons emerge among the various ethnic groups, religious beliefs, ideological causes, and economic groups. Many of them have legitimate claims on society, and some condemn many other people as sexist, racist, immoral, greedy, or homophobic. Other people react adversely to being criticized or denounced. Many people assert that they have fundamental rights that cannot be compromised, even if those rights conflict with the rights of other people. At times, these conflicts appear to threaten the nation's social fabric.

These social conflicts matter to states and communities because those governments must try to establish policies that will satisfy the conflicting demands of different racial, cultural, religious, and economic groups. Furthermore, states and communities must find ways to satisfy these demands in the face of political-economic forces that often obstruct significant action on controversial problems. Some observers worry that the most severe social conflicts will gradually erode the foundations of state and community governments themselves. When governments have difficulty in managing conflict, they are often unable to make decisions and are often unable to sustain a consistent course of action for any significant length of time.

These concerns are especially appropriate at the local level. In many parts of the country, wealthier citizens have created their own local governments, from which poorer citizens are excluded. The results are large variations in wealth and tax resources from one locality to another, with some localities being too poor to cope with the problems they face. Getting the many local governments to work together on broad issues is often very difficult, and efforts to merge local governments when some are much wealthier than others very often fail.

In addition, the growing importance of global economic forces has made many state and local officials fearful of doing anything that would antagonize business interests. Officials worry that major companies may relocate elsewhere unless they are given preferential treatment. Ordinary citizens and owners of small businesses may be unhappy, however, if their officials seem more interested in those large companies than in local residents and small businesses of the area. This complaint has been raised not only by members of the Occupy Wall Street movement but also by the owners of small businesses.

SUMMARY

1. Recent decades have seen a dramatic reform and rejuvenation of state and local governments in the United States, although the pace and extent of reform varies from place to place.
2. One of the most important state and local government responsibilities in recent years has been responsibility for state and local political economies.
3. As state and local governments carry out their responsibilities, they become focal points for important political conflicts, especially conflicts over political ideology and group benefits.
4. Because of budget squeezes and administrative reform movements, state and local governments have made increasing efforts to assess the efficiency of their operations and to improve those operations.
5. As state and local governments become increasingly important to our lives, we increasingly need an effective system of citizen participation in order to keep government accountable to the people.

STUDY QUESTIONS

1. Why are state and local governments important in the American political system? Why have they grown so much over the years?
2. What broad forces influence state and local government decision making?
3. Reformers have often called for modernizing state and local governments over the years. Do you think the growth of state and local governments may have increased the need for modernization?

KEY TERMS

Ideological spectrum   The traditional left–right spectrum, in which liberal (or left-leaning) ideological positions are on the left side of the spectrum and conservative (or right-leaning) ideological positions are on the right side. Liberals often favor a greater governmental role and greater efforts to aid disadvantaged people. Conservatives often favor a smaller governmental role and letting private charities do more to care for the needy.

Individualistic political culture   A viewpoint that believes government exists to distribute favors to individual people and believes politics should be dominated by professional politicians. Citizens have only a limited role in the political process.

Moralistic political culture   A viewpoint that believes government should seek to achieve moral goals in the public interest. Places a high value on citizen participation and government taking an active role in society.

Political culture   People's attitudes, beliefs, and expectations about what governments should do, who should participate, and what rules should govern the political game.

Political economy   The interaction between public policy and the economy. The condition of a state or local economy will affect revenue raising and, consequently, many public services. Public officials may also select policies in the hope that they may improve the area's economy.

Redistributive policies   Policies that provide extensive public services for people on the low end of the income scale and finance those services with revenues collected from people at the middle and upper ends of the income scale. These policies try, to some degree, to equalize the distribution of wealth.

Traditionalistic political culture   A viewpoint that believes government's purpose is to preserve the existing social order. Political power is best exercised by the limited number of people that have traditionally been influential, and government will play a fairly limited role in society.

THE INTERNET CONNECTION

The Council of State Governments is a nonpartisan organization that gathers and distributes a wide variety of information about state and local government, with a primary emphasis on state government. You can find this organization at **www.csg.org**. Its best-known publication, *The Book of the States,* is a valuable source of ideas and data. Another valuable information resource is **www.governing.com**; it is connected with *Governing Magazine,* which covers many issues involving states and localities. Many major news organizations can also be reached through the Internet, although some may allow only limited access unless you pay a fee. Can you find a Web site for your own state's government? What kinds of information does it contain? Is it easy to use? What else does it offer besides information? Can you use it to apply to the state university system, for example?

CAREER PROSPECTS IN STATE AND LOCAL GOVERNMENT

What kind of career can you build for yourself in state and local government? You can build virtually any career that you are likely to think of if you want to work in the public sector. From a stock clerk in a government purchasing office to a physician in a public hospital, more than 17 million state and local government employees work at nearly as many varied tasks as do employees in the private sector. To give you a better idea of state and local employment possibilities, we have outlined here several career categories in state and local politics. Following this list you will find a list of related occupations and career areas that are not normally thought of as public-sector occupations, even though many jobs in these areas are found in the public sector as well as the private sector. For information on salaries and employment opportunities for specific types of careers, consult the latest edition of the *Occupational Outlook Handbook* (Washington, DC: Bureau of Labor Statistics, biennial) and the Bureau of Labor Statistics Web site at www.bls.gov. Information regarding job opportunities in individual state and local government agencies is increasingly available at agency Web sites.

One useful way to test whether you might like a particular job is to take an internship in the area. This will enable you to gain college credit while exploring a career possibility. Internships are also useful when you start looking for a job: Having a work record, especially one in the type of work you want to do, can be a very big advantage, and the contacts you make while doing your internship can help significantly, too.

Administrator

(Chapters 6, 7, 9, 10, 12–17)

The term *administrator* refers to the highest level of permanent employee below the level of politically appointed executives. Administrators seek to ensure that all parts of their agency work together and carry out the policies set by elected or appointed political leaders. Although some agency administrators are brought in from outside sources, many work up through the agency ranks. Most administrators have training in a related professional occupation (engineering, for example, in the Transportation Department or social work in the Welfare Department). Increasingly, administrators bolster their professional experience by acquiring a master's degree in public administration or public policy or a graduate degree in their field of specialization. Salaries and benefits tend to be reasonably generous, especially in large agencies. Salaries and benefits in smaller and poorer local governments are often lower. The position of administrator is not entry level. Opportunities for promotion to the administrative level will be limited by the currently slow growth rates of government and the existence of large numbers of managerial personnel competing for administrative jobs. However, many state and local administrators are nearing retirement age, so opportunities will be developing. Incomes vary widely by region and type of agency.

Budget Analyst

(Chapters 6, 7, 9, 10, 12–17)

Most large units of government have a budget specialist (sometimes more than one) who helps prepare budget documents, tries to forecast future revenues and program costs, sometimes controls the release of budgeted funds, and usually is one of the major financial advisers in the particular governmental unit. Because analysts control agency spending, they find themselves in the thick of many political battles. Qualifications include a college degree and substantial training in, or at least understanding of, accounting practices. A master's degree in public administration, business, or accounting is desirable.

Corrections Officer

(Chapter 11)

Corrections officers work as guards in jails, prisons, and other correctional facilities. The minimum education requirement is a high school diploma, although some college course work in criminal justice, criminology, psychology, and sociology is increasingly required. If the incarcerated population continues to rise as it has in recent decades, employment prospects in the corrections field will be expected to grow much faster than the average.

Court Administrator

(Chapter 11)

The increasing complexity of running the nation's courts has given rise to a relatively new court administrator position in public administration. This professional organizes the calendar for courts, hires the personnel (such as clerical staff), and oversees the day-to-day administrative details of the court's operations. Although legal training is not a prerequisite, many court administrators are trained as lawyers before moving into administration. If judicial case loads continue to rise as they have in recent decades, and if the judicial reform movement keeps pressing for modernizing and professionalizing state and local court systems, it seems likely that the demand for court administrators will continue to grow.

Economic Developer

(Chapter 17)

So intensive is the demand for people to spearhead and oversee economic development projects that many communities have begun hiring certified industrial and economic developers (CID/CED). Economic developers need an understanding of their local communities as well as training and experience in development financing tools, zoning processes, accounting, and marketing. Excellent communications skills are necessary. Certification for the CID/CED is handled by the American Economic Development

Council, which demands five years of work experience in economic development plus appropriate course work.

Employment is found throughout the country in a variety of private and public institutions such as banks, chambers of commerce, port authorities, and state government agencies. Because of the widespread perceived need for communities to do whatever is feasible and reasonable to attract industry, the demand for economic developers seems likely to continue growing over the near future. For more information, write to the: American Economic Development Council, Schiller Park, IL 60176.

Firefighter

The minimum educational qualification for a firefighter is usually a high school diploma. Most firefighting jobs are found at the municipal level. Employment tends to be stable, layoffs are infrequent, and fringe benefits are generous, especially in unionized states. Employment opportunities are expected to grow at a below average rate.

Forester and Conservation Scientist

(Chapter 16)

An important area of environmental protection involves forest management and conservation in order to protect the nation's forests, soils, and wildlife. Many local governments in urban areas also employ environmental and horticultural specialists who care for trees and other plants in parks, near public buildings, and in other settings. Training qualifications usually include at least a bachelor's degree in forestry or range sciences. Employment opportunities are expected to grow as fast as the average.

Health Services Manager

(Chapter 13)

Health services managers are needed to run hospitals, nursing homes, health maintenance organizations, rehabilitation centers, urgent-care facilities, and the offices of doctors, dentists, and chiropractors. Because of the growing complexity of medical and health care provisions, professional managers have been increasingly taking the responsibility for management of health care facilities out of the hands of medical

personnel such as physicians and nurses, whose specialty is medical and health care treatment rather than management. Health services personnel range from executive directors in charge of an institution to internal managers to specialized staff.

The responsibilities of health care managers include budgeting, personnel administration, information management, marketing, strategic planning, systems analysis, and labor relations. Managers need a knowledge of management principles and most likely hold a master's degree in health administration (MHA), in business administration (MBA), or in public administration (MPA) with a health services concentration.

Inspector, Licensor, and Compliance Officer

(Chapters 6, 7, 10, 11, 13, 16, 17)

A great many people are employed at all levels of government to carry out a variety of inspection, licensing, regulatory, and compliance functions, including health inspectors, consumer safety inspectors, food inspectors, environmental health inspectors, motor vehicle inspectors, traffic inspectors, occupational safety and health inspectors, wage-hour compliance inspectors, equal opportunity representatives, and building inspectors. Training and job requirements vary greatly because of the great diversity of functions. Employment growth is expected to be faster than average.

Legal Assistant or Paralegal

(Chapters 10, 11)

These professionals do significant background investigatory work for the preparation of cases. They work in a variety of settings ranging from private law firms to community legal services agencies, where they help provide legal aid to people of limited means.

Legislative Aide

(Chapter 8)

Every legislature hires people to do a variety of specialized and professional tasks, ranging from policy research to putting into legal form the ideas for bills that legislators present. Some of these positions require legal training, some require computer training, and others require training in accounting. For policy analysts, a master's degree in policy analysis, public affairs, or public administration is highly desirable. These analysts may work for committees, for a Democratic or Republican caucus, or even for a specific legislator. One convenient way to test whether you would like to work as a legislative aide is to do an internship with your legislator or participate in some committee of the legislature.

Librarian
(Chapters 10, 14)

As you inevitably discover when you begin working on your term papers, librarians play an extremely valuable role in helping to find resource materials that address important issues in our complicated society. A master of library science degree is required for most professional-level librarians. These jobs are expected to grow more slowly than average.

Lobbyist
(Chapters 3, 4, 6–17)

Although no state has a lobbying industry as large as the one that deals with the federal government, lobbying at the state and local levels is important and most likely will continue to be so. There will be a continuing need for people who can effectively represent clients before state legislatures, city councils, and regulatory agencies. Lobbyists represent every conceivable sector of society, from welfare recipients to multinational corporations. Some lobbyists work for large organizations; others are self-employed persons who hire themselves out to clients. Effective lobbying requires excellent communication and interpersonal skills, intimate knowledge of the government agencies being lobbied, and a willingness to work long hours. Although there are no formal requirements for becoming a lobbyist, lawyers and former legislators have some distinct advantages over other candidates.

Mediator and Arbitrator
(Chapters 4, 6, 10)

When labor–management negotiations reach an impasse, mediators are often hired to meet with each side, listen to their demands, and make suggestions that facilitate a compromise to which both can agree. Arbitrators do comparable kinds of work, but unlike mediators, they are given the power to impose a solution on the two parties if a mediated agreement cannot be reached. Most states have a department of mediation or arbitration services that keeps a list of persons qualified to serve as mediators or arbitrators in contract disputes. Mediators usually have considerable experience in contract negotiations or a professional degree in personnel management or industrial relations. Arbitrators usually have a law degree.

Personnel and Labor Relations
(Chapters 7, 10)

With more than 17 million employees, some of them unionized, state and local governments rely heavily on personnel officers and labor relations specialists. Personnel officers manage the procedures for hiring, promotion, and dismissal. Labor relations specialists help manage relations between government agencies and the collective bargaining agents of their employees. Related jobs include compensation analysts, employee-benefits managers, and training specialists. The goal behind these positions is to provide a competent and productive work force. Because of the diversity of these jobs, training and other requirements vary widely. For entry-level positions, undergraduate course work in personnel or labor relations is helpful, as is a degree or certificate in the field.

Police Work
(Chapters 6, 10, 11)

Police-related occupations include police officers, state highway patrols, detectives, and investigators. The ability to handle people is a prime prerequisite for these jobs. Qualifications include excellent physical condition and the ability to pass competitive written examinations. Although small communities require only a high school diploma for police officers, some college education and often a college degree is increasingly required in metropolitan areas, especially for people who want to move up into middle-level positions or above. Many universities offer degrees in criminal justice or criminology. Many large, private organizations also have private security forces, which currently employ more people than do governmental law enforcement organizations; the training requirements for private firms vary considerably from place to place.

Public Education Employment

(Chapter 14)

The major professional occupations in public education are teachers, principals, and central-office administrators (that is, superintendents, data processors, purchasing officers, and curriculum development specialists). These professionals bear the primary educational responsibility for preparing the next generation of American citizens to live in an increasingly competitive and complex world. To work effectively, these professionals need excellent communication and interpersonal skills.

Requirements for teaching positions include teacher certification and undergraduate course work in education. Teachers in middle schools and high schools must usually have coursework in the subjects they plan to teach. Principals, superintendents, and other high-level administrators also need several years' teaching experience, graduate training in school administration, and certification.

Public Relations Specialist

(Chapters 4–6, 8–11, 17)

Most large organizations, public or private, use public relations tactics to promote their image and maintain positive relations with the public. In addition, many agencies need to inform the public regarding hazards to public safety, proposed governmental actions, and so forth. In government agencies, public relations is often the responsibility of offices of public information. These offices produce news releases, pamphlets, multimedia shows, and other materials designed to further the goals of their agencies. Major employment qualifications usually consist of a college degree plus public relations experience. A bachelor's or master's degree in journalism or public relations is helpful. Public relations professionals need highly developed writing and speaking skills as well as the ability to work with people.

Recreation Worker

(Chapters 6, 7, 10, 16)

These workers organize leisure and recreational activities in a wide variety of settings, ranging from city recreation departments to wilderness areas. Although one can enter the field with less than a bachelor's degree, a college degree and some specialized training are usually required to move up to supervisory and managerial positions.

Social Worker

(Chapter 13)

Demand for social workers has been strong in recent decades because of several societal forces discussed in the text, including the aging of the population; the existence of a large, impoverished subpopulation; the change of the population from predominantly rural to predominantly metropolitan; and the need to offer protection services for abused and neglected children, the handicapped, and the disabled. Effective social workers need a variety of important skills: communication skills, knowledge of principles of behavior, ability to work with people, and familiarity with relevant social legislation and administrative rules. The main training qualifications for social work are a bachelor's degree in the social sciences or social work (BSW) or even more likely, a master's degree in social work (MSW).

Urban and Regional Planner

(Chapters 6, 7, 10, 15–17)

City planners, urban planners, and regional planners advise local and regional officials on decisions involving the growth and redevelopment of cities, suburbs, regions, metropolitan areas, and rural communities. Because planners are called on to make recommendations concerning land use, environmental issues, health issues, and economic development, planners must combine a broad knowledge of public issues with a technical ability to apply contemporary tools of statistical and policy analysis. Good political skills are also helpful. Most planning jobs require a master's degree in urban or regional planning. Planners may also be certified by the American Institute of Certified Planners, a branch of the American Planning Association.

Related Occupations

The following occupations are not distinctly public service careers, since the majority of people working in them are employed in the private sector. Nevertheless, substantial numbers of these people also work in the public sector where their skills are needed.

Accountant and Auditor

These professionals prepare financial reports, analyze financial data, and provide the up-to-date financial data that governments need in order to make responsible decisions. Job requirements may include certification as a public accountant.

Lawyer

Given the complexity of life today, the large number of laws enacted by legislatures and the even larger number of rules issued by regulatory and administrative agencies, lawyers continue to be employed widely by state and local governments in a variety of capacities. Minimum requirements are the LLB degree and passage of the state bar examination. Eighty percent of lawyers work in the private sector, and the majority of public-sector lawyers work at the local level. Lawyers also seem to have an edge working as lobbyists. Also being a private practice lawyer is often considered a good starting place for a career in elective politics.

Energy-Related Careers

Continuing uncertainty and conflict regarding energy issues are likely to mean a continuing need for educated people in many energy-related occupations. In the public sector, energy-related employment opportunities are likely to be found in federal agencies such as the Departments of Energy, Interior, Treasury, Commerce, Transportation, State, Agriculture, and Defense. State-level counterparts of some of these departments will also need energy-related workers.

Environment-Related Careers

For the foreseeable future, there will be no reduction in the need to protect the air, water, and atmosphere from further degradation. Moreover, many states and localities are now wrestling with the issue of global warming. Accordingly, there will continue to be a need for people to serve in a variety of environmentally related occupations. Some of these include forester, range manager, recreationist, soil conservationist, soil scientist, wildlife conservationist, zoo keeper, landscape architect, urban planner, civil engineer, and biologist.

General Considerations on Public Employment Prospects

Because job prospects are heavily influenced by population trends and business conditions, a person should be aware of these when planning a career. In general, it seems likely that professional-level jobs for college graduates will enjoy better growth in affluent areas rather than in poor areas and in fast-growing areas rather than in slow-growing areas. To find relatively current information regarding economic conditions and growth rates in individual states and localities, contact the Bureau of the Census at www.census.gov. The Bureau's Statistical Abstract and State and Metropolitan Area Databook provide similar information and are available at many libraries. Many agencies now have information regarding employment opportunities on their Web sites, and that information is likely to be more specific: education requirements, salary range, and so forth.

NOTES

1. Donald Kettl, "Innovation Freeze," *Governing* 17 (October 2003): 12. For evidence of a similar pattern over a much longer time period, see Jack Walker, "The Diffusion of Innovations Among the American States," *American Political Science Review* 63 (1969): 880–899.
2. David E. Osborne, *Laboratories of Democracy* (Cambridge, MA: Harvard Business School Press, 1988); David Osborne and Peter Plastrik, *Banishing Bureaucracy*, reprint ed. (New York: Plume, 1998); George Beam, *Quality Public Management* (Chicago: Burnham, 2001).
3. Charles Press and Charles Adrian, "Why Our State Governments Are Sick," *Antioch Review* 24, no. 2 (1964): 154–165.
4. James Nathan Miller, "Our Horse-and-Buggy State Legislatures," *Reader's Digest* (May 1965): 49–54.
5. Roscoe C. Martin, *The Cities and the Federal System* (New York: Atherton Press, 1965), pp. 45–47.
6. Coleman Ransone, "Scholarly Revolt in Dullsville: New Approaches to the Study of State Government," *Public Administration Review* 26, no. 4 (December 1966): 343–352.

7. See David C. Nice, "Revitalizing the States: A Look at the Record," *National Civic Review* 72, no. 7 (July–August 1983): 371–376; Ann O'M. Bowman and Richard C. Kearney, *The Resurgence of the States* (Englewood Cliffs, NJ: Prentice-Hall, 1986); Carl E. Van Horn, *The State of the States* (Washington, DC: Congressional Quarterly Press, 1989).

8. Advisory Commission on Intergovernmental Relations, *In Brief: State and Local Roles in the Federal System* (Washington, DC: U.S. Government Printing Office, 1981), p. 3. Also see Advisory Commission on Intergovernmental Relations, *The Question of State Governmental Capability: An Authoritative Catalogue of State Action to Modernize State Governments in Recent Decades,* Report A-98 (Washington, DC: U.S. Government Printing Office, 1986).

9. David E. Osborne and Ted Gaebler, *Reinventing Government: How the Entrepreneurial Spirit Is Transforming the Public Sector* (Reading, MA: Addison-Wesley, 1992); David Osborne and Peter Plastrik *Banishing Bureaucracy* (New York: Plume, 1997).

10. For examples, see Michael Cooper, "Cities Face Tough Choices as U.S. Slashes Block Grants Program," *New York Times*, December 21, 2011 (electronic edition); Christine Vestal, "Medicaid: A Year of Excruciating Decisions," *Stateline*, January 11, 2012 (electronic edition); Brian Sigritz, "State Budgets in 2009 and 2010: In the Midst of Arguably the Worst Economic Downturn Since the Depression, States Experience Record Declines in Revenue and State Spending," in *Book of the States*, vol. 42 (Lexington, KY: Council of State Governments, 2010), pp. 381–385.

11. John Macdonald, *Calling a Halt to Mindless Change* (New York: American Management Association International, 1998).

12. Josh Goodman, "Do States Control Their Fiscal Destiny? Not as Much as They May Think," *Stateline*, May 23, 2011 (electronic edition).

13. See Jeffrey Cohen, ed., *Public Opinion in State Politics* (Stanford: Stanford University, 2006); Jeffrey Jones, "Ideology: Three Deep South States Are the Most Conservative," *State of the States*, Gallup Poll, February 3, 2010 (electronic edition); David Nice, *Policy Innovation in State Government* (Ames: Iowa State University Press,

1994), pp. 27–29, 50–62; Gerald Wright, Robert Erikson, and John McIver, "Public Opinion and Policy Liberalism in the American States," *American Journal of Political Science* 31 (1987): 980–1001.

14. Heather Knight, "UC Officials to Review Nonviolent Protest Policies," *SFGate*, November 21, 2011 (electronic edition).

15. Daniel J. Elazar, *American Federalism: A View From the States*, 2nd ed. (New York: Thomas Y. Crowell, 1972), chapter 4, especially pp. 100–101. For another discussion of American political thinking, see Philip Abbott, *Political Thought in America* (Itasca, IL: Peacock, 1991). For another, more recent assessment of state civic cultures and their impact, see Tom Rice and Alexander Sumberg, "Civic Culture and Government Performance in the American States," *Publius* 27, no. 1 (1977): 99–114.

16. This was recently found in a survey of Illinois residents. See Ellen B. Dran, Robert B. Albritton, and Mikel Wyckoff, "Surrogate Versus Direct Measures of Political Culture: Explaining Participation and Policy Attitude in Illinois," *Publius* 21, no. 2 (Spring 1991): 15–30. Numerous earlier studies also confirmed the higher participation rates of people in the moralistic culture. Ira Sharkansky, "The Utility of Elazar's Political Culture: A Research Note," *Polity* 2, no. 1 (Fall 1969): 66–83. This pattern of participation rates was also found in another study that was generally supportive of Elazar's theory on the geographic dispersion of the cultures. See Timothy D. Schlitz and R. Lee Rainey, "The Geographic Distribution of Elazar's Political Subcultures Among the Mass Population: A Research Note," *Western Political Quarterly* 31, no. 3 (September 1978): 410–415. In support of Elazar's theory, see Robert L. Savage, "Looking for Political Subcultures: A Critique of the Rummage-Sale Approach," *Western Political Quarterly* 34, no. 2 (June 1981): 331–336.

17. Eric B. Herzik, "The Legal-Formal Structuring of State Politics: A Cultural Explanation," *Western Political Quarterly* 38, no. 3 (September 1985): 413–423.

18. Sharkansky, "The Utility of Elazar's Political Culture."

19. David Young Miller, "The Impact of Political Culture on Patterns of State and Local Government

Expenditures," *Publius* 21, no. 2 (Spring 1991): 83–100.

20. Charles A. Johnson, "Political Culture in American States: Elazar's Formulation Examined," *American Journal of Political Science* 20, no. 3 (August 1976): 491–509.

21. John G. Peters and Susan Welch, "Politics, Corruption, and Political Culture: A View from the State Legislatures," *American Politics Quarterly* 6, no. 3 (July 1978): 345–356.

22. See Ibid; David C. Nice, "Political Corruption in the American States," *American Politics Quarterly* 11, no. 4 (October 1983): 507–517.

23. David Lowery and Lee J. Sigelman, "Political Culture and State Public Policy: The Missing Link," *Western Political Quarterly* 35, no. 3 (September 1982): 376–384.

24. For a pessimistic attempt to do this see Peter F. Nardulli, "Political Subcultures in the American States: An Empirical Examination of Elazar's Formulation," *American Politics Quarterly* 18, no. 3 (July 1990). For a survey of Illinois residents that was able to classify people into the types, see Dran, Albritton, and Wyckoff, "Surrogate Versus Direct Measures of Political Culture," pp. 15–30.

25. The southern states continue to be among the most conservative states, however. See Jones, "Ideology: Three."

26. One attempt to update Elazar's categorization through 1980 found several states that no longer fit Elazar's original classification. Only two states, for example, were able to be labeled moralistic, whereas Elazar had originally put nine states into that group. See David R. Morgan and Sheilah S. Watson, "Political Culture, Political System Characteristics, and Public Policies Among the American States," *Publius* 21, no. 2 (Spring 1991): 31–48. One study, for example, finds 10 versions of regional subcultures. See Joel Lieske, "Regional Subcultures of the United States," *The Journal of Politics* 55, no. 4 (November 1993): 888–913.

27. John White, *The Values Divide* (New York: Chatham House, 2003).

28. Matt Bai, "The Tea Party's Not-so-Civil War," *New York Times*, January 12, 2012 (electronic edition).

29. David Cole, *No Equal Justice* (New York: New Press, 1999).

30. Arthur M. Schlesinger, Jr. *The Disuniting of America* (New York: Norton, 1992).

The Constitutional Environment of State and Local Governments

CHAPTER PREVIEW

Chapter 2 outlines the constitutional environments within which state and local politics takes place. In this chapter, we will discuss:

1 The constitutional framework for state and community politics.

2 The criticisms of state constitutions and some of the responses to those criticisms.

3 The politics of constitutional reform.

4 The relevance of state constitutions to contemporary social conflict.

Introduction

In November of 2003, the Massachusetts Supreme Judicial Court ruled that gays and lesbians had the right to marry, according to the state's constitution. The decision provoked a storm of criticism, and a number of state officials and some interest groups began drafting proposals to overturn the court's ruling. Marcia Kadish and Tanya McCloskey feared that one or more of those proposals might be adopted at some point, but they also wanted to get married.

In May of 2004, they applied for a wedding license and sought a waiver of the customary three-day waiting period. As soon as they received the license, they married one another. At approximately the same time, a mayor in upstate New York and county board members in Oregon's most populous county also approved issuing wedding licenses to same-sex couples, as did local officials in San Francisco.

As Ms. Kadish and Ms. McCloskey had feared, opponents of same-sex marriages did not take long to mobilize. New York's attorney general declared that state law there did not permit same-sex marriage. Oregon's attorney general offered a middle-of-the-road decision: He said that gay marriage was not allowed under the state's marriage laws, but that the state law banning gay marriage possibly violated the state constitution. He asked local officials to stop issuing the licenses until the state supreme court ruled on the issue.[1]

In the aftermath of the Massachusetts court ruling, 15 states fairly quickly adopted constitutional amendments that, in effect, prohibited same-sex marriages. By 2010, the number had risen to 29. Hawaii adopted a constitutional amendment giving the state legislature the authority to limit marriage to opposite-sex couples. Conversely, the California Supreme Court struck down two state laws limiting marriage to couples of the opposite sex. The court ruled that the laws conflicted with a basic constitutional right to create a family.[2]

The controversy over same-sex marriage illustrates the way in which constitutional issues may become entangled with our everyday lives. What rights do you have if you are stopped by the police? How much must you pay in taxes? How much does the law protect you from discrimination? How readily can your state or community adapt to changing conditions? Your state constitution may make a significant difference in these and many other issues, although many other forces are also at work.

Whenever people want something done in state or local politics, they may decide to pursue their goals via the state constitution. That may be required in some instances—for example, if people are unhappy with a provision of the state constitution itself. However, even if an issue can be managed without changing the state constitution, some people may want a provision written into the state constitution, for reasons we will examine shortly. As a result, state and local politics is frequently entangled with constitutional politics. Consider a number of developments in recent years:

- California voters defeated a spending limitation measure supported by Governor Arnold Schwarzenegger; the proposed amendment would have given the governor additional powers to cut spending unilaterally. Voters later rejected several proposed constitutional amendments designed to help with the state's financial problems.
- Oregon defeated a proposal to raise taxes on tobacco products; the revenues produced would have helped finance health care for children who lack health insurance.
- A number of states considered proposals to allow gambling statewide or in some parts of the state.
- Voters in several states approved amendments limiting the government's authority to use eminent domain powers (which enable governments to force someone to sell a parcel of property) for economic development programs. Reformers are trying to promote adoption of similar proposals in several other states. [3]

This chapter provides a context for examining the role of state constitutions and judges in shaping state and local government operations. First, we will look at state constitutions, controversies regarding state constitutions, and the constitutional reform movement. Then, we will examine the growing importance of state constitutions in coping with our contemporary social conflicts.

STATE CONSTITUTIONS

A constitution establishes the structure of government and prescribes the fundamental rules of the game of politics. Constitutions may be unwritten (as in the case of Great Britain) or written (as in all 50 American states). Because the constitution outlines government structures and the basic rules of the political game, it is the **fundamental law** of a state and takes precedence over the **statutory laws,** that is, ordinary laws passed by the legislature or adopted by the voters. If the statutory laws contradict the constitution, judges may declare them unconstitutional and not enforce them in the courts. This feature of constitutional government is called **judicial review**. It is partly because of judicial review that judges today play a major role in many public policy decisions.

The notion that the constitutional law is superior to the statutory law is called the *higher law tradition of constitutionalism.*[4] Under this tradition, the constitution should be a brief charter that sets the framework of government and prescribes the basic civil liberties of the citizens. Those civil liberties may be based on enduring moral principles that people want to preserve, regardless of the momentary whims of the public. Because the constitution is seen as higher law, it is deliberately made difficult to amend. It is meant to "endure for ages to come," as the Supreme Court stated in one of its most famous decisions.[5] The U.S. Constitution has all these elements. It is brief, succinct, rather vague in many places (could anyone, for example, provide a universally acceptable definition of the phrase "due process of law"?), and difficult to amend. Congress is slow to initiate new amendments to that document, even when powerful public pressures clamor for amendment. In the early 1990s, there was strong public support for a proposed constitutional amendment that would overturn a recent Supreme Court ruling that had protected burning of the American flag as a form of free speech. Speaking against the proposed amendment, Senator David Durenburger (R, MN) gave a classic higher law argument: when he claimed that the Constitution contains principles that should and must endure far into the future. If a problem can be managed by ordinary legislative action or administrative discretion, those options are preferable to constitutional change.

CRITICISMS OF STATE CONSTITUTIONS

In contrast to this higher law tradition, many state constitutions historically followed a different tradition, a **positive law** tradition of constitutionalism. Under the positive law approach, the state constitution may appropriately contain policy provisions that the higher law tradition would provide for by statute rather than by constitutional provision. The practical consequences of these two traditions are illustrated in Table 2.1, which compares the federal

TABLE 2.1

Differences Between the Federal and State Constitutions

	Federal	The Average State Constitution
Length	About 8,700 words	About 24,300 words
Frequency of Amendments	Seldom. Only 16 amendments since 1800.	Frequent. The average state passes at least one amendment every two years.
Focus	Broad focus on setting fundamental law, with emphasis on the structure of government, the powers of government, and citizens' rights.	Narrow focus on details that might be better left to ordinary statutory law.
Legal Theory	The federal government possesses only those powers specified in the Constitution.	The state governments possess any powers that are not specifically prohibited.
Supremacy	The Constitution is the supreme law of the land.	State constitutions are subordinate to the federal Constitution and to federal law, but are superior to ordinary state laws.

Sources: Book of the States, vol. 37 (Lexington, KY: Council of State Governments, 2005), p. 10; Malcolm Feeley, and Samuel Krislov, *Constitutional Law*, 2nd ed. (Glenview, IL: Scott, Foresman/Little, Brown, 1990); Thomas Marks and John Cooper, *State Constitutional Law in a Nutshell* (St. Paul, MN: West, 1988).

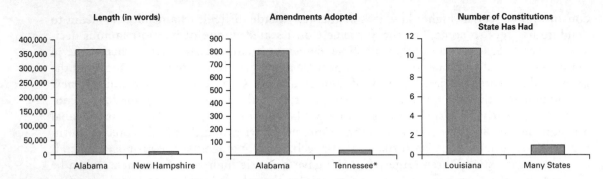

FIGURE 2.1
Highs and Lows in State Constitutions

Source: The Book of the States, vol. 42 (Lexington, KY: Council of State Governments, 2010), p. 11.

*A few current state constitutions have been amended fewer times than Tennessee's, but those constitutions have been adopted comparatively recently. The number of amendments to the current (relatively recent) constitutions excludes amendments to earlier constitutions.

and state constitutions. The federal Constitution is concise (although unclear at times), and it focuses on prescribing the fundamental law. In contrast, many state constitutions are long and contain numerous policy provisions. The state constitutions have been criticized as being archaic documents reflecting the biases of 100 or more years ago. For example, for many years Alabama's constitution contained a ban on interracial marriages.[6] Many state constitutions contained language indicating that public officials and other people serving in government were to be men, although much of that language has been changed in recent years. In addition, reformers charged that many state constitutions place too many restrictions on state legislatures, create fragmented executive branches and inefficient court systems, and hamper the operations of local governments.[7]

As we discuss state constitutions, bear in mind that they are far from identical to one another. As Figure 2.1 indicates, state constitutions range from relatively brief to considerably lengthy. The amount of constitutional change has also varied from state to state, with some states having considered and/or adopted several hundred amendments while other states have only considered a few dozen. Moreover, some states have had six or more different constitutions over the years, while others have largely stayed with the original document (with some amendments).

Too Long and Too Detailed

Although the U.S. Constitution has only about 8,700 words, the average state constitution has about 27,000. Alabama's is the longest with about 360,000 words. Such an impressive length, combined with complex legal language, makes the document very difficult for the average person to understand. The longer constitutions also include numerous public policy provisions, or **super legislation**, as it has been sometimes called.[8] Super legislation refers to provisions in a constitution that many reformers think should be left to statutory law. For example, constitutions in several states contain so-called right-to-work provisions that inhibit labor unions from building their memberships. Conversely, some state constitutions try to guarantee that workers should have the right to unionize if they wish.[9] A number of state constitutions contain provisions establishing environmental rights, such as the right to a clean environment. Many state constitutions include guidelines for state or local revenue systems and for government borrowing. Many state constitutions have contained provisions regarding gambling; for many years, many of the provisions prohibited gambling, but in recent years, the trend has been allowing at least some types of gambling. Because these provisions are written into the constitution itself, they become super legislation that is more difficult to adapt to changing times and changing public opinion than is statutory legislation.[10]

Another example of complications produced by constitutional detail developed recently in Mississippi. As Governor Haley Barbour came to the end of his term, he pardoned 215 criminals (most of whom were already out of prison, having served their sentences). However, the Mississippi constitution provides that pardons must be announced in newspapers where the offenders were convicted and were in custody for 30 days. Some of the offenders receiving the pardons may not have met that requirement, although some of them may have fallen short by only a few days. As a result, the legal status of some of the pardons has come into question, and the state courts will have to sort out which pardons were given correctly and which were not. Some pardoned inmates had to remain in custody until the legal questions were sorted out, and most of the pardon recipients may face months of uncertainty.[11] The situation in Mississippi demonstrates that constitutional details may affect people's lives and produce legal disputes regarding whether an action conforms to the various constitutional provisions.

Because of these considerations, many reformers advocate shorter constitutions that deal only with the fundamental structures and powers of government, although many people in some states obviously disagree. States with the weakest political parties tend to be the states with the longest constitutions.[12] When political parties are weak, it is easier for specific interests to get favorable provisions written into constitutions. Defenders of the positive law tradition contend that important policies may need and deserve constitutional protection. If weak political parties increase the risk of unpredictable behavior by public officials, or if people fear the power of interest groups or the incompetence or dishonesty of public officials, protecting important policies in the constitution may seem particularly attractive.

Legislative Restrictions

Many constitutions put such rigid restrictions on the state legislatures that those bodies find it difficult to establish state policies. Some of the most significant restrictions are the ones on the financial powers of the legislatures. Most constitutions limit the amount of debt the state may incur. Many state constitutions prohibit some revenue-raising options (such as having an income tax), and many limit the use of one or more revenue sources. Most state constitutions also limit or prohibit state aid to private schools; many of those provisions date to the late 1800s, but they have helped discourage some twenty-first century education reforms.[13] Changing those provisions requires a constitutional amendment, although officials in a number of states have developed methods for circumventing the limits. State constitutions often exempt some property (such as church-owned property) or business transactions from taxation. The legislatures cannot change those policies without a constitutional amendment.[14] Not surprisingly, many proposed constitutional changes in recent years have involved taxation and finance,[15] though a considerable number of those proposals have emphasized more restrictions rather than more flexibility.

The Earmarking Controversy

Not only do most constitutions limit the state's debt and restrict the legislature's ability to raise taxes, but they also earmark certain revenues (those raised from specific taxes or fees) to be spent only in specific **dedicated funds** (funds set aside for specific activities). One of the most important **earmarked revenues** is the state gasoline tax, which is typically earmarked for road and highway programs. This fund can be spent only for road and highway maintenance or construction, either at the state or local level. The revenues from fishing and hunting licenses are often earmarked for conservation and natural resources programs, and several states earmark lottery revenues for education.[16]

Why earmark funds? Because, say its advocates, legislatures cannot be trusted to keep their commitments. Legislators serve at the will of the people and can easily turn their backs on important programs if public opinion shifts in another direction, powerful interest groups complain, or a large number of new legislators are elected. It can be very difficult for a public body to keep a sustained, decades-long commitment to a project if it has to rely on annual appropriations. It is unlikely, for example, that the Interstate Highway System, which took 40 years to build and was built almost solely with earmarked federal and state motor-fuel taxes, would be as extensive as it is today if it had had to rely entirely upon annual appropriations from general revenues in competition with many other programs.

However, some critics complain that earmarking sometimes fails to produce its expected results.[17] Earmarking revenues for a program does not guarantee higher funding in future years. Knowing that the earmarked revenues were guaranteed, future legislatures might shift some of the nonearmarked revenues (which they had previously used to support a program) to some other purpose. In fact, this has been a common practice with lottery revenues. Several states in the 1980s and 1990s persuaded their residents to pass constitutional amendments adopting lotteries, on the promise that the lottery revenues would be earmarked for public education. However, it is not clear that those lotteries have consistently expanded total education funding.

Moreover, earmarked revenues may fail to keep pace with rising program costs. When oil prices surged in 2008, many families cut back on driving, which reduced motor-fuel tax revenues. At the same time, higher petroleum prices increased the cost of asphalt paving materials. The combination left many state and local road programs in difficult financial shape and contributed to a growing backlog of road and highway maintenance and improvements.

Earmarked revenues and dedicated funds also inhibit the legislature's ability to alter policy priorities when conditions change. Since the constitutionally earmarked revenues roll into the dedicated fund perpetually (unless the constitution is amended), the legislature cannot readily do its job of providing a forum for debate on whether the program ought to be reduced in scope or altered significantly.

This, of course, was exactly the case with the Interstate Highway System. Started in 1956, the bulk of the system was completed by the mid-1970s, with the uncompleted remainder being predominantly the urban portions. Building those portions sometimes obliterated entire neighborhoods, and small businesses displaced by the construction often failed because their neighborhood customer base no longer existed. Public transit systems deteriorated in virtually every city in the country, and critics charged that the new freeways were speeding up the decline of the central cities.

Despite these major issues, it was largely pointless for most state legislatures to debate whether or not it might be good public policy to alter the original 1956 Interstate Highway plans in order to create a transportation system less heavily dependent on freeways, automobiles, and imported oil. This debate was largely pointless because 90 percent of the money came from the earmarked federal gasoline tax and only 10 percent from state funds; this was a deal too good for most legislators to pass up. If you had been a suburban legislator in 1970, you might have been able to talk your constituents into scaling back freeway construction if they were going to have to provide the funds for it themselves and if you had a proposal for a better and less costly method of easing their traffic congestion problems. But it would have been impossible to convince them of that when 90 percent of the costs were going to be paid by motorists all over the country, and when your constituents themselves would lose this gift from the rest of the country if the funds were not spent on new freeway construction.

Too much earmarked revenue and too many dedicated funds can prevent the legislature from carrying out its major role of establishing and periodically updating the state's policy priorities. Although there has been a general decline in reliance on earmarking over the past few decades, the average legislature still lacks control over a fifth of its budget because of earmarked funds.[18] Note, however, that citizens who lack confidence in the legislature may *prefer* limits on its power and influence. As we will see in Chapter 8, that lack of trust may have other consequences for legislatures as well. People may also prefer a predictable flow of funds to programs they support rather than flexibility that may jeopardize future funding.

Fragmented Executive Branches

Most state constitutions provide numerous independent administrative agencies and departments that are not directly accountable to the governor. The typical state constitution also provides for several independently elected state officials. Consequently, the executive power is fragmented into a number of different offices, making it harder for the governor to provide strong leadership. Some political reformers prefer that the state executive branch be modeled after the business corporation. In the corporation, all administrative units are ultimately accountable to a chief executive, who in turn, answers to a policy-making board of directors. By analogy, the governmental reformers view the governor as the corporate chief executive and the legislature as the policy-making board of directors. Reformers want state executive power to be integrated and accountable to a limited number of policy makers.

The reformers have made some progress in unifying the executive branch in many states. The number of elected state executives has gradually declined, but many states still elect attorneys general, treasurers, and secretaries of state. In some states we also find executives, whether independently elected or appointed by boards, heading departments with such major responsibilities as education, agriculture, and insurance regulation.

Critics of the reformers' ideal of a more integrated executive branch worry that placing too much power in the hands of the governor may lead to abuses—a concern that may have been reinforced by the wave of corporate scandals in recent years. An independently elected attorney general may be a much better watchdog over the governor's office than an attorney general appointed by the governor. In addition, independently elected executives give citizens more access points. If the governor ignores your ideas, an independent education officer may be willing to listen.

Inefficient Court Systems

Traditionally, the typical state and local court system was not tightly integrated. Rather, it comprised dozens of courts that were relatively independent of each other. No one body ensured the enforcement of high judicial standards. The procedures by which cases were given to one court rather than another were sometimes unclear and confusing and sometimes subject to manipulation. In civil cases, when one person sues another, conflict or confusion over which court had jurisdiction sometimes delayed the case. In criminal cases, when a person was tried for breaking the law, the fragmented court systems were not tied into the correctional system; law enforcement, adjudication, and corrections were not integrated. This compounded the already difficult task of creating a corrections system that actually corrected the antisocial behavior of criminals.

Although state and local court systems in a number of states have been reformed over the years, the criminal justice system as a whole remains rather loosely jointed. Many important officials in the system, including judges, prosecutors, and sheriffs, are elected by the voters and may have very different views regarding criminal justice policies. A state may adopt tough new criminal sentencing standards without increasing the capacity of the prison system. With more than two million Americans in prison or in jail (the largest prison/jail population of any country in the world), and with five million more on probation or parole,[19] poor coordination among different parts of the criminal justice system can produce overcrowded prisons and jails (a potentially dangerous situation), prisoners that must be shipped to other parts of the country, and financial pressures to release prisoners early.

Bear in mind that state constitutions are not the only reasons why different parts of the criminal justice system are not always very well coordinated. Citizens and elected officials may favor severe punishment for lawbreakers without being willing to pay for secure prisons and jails.

Hamstrung Local Governments

Most constitutions restrict how much debt local governments can incur and also limit local authority to raise revenues. Those limitations, in turn, may undercut local governments' ability to provide public services efficiently. Many state constitutions prescribe the forms of government allowed for localities, making it impossible for residents to choose the type of local government they want. Traditionally, local governments were legally creatures of the states and possessed only those powers that the state constitutions and legislatures permitted them to have.

Many reformers advocate giving local governments more financial flexibility, giving local officials enough authority to meet their responsibilities, and giving local residents a form of home rule that would allow them to choose the type of local government they want and expand or restrict its legal powers as they think best. As we will see later in the chapter, the reformers have made some progress over the years, but the results have not always been as dramatic as they had hoped. In addition, many states have adopted new restrictions on local governments' financial powers in the last 35 years.

THE MODEL STATE CONSTITUTION

A number of reformers have recommended the systematic overhauling of the worst state constitutions. These proposals come from various places—the National Municipal League, the Council of State Governments, public administration specialists, and citizen groups such as the League of Women Voters. The ideal sought by these reformers is a constitution similar to the **model state constitution** drafted by the National Municipal League.[20] The model constitution is short; it stems from the higher law tradition of constitutionalism rather than the positive law tradition. It deals in fundamental principles of government instead of specific legislative details. It provides a bill of rights to protect the civil liberties of its citizens. Rather than a large number of elected executive offices, it permits only the governor and lieutenant governor to be elected, with the other major state executives being appointed by the governor. The legislature is granted considerable authority and flexibility as the chief policy-making and taxing body in the state. In short, as Figure 2.2 shows, the model state constitution is quite different from many state constitutions, which are subject to the five criticisms just outlined.

Traditional Constitution's Organization

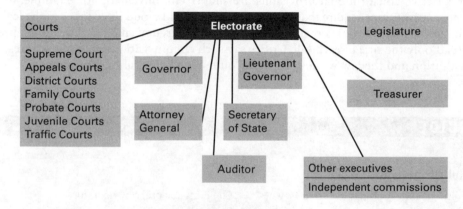

Model State Constitution's Organization

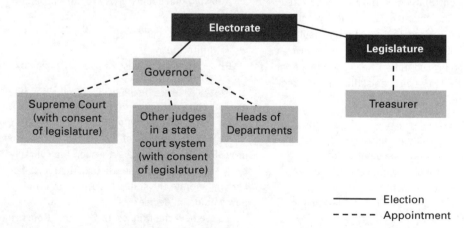

FIGURE 2.2

The Model State Constitution

In contrast to the traditional constitution's large number of elected offices and the fragmentation of authority, the model state constitution concentrates responsibility in the governor and legislature.

Source: Adapted from *Model State Constitution,* 6th ed. (New York: National Municipal League, 1963).

THE POLITICS OF CONSTITUTIONAL CHANGE AND REFORM

In later chapters, we will see that constitutional reform has not always improved governments as much as expected. For now, it is sufficient simply to understand the reformist critique of state constitutions: Unreformed constitutions create an inefficient, anachronistic governmental structure that is unable to respond effectively to changing conditions. Reformers urge that the constitutions be changed. Practical politicians attempt to get around the more cumbersome constitutional restrictions in several ways.

Circumvention and Interpretation

Many restrictive constitutional provisions are simply circumvented. For example, although some state constitutions require that a proposed law be read aloud three times in the legislature before it can be approved, this requirement is regularly circumvented by having the presiding officer read only the title of each bill. Critics say such circumvention encourages disrespect for the constitution and the law without changing outmoded constitutional provisions.

▶ **YOU DECIDE**

Constitutional Circumvention

A common criticism of state legislatures is that they frequently lump many unrelated items together in one law. This enables legislative leaders to write into law some pet provisions that would most likely be voted down if voted on individually. To curb this practice in Minnesota, the Minnesota Constitution stipulates that "No law shall embrace more than one subject, which shall be embraced in its title." The title of one law passed by the Minnesota legislature in 1982 embraced the following:

    Collection of taxes
    Distribution of campaign funds
    Interest rate limits on municipal bonds
    Provisions to withhold income tax refunds
      from child support debtors
    Requiring the registration of rental housing in
      Minneapolis
    Provisions for residential energy credits
    Sale of unstamped cigarettes to members
      of Indian tribes
    Lease and sale of equipment by local governments

    Eligibility for property tax refunds
    Restrictions on tax increment financing
    Issuance of bonds to promote tourism
    Allowing one county a levy for fire protection
      purposes
    Allowing another county to exceed its levy
      limitation
    Providing for the lease of hydroelectric power

In your view, is the inclusion of all these topics in one law consistent with the constitutional provision that a law embrace no more than one subject? Or is this a circumvention of the quoted constitutional provision? If you were a state supreme court justice being asked to determine whether the topics listed here did violate the state constitutional provision, how would you decide?

To see how the Minnesota Supreme Court ruled, see the Highlight box on page 32. ◼

Source: Minnesota Laws, 1982, ch. 523, An Act Relating to the Financing of Government in This State.

The most common way of adjusting rigid constitutional language to the needs of the times is by filing lawsuits that encourage the courts to interpret the constitution. People may also try to put new judges and attorneys general in office. Judicial and attorney general interpretation does not change the wording of the constitution, but it changes the way in which the constitution is applied. Kentucky's constitution, for example, limits state salaries to $12,000 per year. This may have been a reasonable sum in 1949 when it was last changed by constitutional amendment, but it is quite unreasonable today. Kentucky courts got around this limit, however, by a so-called rubber dollar ruling that permitted the dollar limit to be adjusted for inflation.[21]

Interpretation issues also arise when different provisions in the state constitution conflict with one another. In a recent case in Nevada, the state supreme court had to decide whether a constitutional requirement that tax increases be approved by a two-thirds majority of the legislature conflicted with a provision mandating funding for education. The court ruled that the education provision overrode the two-thirds majority requirement, at least for the 2003 legislative session.[22]

Amendment

Amending a constitution is a two-step process requiring initiation first and then ratification. The most common procedure for initiation is for both houses of the legislature to pass the amendment (some states require a three-fifths or a two-thirds majority, while others require only a simple majority). Eighteen states permit citizens to put a constitutional amendment directly on the ballot if they can gather enough signatures on a petition (Illinois' initiative mechanism is limited to the article on the state legislature). Most of the constitutional initiative states are in the West, Midwest, or South.

Ratification usually requires a majority of all those people voting on the amendment. But some states make amendments difficult to pass by requiring the approval of two sessions of the legislature in order to initiate the amendment, limiting the number of amendments that may be put on the ballot in any election, or requiring more than a simple majority vote for initiation or ratification.

During the period from 2000 to 2009, constitutional amendments that were proposed by the state legislatures were considerably more likely to win ratification than were amendments proposed through the initiative process. The differences are sometimes striking: For 2006–2007, amendments from legislatures were ratified 87 percent of the time, but only 33 percent of the citizen-initiated amendments were ratified.[23] What might account for the difference? One possible reason is that members of the legislature are reluctant to propose amendments that are not very popular. Proposing amendments that are defeated by the voters might suggest that legislators are out of step with public sentiments. In addition, proposal by initiative allows a small fraction of the citizenry to propose amendments. That small fraction may be out of step with most voters at times.

Some evidence indicates that constitutional amendments are sometimes scheduled for voter approval (or disapproval) based on the election calendar. Voters in 11 states approved constitutional amendments prohibiting same-sex marriage in the November 2004 election, and some strategists believe that the presence of those proposals on the ballots helped to boost turnout by conservative Republicans. Groups in a number of states tried to use the same tactic to affect turnout in the 2008 elections.[24]

Constitutional Conventions

Constitutions can also be completely rewritten by **constitutional conventions**. Unlike the federal Constitution, which has never been rewritten (unless we consider the change from the Articles of Confederation to the Constitution), the 50 state constitutions have been rewritten 97 times since independence in 1776. Louisiana has had 11 different constitutions, and Georgia is close behind with 10. Bear in mind that a "new" constitution may include many provisions that are identical or similar to the previous document, but a new constitution may include a considerable number of new provisions. The great bulk of constitutional rewritings took place in three relatively short periods, periods of great national turbulence. Following the Declaration of Independence in 1776 and the Revolutionary War, 10 constitutions were revised. The second turbulent period was the one immediately preceding and following the Civil War, when 52 constitutional revisions occurred. And the third period took place from the 1960s to the early 1980s, when 11 constitutions were rewritten. This recent flurry of constitutional revision seems to have come to an end, and even the number of ordinary constitutional amendments has dropped off since the 1970s.[25] However, amendment proposals and adoptions on financial matters continue to be relatively common.[26]

The process of rewriting a constitution requires several steps, which in turn take several years to carry out. First, a constitutional convention must be called. In some states, the legislature can call the convention whenever its members desire.

In most states, however, the legislature must vote to have a referendum on the question of whether a convention should be held. The referendum requirement takes additional time. If the legislature approved the referendum in 2000, for example, the second step would be to put the question of a constitutional convention on the general election ballot for voter approval in 2000 or 2001. The third step would be for the legislature in its 2002 session to provide for holding the convention and electing the delegates. The fourth step would be the elections and convention. These would take place in 2002 and 2003. The fifth and most crucial step would be ratification by the voters at the 2003 general election. If approved, the new constitution would take effect in 2004. Thus, the very shortest period of time it would take to substantially rewrite the constitution would be four years. Because it is difficult and time-consuming to establish a constitutional convention, 14 states require that a call for a convention be put on the ballot periodically. Illinois, for example, requires that this question be put before the voters every 20 years. Hawaii requires it every nine years.

Constitutional conventions in the modern era have generally been nonpartisan. The delegates are usually elected on ballots that do not identify their party affiliation (although

---

◤ HIGHLIGHT

Constitutional Circumvention: Ruling

In 1986, the Minnesota Supreme Court struck down as unconstitutional a law, similar to the one on page 30, that embraced many different subjects. ■

some of the delegates normally have party affiliations); and once the convention starts, the delegates tend to perceive themselves as "idealistic statesmen" concerned about the good of the state as a whole rather than as representatives of a political party.[27] Delegates are now more likely than in the past to accept the higher law rather than the positive law tradition of constitutionalism.[28]

Also, conventions today usually are limited to making proposals on specified constitutional provisions only. Although an unlimited convention can do a more thorough job of overhauling the constitution, the more radically the constitution is revised, the less likely it is to be approved by the voters.[29] Because of this, constitutional reformers tend to prefer more limited reforms that have a better chance of being adopted. Slightly more than half of the constitutional conventions since 1960 have been limited in scope.

One of the most successful unlimited constitutional conventions in recent years was Hawaii's, held in 1978. It put curbs on state expenditures, provided for open meetings of the state legislature, created an intermediate appellate court, added a privacy provision to the state bill of rights, and replaced all male gender words with words having no reference to gender. One of the most noteworthy features of Hawaii's new constitution is the way in which its provisions were approved by the voters. Incorporated into 34 proposals were 116 changes so that the voters could vote separately on each proposal. Submitted to the voters in 1980, all 34 proposals passed.[30]

The ease of getting Hawaii's new constitution adopted by the voters, however, was extraordinary. In recent years, North Dakota, Arkansas, Maryland, New Mexico, and New York have all held extensive constitutional conventions only to have the proposed constitution rejected by the voters.

Constitutional Revision Commissions

Another approach to broad constitutional change is the **constitutional revision commission**. The commission may be either a preparatory commission or a study commission. The study commission meets, studies the constitutional problems, and proposes a number of changes to the legislature. Utah has found such commissions to be so useful that in 1977 it created a permanent Constitutional Revision Commission to propose changes on a regular basis. In contrast to the study commission, which reports to the legislature, the constitutional preparatory commission actually conducts the background work for a constitutional convention. Since the convention meets for a very limited period, it needs as much prior preparation as possible. New Hampshire created a constitutional study commission in 1983 that held public hearings in different locations throughout the state to consider proposals for change. With this groundwork laid, a limited constitutional convention was held the following year. It put 10 proposed changes before the voters, six of which were accepted.[31]

Although constitutional study commissions have become very useful and popular, they are not without their drawbacks. One drawback lies in the fact that many state constitutions prohibit amendments dealing with more than one specific subject. Thus, for example, it becomes constitutionally impossible to use a single amendment to reorganize the entire executive branch. One proposal to remedy this has been the **gateway amendment**, which changes the constitution so that subsequent amendments can cover more than one subject and can pass with a smaller majority.

CONSTITUTIONAL REFORM AND SOCIAL CHANGE

As we saw at the beginning of this chapter, our state constitutions are deeply enmeshed in the nation's various social conflicts. Throughout most of the twentieth century, state constitutional law took a backseat to federal constitutional law in dealing with dramatic social change. Nowhere was this more true than in the example of the civil rights movement of the 1950s and 1960s, which successfully broke the system of government-supported racial segregation in the South and in some other parts of the country. Civil rights advocates had no success challenging segregation under state law because the constitutions of the southern states permitted segregation. Consequently, civil rights advocates used the federal courts to charge that segregation practices violated several provisions of the U.S. Constitution, especially the Equal Protection Clause, the Due Process Clause, and the Commerce Clause. In this way, they were fully in keeping with the higher law tradition of constitutionalism. As a result of this history, we grew accustomed to thinking of the federal constitution and the federal courts as more progressive than state constitutions and state courts when dealing with issues of social change.

Expanding State Bills of Rights

Today, however, this perception is no longer accurate. Two developments in particular are putting state constitutional law in the forefront of issues dealing with contemporary social conflict. First, because of widespread constitutional reform, most states have reduced the most glaring constitutional weaknesses identified earlier. With the issue of legal segregation settled and constitutional reformers increasingly adopting the higher law tradition of constitutionalism, states began expanding their bills of rights to include many provisions not found in the federal Constitution. Some of this is summarized in Table 2.2, which outlines selected provisions from bills of rights in a number of states.

We can make several observations about Table 2.2. First, the provisions relating to environmental rights, economic rights, and natural rights have no parallel in the federal Constitution. The natural rights provisions from Montana and New Hampshire are particularly noteworthy. The New Hampshire provision is so grounded in the philosophy of natural law and natural rights that it reads almost as though it came directly out of Thomas Hobbes's *Leviathan*. In the U.S. Constitution, the only allusion to natural rights does not come until the Ninth Amendment, which admits that people may have rights in addition to those specifically mentioned in the Constitution.

Although some of the bill of rights provisions in Table 2.2 lean in a liberal direction, it is obvious that not all of them do. This is especially true of Florida's prohibiting public employees from striking and Idaho's prohibition on the licensing and registration of firearms. A number of other state constitutional provisions also lean in a conservative direction; tax limitations and limits on borrowing are often dear to conservative hearts.

Some of the provisions, especially the bans on interracial marriage in Alabama (recently repealed) and South Carolina, are clearly unenforceable because they violate the federal Constitution. Some others, such as the environmental rights in Massachusetts, the private property right in Louisiana, and the human labor right in New York, are so vague that it is hard to envision how they would be enforced. In sum, however, the overall impact of state bills of rights today is to expand the notion of rights and liberties far beyond what the federal Constitution guarantees. Note, however, that a state constitutional provision that protects a

TABLE 2.2

State Bill of Rights Provisions Not Found in the Federal Constitution

Environmental Rights Provisions

Massachusetts	People shall have the right to clean air and water and freedom from excessive noise.
Hawaii	All public natural resources are held in trust by the state for the benefit of the people.
Virginia	The state's natural oyster beds shall not be leased, rented, or sold, but shall be held in trust for the benefit of the people.
California	People shall have the right to fish upon and from public lands and waters.
Washington	State's waters shall be deemed a public use.

Economic Rights Provisions

Hawaii	Public employees may organize for collective bargaining.
Florida	Public employees may not strike.
New York	Workers on public works projects shall be paid no less than the prevailing wage of the locality.
Louisiana	People have the right to own and enjoy private property.
New York	Human labor is not a commodity or an article of commerce.

Natural Rights Provisions

Montana	Human dignity is inviolable.
New Hampshire	Upon entering society, people surrender some natural rights in order to ensure the protection of society.

Provisions Related to Racial and Cultural Relations

N. Carolina	Secret political societies shall not be tolerated.
S. Carolina	Prohibits marriages between whites and blacks.
Alaska	Public schooling shall always be conducted in English.
Colorado	The assignment or transportation of a pupil to a public school for purposes of achieving racial balance is prohibited.
Several states	Marriage of same-sex couples is prohibited.

Criminal Justice Provisions

Michigan	The death penalty is prohibited.
Georgia	Whipping as a punishment for crime is prohibited.

Other Provisions

Arizona	No child under age 14 years old shall be employed during public school hours.
N. Carolina	Atheists are guaranteed the right to hold public office.
Tennessee	Persons may not be forced to perform any service to the public on their religion's day of rest.
Idaho	The registration or licensing of firearms is prohibited.

Sources: Mark L. Glasser and John Kincaid, "Selected Rights Enumerated in State Constitutions," *Intergovernmental Perspective* 17, no. 4 (Fall 1991): 35–44; *Time Almanac 2005* (Needham, MA: Information Please, 2004), p. 371.

right in one state will make little difference in other states lacking that provision.[32] If one state recognizes the right of same-sex couples to marry, constitutional provisions in other states may prohibit the practice.

Trends in Constitutional Interpretation

A second development relating state constitutions to contemporary social change comes from changing trends in how judges interpret constitutions. We saw that a key component in the success of the civil rights movement of the 1950s and 1960s was the willingness of liberal federal judges to make progressive interpretations of the U.S. Constitution. In recent years, however, federal judges have become less liberal. Republicans will have controlled the presidency for 28 of the most recent 43 years (through 2011); and they appointed a large number of conservative judges to the federal courts. As the federal courts slowly became less venturesome in tackling difficult social issues, state courts became more so.[33] This is especially the case regarding issues of civil liberties. Four states, for example, include a right to privacy in their bills of rights.[34] A number of state courts have taken up the slack as the U.S. Supreme Court has backed off from the civil libertarian posture it advanced during the 1960s and 1970s. Constitutional law in California and Oregon now provides much more expansive protection of freedom of speech than does federal constitutional law. New York and some other states now have more expansive protections of defendants' rights in some areas.[35] Eighteen states have broader protections against sex discrimination than does the federal Constitution.[36]

In sum, the general principle evolving is that state courts may not set lower standards for human rights than those established under U.S. constitutional law, but they may set higher standards if they choose. We can expect to see state constitutional interpretations also continue to touch on social conflict issues such as those discussed in this chapter—affirmative action, education policies, same-sex marriages, crime, and others. All of these developments will be encouraged by recent federal court rulings granting more flexibility to the states on some issues.

LOCAL "CONSTITUTIONS"

Constitutions provide a structure of government and some delineation of its powers for the national government and the states. The national government can propose amendments to its federal Constitution, subject to state ratification, and the states can propose amendments to their constitutions, usually subject to voter approval. At the local level, the situation is more complex. For city governments and some counties, the local equivalent of a constitution is the charter. For much of our history, a local government with a charter did not have the power to change it. Under home rule, cities and some counties do have the power to revise their charters, usually with voter approval and often subject to various limitations by the state. Without home rule, charter revisions must normally be adopted by the state legislature.

Other local governments, such as school districts and many counties, usually do not have charters. Instead, their structure of government and powers are defined by state laws, either ordinary statutes or the state constitution. Adopting changes will, therefore, require action at the state level. We will explore the local situation in more detail in Chapter 7.

SUMMARY

1. Under the higher law tradition of constitutionalism, a constitution is viewed as fundamental law that takes precedence over statutory laws. Under the positive law tradition, the constitution may appropriately include public policy provisions if people think they are particularly important.
2. The state constitutions have been heavily criticized for five weaknesses: they are too long and too detailed; they place too many restrictions on state legislatures; they create ineffective, fragmented executive branches; they create outmoded, ineffective court systems; and they hamstring local governments.
3. The National Municipal League has drafted a model state constitution that it encourages the states to adopt. It follows the higher law tradition.
4. Many detailed constitutional provisions are evaded or modified through circumvention or judicial interpretation. In some cases, however, constitutional amendments may be needed to change individual provisions.
5. The two major strategies for more broadly overhauling state constitutions are constitutional conventions and constitutional revision commissions. Although a fifth of the states have rewritten their constitutions since 1965, many constitutional conventions are not successful in getting their new constitutions adopted by the voters. Limited conventions have been more successful at getting their constitutions adopted than have unlimited conventions.
6. Both bills of rights of state constitutions and judicial interpretations of state constitutions are becoming increasingly important in the struggles over the nation's contemporary social conflicts.

STUDY QUESTIONS

1. Why are most state constitutions longer than the federal Constitution? What flaws do critics see in many state constitutions? Do you agree with the critics?
2. How can a state constitution be changed? What are the advantages and disadvantages of each approach to changing the state constitution?
3. Why have state constitutions become more important in addressing important social conflicts and protecting people's rights?

KEY TERMS

Constitutional convention A convention that drafts a new constitution and proposes it to voters for ratification.

Constitutional revision commission A commission appointed by the legislature to study the constitution and make recommendations for change. The revision commission may be either a study commission (which presents its results to the legislature) or a preparatory commission (which presents its results to the constitutional convention).

Dedicated funds A portion of a budget set aside for a specific purpose, such as education. Those funds cannot be spent for anything else.

Earmarked revenues Revenues raised from specific sources (such as gasoline taxes) that can only be spent for related purposes (such as roads and highways).

Fundamental law The law of a constitution, with particular emphasis on the structure of government, what officials it will have, and how they will be chosen. Fundamental law also usually includes an outline of the most important rights that people have.

Gateway amendment A constitutional amendment that makes it easier to pass future constitutional amendments.

Judicial review The power of courts to evaluate the constitutionality of acts of other members of government, including the governor, state legislators, local officials, state administrators, and lower courts.

Model state constitution A proposal for constitutions advanced by the National Municipal League that would concentrate authority in the governor and legislature and would reduce the number of

elected executives. It would also contain relatively few public policy provisions.

Statutory law A law enacted by a legislature (in contrast to constitutional law).

Super legislation Detailed public policy provisions of a constitution that should, according to the higher law tradition, more properly be a part of ordinary statutory law.

THE INTERNET CONNECTION

State attorneys general play critical roles in interpreting their state constitutions and in enforcing their provisions (along with numerous other duties). You can contact the National Association of Attorneys General at

www.naag.org. For more information on state constitutions, see the Center for State Constitutional Studies at Rutgers University. You can find it at **www-camlaw .rutgers.edu/statecon**.

NOTES

1. See Theo Emery, "Same-sex Couples Begin Marrying in Massachusetts," *Moscow-Pullman Daily News*, May 17, 2004, p. 5A; Tomas Tizon, "Oregon County to Keep Marrying Gay Couples," *Moscow-Pullman Daily News*, March 16, 2004.

2. John Dinan, "State Constitutional Developments in 2005," in Keon Chi, ed., *The Book of the States,* vol. 38 (Lexington, KY: Council of State Government, 2006), pp. 3, 6; John Dinan, "State Constitutional Developments in 2009," *The Book of the States,* vol. 42 (Lexington, KY: Council of State Governments, 2010), p. 4; Adam Liptak, "California Supreme Court Overturns Gay Marriage Ban," *New York Times*, May 16, 2008 (electronic edition).

3. Janice May, "State Constitutions and Constitutional Revision, 2000–2001," *The Book of the States* 34 (2002), pp. 3–11; Dinan, "State Constitutional Developments in 2005," pp. 3–16; John Dinan, "State Constitutional Developments in 2007," *The Book of the States*, vol. 40 (2008), pp. 3–9; Dinan, "State Constitutional Developments in 2009," pp. 4–9.

4. John J. Carroll and Arthur English, "Traditions of State Constitution Making," *State and Local Government Review* 23, no. 3 (Fall 1991): 103–108.

5. *McCulloch v. Maryland* 4 L.Ed. 579 (1819).

6. May, "State Constitutions," pp. 5–6.

7. This agenda for reform appears in a number of critiques. The one relied on most heavily here is: Committee for Economic Development (1968). A more recent summary of the constitutional reform agenda can be found in Advisory Commission on Intergovernmental Relations, *The Question of State Government Capability*, Report A-98 (Washington, DC: U.S. Government Printing Office, 1985): 35–44. For a good overview of state constitutions, see Thomas Marks and John Cooper, *State Constitutional Law in a Nutshell* (St. Paul, MN: West, 1988).

8. Lawrence M. Friedman, "An Historical Perspective on State Constitutions," *Intergovernmental Perspective* 13, no. 2 (Spring 1987): 10.

9. John Dinan, *The American State Constitutional Tradition* (Lawrence, KS: University Press of Kansas, 2006), pp. 195–204.

10. Dinan, *The American State,* pp. 213–270.

11. Campbell Robertson, "Mississippi Governor, Already Criticized on Pardons, Rides a Wave of Them Out of Office," *New York Times*, January 10, 2012 (electronic edition); Campbell Robertson, "Mississippi: Some Pardons by Barbour Are Halted," *New York Times*, January 11, 2012 (electronic edition); "Vague Advice Threatens Dozens of Barbour's Pardons," *New York Times*, January 20, 2012 (electronic

edition). People already released from prison may want a pardon in order to find better jobs or to regain the right to vote.

12. David C. Nice, "Interest Groups and State Constitutions: Another Look," *State and Local Government Review* 20, no. 1 (Winter 1988): 21–26. Also see Lewis A. Froman, Jr., "Some Effects of Interest Group Strength in State Politics," *The American Political Science Review* 60, no. 4 (December 1966): 956.

13. Kavan Peterson, "School Vouchers Slow to Spread," *Stateline* (electronic edition), May 5, 2005.

14. For a useful discussion of a number of legal issues surrounding state and local finances, see M. David Gelfand, Joel Mintz, and Peter Salsich, *State and Local Taxation and Finance in a Nutshell*, 2nd ed. (St.Paul, MN: West, 2000). For a discussion of state constitutions as limitations on state governments, see Kermit Hall, "Mostly Anchor and Little Sail: The Evolution of State Constitutions," in Paul Finkelman and Stephen Gottlieb, eds., *Toward a Usable Past: Liberty Under State Constitutions* (Athens: University of Georgia, 1991), pp. 388–417.

15. Dinan, "State Constitutional Developments in 2007," pp. 5–9; Dinan, "State Constitutional Developments in 2009," pp. 6–9.

16. Irene Rubin, *The Politics of Public Budgeting*, 4th ed. (New York: Chatham House, 2000), pp. 41–42, 141–143.

17. Ronald K. Snell, "The Trouble with Earmarking," *State Legislatures* 17, no. 2 (February 1991): 33–35.

18. Steven D. Gold, "The Pros and Cons of Earmarking," *State Legislatures* 13, no. 6 (July 1987): 30.

19. Darryl Fears, "New Criminal Record: 7.2 Million," *Washington Post*, June 12, 2008, p. A9; *Statistical Abstract of the United States, 2011–2012* (New York: Skyhorse, 2011), p. 215.

20. National Municipal League, *Model State Constitution*, 6th ed. (New York: National Municipal League, 1963). For more recent developments, see www-camlaw.rutgers.edu/statecon.

21. Thomas Parrish, "Kentucky's Fourth Constitution a Product of the 1890 Times," *State Government: CQ's Guide to Current Issues and Activities*, Thad L. Beyle, ed. (Washington, DC: Congressional Quarterly Press, 1991), p. 47. Also see Carl Chelf, "The Kentucky Constitution," in

Joel Goldstein, ed., *Kentucky Government and Politics* (Bloomington, IN: Tichenor Publishing, 1984), p. 29.

22. Alan Greenblatt, "Courting a Supermajority," *Governing* 17 (October 2003): 61.

23. Dinan, "State Constitutional Developments in 2005," p. 3; Dinan, "State Constitutional Developments in 2007," p. 4. Dinan, "State Constitutional Develop-ments in 2009," p. 5.

24. Dinan, "State Constitutional Developments in 2005," p. 4; Dinan, "State Constitutional Developments in 2007," pp. 8–9 .

25. Janice C. May, "State Constitutions and Constitutional Revision: 1988–89 and the 1990s," *The Book of the States: 1990–91* (Lexington, KY: Council of State Governments, 1990), pp. 20–39. May writes that constitutional revision in the late 1980s had declined to "its lowest level in 40 and even 50 years," p. 20. Amendment initiatives, however, have not declined. See Janice May, "State Constitutions...," 2000–2001," p. 3.

26. Dinan, "State Constitutional Developments in 2005," pp. 3, 5, 7–8.

27. Wayne R. Swanson, Sean A. Kelleher, and Arthur English, "Socialization of Constitution Makers: Political Experience, Role Conflict, and Attitude Change," *Journal of Politics* 34 (February 1972): 183–198.

28. Carroll and English, "Traditions of State Constitution Making," p. 106. The authors discovered this in their survey of delegates to Arkansas's constitutional conventions of 1970 and 1980.

29. Albert L. Sturm, *Trends in State Constitution Making: 1966–1972* (Lexington, KY: Council of State Governments, 1973). Of 14 constitutional conventions from 1966 to 1975 described in *The Book of the States*, five were limited to specific subject matters, and all five were successful in getting all or most of their suggested provisions adopted by the voters (Louisiana, Rhode Island, Tennessee, New Jersey, Pennsylvania). Of the nine states with unlimited constitutional conventions, the new constitutions were adopted by only three states (Montana, Illinois, and Hawaii). See *The Book of the States: 1974–75* (Lexington, KY: Council of State Governments, 1974). Also see the editions for 1972–73, 1970–71, and 1968–69.

30. Norman Meller and Richard H. Kosaki, "Hawaii's Constitutional Convention—1978," *National Civic Review* 69, no. 5 (May 1980): 48–57.

31. Friedman, "An Historical Perspective on State Constitutions," pp. 9–13.

32. For a discussion of the varying possibilities found in state constitutions, see Paul Finkelman and Stephen Gottlieb, eds., *Toward a Usable Past: Liberty Under State Constitutions* (Athens: University of Georgia, 1991).

33. Mark L. Glasser and John Kincaid, "Selected Rights Enumerated in State Constitutions," *Intergovernmental Perspective* 17, no. 4 (Fall 1991): 31–34.

34. Stanley M. Mosk, "The Emerging Agenda in State Constitutional Law," *Intergovernmental Perspective* 13, no. 2 (Spring 1987): 19–22.

35. Steven Pressman, "Protecting Rights in State Courts," *Editorial Research Reports*, May 27, 1988, pp. 278–279.

36. John Kincaid and Robert F. Williams, "The New Judicial Federalism: The States' Lead in Rights Protection," *The Journal of State Government* (April–June, 1992): 50–52; Dorothy Beasley, "State Bills of Rights: Dead or Alive," *Intergovernmental Perspective* (Summer 1989), pp. 13–17.

The Intergovernmental Framework for State and Community Politics

CHAPTER PREVIEW

In the previous chapter, we saw how constitutions structure and sometimes limit what state and community governments can do. In this chapter, we examine the dynamics of federalism, or intergovernmental relations, as it is increasingly being called. We shall discuss:

1 The allocation of powers among the national, state, and local governments.

2 The evolution from dual federalism through cooperative federalism to the New Federalism and, according to critics, coercive federalism.

3 Other intergovernmental politics.

4 Intersectional rivalries.

5 The implications of competitive federalism for state-community political economies.

Introduction

Hurricane Katrina, which struck the Gulf Coast in 2005, presented a crucial test for national, state, and local governments, as well as the private sector. By most accounts, they did a poor job. Many actions that could have prevented or reduced the amount of suffering and damage had not been taken. After the worst of the storm passed, rescue and recovery efforts were pitifully slow. Health care facilities ran out of supplies, and many people were stranded without food or safe drinking water. Law enforcement collapsed in some areas, and veteran journalists began crying while reporting on the extent of the human toll and physical destruction.

The faulty response to Katrina continues today. Although a considerable amount of rebuilding has taken place, considerable damage has still not been repaired, and many levees and dikes in flood-prone areas have not been adequately upgraded. Many of the capabilities needed to respond more effectively to the next major hurricane still do not exist.[1] Many people are still going from agency to office to bureau looking for help from someone, somewhere.

The Katrina saga draws attention to one of the most important principles of intergovernmental relations in America: When people do not get what they want from one part of the system, they are likely to go to another part in hopes of a more positive response. People may have more allies in the national arena than locally (or vice versa); officials in one branch of government may be more sympathetic than officials in another branch. People will try to expand, maintain, or reduce the **scope of conflict** in order to win the policy outcome they desire. When people argue about whether an issue is properly the responsibility of the national government, state governments, local governments, or the private sector, this is almost always what is happening.[2]

Controversies regarding which levels of government should do what go to the heart of one of the most basic principles of government in America—federalism. **Federalism** is a form of government with two or more levels; each level has the ability to make some important decisions on its own. Federalism is distinguished from **unitary government** (such as that of the United Kingdom for a number of years), in which all governmental authority resides at the national level, and confederacy (such as the Confederate States of America, 1861–1865), in which individual states have the ultimate authority. At many points in American history, conflicts have erupted over how our federal system should function; these conflicts have almost always been entangled with public policy disputes.

- In 1832, during arguments regarding national government tariffs, John C. Calhoun convinced a South Carolina convention to proclaim the Nullification Ordinances. Calhoun argued that the U.S. Constitution was a compact among state governments rather than a charter from the people. This **compact theory** proposed that the states, as creators of the national government, could nullify a law of Congress; this would give states (possibly as a group, possibly individually) a virtual veto over national government programs. Eventually the quarreling sides compromised and left the underlying constitutional question unresolved.

- From 1861 to 1865, in order to keep 11 southern states in the Union, the nation fought its bloodiest war, which claimed the lives of roughly 600,000 soldiers. As a result, slavery was abolished and the Union preserved. However, racial discrimination continued in the South for generations, in part because state and local governments ignored national laws for many years.

- In the 1930s, the nation faced the Great Depression, its sharpest challenge since the Civil War. Unemployment rates climbed to 25 percent and millions of people lost their homes and their savings. Violence erupted in some areas as farmers tried to fight the loss of their farms, workers clashed with businesses, and people tried to rid their communities of unemployed drifters. The states, local governments, and private charities lacked the resources to cope with the many problems. Finally, under the New Deal presidency of Franklin Roosevelt, the federal government took steps to help the needy, regulate business, and stimulate the economy. These actions and subsequent developments gave the federal government a much larger role in shaping domestic policy making.

- In recent years, many researchers have concluded that the global climate is gradually warming and that greenhouse gases produced by burning fossil fuels are at least partly responsible. However, the national government, especially under the George W. Bush administration, declined to take much action to correct the situation. Many state and local governments, as well as some private companies, have begun efforts to reduce production of greenhouse gases on their own, although how far they can proceed without national government assistance remains unclear. The Bush administration sometimes tried to block state and local initiatives to fight global warming while declining to do much on its own.[3] Even after Bush has left office, many congressional Republicans continue to oppose policies to combat global warming.

Americans have argued over the preferred distribution of responsibilities among governments on many other occasions as well, including the continuing discussions over homeland security since the

September 11 terrorist attacks, education reform, and health care. The You Decide exercise below gives you a chance to determine how power should be distributed among the three levels of government.

THE EVOLUTION OF FEDERALISM

Federalism today is very different from federalism in 1787, when the Constitution was written. Federalism has evolved through different stages,[4] which have led us from a *dual federalism* concept of state-national relations through *cooperative federalism* and to *creative federalism*, the *New Federalism, coercive federalism,* and an attempt to return to creative federalism. At issue in these concepts is the question raised in the accompanying You Decide exercise. How should power and responsibilities be divided (or shared) among the federal, state, and local governments?

▌ YOU DECIDE

How Should Power Be Divided Among the Federal, State, and Local Governments?

Here is an illustration of three empty glasses. Each glass has a scale from 0 to 100, with 0 meaning empty or no power, and 100 meaning full or all of the power.

If you had 100 units of power to distribute among the federal, state, and local levels of government, how many units of power would you put in each?

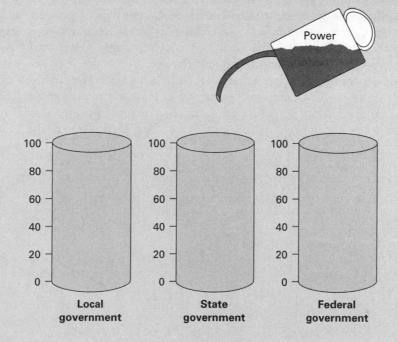

To see how a sample of American citizens responded to this question, see page 45. ■

Dual Federalism: Up to the Mid-1930s

In the early years of our country's history, **dual federalism** was a very influential view of the relations between the state and national governments. According to dual federalism, each of the two levels of government had its own separate source of authority and areas of responsibility.[5] The states were not supposed to interfere in federal responsibilities, such as foreign affairs, and the federal government was not supposed to intervene in areas of state responsibility, such as education. Local government was largely ignored in discussions on dual federalism.

Federal Government Responsibilities

Dual federalism often emphasized that the federal government had only those powers delegated to it by the Constitution. Included among those **delegated powers** (or **enumerated powers**) are the powers to coin money, to regulate foreign and interstate commerce, to establish a post office, to declare war, to provide for defense, and to spend money to promote the general welfare of the United States. However, that limited authority was eventually expanded, in part because of some constitutional provisions that may be interpreted more broadly.

One of those provisions, the **Necessary and Proper Clause**, grants Congress the power to make all laws "necessary and proper for carrying into execution" the enumerated powers. Loose constructionists, who prefer a broad interpretation of national powers, argue that this clause gives the federal government implied powers to act even if such actions have not been specifically enumerated. Strict constructionists generally reject that argument and prefer a narrow interpretation of national powers.

A second clause is the **National Supremacy Clause** (Article VI, Section 2), which provides that the Constitution and laws and treaties made under its authority are the supreme law of the land. All judges must obey those requirements, regardless of what any state constitution or state law says. This provision has sometimes supported expanding national power, although occasionally critics argue that the provision does not apply to national laws that exceed the constitutional authority of the national government.

A third constitutional clause that eventually facilitated the expansion of the federal government's power is the **Commerce Clause**.[6] In a very early interpretation, the Supreme Court ruled that the authority to regulate interstate commerce belongs exclusively to Congress. However, it was not until the catastrophe of the Great Depression of the 1930s that Congress was willing and able to use the Commerce Clause to expand national authority very much.

A fourth major constitutional provision is the **General Welfare Clause**, which gives the national government the authority to tax and spend to provide for defense and promote the general welfare. The federal courts have generally held that this provision gives the national government very broad legal authority to raise and spend money—broader than its authority to pass laws. National officials were not usually willing to use that authority very much in the pre-1937 era, however, except in wartime.

Over the years, these constitutional clauses (Necessary and Proper, National Supremacy, Commerce, and General Welfare) eventually served to expand federal power in domestic policy making, when that inclination was present. Some observers believe that this expansion has reduced the power of the states in policy making, but the reality is considerably more complex than that.

State Government Responsibilities   In the dual federalism era, the states enjoyed considerable freedom from federal intrusion because of the strict constructionist argument that the Tenth Amendment of the Constitution reserves all powers not specifically granted to the national government "to the states respectively, or to the people." Accordingly, these are called the **reserved powers**. From one perspective, dual federalism and the reserved powers gave the states and their local governments primary responsibilities over most domestic matters. Many state officials, however, contend that the primary source of their authority is the people of their individual states. At any rate, states and localities continue to administer the election process; conduct most court trials; operate the public school systems; and maintain most of our public services, such as streets, sewers, water supply, public recreational facilities, and public health facilities. Note, however, that most state governments did not actually provide many public services throughout the 1800s. Most years, the states were the smallest level of government in spending and in employment. Having the legal authority to act does not always provide the will or the resources (such as money) to act.

State legal supremacy in these areas began to break down starting in the 1930s, when Congress responded to the Great Depression with a broad array of laws that started the national welfare system and established federal regulatory control over much of the economy. Congress based its authority to pass these laws on the Constitution's Commerce Clause, which gives Congress exclusive authority to regulate interstate commerce, and the General Welfare Clause, which enables Congress to raise and spend money (but not necessarily pass laws) to promote the general welfare. There was also the more mundane reality that the states and local governments were completely overwhelmed by the Depression. For the first four years of the New Deal, the Supreme Court struck down a number of its programs as unconstitutional. But the Court finally capitulated in 1937 and acknowledged that Congress's commerce powers gave it extensive powers to regulate the economy.[7]

HIGHLIGHT

Dividing Power Among Governments

When Americans were asked to fill each level of the government's glass with power, they gave 30 percent of the power to the local glass, 31 percent to the state glass, and 39 percent to the federal glass. ■

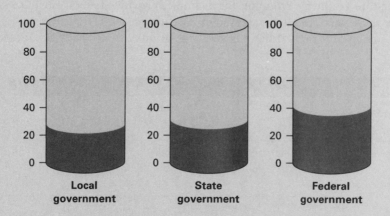

Source: Advisory Commission on Intergovernmental Relations, *Changing Public Attitudes on Government and Taxes: 1991* (Washington, DC: Advisory Commission on Intergovernmental Relations, 1991), pp. 14–15.

What About Local Governments? Local governments were omitted from dual federalism because they were, in theory, legally subordinate to state governments during the period when dual federalism was most influential. This omission was unfortunate because local governments often had considerable informal autonomy and influence and made many important policy decisions during this era. They also spent more money and employed more people than state governments did for most of our early history. In some parts of the country, some local governments began operating before there were state governments in the area.

Cooperative Federalism: The Mid-1930s to the Mid-1970s (or Later?)

As the federal government's policy-making role grew in the 1930s, it led to a new arrangement, called **cooperative federalism**, because the three levels of government (federal, state, and local) now began working cooperatively on programs to cope with the nation's domestic problems. In time, however, the federal government gained considerable influence over many aspects of the new federal partnership. That expanded influence came through four devices: (1) grants-in-aid, (2) federal court orders, (3) preemptive legislation, and (4) unfunded mandates. Less noticed in many circles was a dramatic increase in state governmental activities.

The Grant-in-Aid System One major device for implementing cooperative federalism is the grant-in-aid. A **grant-in-aid** is a payment from the federal government to a state or local government (or from a state government to a local one) for some activity, such as building and maintaining highways. As shown in Table 3.1, there are two major types of federal grants to state and local governments—categorical grants and block grants. A third type, **general revenue sharing**, existed from 1972 to 1986 nationally. It gave about $5 billion yearly to state and local governments to spend as they saw fit, but national revenue sharing was eliminated in a set of budget cuts in 1986. A number of states still have a similar grant for some local governments.

Categorical Grants A **categorical grant** is a federal payment to a state or local government (or a state grant to a local government) to carry out a specific, narrowly defined activity. The Interstate Highway Program, for example, provides federal funds to states to build and maintain the Interstate Highway System. For many years, funds from this categorical grant could not be used for any other purpose. The grants usually have extensive federal guidelines

TABLE 3.1

Types of Federal Aid

Type of Aid	Percent of Total
Categorical grants (e.g., Interstate Highway Program)	88
Block grants (e.g., Education Block Grant)	10
General purpose	1

Note: Totals do not add up to 100% due to rounding error.

Sources: Characteristics of Federal Grant-in-Aid Programs to State and Local Governments (Washington, DC: Advisory Commission on Intergovernmental Relations, 1995), p. 7; *Special Analyses of the Budget of the United States Government: FY 1990* (Washington, DC: U.S. Government Printing Office, 1989), p. H-25.

stipulating how the programs should be run. They may also contain matching provisions that require the recipient governments to match a certain percentage of the federal grant. In the Interstate Highway Program, a state has to contribute only $10 for every $90 contributed by the federal government.

Categorical grants may be project grants, formula grants, or open-ended reimbursements. In a **project grant**, a state or local agency makes a grant application to some federal agency; the application describes a specific activity which the recipient will carry out with the funds. The granting agency has some discretion to decide which applicants will get the money. In a **formula grant** (for example, the Interstate Highway program), the aid is distributed automatically to state or local governments according to a formula drawn up by Congress. In an **open-ended reimbursement** program (for example, unemployment compensation, which gives short-term cash grants to workers who have lost their jobs), states and communities are reimbursed for a share of the expenses they incur implementing the program. These programs are open-ended because their costs vary greatly with the economy, rising in times of recession, but dropping in periods of economic boom. If an open-ended grant expands too rapidly, however, the granting level of government is likely to impose some form of cost controls.

Block Grants In contrast to the categorical grant, which can be used only for a very specific purpose, a **block grant** is one that can be used for a wider variety of purposes and usually has fewer federal guidelines on how programs are to be administered, at least initially. Block grant funds can be spent for any number of purposes within a specified functional area, such as law enforcement or health care. Most block grants have been formed through the consolidation of several specific categorical grants. For example, in 1981 Congress consolidated 38 specific educational categorical grants into one education block grant that increased state flexibility and responsibility for administering federal education dollars.

Because of this greater flexibility, state and local elected officials generally prefer block grants to categorical grants (assuming the amount of funding remains the same). A recent analysis identified 24 block grant programs, 12 of them established during the 1980s.[8] Giving state and local officials more flexibility in using grant funds seems to weaken federal enthusiasm for the grant, perhaps in part due to greater uncertainty regarding how the funds will be used. As a result, funding for block grants tends to decline over time, and federal officials gradually reduce recipient flexibility in using the funds.[9]

The Impact of Grants In 2009, the federal government spent roughly $538 billion on grants. The states spent approximately $479 billion on grants the previous year.[10] Because some of these grants-in-aid have matching features, governments receiving grants are sometimes under considerable pressure to spend some of their own money to meet the policy goals established by the government providing the grants. This sometimes shifts substantial power to set policy goals from the states to the national government and from local governments to the states, according to some critics.

The centralizing influence of grants should not be overstated, however. Many grants have comparatively small amounts of money; states and localities can and do decline to accept grants that are not sufficiently attractive. For example, roughly half of the states no longer take federal grants to support sexual abstinence education, in part due to doubts regarding the effectiveness of the program and in part due to uncertainties regarding funding levels.[11] In addition, grants are subject to **fungibility**; that is, grant money may sometimes be used to replace state or local revenues that the recipient planned to spend anyway. National grant guidelines are not always enforced very vigorously, and the ultimate sanction—withholding grant funds—is not one that federal agencies or members of Congress are willing to employ very often. Withholding grant money may harm the programs receiving support and usually generates a storm of criticism from people in the affected areas. State and local governments lobby vigorously to change grant provisions that their officials dislike.[12] In addition, state and local officials who dislike a federal policy may drag their feet or put forth only very limited efforts to carry it out.[13]

Note, too, that a grant may give a state or locality financial resources that the recipient government could not have raised on its own. In those cases, the national grant may give the recipient government considerably more policy impact and flexibility than it would have had otherwise.

Federal Court Orders As cooperative federalism began to mature, the Supreme Court and other federal courts increasingly issued orders to states to undertake actions to meet national policy goals. The landmark precedent was probably *Brown v. Board of Education*[14] (1954) in which the Supreme Court ordered states to begin desegregating their public schools. Another landmark decision came in 1973, when the Supreme Court made it unconstitutional for states to prohibit abortion in the first three months of pregnancy.[15] The Supreme Court required states to reapportion their state legislatures on the basis of one person, one vote.[16] In 1988, the Court upheld a federal law denying highway grants to states that refused to adopt a 21-year-old minimum drinking age.[17]

In one of the more visible cases of Supreme Court activism, the Court intervened in the 2000 presidential election and ordered officials in Florida to stop recounting of presidential ballots. This decision effectively granted George W. Bush the presidency. While sometimes willing to uphold federal laws that restricted states, the Supreme Court also grew increasingly willing to strike down state laws as unconstitutional.[18] In addition, however, the Court has struck down some federal laws as being too intrusive into state responsibilities, particularly in recent years. The cases tend to involve federal policies that conservatives do not support a great deal.[19]

Preemptive Legislation The latter years of cooperative federalism also saw a dramatic increase in preemptive laws passed by Congress. A *preemptive law* is a *federal law that actually displaces a state law on the same subject*. Most federal environmental protection laws, for example, take precedence over corresponding state laws. From the beginning of the nation's history up to 1969, Congress had preempted only 206 state laws. In the next 22 years, it preempted more than 233.[20] Several recent examples of preemptive legislation include a law shifting many major class-action lawsuits to the federal courts, a law prohibiting many suits against gun manufacturers and distributors, and laws dealing with vaccines.[21] Much preemptive legislation is pushed by big businesses that prefer uniformity in the regulations they obey rather than separate regulatory standards in each of the 50 states.[22] Other preemptive legislation is pushed by groups that are unhappy with the actions (or inaction) of various state and local governments.

Unfunded Mandates Finally, the latter years of cooperative federalism saw a dramatic increase in the congressional practice of requiring states and/or localities to carry out certain activities without providing all the funds necessary to carry out those activities. This is the practice of unfunded mandates. The 1990 Americans with Disabilities Act (ADA), for example, required all public buildings to be made accessible to handicapped people, and it required public bus companies to provide transit services for people in wheelchairs. In 2005, federal legislation required the states to begin work on a more accurate and reliable system for issuing official documents that people use to identify themselves—an effort that may be very expensive.[23]

The sum total of mandates has been extensive. During the 1980s and early 1990s, state or local governments were required by federal law, among other things, to remove asbestos from public schools, implement stricter water pollution regulations, establish programs to protect workers against certain dangerous chemicals, and make reports on measures to protect more than 150 newly endangered species.[24] As the costs for these mandated expenditures go up, the ability of state and local governments to set their own policy priorities among other programs goes down.[25]

Bear in mind that many state and local officials may agree with a mandated policy, although they may not always want to admit that. Especially when a mandate calls for some controversial action, state and local officials may enjoy a measure of political protection that the mandate provides. A governor will be able to tell irate citizens that an action is required by a federal mandate: "It isn't my fault." State governments also impose unfunded mandates on local governments. Whenever the national government (or a state government) is short of money, unfunded mandates are an appealing way to support a policy while shifting the cost to lower levels of government.

The Centralizing Effects of Cooperative Federalism As can be seen from this short review, cooperative federalism included a major expansion of national government influence in domestic policy making. At the same time, the scope of state government activity expanded as well, with greater state activity in fields ranging from transportation and environmental protection to education and health care. Local governments grew more financially dependent on higher levels of government. By the 1980s, the combined impact of grants-in-aid, federal court orders, preemptive legislation, and unfunded mandates had given the federal government a major role in most domestic policies. State officials sometimes complained that the states were increasingly reduced to becoming administrative units responsible for carrying out the national government's will (although an examination of state policies during this period shows considerable variety among the states). Critics complained that cooperative federalism had become coercive federalism.[26]

The New Federalism(s): Mid-1970s to the Present

Criticisms of Cooperative Federalism The most dramatic expansion of federal power took place in the 1960s and 1970s. The federal government increasingly claimed power to set policies in controversial issues such as abortion, affirmative action, environmental protection, and occupational safety. As federal involvement grew, particularly in policy areas that were controversial, a backlash to that involvement gained strength. The backlash was part philosophical and part political.

Philosophical Backlash To some critics, the federal system had become too complicated to function well or to enable citizens to exercise democratic control over it. Critics argued that many citizens had difficulty keeping track of what was happening. To take a recent example, a survey of parents with children in the public schools found that 78 percent of them admitted to knowing very little (44 percent) or nothing at all (34 percent) about the highly publicized

No Child Left Behind education reforms.[27] The many participants in any given program may create delays and cause people to obstruct one another's work. A number of observers suggested that the public might be served better if the complexity were reduced. From these philosophical perspectives, the nation badly needed to sort out responsibilities on a pragmatic basis. To reduce complexity and improve program administration, it was essential to decide what functions could best be done at the federal level and which could be done best by state and local governments.[28]

The calls for simplification and sorting out confront a number of practical difficulties.[29] Much of the complexity of our federal system stems from having over 87,000 different governments (the vast majority of them local) and more than 500,000 elected officials. As we will see later in the book, proposals to simplify that aspect of the system are rarely adopted. Moreover, how do we decide which level of government should be in charge of which responsibilities? Those decisions are almost never politically neutral, for the balance of political forces, financial resources, and political incentives may be very different in the national arena, a particular state, and any given locality. For example, if civil rights policies had remained state and local responsibilities in the 1950s and 1960s, we would have seen a continuation of racial segregation in many areas of society.

Note, too, that a major reason for the emergence of cooperative federalism is the growing cost of meeting public expectations. Many local governments would never have been able to afford a significant section of interstate highway or a major university, just as many localities could not afford to help the needy during the Great Depression. Many people value local government, yet they want government to do a number of things that many localities cannot do alone.

A good deal of governmental complexity also reflects the complexity of the broader environment. Social problems have many aspects; transportation needs take many forms. States and localities are swept by global economic forces that are beyond their control and difficult to understand at times. Terrorists might strike in any number of places and could use any of a number of different weapons. There is little realistic hope of making the world much simpler in the foreseeable future.

Political Backlash   The most potent complaints against cooperative federalism, however, were the political ones. Many people simply objected to the substance of what the federal government was doing. Since many of the federal initiatives in the environment, civil rights, and other policy areas were supported primarily by liberal Democrats in Congress and the White House, political opposition began to grow among conservative Republicans. Many of these complaints found expression by Ronald Reagan when he ran for the presidency in 1980 on the promise to "get the federal government off your backs."[30] As these developments took place, support for a powerful national government, at least in the abstract, began to erode. However, support for many individual federal programs remained fairly strong.

Public opinion polls in the late 1960s and 1970s found that the federal government suffered a significant loss of public confidence (along with many other institutions, such as big business and organized religions). A number of studies found the greatest public confidence in local government, the lowest public confidence in the federal government, with the states in an intermediate position. However, the magnitude of the differences has varied considerably over the years. In 1999, public confidence in local government remained the highest, and public confidence in the national government was lowest, but the differences were rather small (see Table 3.2). Moreover, many people feel uncertain regarding governmental powers.

TABLE 3.2				
Public Confidence in Each Level of Government, 1999				
	A Great Deal (%)	Quite a Lot (%)	Some (%)	Very Little (%)	Can't Say/No Answer (%)
Local	9	24	43	22	2
State	8	23	45	22	2
Federal	8	20	43	27	2

Source: Statistical Abstract of the United States, 2001 (Washington, DC: U.S. Government Printing Office, 2001), p. 249.

The evidence also indicates, however, that wealthier people are more confident in local government than are the poor, and that poor people are more confident in the national government. Wealthy people are likely to live in wealthy localities where funding services is easier, and competition among local governments often makes them more responsive to wealthy people than to the poor.[31]

Reagan's New Federalism Given the weakened public support for the federal government and frequent Republican successes in national elections since 1980, it is not surprising that these years have seen two frontal assaults on cooperative federalism. The first assault came in 1981 when the Reagan administration (1981–1989) proposed a **New Federalism** in which, the president proclaimed: "It is my intention to curb the size and influence of the federal establishment."[32] The key to this curbing of the federal government was devolution, or spinning off the federal government's responsibilities to state and local governments and to the private sector. Devolution had three components: the budget, regulation, and the private sector.

Budgetary Devolution Reagan sought to spin off substantial federal budgetary responsibilities to state and local governments by consolidating 77 categorical grants into nine new block grants, which would be administered by the states with minimal federal strings attached, and by making severe budget cutbacks in social service programs in an effort to shift more of the burden for these services onto the states. He also unsuccessfully proposed a complete federal government takeover of Medicaid, a very expensive and rapidly growing program of health care for the indigent, the elderly, and people on welfare. In exchange, the states would take over responsibility for Food Stamps, Aid to Families with Dependent Children (AFDC), and 43 other categorical programs.

The Reagan administration initially hoped to cut the total amount of federal grants almost in half, which would have consequently cut much of the federal government's ability to influence budget priorities for the states and reduced overall funding for some programs in a number of states. As during most presidencies, however, the Reagan administration's proposals provoked a mixed reception.

He scored some early successes on his block grant and social services cutback proposals, but Congress rejected his more drastic proposals. State and local officials resisted having sole responsibility for Food Stamps and AFDC. Many of them viewed poverty and welfare as national problems, and for years some of them had urged the federal government to assume full financial responsibility for the major welfare programs. Reagan's proposal to devolve Food Stamps and AFDC onto the states directly contradicted this goal. Against opposition from the states, Reagan succeeded in somewhat cutting federal grants-in-aid. However, federal aid began to grow again and now exceeds $500 billion, with funds allocated to several hundred different grants.

Regulatory Devolution   A second aspect of Reagan's New Federalism was regulatory devolution. Between 1965 and 1980, there was a dramatic increase in federal laws, administrative agency rules, and court orders that expanded regulation in several aspects of the economy, ranging from environmental protection to civil rights and occupational health and safety. Because these new regulations added to the cost of doing business, American business leaders bitterly resented many of them. Thus, the Carter administration (1977–1981) took some early steps toward deregulation by phasing out federal controls over the price of petroleum and natural gas and by deregulating the airline industry. President Reagan made further reductions of federal regulatory activities and sought legislation that would shift major regulatory responsibilities to the states, especially in environmental protection. A series of major corporate scandals beginning in the mid-1990s, however, along with growing concerns over global warming and rising petroleum prices, has led some observers to call for greater regulation of some aspects of business activities.

Devolution to the Private Sector   When the Reagan administration cut funds for social programs in the early 1980s, it called on the private sector to take up the slack. In cutting social expenditures, for example, Reagan argued that some federally funded programs providing food and shelter for the destitute could be replaced by volunteers from churches and nonprofit organizations.[33]

He also called for creation of *urban enterprise zones*. These would be city neighborhoods in which taxes and regulatory restrictions (such as occupational safety and minimum wages) would be relaxed for companies that moved facilities into those neighborhoods and created jobs there. This reliance on the private sector to accomplish public goals did not, of course, begin with Reagan. But he pushed for this objective more strongly than any other recent president.

Assessing Reagan's New Federalism   Did Reagan's New Federalism achieve his goal of returning more power and authority to the states and communities?

On balance, he achieved a partial victory. He temporarily slowed the growth rate of many domestic social programs, reduced the number of federal grant-in-aid programs, got nine new block grants passed, terminated general revenue sharing, and provoked an ongoing debate over the delineation of federal from state and local responsibilities. Furthermore, because of the huge budget deficits built up during the Reagan–Bush years, there was only limited room for his successors in the White House to expand the federal government's domestic policy role through federal grants.

Nevertheless, Reagan's victories were only partial victories. Most of his accomplishments came in his first two years. However, Democrats regained control of Congress in 1987, Reagan's influence was weakened by scandals in his administration, and Reagan's successor, George H. W. Bush, was generally much less interested in domestic policy. With Bush's assistance, the Clean Air Act was rewritten in 1991 and it put substantial federal regulations in place on the environment. Funding for social programs and federal grants began to rise again and grew to record numbers in subsequent years.[34]

Some analysts have noted that President Reagan, like most presidents, was not consistent in his approach to federalism. In particular, the administration supported or accepted new federal mandates and regulations to stop states and localities from pursuing policies that conflicted with the administration's ideological agenda.[35]

In sum, the New Federalism of the Reagan and first Bush administrations did not dismantle the federal government's domestic policies, but it did reduce some programs that conflicted with conservative ideology, while sometimes expanding federal policies in conservative directions. Ironically, as the New Federalism pushed for more conservative social policies, some states liberalized their own social service expenditures to make up for the federal budget cutbacks. One study examined the responses of 14 states to federal cuts in social services. Of the 14 states, 13 either increased their own expenditures to make up for the federal cuts or adopted stronger policy-making roles than they had previously had.[36] The net result of Reagan's New Federalism was somewhat less spending on social services and welfare, but it clearly did not bring about the extensive reductions in the overall size and scope of government in welfare and domestic policy and the federal grant system that he had originally envisioned.

The New Federalism II   The second assault on cooperative federalism was launched by Republicans in Congress when they took control there in 1995. One of their first acts was legislation that sought to restrict the federal government's ability to impose new unfunded mandates on the states and localities. Additionally, they passed a block grant program that gave the states more responsibility for AFDC (which was renamed Temporary Assistance to Needy Families), a major cash assistance program for poor families with children. They also proposed that the nation's two largest public health programs, Medicare and Medicaid, be turned over to the states for implementation, although Medicaid has always been administered by the states. Given the immense and rising costs of Medicare and Medicaid, state officials have been extremely wary of proposals that might shift a larger share of the cost of those programs to the states. There seems to be little likelihood of any major change at present.

The agenda of the congressional Republicans included greater competition among the states in the provision of public services. In theory, the hope was that competition between the states would improve public services.

Political scientist Paul Peterson, however, raises some questions about this assumption. To Peterson, interstate competition might improve delivery of some services such as education, public safety, or transportation, which are distributed somewhat evenly to all members of society (although education funding varies considerably from place to place). He doubts, however, whether interstate competition will improve redistributive services such as social welfare or regulatory services like environmental protection. Interstate competition in these areas will most likely reduce the levels of social services and weaken the enforcement of environmental regulations.[37] His concern is born out by the declining purchasing power of welfare benefits since the mid-1970s and the dramatic decrease in the number of people receiving assistance from AFDC/Temporary Assistance to Needy Families since 1995—a decline that is far larger than the decline of the poverty rate since then.[38]

President Clinton's record on intergovernmental issues was a mixed one, partly because of numerous disagreements between him and congressional Republicans. However, he tried to give states and localities more flexibility on a number of occasions, including granting waivers of federal rules and regulations in order to allow states to experiment with new program strategies, and being attentive to state and local concerns. His administration also pushed for and won increases in grant funding.[39]

George W. Bush's record on federalism was also mixed. Some of his initiatives, including education reforms and antiterrorism efforts, increased the federal government's role in education policy making, law enforcement, and airport security. His administration filed a legal brief in favor of striking down the University of Michigan's affirmative action program. His first attorney general, John Ashcroft, also tried to overturn Oregon's law permitting physician-assisted suicide under specified conditions; Ashcroft's initial effort was unsuccessful.[40] In addition, President Bush responded to news of same-sex marriages by supporting a constitutional amendment defining marriage as being between a man and a woman, a proposal that would intrude into what has traditionally been a state responsibility.

Bush's administration worked to block state and local efforts to combat global warming and at least one state's proposal for higher mileage standards for cars and light trucks. Moreover, his education reforms apparently generated higher costs for state and local governments than the amount of federal aid received. A number of states, however, had already begun their own efforts to evaluate the performance of students, teachers, and schools, as the law required.

Overall, President Bush seemed to be concerned that federal policies not pose additional undue burdens on the states.[41] When state and local education officials complained about the administration's education reforms, administration officials eventually responded by giving them more flexibility regarding several aspects of the policy.[42]

Ironically, Bush's proposals to streamline some federal environmental regulations drew criticism from some state and local officials who worried that the new regulations would weaken environmental protection efforts. State and local officials have complained that national government efforts to protect homeland security remain unfocused and that federal funding for local homeland security efforts is not reaching many localities. Part of the latter complaint stems from state officials who want to retain the homeland security funds for state programs, rather than passing most of them along to local governments.[43] In addition, some evidence indicates that the administration's penchant for secrecy left local governments without very good information regarding homeland security risks,[44] although the sensitive nature of some information regarding terrorists may make circulating that information dangerous for intelligence officers.

The Obama administration has also produced a mixed record in its relationships with state and local governments. The health care reforms adopted in 2010 set off a howl of protests from conservatives who criticized almost every aspect of the reforms and legal challenges from a number of state attorneys general, almost all of them Republicans. Governor Scott Walker in Wisconsin chose to return $38 million in federal grants to help the state develop one facet of the health care reform rather than participate in the new policy.[45] Conservative opposition produced some strange dynamics in the 2012 Republican presidential nomination contest, however, because the leading Republican contender, Mitt Romney (as this is being written), helped institute health care reforms in Massachusetts that are very similar to the 2010 federal law.

The Obama administration continued with the Bush administration's efforts to have more rigorous evaluation of educational performance, in spite of continuing complaints from some state and local officials. In addition, Obama has continued many of the Bush administration's homeland security efforts.

Overall, scholars disagree regarding how much flexibility states and localities have gained in recent years and over whether they have actually gained any at all. Some believe that big changes have occurred, but others, especially adherents of *coercive federalism,* conclude that, on balance, the federal role in many domestic programs remains at least as large as it was in the 1970s, with many unfunded mandates remaining in force and some new ones appearing. A review of the Unfunded Mandates Reform Act of 1995 concluded the law included so many exemptions and loopholes that it rarely blocked enactment of new mandates.[46] In addition, the federal government has continued to adopt new preemptive legislation in a variety of policy areas, from banning sales taxes on Internet commerce to banning partial-birth abortions.[47] Moreover, many states and localities face costs and needs that are growing faster than are revenues. State and local autonomy that makes sense when revenues are reasonably abundant may be less practical when revenues are tight relative to needs. At any rate, all three levels of government remain involved in all major domestic programs; many elements of cooperative federalism continue to exist.[48]

OTHER INTERGOVERNMENTAL POLITICS

Federalism traditionally referred to the formal relationship between the national and the state governments, with local governments being added to the picture since the 1930s. In addition, there are so many other ways in which governments (and private organizations) interact with each other that scholars use the term **intergovernmental relations (IGR)** to refer to this phenomenon.[49] Four of these patterns of interaction deserve notice. They are relationships between local governments and higher levels of government, the relationships among states, the role of private organizations in the intergovernmental system, and relationships among local governments.

Local Governments and Higher Levels of Government

The evolution of cooperative federalism and related developments have had the long-term effect of eroding local autonomy. In federal–local relations, this has sometimes taken the form of weakening the general-purpose local governments. In state and local relations, a long-term centralization process has eroded much of the local autonomy that once existed.

Federal and Local Relations   Until the 1930s, the federal government had little direct involvement with local governments. To cope with the Great Depression, as we saw earlier in the chapter, the federal government gave grants-in-aid directly to cities and some other local governments. This practice expanded during the 1960s and 1970s. City governments became very dependent on federal funds to ward off economic recessions and on federal employment funds to hire public service workers. When federal aid to localities was cut back during the Reagan years, many cities were forced to make significant cutbacks and to raise their own taxes and fees.

State and Local Relations   Communities rely strongly on the states for their legal authority. City governments have traditionally been treated as creatures of the states, and the legal principle known as **Dillon's Rule** holds that city governments' powers must be interpreted very narrowly. Because of Dillon's Rule, cities are usually permitted to exercise only those powers granted to them by their state constitutions or their state legislatures. Boulder, Colorado, relearned this lesson the hard way in 1982 when the Supreme Court struck down that city's attempt to regulate cable television.[50]

Probably the most visible impact states have on local governments is financial. State governments provide general and categorical aids to local governments. State aid totaled more than $430 billion annually by 2007.[51] Local governments today are, on average, heavily dependent on the states for funds, although the dependence varies considerably from one locality to another. As the recession that began in 2007–2008 triggered declines in state revenues, many states reduced grants to local governments. Those reductions, coupled with declines in local tax revenues, meant considerable difficulty for many localities.[52]

The states often determine how much debt local governments can have, what sources of revenue they may use, and how much local governments may increase their property taxes and other taxes from year to year. States use mandates to shape many local government activities, and state courts may hear challenges to the actions of local governments.

Although local autonomy generally eroded in the twentieth century, it must not be concluded that local governments are irrelevant. Many political careers begin in local government, and local communities remain the key political bases of many state legislators, congresspersons, and, in some instances, statewide officials. Local leaders are able to call on their elected officials or congresspersons to exert influence on the administration of national and state policies. Moreover, many states have acted to give at least some localities greater flexibility to deal with local problems and to work cooperatively with their local governments. State officials are also unwilling to exercise their authority over local governments when a political uproar may result.

Interstate Politics

Relationships between or among states are an important feature of intergovernmental relations. Some interstate relationships are structured by the U.S. Constitution. The Supreme Court has jurisdiction over legal conflicts between states, although it sometimes declines to use that authority. The Full-Faith-and-Credit Clause provides that each state should recognize the official acts of other states. Thus, people divorced in one state do not find their divorce nullified when they cross into another state (at least, not very often). However, compliance with the provision is not always forthcoming; states often failed to grant full faith and credit in matters such as alimony and child support. The Privileges-and-Immunities Clause prohibits a state from discriminating against nonresidents, with some significant exceptions, such as tuition at public universities. In addition to these clauses, the Constitution also contains a Rendition Clause that requires governors to return fugitives from justice to the state from which they fled. If a governor refuses to return a fugitive, however, the Supreme Court is unlikely to intervene. These constitutional provisions give the states considerable flexibility in dealing with their neighbors.

Interstate Compacts   One popular mechanism for resolving interstate problems is the *interstate compact.* This is an agreement made by two or more states and ratified (actively or passively) by Congress. Interstate compacts are commonly used to settle problems in corrections, education, transportation, or natural-resources management. Compacts are not very useful for most controversial issues because each participating state must approve the compact, and reaching agreement on controversial issues is often impossible. Even after a compact is adopted, there still may be problems gaining agreement on individual decisions and actions.

Informal Cooperation   In addition to compacts, state officials often work informally with officials in other states, in activities ranging from seeking advice to sharing information and emergency assistance. There are now many organizations of state officials (governors, for example) that provide opportunities for members to exchange ideas and experiences dealing with various problems.

Generally speaking, state governments have considerable discretion in dealing with one another. While interstate relations are often cordial when a spirit of cooperation exists, that spirit is sometimes lacking.[53]

The Private Sector and Intergovernmental Relations

Beginning in the 1950s, observers of American federalism began calling attention to the actual and potential roles of private organizations in the federal system. Much of the work of government has always been done by private organizations, which range from defense contractors to private auditing firms and automobile manufacturers producing police cars. Some observers felt (and still feel) that giving private organizations a larger role in providing services will bring an infusion of new ideas, talent, and cost savings to efforts to improve our quality of life. Some skeptics worry that bringing more private organizations into governing will produce an increase in interest group influence, create more confusion regarding who is responsible for what, and provide more opportunities for corruption as organizations interested in making money will try to siphon off as much money as they can from federal, state, and local budgets. We will return to this controversy in Chapter 10.

For now, bear in mind that any discussion of our federal system that fails to include the many private organizations that are involved in fighting poverty, helping the environment, reducing the crime rate, helping people to travel from one place to another, or fighting disease, or any other public need, will not give you a complete picture of what is actually happening. At their best, the private actors can provide additional skills, more people willing to help, lower costs, and greater flexibility, among other things. The proliferation of private actors means that state and local (and national) officials must be able to work carefully with many private sector actors whose goals may not agree with the officials' goals. Achieving coordinated action may take months or even years.

Interlocal Relations

Another important aspect of intergovernmental relations involves relationships among local governments. These relationships take a great many forms and range from friendly and cooperative to openly or covertly hostile. For example, a local government may purchase a service from another local government, as in the case of trash collection or sewage treatment, or two or more localities may share a facility in order to reduce expenses. Local officials from different governments may work together on issues of mutual concern, such as law enforcement or traffic management. In an emergency, a city may provide a neighboring community with assistance to combat a major fire or to treat victims of a major accident. We saw dramatic examples of that emergency aid during and after the September 11 terrorist attacks and again after Hurricane Katrina.

On the conflictual side, officials in one community may try to lure a major employer or wealthy citizens away from other communities to enhance the local tax base. People in one community may create a problem, such as pollution, that affects people in other communities. Action on a shared problem may be blocked because one or more local governments refuse to cooperate with their neighbors. Denver, Colorado, has been working on creating a multilane highway encircling the city for years. The most recent snag in the project has been the fierce opposition from the city of Golden, Colorado. Opponents of the highway project fear that it would adversely affect their quality of life.[54] Although these conflicts can be resolved locally, as we will see in Chapter 6, sometimes they require state or national assistance to reach a resolution.

Regional Politics

Sectional rivalries, which have emerged periodically throughout American history, are an important feature of American federalism. The best-known regional rivalries in recent years are the sunbelt–frostbelt and the East–West rivalries. One component of these conflicts has been the long-term demographic and economic decline of a number of upper midwestern and northeastern **frostbelt** states in comparison with the more rapidly growing **sunbelt** and western states. The problem is especially acute in the upper midwestern (north central) region, whose economies were severely hampered by the decline of industrial manufacturing.

People from the Northeast and upper Midwest argue that their economic problems are compounded by the way in which federal expenditures and tax burdens are spread around the country. The residents and businesses of each state pay various taxes and fees to the federal government. The federal government then spends money in the states so that each state's economy may receive from the federal expenditures either more or less money than its residents send to the federal government in taxes. If we rank the states from those that gain the most federal spending relative to their contributions to the federal treasury to those that receive the least federal spending relative to their revenue contributions, a fairly clear pattern emerges. New Mexico and Alaska made out best from this viewpoint since they received more in federal expenditures relative to federal revenues paid than did any other state. New Jersey and Connecticut made out the worst since they contributed considerably more in federal revenues than they received in federal spending.

As Figure 3.1 shows, of the 10 states that receive the most federal spending relative to federal revenues contributed, most are sunbelt states or western states. By contrast, most of the ten states that pay the most in federal revenues relative to federal spending received are in the Northeast or upper Midwest. This pattern has existed for years, and it led some vocal frostbelt leaders to charge that they were not getting a fair deal from fiscal federalism.

To improve their share of federal funds relative to revenues, frostbelt leaders began to form multistate associations. The Northeast Coalition of Governors and the Northeast-Midwest Coalition of Congressional Members, in particular, sought to get a greater share of federal grants-in-aid spent in their regions. Southerners reacted by forming their lobbying organization, the Southern Growth Policies Board. Southerners and westerners respond to northern complaints about the distribution of federal expenditures by pointing out that their (the southern and western states) rapid growth in recent decades has imposed numerous costs on them, such as substantial investments made in construction projects for roads and schools to handle the rapidly expanding population. Nor has the prosperity gap between the South and the rest of the nation been closed, although the gap has narrowed. Per capita income in the average southern state still lags behind the rest of the nation.[55] Westerners also note that some of the federal spending they receive is for the care of federally owned land, which is mostly found in western states.

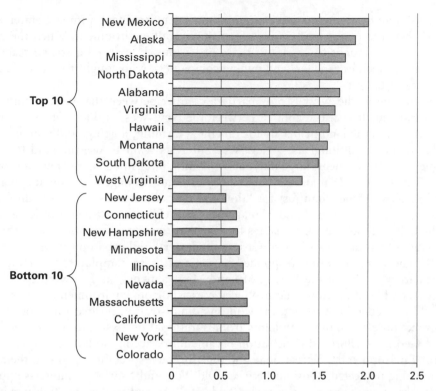

FIGURE 3.1
Federal Expenditures Divided by Federal Taxes, 2004

Source: Curtis Dubay, *Special Report,* No. 139, March 2006 (Tax Foundation: http://www.taxfoundation.org/ publications/show/ 274.html), pp. 2–3.

REGIONAL CONFLICT

Western concerns attracted national attention in July 1979 when the Nevada legislature passed a resolution demanding that 49 million acres of federal land in Nevada be turned over to the state. Termed the **Sagebrush Rebellion,** the idea quickly spread and similar legislation was introduced in other western states where the federal government was a big land owner.[56] Three issues prompted this Sagebrush Rebellion and they are likely to remain important in western politics. They are land, energy, and water.

Land Issues

Land is an issue because the federal government owns over half of the land in five western states and over a third of the land in 10 states. Until 1976, the federal government leased its land mostly for traditional uses such as mining, logging, and grazing livestock, and people who leased the land had considerable freedom to use it as they saw fit. This arrangement changed with the federal Land Policy and Management Act of 1976, which sought to protect the environmental quality of these federally owned lands. Ten-year leases were replaced by one-year leases, and the tenants were required to file environmental impact statements indicating how their use of the land would affect the overall environment. When the Bureau of Land Management sought to carry out those provisions, it sparked a strong reaction from traditional users (such as ranchers and mining companies), who sought to get the federal government "off our backs."

The land issue in the West is only partly a conflict between the western states and the federal government. It is also a conflict between the New West and the Old West. Old West interests seek to use the land primarily for ranching, farming, logging, and mining, which are called "dominant" traditional uses. New West interests want to use the land for industrial and commercial development, large numbers of homes, intensified energy exploration, and/or recreation. Under its 1976 mandate, the Bureau of Land Management is managing the land for "multiple uses" rather than just for "dominant" traditional uses, a situation that angers Old West interests. Bureau of Land Management and U.S. Forest Service officials also resist turning the federal land over to the states for fear that the states will not protect the environmental quality of the land as it is used for more industrial and urban purposes.

The Reagan administration responded to some of these complaints by clamping down on the regulatory efforts of the Bureau of Land Management[57] and slowly began increasing the sale of federal lands, actions that produced criticism from environmental and recreational groups.[58] As the federal courts and the Clinton administration pushed for stronger environmental protection efforts, the complaints from traditional users surfaced again, only to subside as the George W. Bush administration became more accommodating toward traditional users again. Environmental, recreational, and tourism interests complained that their concerns were again being neglected. Tensions between Old West and New West interests appear to be continuing, although they may be crowded aside in 2008 and beyond by high fuel prices and broader worries about the economy.

Energy Issues

Energy issues are also prominent in conflicts between eastern states and western states. Most of the nation's energy-producing areas are found in the West or southwestern-south–central states. There are some traditional energy states in the eastern United States, such as Kentucky, Pennsylvania, and West Virginia, but a great deal of energy extraction is from western states.[59]

The disproportionate concentration of energy resources in a few states creates a serious issue for intergovernmental politics. When the energy shortages of the 1970s produced an **energy crisis**, oil, coal, and natural gas companies responded by dramatically expanding their energy explorations. These efforts were also fostered by environmental policies emphasizing cleaner-burning fuels, such as low-sulfur coal (much of which is in western states). Each coal-mining site or energy-processing plant brought in new people who needed houses, schools, and public services while they worked in the energy production enterprises. Some communities experienced dramatic growth in a short period of time.

To pay for these expanded services, some energy-producing states drastically increased their **severance taxes** (the tax on resources extracted from the ground). Louisiana, for example, sharply increased its tax on natural gas that was piped out of state, and Montana increased its coal tax to 30 percent of the value of the coal that was mined. Energy-consuming states bitterly complained that these increases were a blatant attempt by energy-producing states to gouge the rest of the country by exporting their tax burdens. In 1981, the Supreme Court voided the Louisiana tax on natural gas because it exempted Louisianans,[60] but the Court let stand the Montana tax because it fell on Montanans as well as non-Montanans.[61]

By the mid-1980s, the energy shortage was replaced by an energy glut (partly due to the economic slowdown of the early 1980s), and the price of oil fell by 50 percent. This development greatly eased the financial problems of energy-consuming states, but it wreaked financial havoc in many parts of the West. Some of the energy boomtowns created a decade earlier faced the prospect of becoming ghost towns still burdened with the task of paying for the school buildings, water systems, and other public facilities they built to accommodate their then-growing populations. Some of them no longer had the population and tax base required to raise the needed revenues. States such as Texas and Oklahoma, that relied heavily on energy taxes to expand their public facilities and services in the 1970s, suddenly found their tax base shrinking in the mid-1980s as the price of oil dropped. By the 1990s, however, energy prices improved and the economic prospects of these states began to look better for a time.

Petroleum prices soared after the U.S. invasion of Iraq during George W. Bush's presidency, and many observers began to worry that price hikes for gasoline and diesel fuels might trigger an economic slump, which they did (along with several other forces). The widely dispersed populations of some western states, such as Wyoming and Montana, are particularly sensitive to fuel price hikes, as are the airlines, trucking companies, and many Americans who commute long distances to and from work every day. Homes and businesses that heat with oil are also sensitive to petroleum price increases; many of those homes and businesses are in the northeastern part of the country. With gasoline prices now at roughly three and one-half dollars per gallon in a number of states and with diesel fuel costs of approximately four dollars per gallon, many state economies are under great strain.

The complexity of our federal system and energy politics surfaced again with the controversy over constructing an oil pipeline from the large tar sands projects in northern Canada to the Gulf Coast of the United States. Members of Congress adopted a 60-day time limit on review of the project, but opposition from people in Nebraska erupted over concerns that the pipeline would endanger the source of much of Nebraska's water and mar the beauty of the state's Sandhills region. The time limit ended before a revised route was developed, so President Obama, forced by the congressional deadline to issue a decision, refused to approve the project in January of 2012. A number of Republican officials and candidates blasted the president's decision, but he left open the possibility of approving a revised plan if it resolves the problems raised by the earlier route.[62]

Water Issues

Although the West is energy-rich, many parts of it are water-poor. The West traditionally has sought to meet its water needs through federally sponsored projects that dammed up rivers and moved large volumes of water long distances through aqueducts to growing urban populations. Some urban locations became overdeveloped in relation to their local water supplies. They have depended greatly on federally funded projects, for which eastern state residents help to pay, to help meet their water needs.

Because of urbanization, industrialization, and the desire to exploit natural resources, many competing interests want access to scarce western water rights. However, a survey of legislators and the public in four western states found no support for reallocating existing water supplies among competing users.[63] Rather, they wanted to increase the water supply.

In 1980, Arizona passed legislation that sought simultaneously to increase water supplies and to decrease consumption through conservation.[64] Crucial to this plan was the Central Arizona Project, a huge system of aqueducts to pipe water from hundreds of miles away into Arizona at a cost to federal taxpayers of $180 million per year. Promoting long-term water conservation in the West has proven difficult and population growth in many arid locations continues.

Several questions arise about water politics. From how far can water actually be transported to the West? From the Mississippi River? From the Great Lakes? From the Columbia River to southern California? From British Columbia? Even if such feats were technologically possible, would they make sense as public policy? Will nonwestern states continue to be willing to pay the costs for projects that will benefit mainly the West? Worried about possible efforts to tap the Great Lakes, the states surrounding the lakes in 1985 adopted the Great Lakes Charter, which sets up a plan for managing the use and diversion of Great Lakes' waters.[65] A new agreement in 2005, reaffirmed in 2008, underscored the principle that the water of the Great Lakes is for the states and provinces in the area and should not be diverted to other parts of North America.[66] People in the Pacific Northwest have also been unreceptive to proposals to transfer water from their states to the more arid southwestern states. Nevertheless, the population in many parts of the Southwest continues to grow, and meeting its water needs continues to be a concern.

The water needs of the Southwest were underscored by the mortgage problems that were part of the recession that began in 2007–2008. Three of the four largest concentrations of problem mortgages are located in the Southwest: southern Arizona, southern California, and southern Nevada, particularly the Las Vegas area.[67] With many people struggling to retain ownership of their homes, any conservation-related responses to the water problems that might place additional costs on homeowners are likely to trigger opposition.

The Scope of Intergovernmental Conflict in the West

One of the most important aspects of these political conflicts has been their periodic expansion from the private sector, local level, and state level to the federal level, and recurring efforts to reverse that development. State governments have been unable to resolve the competition for use of land and water, so some of the interests have turned to the federal government. As these interests looked to Washington for help, the Bureau of Land Management and the Forest Service played a stronger role as mediator of various land uses, with some involvement by environmental and business groups. But it was just this role that helped precipitate the Sagebrush Rebellion. And under the Reagan administration, the Bureau of Land Management became less aggressive than it had been in earlier years. These disagreements continued into the Clinton administration. When Clinton created the Escalante-Grand Staircase National Monument in southern Utah, some Old West interests criticized the decision as more federal control. However, New West interests concerned about the environment and the vital tourist industry in southern Utah praised the decision. When President George W. Bush took office, environmental controls were loosened again, and environmental groups pressed state and local governments to do more to protect the environment.

During the Obama administration, White House again pressed more vigorously for environmental protection. However, the Republican gains in Congress following the 2010 elections led to considerable conflict over environmental policy.

INTERGOVERNMENTAL IMPACT ON STATE AND LOCAL POLITICAL ECONOMIES

It is apparent from our review here that federalism and intergovernmental relations have important consequences for the ability of state and local governments to deliver public services and facilitate economic growth in their private sectors. Two of these consequences are very important: (1) the forces for interregional conflict, and (2) the strengths and weaknesses of the intergovernmental system in dealing with regional and state diversity.

Cooperation versus Conflict

Underlying much of what occurs in intergovernmental politics is the fact that the states and regions differ widely in their economic resources and assets, as well as their political values. The West has an abundance of energy resources, but it is the nation's driest region and lacks the water to develop its resources. Moreover, the rapidly growing urban centers of the West increasingly face the same environmental, social, and traffic problems that have traditionally faced the Northeast and upper Midwest. The Northeast and Midwest regions have the most extensive network of factories and productive capacity, including many skilled workers, but they have been hit hard in recent years by foreign competition and by American companies shifting production overseas. The South has benefited immensely from population and economic growth in recent years, but it is still the poorest region and includes a number of the most conservative states in the country.[68]

Not only are there disparities among regions, but there are also dramatic disparities within regions. The sunbelt includes impoverished rural Mississippi as well as dynamic growth centers in Virginia, Texas, and Florida. The northeastern–midwestern frostbelt includes not only Detroit, whose unemployment rates exceeded 20 percent during the early 1980s, but also one of the nation's highest concentrations of dynamic high-technology industry in the Boston suburbs near Harvard University and the Massachusetts Institute of Technology. The West includes relatively liberal states, like California and Hawaii, and quite conservative states, such as Idaho and Wyoming.

These disparities create forces both for cooperation and for conflict among the states. Interstate cooperation has been enhanced by the emergence of regionally based economies. States are still the dominant political units for dealing with local economies, but state officials have sometimes been forced to band together to cope with economic issues that overlap state boundaries. The Great Lakes, for example, are an economic asset to eight different states, and there are many questions on managing water rights, navigation rights, invasive species of fish, and other matters that no single state can manage alone. Similar overarching economic interests exist in other regions also. Hence, the devices of cooperation discussed earlier are used more and more frequently; they include interstate compacts, regional commissions, informal sharing of ideas and information, and regional lobbying.

Working against interstate cooperation, however, are other forces leading the states into conflict with each other. The widespread desire for economic growth sometimes leads states into bidding wars that offer concessions to companies to locate or expand in their states. These bidding wars involve extensive tax concessions; the promise of low tax rates; minimal regulation of the environment, health, and safety; construction of infrastructure, such as highways, rail lines, and water systems; and the promise to enact right-to-work laws that make it difficult for unions to organize employees, among other things.

Free market competition is, of course, one of the basic values of the American culture, and it has the benefits of promoting greater efficiency and a wider variety of products. But an unbridled competition between cities and states to attract industry also has serious unhealthy consequences. Because economic resources and assets are not evenly divided across the country, some places will make out poorly while others will prosper handsomely. In the 1980s and 1990s, for example, increasing numbers of cities tried to entice service industries and high-technology industries in computers, software, biomedical engineering, and genetics. A critical resource needed for this strategy to succeed was a major research university, such as Harvard or MIT outside of Boston or the University of California and Stanford near that state's famous Silicon Valley, which had an early start in making silicon chips for computers. States without major research universities to provide personnel and other attractions to high-technology companies could well invest large sums of money into the competition and get very little payoff.[69]

Unbridled bidding wars for industry might also drastically weaken the ability of states to carry out their constitutional responsibilities to raise revenues for public services and to regulate the public health, safety, and environment. A state or city that gives away too many tax concessions to attract new industries may find itself financially strapped for police, fire, education, welfare, and other services. Or neighboring states or communities may find themselves being played off against each other by a major industry threatening to relocate out of elsewhere. For example, Oregon found itself for years in a weak position to force paper mills to clean up the pollution they dumped into the Columbia River, because the companies threatened to move their operations into neighboring states.[70] Federal action was needed to enforce environmental regulation.

In light of these experiences, competition among states is likely to weaken environmental protection regulations and to reduce overall expenditures for social services.[71] Social services are essentially redistributive services that take taxes from middle- and upper-income people and redistribute them through social services to lower-income and poor people. If states are put in competition over social services, there will be a natural tendency to hold taxes down by keeping social service expenditures as low as possible. This is because no state will want to look much more profligate than its neighbor, although that concern may be countered by other political values.

Environmental regulations may be weakened for the same reasons. If business corporations think regulations are too rigid in one state, they will threaten to move their operations to states where the regulations are more lax. In order to prevent that from happening, each state will have a powerful incentive to promote weak rather than strong environmental regulations. However, weakening environmental protections too much may harm tourism-related businesses, agriculture, the fishing industry, and other firms tied to the environment, not to mention general public health. Moreover, the giveaways to various businesses may fail to produce long-run economic benefits if those companies eventually relocate or outsource production overseas.[72]

If these policy dynamics develop, and they clearly have for some social programs—although not equally across all states—we will eventually see more pressure for federal involvement. The history of the federal system shows that when people are unhappy with the decisions made by one government, they are likely to demand action by some other government, often another level of government.[73] Some states and localities made more efforts to protect the environment as the George W. Bush administration loosened environmental controls. Conversely, some state governments are now pressing for weaker environmental controls in response to the Obama administration's stronger efforts to protect the environment. Overall, this dynamic has helped to produce the overlapping responsibilities of governments in the American political system and is a powerful obstacle to efforts to sort out responsibilities by different levels of government. Even if a sorting process could ever be carried out, the clear separation of duties would begin to erode as soon as people were unhappy with a local, state, or federal decision.

Although much of this chapter has focused on the influence of higher levels of government on lower levels, keep in mind that lower levels are far from helpless. State and local officials lobby higher levels of government, and that lobbying is often influential. Legislators who represent an area often defend its interests at higher levels of government, and private groups with an interest in the state or locality will add their voices. Agencies at all levels find that life is often easier if they adapt somewhat to the local political climate; failure to do so will mean additional criticism and conflict. Passive resistance, delaying tactics, and half-hearted compliance are also highly effective in blunting initiatives by higher levels of government.[74]

SUMMARY

1. The Constitution divides authority (though not very clearly) between the national and state governments. The national government possesses those powers delegated to it by the Constitution. All other powers not otherwise forbidden are reserved to the states or to the people.

2. Although the federal government is restricted to exercising only delegated powers, some constitutional provisions have permitted the Supreme Court to make a loose constructionist interpretation of those delegated powers. The most significant constitutional clauses used by the loose constructionists are the Necessary-and-Proper Clause, the National Supremacy Clause, the Commerce Clause, and the General Welfare Clause.

3. Although the states are given the reserved powers, a number of constitutional provisions put limits on the states' exercise of those powers. The most significant constitutional clauses are the Commerce Clause, the **Equal Protection Clause**, and the **Due Process Clause**. Many state constitutions also contain limits on state powers.

4. Federalism evolved from dual federalism to cooperative federalism and competitive federalism. Part of that development has included a recognition of the importance of local governments in the federal system. The major mechanisms for cooperative federalism have

been grants-in-aid, court orders, preemptive legislation, and mandates.

5. President Reagan sought a New Federalism in the 1980s that would devolve federal responsibilities to the states and the private sector for many social services and for much governmental regulation. He had some successes, but not as many as he wanted. His ideas influenced congressional Republicans in the 1990s and today, and continue to be discussed. Federal grants have grown dramatically since the Reagan administration.

6. In addition to state and national relations, there are also several other forms of intergovernmental relations: national–local, state–local, interlocal, and interstate. Over the long term, the changes in intergovernmental relations have caused local autonomy to decline. Scholars have also become more aware of the important role that many private organizations play in our federal system.

7. Two patterns of interregional conflicts are sunbelt–frostbelt and East–West.

8. State and community political economies are greatly affected by contemporary intergovernmental relations. Fiscal federalism redistributes income from the richer states to the poorer states. The competition for economic growth often pits regions, states, and communities against each other.

STUDY QUESTIONS

1. How has the federal system changed over the years? Why has it changed?
2. How do higher levels of government try to influence the actions of lower levels of government? What difficulties may those efforts encounter?
3. Why have some reformers tried to reduce national involvement in domestic policy making? How successful have those efforts been?
4. Why are regional conflicts important in intergovernmental relations?

KEY TERMS

Block grant   A grant that can be used for almost anything in a broad functional area, such as education or transportation. A block grant may be created by consolidating several categorical grants into a single grant.

Categorical grant   A grant-in-aid given for a specific purpose, such as building airports or improving foreign language instruction in high schools. Also called *categorical aid.*

Commerce Clause   The provision in Article II, Section 8, of the Constitution that grants Congress the authority to regulate interstate and international commerce.

Compact theory   The theory of John C. Calhoun that the U.S. Constitution was a compact between the state governments rather than a charter from the people. This theory could be used to justify the states defying the national government.

Cooperative federalism   The theory of federalism in which federal, state, and local levels of government cooperate in domestic policy making. This theory largely replaced *dual federalism.*

Delegated powers   See *enumerated powers.*

Dillon's Rule   The principle that city government powers must be interpreted very narrowly. This rule gives the states considerable authority over localities and sometimes has left local governments unable to deal with local problems on their own.

Dual federalism   The concept of federalism in which the state and national levels of government have separate areas of authority. Local governments were largely ignored. Popular until the 1930s. Distinct from *cooperative federalism.*

Due Process Clause   The provision of the Fifth and Fourteenth Amendments that protects a person from deprivation of life, liberty, or property without due process of law.

Energy crisis   A situation in the 1970s when petroleum and natural gas sources were scarce and prices for them increased precipitously. Oil prices also surged in 2008.

Enumerated powers   The powers specifically granted to Congress and/or the national government more generally by the Constitution. Also called *delegated powers.*

Equal Protection Clause   The provision of the Constitution's Fourteenth Amendment that forbids any state to deny any person in its jurisdiction the equal protection of the laws. Sometimes used to stop states from discriminating against nonresidents, although a number of exceptions have been allowed.

Federalism   A formal or informal allocation of authority between a national government and one or more levels of subnational governments. Responsibilities may be clearly divided or may be shared among levels of government.

Formula grant   A grant-in-aid in which the funds are dispensed according to a formula specified by law. When the formula is adopted, officials at the receiving level of government know how much funding they will receive.

Frostbelt   The Northeast and Midwest.

Fungibility   The tendency for grant money given to one program being used to replace money the recipient planned to spend on the program. The freed-up money may then be spent on a different program. This phenomenon limits the influence of grants-in-aid over the policies of the lower level of government.

General revenue sharing   A program in which the federal government turned funds over to state and local governments to use as they saw fit with very few federal guidelines on how the money was to be spent. Many states have similar programs.

General Welfare Clause   This clause of the U.S. Constitution gives Congress the authority to enact and collect taxes, duties, imposts and excises to pay for the debts and provide for the common defense and general welfare of the U.S. This provision has been used to support expansion of the federal government.

Grant-in-aid   A federal payment to a state or local government, or a state payment to a local government to carry out an activity or to run a program.

Intergovernmental relations (IGR) A term used for contemporary federalism in which many different layers of government interact with each other in a complex system. May also include private organizations.

National Supremacy Clause The provision in Article VI of the Constitution that makes the Constitution and all legislation passed under its authority the supreme law of the land.

Necessary and Proper Clause The clause in Article I, Section 8, of the Constitution that gives Congress power to pass all laws necessary and proper for carrying into execution the enumerated powers.

New Federalism Attempts by the Nixon and Reagan administrations, and congressional Republicans since that time, to turn federal responsibilities over to the states, in part by giving the states more flexibility in spending federal grants. The Reagan administration added the concept of "devolution" and made sharp cutbacks in federal aid to states and communities.

Open-ended reimbursement A grant-in-aid in which the federal government automatically reimburses state or local governments for a share of whatever program funds are spent. Primarily used for entitlement programs, such as unemployment compensation, in which the funds spent will vary greatly with economic conditions.

Project grant A grant-in-aid in which the recipient government has to make an application to the granting agency, and the granting agency has considerable discretion in deciding which applicants will receive the grant.

Reserved powers The powers reserved to the states or to the people of the United States by the Tenth Amendment to the Constitution.

Sagebrush Rebellion The rebellion of many states in the West against federal ownership and management of significant amounts of western land. Partly a reaction to federal environmental protection policies.

Scope of conflict The size and location of a political conflict—where it is addressed, and who gets involved. It may be private, local, state, or federal. It may involve one or more chief executives, legislatures, courts, and/or agencies, as well as various interest groups and parties. The scope of conflict dictates what sorts of policies are chosen. People who are unhappy with a decision often try to change the scope of conflict to another arena where they hope to get a different decision.

Severance tax A tax levied on natural resources extracted from the earth. Much of the cost of the tax can be passed on to customers in other states or even other countries.

Sunbelt The South and Southwest.

Unitary government A system of government in which all governmental authority resides in the national government. If lower levels of government exist, they have no independent authority.

THE INTERNET CONNECTION

For more information on intergovernmental relations, especially from state and local perspectives, see **Governing.com**. Many intergovernmental lobbying organizations, such as state teachers' associations, can also be found on the Web.

NOTES

1. Lara Jordan, "Federal Fixes for Hurricane Season Could Bring New Problems for States," *Moscow (ID)-Pullman Daily News*, May 23, 2006, p. 9A; Donald Kettl, "Potomac Chronicle: It's Broke—Fix It," *Governing* 19, no. 7 (April 2006): 24; John Kincaid, "Federal-State Relations: Federal Dollars Down, Federal Power Up," in *The Book of the States*, vol. 38 (Lexington, KY: Council of State Government, 2006), pp. 19–20; Jonathan Walters and Donald Kettl, "The Katrina Meltdown," *Governing* 19, no. 3 (December 2005): 20–25.

2. E. E. Schattschneider, *The Semisovereign People* (New York: Holt, Rinehart and Winston, 1960).

3. Josh Goodman, "Greenhouse Gumption," *Governing* 19, no. 8 (May, 2006): 60–63; John Kincaid, "State-Federal Relations: Dueling Policies," in *Book of the States*, vol. 40 (Lexington, KY: Council of State Government, 2008): 19; Dina Cappiello, "Regulation

of Greenhouse Gases Rejected," *Moscow, ID/Pullman Daily News,* July 12–13, p. 5C.

4. Joseph Zimmerman, *Contemporary American Federalism,* 2nd ed. (Albany, NY: State University of New York Press, 2008); David Robertson, *Federalism and the Making of America* (New York: Routledge, 2012); David Nice and Patricia Fredericksen, *The Politics of Intergovernmental Relations,* 2nd ed. (Chicago: Nelson-Hall, 1995), ch. 1; David Walker, *The Rebirth of Federalism,* 2nd ed. (New York: Chatham House, 2000), chs. 1–6.

5. See Zimmerman, pp. 71–72; *Contemporary American* Daniel J. Elazar, *The American Partnership* (Chicago: University of Chicago Press, 1962), p. 20.

6. Gibbons *v. Ogden,* 6 L.Ed. 23 (1824).

7. *National Labor Relations Board v. Jones and Laughlin Steel Corp.,* 300 U.S. 1 (1937).

8. For the position of the National Governors' Association supporting the consolidation of categorical grants into block grants, see "Governors' Bulletin," no. 80–20 (Washington, DC: National Governors' Association, May 16, 1980). For some recent statistics on grant programs, see Walker, *The Rebirth of Federalism,* 2nd ed., pp. 4–7.

9. Kenneth Finegold, Laura Wherry, and Stephanie Schardin, "Block Grants: Historical Overview and Lessons Learned," Urban Institute, April 21, 2004 (**http://www.urban.org/url.cfm?ID=310991**).

10. *Book of the States,* vol. 42 (Lexington, KY: Council of State Governments, 2010), p. 46; *Statistical Abstract of the United States,* 2011–2012 (New York: Skyhorse, 2011), pp. 268–269.

11. Kevin Freking, "States Turn Down Abstinence Grants," *Moscow, ID/Pullman Daily News,* July 10, 2008, p. 3A.

12. For an excellent history of the origins and development of block grants, see Timothy J. Conlan, "The Politics of Federal Block Grants from Nixon to Reagan," *Political Science Quarterly* 99, no. 2 (Summer 1984): 247–270. See also *Characteristics of Federal Grant-in-Aid Programs to State and Local Governments* (Washington, DC: Advisory Commission on Intergovernmental Relations, 1995); recent information on grants can be found in the *Statistical Abstract of the United States 2008* (Washington, DC: Bureau of the Census, 2008), pp. 265, 270.

13. For an example of considerable state foot dragging, see Jeffrey Hill and Carol Weissert,

"Implementation and the Irony of Delegation: The Politics of Low-Level Radioactive Waste Disposal," *Journal of Politics* 57 (1995): 344–369; for a discussion of the importance of bargaining in grant administration, see Robert Agranoff and Michael McGuire, "Another Look at Bargaining and Negotiation in Intergovernmental Relations," *The Journal of Public Administration Research and Theory* 14 (2004): 495–512.

14. *Brown v. Board of Education,* 347 U.S. 483 (1954); 349 U.S. 294 (1955). For a discussion of federal court intervention in state programs, see Charles Wise and Robert Christensen, "A Full and Fair Capacity: Federal Courts Managing State Programs," *Administration and Society* 37 (2005): 576–610.

15. *Roe v. Wade,* 410 U.S. 113 (1973).

16. *Baker v. Carr,* 369 U.S. 186 (1962); *Reynolds v. Simms,* 377 U.S. 533 (1964).

17. *South Dakota v. Dole,* 483 U.S. 203 (1987).

18. David M. O'Brien, "The 'Rehnquist Court' and Federal Preemption: In Search of a Theory," *Publius: The Journal of Federalism* 24, no. 4 (1993): 15–31.

19. For a discussion and critique of some of these cases, see John Noonan, *Narrowing the Nation's Power* (Berkeley: University of California, 2002).

20. Advisory Commission on Intergovernmental Relations, *Federal Statutory Preemption of State and Local Authority* (Washington, DC: Advisory Commission on Intergovernmental Relations, 1992).

21. Kincaid, "State-Federal Relations: Continuing Regulatory Federalism," p. 23.

22. Ellen Perlman, "The Gorilla that Swallowed State Laws," *Governing* (August 1994): 46–48; Joseph Zimmerman, "Congressional Preemption and the States," in *Book of the States,* vol. 38 (Lexington, KY: Council of State Governments, 2006), pp. 26–29.

23. Kincaid, "State-Federal Relations: Dueling Policies," p. 21.

24. *The New York Times,* May 21, 1990, p. A11. *The New York Times,* March 24, 1992, p. A1.

25. For discussions of limitations on grant impact, see John Chubb, "The Political Economy of Federalism," *American Political Science Review* 79 (1985): 994–1015; George Hale and Marian Palley, *The Politics of Federal Grants* (Washington, DC: CQ Press, 1981), pp. 113–116; David Nice and Patricia Fredericksen, *The Politics of Intergovernmental Relations,* 2nd ed. (Chicago: Nelson-Hall, 1995), pp. 64–66.

26. Thomas R. Dye, "Federalism: A Return to the Future," *Madison Review* 1, no. 1 (Fall 1995): 2; Kincaid, "State-Federal Relations: Continuing Regulatory Federalism," pp. 21–24.

27. Ben Feller, "No Parent Left Behind?" *Moscow-Pullman Daily News*, March 3, 2004, p. 10A.

28. See Edward C. Banfield, "Making a New Federal Program: Model Cities, 1964–1968," in Allan P. Sindler, ed. *Policy and Politics in America* (Boston: Little, Brown and Co., 1973), pp. 160–198; Martha Derthick, *New Towns in Town: Why a Federal Program Failed* (Washington, DC: Urban Institute, 1972); Paul R. Dommel, "Distribution Politics and Urban Policy," *Policy Studies Journal* 3, no. 4 (June 1975): 370–374; Jeffrey L. Pressman and Aaron B. Wildavsky, *Implementation* (Berkeley, CA: University of California Press, 1973); Helen W. Smookler, "Administrative Hara-Kiri: Implementation of the Urban Growth and New Community Development Act," *Annals of the American Academy of Political and Social Science* 422 (November 1975), pp. 133–137; David B. Walker, "The Federal Role in the Federal System: A Troublesome Topic," *National Civic Review* 72, no. 1 (January 1983): 6–23.

29. See Morton Grodzins, *The American System* (Chicago: Rand McNally, 1966), pp. 307–316; Nice and Fredericksen, *The Politics of Intergovernmental Relations*, pp. 230–237.

30. Ronald Reagan, "Inaugural Address," January 20, 1981 and speech to the National Governors Association, August 8, 1988.

31. *Washington Post National Weekly*, March 27–April 2, 1995, p. 37. See George Gallup, *The Gallup Poll* (Wilmington, DE: Scholarly Resources, 1998), pp. 95–98; Nice and Fredericksen, *The Politics of Intergovernmental Relations*, pp. 227–228.

32. Ronald Reagan, "Inaugural Address," January 20, 1981.

33. For a careful analysis of the flaws of that argument, see Julian Wolpert, *Patterns of Generosity in America: Who's Holding the Safety Net?* (New York: Twentieth Century Fund Press, 1993).

34. Spending on federal grants grew from $154 billion in 1991 to $236 billion in 1996. *Statistical Abstract of the United States, 1996*, p. 300.

35. See Robertson, *Federalism and the Making of America*, pp. 151–152; Timothy Conlan, *The New Federalism* (Washington, DC: Brookings, 1988); David Beam and Timothy Conlan, "The Growth of Intergovernmental Mandates in an Era of Decentralization and Deregulation," in Lawrence O'Toole, ed. *American Intergovernmental Relations,* 2nd ed., (Washington, DC: CQ Press, 1993), pp. 322–336.

36. Richard P. Nathan and Fred C. Doolittle, "The Untold Story of Reagan's 'New Federalism'," *Public Interest*, no. 77 (Fall 1984): 96–105.

37. A. F. Sulzberger, "Businesses Stand to Gain Most in Rivalry of States," *New York Times*, April 7, 2011 (Web edition).

38. Paul E. Peterson, "Who Should Do What? Divided Responsibilities in a Federal System," *Brookings Review* 13, no. 2 (Spring 1995): 6–11. L. Jerome Gallagher, *A Shrinking Portion of the Safety Net: General Assistance from 1989 to 1998* (Washington, DC: Urban Institute, 1999), p. 6; Mark Rom, "Transforming State Health and Welfare Programs," in Virginia Gray, Russell Hanson, and Herbert Jacob, eds. *Politics in the American States,* 7th ed., (Washington, DC: CQ Press, 1999), p. 361.

39. For a discussion of the various currents at work during the Clinton years, see Walker, *The Rebirth of Federalism*, 2nd ed., pp. 156–168.

40. See *State of Oregon and Peter A. Rasmussen, et al., v. John Ashcroft, et al.* (Civil No. 01-1647-JO). David Brater, "So, Now Bigger Is Better?" *Washington Post National Weekly Edition*, January 20–26, 2003, p. 21; Brad Cain, "Advocates of Assisted Suicide Cheer Supreme Court Ruling," *Moscow, ID/Pullman Daily News*, January 18, 2006, p. 4A.

41. See John Kincaid, "State-Federal Relations: Continuing Regulatory Federalism," in *The Book of the States* (Lexington, KY: Council of State Governments, 2002), pp. 25–29.

42. Paul Foy, "States Are Rebelling Against New Federal Education Rules," *Moscow-Pullman Daily News*, February 18, 2004, p. 9A; Ben Feller, "Testing Law Eased Once Again," *Moscow-Pullman Daily News*, March 29, 2004, p. 1A.

43. Donald Kettl, "Unconnected Dots," *Governing* (April 2004), p. 14.

44. Susan MacManus and Kiki Caruson, "Code Red: Florida City and County Officials Rate Threat Information Sources and the Homeland Security Advisory System," *State and Local Government Review* 38 (2006): 12–22.

45. Jason Stein, "State to Return $11 Million Federal Grant in Dispute Over Health Care Law,"

Milwaukee Journal Sentinel, January 20, 2012 (Web edition).

46. *Federal Mandates: Few Rules Trigger Unfunded Mandates Reform Act* (Washington, DC: United States Government Accountability Office, 2011), report GAO-11-385T.

47. See Kincaid, "State-Federal Relations: Dueling Policies"; Walker, *The Rebirth of Federalism*, chs. 9–11.

48. Robert Agranoff and Michael McGuire, *Collaborative Public Management* (Washington, DC: Georgetown University, 2003).

49. For a valuable overview of numerous aspects of intergovernmental relations, see Laurence O'Toole, *American Intergovernmental Relations* (Washington, DC: CQ Press, 2007).

50. *Community Communications Company, Inc. v. City of Boulder*, 102 S.Ct. 835 (1982). For a recent overview of state-local relations, see Joseph Zimmerman, "Evolving State-Local Relations," in *The Book of the States* (Lexington, KY: Council of State Governments, 2002), pp. 33–39.

51. *Statistical Abstract*, 2011–2012, p. 286.

52. Rob Gurwitt, "As States Cut Aid, Localities Learn to do Less with Less," *Stateline*, October 3, 2011 (Web edition).

53. See Joseph Zimmerman, *Contemporary American Federalism*, 2nd ed., ch. 7; Joseph Zimmerman, "Trends in Interstate Relations: Political and Administrative Cooperation," in *The Book of the States* (Lexington, KY: Council of State Governments, 2002), pp. 40–47.

54. Kirk Johnson, "No Closure for Denver's Beltway Loop," *New York Times*, January 16, 2012 (Web edition).

55. *Statistical Abstract*, 2011–2012, pp. 460–461.

56. See *The National Journal*, November 11, 1979, p. 1928.

57. See *The New York Times*, February 14, 1983, p. 1, and June 18, 1982, p. 11. State complaints were not totally put to rest, however. Alaskans, in particular, got upset in the 1980s when the amount of National Park land was expanded in that state; See *The New York Times*, August 4, 1986, p. 1.

58. Frank J. Popper, "The Timely End of the Sagebrush Rebellion," *The Public Interest* 76 (Summer 1984): 61–73.

59. *Statistical Abstract*, 2011–2012, pp. 574–576, 578.

60. *Maryland v. Louisiana*, 451 U.S. 725 (1981).

61. *Commonwealth Edison v. Montana*, 453 U.S. 609 (1981).

62. Jim Malewitz, "Obama Decision Denies Keystone XL Permit," *Stateline*, January 19, 2012 (Web edition).

63. John C. Pierce, "Conflict and Consensus in Water Politics," *Western Political Quarterly* 32, no. 3 (September 1979): 307–317.

64. Michael F. McNulty and Gary C. Woodward, "Arizona Water Issues: Contrasting Economic and Legal Perspectives," *Arizona Review* 32, no. 2 (Fall 1984): 1–13.

65. Larry Morandi, "Not for Sale," *State Legislatures* 13, no. 1 (January 1987): 16–19.

66. Gretchen Ehlke, "Great Lakes Governors Sign Agreement on Water Protections," *Moscow-Pullman Daily News*, December 14, 2005: 10A.

67. We will examine this issue in greater depth in chapter 15.

68. Jeffrey Jones, "Ideology: Three Deep South States Are the Most Conservative," *Gallup Poll*, February 3, 2010 (Web edition).

69. See Aaron S. Gurwitz, "The New Faith in High Tech," *The Wall Street Journal*, October 27, 1982.

70. Council on Environmental Quality, *Environmental Quality Annual Report: 1973* (Washington, DC: U.S. Government Printing Office, 1973), pp. 43–71.

71. See John Donahue, *Disunited States* (New York: Basic Books, 1997); Peterson, "Who Should Do What? Divided Responsibilities in a Federal System," pp. 6–11.

72. Greg Leroy, *The Great American Jobs Scam* (San Francisco: Berrett-Koehler Publishers, 2005).

73. E. E. Schattschneider, *The Semisovereign People* (New York: Holt, Rinehart, and Winston, 1960).

74. Grodzins, *The American System*, chs. 8–9; Helen Ingram, "Policy Implementation Through Bargaining: The Case of Federal Grants-in-Aid," *Public Policy* 25 (1977): 499–526.

Channels of Citizen Influence: Participation, Public Opinion, and Interest Groups

CHAPTER PREVIEW

If democracy is to have any meaning, there must be channels through which ordinary citizens can influence government policies. This chapter examines three aspects of this process. We will discuss:

1 The patterns of political participation and the attempts to increase participation over the years.

2 The influence of public opinion on government and public policy.

3 Interest groups—their types, tactics, and patterns of influence.

Introduction

A long-standing controversy in American politics centers on the questions of how much influence citizens should have in the governmental process and how that influence should be exercised. Moreover, political currents beginning in one part of the political system may spill over into other parts. In 2011, people from a variety of backgrounds began a series of demonstrations to criticize the growing economic inequality in the United States, the plight of people who are unemployed, and a number of other issues. In some places, they blocked traffic to attract attention, and they set up tent communities in local parks in a number of cities. The protesters began to use the label of "Occupy Wall Street" (or, at times, Occupy Some-other-community).

As has happened to many other groups in our history, the Occupy movement began to annoy some people. Demonstrators who blocked traffic angered commuters, and tent camps began to take a toll on the condition of local parks. Also, homeless people joined the informal communities in some parks, and they brought problems associated with alcohol and drugs. Eventually, local officials tried to move demonstrators out of parks and off of busy streets. A number of demonstrators were arrested.[1]

Although police interactions with the demonstrators were often peaceful, there were some clashes between the two groups. Police sometimes resorted to tear gas, and demonstrators and police suffered injuries in some clashes. In addition, some officers of the campus police at the University of California at Davis used pepper spray on some peaceful demonstrators who were sitting on the ground. Two officers who used the pepper spray were suspended while an investigation was conducted. Police at the University of California at Berkeley struck demonstrators with riot batons. Tensions were high on both sides, but it has begun to subside in at least some areas.[2] Although the number and size of demonstrators have declined, more Americans are now thinking about conflicts between the wealthy and the poor.[3]

Understanding participation in state and local politics is important because it goes to the core of what democracy is about: People who know how to participate in government and who have the means to do so are in a better position to protect their interests and advance causes they support. People who do not know how to participate or who lack the means risk being ignored when important decisions are made.

How do the channels of participation work and who benefits from them? In order to deal with this question, this chapter will first explore the patterns of political participation and then examine two facets of citizen influence—public opinion and interest groups. In Chapter 5, we will examine three other channels of citizen influence—political parties, election of public officials, and direct democracy.

POLITICAL PARTICIPATION

Political participation is any activity that seeks to influence the selection of government officials or the actions that public officials take.[4] In addition, actions to tackle a problem directly, such as picking up trash at a city park or organizing a neighborhood watch system to reduce crime, can be politically relevant.

Political participants can be classified as gladiators and spectators, to use the terminology of Lester Milbrath.[5] **Spectators** compose the 50 to 60 percent of the population that votes fairly regularly, pays some attention to political news, and displays political support through activities such as flying the flag and attending patriotic events. Spectators may also talk about politics with their friends and neighbors at times. The **gladiators** do the same things that spectators do, plus they invest time and money in more demanding political activities, such as joining an interest group or making a campaign contribution. There are many ways to get involved; Table 4.1 displays several major ways in which people can become politically active. For a more complete overview, see *MoveOn's 50 Ways to Love Your Country* and Paul Simon's *Fifty-two Simple Ways to Make a Difference*.[6]

While most American adults report having voted in the previous presidential election, official turnout statistics show that barely half the adult population actually voted. A substantial portion of the public discusses politics with other people and/or tries to persuade other people how to vote from time to time. Far fewer people are likely to give money to a campaign, attend a campaign rally, or work for a political party, a campaign, or an interest group. Voting turnout declined since the early 1960s, a development that concerns many Americans, although there has been a slight rebound since 1996. Turnout in state and especially local

TABLE 4.1

Some Modes of Participation

Spectator Activities

Vote

Read or watch political news coverage

Discuss politics with friends, family, and/or coworkers

Gladiator Activities

Send letters or e-mails to public officials or contact by phone

Give money to a campaign, political party, or interest group

Volunteer to work for a party, campaign, or interest group

Run for public office

elections is usually considerably below turnout in presidential elections, especially if the state or local elections are held in nonpresidential years. Note, too, that if we compare the proportion of people who claim to have voted with actual turnout, we find that some people are claiming to have voted when they actually have not.[7]

Given the importance of effective participation to a meaningful democracy, there are several questions we want to explore about these patterns of political participation. In what ways do the participators differ from the politically inactive? Why do some people avoid taking part in the political life of their states or communities? Why have some types of participation declined over time? And how much impact does political participation have on America's state and community political systems?

Who Participates?

The standard measure of political participation is the percentage of eligible voters who vote in an election. Researchers regularly find that voter turnout is higher among people of higher socioeconomic status and people with strong organizational ties (which tend to be more common among better-educated, wealthier people). As Figure 4.1 indicates, voter turnout is higher among the upper socioeconomic classes than among people with less education and lower incomes. Socioeconomic status appears to have more influence on voter participation in the United States than in a number of other countries.[8]

Voter turnout is also higher among middle-aged and older people than among young people, especially in nonpresidential election years. The turnout gap by age has increased in recent decades.[9] For many years, voter turnout among women was lower than turnout among men, but women gradually narrowed the gap and in recent years have been somewhat more likely to vote than have men. In a similar fashion, voter turnout among African Americans was considerably lower than turnout among whites for many years, but the gap has narrowed considerably in recent years. Turnout among Hispanics remains relatively low, however.

Higher socioeconomic status is also associated with the more demanding political activities. Leadership positions in campaigns and in interest groups are held disproportionately by

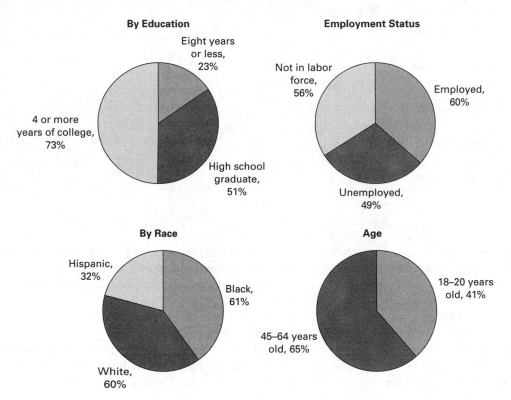

**Percentage of Eligible Voters Who
Claim They Voted in the 2008 Presidential Election**

By Education

Eight years or less, 23%

4 or more years of college, 73%

High school graduate, 51%

Employment Status

Not in labor force, 56%

Employed, 60%

Unemployed, 49%

By Race

Hispanic, 32%

Black, 61%

White, 60%

Age

18–20 years old, 41%

45–64 years old, 65%

FIGURE 4.1
The Socioeconomic Bases to Participation

Source: U.S. Census Bureau, *Statistical Abstract of the United States, 2011–2012* (New York: Skyhorse, 2011), p. 260. Note that self-reported turnout rates are usually somewhat inflated.

people with college degrees and people who have ties to various organizations; elected officials tend to be above the average socioeconomic level of their constituents.

Many observers are concerned by the large number of Americans who avoid virtually all conventional modes of political participation. Many people don't vote or pay much attention to politics in the news, or have any significant contact with major political groups.[10] However, many people who don't engage in conventional types of participation regularly engage in a variety of activities that either support the political system or place demands on it. They work, obey laws, pay taxes, use public services, collect benefits from government programs, raise families, send their children to school, serve in the armed forces, support the national economy through their purchases, and engage in a variety of other activities that are politically relevant. In addition, political interest and activity may vary over time; someone who is not involved this year may become involved next year because of a new issue or new candidate.

Why Do Some People Not Participate?

Socioeconomic Factors Research on political participation shows that the nonparticipants tend to be heavily concentrated among poor people, those who work in less prestigious occupations, and those with little education. Raymond Wolfinger and Steven Rosenstone sorted out the relative association of various socioeconomic variables with nonvoting and concluded that education was the most important of these variables.[11] Thus, poor people vote less often than middle-class people, not primarily because they are poor but because they have much less education. Less-educated people are more likely than middle-class people to lack the confidence and the communications skills needed to engage in community organizing, campaign work, and lobbying. They are less knowledgeable about political issues and candidates than college-educated people are, and they are less likely to have internalized a **sense of civic duty**, the belief that they have a community obligation to vote and to take part in community affairs.[12]

One form of political participation not explained very fully by socioeconomic status, however, is the contacting of local or state officials about personal or neighborhood problems. This is especially so in neighborhoods with serious needs. In such neighborhoods, people of low socioeconomic status are just as likely to bring their complaints to local officials as are people of higher status.[13]

For most forms of political activity, however, the poor and undereducated have the lowest participation rates, and this is one of the great paradoxes of American society. If poor people are most in need of governmental benefits and if political participation is a way of gaining those benefits, why then do the poor not participate more actively? Three explanations have been advanced: (1) individual psychological and skill barriers, (2) legal and political barriers, and (3) lack of organizations to mobilize the poor.

Psychological and Skill Factors Play a Part Psychological and skill barriers discourage poorer, less-educated people from participating. As just indicated, the poor often lack the self-confidence that comes with education. They do not work in the highly verbal or analytical occupations that businesspeople, union organizers, lawyers, doctors, or other professionals do. Moreover, less-educated people are likely to have more trouble understanding political discussions when more complex language is used. Thus, persuasion tactics, organizing activities, and seeking cooperative solutions to common problems are not second nature to the poor as they are to the more educated.

If poor people with little education attend a city council meeting and clash with an articulate lawyer, for instance, they are likely to lose the argument and come away with bruised egos and feelings of discouragement. Repeated experiences such as this reduce one's **sense of political efficacy**, a term used by political scientists to describe a person's belief that one's participation in politics can have some impact. Voting research has demonstrated that the lower a person's sense of political efficacy, the less likely that person is to vote.[14] Some aspects of efficacy declined considerably from the late 1950s through the early 1990s.[15]

How the various psychological factors affect participation is rather complicated. Using voter turnout as a measure of participation, Arthur Hadley divided nonvoters into six different types,[16] five of which result from psychological factors. First, the largest group of nonvoters are the *positive apathetics*, about 35 percent of his sample of nonvoters. These people are contentedly involved in their jobs and family lives and perceive politics as irrelevant. Second, about 13 percent of the nonvoters are the *bypassed*, people who have such low levels of information that they do not bother to participate. A third category of nonvoters, about 6 percent, is composed of the *naysayers,* those who have philosophically rejected voting. Fourth are the *cross-pressured,* about 5 percent of the nonvoters. They feel some pulls in favor of the Democrats and some pulls favoring Republicans and try to escape the conflict by not voting.

A fifth category of nonvoters (about 22 percent) is the *political impotents* who have an extremely low sense of political efficacy. The political impotents do not think that they can influence political outcomes. Anthony Downs applies a form of cost–benefit analysis to explain this form of nonvoting. With thousands of voters deciding a typical legislative race, for example, an individual's chance to affect the outcome is negligible. If a person thinks that his or her life will be the same no matter who wins, even the minimal cost of taking a few minutes to stop and vote may outweigh the apparently nonexistent benefits, especially if one has no sense of civic duty to nag the conscience. By contrast, a hard-fought contest or a campaign that raises issues about which people feel strongly may motivate more voters to come to the polls.[17]

Other motivational factors include an interest in politics. Generally speaking, people who are more interested in politics tend to be more active in politics; although a significant number of uninterested people are willing to vote, usually they do not do much more than that. People who believe that an election will be a close contest are also more likely to vote, as are people who feel more concerned about the outcome of the election. Strong party loyalties are also a strong motivator; political independents are likely to stay home on election day, unless they lean toward one of the parties.[18]

One other psychological factor affecting turnout is a feeling of being rooted in an area and having a stake in what happens there. When people are new to an area, they are often unfamiliar with state and local political figures and political organizations. As those people settle in, learn about the local political environment, and begin to care more about the community and the people in it, they are more likely to be politically active. This is part of why voter turnout among young people tends to be low; they tend to be more mobile.

Legal and Practical Factors Play a Part   The sixth category of nonvoters found by Hadley is the *physically disenfranchised.* Composing about 18 percent of nonvoters, some of these people are knowledgeable and have a relatively high sense of civic duty. Yet they either do not meet voter registration requirements, or physical or health reasons keep them from going to the polls.

Historically, there were many legal barriers to voting. In colonial times, property requirements were common, but these have now been stripped away. Until the passage of the Nineteenth Amendment to the Constitution in 1920, most states denied women the right to vote. And until the ratification of the Twenty-Sixth Amendment in 1971, few states permitted 18-year-olds to vote.

The most tumultuous voting discrimination was against racial minorities prior to the passage of the Voting Rights Act of 1965. The historical experience of the racial minorities—especially African Americans before 1965—best illustrates how legal impediments have been used to deny the vote to large minority groups.

Although the Fifteenth Amendment (1870) guaranteed racial minorities the right to vote, southern states (as well as some other states and localities) applied several discriminatory devices that nullified the Fifteenth Amendment in practice after Reconstruction ended. The *poll tax* reduced turnout among minorities and the poor because it had to be paid each election year, and it accumulated for every year it was not paid. Records indicating that some people had paid the tax sometimes mysteriously disappeared, and some people did not receive notices that the taxes were due. The poll tax was finally prohibited by the Twenty-Fourth Amendment in 1964.

Many states also required voters to pass *literacy tests*, which were graded unfairly to stop minorities from voting. Other states, such as Texas, had *White primaries*. African Americans were allowed to vote in the general election but not in the primary election of the Democratic Party. Because Texas was a one-party Democratic state in those days, the Democratic primary really determined who got elected to office. The White primary was struck down by the Supreme Court in 1944.[19]

When African American voters became numerous enough to determine local elections, local communities often changed their boundaries or gerrymandered election districts to dilute the impact of these voters. One flagrant case of this was Tuskegee, Alabama, which in the 1950s changed its boundaries from the shape of a square to a 28-sided polygon in order to dilute African American voting in city elections. This practice was struck down by the Supreme Court in 1960.[20]

The key that finally enabled racial minorities to enter the electorate as full citizens was the **Voting Rights Act of 1965**. This law and its later amendments set up provisions for eliminating the literacy test, placing federal registrars and poll watchers in counties with the worst records of voting discrimination, and requiring federal government approval before changes in the voting laws could take effect (see the Highlight feature below). The results of this act have been dramatic. Since 1965, voter turnout and office-holding by African Americans have increased not only in the South but throughout the country. In 1969, only 1,185 African American

HIGHLIGHT

The Voting Rights Act

1. *A Triggering Formula*
   The provisions of the act would apply to any state, county, or municipality that had (a) used a literacy test for voter registration in 1964 and (b) experienced less than a 50 percent turnout in the 1964 presidential election. This was called the triggering formula.

2. *Voting Examiners*
   The U.S. Department of Justice was authorized to use federal voting examiners to register people in any jurisdiction identified by the triggering formula.

3. *Literacy Tests*
   The Department of Justice was authorized to suspend literacy tests in any jurisdiction identified by the triggering formula.

4. *Preclearance Requirement*
   Voting laws, municipal boundaries, and election districts could not be changed in any community identified by the triggering formula unless the change was cleared in advance by the Department of Justice or a three-judge district court panel in Washington, DC. The object of this provision is to prevent dilution of the minority vote by gerrymandering election districts or by annexing substantial white subdivisions.

5. *Enforcement Machinery*
   The act gave the attorney general considerable authority to prosecute violations and stipulated fines and imprisonment for convictions. ■

officials had been elected throughout the United States; by 2002, this number had increased to 9,430.[21] In a similar manner, the growth of America's Hispanic population and Hispanic voting has produced a dramatic increase in the number of Hispanic elected officials, to 4,932 by 2006.[22] As we will discuss in Chapter 9, the Voting Rights Act has become a major issue in drawing boundaries for state legislative districts and city councils.

New Barriers to Voting   Ironically, as a number of traditional legal barriers to voting were overcome, there was a decrease in the percentage of the voting-age population who actually turned out and voted. In part, this occurred because the ranks of some legally ineligible adults, such as felons, noncitizens, the "mentally incompetent," and people living overseas, have grown considerably since 1972.[23] The number of people who are legally eligible to register but fail to do so has remained distressingly large.

Our low turnout rate has led some critics to push for relaxing voter registration requirements and making voting more convenient. One analysis estimated that voter turnout would increase by 9 percent if all states relaxed their registration laws to the level of the most lenient states.[24] However, while the proportion of the voting-age population that has registered has risen, turnout among registered voters declined through the late 1990s,[25] although there has been a slight rise in turnout since then.

In an effort to make voting more convenient, Oregon instituted a mail-in election in 1995, and mailed out ballots to all its registered voters. A number of other states have relaxed their rules for using absentee ballots in order to make voting more convenient.[26] If this practice gains wider acceptance, many voters will not have to go to the polls to cast their votes. They will simply return the ballot through the mail. So far, however, the effects on turnout appear to be rather modest.

Some critics worry that people may vote early using mail-in ballots and, consequently, be unable to consider late-breaking information in their voting decisions. Critics also worry that more widespread use of mail-in ballots will increase opportunities for voting fraud. In a 1997 mayoral election in Florida, a substantial number of ballots were forged or illegally obtained, which led the courts to overturn the results of the election. Four years earlier, absentee ballot irregularities in another local race in Florida led the courts to order holding a new election.[27]

Motor Voter   Reformers have also tried to make voter registration easier and more convenient. In 1993, Congress passed the Motor Voter Bill, which requires each state to register people to vote when they apply for a driver's license. Not all states have implemented motor voter in the same way, however. In some instances, people may be allowed to register if they ask to, but license bureau personnel will not raise the possibility themselves. In other cases, bureau personnel ask each customer if he or she is registered and take the initiative in encouraging people to register.

Some states allow voters to register at the polling places on election day, whereas one state (North Dakota) has no registration requirement at all. Many states permit setting up temporary registration desks in various locations, including stores and college campuses. So far, the combined effects of these efforts to increase turnout have produced only modest results nationwide. From 1996 to 2000, turnout nationwide rose, but only by a small amount, about half a percentage point. From 2000 to 2004, turnout rose by roughly five percentage points; however, turnout grew more rapidly in the so-called battleground states where the presidential campaigns focused more of their attention.[28] Turnout continued to grow, but at a modest pace, through 2008.[29]

A number of other legal factors influence turnout. Nonpartisan elections, which are common at the local level, attract fewer voters than do elections where the parties are officially involved. The election calendar also plays a role: Holding state elections at the same time as presidential elections yields higher turnout than holding state races in other years. Holding local elections at the same time as state or federal elections produces higher turnout than does scheduling local elections separately. Cities with an elected mayor usually have higher turnout in city elections than do cities with a city manager form of government.[30]

One of the most recent legal controversies regarding voting is the voter identification laws that have been proposed in a number of states and adopted in roughly a dozen states. These laws require voters to show some specified type(s) of identification, probably one issued by government, with a photograph of the person on it. Anyone without that identification would not be allowed to vote. Critics of the voter identification laws charge that they are an effort to block voting by poorer people and racial minorities. Advocates of the laws contend that they are simply trying to make elections more honest.[31]

Mobilizing Organizations Play a Part A third factor reducing political participation, especially among the poor, is the lack of organizations to mobilize them. Among working-class people in some parts of the country, labor unions make strenuous efforts to mobilize their members to participate. However, the nation's unions have lost membership over the years, a development that has weakened their abilities to mobilize voters. Many more organizations encourage involvement by middle- and upper-class professionals.

The importance of union-organizing activities can be seen in a study comparing voter turnout in different states and the extent of unionization in each state. Researchers found that higher levels of unionization were associated with higher turnout, although other factors, especially education levels, also affected turnout rates.[32] A potentially very important mobilization effort taking place recently focuses on Hispanics. With the very large Hispanic population in the Unites States and their traditionally low turnout rate, successfully mobilizing them could affect the outcomes of thousands of elections.[33]

Competitive parties and hard-fought campaigns also help to mobilize voters. When elections are closely contended, the parties and candidates have a stronger incentive to find their supporters and encourage them to vote (and possibly help the campaign in other ways, such as making a financial contribution or putting a campaign sign in the front yard).[34]

Mobilization activities are important, in part, because participation is not a high priority for many people. As a result, many people may not participate without some degree of encouragement. Many mobilizing groups seek to defend the interests of people who are already relatively well-off (such as business and professional interests), and mobilizing groups often target people who are easier to mobilize. As a result, wealthier and better-educated people who have been politically active in the past are more likely to be encouraged to become involved again. Poorer and less-educated citizens are more difficult to mobilize because they are less inclined to participate. Consequently, many groups devote little or no effort to getting them involved.[35]

As we will see shortly, some researchers believe that the last 50 years have seen a decline in some of the intermediary associations, such as unions and other groups, that stimulate citizen activity, although scholars disagree regarding the extent of the decline. Not only do many intermediary groups stimulate activity, but they also help their younger members develop participatory skills that stick with them as adults.[36] Those added skills further encourage participation. Involvement in a larger number of these groups also seems to increase political tolerance and produce greater acceptance of election outcomes.[37]

TABLE 4.2

Highs and Lows in Voter Turnout, 2008

Highs (%)		Lows (%)	
Minnesota	71	Hawaii	47
Maine	70	Texas	49
New Hampshire	70	Utah	50

Source: U.S. Census Bureau, *Statistical Abstract of the United States, 2011–2012* (New York: Skyhorse, 2001), p. 261. The turnout rate is the percentage of voting-age adults claiming to have voted in the election.

The combined effect of all the influences on participation is that participation rates vary considerably from one person to another, from one area to another, and over time. One convenient way to compare across jurisdictions uses voting turnout (see Table 4.2). Note that the states with the highest voting turnout have politically competitive parties with relatively progressive political traditions and high levels of education. The states with the lowest turnout are mostly in the western or southern parts of the country, where strong political parties are rare and where many people are new to these states. Newcomers tend to participate less until they become more familiar with state and local political matters.

Turnout statistics should be treated with some caution, for states differ in the proportion of the voting-age population that is actually eligible to vote. Some states, such as California and Florida, have unusually large noncitizen populations, and both prohibit voting by convicted felons.[38] Banning voting by convicted felons has provoked criticism from groups that point out that the policy tends to especially reduce voting by African Americans, Hispanics, and poorer people.

Why Does Participation Matter?

Participation matters because people who are politically active are communicating their preferences to public officials and are wielding rewards and punishments, such as votes and campaign contributions, that may affect officials' careers. As a result, officials are more likely to share the issue concerns of the public where citizens are more active and to particularly focus on the opinions of the more active when making policy.[39] In addition, in states where proportionally fewer poor people vote, public policies are less likely to respond to the needs of the poor.[40] The low levels of political participation by young people similarly increase the risk that their needs and concerns will be overlooked (see Figure 4.2).

Participation also matters because people's willingness to invest time and energy in public affairs affects the ability of states and communities to deal effectively with their public problems. If people do not mobilize and express their preferences, officials may conclude that people are not interested or may misinterpret public sentiments. If very few people will help run or support campaigns, voters may not have very many choices on election day. If people fail to speak up when they see problems, other people may not be aware that the problems exist. Note, too, that the current generation of public officials cannot serve forever; if few people participate today, there will be few people honing their political skills to prepare for office in the future.

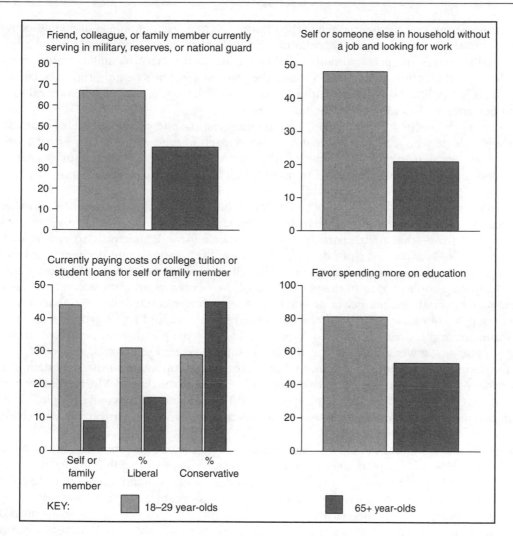

FIGURE 4.2
But Why Should I Bother? Age, Life Circumstances, and Policy Views

Source: Martin Wattenberg, *Is Voting for Young People?* (New York: Pearson Longman, 2007), pp. 143, 145.

The Propensity for Exit, Not Voice As we will see in Chapters 6 and 7, many of our localities face serious problems: drugs, crime, unemployment, poverty or economic stagnation, and stresses on public services such as schools, public safety, and public recreation. According to Albert Hirschman,[41] people who become dissatisfied with these developments have three basic options—exit, voice, or loyalty. Exit is the option of looking elsewhere for services. If you are very affluent, you can afford to substitute private services for public services. You can send your children to private schools, join the YMCA or a private recreational club, hire private security forces to protect your block, your street, or your business, or move to a nicer area. Obviously, only the fairly affluent can afford to do all these things. However, even middle-class people can exit from an area's problems by moving to a safer, more pleasant, and more prosperous environment, often in the suburbs. As increasing numbers of people exercise the exit option, central city neighborhoods and poor rural areas lose people who have the financial resources and personal skills to help the community attack its major problems.

Voice is the option of fighting to attack the problems in one's neighborhood or community. This is a political option that requires people to work together—even when they disagree with one another—to solve their common problems.

Loyalty is the practice of staying in communities in spite of the problems that exist. Some people may hope that a problem will resolve itself in time without their efforts. Other people suspect that other places have equally serious problems, so staying put is a reasonable choice. Some people are unable to move, often for economic reasons.

Bowling Alone and the Decline of Social Capital Compounding the consequences of the exit strategy is a long-term decline in what Robert Putnam calls "social capital," the "networks, norms, and trust—that enable participants to act together more effectively to pursue shared objectives."[42] Over the last three decades, there have been membership declines of 25 to 50 percent in community groups as diverse as PTAs, Elks clubs, unions, and even bowling leagues.

As fewer people engage in the public lives of their communities, these communities see their social capital decline. Fewer people belonging to fewer community groups means that fewer people step forward to confront community problems, and fewer groups help to link government and individual citizens. As more and more people absorb themselves in their private pursuits, fewer people tend to the public sphere. Not all scholars agree on the extent of the decline, and some evidence showed an increase in involvement in the aftermath of the September 11, 2001, attacks, although the increase faded over time.[43] Martin Wattenberg's recent analysis finds a disturbing pattern of political disengagement by young people[44]; if that pattern continues, many organizations will face increasing difficulty in attracting participants.

Professionalizing Politics Finally, as large numbers of people exit the problems of the inner city and large numbers of people disengage from community life in general, public affairs are increasingly handled by professionals, particularly in larger communities. Traditional American politics by part-time amateurs has given way to public problem-solving by experts, leaving many people to function primarily as clients outside the problem-solving process. These clients sometimes donate checks to large interest groups that they favor, but few clients have any face-to-face involvement with other people in resolving public problems. The result, according to Harry Boyte, is a population that has been socialized to make moralistic judgments about politics as sleazy, immoral, and corrupt. In reality, successful politics requires different interests to compromise with each other in order to achieve common goals. But compromise is a dirty word in the minds of people brought up to disengage from politics and to view politics essentially in personal and moralistic terms.[45] In this sense, declining participation contributes to the emergence of a political system where it becomes increasingly difficult to solve problems through compromise.

It would be unrealistic to expect too much in the way of political participation from average people. After all, most of us have our hands full simply raising our families and doing our jobs, and there is often little time or energy left for most of us to become gladiators on very many fronts. In addition, many Americans move periodically and, therefore, do not develop community roots that, when present, tend to encourage participation.[46] But the growing number of people who *never* act as gladiators and seldom engage in spectator activities raises disturbing issues about the quality of democracy in many of the nation's communities. A community can tolerate some people following the exit option and still thrive.

However, if large numbers of people follow the exit option, the community will wither unless it can attract large numbers of new residents. If only a very few people join a Lions Club, a labor union, or a PTA, then the community does indeed lose social capital and that will hinder its abilities to confront its problems. Finally, in the complicated world that we inhabit, some professionalization of politics is inevitable. But democracy cannot survive if *everybody* leaves decision making to the professionals. In short, some level of gladiator activity by ordinary people is essential if our states and communities are to have a meaningful democracy. And the declining participation of people in these activities over the past two generations poses disturbing questions.

What Are the Channels of Participation?

Much of the rest of this chapter and the next is devoted to exploring the various ways in which people participate in the political process. Political scientists identify *linkages* between the individual citizen and the governing officials. These linkages can be thought of as channels through which individuals have input into the governing process. The major channels to be examined in these two chapters are (1) public opinion, (2) interest groups, (3) political parties, (4) elections, and (5) direct democracy. For any of these channels to serve as effective means of allowing citizens to influence government policy, two conditions must prevail. The channels themselves must effectively influence government policy, and the channels must be responsive to citizen demands.

PUBLIC OPINION

Public opinion refers to people's views on politically relevant issues.[47] If democracy has any meaning at all, there must be some correlation between public opinion and government policy, although different conceptions of democracy call for different amounts of correspondence between opinions and policy. By this criterion, how democratic are the American states?

Fifty years ago, the preponderant research would have concluded, probably not very! Most research until that time had concluded that a state's per capita income and its level of economic development had a bigger impact on the kind of policies it adopted than did any political factors, including public opinion, although most early research did not have very good measures of opinion.[48] Newer research, however, has found that public opinion has a much greater impact on public policy than previously thought. Researchers have found a consistency between preferences expressed in public opinion polls and public policies on about two-thirds of all public opinion preferences. They have also identified many instances (but not all) in which public opinion directly influences policy outcomes.[49]

One team of researchers used numerous surveys to rate each state on an index of political ideology. When this index was correlated with policy outcomes, the researchers found that public opinion had a greater impact on public policy than did socioeconomic variables such as per capita income or level of education. In short, states with the most liberal populations also have the most liberal policies, and states with the most conservative populations have the most conservative policies.[50]

How Does Public Opinion Influence Policy?

In Theory Several theoretical models describe how public opinion might influence public policy.[51] The first model is the *rational activist* model,[52] which holds that people choose their elected officials rationally on the basis of their issue positions. However, a basic flaw in this model is that many voters in state and local elections seldom know very much about the candidates' stands on a range of issues.[53] Governors are relatively visible, but most state and local races generate little public interest and attract little media coverage. Both conditions often mean voters will not be well informed about the candidates. Moreover, many state and especially local races are not very competitive; we often find elections in which there is only one candidate for a given office. When people do know where the candidates stand on issues, however, they are quite likely to vote for the one who shares their political beliefs. Note, too, that many special district local governments are headed by officials who are not elected.

A second model holds that public opinion may influence policy decisions because public officials believe that they have a duty to respond to public sentiments. Although some evidence indicates that state and local leaders can accurately gauge public opinion on some specific issues,[54] that is more difficult on issues that attract limited public attention. Moreover, public opinion is sometimes inconsistent or unclear.[55]

Not all officials place equal emphasis on responding to public opinion, either; officials who do not care about being reelected or who have more confidence in their own judgment than in the public's may be less responsive to public sentiments.[56] Assuming that public opinion polling is done competently, the growing use of polls in states and localities means that more information regarding public preferences is available to officials now than it was in the past.[57] Bear in mind, though, that poorly done polls may give very misleading information about public sentiments.

The third model is a *sharing or consensus* model. In this view, elected officials often share the same values that their constituents hold, in part because many officials have deep roots in their communities and share the local culture. When those officials make decisions, they automatically bring the values of their constituents to bear on the policy questions before them. The officials reflect popular opinion not because they fear voter retaliation but because they share that opinion.[58] This type of linkage does not require citizens to pay close attention to officials' actions in order to create a bond.

In Practice   Given these theoretical models, is there any evidence showing how, in practice, public opinion affects policy? Four important generalizations can be made. First, the policies adopted by a state appear to be influenced to some extent by the broad political values of the state's population. Studies correlating state policy outcomes with public opinion tend to find a strong relationship.[59] For example, states at the conservative end of the opinion spectrum (Idaho, North Dakota, Mississippi, and Oklahoma, as examples) are not usually the standard bearers for liberal policies on abortion, welfare spending, or civil rights. Conversely, the states at the liberal end of the spectrum (such as Vermont, Connecticut, New Jersey, and Massachusetts) tend to have more liberal policies in these issue areas. The correlations are far from perfect, but a strong pattern exists. What people think makes a difference on public policies that get adopted.

A second aspect of the evidence is that public opinion has its strongest impact on issues that are highly visible and emotional. This can be seen most clearly in the history of the civil rights movement.[60] An attempt to correlate public opinion in the states with policy outputs found the strongest correlations in the area of prohibiting racial discrimination in public accommodations.[61] Where public opinion was strongly against this, it was difficult to enact. On a less visible issue, however, many people may not be aware of the issue or may not have an opinion regarding what to do about it. Fewer people will contact public officials, and those officials will have a more difficult time determining what the general public wants. In that case, public opinion may have very little influence.

A third generalization concerns the **intensity problem.** We often find that some people feel more strongly about an issue than do others. On gun control, for example, an individual legislator may find that two-thirds of the constituents favor stricter controls but are not excited about it. The other one-third may oppose tighter controls vociferously and may agitate for the defeat of legislators who support those controls. Since the minority feels much more intensely about its position than does the majority, the legislator may lose votes by going along with the majority public opinion. Anne Hopkins found that gun permit legislation typically was not passed until more than 70 percent of people supported it.[62] People who feel strongly about an issue are more likely to notice what an official does, remember it at the next election, and act on their opinions.

A fourth generalization is that some parts of the public have more influence on public policy than do others. Legislators identify **attentive constituents** in their districts[63] who are politically aware and paying attention to what officials do. The legislators not only respect the opinion of these constituents but also actively seek their advice. These attentive constituents have more effect on public policy than does the public at large, in part because the attentive citizens are more likely to notice what legislators decide and in part because those citizens tend to be politically active. The tendency for young people to pay little attention to political news puts them at a significant disadvantage when policy choices are made.[64]

Finally, it is important to keep in mind that finding a correlation between public opinion and public policy does not always tell us which caused which. Comparing 1930s survey data with later public policy changes, Robert Erikson studied public opinion on capital punishment and argued that public opinion preceded the public policy. That is, states with the strongest antideath-penalty feelings in the 1930s were the first states to abandon capital punishment in later decades.[65] However, examples can also be found where the policy shapes opinion. Scholars have noted, for example, that public opinion on foreign policy tends to change in response to the government's policies,[66] at least for a while.

In summary, public opinion's influence on public policy cannot be ignored. It is difficult for legislators to enact policies that violate deeply held values of a substantial majority of the population. Public values help establish the overall boundaries within which policy makers have much discretion, but outside of which they cannot act without risk. On the day-to-day operations of government that are less visible and less emotional than civil rights or gun control, policy makers find themselves responding more to other channels of influence than to public opinion.

INTEREST GROUPS

One of the most-discussed channels of citizen influence is the political **interest group,** any organization that tries to influence government decisions. Interest groups are sometimes confused with political parties, but the two differ in several respects. *Interest groups do not run candidates for office.* It is true that candidates are *endorsed* by interest groups, such as labor unions, gun clubs, environmental groups, and business associations, and some groups will encourage people sharing their views to run for office, but the candidates are *not nominated* by interest groups, at least not officially. They are nominated by political parties (in partisan elections), and they appear on the ballot with their party designation. Also, interest groups do not organize the government once the election is over; parties do. The legislature (except for Nebraska's) is formally divided between the Republican and Democratic parties, not a series of interest groups. In addition, many interest groups alternate between being involved in the political process and not being involved, particularly groups that have important, nonpolitical objectives—making money or saving souls, as examples. Finally, whereas parties represent geographic entities, interest groups usually represent functional entities that may be widely dispersed, although some of them may be concentrated in certain geographic areas.

Kinds of Interest Groups

There are many different interest groups. Traditionally, the five interest groups that have been important in state politics are business, labor, education, farmers, and local government groups.[67] However, there has been a dramatic expansion of interest groups over the past several decades. The explosion in interest group activity can be seen in the fact that the number of organizations registered to lobby before state legislatures increased from an average of 195 per state in 1975 to more than 600 per state in 1990, then rose to 694 by 1997.[68] Table 4.3, relying on a recent, exhaustive study of interest groups in the 50 states, lists the groups most frequently listed as influential in state politics. This table shows three broad categories of groups: economically motivated groups (business and labor), professional groups, and public sector groups. Some groups fall into more than one category.

Economically Motivated Groups First, and most influential on state policy making, are the economically motivated groups (groups that have a direct economic interest in government policy). Government policies will either cost or save their members money. Business and labor are the most obvious examples. Table 4.3 shows that of the groups that were consistently ranked as among the most effective in influencing state politics, most were economically motivated business or labor groups.

Business groups tend to focus on state taxation and spending policies and regulations. They seek to minimize business taxes and to channel government spending into areas that will benefit the business community. The business groups identified as most influential are usually general business groups such as chambers of commerce and associations representing specific industries like bankers, manufacturers, utilities, or the construction and real estate development industries.

TABLE 4.3

Most Influential Interest Groups in the States, 2006–2007

Interest Represented	Category of Group	Number of States in Which a Group Ranks at Highest Level of Effectiveness
General business organizations	Business	39
School teachers	Labor/professional/ public sector	31
Utilities	Business	28
Manufacturers	Business	25
Hospital and nursing home associations	Business	24
Insurance	Business	22

Source: Adapted from Anthony Nownes, Clive Thomas, and Ronald Hrebenar, "Interest Groups in the States," in Virginia Gray and Russell Hanson, eds. *Politics in the American States,* 9th ed. (Washington, DC: CQ Press, 2008), p. 117.

Labor organizations are also economically motivated. Their main purpose is to improve the working conditions and economic status of their members. In recent years, they have devoted considerable attention to job losses and the plight of workers whose jobs have been moved out of the country. But unions also have generally fought for social welfare policies that have served a broad cross-section of people regardless of whether they are union members. Included among those policies are Social Security, unemployment compensation, and Medicare and Medicaid.

Unions have had a difficult time in recent years. The decline of the manufacturing sector of the American economy saw corresponding declines in the membership of industrial unions such as the United Auto Workers (UAW) and the United Steel Workers (USW)[69] (although *total* union membership has declined less substantially than the proportion of workers who are unionized). These problems were compounded by the Reagan and George H. W. Bush administrations, which influenced labor-related federal agencies to be less helpful to unions.[70] Businesses have also employed a variety of tactics to discourage unionization; one of the most extreme methods is to fire employees who advocate unionization.[71] American culture's emphasis on individualism may also discourage union involvement at times.

As traditional labor unions in the private sector have lost influence over the past generation, government employee unions have gained influence. When legislators and knowledgcable observers in states are asked to identify the most significant interest groups in their states, they often include public employee organizations and unions, especially teachers' associations and state employee associations. The most important of these associations are the NEA (National Education Association), the AFT (American Federation of Teachers), and the AFSCME (American Federation of State, County, and Municipal Employees). The 50-state interest group study found that teachers' organizations are among the most effective interest groups in 31 of the 50 states (see Table 4.3). One sign of the growing importance of public sector unions is the recent conflict among different unions regarding which ones should organize which groups of workers.[72]

Several of the Republican governors elected in 2010 pushed for laws to reduce the power and influence of public employee unions, partly in hopes of reducing spending pressures and partly because many public employee unions often support Democratic Party candidates. These efforts triggered a backlash in some states, with Ohio voters overturning the antiunion legislation there and Wisconsin groups gathering enough signatures to trigger a recall election for the governor.[73]

Professionally Motivated Groups   The second most influential category of interest groups is the *professionally motivated group,* whose primary purpose is to provide services to its members. The state medical association, for example, might distribute medical journals to members, or sponsor conferences on important medical issues and problems. Although the primary purpose of these groups is to further the professional concerns of their members, the groups do not hesitate to press for economic advantages as well. Thus, doctors' groups, nursing homes, and hospitals are very vocal on issues such as state policies toward health maintenance organizations and funding for health care for the poor and the elderly, while trial lawyers are very vocal on issues such as automobile insurance and rules regarding litigation. The 50-state study found that teachers', doctors', and lawyers' groups were the professional groups ranked as the most influential in the states.

Public Agency Groups   A third category of interest groups is the public sector group, an organization of public agencies. The seven most prominent are the Council of State Governments, the United States Conference of Mayors, the National Governors' Association, the National Conference of State Legislatures, the National Association of County Officials, the National League of Cities, and the International City/County Management Association. Also influential are associations of specialists in fields ranging from education and law enforcement to conservation and transportation. These groups help public officials to exchange ideas, to lobby collectively at the local, state, regional, and national levels, and to get up-to-date information about the latest developments and concepts that affect their own public agency. Because public-sector lobbyists are often knowledgeable and are directly involved in program operations, they are more likely to be approached by state legislators seeking advice than are private-sector lobbyists.[74]

Ideological/Cultural Groups   A final category of interest groups is the ideological/value-oriented group, such as the Sierra Club, the Audubon Society, Common Cause, religious organizations, and similar groups that claim to represent a public interest not embodied by the economic or professionally motivated interest groups. Because they claim to speak for the public interest and to support policies that will benefit everyone or at least a large majority of people, ideological groups are sometimes called **public interest groups.** The Sierra Club and Ducks Unlimited, for example, try to protect the environment and wildlife. Unlike a labor union or a medical association, the ideological/cultural group offers its members no direct economic or professional benefits; rather, members are attracted by an ideological concern or a commitment to the group's ideals—protecting the environment, fighting governmental corruption, encouraging a higher level of morality, or protecting the rights of gun owners. One of the most dramatic developments in this interest group sector is the mobilization of conservative religious groups in recent years on issues ranging from abortion to the teaching of evolution. That mobilization has led other religious groups to assess how to present their views more effectively.[75]

Another recent development in this sector is the Occupy Wall Street movement, which has appeared in a number of cities and expressed concerns regarding the power of large corporations and economic inequality. We cannot yet assess its impact on public policies, but it has fostered more discussion on the issues it has raised.

Finally, some groups overlap into more than one category. Racial minority groups, women's groups, and gay rights groups are examples. To the extent that they promote civil rights and civil liberties for all citizens, they function as ideological groups. To the extent that they promote policies aimed at the economic advancement of their own members, however, they function as economically motivated groups.

Interest Group Political Tactics

Interest groups use a wide variety of tactics in pursuing their goals.[76] Some of the most common group tactics are *public relations, electioneering,* and *lobbying.* **Public relations** activities normally try to create a favorable climate of opinion within which the interest group can operate. Public utilities companies, for example, sometimes run advertisements emphasizing how hard people in the companies are working to provide reliable supplies of electricity or natural gas. Public relations activities sometimes try to draw attention to a problem for which the group wants action. The oil and natural gas industry and the petroleum industry are currently waging a major public relations campaign to press for greater freedom for their operations, in part to help the economy.

Public relations activities can be very expensive unless a group can find a way to attract free news media coverage. One method of doing that is by finding a celebrity to speak for the group. The National Rifle Association employed that tactic when it chose Charlton Heston, an award-winning actor, to be its president. Robert Redford has sometimes spoken on behalf of environmental groups. A group may also engage in dramatic public behavior, such as a demonstration, in hopes of attracting media coverage. The Occupy Wall Street movement is one of the most recent examples of that tactic.

A key difficulty in public relations campaigns is getting people to pay attention to the group's message. People may mute the sound of a television commercial or throw out a political mailing without reading it. Many people pay little attention to political news coverage. Even if a group can capture people's attention, there is no guarantee that they will respond favorably to the group's message.

Electioneering is the tactic of trying to elect officials who are sympathetic to your point of view. Thus, farmers' groups are partial to rural-based candidates for office, business groups lean toward conservative candidates, labor unions favor economic liberals, and teachers' associations unite behind candidates who support public schools.

Electioneering takes many forms. A group may encourage a friendly candidate, possibly even a member of the group, to run for office. Members of the group may volunteer to work in the candidate's campaign, performing tasks ranging from calling potential voters on the telephone to distributing literature door to door to advising the candidate on political strategy. Members may give money to the candidate's campaign or write letters to the editors of local newspapers in praise of the favored candidate or criticizing the opposition.[77]

Interest groups also help candidates by forming **political action committees (PACs)**. A PAC collects money to use as a campaign contribution in an effort to get friendly people elected to public office. Many states prohibit unions or corporations from directly contributing money to campaigns. But unions or corporations can legally set up a PAC that will collect money from potential contributors, including members of the group. In this way, the PAC can effectively give the union or corporation political influence without violating the law. An estimated 12,000 PACs are active in the United States.[78]

Most individual contributions to PACs tend to be relatively small, ranging from about $10 to $200.[79] But when these sums are multiplied by thousands of contributors, they give PACs considerable clout in campaign finance. PAC contributions as a percentage of all campaign fund-raising have grown steadily since the mid-1970s, when federal legislation stimulated the growth of PACs. PAC money for state legislative races often goes primarily to incumbent legislators and to legislative leaders. PAC leaders look on their contributions as ensuring their access to the law makers.

As the role of PACs in elections has grown, political reform groups such as Common Cause have pushed the states to limit the amount of money a PAC may contribute to a campaign. Today, most states have adopted some limit on PACs,[80] but few observers expect the influence of PACs to decline. Nor, in the view of some observers, *should* PACs be prohibited from making campaign contributions. The nation's foremost observer of campaign contributions has argued that PACs dramatically expand the number of people contributing to the campaigns and perform a number of other positive roles in the democratic process.[81] Ending financial contributions by PACs might result in even more candidates who cannot raise enough money to support an adequate campaign.

A number of decisions by the U.S. Supreme Court have given groups much more freedom to spend money to influence elections. If that spending is officially separate from the candidates' campaign organizations, groups, including corporations and labor unions with large bankrolls, can spend huge amounts of money to try to influence election outcomes.[82] In addition, a number of lawsuits are currently trying to persuade various courts to strike down financial disclosure requirements.[83]

Lobbying is the tactic of trying to influence a legislature or some other governmental body. Lobbying is done directly by interest groups, by individuals, and by professional lobbyists who make a career of representing the interests of various groups before legislatures and other governmental organizations. Much lobbying is defensive in nature, seeking to prevent new legislation that might undo some existing privilege or right.

The 50-state interest group study identified five types of lobbyists.[84] First are the *contract lobbyists*—people who are paid a fee by one or many clients to look after those clients' interests in the legislature and state agencies. Extremely effective contract lobbyists can command fees of $100,000 or more, but the vast majority earn far less than that. Instead of paying for a contract lobbyist, many larger organizations (such as large businesses) prefer to have their own *in-house lobbyists*. These are regular employees of the organization who carry titles such as government relations officer and spend most of their work time on lobbying and governmental relations activities.

Third are the *government legislative liaisons*. Like the in-house lobbyists, they are regular employees, but of a government organization. They spend their workday furthering the interests of their agency or department in the legislature and other governmental bodies. Also, like the in-house lobbyists, they have titles such as legislative liaison officer rather than lobbyist. A fourth type of lobbyist is the *citizen or cause lobbyist*. They are often volunteers or highly committed representatives of environmental organizations, organizations for the handicapped, or other cause groups. Finally, a small number of *hobbyist lobbyists* exist. These are individual citizens who stalk the legislative corridors pushing for some pet project or policy proposal.

One other important type of lobbyist is the *legislator lobbyist*, who is simultaneously a member of the interest group and a member of the legislature (or other decision-making body). A banker who serves in the state legislature may try to protect banking interests in the course of doing legislative work. A realtor who is elected to the city council may do the same thing for the real estate industry. The many part-time offices in state and especially local government create many opportunities for interest groups to put their members into office while maintaining their ties to the group.

Lobbyists have the reputation of being wheeler-dealers who get what they want by wining and dining legislators and making under-the-table payoffs of one sort or another. Unfortunately, this type of activity was widespread at one time. Lobbyists in the early history of Wyoming, for example, paid off legislators for voting in favor of the lobbyists' interests.[85]

Today, by contrast, lobbying has become more sophisticated. The most important resource of the professional lobbyist today is information about issues before the legislature. Effective lobbying firms often supplement the presentation of information to legislative committees with elaborate media campaigns to build up public opinion for the lobbyist's position (or prevent the development of broad public opposition), and also with detailed grass roots campaigns aimed at putting pressure on legislators from constituents in their own districts.

Modern lobbying also includes monitoring governmental decision makers, from governors and city council members to regulatory agency personnel, in order to advise the group's members of looming developments in government that may affect the group's interests.[86] Monitoring legislative and administrative activities in recent years has become easier as more legislative and administrative information can be accessed through the Internet, although politically sensitive information is not always available on governmental Web sites.

Lobbyists also seek to link their informational presentations with local grass roots support. The California Association of Realtors, for example, maintains a "legislative tree" that lists any personal, professional, or social connections that individual realtors in the state may have with specific legislators.[87] In this way, the Association is not limited to making a formal presentation to a legislative committee. It can enlist the support of an individual realtor who has some personal link to a key legislator. Many interest groups now use e-mail in order to mobilize grass roots activists quickly in response to new lobbying opportunities and in an effort to recruit new members. Rank and file group members can also use e-mail to influence the leaders of their groups and public officials, as well as share information among the rank and file.[88]

The professionalization of lobbying does not mean that money has lost its importance. But the money is more likely to come in the form of a campaign contribution of some sort than it is in the form of an implicit or explicit bribe. Campaigning for state office is becoming increasingly expensive, and political action committees, as we saw earlier in the chapter, have an important role in campaign finance. Just how much difference a campaign contribution makes in an official's decision is very difficult to calculate. Many lobbyists feel that it does make a difference, so they arrange for contributions to officials whom they think will be important to them. One long-time lobbyist in California was quoted:

> If everything else is equal and your opposition has a significant advantage in contributions, you are going to lose. It has to be equal on the merits, but I've seen votes change because of money.[89]

Finally, despite the widespread belief that PAC contributions corrupt the officials who accept them, most of the evidence for this belief is sporadic and anecdotal. Although some campaign contributions certainly are little more than vote-buying exercises, most scholarly studies seeking to tie campaign contributions to legislative voting patterns have failed to find any systematic link. However, many studies find that campaign spending influences the outcome of elections, and some research finds that campaign contributions affect which issues receive attention and which people will have access to public officials.[90] If a group can elect friendly officials and gain their attention, it will not need to change their minds.

From a representational standpoint, a problem regarding interest group contributions is the tendency for some candidates to receive many campaign contributions from outside the state, locality, or district they seek to represent. To take an extreme case, an examination of the Utah state legislature found that one-third of the members elected in 2010 did not receive any campaign contributions at all from their local constituents![91] That does not necessarily indicate anything illegal, but the groups giving the money may divert officials' attention away from the people who vote for them. More dramatically, periodic scandals regarding interest group money reinforce the view that it sometimes has a corrupting influence.

Some groups are also very creative in developing new ways to use funds to influence public officials. A publisher of educational materials, for example, created a nonprofit foundation that, in turn, has financed international travel and lodging by a number of state education officials. The trips enable U.S. education officials to learn more about educational practices in other countries, but they also meet with leaders of the publishing company. The practice has raised eyebrows in some states, but executives of the publishing company deny that they are trying to encourage the officials to buy more products from their company.[92]

Do Interest Groups Affect Public Policy?

How much influence interest groups have on public policy is difficult to determine. We can approach the problem, however, by asking: (1) What resources can interest groups bring to bear on influencing public policy? (2) In which states are interest groups the strongest? and (3) How effective have states been in regulating the influence of lobbying groups?

The Resources for Interest Group Influence   Some groups have more of the resources needed for strength than others. Among the most important resources are size of membership, unity, leadership and organization, intensity, money, and access.

A *large membership* can be a source of interest group strength. Cities and states with large labor union memberships, for example, usually have public policies that are pro-union.[93] The size of groups is important because their members are a source of campaign contributions, campaign workers, potential lobbyists during the legislative session, and votes.

Although large memberships can be an asset for group influence, they can also present a problem: A larger group may have more differences of opinion among its members. Open disagreement among the members is likely to weaken the group's influence and may even cause some members to leave the group. Large groups may sometimes be unable to take a position on some issues or may be restricted to vague positions as the price of maintaining group unity. Some scholars argue that the large membership groups tend to win symbolic benefits for their members, whereas the small membership groups tend to win tangible benefits.[94]

The *leadership and organization* of an interest group are also vital to success. The AFL-CIO has been powerful in the Northeast and Midwest not only because of its size but also because it enjoys capable leadership. The National Rifle Association also benefits from its active leaders and well-established communications network. Organization helps a group survive, an important consideration in view of the slowness of governmental decisions at times and the possible emergence of new concerns in the future. Some observers argue that group leadership over the long term tends to gravitate into the hands of a small circle of staff and self-perpetuating leaders. Roberto Michels called this the **iron law of oligarchy**.[95] Groups may have a tendency to become less democratic and more oligarchic over time.

Intensity is another important group resource. If members of a group feel strongly about the group's goals, they are more likely to give money, write letters, and support the group's efforts in other ways. If people do not care very much about what the group is doing, they are unlikely to do anything to support its efforts.

Money is very helpful for groups. It can be used to help friendly candidates, finance public relations campaigns, hire skilled lobbyists, and manage many other tasks. Moreover, money can be stored for future use and can be transferred from one state or locality to another.

In addition, *access*—the ability to receive a respectful or even friendly hearing from public officials—helps a group succeed. In a Republican-dominated state, business groups are likely to have more access than labor unions and are more likely to get a better reception among elected officials. In a Democratic-controlled legislature of the Northeast or Midwest, however, the reverse may often be true. Public officials will invite groups with the greatest access to offer their opinions, as noted earlier in the chapter.

Other resources can also be important. One is having a role in the implementation of a policy. Many public policies are carried out by a complex web of public and private organizations.[96] If a private group helps to carry out a policy, or if a group's members work in a public agency involved in policy execution, they may be able to mold the policy to better fit the group's desires.

State Differences in Interest Group Strength   In addition to a group's resources and tactics, interest group influence is determined by the overall political and economic environments of the states. Table 4.4 lists the states where groups have the greatest impact, according to a recent

TABLE 4.4

Comparative Interest Group Strength in a Few States

Strong← Overall Impact of Interest Group →Weak

Dominant (4)	Dominant/Complementary (26)	Complementary (16)	Complementary Subordinate (3)
Alabama	California	Montana	Michigan
Florida	Mississippi	Pennsylvania	Vermont

Source: Adapted from Anthony Nownes, Clive S. Thomas, and Ronald J. Hrebenar, "Interest Groups in the States," in Virginia Gray and Russell Hanson, eds. *Politics in the American States,* 9th ed. (Washington, DC: CQ Press, 2008), p. 121.

assessment, and the states where groups have the least impact. In the high-impact states, policy making is strongly influenced by some interest groups, although not all groups are necessarily influential. At the other extreme, interest groups have some influence on public policies but may be overwhelmed by general public opinion, the political parties, and/or public officials.

The distribution of interest group strength is not random. Generally speaking, the states with stronger interest groups tend to have *less complex social and economic systems than do the states with weak interest groups.* That is, strong interest group states tend to have lower per capita incomes, lower population densities, lower levels of education among the adult population, and less industrialized economies, and they are more likely to have state economies dominated by a single industry.[97] *The weaker interest group states also tend to have stronger political parties, although that relationship is not nearly as pronounced as it was two decades ago.* The weak interest group states additionally tend to have Moralistic political cultures, stronger governors, and more professional legislatures than the strong interest group states. Regionally speaking, interest groups tend to be stronger in the South and weaker in the Northeast and upper Midwest. In general, the more diversified a state's economy is, the more affluent its population is, and the stronger its political party system and governing institutions are, the less likely that state is to be dominated by a single interest group or a single combination of groups. However, some large, diverse states, such as California, Illinois, and Ohio, still have fairly powerful interest groups.[98]

Interest Group Regulation

Scandals in a number of states and localities, as well as in national politics, have triggered efforts to regulate group activities. How effective have the states been in regulating interest groups to curb the growing influence of PACs and minimize corrupt practices? Critics (including many citizens) are not entirely happy with the results. Most states have laws to limit campaign contributions, to force the disclosure of the names of contributors, and to require the registration of lobbyists. From all appearances, these laws have had relatively limited influence.

If the law limits how much a group can donate to candidates' campaigns, the group can encourage its members to give individually.[99] Groups can also circumvent contribution limits by running advertisements that are not officially part of the candidates' campaigns but attack their opponents.

Lobbyist regulation laws have been equally easy to circumvent. California passed one of the most stringent lobbying regulation acts in 1974, requiring lobbyists to register with the secretary of state and to make detailed reports on their income and expenditures. Despite these seemingly strict provisions, one California analyst commented, it "has not significantly altered lobbyist activity in Sacramento [the capital], although wining and dining has been drastically curtailed."[100] Disclosure of lobbying activity and campaign contributions has limited impact, in part because the disclosure reports often get little or no attention from the public or the mass media. Final reports may not be filed until after the election is over.

Efforts to regulate lobbying practices have fluctuated over the years. A dramatic scandal may lead to new reforms, but as time goes by, enforcement efforts may weaken, especially if the enforcement causes embarrassment to members of one or both parties. Where lobbying practices are honest, noncorrupt, and aboveboard, this desirable situation seems to stem more from a broad climate of a moralistic culture in the state than from specific laws to regulate lobbying behavior.[101]

CONCLUSION

Table 4.5 summarizes the preceding discussion. Public opinion and interest groups are rated as channels of political participation by their policy impact, the ease with which a citizen can use the channel to affect public policy, and the responsiveness of the channels.

For policy impact, public opinion's effectiveness varies considerably. Its impact is weakest on issues that attract little public interest or attention and on the details of policies about which many people may know little. Public opinion is most effective on visible and highly emotional issues. As discussed earlier in the chapter, there is some evidence that elected public officials share a consensus of values with many of their constituents, at least on some issues. By contrast, interest groups may be most influential on issues that attract little attention from the media or the general public and on issues that do not generate conflict among groups. When powerful groups oppose one another, none of them may be very successful.

How readily can an outsider influence public opinion or the interest group system to shape state policies? Public opinion may be easy to manipulate in some cases. Outsiders can alter public opinion when they have charismatic appeal or large sums of money and when the issue is interesting enough to attract public attention, but does not involve strongly held beliefs, which are usually resistant to change.

TABLE 4.5

Public Opinion and Interest Groups as Conventional Channels of Political Participation

Channel	Policy Impact	Ease with Which an Outsider Can Use This Channel to Change Public Policies	Most Responsive to Whom?	Least Responsive to Whom?
Public opinion	Variable: more on visible issues, broad contours of policy	Difficult (unless outsiders have money and many people lack opinions)	Intense opinions, people whose views are shared by many others	Less-educated, people, less attentive, and less active
Interest groups	Variable: more on less-visible issues, specific provisions of policy	Difficult, but possible	Existing institutions, group members, businesses, professions	Poor and unorganized people

Most established interest groups are not easily accessible to manipulation by outsiders. Yet, if enough outsiders feel strongly enough about a policy, they are free to organize their own interest group. In the environmental politics of the 1970s, many environmentalists formed ad hoc interest groups, which exerted influence on environmental policy making. Since then, conservatives have formed new groups in a number of states to promote conservative viewpoints.

Finally, and most important from the point of view of representative democracy, Table 4.5 examines the responsiveness of these channels. Public opinion is more effective in transmitting the concerns of people who pay attention to politics, are well informed, decide what they want, and become involved enough in politics to give officials an incentive to respond to them. Better-educated people are often better able to meet those requirements. Interest groups tend to overrepresent business and professional people and tend to underrepresent the poor.[102]

To place interest groups and public opinion in a broader comparative context, we need to examine the other channels of political influence. We will do this in the next chapter.

SUMMARY

1. Several patterns of participation arise in conventional political activities. Participation is concentrated among a small part of the population and is disproportionately an upper-status and middle-status phenomenon. This is especially true for demanding gladiator activities. Poor and less-educated people do not participate nearly as much as do affluent, well-educated people. Young people participate less than people who are middle-aged or old. To explain these patterns of participation, scholars have focused on psychological and skill barriers among the poor, political barriers, the lack of mobilizing organizations, the indifference of the governing institutions to the concerns of the poor, and low political interest among the young.

2. Three models try to explain the impact of public opinion on public policy—the rational activist model, the role-playing model, and the sharing or consensus model. Public opinion appears to have its strongest voice in issues that are visible and emotional. In deciding how much importance to attach to public opinion on a given issue, legislators have to cope with the intensity of voters' reactions. Policy makers also tend to be more responsive to their attentive constituents than they are to constituents in general. Even when public policy does correlate with public opinion, it often is not possible to know which one caused the other.

3. Interest groups are organizations that try to influence government decisions. A distinction can be drawn between economically motivated groups, professionally motivated groups, public interest groups, and ideological groups. Interest groups engage in a variety of tactics to influence government decisions—public relations, electioneering, and lobbying.

STUDY QUESTIONS

1. How active are people in politics? What kinds of activities generate the most public involvement? What factors influence how active a person is likely to be in politics?

2. How effectively does public opinion guide public policy decisions? What kinds of opinions are most likely to be influential in the political arena?

3. Evaluate interest groups as vehicles of representation. What kinds of interests are most likely to be organized? Why are some groups more influential than others? What tactics do groups use to promote their agendas?

KEY TERMS

Attentive constituent   The citizen who pays attention to political news and is, therefore, likely to learn about the actions of public officials.

Electioneering   The interest group tactic of trying to get favorable or sympathetic people elected to public office.

Gladiator   A person active in the more demanding types of political activities, including campaigning for a candidate, contributing to a political party, and serving as an officer in an interest group.

Intensity problem   Officials' difficulty in deciding whether they should support the preferences of a smaller group that feels very intensely about an issue or the larger group that feels much less intensely about it.

Interest group   Any organization of people who try to influence government decisions. This includes many organizations that primarily exist to serve some other purpose—manufacturing automobiles, saving souls, or helping the sick get well.

Iron law of oligarchy   The tendency of groups to become less democratic over time and to fall under the dominance of a small number of leaders.

Lobbying   The interest group tactic of trying to influence a decision of the legislature or some other governmental body.

Political action committee (PAC)   A group that collects money from various sources and uses it to make campaign contributions and to try to influence election outcomes.

Political participation   Individual or group activity that seeks to influence the selection of government officials or the actions of government.

Public interest group   An interest group that claims to represent a widely held interest. Members of the group do not expect their efforts to produce benefits just for the membership.

Public opinion   The general population's views on politically relevant issues.

Public relations   The use of the media to create a favorable public opinion. This includes generating agreement with the group's political values as well as drawing attention to an issue.

Sense of civic duty   The belief that one has a moral obligation to vote and take part in political activities.

Sense of political efficacy   The belief that an individual's participation in politics can have some effect. This typically includes the belief that the person can understand what is happening, knows how to become involved, and that the political system will respond to his or her efforts.

Spectator   A person whose main political activities are voting and observing politics. The spectator rarely engages in more demanding activities, such as joining an interest group, making a campaign contribution, or writing to a public official.

Voting Rights Act of 1965   This law was very effective in striking down the legal barriers that had prevented the majority of racial minorities in the South from registering and voting.

THE INTERNET CONNECTION

The League of Women Voters is a nonpartisan group that encourages voter participation and tries to help people learn about candidates and issues. You can contact this group at **www.lwv.org**. Many other interest groups also have Internet sites, where you can find information about the groups and their policy priorities. Can you find any groups that share your interests and your points of view?

NOTES

1. Karen Matthews, "Occupy Protesters March Nationwide; 300 Arrested," *Moscow, ID/ Pullman, WA Daily News*, November 18, 2011, p. 5A; Katharine Seelye, "A Day of Protests as Occupy Movement Marks Two-Month Milestone," *New York Times*, November 17, 2011 (Web edition); David Sharp, "Evictions Sweep Away Occupiers," *Pullman, WA, Daily Evergreen*, February 7, 2012, p. 4.

2. Heather Knight, "UC Officials to Review Nonviolent Protest Policies," *San Francisco Chronicle*, November 21, 2011, p. A-9; Matthews, "Occupy Protesters...."

3. Rich Morin, "Rising Share of Americans See Conflict Between Rich and Poor," *Pew Research Center* (Web document), January 11, 2012; David Carr, "The Occupy Movement May be in Retreat, But Its Ideas Are Advancing," *New York Times*, February 9, 2012 (Web edition).

4. Sidney Verba and Norman Nie, *Participation in America* (New York: Harper & Row, 1972), p. 2.

5. See Lester W. Milbrath and M. L. Goel, *Political Participation: How and Why Do People Get Involved in Politics?* 2nd ed. (Chicago: Rand McNally, 1977), pp. 19–21. Also see Robert Lane, *Political Life: Why People Get Involved in Politics* (Glencoe, IL: Free Press, 1959).

6. *MoveOn's 50 Ways to Love Your Country* (Maui, HI: Inner Ocean Publishing, 2004); Paul Simon, *Fifty-two Simple Ways to Make a Difference* (Minneapolis: Augsburg Fortress, 2004). Be advised that MoveOn is a relatively liberal group, but the techniques discussed in the book apply to any political viewpoint.

7. See *Statistical Abstract of the United States 2008* (Washington, DC: Bureau of the Census, 2008), 256–257; *The ANES Guide to Public Opinion and Electoral Behavior* (American National Election Study, November 28, 2007; Web document).

8. For recent evidence, see Russell Dalton, *Citizen Politics*, 3rd ed. (New York: Chatham House, 2002), pp. 49–56.

9. Martin Wattenberg, *Is Voting for Young People?* (New York: Pearson Longman, 2007), ch. 4.

10. For a recent discussion, see Thomas Patterson, *The Vanishing Voter* (New York: Vintage, 2003).

11. Raymond E. Wolfinger and Steven J. Rosenstone, *Who Votes?* (New Haven, CT: Yale University Press, 1980), pp. 23–30.

12. The importance of a sense of civic duty to voting is discussed in the work of William Riker and Peter Ordeshook, "A Theory of the Calculus of Voting," *American Political Science Review* 62, no. 1 (March 1968): 25–42.

13. This was the major finding of Elaine B. Sharp's study of citizen-contacting in Kansas City, Missouri, in 1982–1983. See her "Citizen Demand Making in the Urban Context," *American Journal of Political Science* 28, no. 4 (November 1984): 654–670.

14. Angus Campbell et al., *The American Voter* (New York: Wiley, 1960), ch. 4.

15. *The ANES Guide to Public Opinion and Electoral Behavior* (American National Election Study; November 11, 2007, Web document).

16. Arthur T. Hadley, *The Empty Polling Booth* (Englewood Cliffs, NJ: Prentice-Hall, 1978), pp. 67–103.

17. Anthony Downs, *An Economic Theory of Democracy* (New York: Harper & Row, 1957), ch. 14; Campbell et al., *The American Voter*, ch. 4.

18. See John Bibby, *Politics, Parties, and Elections in America*, 5th ed. (Belmont, CA: 2003), pp. 314–315; William Flanigan and Nancy Zingale, *Political Behavior of the American Electorate*, 10th ed. (Washington, DC: Congressional Quarterly, 2002), p. 44; Thomas Patterson, *The Vanishing Voter* (New York: Vintage, 2003), pp. 42–43.

19. *Smith v. Allwright*, 321 U.S. 649 (1944).

20. *Gomillion v. Lightfoot*, 364 U.S. 339 (1960).

21. Bureau of the Census, *Statistical Abstract of the United States, 1995* (Washington, DC: U.S. Government Printing Office, 1995), p. 287; *Statistical Abstract of the United States, 2008* (Washington, DC: U.S. Government Printing Office, 2003), p. 255.

22. *Statistical Abstract 2008* (Washington, DC: U.S. Census Bureau, 2008), p. 255.

23. Michael McDonald and Samuel Popkin, "The Myth of the Vanishing Voter," *American Political Science Review* 95 (2001): 963–974.

24. Wolfinger and Rosenstone, *Who Votes?* p. 73.

25. See the figures in *The New York Times Almanac* (New York: Penguin, 2006), p. 120.

26. Josh Goodman, "Pushing the Envelope," *Governing*, May, 2008, pp. 40–41.

27. Norman Ornstein, "The Risk with Absentee Ballots," *Washington Post National Weekly Edition*, December 4, 2000, p. 21.

28. *Statistical Abstract of the United States, 2001* (Washington, DC: U.S. Government Printing Office, 2001), p. 251. Bureau of the Census Web site, 2005; Center for the Study of the American Electorate, 2005.

29. *Statistical Abstract, 2011–2012* (New York: Skyhorse, 2011), p. 261.

30. See John Bibby and Thomas Holbrooke, "Parties and Elections," in Virginia Gray and Russell Hanson, eds. *Politics in the American States*, 8th ed. (Washington, DC: CQ Press, 2004), pp. 92–95; Albert Karnig and B. Oliver Walter, "Municipal Voter Turnout During the 1980s:

The Case of Continued Decline," in Harry Bailey and Jay Shafritz, eds. *State and Local Government and Politics,* (Itasca, IL: Peacock, 1993), pp. 26–38.

31. Alexander Keyssar, "The Strange Career of Voter Supression," *New York Times*, February 12, 2012 (Web edition).

32. Benjamin Radcliff and Patricia David, "Labor Organization and Electoral Participation in Industrial Democracies," *American Journal of Political Science* 44 (2000): 132–141; Gerald W. Johnson, "Research Note on Political Correlates of Voter Participation: A Deviant Case Analysis," *American Political Science Review* 65, no. 3 (September 1971): 768–776. One study found that African American voting increased when outside organizers and federal registrars appeared. See Lester M. Salamon and Stephen Van Evera, "Fear, Apathy, and Discrimination: A Test of Three Explanations of Political Participation," *American Political Science Review* 67, no. 4 (December 1973): 1288–1307.

33. For example of one of those efforts, see Pat Muir, "Yakima Sees New Latino Vote Effort," *Moscow, ID/Pullman Daily News,* August 7, 2008, p. 3A.

34. Bibby and Holbrooke, "Parties and Elections," (2004), pp. 94–95.

35. Steven Schier, *By Invitation Only* (Pittsburgh: University of Pittsburgh, 2000).

36. Henry Brady, Kay Schlozman, and Sidney Verba, "Prospecting for Participants: Rational Expectations and the Recruitment of Political Activists," *American Political Science Review* 93 (1999): 153–168; Henry E. Brady, Sidney Verba, and Kay Lehman Schlozman, "Beyond SES: A Resource Model of Political Participation," *American Political Science Review* 89, no. 2 (June 1995): 271–294; Alan Gerger and Donald Green, "The Effects of Canvassing, Telephone Calls, and Direct Mail on Voter Turnout: A Field Experiment," *American Political Science Review* 94 (2000): 653–664.

37. See Allan Cigler and Mark Joslyn, "Groups, Social Capital, and Democratic Orientations," in Allan Cigler and Burdett Loomis, eds. *Interest Group Politics,* 6th ed., (Washington, DC: Congressional Quarterly, 2002), pp. 37–54.

38. See Michael McDonald, "The Turnout Rate Among Eligible Voters in the States," *State Politics and Policy Quarterly* 2: 199–212.

39. Larry Bartels, *Unequal Democracy* (New York: Russell Sage Foundation, 2008), pp. 259–277.

40. Kim Hill and Jan Leighley, "The Policy Consequences of Class Bias in State Electorates," *American Journal of Political Science* 36 (1992): 351–365; Sidney Verba and Norman Nie, *Participation in America* (New York: Harper and Row, 1972).

41. Albert O. Hirschman, *Exit, Voice and Loyalty: Responses to Decline in Firms, Organizations and States* (Cambridge, MA: Harvard University Press, 1970).

42. Robert Putnam, "Tuning In, Tuning Out: The Strange Disappearance of Social Capital in America," *PS: Political Science and Politics* 27, no. 4 (December 1994): 664–683.

43. Michael Traugott, et al., "Civic Engagement in the Post-9/11 World," *PS: Political Science and Politics* 35, no. 3 (September 2002): 11–16.

44. Wattenberg, *Is Voting for Young People?*

45. Harry Boyte, "Civic Education as Public Leadership Development," *PS: Political Science and Politics* 26 (December 1993): 763–769.

46. This may be a particular handicap for younger people. See Benjamin Highton and Raymond Wolfinger, "The First Seven Years of the Political Life Cycle," *American Journal of Political Science* 45 (2001): 202–209; Eric Plutzer, "Becoming a Habitual Voter: Inertia, Resources, and Growth in Young Adulthood," *American Political Science Review* 96 (2002): 41–56.

47. M. Margaret Conway and Frank B. Feigert, *Political Analysis: An Introduction*, 2nd ed. (Boston: Allyn and Bacon, 1976), p. 130.

48. Thomas R. Dye was one of the most persistent and influential advocates of this view. See his *Politics, Economics, and the Public: Policy Outcomes in the American States* (Chicago: Rand McNally and Company, 1966). Dye, in this book, does not directly test public opinion as a possible independent variable; rather, he uses measures such as interparty competition and voter turnout, which presumably reflect public opinion partially.

49. Robert Erikson, Gerald Wright, and John McIver, *Statehouse Democracy* (New York: Cambridge, 1994); Robert Weissberg, *Public Opinion and Popular Government* (Englewood Cliffs, NJ: Prentice-Hall, 1976), p. 137. The best recent overview of public opinion and state politics is Jeffrey Cohen, ed., *Public Opinion in State Politics* (Stanford, CA: Stanford University, 2007).

50. Gerald C. Wright, Jr., Robert S. Erikson, and John P. McIver, "Measuring State Partisanship and Ideology with Survey Data," *Journal of Politics* 47, no. 2 (May 1985): 469–489. The validity of this measure of political ideology was affirmed by Thomas M. Holbrook-Provow and Steven C. Poe, who found high correlations between this measure and four other measures of ideological leaning in the states. See their "Measuring State Political Ideology," *American Politics Quarterly* 15, no. 3 (July 1987): 399–414.

51. David Held, *Models of Democracy,* 3rd ed. (Stanford, CA: Stanford University Press, 2006); Robert Erikson, "The Relationship Between Public Opinion and State Policy: A New Look Based on Some Forgotten Data," *American Political Science Review* 20, no. 1 (February 1976): 25–37; Robert Erikson and Kent Tedin, *American Public Opinion,* 6th ed. (New York: Longman, 2001), chs. 7–11.

52. Norman R. Lutbeg, *Public Opinion and Public Policy,* rev. ed. (Homewood, IL: Dorsey Press, 1974), p. 4.

53. Warren E. Miller and Donald E. Stokes, "Constituency Influence in Congress," *American Political Science Review* 57, no. 1 (March 1963): 15–56.

54. Lutbeg, *Public Opinion and Public Policy,* p. 8.

55. Roberta S. Sigel and H. Paul Friesema, "Urban Community Leaders' Knowledge of Public Opinion," *Western Political Quarterly* 18, no. 1. (December 1965): 881–895; Paul Friesema and Ronald Hedlund, "The Reality of Representational Roles," in Norman Lutbeg, ed. *Public Opinion and Public Policy,* 3rd ed. (Itaska, IL: Peacock, 1981), pp. 316–320; Robert Erikson, Norman Lutbeg, and William Holloway, "Knowing One's District: How Legislators Predict Referendum Voting," *American Journal of Political Science* 22 (1978): 511–535.

56. See Kenneth Prewitt, "Political Ambitions, Volunteerism, and Electoral Accountability," *American Political Science Review* 64, no. 1 (March 1970:) pp. 5–17; James Kuklinski and Donald McCrone, "Electoral Accountability as a Source of Policy Representation," in Norman Lutbeg, ed. *Public Opinion and Public Policy* (Itaska, IL: Peacock, 1981), pp. 320–340.

57. For a useful guide to doing surveys at the local level, see Thomas Miller and Michelle Kobayashi, *Citizen Surveys* (Washington, DC: International City/County Manager Association, 2000).

58. David R. Morgan, "Political Linkage of Public Policy: Attitudinal Congruence Between Citizens and Officials," *Western Political Quarterly* 26, no. 2 (June 1973): 219–223. Eric Uslaner and Ronald E. Weber, "U.S. State Legislators' Opinions and Perceptions of Constituency Attitudes," *Legislative Studies Quarterly* 4 (November 1979): 563–585.

59. Kim Quaile Hill and Angela Hinton-Andersson, "Pathways of Representation: A Causal Analysis of Public Opinion-Policy Linkages," *American Journal of Political Science* 39, no. 4 (November 1995): 924–935.

60. Miller and Stokes, "Constituency Influence in Congress," pp. 45–56.

61. Ronald E. Weber and William R. Shaffer, "Public Opinion and American State Policy Making," *Midwest Journal of Political Science* 16, no. 4 (November 1972): 683–699.

62. Anne H. Hopkins, "Opinion Publics and Support for Public Policy in the American States," *American Journal of Political Science* 18, no. 1 (February 1974): 167–177.

63. G. R. Boynton, Samuel C. Patterson, and Ronald D. Hedlund, "The Missing Links in Legislative Politics: Attentive Constituents," *Journal of Politics* 31, no. 3 (August 1969): 700–721.

64. See Wattenberg, *Is Voting for Young People?,* chs. 1–3.

65. Erikson, "The Relationship Between Public Opinion and State Policy," pp. 25–37.

66. See Weissberg, *Public Opinion and Popular Government,* pp. 159–162.

67. Clive Thomas and Scott Hrebenar, "Interest Groups in the States," in Virginia Gray and Russell Hanson, eds. *Politics in the American States: A Comparative Analysis,* 8th ed. (Washington, DC: CQ Press, 2004), pp. 118–121.

68. David Lowery and Virginia Gray, "The Density of State Interest Group Systems," *Journal of Politics* 55, no. 1 (February 1993): 191–206. See also Burdett Loomis and Allan Cigler, "Introduction: The Changing Nature of Interest Group Politics," in Allan Cigler and Burdett Loomis, eds. *Interest Group Politics,* 6th ed. (Washington, DC: Congressional Quarterly 2002), p. 2; David Lowery and Holly Brasher, *Organized Interests and American Government* (Boston: McGraw-Hill, 2004), pp. 75–77.

69. Between 1968 and 1989, USW membership dropped from 1,120,000 to 421,000 and UAW membership dropped from 1,473,000 to 771,000. *Statistical Abstract of the United States, 1971* (Washington, DC: U.S. Government Printing Office, 1971), p. 234; *Statistical Abstract of the United States, 1995* (Washington, DC: U.S. Government Printing Office, 1995), p. 443.

70. Jack Barbash, "Trade Unionism from Roosevelt to Reagan," *Annals of the American Academy of Political and Social Science*, no. 473 (May 1984): 21.

71. Michael Goldfield, "Labor in American Politics: Its Current Weaknesses," *Journal of Politics* 48, no. 1 (February 1986): 2–29.

72. Jonathan Walters, "Solidarity Forgotten," *Governing* 19, no. 9 (June 2006): 28–35.

73. John Gramlich, "After a Contentious Political Year, Republicans May Moderate Their Approach," *Stateline,* January 9, 2012 (Web edition); Daniel Vock, "In Wisconsin, Assessing a New Labor Law's Impact," *Stateline,* February 13, 2012 (Web edition).

74. Anthony Nownes, "Solicited Advice and Lobbyist Power: Evidence from Three American States," *Legislative Studies Quarterly* 24 (1999): 113–123.

75. David Gushee, ed., *Christians and Politics: Beyond the Culture Wars* (Grand Rapids: Baker, 2000).

76. Anthony Nownes, Clive Thomas, and Ronald Hrebenar, "Interest Groups in the States," in Virginia Gray and Russell Hanson, eds. *Politics in the American States* (Washington, DC: CQ Press, 2008), pp. 106–110.

77. See Paul Herrnson, Ronald Shaiko, and Clyde Wilcox, eds., *The Interest Group Connection* (Washington, DC: CQ Press, 2005), Part I.

78. Clive S. Thomas and Ronald J. Hrebenar, "Political Action Committees in the States: Some Preliminary Findings," A paper presented at the American Political Science Association annual convention (Washington, DC: September, 1991).

79. Larry Sabato, *PAC Power: Inside the World of Political Action Committees* (New York: Norton, 1984), pp. 197–198.

80. Candace Romig, "Placing Limits on PACs," *State Legislatures* 10, no. 2 (January 1984): 22.

81. Herbert E. Alexander, *The Case for PACs*, A Public Affairs Council Monograph (Los Angeles, CA: The Public Affairs Council, 1983).

82. Floyd Abrams, "Citizens United Decision," *New York Times*, January 16, 2012 (Web edition);

83. "Attacks on Disclosure," *New York Times*, February 10, 2012 (Web edition).

84. Clive Thomas, Ronald Hrebenar, and Anthony Nownes, "Interest Group Politics in the States: Four Decades of Developments—the 1960s to the Present," *Book of the States 2008* (Lexington, KY: Council of State Governments 2008), p. 325.

85. Clive S. Thomas and Ronald J. Hrebenar, "The Wheeler Dealer Lobbyist: An Endangered Species in States Capitals?" *Comparative State Politics* 13, no. 2 (April 1992): 32.

86. Randy Welch, "Lobbyists, Lobbyists All Over the Lot," *State Legislatures* 15, no. 2 (February 1989): 21.

87. John C. Syer and John H. Culver, *Power and Politics in California*, 4th ed. (New York: Macmillan, 1992), p. 63.

88. Christopher Bosso and Michael Collins, "Just Another Tool? How Environmental Groups Use the Internet," in Allan Cigler and Burdett Loomis, eds. *Interest Group Politics*, 6th ed. (Washington, DC: CQ Press, 2002), 95–116; Marilyn Cohodas, "Digital Activism," *Governing* 13, no. 11 (August 2000): 70.

89. Cohodas, "Digital Activism," p. 63.

90. Jay K. Dow and James Endersby, "Campaign Contributions and Legislative Voting in the California Assembly," *American Politics Quarterly* 22, no. 3 (July 1994): 334–353; Alan Rosenthal, *The Decline of Representative Democracy* (Washington, DC: CQ Press, 1998), pp. 222–224; Gary Jacobson, *The Politics of Congressional Elections,* 4th ed. (New York: Longman, 1997), pp. 38–65; Sott Ainsworth, *Analyzing Interest Groups* (New York: Norton, 2002), pp. 199–200.

91. "Lawmakers Rely on Special Interest Donations," *Moscow, ID/Pullman, WA Daily News*, November 22, 2010, p. 3A.

92. Michael Winerip, "Free Trips Raise Issues for Officials in Education," *New York Times*, October 9, 2011 (electronic edition).

93. See Weber and Shaffer, "Public Opinion and American State Policy Making," pp. 683–699.

94. This argument is especially made by Thomas R. Dye and L. Harmon Zeigler, in *The Irony of American Democracy: An Uncommon Introduction to American Politics*, 4th ed. (North Scituate, MA: Duxbury Press, 1978), pp. 209–210.

95. Roberto Michels, *Political Parties: A Sociological Study of the Oligarchical Tendencies of Modern Democracy*, trans. Eden Paul and Cedar Paul (New York: Free Press, 1962).

96. For an example at the local level, see Robert Agranoff and Michael McGuire, *Collaborative Public Management* (Washington, DC: Georgetown University, 2003).

97. Sarah McCally Morehouse, *State Politics, Parties and Policy* (New York: Holt, Rinehart & Winston, 1981), pp. 108–113, 491–492.

98. Anthony Nownes, Clive Thomas, and Ronald Hrebenar, "Interest Groups in the States," in Virginia Gray and Russell Hanson, eds. *Politics in the American States*, 9th ed. (Washington, DC: Congressional Quarterly Press, 2008), p. 121; Thomas and Hrebenar, "Interest Groups in the States," in Virginia Gray and Russell Hanson, eds. *Politics in the American States*, 8th ed. (Washington, DC: CQ Press, 2004) pp. 121–122.

99. William P. Browne and Delbert J. Ringquist, "Michigan Interests: The Politics of Diversification," in Ronald J. Hrebenar and Clive S. Thomas, eds. *Interest Group Politics in the Midwest* (Ames: Iowa State University Press, 1993).

100. Michael J. Ross, *California: Its Government and Politics* (North Scituate, MA: Duxbury Press, 1979), p. 66.

101. This was the conclusion reached by observers of interest groups in Iowa and North Dakota. See Charles W. Wiggins and Keith E. Hamm, "Iowa: Interest Group Politics in an Undistinguished Place," A paper presented at the 1987 meeting of the Midwest Political Science Association, Chicago, April 1987, pp. 5–6. Also see another paper presented at the 1987 meeting: Theodore B. Pedeliski, "Interest Groups in North Dakota: Constituency Coupling in a Moralistic Political Culture," pp. 26–28.

102. E. E. Schattschneider, *The Semisovereign People* (New York: Holt, Rinehart, and Winston, 1960); Kay Schlozman and John Tierney, *Organized Interests and American Democracy* (New York: Harper and Row, 1986), ch. 4.

Channels of Citizen Influence: The Ballot Box, Parties, and Direct Action

CHAPTER PREVIEW

This chapter explores several more channels of citizen input that may enable citizens to influence the actions of state and local governments. We will discuss:

1 The election process.

2 Political parties.

3 Direct democracy devices, such as initiative, referendum, and recall.

4 Direct action tactics, such as protests, demonstrations, and sit-ins.

Introduction

The most dramatic feature of the 2010 election in many parts of the country was probably the Tea Party, a movement that emerged from a number of roots, including traditional economic conservatism, the decline of opportunities for advancement for many people in the current economy, the recession, and a personal dislike of President Obama, who had been repeatedly accused of not being a "real American" and not genuinely eligible to be president due to the conspiracy theory that he was not actually born in the United States (although a wealth of evidence shows that he was born in Hawaii). Tea Party supporters repeatedly pressed the Republican Party to nominate more conservative candidates, who would cut government spending and reduce the level of governmental borrowing.[1]

Political observers and analysts have described the Tea Party in a number of ways. Some suggested that the Tea Party was a spontaneous, grassroots movement that appeared all over the country and lacked much in the way of overall organization or leadership. Others noted that a small number of very wealthy leaders had in fact helped the Tea Party get started and kept it going:

media mogul Rupert Murdoch and brothers David and Charles Koch. They have given millions of dollars and, in Murdoch's case, enormous media coverage to the Tea Party and its ideas. Some observers believe that the Tea Party played a major role in the dramatic Republican gains in the 2010 election. Other analysts have concluded that the 2010 election was largely a result of a weak economy, President Obama's low approval rating, unhappiness with various aspects of the 2010 health care reforms, and some elements of racial resentment.[2]

At any rate, the 2010 election revealed, yet again, that national political dynamics can spill over into state and local politics. The Republican Party rode that tide to win control of a number of governorships and several hundred state legislative seats. Elements of the Tea Party continue to be active, although they are overshadowed by the presidential nomination and election processes of 2012. They still oppose tax increases and push for tax reductions, however. Because Tea Party supporters tend to be older than the average Americans, they also tend to oppose cuts to Social Security and Medicare.

THE BALLOT BOX

In a representative democracy such as that in the United States, the election process is the central means by which people are expected to hold the government accountable.

Elections are regulated by the states and generally administered by local governments. In all states, you must meet minimal requirements in order to vote. You must be a U.S. citizen, 18 years of age, and a resident of your state for a given period. Except for North Dakota, all states also require you to register in order to vote.

Except for the Nebraska Legislature and most judgeships, state elections usually use a partisan ballot on which the political party of each candidate is indicated near his or her name. Consequently, voters can easily determine whether they are voting for a Democrat, a Republican, or a member of another party.

At the local level there is a much wider variety of election systems. In general, local election systems can be categorized as either *reformed* or *unreformed*. A **reformed election system** tends to have nonpartisan, at-large elections, which are held at times separate from state or national elections, and the chief executive is appointed by the city council, county commission, or school board, not elected by the voters. In nonpartisan elections, the ballots do not list the party designation of the candidates (although some voters may sometimes learn the party affiliations of some candidates). In at-large elections, city council members are elected from the entire city. They are distinguished from **ward elections** or **district elections,** in which the council members are elected from neighborhood areas usually called *wards* (sometimes *districts*). Reformed elections also try to protect against voter fraud by voter registration, voting machines, election judges from all parties and factions, and safeguards in counting the ballots.

An **unreformed election system,** in contrast, tends to be partisan, with officials chosen by ward rather than at-large. These elections are held at the same time as statewide elections, and while they traditionally lacked effective protection against voter fraud, that is much less true today. Reformed election systems predominate in suburbs and in the Far West. Unreformed election systems predominate in many parts of the East, the Midwest, and the South.

One consequence of reformed election systems is reduced voter turnout. Most of the reform devices slightly increase the difficulty and/or decrease the attractiveness of voting. Eliminating parties from the ballot makes voting more confusing and less interesting to partisans and discourages party efforts to mobilize voters. Local-only elections often generate little interest, as do local elections without an elected chief executive. Since nonvoting tends to be highest among the poor and less educated, especially if no one encourages them to vote, one frequent effect of reformed election systems is to reduce even more the influence of poorer and less educated people in the election process.[3] These considerations are discussed more fully in Chapter 6.

Elections as Instruments of Accountability

Do elections hold governing officials accountable to the voters? Two general propositions can be made. First, elections are often instruments of **retroactive accountability**; they hold public officials accountable after the fact. They are less often instruments of **proactive accountability**, in which voters would assess the policy views of candidates and vote for the candidates who share their (the voters') beliefs. Voters often have an easier time judging officeholders on past performance.[4]

Although gubernatorial elections sometimes do present voters with relatively clear choices, as do some mayoral races, in many elections, voters simply do not know enough about the candidates to choose one set of future policies over another. The winners will have to face reelection two or four years later, and at that time the voters will make a retroactive judgment about whether they are dissatisfied enough to replace the incumbent. These judgments are easier to make in the case of relatively visible officials, such as governors, than in the case of less visible officials, including many at the local level.

Second, contrary to some conventional wisdom, the available evidence suggests that elections are better instruments of accountability at the state level than they are at the local level. Kenneth Prewitt's research on local government officials found that many of them did not worry about being defeated at the polls if they angered their constituents.[5] A fourth of them got their council positions through appointment rather than election. During elections, voter turnout was so small that the average candidate could win by getting the vote from as little as 6 to 8 percent of the population. Once in office, 80 percent were reelected when they chose to run again. The offices had low salaries, which made them relatively unattractive, and few council members cared to run for higher office. These problems appear to be especially acute for localities with reform-style governments.[6] A considerable number of special-purpose local governments are also headed by appointed officials, not elected ones.

Many local officials are essentially volunteers doing a civic duty, not professional politicians attempting to build a career. We can call this phenomenon **volunteerism**. These voluntary public officials follow their own judgments and the judgments of trusted associates. Despite the election process, these officials are, in practice, not very accountable to the public. That is, the volunteers don't have to worry about displeasing the voters, because they (the officials) don't care about being ousted from office. The clearest indication of that sentiment is the large number of state and local officials who refuse to run for another term when they are eligible. Even when the volunteers are ousted, they are often replaced by other volunteers, who also have no strong incentive to worry about public sentiments.

In this type of environment, the electorate can make its will felt only intermittently when voters occasionally rise in rebellion against a particularly unpopular decision. Usually, this occurs retroactively, as when a neighborhood group is upset by the cost of a major project and votes out the local council members at the next election. By this time, however, the unpopular action may already be underway and cannot easily be reversed. The problem of holding local elected officials accountable to the public is also complicated by the fact that most local governments are severely constrained by state and federal rules and regulations in what they can do (see Chapters 6 and 7). Moreover, media coverage of local government is rather limited in many communities and seems to be declining in many areas; voters cannot readily hold officials accountable without information regarding their actions.

Local elections are also hampered by a lack of candidates in many jurisdictions, especially the smaller ones. Guy, Tennessee (population about 500), recently provided an extreme example of that problem in an election for town aldermen. No candidates filed to run, although one incumbent, who was reelected by write-in votes, apparently didn't notice that the deadline for qualifying on the ballot had passed. Even worse, officials in Brinson, Georgia (population 225), forgot to hold town council elections—an occurrence that strongly suggested a low level of interest in running for the positions.[7] Many local offices in smaller jurisdictions pay little or no money, but make many demands on the officials' time. The resources available to deal with policy problems are often quite limited, and the public often has unrealistic expectations regarding how cheaply and quickly things can be done. As a result, few candidates want to run for those offices, and few people want to stay in those offices for very long.[8]

In contrast to local-level elections, state-level elections provide more opportunity for accountability to the voters. Although people do not follow state affairs any more closely than they follow local ones,[9] state elections usually have higher turnout rates than local elections. Higher turnout may make those candidates more attentive to the concerns of a broader spectrum of the population than do local officials. Finally, the governor is usually the most visible state official and, as such, is an "easy target of discontent" when things do not seem to be going well in a state.[10] This can occur when people perceive their state economy is slumping or some major program, such as education, has serious problems. When this happens, governors tend to see downturns in their public opinion ratings and their vote totals at reelection time.[11] Governors are even more likely to become targets of discontent if they pushed for an unpopular increase in state sales or income taxes.[12] For an overview of the factors that often influence voters' decision, see the following Highlight.

HIGHLIGHT

Why Do People Vote as They Do?

Many studies have tried to determine what factors influence people's voting decisions. Some of the most important factors are:

Party Loyalty   Most Americans feel some degree of preference for one or the other of the major parties. They will usually vote for the candidates of that party, in part because the party label is easy to remember and because the ballot tells them which candidates belong to which party in partisan elections. The party labels also serve as a rough guide to the candidates' political values.

Issues   When voters can tell candidates apart on an issue that they (the voters) care about, they are very likely to vote for the candidate who shares their policy position. This is normally much easier with highly visible offices, such as governors, than for other offices, such as hospital boards and county commissions.

Candidate Qualities   For important offices, such as governor, voters often prefer candidates with previous governmental experience. Voters also prefer candidates who appear to be trustworthy and concerned about public needs. Voters may not know much about many of the candidates on the ballot, however.

(continues)

(continued)

Incumbency If an incumbent (an official already in office) runs for reelection, he or she is much more likely to win than is the challenger most of the time. Incumbents usually have a variety of advantages over challengers: incumbents are usually better known, more experienced in campaigning, and better financed.

Money Candidates with more money usually attract more votes. Money is especially important for candidates who are not well known.

National Political Tides Sometimes national political forces sweep through state and local elections. People who are unhappy with the president or unhappy with the condition of the country may vote against the president's party in state and local elections, as happened in 2010. ■

Elections as Channels of Citizen Input

Related to the issue of elections as instruments of accountability is the question of whether citizens can use the election process as a means to get the government to enact favorable policies. This is especially important for low-income people, who—as we saw in Chapter 4—have lower voter turnout than do middle-income people and are usually represented by few, if any, interest groups. If more low-income people voted, could they get more favorable policies and programs from government?

Early research on this question during the 1960s was not very encouraging.[13] Researchers found that voter turnout rates had virtually no effect on funding of services for the poor and did not affect whether the state was controlled by Democrats (who presumably would be more favorable to low-income voters) or by Republicans.[14]

However, a more recent analysis compared the states by how well low-income voters were represented at the polling place on election day. Low-income people consistently received better welfare-type benefits in the states where they had the best voter turnout. Where their turnout was especially poor, they fared badly. In addition, recent research comparing people who consistently vote from one election to another and people who consistently do not vote found that consistent nonvoters tend to have more liberal views on some issues than do the consistent voters.[15]

What is true for low-income voters is also true for other categories of people. When a distinctive category of people goes from practically no voter turnout to a relatively high turnout, the political system is likely to become more responsive to their concerns. Quantum leaps in voter turnout for distinct categories of people happened twice in the twentieth century—following the Nineteenth Amendment's enfranchisement of women in 1920 and following enfranchisement of racial minorities after the Voting Rights Act of 1965. Enfranchisement was gradually followed by the emergence of increasing numbers of minorities and women performing the more demanding types of political activity, such as making campaign contributions or distributing campaign literature. That, in turn, fostered adoption of public policies aimed at their concerns.

The right to vote does not necessarily give a particular category of people a great deal of influence in public policy making, but the absence of the right to vote virtually ensures that their influence will be minimal. How influential they can be depends on several factors in addition to the right to vote—whether they are united, whether their leaders can mobilize them to vote, whether their leaders are effective, and whether the political system has the resources to meet their demands, among other considerations. A group's political leanings can also shift over time, as has happened with American Catholics. They have shifted from a strongly Democratic leaning to a pattern of supporting both parties and even leaning Republican in some recent elections.[16]

Financing State and Local Elections

Money is important in elections. Parties and candidates need money to produce bumper stickers, put out brochures, hire pollsters, buy advertisements (and the services of the professionals who make them), pay for television time, and do all the other things necessary to run an effective campaign today.[17] A governor's race can easily cost several million dollars, and statewide campaigns in larger states can cost much more.[18] The 2006 gubernatorial campaigns in California cost $137 million, and the 2009 campaigns for governor in Virginia cost $53 million. The 2009 New Jersey governor's race also cost $53 million. In a recent New York City mayoral election, the winning candidate, Michael Bloomberg, spent about $70 million—a new record for a local campaign. The 2004 election campaigns (national, state, and local) also set a new record: $4.3 billion.[19]

Where this money comes from is vitally important. Since big contributors will usually expect to gain access to the candidates they support, the public at large has a key interest in seeing who the contributors are, in broadening the contribution base as much as possible, and in limiting the potential for corrupt relationships between contributors and candidates. However, many Americans are unwilling to make significant campaign contributions to candidates or to the political parties, a situation that forces candidates to rely on the proportionally small number of people who will contribute (unless a candidate is wealthy enough to finance his or her own campaign, a phenomenon that has appeared in a number of states over the years).

Reform of Campaign Finance In the wake of the Watergate scandal in the Nixon administration (1972–1974), many states enacted campaign finance legislation, and all states now have some regulation of political financing. The most common provisions are disclosure of contributors (50 states), limits on campaign contributors (37 states limit contributions by individuals; 45 have limits or bans on contributions by corporations; and 38 states have restrictions on direct labor union contributions), and limits on campaign expenditures (nine states).[20] States with stronger interest groups are less likely to adopt strict limits on contributions from corporations, banks, and labor unions.[21]

About half of the states provide some public funding for campaigns. Most of those systems offer an income tax check-off provision whereby taxpayers can earmark a small portion of their income taxes to a public campaign fund. Several states, however, fund their systems by allowing taxpayers the option of increasing their own income taxes by a small amount, an approach that usually generates relatively little money. And seven states provide either income tax credits or income tax deductions for a portion of campaign contributions.[22] (The Where Do I Fit In? exercise on pp.104–105 gives you a chance to examine the incentives it would take to get you to contribute.) Connecticut has taken the unusual step of financing statewide campaigns with unclaimed property.[23]

Campaign finance regulations were tightened in 2002 when Congress passed and the president signed the McCain–Feingold bill. The new law prohibits the national parties from raising or spending **soft money** (money raised and spent for party-based campaigning as well as voter registration and mobilization efforts; this money was previously exempt from many campaign finance laws and was used to channel large sums of money from the national parties to state and local parties). McCain–Feingold does allow limited soft money donations to state and local party organizations, but that money cannot be used for advertisements for or against federal candidates.

Goals of Reform   Three essential goals underlie many finance reform provisions. First, financial disclosure requirements are intended to let voters know if the candidates themselves have any potential conflicts of interest between their governmental responsibilities and either their sources of income or their campaign contributions. Some citizens, for example, might want to vote against candidates who obtain most of their campaign funds from labor union political action committees; other voters might want to do the opposite.

WHERE DO I FIT IN?

What Would It Take to Get You to Contribute?

The integrity of the democratic process is undermined to the extent that campaign finance is left to wealthy individuals, interest groups, and political action committees. Few Americans ever contribute to political campaigns. The democratic process in most states would probably be healthier if more people contributed or if there were a broader base of contributions. As a student, you may not have the spare funds now to contribute to political causes. But a few years after graduation, your finances will stabilize and you will find yourself with the discretionary income to support causes and candidates. Listed below are several steps proposed by various groups to encourage a broader range of participation in campaign finance. Assuming you had an extra $100 above and beyond your normal spending needs, what would it take to get you to contribute half of that $100 to a political campaign for a candidate or party of your choice?

	Yes	No
1. No special incentive needed. I would willingly contribute. *Rationale:* _____	❑	❑
2. A state tax credit for one-half of the contribution, so that the $50 contribution would actually cost me only $25. *Rationale:* _____	❑	❑
3. A state tax credit for one-half of the contribution and an additional federal tax credit for the other half so that the $50 contribution would actually cost me $0. *Rationale:* _____	❑	❑
4. I would not contribute $50, but I would willingly earmark $1 of my state income tax refund to a public campaign fund distributed to the candidates of my party. *Rationale:* _____	❑	❑

Second, contribution limits aim to reduce the influence of wealthy contributors. If a state legislative candidate is limited to accepting no more than $5,000 from a single source (whether an individual or a political action committee), that candidate is probably less vulnerable to undue influence from that contributor than if a donor is allowed to give $200,000 to a candidate. Third, public financing provisions are designed to give the average voter an incentive to make campaign contributions, in the hope that such contributions will offset the influence of PACs and wealthy individuals.

Does Campaign Finance Reform Work? Reforms have probably curbed some of the worst abuses in campaign finance, but the results have been less than the reformers had hoped or

	Yes	No
5. I would not contribute $50 or earmark $1 of my state income tax refund for candidates of a particular party, but I would willingly earmark $1 of my state income tax refund to a public campaign fund distributed equally to all candidates of all parties. *Rationale:* _____	❏	❏
6. I would not make any of the aforementioned contributions, but I would support tax dollars from the general fund being spent on public funding of campaigns, with equal amounts going to all candidates for the office. To hold down the number of frivolous candidacies, candidates would have to get a minimum percentage of the vote. *Rationale:* _____	❏	❏
7. None of the aforementioned tax concessions or public funding proposals appeals to me, but I would contribute if it were likely to lead to an appointment to some public advisory commission for me. *Rationale:* _____	❏	❏
8. I would contribute $50 if I found a candidate or cause that I truly believed in but not otherwise, regardless of any incentives. *Rationale:* _____	❏	❏
9. I would not contribute the $50, and I would not support any of the public funding or tax incentives listed. *Rationale:* _____	❏	❏

Having decided what incentives, if any, would be needed to get you to contribute under these ideal conditions in which you had a spare $100, what percentage of the people in your state do you think would support each of the nine options? What percentage of your classmates? How many of the options exist in your state? What are some of the advantages and disadvantages of each option? ∎

their opponents feared. Implementation has been plagued with problems. One of the major difficulties stems from the ingenuity of campaign contributors and fund-raisers. They are often able to find new avenues to circumvent funding regulations when reformers close down old avenues.[24]

Another major implementation problem lies in the underfunding and understaffing of the watchdog agencies set up to enforce campaign finance laws.[25] The fundamental problem for these agencies is that for their budgets and authority they rely on the very people they oversee—governors, legislators, and other state officials. When watchdog agencies get tough about exercising their authority, legislatures tend to cut those agencies' budgets.[26] Disclosure rules also lose effectiveness because campaign finance reports often receive little or no attention from the news media or the public. In addition, some reports are not filed in final form until after the election is over. As a result, disclosure is probably less effective than reformers had hoped.

Despite these obstacles to campaign finance reform, reforms have been a recurring concern in recent years. As noted above, several states enacted provisions ranging from expenditure limitations to income tax check-offs that let voters earmark a dollar or two of their income taxes to a public fund that helps finance state elections. Unfortunately for the reformers, however, citizen participation in the check-off programs has declined over time in a number of states,[27] and the funds provided are generally not enough to finance an adequate campaign. In addition, many candidates and potential candidates lose each year (or decide not to run at all) because they cannot raise enough money to support a genuine campaign.

Effective implementation of many campaign finance regulations has also been undercut by a number of U.S. Supreme Court cases creating enormous loopholes in many campaign finance laws. In the most notorious of those cases, *Citizens United v. Federal Election Commission,* a very divided Court ruled that organizations, including corporations and labor unions, could spend as much money as they desired to publicize their beliefs, as long as the organizations avoid having direct, formal relationships with candidates' campaigns. The ruling helped bring about the creation of so-called super political action committees, which can raise unlimited amounts of money in contributions of any size. These groups are not required to disclose the sources of their funds,[28] although they may do so voluntarily.

Although the *Citizens United* decision applied only to national elections, apparently, it raised questions about campaign finance laws in a number of states. These questions were underscored in June of 2010 when the Court struck down an Arizona law providing additional public campaign funds to candidates who had agreed to accept public funds but were being greatly outspent by candidates with larger campaign treasuries from private sources. This decision was handed down when the state was in the middle of its party primaries. Campaign finance laws in almost half the states that prohibit "independent spending" by corporations and/or labor unions will probably not be enforced as vigorously as they might have been before the *Citizens United* decision. One aspect of the ruling that is troubling to people in a number of states is that it opens the door much wider to permit organizations from outside of the state to spend large sums to influence its elections.[29]

GETTING THE VOTES COUNTED

The 2000 presidential election in Florida cast an embarrassing light on election administration in the United States. After a preliminary tabulation of the vote, George W. Bush, the Republican candidate, was declared the winner of the state's electoral votes. That would have given Bush the White House. However, Democrat Albert Gore's campaign called for a recount in several counties, in part because of the closeness of the vote and in part because of reports of election problems, including people who were improperly denied the right to vote, confusing ballot forms, and ballots (especially punch-card ballots) that had not been properly counted.[30]

After legal wrangling over the election subsided, a team of researchers and journalists began reviewing the Florida ballots. They found that under some tabulation rules, Bush appeared to be the winner, while under other tabulation rules, Gore appeared to be the winner. They also found that the number of ballots counted for most counties did not match the number of ballots in the official records.[31]

After the Florida debacle, officials at all levels of government called for election reforms to prevent similar problems from happening again. However, sustaining interest in more accurate voting systems has been difficult, especially in light of the 2001 terrorist attacks, the wars in Afghanistan and Iraq, and the erratic performance of the U.S. economy, especially the recession that began in 2007–2008. Congress passed the Help America Vote Act in 2002. The Act called for statewide voter lists and greater voter access for voters with disabilities.[32] A number of reformers called for widespread use of more accurate, electronic voting systems, but producing the money to buy that equipment has not been easy.[33]

Touch-screen voting systems, which initially appeared to be the preferred replacement for the older, punch-card ballots, also proved to have problems of their own. Manufacturers of the touch-screen voting equipment were slow to have their equipment certified for accuracy by outside authorities. In addition, in California's March 2004, primary, *all the manufacturers* of California's touch-screen voting equipment tried to change their equipment's hardware and/ or software just before the election. Some of the equipment also malfunctioned on election day. Several studies also raised questions about the electronic equipment's vulnerability to tampering, especially if the machines did not produce a paper printout confirming how each voter had voted. This was especially true for one brand of voting machines.[34] A number of jurisdictions that had purchased touch-screen voting machines abandoned them in favor of older technologies.

Despite the problems with touch-screen machines, election administration made some progress from 2000 to 2008. However, some jurisdictions continued to have problems with registration errors (people who have registered but are told they have not when they try to vote), people who requested absentee ballots but did not receive them, and people who turned away from voting because lines at polling places were too long.[35] The most recent battles over election administration are proposals and laws that require specific types of identification with a photograph of the person identified in it. Advocates say that the requirement will reduce ballot fraud, but critics charge that the identification requirements are actually an effort to reduce turnout, particularly among the poor and racial minorities.[36]

Election administration problems will probably always exist to some degree, but election officials are generally trying to do a good job of tabulating votes. Some glitches continue, as in the case of Harris County, Texas, which issued election manuals that included the state's voter ID law a year before it took effect. Georgia launched an effort to stop noncitizens from voting, but a U.S. Justice investigation of the effort concluded that it was biased against minorities and often erroneous: Half of the people identified as noncitizens were actually citizens.[37]

POLITICAL PARTIES

Political parties make several contributions to a representative democracy: They nominate candidates for public elective office, help those candidates win elections, educate the public about the candidates and the issues of the day, and organize the government once the election is over, or at least they try to. The parties face a number of difficulties in performing these tasks, however, and they face competition from other organizations as well. We can explore this situation by examining the political party as a **tripartite organization**: the party in its organization, the party in the electorate, and the party in government.[38]

Party Organization

Party organization refers to the structures and people that help to nominate the party's candidates for office and work to get them elected. The party structure, or organization, is divided into semi-independent units at different levels of government (see Figure 5.1).The highest levels traditionally exerted relatively little influence over the lower levels. This tendency for each level of the party to have considerable autonomy has been labeled **stratarchy** and results from inadequate communications, the need to adapt to varying state and local political climates, the limited rewards available for party service, and the role that many lower-level party officers play in selecting higher-level officers.[39]

The National Party Organizations The formal authority of the national convention and national committee over the state and local parties has traditionally been limited to setting the rules for seating each state's delegates to the national convention. If two competing delegations both demand to be seated, the national convention must decide which delegation is legitimate. Since the late 1970s, however, the national party organizations have distributed considerable sums of money to the state parties; the national Republican Party organizations distributed approximately $184 million during the 1999–2000 campaign season, and the

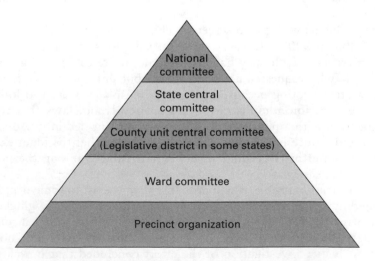

National committee

State central committee

County unit central committee
(Legislative district in some states)

Ward committee

Precinct organization

FIGURE 5.1
Political Party Organization

Democratic committees provided $227 million. Much of that money was channeled to states that were particularly important in the presidential election in 2000.[40] However, the 2002 campaign finance reforms yielded a dramatic decline in national party financial aid to state parties—to $38 million in the Republican Party and $66 million in the Democratic Party.[41]

In addition to money, national party organizations provide a wide range of services to the state parties, from public opinion polling to helping develop campaign themes and campaign commercials.[42] This expanded assistance has fostered stronger ties between the national and state party organizations. New restrictions on soft money contributions may weaken those ties somewhat, although we do not yet have enough experience with the new law to tell. The amount of money distributed by the national party committees is not impressive compared with the volume of money being spent by the new Super PACs in the 2012 presidential nomination process so far.

The State and Local Structures The leading party organization officials are likely to be the state and the county chairpersons. Despite negative stereotypes of political party leaders, state chairpersons are usually successful, well-educated people who often are attracted to politics because of their philosophical and ideological concerns. They administer the party organization and try to boost the party's image. The state chairs may also try to recruit candidates and serve as diplomats between the party and various groups, such as farmers, labor union members, or religious conservatives, who are allied with the party.[43] If the state chairperson is the most significant state party official, the county chair (legislative district in some states) is probably the most important party official at the local level.

The precinct is the basic level of political organization in most states. There is one precinct for each polling place. The precinct chairperson's job is to keep a list of all voters in the precinct; to identify which ones are Republicans, Democrats, or Independents; try to convince people to support the party's candidates; and to get the voters from his or her party to the polls on election day, although not all precinct chairpersons will do that much work. The precinct chairperson is normally elected at the precinct caucus or mass meeting or, in some states, in primary elections. In many communities, a number of precinct positions are vacant because of the limited rewards of the job.

Nominating Candidates Perhaps the most important role of the party organization is the nomination of candidates for public office, but many nominations are difficult for the party organizations to control. Most candidates are nominated through varying combinations of conventions and **primary elections**. The nominating convention is usually dominated by party activists, and it endorses candidates for the party nomination. In most states, however, the official nomination comes not from the convention but from the primary election. In states with a **challenge primary**, if no candidate gets enough votes to win endorsement at the convention, or if the losing candidate at the convention thinks he or she can do better in the primary, then a primary election is held to determine the nominee. Connecticut has a challenge primary. The losing candidate at the convention can challenge the winner to a primary election only if the loser received at least 20 percent of the vote at the convention.

Other states permit the state parties to make a nonbinding endorsement, which is followed by the primary. Usually the parties will try to endorse candidates who are likely to please the voters. For a number of years, convention-endorsed candidates usually won the primary.[44] Since 1970, however, endorsees have had a more difficult time when challenged in the primary. In Minnesota, for example, the Republican Party convention in 1994 refused to endorse the incumbent Republican governor and endorsed a conservative extremist who was then defeated by the governor in the ensuing primary.[45]

There are several different types of party primaries. In relatively **closed primary** states, you must declare a party affiliation before voting and are allowed to vote only in that party's primary. In the purest form of closed primary, a record of your party affiliation is kept; you must change your party declaration ahead of time in order to vote in the other party's primary. In the more lenient closed primary states, you can change your party affiliation on election day or the day before. Some closed primary states permit independents to vote in a party primary if they are willing to declare a party affiliation.

In the **open primary** states, you can vote in either (but not both) the Republican or Democratic primary, and declaring a party affiliation is not necessary. A number of states combine elements of open and closed primary systems in a variety of ways. Washington, California, and Alaska formerly had the **blanket primary**, which allowed you to vote in the Republican primary for some offices and the Democratic primary for other offices; you could not vote in both party primaries for the same office. The blanket primary was declared unconstitutional in 2000.

Finally, Louisiana has a **Cajun primary**, in which all the candidates for a particular office are grouped together, and the top two vote-getters become the nominees for the general election, regardless of their party affiliations. Both could be Democrats or both Republicans. If the top vote-getter receives more than 50 percent of the primary vote, however, he or she wins the office and no general election is held. Washington adopted a somewhat similar primary after its blanket primary law was overturned, but the nominees must still compete in the general election. In 2010, California voters approved adoption of a very similar system, in part with the hope that it may help increase nomination of more middle-of-the-road candidates.[46]

A number of states, mostly in the South, provide that if no candidate receives a majority of the party's vote for a particular nomination, a **runoff** election must be held between the two candidates of that party with the most votes. Having a runoff primary law may encourage even more candidates to run in hopes of placing first or second in the first round of voting and then winning the runoff.

Criticisms of Primaries   Party leaders dislike the open primary and the Cajun primary because they allow members of one party to cross over and vote for the weakest candidates in the other party's primary.[47] The open primary was given a boost in 1986 when the Supreme Court ruled that the closed primary violated a party's right to determine its own membership.[48] The Republican Party of Connecticut had wanted to allow Independents to vote in its primary elections but was prevented from doing so by that state's closed primary law. The ruling has apparently had little impact on other state primary laws to date, however. Some strategists believe that the open primary has increased appeal as the proportion of independents among the American public has grown.[49]

Critics of the primary in general complain that it is an expensive way to nominate candidates, especially in jurisdictions with many voters. A candidate may spend as much money seeking the nomination as in the general election. Primary battles may create or increase lasting divisions within a party or may produce candidates who are out of step with most of the party and unable to work with party colleagues. The extra labor and expense of primary campaigns may also hamper a party's ability to recruit candidates to run against incumbents who are favored to win.[50] Voters, however, do not appear to trust the parties enough to dispense with primaries.

Electing the Party Nominees   The main value of the party to the nominated candidate is the party label. For all practical purposes, candidates usually cannot get elected to the governorship or the state legislature (except in Nebraska or Louisiana) without being nominated by the Republican or Democratic Party, although some states have occasionally elected major officials who were not affiliated with either of the major parties.

Whether the party organization will contribute much assistance beyond the party nomination varies greatly from state to state, depending on the strength or weakness of the state party system, whether a particular candidate is perceived to have much chance of winning, and whether the candidate is on good terms with party leaders. Historically, the parties helped candidates a great deal, especially where **political machines** could mobilize hundreds or even thousands of local campaign workers to help candidates win elections.[51]

In most of the country, however, machine politics is a thing of the past. Victory in a statewide race, or even a big-city mayoral race, depends much less on an army of precinct workers making personal contact with voters than it does on television appearances, imaginative advertising in the media, favorable endorsements by influential interest groups and celebrities, travel to meet with all sorts of groups, and computerized information banks for direct mailings to target groups. These activities require the expertise of professional campaign management firms. To a significant extent, these firms displaced the parties as campaign managers for a time.[52]

Eventually the parties responded to this situation by developing fund-raising and campaign service functions that put the party organizations into an important *broker* position between potential contributors and candidates for the party endorsement. The Republicans discovered this new broker role first, and the Democrats followed suit.

State party organizations have emulated the brokerage role of the national parties. They coordinate PAC contributions to their parties' nominees. Further, as the recipients of funds coming from the national parties, they often can afford to provide media consulting, public opinion polling, and other campaign services to party nominees that the candidates themselves might not be able to afford.[53]

The most striking development in recent years has been the use of this brokering role by the political party leaders in the state legislatures. Forty states now have PACs run by the legislative parties or the legislative leaders. These PACs play a significant role in recruiting candidates, helping finance their campaigns, and providing them with valuable campaign services, from developing campaign commercials to training candidates and campaign managers in various aspects of campaigning. Those activities help to strengthen the parties in state legislatures and contribute to party discipline.[54]

The net result of these developments today is a greatly transformed political party organization[55] that has access to considerable sums of money. These sums and the influence they bring make the party organization the target of different ideological movements that seek to use the party as a tool to achieve their own political ends. In some states, such as California, Minnesota, and New Jersey, the political parties have become sharply polarized along ideological lines, with the Democratic organizations heavily influenced by the ideological left and the Republican organizations heavily influenced by the ideological right. While the ideologically oriented activists may provide campaign assistance, their political beliefs may seem extreme to many voters and other party members. Candidates may feel conflicting pulls from the ideological activists and the electorate. The candidates may also feel conflicting pulls from various interest groups, on one side, and the voters.

Although the parties have become more active in campaigns in recent years, most candidates must still raise most of their campaign funds themselves; the cost of campaigns for America's many elected offices remains much higher than the parties can afford. Unfortunately, the result is that many candidates each year do not have enough funds to have much chance of winning. Even worse, elections for many significant offices are uncontested,[56] in part because the cost of running discourages some potential contenders. Candidates may also prefer a campaign organization that they can control rather than relying too much on the party. In practice, major campaigns often involve a complex mix of individual candidate organizations, the parties, and a wide variety of groups that sometimes work closely with a favored candidate and sometimes raise issues that a candidate would rather not face during the campaign.

The Party in the Electorate

These changes in party organization have been accompanied by equally dramatic changes in the *party in the electorate*, which refers to the mass of people who identify themselves to varying degrees as Republicans or Democrats. Beginning in the early 1960s, party loyalties became progressively weaker, and a growing number of people regarded themselves as political Independents rather than as Democrats or Republicans. However, party loyalties apparently stabilized somewhat in the 1970s and, according to some measures, have regained some of their earlier influence among voters (but apparently not among nonvoters).[57]

A second important change has been a powerful growth of Republican strength in the South. Historically, the South was solidly Democratic, a reaction to the fact that it was the Republican Party that had promoted the Civil War, ended slavery, and imposed Reconstruction on the South. Today, the South has become a competitive two-party region, with some southern states leaning toward the Republican Party. In 1994, Republicans for the first time captured a majority of congressional seats in the South. These Republican candidates benefited from a growing Republican allegiance among southern whites. These Republican gains, however, have been partially offset by a growing electoral strength of African American Democrats and a tendency of many whites to vote a split ticket,[58] voting for Republican presidential candidates but for Democratic candidates in state races.

A third important development in the party in the electorate is a growing ideological polarization of the voting coalitions that support each party in a number of states.[59] The most polarized states were Utah, California, and Connecticut, where large numbers of the people identified themselves as either liberal Democrats or conservative Republicans. The least polarized states were found in the South where far fewer people split along liberal–conservative lines. Researchers also found that the more polarized a state's population was ideologically, the less it engaged in ticket-splitting and the less likely it was to swing sharply back and forth between the parties by electing Democrats in one election and Republicans in another.

Amid these profound changes in the party in the electorate, there are also some important continuities with the past. The socioeconomic character of the Republican and Democratic voter coalitions continues to have many of the same class, racial, and religious splits that they have had since the 1930s. In both education and income, upper-status people are more likely to be Republican, although the most highly educated people are closely divided between the parties. There are also key differences by race and religion. African Americans and Jews are more likely to be Democrats, whereas whites and Protestants (especially non-southern, white Protestants) are more likely to be Republicans. However, Republicans have made some gains among Catholics, and Hispanics are a growing presence in both parties. Many observers have also noted a partisan split between men and women, with men leaning toward the Republican side and women leaning toward the Democratic side.[60]

The Party in Government

The last component of the tripartite political party is the *party in government*, which refers to public officeholders such as governors and legislators. Party success appears to vary considerably from state to state, with some states being closely divided between the parties most of the time and other states leaning toward one party or the other. Party fortunes may also vary from one office to another within a state and over time, as growing Republican success in the South illustrates. In addition, a state party's elected officials may work together well or may fight frequently. The variations in party control raise two important questions: Does it make any difference in policy outcomes whether strong competition exists between the parties? Does it matter which party controls the government?

Two-Party Competition: Does It Make Any Difference?

According to American democratic theory, strong two-party competition encourages the parties to respond to the needs and wants of the majority of the voters. V. O. Key argued also that the parties' attempts to satisfy constituent needs would force the states with competitive, well-organized parties to give more generous benefits to the needy than the states that lacked competitive, strong parties. People who are well off have other ways to voice their concerns, but poorer people have few alternatives to their votes.[61]

Many scholars have tried to assess whether two-party competition leads to more generous government benefits. Scholars have identified two general patterns regarding party competition. First, two-party competition tends to be keenest in states that have large populations, high educational levels, substantial socioeconomic diversity, and strong political party organizations. With few exceptions, the one-party states tend to lack these characteristics.[62]

Second, the two-party states provide more generous welfare benefits and educational benefits than do the one-party states. Early studies attributed this to the greater wealth of the competitive states, not to their greater competitiveness.[63] More recent studies, however, have discovered that competition, especially when combined with high turnout, did affect education and welfare policies. In addition, party competition has more effect when many state legislative districts are competitive rather than simply statewide, for a state may be competitive in state elections but have many legislative seats that are very safe for one party or the other.[64] Also, competitiveness varies from year to year, depending on whether there are national election tides, as there were in 2010, and in which direction they are running. For example, the 2010 elections showed pro-Republican tides running in many parts of the country, due in part to the faltering economy and President Obama's relatively low popularity.[65]

Democrats or Republicans: Does It Make Any Difference?

Does it matter which party controls a state? In most states, the answer to that question clearly is yes. Two important differences exist between the parties. First, in many states, the party leaders differ sharply in ideology. Surveys of Republican and Democratic delegates to the national conventions generally find that the party leaders differed from each other much more than did the party supporters. On average, Democratic voters lean slightly liberal and Republican voters lean slightly conservative. In contrast, the Democratic leaders are usually very liberal and the Republican leaders are very conservative.[66]

TABLE 5.1

The Social Basis of Partisanship (Presidential Vote, 2004)

	Democratic Voters (%)	Republican Voters (%)
Education		
College graduate	51	49
High school	57	43
Less than high school	72	28
Race		
White	44	56
African American	99	1
Sex		
Male	52	48
Female	57	43
Union Household	60	40
Nonunion Household	54	46
Year of Birth		
1975 or later	65	35
1959 to 1974	56	44
1911–1926	52	48

Source: U.S. Census Bureau, *Statistical Abstract 2011–2012* (New York: Skyhorse, 2011), p. 245.

Second, Democratic leaders differ sharply from Republican leaders on issues, in part because Democrats draw their voting strength from different social groups than do Republicans (see Table 5.1). As a result, some groups are likely to be more influential when Democrats control a state than when Republicans do. For example, Robert Erikson's research on civil rights legislation outside the South revealed that civil rights laws were three times as likely to get passed when the Democrats controlled the legislature as when it was controlled by Republicans or divided between Republicans and Democrats. Democratic governments also tend to spend more than Republican governments. However, Democrats in power do not make a state any more redistributive. They do not take from the rich and divide it among the poor. Nevertheless, Democrats tend to enact less conservative policies than Republicans.[67]

In addition, the ideological leanings of each of the parties vary considerably from state to state. When Congress renewed the Voting Rights Act in 2006, virtually all of the votes against the bill came from more conservative Republicans, primarily from the South.[68] Where the Democratic and Republican parties are relatively liberal, we often find more liberal public policies than are found in states with more conservative parties.[69] For these reasons, it is important to know how the parties fare in their quest for control over state government (see Table 5.2). In recent years, the Democrats have gained strength on the Pacific Coast and the Northeast. Republicans have gained ground in the Rocky Mountain and Intermountain states and in the South.[70]

We have also found that many states have had divided party control in recent decades, with one party controlling the governorship and the other party controlling at least one house of the legislature. When that occurs, states with highly polarized parties will have considerable

TABLE 5.2						
Party Control of State Legislatures and Governors' Offices						
	State Legislatures			Governors		
	D*	S/T	R	D	I	R
1997	20	11	18	17	1	32
2005	19	10	20	22	0	28
2007	23	10	16	28	0	22
2011	15	8	26	20	1	29

*For the legislatures, D = Democratic majority in both houses of the legislature; S/T = Split party control (i.e., one house Democratic and the other house Republican) or party control of one or both chambers equally divided between the parties; R = Republican majority. Nebraska's legislature is nonpartisan. For governors, D = Democrat; I = Independent; R = Republican.

Source: Statistical Abstract of the United States, 2012 (Washington, DC: U.S. Bureau of the Census, 2012), p. 261; "2006 Post-Election Partisan Composition of State Legislatures," National Conference of State Legislatures Web document, November 16, 2006; Alan Greenblatt, "Legislatures: Democrats to Control 23 States," governing.com Web document, November 9, 2006.

conflict over policy decisions. By contrast, if the two major parties in a state are relatively similar in their political values, divided party control is less likely to trigger partisan wrangling.

When a party sweeps to victory in state elections, especially if the victory follows a campaign season in which the party candidates discuss their issue positions a great deal and generally agree on their goals, the winners may feel that they have a mandate to push through their agenda, regardless of how other people may feel. Many Republicans felt that they had a mandate after the 2010 election, which produced a dramatic increase in the number of Republican state legislators in many states and many new Republican state executives, including nearly a dozen governors. In Indiana, Ohio, and Wisconsin, Republicans pushed through legislation to weaken public employee unions. Florida's new governor blocked a high-speed rail project favored by many people in the state. Republican officials in a number of states rejected revenue increases and cut spending on many state programs.[71]

The aggressive action by Republican officials did not please everyone. Voters in Ohio repealed the legislation designed to weaken public employee unions. Citizens in Wisconsin gathered more than enough signatures to force a vote on whether to remove the governor from office before his term ends. Florida's governor became more conciliatory toward some other state leaders after his popularity slumped to alarming levels. Governors in several other states saw greater value in compromise since 2012.[72]

DIRECT DEMOCRACY

Direct democracy refers to the *initiative*, the *referendum*, and the *recall*. If an elected official becomes controversial and displeases voters, they may attempt to recall that official. The recall process begins with a petition drive calling for a vote on whether the official should remain in office. If enough valid signatures are obtained, a special election determines whether that official should be removed before the term of office expires. For example, voters in Sheboygan, Wisconsin, voted in February of 2012 to remove their mayor after incidents involving alcohol and personal misconduct became public. Voters in Bell, California, voted to remove their mayor and city council for enriching themselves from the public treasury. Bell is a working-class community, but the mayor was quietly receiving $800,000 per year, and city council members were paid $100,000 for their part-time work.[73]

If the legislature fails to pass a desired policy, the best known type of **initiative** lets citizens draft legislative proposals and, if they gather enough petition signatures, put these proposals on a ballot, where they can be decided directly by the voters in a **referendum**. The initiative, thus, is a political safety valve that allows people to act directly when legislatures fail to act as people desire on hot issues. There is some evidence that the existence of this safety valve keeps the legislatures in touch with public preferences.[74]

Initiatives can be either direct or indirect. Under the *direct* initiative, people draft a proposal, gather signatures on a petition, and put the petition on the ballot. Not all petitions gain enough signatures to be put on the ballot, and almost 60 percent of those put on the ballot are rejected by the voters.[75] Under the *indirect* initiative, people also draft a proposal and gather signatures, but it must be submitted first to the legislature. If the legislature does not act by the end of the legislative session, the petition goes on the ballot in the next general election. Legislative bodies may refer a proposal to the public for a referendum, either because a public vote is always required for that particular matter (such as constitutional amendments in almost all of the states) or because members of the legislature are uneasy about deciding the matter themselves. If a public vote decides the issue, legislators may be able to shield themselves, to some degree, from political blame.

Direct democracy came into existence at the start of the twentieth century and has been primarily a western phenomenon. The seven states of California, Oregon, Washington, Colorado, North Dakota, Oklahoma, and Arizona account for 80 percent of all initiatives in recent years.[76] The initiative and referenda have become especially popular in California, where voters faced 28 referendum proposals in 1990 alone. To help the voters cope with these issues, the state published a voter's pamphlet that ran to 222 pages.[77] When one group gets an initiative qualified for the ballot, opponents may place a contrary proposition on the same ballot. California's 1988 ballot included a proposal providing public funding for election campaigns and a proposal *prohibiting* such funding. Voters passed both measures; the California Supreme Court opted for the campaign funding proposal that received the most votes. However, a federal court struck down portions of that law as unconstitutional. From 1996 through 2005, California had 75 initiative efforts. Oregon had 66 during that same period and Colorado, 41.[78]

More recently, voters in Ohio overturned a law designed to weaken public employee unions. Voters in Mississippi rejected a proposal to ban all abortions and many forms of contraception. Citizens in Maine approved a proposal to allow people to register to vote on election day, a policy they had maintained for a number of years.[79]

Criticisms of Direct Democracy

Critics of the initiative, referendum, and recall complain that they have often been transformed from a safety valve for average citizens into an expensive contest between well-heeled interest groups. Millions of dollars are spent to hire professional signature gatherers and public relations experts to prepare television advertisements. In 2005, total spending on California's eight initiative and referendum proposals reached approximately $250 million.[80] Some of the money for initiative and referendum efforts may come from out of state. Moreover, some groups are willing to mislead people in order to gain a political advantage.

Voter participation in referendum votes is quite variable, with high-interest issues attracting significant turnout, but low-interest issues attracting relatively few voters. Referendum advocates also face a painful dilemma: Specific proposals may be harder to pass, but vaguer proposals may be modified in unexpected ways by officials charged with implementing them.[81] In addition, people who are unhappy with the results of an initiative may challenge the outcome in court.

These problems have led many scholars to become disillusioned with the initiative. As the Highlight feature shows, direct democracy does not have a consistent ideological impact.

HIGHLIGHT

Direct Democracy in Practice

Direct democracy is a two-edged sword that can have either liberal or conservative outcomes:

Liberal Outcomes

In 2011, Ohio voters overturned a law designed to weaken public employee unions, and Mississippi voters rejected a proposal to, in effect, outlaw abortion and several types of contraception.

In 2008, Colorado voters rejected an anti-abortion proposal, in part because it did not make exceptions for rape victims or the health of the mother.

In 2000, California, Michigan, and Washington voters defeated school vouchers.

In 2000, Florida voters approved creating a high-speed railroad system.

In 1996, Arizona and California voters approved the legislation of marijuana for medical purposes.

In 1992, Oregon voters defeated an antigay initiative to amend the state constitution.

In 1986, voters in Massachusetts, Oregon, and Rhode Island defeated measures to outlaw abortion or to prohibit state funds for abortions.

In 1982, voters in eight states passed propositions calling for a freeze on nuclear weapons possessed by the United States and the USSR.

In 1978, voters in four states refused to set tax and spending limits on their state governments.

In 1976, Colorado voters refused to repeal the state Equal Rights Amendment and the state sales tax.

Conservative Outcomes

In 2010, voters in Arizona, Missouri, and Oklahoma approved proposals saying that individuals and businesses could not be required to participate in a government health care system (a gesture of opposition to the 2010 national health care reforms).

In 2008, Florida voters approved an amendment defining marriage as that between a man and a woman.

Also in 2008, Maine voters rejected a proposal to enact a sales tax to finance comprehensive health care coverage.

In 2004, several states' voters approved bans on same-sex marriages.

In 2000, California voters approved a ban on same-sex marriages.

In 2000, voters defeated environmental protection measures in Arizona, Colorado, Maine, and Missouri.

In 1996, California voters repealed the state's affirmative action programs.

In 1992, Colorado voters approved an initiative that would prohibit the categorization of gays and lesbians as a protected class of people.

In 1986, Vermont voters rejected a state Equal Rights Amendment.

In 1982, voters in Arizona rejected a call for a nuclear freeze.

In 1978, voters in 11 states set tax and spending limits on their state governments.

In 1978, voters in Miami, Saint Paul, and several other cities repealed gay rights sections of their cities' human rights ordinances. ∎

The initiative process introduces an element of political instability and gives the legislators a reason to avoid action on controversial issues in the hope that they will be dealt with through an initiative.[82] Howard Hamilton's research on referenda in Toledo, Ohio, found that direct democracy is governance by an active minority and that "minority may be far from a mirror image of the populace."[83] There is no way to balance the intense wishes of a minority with the less intense wishes of the majority. Some observers believe that the rights of minorities are bound to suffer, unless they have considerable money.[84] However, research on initiatives in California finds that minority groups are only slightly less likely to be on the winning side in referenda than are whites and are usually on the winning side.[85]

Referenda also suffer from the problem that voters are presented with a yes or no choice. Unlike in the legislature, there is no opportunity for amending the proposal on the ballot or for expressing support for some provisions but not others, unless people are willing to launch another initiative and referendum effort.

Despite its shortcomings, direct democracy is not likely to be dropped where it exists. If anything, its use is growing. The 1980s saw more initiatives passed than any decade since the 1930s, and more than 450 initiative votes were held from 1996 to 2005. Two-thirds of Californians in a 1982 poll thought that people should vote on important issues directly rather than having them dealt with by the legislature, and two-thirds of Americans in a 1987 Gallup Poll favored a recall provision for members of Congress.[86] Proponents argue that the threat of an initiative may goad the legislature into acting when it would not have otherwise.[87] However, initiative activity began to slow after 1996.[88]

Supporters of direct democracy disagree with the charge that initiatives and referenda are dominated by big spenders; some proposals with major financial backing have been rejected by the voters.[89] In an era when many citizens lack confidence in public officials, direct democracy appears to be an attractive alternative to relying on the governor and legislature. In addition, repeated use of direct democracy mechanisms gradually helps voters to learn about government and politics.[90]

DIRECT ACTION

Direct action is not an electoral activity (although it may be combined with electoral activity). Rather, it is the attempt to influence public policy outcomes through the use of tactics such as citizen contacting, group protests, civil disobedience, labor strikes, rent strikes, sit-ins, and takeovers. *Citizen contacting* refers to the communications of demands or grievances by citizens to public officials, both elective and appointive. That may be done in person or in writing. *Protest* occurs when a group complains about something by staging a march down a main thoroughfare, confronting a mayor in his or her office, or even passing out leaflets in a shopping center.[91] A common protest tactic during the 1960s was for groups of African Americans to gather in a mayor's office and demand more jobs for teenagers in their communities. In 2011 and 2012, the Occupy Wall Street movement conducted a number of protests, including group marches, picketing, and creating tent communities in public parks. Officials in some communities eventually forced the removal of the tent communities, and supporters of the movement clashed with police in some cities.[92]

Civil disobedience occurs when someone deliberately breaks a law for the purpose of turning public opinion against the law. The most famous American advocates of civil disobedience are probably philosopher and author Henry David Thoreau, who went to jail for refusing to pay taxes in support of slavery and the Mexican-American War, and the Reverend Martin Luther King, Jr., who led a variety of protest activities, including civil disobedience, in the 1950s and 1960s. The Occupy Wall Street movement conducted a number of civil disobedience actions, including conducting public marches without a permit and the continued occupation of some parks without permits.

A *labor strike* occurs when a group of employees refuse to work until management agrees to collective bargaining or other demands; state and local government employees have used this tactic at times, although some jurisdictions prohibit strikes by public employees generally or by employees with especially vital jobs, such as firefighters. A *rent strike* is the refusal to pay rent to a landlord until some grievance has been met. Tenants pay the rent to an escrow account held by an attorney until the landlord complies.

A *sit-in* is the tactic of people simply sitting in a place where they are not supposed to be until someone in charge responds to their demands. In the 1950s and early 1960s, integrated groups of college students occupied segregated lunchroom counters. The lunchroom business could not go on until the manager responded by serving the demonstrators or having them removed. When the demonstrators were convicted of violating the local segregation ordinances, they expanded the scope of the conflict by appealing to the federal courts, which usually declared the segregation ordinances unconstitutional.

A *takeover* is similar to a sit-in. A group simply occupies a facility and refuses to give it up. This tactic was used by labor unions early in the twentieth century and by some Vietnam War protestors who took over college buildings in the late 1960s. A more subtle form of takeover may occur when members of a group move into a neighborhood or small community to give the group effective control. One of the more ambitious takeover attempts began in 2003 when an organization called the Free State Project announced that 20,000 of its members would move to New Hampshire. That state was chosen because it already reflected their political beliefs in very limited government. Some long-term residents of the state, however, expressed concern that the group would push for fewer restrictions on gambling and on the medical uses of marijuana.[93]

The most extreme forms of direct action involve political violence. Political violence comes in many forms, from destruction of property to assaults and even assassination. Attacks on property range from minor vandalism to arson and bombings, which have been used in attempts to close abortion clinics. Violence against people has ranged from roughing up tax collectors in the colonial era to killing African Americans in the South who wanted to vote and be treated as human beings. Nor are these incidents limited to the distant past. Two candidates for sheriff in eastern Kentucky were shot to death in 2002, and a county clerk who was campaigning was attacked in a hail of gunfire. Investigators found 33 bullet holes in his car. A private investigator working for another candidate was shot six times but survived.[94] State and local officials have had similar encounters in a number of other states in recent years. Recent investigations have targeted environmental radicals who have used firebombs to stop logging, expansion of a ski resort, and other activities they oppose in western states.[95]

These direct action tactics are normally used to achieve some broader goal, such as greater leverage for bargaining. By demonstrating in front of a city hall where they receive television and newspaper attention, protesters can make mayors and city councils uncomfortable and put pressure on city officials to negotiate with protest leaders. Direct action may be used to encourage inactive people to become involved in the issue. Another common objective is to change policies. Protesters may want more minority police or firefighters hired by the city, or more generous funding for some program. Anti-abortion advocates often demonstrate for the purpose of pressuring state legislators not to liberalize state abortion laws, and women's movement groups often demonstrate for the opposite purpose.

A Successful Example of Direct Action in Practice

One of the most successful uses of direct action tactics came with the civil rights movement. Although civil rights activities had occurred for decades, they did not draw broad public interest until the 1950s and early 1960s. African American leaders organized boycotts, demonstrations, and sit-ins that sought to enable them to vote and to eliminate racial discrimination in various public facilities, from restaurants and hotels to insurance companies and banks. A key strategy was to expand the scope of the conflict beyond local southern communities to the federal level, which culminated with the Civil Rights Act of 1964 and the Voting Rights Act of 1965. Among other provisions, the 1964 act prohibited racial discrimination in public accommodations, such as hotels and restaurants. The 1965 act was adopted to defend the voting rights of African Americans throughout the South; that law was an effort to enforce the Fifteenth Amendment to the U.S. Constitution.

The civil rights movement did not eliminate all the inequities that African Americans suffered and continue to suffer; nor did it end all racial discrimination. However, it did give them increased access to many institutions, services, and opportunities that previously had been closed to them. It also helped them gain access to the political process.

What Does Direct Action Accomplish?

Analyses of whether direct action is an effective strategy have produced mixed conclusions regarding its value. Some analysts believe that direct action is a reasonably effective political tactic.[96] Although a single protest action may not produce the desired response, repeated, persistent use of direct action sometimes bears fruit. In the 1930s, direct action may have helped encourage the adoption of policies protecting some of the rights of workers to form unions and policies to help the poor and unemployed. During the 1960s, direct action may have helped spur the adoption of civil rights reforms and programs to help the needy. Environmentalists have used direct action a number of times since the early 1970s, and those efforts have sometimes been followed by new legislation or administrative policy changes.

Direct action tactics carry some serious risks, however. Authorities, whether public or private, may try to stop these tactics by arresting people in the protest group, roughing them up, or even killing some of them. Pro-union workers were targets of violence on a number of occasions over the years, as were abolitionists, civil rights activists, and a number of other groups throughout American history.[97] Fears of responses like that may make many members of a group unwilling to use direct action tactics and/or unwilling to sustain those efforts for very long. Less dramatically, direct action tactics may frighten and antagonize some people who might have responded more positively to other influence tactics.

Direct action tactics may also prove disappointing if the group fails to create permanent institutions to represent the interests of the members over the long term.[98] The most successful transition from direct action tactics to institution building probably occurred in organized labor. What began as movements by militant agitators during the 1880s was transformed in the 1930s into organized labor unions, which are now officially recognized by the government and have the legal right to bargain collectively and to strike. However, those organizations have not been very successful in stopping the decline in the proportion of private-sector workers who belong to unions in recent decades.

Environmentalists and consumer groups have been relatively successful in building political organizations to carry on more conventional politics, although both groups have had difficulty keeping large numbers of members involved over time. But many other groups using direct action have been less successful in building durable political organizations.

SOCIAL CHANGE AND THE BALLOT BOX

How do women, minorities, and the poor fare in the battle of the ballot box? Since white men hold the majority of elected positions in the country, it would seem that women and minorities are at a big disadvantage. In fact, however, they have made significant strides at the ballot box. Lower income people with little education are a different story.

Research on female legislative candidates in recent years finds that when women run as incumbents, their success rate is approximately the same as for male incumbents. In races for open seats, male and female candidates are about equally likely to win. When we examine challengers in state senate contests, women challengers are somewhat more likely to beat male incumbents than are male challengers facing female incumbents.[99] Based on these results, women do as well as men in electoral contests, and may be doing even slightly better, although the success rates of female candidates appear to vary considerably from state to state.

If women are often strong candidates, why do women only hold less than one-fourth of state legislative seats? The most probable reason is that up to the present, incumbents have more frequently been male than female. This may well mean that as the number of female incumbents rises, they will have a larger base to build from for the future. Women also are more likely to need some encouragement to run, whereas male candidates are more likely to be self-starters.[100] Analysts who support having more women in public office have been concerned that the growth in the number of women in state legislatures has been slow and erratic since 2000. Excluding governors, the number of women in statewide elected office has grown slowly and inconsistently, although the number of states that have ever had a female governor continues to increase, if slowly.[101]

Racial minorities have made considerable progress in election to public office in recent decades. The number of African American elected officials in the nation more than quintupled from 1,469 in 1970 to 9,430 in 2002. The number of Hispanic elected officials reached 5,459 in 1994, declined to 4,303 by 2002, and rebounded to 5,240 by 2008.[102] Asian Americans are also a growing presence in state and local politics; they held 73 state legislative seats in 2000.[103] Their most visible success in state politics was perhaps the election of Gary Locke as governor of Washington. He was the first American of Chinese ancestry to serve as governor of any state. Asian Indian-Americans have won governorships in Louisiana and, more recently, in South Carolina.

Who Hasn't Made Progress?

Although women and minorities have made significant gains at the ballot box in recent years, the same cannot be said for low-income and lower-moderate income people. The American electorate continues to be very unrepresentative economically, with poorer people being consistently less likely to vote than are wealthier people and less-educated people being considerably less likely to vote than are highly educated people.[104] The same pattern shows when we examine elected officials. They are usually wealthier and better educated than the people they represent. Moreover, campaigns for major offices are very expensive, and few poor people make large campaign contributions. As noted in Chapter 4, we also have very low turnout among young people.

Does it make any difference that turnout rates are so low among the lowest income groups of the population and among young people? The answer is an emphatic yes. If poor and young people do not turn out at the polls, they do not give political support to legislators who might otherwise be inclined to help them. In states where low-income people have the best voter turnout rates, welfare benefits were above average. In states with the worst turnout rates among low-income people, welfare benefits were below average.[105] Programs benefiting young people (such as education) have not fared as well as programs for older Americans in budgetary decisions in recent years.

In essence, the electoral impact of the contemporary social movements among women and minorities has been in keeping with the historical pattern of American immigrant politics. Americans traditionally organized themselves along ethnic and religious lines rather than class lines. Irish, Jewish, Italian, and other European immigrant politicians of the early twentieth century sought primarily their own upward mobility to the middle class rather than a social revolution.[106] Elected women and minority leaders today largely want the same. But their primary goals are gender based and racially/ethnically based rather than class based.

America does not appear to have effective groups trying to organize and mobilize poorer, less-educated people or young people on any significant scale. With the decline of organized labor, as discussed in the last chapter, a continuing socioeconomic bias in the electorate, and the rising costs of campaigns, poorer and less-educated people remain among the most vulnerable groups in our society.

CONCLUSION

One theme that has pervaded the past two chapters has been that state and local governments are often more responsive to established institutions and to special interests than they are to broader interests, to the interests of isolated citizens who are unrepresented by existing institutions, or to the poorest part of the population. The conventional components of citizen influence (public opinion, elections, political parties, and interest groups) tend to be subject to influence by large, economic-based institutions. These channels of citizen influence are more likely to communicate middle- and upper-class concerns and the concerns of older people to the government than to transmit the concerns of either the poor, young, or isolated individuals. However, large groups of people are sometimes able to influence their public officials, but the process takes effort and persistence.

In contrast to these conventional channels of political influence, the 1960s and 1970s saw significant use of the more unconventional tactics of direct action and independent political action. Those activities have continued since then, although most Americans are not willing to participate in the more demanding types of direct action and often appear to be uncomfortable with them.[107] Many of the tactics of direct action and independent political action seem to depend on face-to-face contacts and the mass mobilization of people in relatively small communities, such as in a business establishment, a small town, a suburb, or a big-city neighborhood. Because these tactics seem most appropriate for community-level politics, we need to make a closer examination of such politics. Chapter 6 will examine the institutions of local government, and Chapter 7 will look into the dynamics of community politics.

SUMMARY

1. The election process is the most fundamental institution of democracy. However, elections were found to be very limited channels for citizen input to public policy for several reasons. Elections do not usually give mandates. At the local level, elected officials are not greatly concerned with the opinions of the mass of the electorate, since reelection is not a worry.

2. Political parties play roles in nominating candidates to office and in organizing the government once the election is over. The parties tend to be decentralized organizations, with the strongest units at the county and state legislative district levels. The 1960s and 1970s witnessed a decline in party loyalties, although they appeared to stabilize and, in some cases, rebound, after the mid-1970s. Despite the earlier declines, recent scholarship attributes more importance to party politics than was thought a few decades earlier. The thrust of policy making, as well, will depend on whether a state is controlled by the Republicans or the Democrats and whether the state parties are relatively liberal or conservative.

3. Direct democracy refers to the initiative, the referendum, and the recall. These controversial practices are most popular in the West. They can be used for either liberal or conservative causes.

4. Direct action strategies were successful during the civil rights movement of the 1950s and 1960s. They have had more limited success, however, in trying to combat such complicated urban problems as slum housing. To be successful, direct action requires excellent leadership, sympathetic outside political actors in the press and in government, and an ability to expand the scope of the conflict beyond the local level to the state and national levels.

5. The social movements of the past two decades have brought more electoral influence to women and minorities than they have to low- and moderate-income people.

STUDY QUESTIONS

1. What are the strengths and weaknesses of elections as instruments for making government respond to public concerns? Under what conditions are elections most likely to make government respond to the public? Least likely?

2. What roles do parties play in state and local politics? How and why have the parties changed during this century? How do they affect policy making?

3. In what ways have the initiative, referendum, and recall given ordinary citizens more influence over government? What difficulties have those direct democracy reforms sometimes produced?

4. Evaluate direct action as an approach to influencing governmental decisions. What difficulties may it create?

KEY TERMS

Blanket primary A primary election in which the ballot lists all the parties. Voters are allowed to vote in the primary of one party for some offices and the primary of another party for other offices. Voters cannot vote in more than one party's primary for the same office. Recently declared unconstitutional by the federal courts.

Challenge primary A primary election held only if more than one candidate receives a significant show of support in their party's nominating convention.

Closed primary A primary election in which only identifiable party supporters may vote. Only Republicans may vote in the Republican primary and only Democrats may vote in the Democratic primary.

Direct action Such political tactics as group protests, civil disobedience, strikes, sit-ins, and political violence. These activities may be directed at public officials or at other people with whom the group disagrees.

Direct democracy The initiative, the referendum, and the recall as political devices.

District election See **Ward election**.

Initiative A political device that lets voters draft legislative proposals and, if they gather enough petition signatures, put their proposals on a ballot, where they can be decided directly by the people. Some states refer the proposal (if it gains enough signatures) to the state legislature. If it fails to act, the proposal is then referred to the voters.

Nonpartisan primary A primary election in which the ballot does not list the nominees by party affiliation, and the nomination goes to the two candidates who get the most votes.

Open primary A primary election in which anyone can vote, regardless of party affiliation, but each voter can vote in only one party's primary for that election.

Political machine A tightly knit party organization that controls the party's nominations for public office and controls many patronage jobs. The people in those jobs are expected to work for the party during campaigns.

Primary election An election held to choose nominees to compete for public office in the general election.

Proactive accountability The idea that elections give winners a mandate to establish a specific line of policy. Voters assess the candidates' positions on issues and vote for the candidate who most shares their political values.

Recall A political device that allows voters to remove from office, before his or her term ends, an official who has invoked popular displeasure. The first phase of the process is gathering signatures on petitions calling for a recall election affecting the official; if enough signatures are gathered, a special election is called on the question of whether the official should be retained in office.

Referendum The practice of allowing voters to vote directly on public policy proposals. Proposals may come from initiatives, from the legislature, or because a law (possibly a constitutional law) requires voter approval for certain decisions. Almost all states require voter approval of state constitutional amendments.

Reformed election system An election system characterized by nonpartisan, at-large elections, preferably held on a different day than other elections.

Retroactive accountability The idea of holding someone accountable after the fact. When an incumbent official runs for reelection, voters assess whether he or she has done a reasonably good job thus far. If the answer is yes, the person is kept in office. If the answer is no, he or she is voted out. This type of accountability is less demanding for voters than proactive accountability.

Runoff A type of primary in which, if no candidate wins a majority of his/her party's votes, or if no candidate wins a majority overall in a nonpartisan primary, then the top two candidates must go through a second round of campaigning and a second round of voting.

Soft money The channeling of campaign contributions from one party organization or campaign to another party organization or campaign, sometimes to circumvent legal regulations of campaign finance, but sometimes to help tie different party or campaign organizations together.

Stratarchy An organization, such as a political party, in which each level of the organization has considerable freedom to act as people in that level prefer. Different parts of the party, then, will not always work together harmoniously.

Tripartite organization The view of the political party as composed of three components: the party organization, the party in the electorate, and the party in government.

Unreformed election system An election system characterized by partisan, ward elections, often held on the same day as elections for other offices.

Volunteerism Refers to elected officials who look on themselves as community volunteers doing a civic duty rather than as professional politicians attempting to build a career. Many of these elected officials are originally appointed to the office, often face only weak opposition when running for reelection, and do not much care whether they are reelected. Common among local officials in smaller jurisdictions but also found in many other offices.

Ward election An election in which city council members are elected from neighborhood units called wards or districts.

THE INTERNET CONNECTION

You can contact the Republican and Democratic National Committees at **www.rnc.org** and **www.democrats.org**. You can also contact many state parties on the Web, as well as organizations that are involved in initiative and referendum campaigns. What kinds of information do they offer? Do they affect your interest in participation?

NOTES

1. Will Bunch, *Backlash* (New York: Harper, 2010).
2. Ibid.; Dan Balz, "Don't Be Too Quick to Mistake Tea Party for Perot Movement," *Washington Post*, April 18, 2010, p. A02; Dan Balz, "What the Tea Party Is—and Isn't," *Washington Post*, September 11, 2011 (Web edition); E. J. Dionne, Jr., "The Tea Party: Populism of the Privileged," *Washington Post*, April 19, 2010, p. A15; Frank Rich, "The Billionaires Bankrolling the Tea Party," *New York Times*, August 28, 2010 (Web edition); Sam Tanenhaus, "History vs. the Tea Party," *New York Times*, January 14, 2012 (Web edition). Racial resentment includes beliefs that African Americans receive preferential treatment and that President Obama is biased in favor of African Americans and against whites.
3. For further discussion of this point, see John J. Harrigan, *Political Change in the Metropolis*, 4th ed. (Glenview, IL: Scott Foresman, 1989), ch. 4.
4. Gerald Pomper, *Elections in America: Control and Influence in Democratic Politics* (New York: Dodd, Mead, 1968), pp. 254–255; Peter Flanigan and Nancy Zingale, *Political Behavior of the American Electorate*, 11th ed. (Washington, DC: CQ Press, 2006), pp. 202–203.
5. Kenneth Prewitt, "Political Ambitions, Volunteerism, and Electoral Accountability," *American Political Science Review* 64, no. 1 (March 1970): 5–17.
6. See the discussion in Alan Saltzstein, *Governing America's Urban Areas* (Belmont, CA: Thomson Wadsworth, 2003), pp. 117–121, and the studies they cite.
7. "Mistake Turns Into Election Blunder," *The Daily Evergreen* (Pullman, WA: January 17, 2002), p. 11; "Town's Election Has Blank Voting Ballots," *The Daily Evergreen* (Pullman, WA: October 11, 2002), p. 12.
8. Charles Mahtesian, "How to Get Rid of Excellent Public Officials," *Governing* 12 (July 1998), pp. 25–26, 28, 30.
9. M. Kent Jennings and Harmon Zeigler, "The Salience of American State Politics," *American Political Science Review* 64, no. 2 (June 1970): 523–535.
10. Dick Kirschten, "The Targets of Discontent," *National Journal* 22, no. 45 (November 10, 1990): 2736–2742.
11. Robert Lowry, James Alt, and Karen Ferree, "Fiscal Policy Outcomes and Electoral Accountability in American States," *American Political Science Review* 92 (1998): 759–774; Randall W. Partin, "Economic Conditions and Gubernatorial Elections: Is the State Executive Held Accountable?" *American Politics Quarterly* 23, no. 1 (January 1995): 81–95.
12. Susan J. Kane and Richard F. Winters, "Taxes and Voting: Electoral Retribution in the American States," *Journal of Politics* 55, no. 1 (February 1993): 27–40. Kane and Winters studied 407 gubernatorial elections from 1957 through 1985.
13. Thomas R. Dye, *Politics, Economics, and the Public: Policy Outcomes in the American States* (Chicago: Rand McNally, 1966), pp. 260–270.
14. Raymond E. Wolfinger and Steven J. Rosenstone, *Who Votes?* (New Haven, CT: Yale University Press, 1980), p. 85.
15. Kim Quaile Hill and Jan E. Leighley, "The Policy Consequences of Class Bias in State Electorates," *American Journal of Political Science* 36, no. 2 (May 1992): 351–365; Noah Kaplan, *Episodic Voting: The Logic of Participation in the Context of Multiple Elections* (Unpublished doctoral dissertation, Columbia University; forthcoming).

16. Monika McDermott, "Voting for Catholic Candidates: The Evolution of a Stereotype," *Social Science Quarterly* 88 (2007): 953–969.

17. For a useful overview of the ingredients needed for a campaign, see Judge Lawrence Grey, *How to Win a Local Election* (New York: M. Evans, 1999).

18. For recent statistics, see Thad Beyle, "Gubernatorial Elections, Campaign Costs and Powers," *The Book of the States*, vol. 43 (Lexington, KY: Council of State Governments, 2011), pp. 130–133.

19. L. Sandy Maisel and Mark Brewer, *Parties and Elections in America*, 5th ed. (Lanham, MD: Rowman and Littlefield, 2008), p. 151.

20. Thomas Holbrook and Raymond La Raja, "Parties and Elections," in Virginia Gray and Russell Hanson, eds. *Politics in the American States*, 9th ed. (Washington, DC: CQ Press, 2008), pp. 64–65.

21. Sarah Morehouse and Malcolm Jewell, *State Politics, Parties, and Policy*, 2nd ed. (Lanham, MD: Rowman and Littlefield, 2003), pp. 87–89.

22. Herbert E. Alexander, *Financing Politics: Money, Elections, and Political Reform*, 4th ed. (Washington, DC: CQ Press, 1992), pp. 127–131; John Bibby, *Politics, Parties, and Elections in America*, 5th ed. (Belmont, CA: Wadsworth, 2003) p. 263; Sarah Morehouse and Malcolm Jewell, *State Politics, Parties, and Policy*, 2nd ed. (Lanham, MD: Rowman and Littlefield, 2003), pp. 143–144; Malcolm Jewell and Sarah McCally Morehouse, *Political Parties and Elections in American States*, 4th ed. (Washington, DC: CQ Press, 2001), pp. 65–70.

23. Susan Haigh, "Connecticut Lawmakers Pass Sweeping Campaign Finance Bill," *Moscow, ID/Pullman Daily News*, December 1, 2005, p. 10A.

24. Herbert E. Alexander, "Political Parties and the Dollar," *Society* 22, no. 2 (January–February 1985): 54.

25. John Bibby and Thomas Holbrooke, "Parties and Elections," in Virginia Gray and Russell Hanson, eds. *Politics in the American States*, 8th ed. (Washington, DC: CQ Press, 2004), p. 66.

26. Herbert E. Alexander, *Reform and Reality: The Financing of State and Local Campaigns* (New York: The Twentieth Century Fund Press, 1991).

27. See Morehouse and Jewell, *State Politics*, p. 143.

28. Floyd Abrams, "Citizens United Decision," *New York Times*, January 16, 2012 (Web edition); "Attacks on Disclosure," *New York Times*, February 10, 2012 (Web edition); Nicholas Confessore and Michael Luo, "Secrecy Shrouds 'Super PAC'; Funds in Latest Filings," *New York Times*, February 1, 2012 (Web edition); Adam Liptak, "Justices Overturn Key Campaign Limits," *New York Times*, January 22, 2010 (Web edition); Adam Liptak, "Justices, 5–4, Reject Corporate Spending Limit," *New York Times*, January 22, 2010 (Web edition).

29. Robert Barnes, "Two Justices Suggest Citizens United Ruling Should Be Reconsidered in Montana Case," *Washington Post*, February 17, 2012 (Web edition); "Court Blocks Campaign Spending Limits," *New York Times*, February 18, 2012 (Web edition); "Montana and the Supreme Court," *New York Times*, February 13, 2012 (Web edition); Fredreka Schouten, "10 States Add Campaign-Finance Laws," *USA Today*, July 23, 2010 (Web edition); Ian Rubina, "Campaign Contributions Ruling Stymies States," *San Francisco Chronicle*, January 25, 2010, p. A4; Jake Grovum, "State Campaign Finance Laws in Crosshairs," *Stateline*, January 25, 2010 (Web edition); David Savage and Jennifer Martinez, "Supreme Court Curbs Arizona Public Funding in Elections," *Los Angeles Times*, June 8, 2010 (Web edition).

30. See *36 Days: The Complete Chronicle of the 2000 Presidential Election Crisis* (New York: *The New York Times*, 2001); Samuel Issacharoff, Pamela Karlan, and Richard Pildes, *When Elections Go Bad*, rev. ed. (New York: Foundation Press, 2001).

31. Peter Slevin, "In Florida, the Media's Still Looking at Ballots," *Washington Post National Weekly Edition* (May 14–20, 2001), pp. 14–15.

32. R. Doug Lewis, "State Election Innovations Could Be Threatened by Continued Push for Federal Mandates," in *Book of the States*, vol. 40 (Lexington, KY: Council of State Governments, 2008), p. 299.

33. Anya Sostek, "The Immortal Chad," *Governing* 16 (January 2002): 26–28; Robert Tanner, "Only Piecemeal Improvements to Election Systems, Report Says," *Moscow-Pullman Daily News*, January 22, 2004, p. 7A.

34. Statewide Election Report, Office of the Secretary of State of California, Kevin Shelley (March 2, 2004); "3 States Mandate More Security for Diebold E-Voting Machines," *Moscow-Pullman Daily News*, May 11, 2006, p. 2A; Will Lester, "Panel Recommends Paper Trail on Electronic Voting Machines, Voter IDs," *Moscow-Pullman Daily News*, September 19, 2005, p. 6A; Anya

Sostek, "No Soft Touch," *Governing* 17, no. 8 (May 2004): 36–41.

35. Ian Urbina, "Hurdles to Voting Persisted in 2008," *New York Times*, March 11, 2009 (Web edition).

36. Alexander Kayssar, "The Strange Career of Voter Suppression," *New York Times*, February 12, 2012 (Web edition); Fredreka Schouten, "More States Require ID to Vote," *USA Today*, June 19, 2011 (Web edition).

37. Mike Morris, "Election Manual Included Voter ID Law Before It's the Law," *Houston Chronicle*, October 31, 2011 (Web edition); Aaron Sheinin, "Handel Defiant After Feds Reject Georgia Voter Screening," *Atlanta Journal-Constitution*, June 1, 2009 (Web edition).

38. Marjorie Hershey, *Party Politics in America*, 13th ed. (New York: Pearson Longman, 2009), pp. 5–13.

39. Samuel Eldersveld and Hanes Walton, *Political Parties in American Society*, 2nd ed. (Boston: Bedford/St. Martin's Press, 2000), pp. 125–126.

40. Bibby and Holbrooke, "Parties and Elections," pp. 78–81; Sarah Morehouse and Malcolm Jewell, "The Future of Political Parties in the States," *Book of the States*, vol. 37 (Lexington, KY: Council of State Governments, 2005), 338–342.

41. Thomas Holbrook and Raymond La Raja, "Parties and Elections," in Virginia Gray and Russell Hanson, *Politics in the American States*, 9th ed. (Washington, DC: CQ Press, 2008), pp. 75–77.

42. John Bibby, *Politics, Parties, and Elections in America* (Belmont, CA: Wadsworth, 2003), p. 82; Jewell and Morehouse, *Political Parties*, pp. 265–271; Bibby and Holbrook, "Parties and Elections," p. 78.

43. Bibby and Holbrook, "Parties and Elections," pp. 69–71; Hershey, *Party Politics*, ch. 3.

44. Sarah Morehouse and Malcolm Jewell, *State Politics, Parties, and Policy*, 2nd ed. (Lanham, MD: Rowman and Littlefield, 2003), pp. 136–138.

45. James P. Melcher, "Party Endorsements in Minnesota in the Wake of the 1994 Elections: Reform Strikes Out," *Comparative State Politics* 16, no. 6 (December 1995): 1–13; Morehouse and Jewell, *State Politics*, p. 136.

46. Jesse McKinley, "Calif. Voting Change Could Signal Big Political Shift," *New York Times*, June 9, 2010 (Web edition).

47. The extent of such party crossover voting is, however, not really known. One study of presidential primaries in Wisconsin from 1968 to 1984 estimated such partisan crossover to be no more than 11 percent of the voters. More numerous were Independents who voted in Republican or Democratic primaries (about 34 to 39 percent of the total). The overwhelming majority of primary election voters were people who belonged to the party in whose primary they were voting. See Ronald D. Hedlund and Meredith W. Watts, "The Wisconsin Open Primary: 1968–1984," *American Politics Quarterly* 14, nos. 1 and 2 (January–April 1986): 55–74.

48. *Tashjian v. Republican Party of Connecticut*, 107 S.Ct. 544 (1986).

49. On the latter point, see David Postman, "Party Ties Mean Less as Voters Shift Their Allegiance," *The Seattle Times* (electronic edition) January 19, 2008.

50. See Hershey, *Party Politics*, 13th ed., pp. 163–167.

51. A 1980 study estimated that the machine controlled 20,000 jobs. David Price, *Bringing Back the Parties* (Washington, DC: CQ Press, 1984), p. 23.

52. Malcolm E. Jewell and David M. Olson, *American State Political Parties and Elections* (Homewood, IL: Dorsey Press, 1982), p. 181.

53. Advisory Commission on Intergovernmental Relations, *The Transformation of American Politics: Implications for Federalism* (Washington, DC: U.S. Government Printing Office, 1986), p. 115; Morehouse and Jewell, *State Politics*, pp. 138–140; John Bibby and Thomas Holbrook, "Parties and Elections," in Virginia Gray and Russell Hanson, eds. *Politics in the American States* (Washington, DC: CQ Press, 2004), pp. 69–70.

54. Frank J. Sorauf, *Money in American Elections* (Glenview, IL: Scott Foresman, 1988), p. 268; Alan Rosenthal, *The Decline of Representative Democracy* (Washington, DC: CQ Press, 1998), pp. 176–183; Morehouse and Jewell, *State Politics*, pp. 199–200.

55. James L. Gibson, Cornelius P. Cotter, John F. Bibby, and Robert J. Huckshorn, "Whither the Local Parties? A Cross-Sectional and Longitudinal Analysis of the Strength of Party Organizations," *American Journal of Political Science* 29, no. 1 (February 1985): 139–161.

56. For example, the typical state had roughly one-third of its state house seats uncontested from 1984 through 1994. See Morehouse and Jewell, *State Politics*, p. 198; Alan Greenblatt, "Whatever

Happened to Competitive Elections?", *Governing* 18, no. 1 (October 2004): 22–27.

57. John Aldrich and Richard Niemi, "The Sixth American Party System: Electoral Change, 1952–1992," in Richard Niemi and Herbert Weisberg, eds. *Controversies in Voting* Behavior, 4th ed. (Washington, DC: CQ Press, 2001), pp. 405–426; William Flanigan and Nancy Zingale, *Political Behavior of the American Electorate*, 10th ed. (Washington, DC: CQ Press, 2002), ch. 3–4.

58. See Harold W. Stanley, "Southern Partisan Changes: Dealignment, Realignment or Both?" *Journal of Politics* 50, no. 1 (February 1988): 64–87. Stanley found that in 1952, barely 14 percent of southern whites called themselves Republican; by 1984, this had increased to almost 40 percent.

59. Robert D. Brown and Gerald C. Wright, "Elections and State Party Polarization," *American Politics Quarterly* 20, no. 4 (October 1992): 411–426; Dan Balz and Jon Cohen, "Poll Shows a Nation Deeply Divided and More Doctrinaire," *Washington Post*, May 5, 2011 (Web edition).

60. Hershey, *Party Politics*, pp. 121–127.

61. V. O. Key, Jr., *Southern Politics in State and Nation* (New York: Knopf, 1949), ch. 5.

62. Samuel C. Patterson and Gregory A. Caldeira, "The Etiology of Partisan Competition," *American Political Science Review* 78, no. 3 (September 1984): 691–707.

63. See especially Dye, *Politics, Economics, and the Public*, pp. 293–297; Richard E. Dawson and James A.Robinson, "Inter-Party Competition, Economic Variables, and Welfare Policies in the American States," *Journal of Politics* 25, no. 2 (May 1963): 265–289; Richard I. Hofferbert, "The Relation Between Public Policy and Some Structural and Environmental Variables in the American States," *American Political Science Review* 60, no. 1 (March 1966): 78–82.

64. Virginia Gray studied competition and policy over time and found that when the competition was unstable, two-party competition affected welfare policy outcomes. See Gray, "The Effect of Party Competition on State Policy, A Reformulation: Organizational Survival," *Polity* 7, no. 2 (Winter 1974): 248–263. Gerald C. Wright used a multiple regression of the logarithms of two-party competition and welfare expenditures and found a curvilinear rather than a linear relationship. That is, increasing the degree of competition did not affect policy outcomes until it became very competitive. Once competition approached the maximum possible level, it began to have significant effect on outcomes. See Gerald C. Wright, "Interparty Competition and State Welfare Policy: When a Difference Makes a Difference," *Journal of Politics* 37, no. 3 (August 1975): 796–803. Finally, Richard I. Hofferbert found that two-party competition combined with high voter turnouts produced higher expenditures for education and welfare. See Hofferbert, *The Study of Public Policy* (Indianapolis: Bobbs-Merrill, 1974), pp. 218–221. On within-state competition, see Thomas Holbrooke and Emily Van Dunk, "Electoral Competition in the American States," *American Political Science Review* 87 (1993): 955–962.

65. Frank Newport, "More States 'Competitive' in Terms of Party Identification," *Gallup Poll*, July 26, 2010 (Web edition).

66. Herbert McClosky, Paul J. Hoffmann, and Rosemary O'Hara, "Issue Conflict and Consensus Among Party Leaders and Followers," *American Political Science Review* 54, no. 2 (June 1960): 406–427; *The New York Times*, August 13, 1980, p. B-2; Jewell and Morehouse, *Political Parties*, pp. 88–92; Hershey, *Party Politics*, pp. 189–191.

67. Robert S. Erikson, "The Relationship Between Party Control and Civil Rights Legislation in the American States," *Western Political Quarterly* 24, no. 1 (March 1971): 178–182; Richard Winters, "Party Control and Policy Change," *American Journal of Political Science* 20, no. 4 (November 1976): 597–636.

68. "House Passes 1965 Voting Rights Act Renewal Over Objections from Southern Conservatives," *Moscow-Pullman Daily News*, July 14, 2006, p. 5A.

69. David Nice, *Policy Innovation in State Government* (Ames: Iowa State University Press, 1994), pp. 29–30, 58, 71, 82–83, 108–109, 119–120.

70. See Alan Greenblatt, "The Gubernatorial Baby Boom," *Governing* 16, no. 4 (January 2003): 20–25; Bob Gurwitt, "New Day Under the Dome," *Governing* 16, no. 4 (January 2003): 26–31.

71. John Gramlich, "In an Era of One-Party Rule, Republicans Pass a Sweeping State Agenda," *Stateline*, June 13, 2011 (Web edition); Annie Gowen, "In Kansas, Gov. Sam Brownback Puts

Tea Party Tenets into Action with Sharp Cuts," *Washington Post*, December 21, 2011 (Web edition); "States Out of Balance," *New York Times*, November 9, 2010 (Web edition).

72. Michael Cooper, "Second Year in, Republican Governors Moderate Tone," *New York Times*, January 31, 2012 (Web edition); John Gramlich, "After a Contentious Political Year, Republicans May Moderate Their Approach," *Stateline*, January 9, 2012 (Web edition).

73. Ian Lovett, "Bell, Calif. Voters Recall Government Officials," *New York Times*, March 9, 2011 (Web edition); Georgia Pabst, "Van Akkeren Defeats Ryan for Sheboygan Mayor," *Milwaukee Journal Sentinel*, February 21, 2012.

74. Elisabeth Gerber examined the passage of legislation requiring parental notification or parental consent before a minor could have an abortion. She compared the existence of such legislation to state-level public opinion surveys and found not only that the legislation was more likely to pass in states where it had popular support, but it was even more likely to pass in such states if they had the initiative. The potential threat of an initiative, thus, may have helped persuade legislators to pass the law. Elisabeth R. Gerber, "Legislative Response to the Threat of Popular Initiatives," *American Journal of Political Science* 40, no. 1 (February 1996): 99–128.

75. Richard Winters, "Party Control and Policy Change," *American Journal of Political Science* 20, no. 4 (November 1976): 597–636; M. Dane Waters, "Trends in State Initiatives and Referenda," in *The Book of the States*, vol. 34 (Lexington, KY: Council of State Governments, 2002), pp. 239–242.

76. Charles M. Price, "The Initiative: A Comparative State Analysis and Reassessment of a Western Phenomenon," *Western Political Quarterly* 28, no. 2 (June 1975): 243–262; Shaun Bowler and Todd Donovan, "The Initiative Process," in Virginia Gray and Russell Hanson, *Politics in the American States*, 9th ed. (Washington, DC: CQ Press, 2008), p. 135.

77. John C. Syer and John H. Culver, *Power and Politics in California*, 4th ed. (New York: Macmillan, 1992), p. 157.

78. Ibid., p. 159; David Broder, *Democracy Derailed* (New York: Harcourt, 2000); Shaun Bowler and Todd Donovan, "The Initiative Process," in Virginia Gray and Russell Hanson, eds. *Politics*

in the American States, 9th ed. (Washington, DC: CQ Press, 2008), p. 135.

79. Katharine Seelye, "Voters Defeat Many G. O. P.-Sponsored Measures," *New York Times*, November 9, 2011 (Web edition); Sabrina Tavernise, "Ohio Turns Back a Law Limiting Unions' Rights," *New York Times*, November 8, 2011 (Web edition).

80. John Matsusaka, "2005 Initiatives and Referendums," in *Book of the States*, vol. 38 (Lexington, KY: Council of State Governments, 2006), p. 300.

81. Ibid., p. 156. See also Alan Rosenthal, et al., *Republic on Trial* (Washington, DC: CQ Press, 2003), pp. 206–209; Elisabeth Gerber, et al., *Stealing the Initiative* (Upper Saddle River, NJ: Prentice-Hall, 2001).

82. William J. Keefe and Morris S. Ogul, *The American Legislative Process: Congress and the States*, 3rd ed. (Englewood Cliffs, NJ: Prentice-Hall, 1973), p. 258.

83. Howard D. Hamilton, "Direct Legislation: Some Implications of Open Housing Referenda," *American Political Science Review* 64, no. 1 (March 1970): 127, 131.

84. Raymond E. Wolfinger and Fred I. Greenstein, "The Repeal of Fair Housing in California: An Analysis of Referendum Voting," *American Political Science Review* 62, no. 3 (September 1968): 787; for a defense of the initiative process, see Charles Price, "Direct Democracy Works," *State Government News* (June/July 1997), pp. 14–15, 35; for additional criticisms, see Charles Mahtesian, "Grassroots Charade," *Governing* 12 (November 1998): 38–42.

85. Zoltan Hajnal, Elisabeth Gerber, and Hugh Louch, "Minorities and Direct Legislation: Evidence from California Ballot Proposition Elections," *Journal of Politics* 64 (2002): 154–177.

86. See Thomas E. Cronin, "Public Opinion and Direct Democracy," *PS: Political Science and Politics* 21, no. 3 (Summer 1988): 613–615; Bowler and Donovan, "The Initiative Process," p. 135.

87. Gladwin Hill, "Initiatives: A Score Card," *Working Papers for a New Society* 4, no. 4 (Winter 1977): 33–37.

88. David B. Magleby, "Taking the Initiative: Direct Legislation and Direct Democracy in the 1980s," *PS: Political Science and Politics* 21, no. 3 (Summer 1988): 603; Waters, "Trends in State," p. 239.

89. John R. Owens and Larry L. Wade studied campaign spending for and against 708 ballot propositions in California between 1924 and 1984. They concluded that "Money has simply been overemphasized as a determinant of voting on direct legislation." See their "Campaign Spending on California's Ballot Propositions, 1924–1984: Trends and Voting Effects," *Western Political Quarterly* 39, no. 4 (December 1986): 688; see also Broder, *Democracy Derailed*.

90. Mark Smith, "Ballot Initiatives and the Democratic Citizen," *Journal of Politics* 64 (2002): 892–903.

91. For a valuable overview of protest activities, see Russell Dalton, *Citizen Politics*, 3rd ed. (New York: Chatham House, 2002), ch. 4.

92. David Carr, "The Occupy Movement May Be in Retreat, But Its Ideas Are Advancing," *New York Times*, February 9, 2012 (Web edition); Karen Matthews, "Occupy Protesters March Nationwide; 300 Arrested," *Moscow, ID/Pullman, WA Daily News*, November 18, 2011; Katharine Seelye, "A Day of Protests as Occupy Movement Marks Two-Month Milestone," *New York Times*, November 17, 2011 (Web edition); Heather Knight, "UC Officials to Review Nonviolent Protest Policies," *San Francisco Chronicle*, November 21, 2011 (Web edition).

93. "Limited Government Advocates Choose New Hampshire for 'Project,'" *Moscow-Pullman Daily News*, October 1, 2003, p. 3A.

94. "Kentucky Political Race Leaves Two Candidates Dead," *Moscow-Pullman Daily News*, May 25–26, 2002, p. 13A.

95. "Three More Plead Guilty in Oregon to Ecoterrorism Spree," *Daily News*, July 22–23, 2006, p. 6A.

96. Frances Fox Piven and Richard A. Cloward, *Regulating the Poor: The Functions of Public Welfare* (New York: Random House, 1971); William Gamson, *The Strategy of Social Protest* (Homewood, IL: Dorsey, 1975).

97. Gamson, *The Strategy of Social Protest*, ch. 6.

98. On the importance of organization building, see Michael Gecan, *Going Public* (Boston: Beacon, 2002).

99. Cited in *State Legislatures* (December 1994): 5; see also Gary Moncrief, Peverill Squire, and Malcolm, *Who Runs for the Legislature?* (Upper Saddle River, NJ: Prentice-Hall, 2001), pp. 95–105.

100. Moncrief, Squire, and Jewell, *Who Runs*, pp. 99, 102.

101. Christine Kelleher, Cynthia Bowling, Jennifer Jones, and Deil Wright, "Women in State Government: Trends and Issues," in *Book of the States*, vol. 38 (Lexington, KY: Council of State Governments, 2006), pp. 414–420.

102. United States Bureau of the Census, *Statistical Abstract of the United States, 2003* (Washington, DC: U.S. Government Printing Office, 2003), p. 268; United States Bureau of the Census, *Statistical Abstract of the United States, 2008* (Washington, DC: U.S. Government Printing Office, 2008), p. 255; *Statistical Abstract of the United States, 2011–2012* (New York: Skyhorse, 2011), p. 259.

103. James Lai, et al., "Asian Pacific-American Campaigns, Elections, and Elected Officials," *PS: Political Science and Politics* 34 (2001): 611–617.

104. Calculated from National Election Studies data preserved in Jan E. Leighley and Jonathan Nagler, "Socio-economic Class Bias in Turnout, 1964–1988. The Voters Remain the Same," *The American Political Science Review* 86, no. 3 (September 1992): 725–736; *Statistical Abstract 2006* (Washington, DC: Bureau of the Census, 2005), p. 263.

105. Kim Quaile Hill and Jan E. Leighley, "The Policy Consequences Class Bias in State Electorates," *American Journal of Political Science* 36, no. 2 (May 1992): 351–365.

106. John J. Harrigan, *Political Change in the Metropolis*, 5th ed. (New York: HarperCollins Publishers, 1993), ch. 3.

107. Dalton, *Citizen Politics*, pp. 64–65.

The Institutions of Local Government

CHAPTER PREVIEW

To understand how state and local governments affect our lives, we need to understand how local government is organized, why it is organized the way it is, and the effects of its organization. We will cover these topics in this chapter by examining:

1 The different types of local governments and the functions they perform.

2 How cities and counties are organized.

3 How machine-style politics came to dominate many localities in the nineteenth century, but has faded since the early twentieth century.

4 How reform-style politics emerged as a reaction to machine-style politics, and the effects of reform-style politics.

5 How the metropolitan challenge has been confronted or, in some cases, not confronted, and how rural areas face a number of the same problems.

Introduction

Charleston, South Carolina, has had a lively history, including warfare, major fires, and hurricanes. In spite of the damage inflicted by those and other events, Charleston is a lovely city with many historic buildings, some of them dating to before the American Revolution. A number of fine old mansions overlook a park and the city's harbor.[1] Many people have contributed to making Charleston such an attractive place, but one of the most important figures is Mayor Joseph Riley, Jr., who has spent approximately half his life as mayor.[2]

Mayor Riley has worked hard to protect the historic character of the city, but he has also tried to serve a wide range of needs and interests. When wealthier people began moving into older neighborhoods and fixing up older homes, he made sure that the city had suitable housing for the poorer residents that were being pushed out of those neighborhoods. He helped the city attract the Spoleto Arts Festival, which brings visitors from all over the world to the city every year. When Charleston was struck by a major hurricane in 1989, he moved quickly to help repair the storm damage and restore vital services.

Unlike some local leaders, who focus almost entirely on their own individual communities, Mayor Riley is concerned about the condition of cities all over the country. He founded the Mayors' Institute on City Design, which holds meetings every year to help mayors learn more about the physical development of their cities and the ways that individual projects can affect that development for years to come. In 2003, he was named as one of the Public Officials of the Year by *Governing* magazine.

We each live in a community. It may be rural, small town, big city, or suburban, but communities affect the quality of our lives and are where we have many significant contacts with government. Those contacts might include the local schools, the local welfare department, local streets, public libraries, or police, among others. Many people develop strong emotional attachments to their communities. The term "community" may be defined and felt in many different ways, however. One person's community may be an entire city; another person may primarily identify with a particular section of a city or county with a strong ethnic or racial character—Italian or Chinese or Irish. During the twentieth century, the United States built up a nationwide assortment of locally delivered public services that became the envy of the world but which also varied a great deal from place to place.

Today, our communities are under great pressure as a result of many forces over which local governments have little control. These include social change, international economic competition, conflicts among ethno-religious and ideological groups, the fraying of stabilizing social institutions such as the family, and huge demographic migrations that have poured more than a hundred million people into the great suburban developments that seem to be popping up everywhere. The recession that began in 2007–2008 has created very great stress on many local governments. Not only have many seen their own revenues decline, but many have also faced reduced financial aid from both the state and the national government. In addition, many local agencies are involved in emergency management and protecting homeland security, especially since the September 11 terrorist attacks.

In Chapters 6 and 7, we want to examine the local governments that try to cope with these pressures. We will begin with some groundwork in this chapter by describing the institutions of local government. Then, in Chapter 7, we will turn to the dynamics of community politics.

Let us begin this excursion into community politics by focusing on (1) the different types of local government, (2) county and city organization, (3) the evolution of reform-style local government, and (4) the metropolitan challenge.

DIFFERENT TYPES OF LOCAL GOVERNMENT

Local government structure is much more complicated than state government structure. Whereas the 50 states all have fairly similar structures of government, the 89,476 local governments come in many forms. Some local governments (counties, municipalities, towns, and townships) are general purpose and perform a wide variety of governmental functions. Others (school districts and other special districts) have much narrower responsibilities and perform only one function or, at most, just a few.[3]

Single-Purpose (Mostly) Local Governments

Special districts are local governments that perform a narrow range of functions. Traditionally, the most numerous type of special district government was the **school district**. However, as Table 6.1 shows, there has been a sharp decline in the number of school districts since the 1940s.

TABLE 6.1						
Number of Governments in the United States						
	1942	**1972**	**1992**	**1997**	**2002**	**2007**
Counties	3,050	3,044	3,043	3,043	3,034	3,033
Municipalities	16,220	18,517	19,296	19,372	19,429	19,492
Townships and towns	18,919	16,991	16,666	16,629	16,504	16,519
School districts	108,579	15,781	14,556	13,726	13,506	13,051
Other special districts	8,299	23,885	33,131	34,683	35,052	37,381
Total local governments	155,067	78,218	86,692	87,453	87,525	89,476
States	48	50	50	50	50	50
Federal	1	1	1	1	1	1
Total all governments	155,116	78,269	82,688	86,743	87,504	87,576

Note: The growth in local governments since 1972 is accounted for by the continuing proliferation of special districts (other than school districts) combined with a dramatic slowdown in the rate of school district consolidations.

Source: Bureau of the Census, *Census of Governments, 1987* (Washington, DC: U.S. Government Printing Office, 1990), p. vi; *Statistical Abstract of the United States, 1998* (Washington, DC: U.S. Government Printing Office, 1998), p. 305; *Statistical Abstract of the United States, 2011–2012* (New York: Skyhorse, 2011), p. 267.

This decline resulted from the movement to consolidate school districts. School districts have been pressed to provide new educational services, costly laboratories, and expensive athletic equipment. Small rural school districts often could not afford these services, and having large numbers of school districts sometimes meant one district might be able to raise large amounts of money for education from its wealthy residents, while an adjacent district was poorly financed. Education reformers spent years pushing to merge smaller districts into larger ones. The trend of school district consolidation, however, has slowed down dramatically since 1982.

Although the number of school districts has declined, the number of nonschool, special districts has more than quadrupled since 1942. These other **special district** governments provide a single service or, at most, a few services. In metropolitan areas, for example, often one special district is used to provide public transit services, another to construct suburban hospitals, another to install sewer systems, another to provide a water supply, and still another to handle housing and renewal activities. Rural areas also use special districts for a variety of purposes, including soil conservation, safe drinking water, and health care.

Because the need for their services is so apparent and their mode of operation so apparently businesslike, the number of special districts (other than for schools) has grown considerably over the years and, as Table 6.1 shows, they are still proliferating today. Special districts are created for a number of reasons: to cope with problems that spread over other local government boundaries, to circumvent limits on the financial powers of city or county governments, or to provide more flexible administration, among other considerations.[4]

Special districts do, however, create two serious problems—coordination and lack of accountability. Especially in metropolitan areas, where governmental coordination is particularly important, the existence of too many special districts can threaten effective governance. Reaching agreement among dozens of local governments on a common course of action is often very difficult. Also, since the officials in charge of special districts are often appointed rather than elected, they are not very visible. Even when special-district officials are elected, the election turnouts are frequently low, and voters often know relatively little about the candidates—although elections may make special districts somewhat more responsible to the public than if none of the officials are elected. Media coverage of many special districts is often very limited. For all these reasons, special districts present serious problems of accountability. Some political reformers favor the consolidation of school districts, but they oppose the continuing growth in other special districts.[5]

General-Purpose Local Governments

The general-purpose local governments are counties, municipalities, towns, townships, and villages. Although they are labeled general-purpose governments, they are not general purpose in the same sense that the state is a general-purpose government. They are often more limited in what they can do, and their grants of authority are much more specific.

In some areas of the country, the **county** is the basic administrative subdivision of the state, and its existence is often specified in the state constitution. It is responsible in most states for the local administration of some major state services, including law enforcement, justice, welfare, roads, agricultural extension services, and, in some states, education. County governments have traditionally been strongest in the South, Southwest, and Midwest, where the historically rural character, low population density, and more elitist nature of local politics facilitated a form of government that covered large geographic areas and required less concentration of authority. Authority was traditionally dispersed through a large number of administrative agencies, many of which had independently elected agency heads. There was often little coordination among the major agencies. The skill levels of county employees varied considerably, and the legislative board of commissioners sometimes made little attempt to control or coordinate the departments. As we will see shortly in the chapter, the traditional image of county government no longer applies in many places.

In New England, the **town** rather than the county has been the predominant form of local government. Towns perform many of the same functions as counties, but they govern a much smaller geographic area, usually 20 to 40 square miles,[6] which encompasses both urban and rural territory. The most distinctive feature of town government is the town meeting. This takes place once a year (or, at times, more often) when the voters meet to establish the town budget for the following year, enact ordinances, and set the town's policies. The town meeting has been proclaimed as America's unique contribution to direct democracy.[7] Between town meetings, day-to-day operations are carried out by elected, traditionally part-time officials. Larger towns sometimes use a representative assembly instead of trying to have meetings with enormous numbers of people attending.

The **township** as a form of government exists primarily in the Midwest. Townships are primarily rural units of government. They perform at the local level many of the functions that the county performs at the countywide level. Thus, a township constable performs local police functions that supplement those of the county sheriff. Townships are governed by a town meeting and township officers similar to those used in the New England towns. As township territory is invaded by growing metropolitan populations, the territory is quite often annexed to suburbs or central cities, which are better able to provide the public services that the urban populations require. A number of states have gradually shifted township functions to other local governments, including counties.

The **municipality** is the form of government in cities. Most Americans live in municipalities. Unlike the counties, which are basic subdivisions of the state, municipalities (or city governments) only come into existence when they are incorporated by a charter. The charter prescribes the basic structure of city government and outlines its powers, much as the state constitution does for the state. The city charter has been a target of the political reform movement.

Local Charters

The legal authority for local government has traditionally differed fundamentally from the legal authority for states. The U.S. Constitution reserves to the states all the governmental powers not given by the Constitution exclusively to the national government or reserved exclusively to the people. Local governments, on the other hand, were traditionally treated as creatures of the state and had only those powers that were specifically given to them by the state constitution, the state legislature, or the state-drafted city charter.

If city officials wanted to do something not specified in the charter, then the courts usually prohibited the city from action by applying **Dillon's Rule**. Dillon's Rule established the principle of law that city governments' powers are very restricted. Cities may exercise only the powers specifically mentioned in their charter. Dillon wrote, "Any fair, reasonable, substantial doubt concerning the existence of power is resolved by the courts against the [city government], and the power is denied." Moreover, the legal authority of state governments is normally superior to that of local governments.[8] Dillon's Rule remains an influential legal doctrine in many states.

The city charter spells out the precise powers that the local government possesses and determines how the government is to be organized. Chartering systems fall into five categories—special charters, general charters, classified charters, optional charters, and home rule charters. *Special charters* arose shortly after independence when the legislatures enacted different charters for each city. As a result, the patterns of city governance had very little uniformity, and the legislatures were more deeply involved in city governance than many people desired. As the number of local governments rose, the task of handling individual charter needs became increasingly burdensome for state legislators.

In reaction, states began enacting a *general charter* for cities that provided uniform patterns of governance, but gave the cities little flexibility. A city of a few thousand people need not be governed in the same way as a city of a million. Consequently, the *classified charter* was established to separate cities by population size. Cities of the largest class usually have the greatest grants of authority.

A number of states provide an *optional charter* system, which allows cities to choose among a number of optional kinds of government. People in one city might prefer an elected mayor with broad authority, while people in another city prefer having a professionally trained city manager.

Most reformers prefer the *home rule charter*, which allows the residents of a city (or in some states, a county) to choose whatever form of government they want, usually within limits set by state law. Such a charter is drafted by a local charter commission and submitted for voter approval through referendum. Home rule provisions vary considerably; they may only give localities the power to alter their structure of government, or they may also allow a locality to add to its legal authority to operate programs or regulate activities. Note, too, that the existence of a state home rule provision does not necessarily mean that all local governments of that type actually exercise home rule powers. Communities may have to request approval to exercise those powers, and gaining approval may be difficult.[9]

About half of the states have enacted *devolution* statutes that give broad grants of authority to at least some local governments, most commonly municipalities. Devolution allows local governments to respond to problems without prior approval from the state government. Bear in mind that with or without either home rule or devolution, state policies usually override local policies. That is a particularly sensitive issue in the case of unfunded mandates, which may require localities to perform a task without providing any financial assistance to help defray the costs.[10] Not surprisingly, local government officials find that they must devote considerable effort to keeping track of their respective state governments and lobbying state officials.[11]

Local governments that do not have charters, such as some special district governments, are normally established and regulated by a combination of provisions in the state constitution and in ordinary statutes. Those laws may apply to all of the special districts of a certain type, such as school districts, or some laws may cover only a single district if its responsibilities are unusual (such as a seaport).

Division of Local Government Responsibilities

There is some overlap in the functions served by the different local governments, and responsibilities vary from state to state and sometimes from one part of a state to another part. But there also is some specialization. Counties (outside of New England) are heavily involved in human and social services, yet they traditionally handled very little in the way of redevelopment activities. However, a number of counties have become increasingly involved in economic development efforts in recent years.[12] Cities have the biggest burden for public safety in urban areas and for the physical maintenance of the urban infrastructure (streets, sewers, water supply, and park space). School districts have the biggest burden for public education, and other special districts share with cities the main burden of redevelopment activity and physical maintenance.

THE ORGANIZATION OF COUNTIES AND CITIES

Counties

Counties are governed by legislative bodies that usually bear the name **county board of supervisors** or **county board of commissioners**. More than 70 percent of these county legislators are elected from districts, with the balance being chosen in countywide, at-large elections.[13] Authority in county governments has historically been very fragmented, with large numbers of independently elected officials.[14]

Although some of the most important public services—such as welfare, public health, sheriff's patrol, county jail—are delivered by county governments, these governments are generally among the most fragmented of all major local governments. The executive power is typically divided among several agencies, which report individually to the county board or their own elected executives rather than to a chief executive. This gives the agencies considerable independence, especially the larger departments, such as welfare and highway maintenance. Over the years, many counties often hired employees with little specialized training, in part because the salaries available for some jobs were too low to attract trained professionals. Some department heads, such as sheriffs, are often elected directly, giving them an independent political base and making them even more insulated from the county board.

In order to reform these weaknesses of traditional county government, reformers have proposed two options for providing better leadership—the county administrator, and the elected county executive. The county administrator or county manager plan has been adopted by about 12 percent of all counties.[15] The administrator, hired directly by the county board, helps the board set the budget and tries to coordinate operations of the various departments. In addition, some administrators have fairly broad supervisory powers over various county agencies. County administrator plans are usually found in the more populous counties. For example, one-third of the counties with 250,000 or more people have some form of the council-administrator plan, compared to only 5 percent of the counties in the 2,500 to 24,999 range.

The elected county executive is similar to the strong-mayor form of city government, which will be discussed shortly. As an elected official, the county executive has more political influence to deal with administrative agencies and with the county board. About 16 percent[16] of all counties have adopted the elected county executive, and they tend to be counties with relatively large populations. In all, 36 percent of the counties with 250,000 or more people have elected chief executives. According to one study of rapidly growing counties, adoption of stronger executive plans was associated with higher levels of county government spending,[17] which probably helped those counties cope with the needs of a rapidly growing population.

Finally, to facilitate the modernization of counties, many reformers pushed for the adoption of county home rule charters, especially in the populous metropolitan areas. Like municipal home rule, county home rule charters let county residents choose the form of county government they want. Currently, about 5 percent of all counties have home rule charters.[18] In addition, reformers have supported changing county hiring systems to place more emphasis on training and expertise, and less on political loyalties.

Adoption of structural reforms within county governments has not entirely solved the problem of dispersed authority, for many county programs are interlinked with the activities of other local governments and with private organizations,[19] and achieving coordinated action on major problems is often difficult. Many county government programs are also subject to various state and federal laws and regulations, which may sometimes give departments a degree of independence from local control. In addition, structural reforms have made less headway in many of the more rural counties, even though those counties are often the most important local governments in their areas.[20]

Municipalities

Municipal government can be described as reformed or unreformed, although some combine features of both types. The reformed municipal government has a city council characterized by several features of the early twentieth-century progressive reform movement, especially nonpartisan and at-large elections. Reform-style cities are also more likely to have city manager or commission forms of government and systems to hire city employees based on their skills and training. Unreformed cities, by contrast, have partisan elections, council members chosen by ward or district, and an elected mayor, whose authority varies considerably from place to place. In unreformed cities, many city employees were traditionally hired because of their political connections rather than their job skills, although this practice is less common today than in the past.

Over time, the **Progressive Movement** to reform city government structure has been resoundingly successful, at least in some respects.[21] Roughly three-fourths of all cities elect their council members through nonpartisan elections, and roughly two-thirds rely on at-large elections.[22] Whether a city uses these reformed structures has an important policy impact. Probably because of their partisan and neighborhood basis and higher voter turnout, unreformed councils respond more effectively to political divisions within the city than do reformed councils. The unreformed councils tend to tax more and spend more money on city services than do reformed councils.[23] In addition, whether a city council is elected at-large or from wards has emerged as a major issue for the equal representation of minority groups, especially African Americans and Hispanics. Critics complain that at-large elections, with their more costly campaigns, reduce the likelihood that minority candidates will be elected.

The Commission   The commission form of government was created in Galveston, Texas, after a tidal wave in 1900 killed 5,000 people. This disaster required emergency action that the weak-mayor form of government was unable to provide, so a commission of prestigious businesspeople was appointed to run the city during the emergency. This commission carried out its task so effectively that the leading citizens obtained a charter change that permanently installed the commission form of government.

   Commission government unites executive and legislative functions in the same people. Each commissioner is the head of a city department, as shown in Figure 6.1. Although this form of government apportioned responsibility clearly enough to take decisive action during the Galveston tidal wave disaster, when virtually everyone recognized the need for emergency action, it had some serious defects when installed on a permanent basis. As department heads, the commissioners tended to defend the interests of their particular departments during the city council meetings. Budget sessions turned into contests in which alliances were established and the department heads left out of the alliance were given budgetary leftovers. Since neither a chief executive nor a legislative body was independent of the existing departments, the commissioners tended to be unreceptive to new spending needs outside of their limited responsibilities, and setting priorities was difficult. Although the commission form of government spread rapidly in the early 1900s, the defects of the system began to appear and it swiftly lost favor. Today, only 1 percent of all cities still maintain the system.

City Manager   The second and more lasting reform-style government is the **city manager,** or the council-manager plan, which is generally conceded to have been created in Staunton, Virginia, in 1908. Where the commission form unites the legislative and administrative functions, the city manager form separates them. It also tries to separate politics from administration. Reformers view the city council as the legislative and political body. It is engaged in the politics of campaigning, lobbying with the state legislature, establishing political support for the city government, and adopting overall city policies. The manager, a trained professional, is hired by and serves at the pleasure of the city council. The manager's job is to administer the policies established by the council and to take charge of all personnel matters, budget preparation, and other administrative details.

   Does the manager form of government really remove politics from administration? No, it does not. To be sure, managers are supposed to be nonpolitical, in the sense of staying out of election campaigns and seeking to protect the city administration from partisan politics, campaign pressures, and patronage.[24] However, in the more commonly understood definition of politics as including the process of policy making, city managers are definitely political.[25] Furthermore, a survey in the 1980s found that up to a third of managers helped council members get reelected.[26] City managers develop most of the policy proposals that city councils adopt.[27] They spend nearly a third of their time on policy making and a fifth of their time on political activities, such as trying to influence state legislators and other elected officials and showing up at community meetings where local issues are debated.[28] Another study of city managers found that they had a strong tendency not only to identify

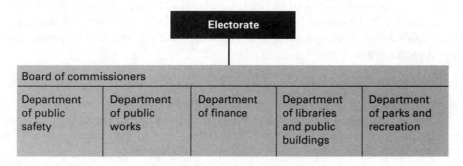

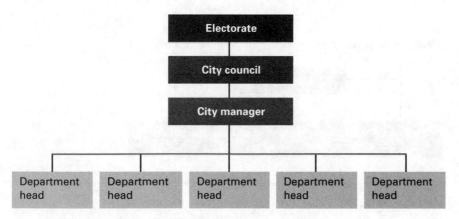

FIGURE 6.1

Manager and Commission Forms of Government

In the commission form of city government, each city council member (commissioner) is also a department head. In the council-manager form, executive and legislative functions are separated. The council theoretically sets policy, whereas the manager theoretically confines himself or herself to administering the city. In practice, as the text discusses, the manager is indeed political.

themselves in ideological terms (24 percent as liberals and 45 percent as conservatives) but also to pursue local policies that reflected their own ideological orientation.[29]

Because city managers are hired and fired by their city councils, managers must usually align themselves with the dominant coalition of their city councils. When the council majority changes, the manager either realigns his or her loyalties or faces dismissal by the council. Moreover, city officials may use the manager as a scapegoat when things go wrong, a practice that can produce rapid turnover during stressful times.

The city manager plan is most commonly found in small and medium-sized cities, especially suburbs, where the populations are less heterogeneous and less divided politically than they are in large cities. A majority of all cities with population of less than 250,000 have the manager form of government. Larger cities, by contrast, tend to have mayor-council governmental systems. In these large cities, the political divisions often become too acrimonious to be handled smoothly by a manager who can be fired at any time. The recent conflicts in Dallas, Texas, the ninth largest city in the United States, illustrate the difficulties with the city manager plan in a large city. With a wide range of groups and opinions, the city has lacked effective executive leadership in recent years.[30]

Mayors The major differences between the city manager and the mayor are that the mayor is elected and typically has deep roots in the community, but the manager is appointed by the council. City managers often have professional training in city management, and often come from another part of the country. Mayors frequently have an independent base of political support, which strengthens their hand in dealing with the council.

Two types of mayor—the weak mayor and the strong mayor—are illustrated in Figure 6.2. The **weak mayor** resulted from the traditional American distrust of strong executives. Because of

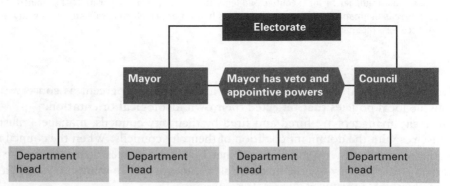

FIGURE 6.2
Strong-Mayor and Weak-Mayor Forms of Government
Under the weak-mayor form of government, the mayor has neither a veto over the council nor the power to appoint department heads. Under the strong-mayor form, the mayor is given both of these powers.

this distrust, city departments were set up to be independent of each other and of the mayor. Often the department heads were directly elected by the people and were given political patronage jobs to hand out. The weak mayor has little appointive power and very limited budget-making powers and often cannot veto measures of the city council. In some communities, the weak mayor is not even elected by the public but is instead picked by the city council from among its members. Bear in mind, however, that a mayor with weak legal authority may still be influential for other reasons, from popularity to being skilled at persuasion.

The **strong mayor**, by contrast, is elected by the public, has broad appointive powers, presides over council meetings, sets the council's agenda (often in consultation with council members), has strong budget-making powers, and has a veto. In large cities, the mayor often has a chief administrative officer or a deputy mayor who runs the day-to-day operations of the city departments and leaves the mayor free to deal with the larger areas of policy and leadership. When that official is a trained administrator, the differences between the mayor-council plan and the city manger plan become much smaller. City administrators are often appointed by the mayor, sometimes with the consent of the city council.[31]

The visibility of mayors and their involvement in controversial issues can lead to tensions and resentment directed against the mayor's office. Irate citizens and officials may resort to angry letters and personal confrontations with the mayor, or the resentment may be expressed in other ways, from demonstrations to voting the mayor out of office. When Mayor Joan Wagnon of Topeka, Kansas, came to work the day after losing a bid for another term, she found a mannequin sitting on a toilet outside her office door and a sign that read, "Flush Wagnon." A city councilman told the police that he and two other officials, another city council member and a county commissioner, had placed the display outside the mayor's door. All three had opposed Wagnon on a number of issues over the years.[32]

THE EVOLUTION OF REFORM-STYLE CITY POLITICS

The evolution of reform-style local government forms, such as county manager, city manager, and strong mayor-councils, was a direct product of the Progressive political reform movement of the early twentieth century. This movement sought to replace boss-dominated, machine-style politics with a style of politics that reformers hoped would be less corrupt and less partisan in nature, and place more emphasis on professional expertise.

Machine-Style Urban Politics

Political machine refers to a local (or, less commonly, state) political party that had organized itself so strongly that it dominates politics in its region. The political machine differs from conventional political parties, however, in several respects. The machine is led by a single boss or a unified central committee. The organization controls the nominations to public office and provides candidates with considerable organized support during campaigns. The machine leaders are often of working-class or lower-class social origins. They usually do not hold public office, although some machine leaders have. The machine's workers are kept loyal through material rewards (such as patronage jobs and government purchases), administrative favors, and psychological rewards (such as fellowship and ethnic recognition).[33]

Machine politics often had an ethnic basis. The rise and decline of machine politics coincided with the massive immigration of Europeans to American cities between 1840 and 1930.

Local political parties began nominating ethnic minorities as candidates in the hope that these ethnic candidates would attract other immigrant voters. This development has been called the balanced ticket or the politics of recognition.[34]

The machine also provided assistance to the newcomers. This assistance was granted on an individual basis to people who could be expected to support the machine's candidates in return. One common favor was finding jobs for people. Some of those jobs were in local or even state government, the so-called patronage jobs, but others were with private companies that needed workers. To keep the patronage jobs, workers were expected to work for the party during election campaigns, to contribute money to the party, and to promote the party's welfare.

Local governments controlled by a machine purchased supplies, from typing paper to police cars, from businesses friendly to the machine. Party workers also helped newcomers who had problems with the police or other governmental agencies and watched for opportunities to help people in other ways, as well. These political favors helped keep the machine in power but also facilitated the upward social mobility of the immigrants and their children. Although the extent of this upward mobility can be questioned,[35] many ambitious immigrants turned to the machine for opportunities when they perceived that other doors were closed.

The oldest and most famous machine was New York City's Tammany Hall, founded in 1789 as a social club. Another well-known machine is in Chicago; it was plagued by internal conflict that erupted in the mid-1970s, but that has subsided somewhat in recent years. Machines also existed in smaller communities and in rural areas.

A very durable political machine is found in Nassau County, New York, which has had a political machine since the 1930s. In spite of the county's considerable wealth, it has had recurring financial problems for years, partly because local officials tend to use government purchasing to reward their political cronies. Those problems led bond ratings firms to downgrade the county's bonds to barely above junk bond status. Exasperated state officials finally created an oversight board to help bring some order to the county's finances, and angry voters also placed a number of new elected officials in charge. Bringing lasting improvements will require numerous changes in the county government's operations.[36]

The Results of Machine Politics

Political machines generally avoided ideological or programmatic politics. Their leaders feared that issue-oriented campaigns would produce too much conflict, and they wanted to control which individuals received specific benefits. As they assisted individuals with their problems, they helped their communities, to some degree, cope with problems such as unemployment.

The machines were generally friendly to lower- and working-class immigrants who secured patronage jobs and political positions. In the process of controlling city government, the machines helped integrate the European immigrants into American society, find them employment, get them into the political system, and get them registered to vote. Sociologist Robert Merton referred to these functions as the *latent functions* of the machines. Latent functions are the side effects or secondary effects produced by an organization with leaders who are primarily interested in something else. In the case of political machines, their *manifest functions* (that is, their main foci of interest) involved gaining control of the government and getting a share of the rewards that came with that control.[37] Some of the machines, however, were not as open to later migrants to the cities, such as African Americans and Hispanics.

The machines also gave a personal touch to government and politics. Campaigns were conducted by people in each neighborhood, and when people needed help with government, their local precinct worker, a neighbor, might accompany them. The personal touch was not always friendly, however; critics and opponents of the machines might experience police harassment, more zealous inspectors, missed garbage collections, or deteriorating streets.

Some political machines also had corruption problems, which unfortunately reinforced the public view that all politicians are unethical and dishonest. Those corruption problems eventually helped ignite a reform movement that affects state and local politics to this day. Unfortunately, the efforts of the reformers have not been altogether successful; corruption problems have surfaced in recent years in communities ranging from Chicago and Detroit to Bell, California, Towns County, Georgia, a number of local officials in New Jersey, Broward County, Florida, and the Las Vegas, Nevada, areas.[38]

THE PROGRESSIVE REFORM MOVEMENT

Many upper-class and upper-middle-class people disliked machine politicians who catered to the lower-class immigrants and "foreigners." Historian Samuel P. Hays has shown that the initiative for progressive reform in the early twentieth century came primarily from the cities' top business leaders and upper-class elite.[39] Some businesspeople-reformers hoped to make direct financial gains by overthrowing the corrupt machine politicians.

However, the reformers also had philosophical reasons for displacing the machine politicians. Historian Richard Hofstadter contends that the typical reformer viewed politics differently than did most machine politicians. The machine politician viewed politics in personal terms. Government was "the actions of particular powers. Political relations were not governed by abstract principles; they were profoundly personal."[40] In contrast, the upper-middle-class reformers looked upon politics as "the arena for the realization of moral principles of broad applications—and even, as in the case of temperance and vice crusades—for the correction of private habits."[41] Reformers also wanted greater expertise in local government, in part because the work of local governments was growing more complex and more expensive.

The Mechanics of Reform

The political reformers devised several mechanisms to eliminate the machines. The most prominent reform mechanisms were the merit system of public employment, reforms of government purchasing, the direct primary, at-large elections, nonpartisan elections, the short ballot, and the city manager and commission forms of government. No one single measure destroyed the machines, and some machine organizations showed a tenacious ability to persist despite the reforms. Nevertheless, the combination of reforms had a detrimental effect on the machines.

The Merit System   If the machine bosses relied on patronage jobs to keep themselves in power, then the obvious antidote was **civil service** and the **merit system**. From the point of view of reformers, it was morally wrong for partisanship to influence who received governmental jobs. Governmental hiring and promotion should be based on skills, training, and relevant work experience. The machine politicians, however, thought that the patronage system helped to get ordinary people involved in the politics and government of their communities.[42]

Reform of Government Purchasing   Political machines traditionally bought products and services from companies friendly to the machine. That practice sometimes caused local governments to pay inflated prices and, in some cases, they received faulty products and services. Reformers pressed for allowing a number of companies to submit competitive bids when a local government needed to buy, for example, police cars or concrete for pavement, and for requiring the lowest qualified bid to receive the contract, regardless of political considerations.

The Direct Primary   The convention system of nominations favored the political machines. Because the bosses controlled the selection of delegates to the conventions, they easily controlled the nominations for public office. The reformers' cure was a system wherein nominations were made directly by the voters in a **direct primary** election, thus weakening the political bosses' influence.

At-Large Elections   Election from wards enabled ward leaders and council members to provide enough services and close personal contact with their constituents to control (or at least strongly influence) their votes. The reformers' rejoinder was **at-large elections**, in which a candidate runs in the city as a whole rather than from a specific district. They hoped that at-large elections would encourage voters and council members to adopt a citywide vision of how the government should operate. With elections conducted at-large, reformers hoped the ward politicians would find it more difficult to give people favors in exchange for their votes.

Nonpartisan Elections   Partisan elections also benefited the bosses. The likely reform was **nonpartisan elections**. With the party designation removed from the ballot, the machine's choices for office would be much less obvious and other endorsing organizations, such as good-government leagues, newspapers, and interest groups, would presumably gain influence.

The Short Ballot   Many machine leaders preferred weak mayors who had little control over city agencies and bureaucracies, many of which were headed by elected officials. Because the department heads and elected officials competed with each other and depended on the machine to keep them in office, it was easy for the boss to control them and, in turn, the city government. The obvious antidotes were the **short ballot** and either the city manager or the commission form of government. The short ballot has the voters elect only those few offices that set overall policy—preferably just the mayor and the city council. It is distinguished from the long ballot, in which a large number of officials, including administrative and even judicial officials, are elected. The more names on the ballot, the more individual voters have to rely on recommendations of endorsing organizations. As the best-organized endorsing organization, the political machine had considerable influence under the long ballot. By substituting a short ballot, the reformers had a better chance to compete with the machines.

Reformed City Government   Finally, the city manager and commission forms of government provided professional administration for city functions and greater emphasis on broad policies rather than personal connections, thereby weakening machine influence. These reforms did not always cause machines to die, but where all the reform mechanisms went into effect, machines found it difficult to survive.

Machines were also weakened by a number of other forces, including federally-and state-supported social programs that replaced machine favors, rising education levels that reduced reliance on the machine's political guidance, and the growing presence of middle-class citizens who disapproved of the machine's usual modes of operation. Some machines were also plagued with internal conflicts that gave reformers an opportunity to press for changes.[43]

The Effects of Progressive Reform

The Progressive reforms, like many other reforms over the years, did not benefit everyone equally. The reforms helped upper- and upper-middle-class people to gain influence in local politics. Correspondingly, low-status voters lost influence. Nonpartisan elections, for example, produce council members of higher socioeconomic status than do partisan elections.[44] One reason for that pattern is that party loyalties help motivate people of lower socioeconomic status to vote.[45] Shifting to nonpartisan elections reduces that motivator considerably.

In addition, nonpartisan elections are often combined with selecting council members at-large. In larger jurisdictions, running an at-large campaign across an entire city or county and without party help can be an expensive proposition. And reform-style politics generally reduced the likelihood that city governments would be responsive to majority demands in the city. One study found that local officials in cities with partisan elections were much more likely to agree with a majority of city residents about the city's problems than were officials in cities with nonpartisan elections.[46] These findings suggest that reform-style politics makes it less likely that the leaders of a city will be responsive to peoples' concerns and interests.

Elected Officials, Reform Style   Many machine politicians saw politics as a career, but many elected officials in reformed local political systems do not. Their approach to public office is **volunteerism.** That is, they regard themselves as volunteers serving as a civic duty. For the most part, they are not interested in higher office and not greatly concerned about reelection. Consequently, they may feel free to follow their own beliefs rather than paying great attention to citizens' opinions,[47] although some voluntaristic officials do pay attention to public sentiments as a matter of principle.

Not all locally elected officials take the voluntaristic approach; people run for office for many different reasons. However, many local officials do not face strong competitive pressures that keep them responsive to city residents. Local officials who run for another term typically have quite high reelection rates—from 70 to 85 percent.[48] Skimpy news coverage of local politics may mean that many voters know relatively little about the candidates except that some (usually the incumbents) have familiar names. In addition, many incumbents face opponents with little political experience and little money for their campaigns. It is not unusual for local races in smaller communities to have only one candidate for each of several offices.[49]

Summing Up: From Machines to Reform Politics

The legacy of progressive reform for today's communities is mixed. Early in the twentieth century, machine politics helped encourage many people, including poorer and less educated people, to be involved in politics. But because the machines were often corrupt and favored a personalized style of politics that could not cope well with contemporary local problems, they have probably outlived their usefulness. The reform-style politics that tends to replace machines has reduced political corruption and produced public employees with higher skill levels.

However, reform politics has been less effective at involving poorer and less-educated people in politics. In addition, removing the parties from local politics, holding local elections separately from national or state elections, and changing from mayoral to city manager plans of government all tend to reduce voter participation in local elections. When citizens are inattentive many problems may result. Public disinterest helped allow political corruption to develop in San Bernadino Country, California, in the 1970s and continue to the present time, although recent investigations and the departures of a number of the city's department heads may help root out the problems.[50]

Recent Reforms of the Reforms

A number of communities have tried to compensate for the problems of reform-style politics. Some cities have created neighborhood councils and citizen advisory committees to give residents more influence in local governance. Some large cities have experimented with little city halls, which are neighborhood offices that serve as an outreach arm for the mayor's office and sometimes increased the accessibility of local services. A number of these were disbanded in the budget-retrenchment years of the early 1980s.

A number of communities have established an **ombudsman** office, which is an independent office responsible for handling citizen complaints about local government services. Its ability to improve services varies, not surprisingly, with the intractability of the problems involved. It is easier, for example, for the ombudsman to get trees trimmed and storm sewers unclogged than to resolve problems associated with abandoned buildings in poor neighborhoods.[51]

The advent of cable television has led many communities to televise major local government meetings. Not enough is yet known to be able to determine whether this development will have a positive or negative impact. A study of such televised meetings in Kansas found that, despite a tendency for members to play to the cameras, televising the meetings increased the feedback council members received from local residents, and the viewers were, disproportionately, people of lower socioeconomic status.[52]

Many local governments are also using the Internet for a variety of purposes, one of which is to help citizens gain access to local agencies and officials. A number of officials have found e-mail to be a useful way to learn more about public sentiments and concerns. These efforts are still developing, and assessing their impact is difficult at this point. However, one major concern regarding Internet access to local governments is the fact that many households still do not have ready access to the Internet. The localities where relatively few people have personal computers at home have generally done little to help foster Internet access to local government agencies and officials, and many localities are developing Internet services on a piecemeal basis rather than according to any overall plan. A major study on political involvement and the Internet found that, as with conventional participation, political activity on the Internet was considerably biased, with poorer people and less educated people being less likely to participate.[53] Privacy advocates have also expressed concern over possible losses of privacy and the dangers of identity theft as more information is placed in computerized records. Clearly, a great deal remains to be done.[54]

THE METROPOLITAN CHALLENGE

The official designation of a metropolitan region in the United States is the **metropolitan statistical area (MSA)**, which consists of any county containing a city or contiguous cities of 50,000 people, plus the surrounding counties that are economically integrated into the central county. Areas lacking a central city of 50,000 can also qualify if their built-up, urbanized area contains 100,000 people. Because the MSA is defined by counties, most MSAs contain substantial rural areas as well as urbanized areas. The extreme case of this is found in the San Bernardino–Riverside (California) MSA, where the sparsely populated rural areas cover a huge space that vastly exceeds the urbanized areas around the cities of San Bernardino and Riverside.

There are more than 300 MSAs, and they contain three-fourths of Americans. The typical metropolitan area is a patchwork of community identities, governing institutions, and private organizations, many of which are involved in various public programs. Metropolitan areas usually lack a central political authority that can speak for the metropolis as a whole. The mayor is usually the most visible spokesperson for the city, just as the governor is typically the most visible spokesperson for the state. But the intermediate metropolitan level typically has no highly visible advocate. Lack of such a visible leader makes it very difficult to create a sizable metropolitan constituency with any interest in metropolitan problems. The lack of such a constituency, coupled with the dispersal of authority across numerous local governments, hampers efforts to tackle metropolitan-wide problems, especially controversial problems.

A typical MSA is built up around a central city, sprawls over into two or more counties, and embraces dozens of municipalities, school districts, and other special districts. Some of the most serious problems (air pollution, crime control, housing, education, transportation, racial discrimination, natural disasters, and combating terrorism) affect all of these governmental jurisdictions and may extend well beyond the metropolitan area. As a result, the past 50 years have seen many attempts to create governmental structures that could deal with metropolitanwide problems with the same authority that mayors and city councils use to deal with individual city problems.

The Hopes for Metropolitan Government

Following World War II (1941–1945), many metropolitan areas appeared headed for trouble because the structures of local government often lagged behind population growth, social and economic changes, and new needs. Rapid suburban growth in this period led to numerous problems, especially local governments' inability to provide the normally expected urban services in the suburban fringes that were not officially part of any city. Central city water and sewer lines, for example, were usually not extended into the new suburban subdivisions outside the city limits, and homeowners often had to rely on private wells and backyard septic tanks. As populations grew, this combination led to inevitable pollution of wells and ground water.

Resolving these problems was difficult because metropolitan areas typically lacked a governmental mechanism for coping on a coordinated, areawide basis with such problems as air pollution, sewage disposal, water supply, solid waste disposal, transportation, and public health, issues that spilled over many local government boundaries. The typical metropolis had several dozen local governments, and new governments were added to cope with new concerns, but without any overall plan of development. That process led to overlapping of responsibilities, intergovernmental conflicts, and important gaps and inequality in services.

Reformers eventually developed a number of strategies for coping with these problems. The more drastic remedies usually fell victim to strong opposition; limited remedies were more easily adopted.[55] The more drastic remedies were consolidation and two-tiered metropolitan government.

City-County and City-City Consolidation   One strategy was to develop one local government, usually achieved by consolidating a county and the cities that it contained. A single countywide council would replace the previous city councils and county board of commissioners, and the city and county service departments would be merged. This synthesis would prevent the formation of new municipalities in the suburbs and would reduce the need for more special districts. Prominent successes in **city-county consolidation** occurred in Nashville–Davidson County, Tennessee (1962), Jacksonville–Duvall County, Florida (1967), Indianapolis–Marion County, Indiana (1969), and Louisville–Jefferson County, Kentucky (2000).[56]

A related approach is consolidating two adjacent cities or towns into one that covers the area of both. This reform is sometimes proposed in smaller communities in hopes of pooling limited resources and coordinating actions across the whole area.

The Two-Tier Government Strategy   A second strategy for metropolitan reform is the **two-tier government**,[57] in which local units perform the governmental functions best suited for the localities, and a regional authority handles the broader functions, such as sanitation, transportation, and regional planning. The inspiration for this strategy came from Canada, where federative forms of metropolitan government were established in Toronto, Ontario, and Winnipeg, Manitoba.[58] A variation of this approach was achieved in Miami–Dade County, Florida, in 1957. The county government was reorganized that year and was given expanded regional service responsibilities for transportation, sewage, water supply, and land-use planning. The existing 26 municipalities continued to provide such local services as police patrolling and zoning.

The Great Hopes Dashed

Proposals for these drastic reorganizations of local government have failed about 75 percent of the time that they were submitted to the electorate for a vote.[59] And with the few exceptions just noted, most of the successes occurred in relatively small metropolitan areas, where the problems were less severe.

Several reasons have been given for the failure of major metropolitan reform. First, many reform proposals encountered severe resistance from suburban voters, who viewed the reform as an attempt by central city politicians to grab their tax base, schools, amenities, and above all their autonomy. Many wealthy suburbanites do not want to pay taxes to help poorer central city residents and do not want to lose control of local zoning and building code decisions that are used to exclude poorer people from some communities. In addition, suburbanites may fear that central city problems will increasingly filter into the suburbs after creation of a stronger areawide government.[60]

Second, resistance often comes from many local political leaders, who fear a loss in their own influence in a reformed system.[61] Suburban leaders may fear that they will lose power to central city politicians (and vice versa); county officials may fear a loss of power to city leaders.

A final reason for the failure of metropolitan reform is that in most metropolitan areas, many people have been relatively satisfied with their existing governmental arrangements. Reform advocates often define the problems as "inefficiency" and "overlapping functions," which have limited meaning to the average voter. They often failed to convince people that

WHERE DO I FIT IN?

Although reformers have often complained that the United States has too many local governments, their large number means that there are many opportunities for involvement in local politics. The thousands of elected local offices generate thousands of campaigns in which people can become involved. The numerous private organizations that help provide many public services provide many more opportunities for involvement in attacking problems. Public hearings and advisory panels provide still more arenas for participation. Journalists covering local governments and politics can help focus attention on important problems and help publicize possible remedies.

The large numbers of local governments also complicate participation in some respects. Finding the best arenas for involvement can be laborious where there are dozens or even hundreds of local governments in a limited area. The need for negotiation and consultation among many local governments and private organizations can produce delays that tax the patience of many people. Even when one local government is sympathetic to a group of citizens, effective action may be blocked by other local governments and/or private organizations. Moreover, local officials may fail to act because they lack financial resources or legal authority. ∎

reorganization would mean better services or lower taxes. Many citizens apparently preferred keeping the numerous, small local governments that seemed relatively accessible rather than creating a large local authority that might be less responsive to small groups[62] (see "Where Do I Fit In?").

By contrast, when voters are unhappy with public services (as in Jacksonville, Miami, and Nashville) and the reformers campaign on the basis of those complaints, major reorganizations have a much better chance of winning. The frequent defeat of reforms over the years has led to emphasizing other, more modest, coping strategies.

Annexation as an Approach to Metropolitan Governance

One simple way to achieve unified metropolitan governance is to let the central city expand by annexing land beyond the central city boundary. In this way, metropolitan growth would be gradually contained within the central city. This, in fact, was what typically happened during the nineteenth century. But early in the twentieth century, many state legislatures began requiring that annexations be approved by dual referendums of the voters, both within the city doing the annexation and within the area to be annexed. In the Northeast and Midwest, suburbanites often voted against annexation in order to keep their distance from the large immigrant populations whom they blamed for the vice and corruption of central city politics.[63] As a result, by the 1930s the central cities of the Northeast and Midwest were mostly encircled by a ring of suburbs. Attempts by central cities to annex noncontiguous land beyond the ring of suburbs were generally frowned upon by the courts.

Following World War II, many states relaxed their annexation restrictions and a new wave of annexation took place, especially in the South and West. That option was, however, not available to the northern and midwestern cities that were surrounded by incorporated suburbs. Even when annexation is legally possible, it may fall victim to opponents who fear that the area to be annexed will generate major costs to the city or bring in people with different political beliefs.

Searching for a New Regionalism

Despite the defeat of most metropolitan reform proposals, the problems of metropolitan America did not go away. In many ways, they worsened. In response, local officials have tried other strategies. Two of the milder regional approaches are metropolitan planning agencies and councils of governments. A **metropolitan planning** agency seeks to develop long-range plans for regional land use and also to develop plans for the extension of major public services (such as roads, public transit, and sewers) into the growing suburban fringes, and modification of existing services to cope with future needs.

A **council of governments** (**COG**) consists of representatives from the counties and municipalities in an area. COGs proliferated rapidly during the 1960s as a consequence of federal funds for planning and requirements that local government grant applications for federal aid be reviewed by a COG-like metropolitan agency to see if they were consistent with their area's metropolitan plans. COGs have often had difficulty in coping with relatively controversial issues, however.[64]

Other modest strategies for coping with areawide problems include transferring responsibility for some policy, such as transportation, to a special district government or, for areas that fall within a single county, to the county government. Creating even more special districts may have the unfortunate side effect of making local politics even more confusing than it was before, especially if the strategy is used a number of times in an area.

Local governments may enter into service contracts with another local government or a private contractor. The contracts take many forms, but a common type involves one local government purchasing a service from another local government or a private company. Another type involves creating a joint facility or project, such as a jail, that is run by a committee representing two or more local governments.[65] Service contracts and sharing facilities or services sometimes save money and may give a community access to skills or equipment that it could not afford on its own. However, purchasing services from others can also produce problems if the contracts are not carefully written and enforced or if a contractor is not as competent as officials hope.[66] Service contracts and joint projects shared among two or more local governments may also help to coordinate the actions of those different governments, at least to some degree.

Local officials may also use informal cooperation and negotiation to address problems that cross jurisdictional boundaries and also to share resources in the event of an emergency. Since the September 11, 2001, terrorist attacks, many local officials have developed informal (or even formal) agreements with officials in neighboring jurisdictions and private organizations to provide assistance to one another in the event of another major terrorist incident. Similar agreements exist for coping with riots, natural disasters, and many other problems.

Officials may also advise one another of upcoming projects, such as major bridge repairs, that are likely to produce effects on nearby communities. Officials often look to their counterparts in nearby communities for advice in coping with problems, too. The great shortcoming of informal cooperation, unfortunately, is that it is often impractical for highly controversial issues, especially if they involve a large number of different local governments.

Bear in mind that problems spill across local boundaries in rural areas and small towns as well. Many of them have struggled with declining populations and a loss of jobs, as well as a shortage of people willing to serve in public office. There, too, major structural reforms have faced considerable opposition. Local officials have often had to rely on more modest reforms, such as service contracts, and informal remedies instead.[67]

SOCIAL CHANGE AND LOCAL GOVERNMENT

MSAs comprise about 20 percent of the land mass of the United States, but they house 80 percent of the American population. With some exceptions—mostly the newer, smaller, metropolises of the West—the typical metropolitan area has many local governments and considerable social and economic segregation. With poorer people living in some communities and wealthier people often living in other communities, economic resources for dealing with problems are separated from the areas where problems are most severe. That separation means that local governments with the most severe problems frequently have fewer financial resources for addressing those problems. In addition, economic segregation may reduce political involvement: Communities with more diverse populations tend to foster more citizen participation.[68] A homogeneous community tends to produce dull politics.

While many central cities and older suburbs have seen their minority and poverty populations growing over the past 40 years, the most dynamic job growth has often occurred in new developments on the fringes of metropolitan areas.[69] Public transportation between poorer communities and these new employment centers is often inadequate, which further limits the job prospects for many poorer people. Some officials recognize that difficulty and are working to improve public transportation, including linking different suburbs together more effectively,[70] but much work remains to be done. That work has become much more important with the higher prices for gasoline and diesel fuel since 2007.

Because major structural reorganizations of local governments are usually doomed to defeat under all but ideal conditions, the most realistic strategies for coping with areawide problems appear to involve relatively modest steps, many of them informal.[71] Some of those strategies involve reviving the economies of older cities, a task that is difficult but not impossible. A successful revitalization program needs skillful leadership, a willingness to make the most of particular opportunities, and a bit of luck (and the willingness to keep trying when one effort fails).[72] We will explore economic development programs in more detail in Chapter 17.

CONCLUSION

In this chapter, we have examined the major governing institutions at the community level. It is important to stress that none of these institutional forms are politically neutral. The reformed structures of city government (commission, city manager, at-large elections, and nonpartisan elections) were promoted by upper-class and upper-middle-class leaders who wanted to reduce the influence of machine politicians and the lower-status European immigrants to whom the machines were responsive. Those reforms have reduced political corruption and increased the skills of local government workers, but also reduced participation in local politics.

The typical metropolitan area in the United States has dozens of local governments, many of which overlap with one another. That situation, according to critics, creates many obstacles to solving large-scale problems. Major attempts at metropolitan reform have often been defeated because many citizens feel reasonably satisfied with existing arrangements and because citizens and leaders in many communities fear that major reforms will reduce their political influence.

Many local governments today lack the authority and effective power to cope comprehensively with major problems. In some cases, informal mechanisms and relatively modest reforms have helped remedy some problems. When those efforts fail, power and authority over some problems (such as pollution control and transportation) have drifted to the federal- and state-level agencies, while power and authority over other problems (such as land use and racial integration) have proved elusive.

SUMMARY

1. There are more than 89,000 local governments (counties, municipalities, school districts, other special districts, towns, and townships) in the United States. The number continues to grow as special districts proliferate.

2. An important distinction about local governments is that some are reformed and some are unreformed. Reformed counties have a county manager or an elected county executive and employees with considerable training. Unreformed counties have no chief executive power, numerous county agencies reporting independently to a board of supervisors or commissioners, and many workers with only limited training. Reformed city governments have city manager or strong-mayor forms of executive, the at-large city council, and nonpartisan elections.

3. Many major problems spread across the boundaries of many local governments. Political reformers have called for major structural reforms, especially in metropolitan areas. Those reforms are usually rejected by the voters, however; more modest reforms, such as metropolitan planning and councils of government, have proven more acceptable to the public. Informal cooperation among local governments is also fairly common, except on controversial issues.

4. The typical metropolis is not well organized to cope with contemporary social problems. Economic resources are often concentrated in jurisdictions with relatively few problems, while other jurisdictions have many problems and limited financial resources. That situation has contributed to growing state and federal involvement in the issues that cannot be resolved locally.

STUDY QUESTIONS

1. Why are there so many local governments in the United States? What are the different types of local governments?

2. Why did reformers dislike the political machines, and how did the reformers attack the machines? How did the unreformed, machine-style local government differ from the reformed local government?

3. The typical metropolitan area in the United States contains roughly 100 local governments. What problems can the many local governments create? How have reformers tried to deal with those problems, and why have they been relatively unsuccessful?

KEY TERMS

At-large election A city council or county commission election in which a candidate runs in the city or county as a whole rather than from a specific district.

City-county consolidation A reform strategy in which the city and its surrounding county are merged into a single government.

City manager A city chief executive who is a professionally trained administrator picked by the city council and serves at the pleasure of the council. City managers oversee city agencies and develop policy proposals to submit to the council.

Civil service A form of recruitment for government jobs in which people are hired on the basis of merit, as measured by their training, work experience, and performance on competitive examinations.

Commission government A form of city government in which the council members (commissioners) also serve as the city's executives, with individual council members in charge of individual departments.

Council of governments (COG) An agency composed of representatives from counties and larger municipalities, usually in a metropolitan area. The council meets to discuss issues facing the various local governments in the area.

County The general-purpose local government that is the basic geographic subdivision of the state and which usually plays a major role in administering many state programs. Used throughout the country.

County board of commissioners See *County board of supervisors*.

County board of supervisors The legislative body for the county in states where towns and governmental units have representatives on the board. Called *board of commissioners* in counties where the representatives come from districts or are elected at-large instead of coming from existing governmental units.

Dillon's Rule The legal principle that city government powers must be interpreted very narrowly.

Direct primary A means of nominating candidates for office. The nominees are chosen directly by the voters at the ballot box. Primaries may or may not be conducted with candidates identified by party.

Merit system (employment) A recruitment method for government jobs that hires and promotes people on the basis of their training and competence to perform specific jobs. See *Civil service*.

Metropolitan planning The attempt to develop long-range plans for land use and the extension of local government services throughout the metropolis.

Metropolitan statistical area (MSA) The official U.S. government definition of a metropolitan area. Prior to 1983, the term used was *standard metropolitan statistical area (SMSA)*.

Municipality A city government.

Nonpartisan election An election in which the party affiliation of the candidates is not printed on the ballot.

Ombudsman An office established to follow up on citizen complaints about government services and to get the complaints resolved.

Progressive Movement An early twentieth-century political movement that sought to replace boss-dominated machine-style politics with a less corrupt and less partisan form of politics.

School district A special-purpose government that runs a school system.

Short ballot An election in which only a few local officials are chosen by the voters.

Special district A government that performs only a single function, such as a waste-control commission or, less commonly, a small number of related functions.

Strong mayor A mayor who has power to appoint the city department heads, oversee the operations of city agencies, and the authority to develop proposals to submit to the city council. The strong mayor often has authority to veto bills passed by the city council.

Town A general-purpose form of local government especially prominent in New England.

Township A form of local government in rural areas, prominent in the Midwest. Traditionally, townships had responsibility for a number of programs, including transportation, but many states have shifted township responsibilities to county governments over the years.

Two-tier government A metropolitan reform strategy that divides public services into those to be performed by a metropolitanwide central government and those to be performed by local governments.

Volunteerism An ethic common in local officials; they believe they are serving as volunteers doing a civic duty rather than as professional politicians building a career. Officials with this viewpoint are often less interested in public opinion regarding local issues.

Weak mayor A mayor who cannot appoint the city department heads and who has little authority over the city council.

THE INTERNET CONNECTION

The International City/County Management Association conducts research on local government in the United States and prepares reference books and training materials to help local officials do a better job. It is an excellent reference source for anyone wanting to learn more about local government. You can contact this association at **www.icma.org**. An increasing number of individual local governments can also be reached on the Web, although the coverage of local Internet sites varies considerably. Pick two or three communities and compare what they offer on the Web. Does one offer more information than another? What services are offered on the Web site?

NOTES

1. The description of the city is derived from *The Beauty and Splendor of North America* (Montreal: Reader's Digest, 1995), p. 399; See *Atlas of America* (Pleasantville, NY: Reader's Digest, 1998).

2. Christopher Swope, "Master of the Public Realm," *Governing* 17, no. 2 (November 2003): 36.

3. For a useful overview of various types of local governments, see David Miller, *The Regional Governing of Metropolitan America* (Boulder, CO: Westview, 2002), ch. 3.

4. Susan MacManus, "Special District Governments: A Note on Their Use as Property Tax Relief Mechanisms in the 1970s," *Journal of Politics* 43 (1981): 207–214.

5. Virginia Marion, *Special Districts, Special Purposes: Fringe Governments and Urban Problems in the Houston Area* (College Station, TX: Texas A&M University Press, 1984). Also see Advisory Commission on Intergovernmental Relations, *The Problems of Special Districts in America*, Report A-22 (Washington, DC: U.S. Government Printing Office, 1964); and Advisory Commission on Intergovernmental Relations, *Regional Decision Making: New Strategies for Substate Districts* (Washington, DC: U.S. Government Printing Office, 1973), ch. 2; Nicholas Bauroth, "The Influence of Elections on Special District Revenue Policies: Special Democracies or Automatons of the State?," *State and Local Government Review* 37 (2005): 193–205.

6. Russell W. Maddox and Robert F. Fuquay, *State and Local Government*, 4th ed. (New York: Van Nostrand, 1981), p. 333.

7. Two students of New England local government argue that, even today, residents in places where town meetings exist are more knowledgeable about local government affairs than are residents in places without the town meeting. See William Doyle and Josephine F. Milburn, "Citizen Participation in New England Politics: Town Meetings, Political Parties, and Interest Groups," in Josephine F. Milburn and Victoria Schuck, eds. *New England Politics* (Cambridge, MA: Schenkman, 1981), pp. 36–37; Tod Newcombe, "267 Years and Counting," *Governing* (December 2010): pp. 33–37 .

8. John F. Dillon, *Commentaries on the Law of Municipal Corporations*, 5th ed. (Boston: Little, Brown and Co., 1911), Vol. I, sec. 237. For overviews of Dillon's Rule and chartering systems, see Thomas Marks and John Cooper, *State Constitutional Law in a Nutshell* (St. Paul: West, 1988), pp. 111–122, 193–207; David Nice and Patricia Fredericksen, *The Politics of Intergovernmental Relations*, 2nd ed. (Chicago: Nelson-Hall, 1995), pp. 147–153; David Berman, "State-Local Relations: Authority and Finances," in *The Municipal Year Book* (Washington, DC: International City/County Management Association, 2008), pp. 45–46; Adam Coester, "Dillon's Rule or Not," *Research Brief* (Washington, DC: National Association of Counties) 2, no. 1 (January 2004): 1–3.

9. David Berman, *Local Government and the States* (Armonk, NY: M. E. Sharpe, 2003), pp. 70–77; David Folz and P. Edward French, *Managing America's Small Communities* (Lanham, MD: Rowman and Littlefield, 2005), pp. 15–23.

10. Berman, "State-Local Relations," pp. 46–47.

11. For example, see Patrick McGreevy, "Cities, Counties Pay Price for Capitol Clout," *Los Angeles Times* (Web edition), September 10, 2007.

12. Katherine Barrett, Richard Greene, and Michele Mariani, "Grading the Counties," *Governing* 15, no. 5 (February 2002): 24.

13. Beverly A. Cigler, "County Governance in the 1990s," *State and Local Government Review* 27, no. 1 (Winter 1995): 57.

14. Ibid.

15. See "Inside the Year Book," in *The Municipal Yearbook* (Washington, DC: International City/County Manager Association, 2002), p. xiii.

16. Ibid.

17. J. Edwin Benton, "The Impact of Structural Reform on County Government Service Provision," *Social Science Quarterly* 84 (2003): 858–874.

18. Berman, "State-Local Relations," p. 48; Berman, *Local Government*, pp. 74–75.

19. Robert Agranoff and Michael McGuire, *Collaborative Public Management* (Washington, DC: Georgetown University, 2003).

20. See Alan Greenblatt, "Regional Agitator," *Governing* 14, no. 4 (April 2001): 25–29; Barrett, Greene, and Mariani, "Grading the Counties," pp. 20–39.

21. See Dennis Judd and Paul Kantor, eds., *American Urban Politics*, 4th ed. (New York: Pearson Longman, 2006), ch. 3.

22. Evelina Moulder, "Municipal Form of Government: Trends in Structure, Responsibility

and Composition," *Municipal Yearbook* (Washington, DC: International City/County Manager Association, 2008), p. 32; Tari Renner, "Municipal Election Processes: The Impact of Minority Representation," *Baseline Data Report* 19 (November–December 1987).

23. Robert L. Lineberry and Edmund P. Fowler, "Reformism and Public Policies in American Cities," *American Political Science Review* 61, no. 3 (September 1967): 701–716; Terry N. Clark, "Community Structure, Decision Making, Budget Expenditures and Urban Renewal in 51 American Communities," *American Sociological Review* 33, no. 4 (August 1968): 576–593.

24. See David Morgan and Robert England, *Managing Urban America*, 4th ed. (Chatham, NJ: Chatham House, 1996), pp. 96–97.

25. See Ibid., pp. 97–99; Folz and French, *Managing America's*, ch. 3.

26. Roy E. Green, *The Profession of Local Government Management: Management Expertise and the American Community* (New York: Praeger, 1989), p. 106. This survey, however, included county managers and council of government directors as well as city managers, so it is not conclusive that city managers were as active in campaigns as were the other types of managers.

27. One survey of more than 1,700 cities found that 94 percent of city managers sought to set the policy agenda for their city councils. Robert J. Huntley and Robert J. McDonald, "Urban Managers: Managerial Styles and Social Roles," *Municipal Yearbook, 1975* (Washington, DC: International City Management Association, 1975), pp. 149–159.

28. Clifford J. Wirth and Michael L. Vasu, "Ideology and Decision Making for American City Managers," *Urban Affairs Quarterly* 22, no. 3 (March 1987): 454–474.

29. David N. Ammons and Chaldean Newell, "City Managers Don't Make Policy: A Lie; 'Let's Face It,'" *National Civic Review* 77, no. 2 (March–April 1988): 124–132. Also see their "Role Emphases of City Managers and Other Municipal Executives," *Public Administration Review* 47, no. 3 (May–June 1987): 246–253.

30. Rob Gurwitt, "Can Dallas Govern Itself?," *Governing* 19, no. 11 (August, 2006): 42–47.

31. *Municipal Year Book* (Washington, DC: International City/County Manager Association, 2008), pp. 27–31.

32. Mike Hall, "Wagnon Lost Key Precincts," *The Topeka Capital-Journal*, March 4, 2001, pp. 1A, 7A.

33. The first four points are taken from Fred I. Greenstein, "The Changing Pattern of Urban Party Politics," *Annals of the American Academy of Political and Social Science* 353 (May 1964): 3.

34. Raymond E. Wolfinger, *The Politics of Progress* (Englewood Cliffs, NJ: Prentice-Hall, 1974), p. 69.

35. Steven P. Erie, *Rainbow's End: Irish-Americans and the Dilemmas of Urban Machine Politics, 1840–1985* (Berkeley, CA: University of California Press, 1988).

36. See "Nassau County, New York," *Governing* 15, no. 5 (February 2002): 24.

37. Robert K. Merton, *Social Theory and Social Structures* (Glencoe, IL: Free Press, 1957), pp. 78–82.

38. Wanda Demarzo and Jay Weaver, "Former Broward Sheriff Ken Jenne Facing Jail," *Miami Herald* (Web edition), September 4, 2007; Ian Lovett, "Bell, Calif. Voters Recall Government Officials," *New York Times*, March 9, 2011 (Web edition); Ken Ritter, "Former Las Vegas Commissioners Face Prison Time for Corruption, Bribery," *Daily Evergreen* (Pullman, WA), August 22, 2006, p. 5; Mike Robinson, "Chicago Mayor Wrestling with One Corruption Scandal After Another," *Moscow, ID/Pullman Daily News*, February 10, 2005, p. 9A; "Towns Co. Sheriff Pleads Guilty, Resigns," *Atlanta Journal-Constitution* (Web edition), August 21, 2007; Jeff Welan and Mark Mueller, "Statewide Sting Catches 11 Officials," *New Jersey Star-Ledger* (Web edition), September 7, 2007.

39. Samuel P. Hays, "The Politics of Reform in Municipal Government in the Progressive Era," *Pacific Northwest Quarterly* 55 (October 1964): 157–166.

40. Richard Hofstadter, *The Age of Reform: From Bryan to F.D.R.* (New York: Knopf, 1935), p. 181.

41. Ibid.

42. William Riordon, *Plunkitt of Tamany Hall* (Boston: Bedford Books of St. Martin's Press, 1994), pp. 11, 13.

43. The authors thank Professor Jeffrey Cohen of Fordham University for calling our attention to the role of internal conflicts, particularly over the choice of new leaders, in weakening the machines.

44. Carol A. Cassel, "Social Background Characteristics of Nonpartisan City Council Members: A Research Note," *Western Political Quarterly* 38, no. 3 (September 1985): 493–501.

45. Sidney Verba and Norman Nie, *Participation in America* (New York: Harper and Row, 1972), pp. 220–224.

46. Susan Blackall Hansen, "Participation, Political Structure, and Concurrence," *American Political Science Review* 69, no. 4 (December 1975): 1181–1199.

47. Kenneth Prewitt, "Political Ambitions, Volunteerism, and Electoral Accountability," *American Political Science Review* 67, no. 4 (December 1973): 1288–1307. For a discussion of why people decide to run or not run for city councils, see Susan MacManus, "The Resurgent City Councils," in Ronald Weber and Paul Brace, eds. *American State and Local Politics* (New York: Chatham House, 1999), pp. 185–190.

48. Timothy Krebs, "The Determinants of Candidates' Vote Share and the Advantages of Incumbency in City Council Elections," *American Journal of Political Science*, 42 (July 1998), pp. 921–935.

49. Norman R. Luttbeg, *Comparing the States and Communities: Politics, Government, and Policy in the United States* (New York: HarperCollins, 1992), pp. 206–207; *Moscow-Pullman Daily News,* October 30–31, 1999, pp. 6C–7C.

50. Albert Karnig and R. Oliver Walter, "Municipal Voter Turnout During the 1980s: The Case of Continued Decline," in Harry Bailey and Jay Shafritz, eds. *State and Local Government and Politics* (Itasca, IL: Peacock, 1993), pp. 26–38; William Fulton and Paul Shigley, "Addicted to Corruption," *Governing* 16, no. 2 (November 2002): 36–43; Elizabeth Daigneau, "San Bernardino Gets Its Due," *Governing* 18, no. 1 (October 2004): 68.

51. Lynn W. Bachelor, "The Impact of the Detroit Ombudsman on Neighborhood Service Delivery," A paper presented at the 1983 meeting of the Midwest Political Science Association, Chicago, April 1983.

52. Elaine B. Sharp and Allen Cigler, "The Impact of Televising City Council Meetings," A paper presented at the 1983 meeting of the Midwest Political Science Association, Chicago, April 1983.

53. Kay Schlozman, Sidney Verba, and Henry Brady, "Weapon of the Strong? Participatory Inequality and the Internet," *Perspectives on Politics*, 8 (June 2010), pp. 487–510.

54. Russell Smith, "The 'Electronic Village': Local Governments and E-Government at the Dawn of a New Millenium," *Municipal Yearbook* (Washington, DC: International City/County Management Association, 2002), pp. 34–41; Christopher Swope, "E-Gov's New Gear," *Governing* 17, no. 6 (March 2004): 40–43.

55. G. Ross Stephens and Nelson Wikstrom, *Metropolitan Government and Governance* (New York: Oxford, 2000), especially pp. 122–124. See also the symposium in the *State and Local Government Review* 2, no. 3 (Fall 2000).

56. See Daniel R. Grant, "Urban and Suburban Nashville: A Case Study in Metropolitanism," *Journal of Politics* 17, no. 1 (February 1955): 82–99; Brett W. Hawkins, *Nashville Metro: The Politics of City-County Consolidation* (Nashville, TN: Vanderbilt University Press, 1966); Alan Greenblatt, "Anatomy of a Merger," *Governing* 16, no. 3 (December 2002): 20–25. For general discussions of methods for dealing with fragmentation, see Lawrence Herson and John Bolland, *The Urban Web* (Chicago: Nelson-Hall, 1990), ch. 12; Nice and Fredericksen, *The Politics of Intergovernmental Relations*, pp. 207–214, and the studies they cite; also "Inside the Yearbook," *Municipal Year Book* (Washington, DC: International City/County Management Association, 2002), pp. xiii–xiv.

57. See Committee for Economic Development, *Reshaping Governments in Metropolitan Areas* (New York: Committee for Economic Development, 1970).

58. See Advisory Commission on Intergovernmental Relations, *A Look to the North Canadian Regional Experience,* vol. 5 of *Substate Regionalism and the Federal System* (Washington, DC: U.S. Government Printing Office, 1973), ch. 3, 6.

59. Vincent L. Marando, "City-County Consolidation: Reform, Regionalism, Referenda, and Requiem," *Western Political Quarterly* 32, no. 4 (December 1979): 409–422.

60. Sharon P. Krefetz and Alan B. Sharof, "City-County Merger Attempts: The Role of Political Factors," *National Civic Review* 66, no. 4 (April 1977): 178. For related discussions of forces promoting or maintaining fragmentation, see Nancy Burns, *The Formation of American Local Governments* (New York: Oxford, 1994); Anthony Down, *Opening Up the Suburbs* (New Haven: Yale, 1973); Miller, *The Regional Governing*, ch. 6–7.

61. Thomas A. Henderson and Walter A. Rosenbaum, "Prospects for Consolidation of Local Governments: The Role of Local Elites in Electoral Outcomes,"

American Journal of Political Science 17, no. 4 (November 1973): 695–720.

62. See Elinor Ostrom, "Metropolitan Reform: Propositions Derived from Two Traditions," *Social Science Quarterly* 53 (1972): 474–493.

63. See Kenneth T. Jackson, "Metropolitan Government Versus Suburban Autonomy: Politics on the Crabgrass Frontier," in Kenneth T. Jackson and Stanley K. Schultz, eds. *Cities in American History* (New York: Knopf, 1972), pp. 442–446.

64. Melvin B. Mogulof, *Five Metropolitan Governments* (Washington, DC: Urban Institute, 1973).

65. Alan Greenblatt, "Little Mergers on the Prairie," *Governing* 19, no. 10 (July 2006): 48–55.

66. Russell Nichols, "Selling Out," *Governing* (December 10, 2010): pp. 39–41.

67. Laurent Belsie, "Town Government... When There's Not Much Town to Govern," in Bruce Stinebrickner, ed. *State and Local Government,* 12th ed. (Dubuque, IA: McGraw-Hill/Dushkin, 2005); *Rural America at a Glance* (Washington, DC: Department of Agriculture, 2006).

68. J. Eric Oliver, "The Effects of Metropolitan Economic Segregation on Local Civic Participation," *American Journal of Political Science* 43 (January 1999): 186–212.

69. Joel Garreaux, *Edge City: Life on the New Frontier* (New York: Anchor Books, 1992).

70. Rob Gurwitt, "Connecting the Suburban Dots," *Governing* 17, no. 1 (October 2003): 36–40.

71. See the symposium in *State and Local Government Review* 32, no. 3 (Fall 2000).

72. For successful examples, see Christopher Swope, "The Return of the Planner," *Governing* 17, no. 8 (May 2004): 30–35; Christopher Swope, "A Wing and a Prayer," *Governing* 17, no. 4 (January 2004): 20–25; Rob Gurwitt, "Atlanta Reaches Out," *Governing* 17, no. 7 (April 2004): 22–27.

The Dynamics of Community Politics

CHAPTER PREVIEW

Having examined the institutions of local government in the previous chapter, in this chapter we go on to explore the dynamics of community politics today. We will discuss:

1 Competing theories for explaining who runs community politics.

2 Who governs in the age of urban restructuring.

3 Urban mayors and other local officials, and the quest for community leadership.

4 Urban mayors and the politics of ethnic change.

5 The challenge of the urban political economy.

Introduction

Michael Sessions is the mayor of Hillsdale, Michigan. Like many other small communities, Hillsdale has had some economic problems in recent years. Mayor Sessions decided to run in the hope that he could do something about those problems. He was elected after running an old-fashioned campaign, in which he personally visited almost every home in the community.[1]

As in many other communities, being mayor of Hillsdale is a part-time job. The mayor's salary is only $250 per month. The mayor spends a considerable amount of time reviewing various reports, attending meetings, appointing people to various committees, and discussing citizen concerns. His other job is also quite time consuming; he is a senior in high school.

Mayor Session's political career presents an image of local politics that many people approve. A candidate with a small campaign budget and considerable concern for the future of the community runs for office and wins. He divides his time between politics and his "regular" job rather than being a professional politician. His community was open to the entry of a new political leader.

Not everyone believes the situation in Hillsdale is common in local politics. According to a number of analysts, many communities are largely dominated by wealthy people who have the money, organization, and political connections to make the important decisions in their communities and to impose their wills on other people. We will explore that issue and several related issues in this chapter. Do rich people have more political clout than the rest of us? If they do, how much more clout do they have, and how is it exercised?

The controversy over money and political influence strikes directly at the fundamentals of our system of government because most of us are not extremely wealthy. What can ordinary citizens do to influence local policies and affect the way public services are delivered to them? Some pessimists think that most people can do very little and that power is concentrated in a very small, closely knit group of elites who dominate the lives of the rest of the people in their communities.[2]

Is this pessimistic view of elite dominance of community life accurate? Was it ever accurate? And whether or not it is accurate, what roles do interest groups, citizens, and political parties play in American communities? Are individual citizens gaining or losing influence over the public services that affect their lives? What are the dynamics of community politics?

To answer these questions, we must approach them from four different perspectives. First, we must examine two opposing theories about the way power is distributed in American communities. Second, we must explore the application of these and other theories to the contemporary scene in which economic change and international competition have undermined the economic security of many, if not most, American communities. Third, we must look at the mayor and other local officials as catalysts for local political change. And finally, we must examine the mayor's role in adapting city politics to three of the most forceful pressures on cities today: (1) the racial and ethnic cleavages that characterize many big cities, (2) the challenge of economic competition and development, and (3) the struggle to cope with possible terrorist threats and other emergencies.

THEORIES OF COMMUNITY POWER

Who really runs American communities? Some people think that community power resides in a core of wealthy persons who secretly control all key decisions. Others think that power is widely dispersed among a variety of interest groups that participate democratically in running the community. These two schools of thought are the *elitist* and the *pluralist* theories of community power. In either theory, power can be defined as the ability of groups or individuals to influence what a government does, although some versions of elitist theory also emphasize the social impact of nongovernmental decisions.[3]

The Elitist Theory of Community Power

The elitist theory was originally developed (in its modern form) by a small group of early twentieth-century European sociologists who viewed society as ruled by a relatively small group of leaders referred to as elites.[4] This view influenced American sociologists and anthropologists, who began conducting community studies during the 1920s and 1930s[5] and who often found that their communities were dominated by a small business elite.

One of the most influential of the elitist studies on local politics was Floyd Hunter's book *Community Power Structure*.[6] Hunter concluded that community politics in Regional City (Atlanta, Georgia) in the early 1950s was controlled by a small, closely knit group of elites. These elites were predominantly the people who ran the major business and economic institutions, many of which were linked together by people who invested in two or more of them, held official positions in two or more of them, or came from different firms but belonged to the same clubs and other organizations.

The elite controlled the city by manipulating local government officials. Further, power was viewed as cumulative in that the individual elite person who became powerful in the economic sphere also began to accumulate power in the social and political spheres. Social and political power might help the elite leader gain more economic power. Political decisions flowed from the elite down to ordinary citizens. Because he viewed Atlanta's power structure as a fairly stable, stratified pyramid, Hunter's theory is called **elitist theory** or **stratificationist theory**.

Hunter came to these conclusions using a research method called the **reputational approach**. He began by asking, "Who runs Regional City?" To identify the leadership, he compiled lists of prominent leaders in civic affairs, business, and society. He then selected a panel of knowledgeable people to examine the lists and to identify the most influential individuals and organizations. From these selections, Hunter identified 40 individuals who, in his opinion, constituted the top power structure in Regional City. Most of these 40 served on the boards of directors of the same corporations and belonged to the same social clubs. Beneath these top 40 leaders were dozens of other important but less prominent persons whom Hunter called *understructure personnel*. They carried out the instructions of the top leaders of the power structure.

Hunter contended that this elite group initiated most of the development that occurred in Regional City and that it successfully kept most projects it disliked from appearing on the decision-making agendas of the local governments.[7] Enterprising newspaper or journal writers lost their jobs when they disagreed with the ruling elite. Social welfare professionals carefully avoided raising issues that might violate the interests of the power structure. Hunter pictured the governor, the U.S. senators, the key state legislators, the party leaders, and most other officials as subordinated to the top power structure. The people for whom ordinary citizens vote, therefore, are not the true policy makers.[8]

This elitist theory rapidly came under criticism,[9] particularly from political scientists who objected to Hunter's conclusion that the political structures were subservient to monolithic economic institutions. Hunter's critics also objected to his assumptions about power and his methods of researching power. By asking knowledgeable observers to identify the most influential leaders, said Hunter's critics, he had not really measured the exercise of power; he had merely measured the reputation for power.[10] To make a valid measurement of power, they argued, one would have to analyze the actual decisions through which power was in fact exercised.

The Pluralist Theory of Community Power

The first major attempt to measure power through a **decision-making approach** was Robert Dahl's study of New Haven, Connecticut, and was reported in his book *Who Governs?*[11] This and several other decision-making studies that followed spelled out the principles of **pluralist theory**.[12] Rather than believing that power is stratified, pluralists generally found that a plurality of power centers exists in a city—labor unions, political parties, banks, manufacturing plants, churches, school systems, and government agencies. These power centers compete with each other democratically, and public policy emerges out of their competition. Most of these power centers are powerful only within particular functional areas. Many of the participants dealing with one policy issue will not be involved in other issues, in part because many people are only interested in a limited range of issues.

Pluralists also reject the elitist implication that some permanent, vague power holders control situations from behind the scenes. Rather, power exists only when it is exercised through specific decisions by specific individuals or groups. Finally, pluralists reject the elitist's belief that power is necessarily cumulative; a person could be politically influential without being economically powerful, or economically powerful but politically unimportant.

Dahl set out to explore the distribution of power and influence in New Haven. He analyzed a number of important governmental decisions during the 1940s and 1950s. Contrary to Hunter's findings, Dahl found that *no significant overlap* existed between the economic, political, and social elites, that economic and social elites had little influence on the decisions he studied, and that power in New Haven was *noncumulative*—that is, power in one functional area did not lead to power in other functional areas.

In the issue areas that concerned him, Dahl conducted extended interviews with 46 top decision makers. He found very few instances in which an individual person was involved in more than one major decision, let alone more than one issue area. The exception to this was the mayor of New Haven, Richard C. Lee. Lee was a supreme political tactician at bargaining with leaders of all the functional power centers in New Haven, plus some others in federal and state agencies that ran programs in the city. Through his bargaining skill, he successfully started and carried out the kinds of programs he thought the city needed to grow and prosper. Dahl perceived Mayor Lee as occupying the critical position in what Dahl referred to as an "executive-centered coalition" of a plurality of interest groups in New Haven. Because this view sees power as noncumulative and dispersed among several power centers, Dahl's theories about community power are called *pluralist* theories. They imply (and sometimes state) that ordinary people are able to exert significant influence over governmental decisions because of the competition among different groups.

Early Refinements of the Two Models of Community Power

Following the publication of the initial studies by Hunter and Dahl, increasingly sophisticated research methods were used to examine every conceivable subtlety of these two models[13] (see Table 7.1 for a summary). Three issues, in particular, kept recurring in these studies: the role of business, the importance of nondecisions, and the great variety of power relationships that exist.

The Role of Business   Subsequent research has raised questions regarding whether top businesspeople operate as a cohesive clique and dominate city public affairs, the picture that Hunter presented in Atlanta. However, it is conceivable that Hunter's observations of Atlanta were accurate for that period and that businesspeople did indeed dominate the city's politics during the early 1950s. Hunter's findings of business dominance are consistent with the overwhelming majority of early anthropological and sociological community studies.

Many other communities in addition to Muncie and Atlanta seem to have had a particular business elite that dominated local affairs. United States Steel Corporation planned and built Gary, Indiana, and exercised considerable influence over its government. The Mellon family, which has had great wealth for years, had disproportionate influence in Pittsburgh. A field representative of the Bank of California eventually gave the bank effective control of the ore-processing facilities in Virginia City, Nevada, and enormous financial leverage over the silver mine owners. That

> ### TABLE 7.1
>
> #### Key Tenets of the Pluralist and Elitist Theories
>
> | Issue | Pluralist Tenet | Elitist Tenet |
> |---|---|---|
> | Locus of political power | In individual actions and individual competence, along with group organizations | In positions of economic and institutional leadership |
> | Structure of power | Divided among competing power centers | Stratified in pyramid form, a small group rules |
> | Nature of power | Not cumulative; power in one area does not necessarily lead to power in a different area | Cumulative; power in one area tends to lead to power in different areas as well |
> | Most common approach to identifying powerholders | Decision-making analysis | Reputational analysis |
> | Exercise of power | Through decisions only (mainly governmental) | Through decisions and nondecisions (including private decisions) |
> | Role of business community | The business community is only one of many competing power centers; the great diversity of business interests makes it impossible to speak of *the* business-community interest | Business is the dominant interest in the community; despite its diversity, there is considerable unity on issues important to top business leaders |

field representative went on to found a new railroad to serve the city and its mines and became tremendously wealthy when very large deposits of silver were discovered under the city.[14] One-company mining towns often stayed under the control of their patrons for decades, and many small localities today have an economy dominated by a handful of businesses.

Business groups gain political influence because they represent a large portion of the tax base in many communities and because they control many jobs. If a major business closes its doors and moves away, the tax base shrinks and people lose their jobs. Local officials cannot afford to antagonize the leaders of those major businesses very often without risking great harm to the community.[15]

Very wealthy individuals and the owners and managers of major businesses can afford to hire experts to produce analyses supporting what the elites want and to draft proposals.[16] Wealthy people also make a considerable share of the campaign contributions each year; as we saw earlier, campaign funds are very important influences over election outcomes, particularly in larger jurisdictions. Wealthy people can more easily afford legal representation, which is vital if they want to fight some action in court.

Wealthy business leaders can also afford to create and support think tanks and legal foundations to help publicize their views and to present them in meetings of local officials, the mass media, and the courts.[17] Wealthy leaders can also afford to buy advertising to present their views and to influence the news media. The ordinary person cannot afford to counter those efforts, by and large.

Divisions Among Business Leaders

Despite the factors that enhance the influence of wealthy people and business leaders, these individuals do not always agree among themselves. Downtown businesspeople may clash with developers who are working on a new shopping mall at the edge of town. Owners of businesses that don't pollute may criticize owners of companies that cause pollution. Different types of businesses may have very different needs; a company burning large quantities of coal usually needs a railroad line to handle the coal, but a computer software firm may be more affected by the number of suitably educated people in the area.

In the years that have passed since the first community power studies were conducted, many sectors of the economy have come to be increasingly dominated by national and international corporations rather than local companies. This means that business leadership in a community is often divided between a local group of business leaders who are very much interested in local affairs and who often have deep roots in the community, and the managers of national and international corporations whose careers and interests impel them to pay more attention to the affairs of their corporation than to local politics. Many of those leaders do not have deep roots in the community where they work and may expect to move on before long.[18] They will be interested in local government actions that affect their companies directly, but may otherwise have little interest in local politics.

The business sector is not only divided between the owners of local businesses and the managers of national/international corporations but it is also divided into several functional categories. Few businesspeople exhibit much interest in public issues that lie beyond their functional sphere. Thus, urban renewal agencies routinely seek out the advice and collaboration of real estate brokers, builders, and the financial community, whereas many other kinds of businesspeople—such as retail merchants, automobile dealers, and shopping center owners— are often quite uninterested, unless a proposed project might attract more customers to, or repel them from, the business's locations. Owners and managers of restaurants and hotels are interested in promoting tourism in the area, but many other businesses may be uninterested in tourism. Owners of factories and retail stores have a strong interest in the local transportation system, which affects shipments of merchandise, but some computer programming firms may care more about the telecommunications system. Utilities seek to promote growth of a community's population, income, and employment, whereas railroads often display little interest in local politics, with some important exceptions.[19]

Because of this divergence of interests, the business community (at least in larger localities) is not necessarily as cohesive in its approach to local politics as the Hunter portrayal suggests. And the resources that businesspeople have to influence public affairs depend on the functional area involved, the issue, the interests of the businesspeople, and the unity with which they can act.

Bear in mind, however, that one or two very large companies may exert considerable influence even without the support of other businesses. If a great many jobs are at stake, if a considerable portion of the local tax base is at risk, or if the community's image may be affected, local officials may feel considerable pressure to go along with what the heads of those companies want. If the officers of a large corporation threaten to close their local office and move elsewhere, local officials are likely to be far more worried than if a few blue-collar workers threaten to move away from the area if their demands are not met.

The practice of having private companies help in delivering public services (see Chapter 10) can also enhance business influence. Once a company becomes heavily dependent on a local government for business, the company's owners and managers have a very strong incentive to elect friendly officials to office and to keep close tabs on their actions. Moreover, the companies helping to provide services may quietly shape the nature of those services, in part by bargaining with public officials regarding how a job should be done.[20]

The Importance of Nondecisions   If subsequent research on the role of business people in city politics cast some doubt on the notion that they consistently form a cohesive, well-organized bloc, it also found flaws in the decision-making approach to analyzing community power. Political scientists Peter Bachrach and Morton S. Baratz charged that the concentration on governmental decisions (especially high-visibility decisions) ignores "the fact that power may be, and often is, exercised by confining the scope of decision-making to relatively 'safe' issues."

> Of course power is exercised when A participates in the making of decisions that affect B. But power is also exercised when A devotes his energies to creating or reinforcing social and political values and institutional practices that limit the scope of the political process to public consideration of only those issues which are comparatively innocuous to A. To the extent that A succeeds in doing this, B is prevented, for all practical purposes, from bringing to the fore any issues that might in their resolution be seriously detrimental to A's set of preferences.[21]

Such an exercise of power is referred to as coming to **nondecisions**. This is a form of "preemptive power" according to Clarence Stone.[22] Only certain kinds of questions are put on the agendas of decision-making agencies. Other kinds of questions are never put on those agendas and hence never reach the point where public decisions about them can be made. In addition, some policy options may be excluded because they are treated as "too extreme" or criticized for creating "class conflict" or being "un-American."

Note, too, that not all important decisions are necessarily made by government. If the owners of a large private company decide to close their doors and eliminate many people's jobs, the community may be seriously affected. Changing the curriculum of a large private school system may affect the quality of the future labor force and the community's culture. Closing a major church or a prolonged strike at a large private company may significantly influence life in a community without ever reaching a governmental decision-making arena.

Furthermore, some people have fewer resources for waging political battles than do others. The people with few resources frequently lose these battles, and they quite often are the poorest people in the city. Many issues stay in the realm of nondecisions because these people lack either the resources or the confidence in the political system to fight for their concerns. In the words of Clarence Stone, "Because people have no taste for waging costly battles they are sure to lose, much goes uncontested."[23] People who are not active in the political process are more easily ignored than are people who are active.[24]

In a related vein, the resources and skills needed to develop a plausible policy proposal (which can help get an issue onto the agenda) are unevenly spread across a community. People who are wealthy, who control large organizations, or who have specialized training have a much easier time generating a policy proposal and amassing evidence on its behalf. The head of a large corporation may be in a better position to develop and press for a major policy initiative than are many city councils, which are often hamstrung by internal conflicts, a lack of staff support, and parochialism.[25]

The Variety of Power Relationships   Finally, pluralists point out that power is (or might be) structured differently in different communities, and the structures may change over time.

Atlanta today is vastly different not only from the New Haven that Dahl studied, but even from the Atlanta that Hunter studied in the early 1950s. For one thing, it has an African American majority today compared to only a minority at the time of Hunter's analysis. Atlanta has had African American mayors for the past two decades, an accomplishment that would have been impossible if the city's power structure were still the same as the one described by Hunter.

Highly stratified power structures are most likely to be found where city leaders share a consensus on the role of government with reformed governmental structures, and where power is not shared extensively with the mass of the people. Highly stratified power structures are also most likely to be found in isolated communities dominated by a single industry, where businesses are owned by people living elsewhere, in small homogeneous communities, and in the South.[26] Pluralist power structures are most likely to be found in metropolitan areas, communities with a heterogeneous population, and communities with a diversity of economic foundations and social cleavages.

Power structures may also shift in the face of a major crisis, which can push aside established patterns of influence. When the state of Rhode Island appointed a retired judge to straighten out the finances of Central Fall, Rhode Island, the judge moved quickly to greatly reduce the mayor's authority and his salary and fired one of his top aides. The judge also has the authority to exercise the powers of the city council if he wishes.[27] More dramatically, many groups in New York City put aside their differences after the September 11 attacks and pooled their efforts to help the city rebuild and to help the many people traumatized by the attacks.

The wave of corporate scandals that has engulfed a number of major corporations demonstrates that power and influence can be very fragile. For a number of years, the leaders of Enron socialized with many important state and local government leaders in Texas. They made generous campaign contributions to many of them, including President George W. Bush, and their political influence appeared to be considerable. However, the company's financial collapse and the many accusations of wrongdoing that accompanied the collapse led many Texas officials to distance themselves as far as possible from Enron's leaders. A number of other business leaders have had similar experiences in recent years. The collapse of the home mortgage market in 2008, with accusations of corruption and incompetence, has eroded the position of a number of leaders of banks and savings and loan companies, in part by greatly reducing their financial power.

Some public officials have also found that power can be fragile. Baltimore mayor Sheila Dixon was driven from office when she admitted being involved in embezzlement and perjury. A member of the Kildeer, Illinois, board of trustees resigned in protest after the board agreed to hire the mayor's brother-in-law as the village administrator. The once-peaceful local politics of Tulsa, Oklahoma, has been replaced by angry wrangling among city council members (sometimes reaching the level of lawsuits against one another) and a major corruption scandal in the city's police department. The mayor of Sheboygan, Wisconsin, was recently driven from office after revelations of drinking problems and sexual harassment accusations became public.[28]

WHO GOVERNS IN THE AGE OF URBAN RESTRUCTURING?

By the end of the 1970s, these four statements reasonably summarized the dispute over community power: The role of business is a great deal more complex than the elitists and pluralists had portrayed it. But the existence of nondecisions and the importance of nongovernmental decisions give business a larger role than pluralists initially admitted. The structure of power relationships varies from place to place and from time to time. Finally, urban bureaucracies in some of the largest cities have considerable power of their own, some of it arising from their ties to similar bureaucratic specialists at the state and federal levels, many of whom administer grant programs used to help support local services.

While these debates over community power were raging, the cities themselves were undergoing a dramatic restructuring that neither elitists nor pluralists could explain very well. Especially prominent were the eruption of riots during the 1960s, the economic decline of many cities, widespread fiscal stress in the late 1970s, a global economic restructuring that wreaked havoc on many old manufacturing cities, and the impressive downtown and economic redevelopment schemes that blossomed across the land. In terms of their ethnic base, their economic base, and their physical appearance, American cities in the last third of the twentieth century experienced one of the greatest restructurings that had occurred to any system of cities in history. At the same time, many rural areas and small towns faced a loss of jobs and population, and officials scrambled for ideas that might stop the decline of their communities. Many localities were also hit very hard by the recession that began in 2007–2008. Many observers, including a number of members of the Occupy Wall Street movement, also noted the growing inequality in the American distribution of income and wealth.

If the stratificationists were correct that a small group of business elites controlled the cities for their own benefit, why would they have collaborated with the economic disinvestment that has been so disastrous for so many central cities and also for many small towns and rural counties? And why did so many of the economic redevelopment schemes appear to originate not in company board rooms but in city halls? If the pluralists were correct in their optimistic view that a plurality of interest groups governed the city through competition and coalitions, then how do we explain the fact poorer people are frequently and recurrently left out of the governing coalition? We might try to explain it by their low rates of political participation, but why are so few people trying to mobilize them? If many local groups have influence, why have so many economic development efforts had so little payoff at the neighborhood level?

These questions are very difficult to answer within the framework of early elitist or pluralist theories. But just as nature cannot tolerate a vacuum, the human mind cannot tolerate unexplainable facts.[29] So it is not surprising that new theories emerged to answer the perplexing question of who governs in the current age of urban restructuring. As cities struggle to cope with the task of urban restructuring and as smaller towns and rural counties struggle to adapt to a changing world, who has the most influence? How is it exerted? And who benefits?

Dominance by Global Capital

One group of analysts, some of them neo-Marxian, believe that communities are increasingly at the mercy of global economic forces. A city needs business activity to prosper, and many business decisions today extend beyond individual communities, states, and countries. Cities must compete with each other to attract employers, and a fundamental problem facing many American cities (especially old manufacturing centers such as Detroit or Gary, Indiana) and smaller towns is that they are less competitive than they once were. The same plight may befall any number of other communities in the near future.[30]

From this viewpoint, the old industrial cities like Detroit and Gary were built a century ago when labor-intensive industrial manufacturing required large numbers of unskilled laborers to be assembled in concentrated areas. It was the job of the city to provide the sewers, streets, and other infrastructure that would enable this concentration of laborers to take place.

For today's automated, capital-intensive factory, however, large concentrations of workers are not as vital as they once were. Automation and computers enable machines and robots to perform many repetitive tasks more efficiently and cheaply than human laborers can.

Not only are many modern factories capital intensive rather than labor intensive, but capital is also mobile; corporations can move the production facilities out of troublesome spots into more receptive locations. Communities, by contrast, are stationary; you cannot move Detroit to the sunbelt. Detroit, in fact, suffered from the loss of capital for years, as corporations closed down plants in the city and built new ones in the suburbs, in the sunbelt, or overseas. Between 1960 and 1976, Detroit lost 200,000 jobs, about 30 percent of all the jobs that had existed only 16 years earlier, in 1960.[31]

In the late 1970s, when General Motors decided to invest $40 billion to build new automobile production plants, there were probably 100 places around the globe that might have been suitable. Detroit spent over $200 million to prepare a site in order to attract the new plants, and critics complained that the city might never recoup the cost of getting the plants. Similar, sometimes more costly, development schemes have taken place in other states and communities, and some of them have involved large amounts of state and/or local funds going to attract companies that are profitable, a practice leading to complaints of "corporate welfare." We will examine some of those efforts in Chapter 17.

The neo-Marxian perspective is consistent with some dynamics of local politics, but much is left unexplained. Not all local issues are economic; many people are interested in noneconomic issues, such as abortion, school prayer, or family violence.[32] The leaders of many large corporations may have little interest in those types of issues and, consequently, leave other people a clear field to influence public decisions. In addition, as noted earlier in the chapter, business interests are not necessarily monolithic. When business leaders cannot agree on a course of action, their influence is likely to be reduced.

Furthermore, when people feel strongly about an issue, they may be willing to stand up even to very large corporations. For example, the managers of police and fire department pension funds in New York City recently submitted questions to three large corporations regarding their dealings with countries that support terrorism. The pension managers, acting at the prodding of their members, clearly intended to remove their pension funds from companies that gave unsatisfactory answers.[33] The enormous amounts of money in state and local government pension funds may give larger localities some leverage over businesses.

People in some communities are also giving more attention to the localized problems that business development may cause. Voters in Inglewood, California, rejected a package of proposals to enable Wal-Mart to build a new store in the city. Residents complained that the new store would generate too much traffic, drive local, independent firms out of business, and aggravate urban sprawl.[34] If economic power alone had been decisive, Wal-Mart would have gotten its way.

Bear in mind, too, that capital is not always very mobile. A company may invest considerable sums in a facility that cannot be moved very readily. In addition, a particular location may have special attractions that make some business leaders unwilling to relocate. In that context, local officials may have significant bargaining leverage over businesses.[35]

A community may also try to revitalize its economy without emphasizing large corporations. The community may instead try to develop smaller local firms with roots in the area; many places have tried this strategy with tourism in recent years. Alternatively, a number of small towns recently began a new initiative to boost their communities by trying to attract new families rather than businesses. The communities are offering families free or nearly free land in neighborhoods with complete utilities (water and sewer lines, access to electric power, streets, and so forth) already in place.[36] This inducement alone is probably not enough to attract many people, but if a community has other assets as well, such as relatively inexpensive housing, an attractive environment for raising children, and jobs within reasonable commuting distance, the tactic may have some promise.

Growth-Machine Theory

To a second school of thought about urban restructuring, the most important force is what sociologist Harvey Molotch called "a growth machine."[37] Molotch argues that local elites with substantial local land holdings dominate community policy making and that these leaders' common interest lies in promoting growth. Growth will make their land more valuable. To safeguard their investments, these local, land-based elites dominate local government and seek to co-opt local political leaders by bringing them into the pro-growth machine.

Growth-machine theory differs from global capital theory in at least two key respects. First, the goal of the growth machine is not to *maximize profit* from selling goods and services in a national or global market, as is the goal of many corporations. Rather, the goal of the growth machine is to *maximize rental return* through renting (or selling) space to the businesses and people who will use the facilities developed by the growth machine.[38] Second, due to its interests in land use rather than in maximizing profit, the growth machine is not composed of the national upper class or even the leaders of the national or international corporations. Instead, the elites of the growth machine are local real estate owners, bankers, developers, construction unions, and local newspapers and television stations whose circulations, ratings, and advertising revenues will expand with growth in the metropolis.

In dealing with the growth machine, city government plays two conflicting roles. First, it must support the growth machine's promotion of economic growth and redevelopment, on the grounds that growth will bring in the jobs for city residents and will make land in the region more valuable, which will increase property tax revenues. Second, since it represents people in local neighborhoods, city government often finds itself playing an intermediary role in the conflicts that arise when neighborhood residents oppose particular redevelopment projects. City officials may also play that intermediary role when different businesses have different interests or priorities. The growth machine perspective alerts us to the possibility that city officials and business leaders may have common goals, in which case determining who is influencing whom is very difficult.[39]

Some communities are also pursuing growth by strategies other than large-scale business and residential development. One approach that is being tried in a number of places, mostly smaller communities, is to promote development that is tied to a local college or university. By adding a limited range of amenities to the attractions offered by the typical college (including sports events, concerts, plays, and guest speakers, among other things), advocates hope to promote development in terms of small businesses and small projects. Some larger communities are trying similar strategies, with the addition of health care facilities and a limited number of large businesses.[40]

Immigrants have provided another unconventional method for economic revival in some declining areas. Utica, New York, lost considerable population in the last 50 years but has recently attracted a considerable number of immigrants from various parts of the world, including many from Eastern Europe. Many of the immigrants have brought skills and energy, reviving older businesses and starting new, small businesses as well.[41] A number of declining communities on the Great Plains have undergone unexpected revivals with the arrival of many Hispanic immigrants (some from outside the United States and some from other parts of the United States), who have reopened businesses, repaired and moved into abandoned or decaying homes, and boosted enrollment in local schools and membership in local churches.[42]

Cities as a Unitary Interest

In contrast to the neo-Marxist and growth-machine interpretations of urban decline and redevelopment is Paul Peterson's concept of *unitary interest,* spelled out in his highly influential 1981 book *City Limits.*[43] The heart of Peterson's theory focuses on the role that city governments can effectively play in the local political economy. Peterson placed great emphasis on the role of investment capital in determining the fate of cities. Cities are in competition with each other to capture as much investment capital as they can. A city also has "export" industries (computer hardware and software in Silicon Valley, health services in Cleveland, casinos and hotels in Las Vegas) that provide many jobs and bring money into the city from people who live elsewhere.

In Peterson's view, the business leaders of the city, its political leaders, and ordinary residents have a *unitary interest* in protecting those export industries and helping attract new investment capital that will help them expand in the future. Thus, it is not a "growth machine" of certain business leaders that impels the mayor to pursue downtown redevelopment; it is simply a mutual recognition of the best interests of all the city's residents.

This argument provides a powerful justification for the economic redevelopment activities of most cities. But, like the other theories, it too has been criticized.[44] The key interests of business leaders sometimes diverge sharply from those of political leaders. Although political leaders may care most about maximizing the city's export industries, the self-interest of most corporate leaders necessarily lies in maximizing the profits of their particular businesses or maximizing their own personal incomes, and in many instances these goals are unrelated to the well-being of the communities in which the corporation resides. Very wealthy individuals may also provide themselves with private services, including schools and security forces, instead of working to improve public services.

Finally, neighborhood residents might or might not benefit from development projects. Certainly the U.S. economy nationally has not benefited everyone proportionally in recent years. Instead, the distribution of income since 1970 has grown more unequal, with the highest income families increasing their income share while the 60 percent of families with the lowest incomes saw their shares declining.[45]

Another facet of conflicts erupting over some economic development involves recent drilling for oil and natural gas in various parts of the country. Some of this exploration has been in communities with little experience in drilling, and some is taking place where people who own the top layer of land do not have the rights to control mineral development beneath that land. Oil and gas exploration in some areas has clashed with residential real estate development needed to cope with population growth. Critics have charged that hydrofracking, which injects a mixture of hot water, chemicals, and sand into rock layers to help release natural gas, has polluted groundwater and may have caused earthquakes in at least one area.[46]

Some critics of the business-growth oriented model argue that strengthening neighborhoods is a more important unitary interest of a city than is downtown redevelopment. If crime rates are low, the middle class is not moving out, city services are good, and schools are excellent, then a city will be a very attractive location for many kinds of businesses. This is precisely the situation in many suburban cities. But simply redeveloping the central-city downtown or putting in an automobile production plant will not necessarily pull in the middle class, improve the schools, reduce the crime rates, or make the neighborhoods better places in which to live. Stronger neighborhoods may not interest some major business leaders, however, who might prefer boosting their companies' profits. At any rate, a single, united economic interest may not exist in some communities.

Different Regimes for Different Cities

One of the strongest critics of the idea of a unitary interest has been Clarence Stone, who argues that each city has a dominant coalition of interests that create an "Urban Regime."[47] The urban regime consists of a working relationship between three power clusters in cities: (1) a pro-growth business elite, (2) the elected city government leaders and their top appointees, and (3) city residents and the variety of neighborhood groups, labor union locals, political party organizations, and other political groups to which the residents belong. The mayor is usually elected to office by the voters. But once in office, the mayor and other top political leaders can gain relatively few additional rewards from the city voters or their representative groups. Instead, it is the business leaders and, to a lesser extent, other institutional elites who control access to many of the things that local officials are likely to want (a thriving city economy, a successful administration, prestige, respect, and possibly future employment at a high salary). Ordinary voters can give a mayor respect, prestige in some respects, cooperation, and their support on some occasions (especially if the mayor and/or city council must submit a proposal to the voters or want to run for reelection or another public office), but those rewards may seem minor compared with what business leaders may be able to offer.

Because they control access to the goals that many mayors and other local officials seek, business and institutional elites exercise *systemic power* over the city government, according to Stone.[48] Their exercise of power will seldom be overt, but the mayor and other city leaders may psychically identify with the top institutional elite rather than with the general public. Local officials will anticipate the reactions of business leaders to city initiatives before the initiatives are taken. And it makes little difference if the mayor is black, white, male, female, Democrat, or Republican. Mayors and other local officials generally "find themselves rewarded for cooperating with upper-strata interests and unrewarded or even penalized for cooperating with lower-strata interests."[49]

What is at work in most cities, according to Stone, is a regime of systemic power. There is no unitary interest binding the general public, business leaders, and city officials. Rather, successful elected officials align themselves with the upper-strata interests of the area and keep themselves in power by convincing a majority of the average voters (which will be a minority of the public in most local elections) that all this will benefit them in the long run.

What is important, in Stone's analysis, is to determine what sort of regime dominates in a given metropolis. The *entrepreneurial* or *corporate regime* is devoted primarily to downtown development policy, and in towns with corporate regimes, local officials will not have much success reorienting the city's priorities toward serving its neighborhoods or its disadvantaged residents. Cities with a *progressive regime,* however, provide greater leeway for local officials to expand services and shift priorities to neighborhoods. In Boston, for example, Mayor Raymond Flynn was able to follow several redistributive policies. He instituted a "linkage" program that required large developers to contribute to a trust fund that the city used for housing and job-training purposes. Flynn also curbed the conversion of apartments into condominiums and required large residential development projects to earmark 10 percent of their space for low- and moderate-income renters.[50] These types of initiatives are more likely to be successful if business leaders believe there are considerable advantages to being in the community and/or personally believe that they have an obligation toward the less fortunate.

The Pluralist Rebuttal

In the final analysis, it may be that there are just too many kinds of communities in the United States, and the local restructuring that has been going on since the 1950s may be too complex for any single theory to explain who governs the city. What is true of one locality might not apply to a different one. Clarence Stone's analysis of the mayor's dependence on growth-oriented business elites for the success of his or her administration is probably accurate for Atlanta and other cities with a corporate-dominated urban regime. Lawrence, Kansas, by contrast, has a strong tradition of citizen activism, and for more than a decade local residents successfully prevented the construction of a downtown shopping mall dearly wanted by the city's local business leaders.[51] The growth machine there was clearly not dominant. Particularly in reasonably prosperous communities, people may regard growth for growth's sake as a threat to their quality of life.

Not only does the nature of the urban regime differ from place to place, but different theories lead us to focus on different aspects of the same event. This is why various observers can look at the same political situation and reach significantly different conclusions. Suppose that a local government spends money attracting a new business to a city. From the growth machine and global capital perspectives, that action looks like local officials caving into pressure from business groups. From the viewpoint of unitary interest theory, if the business brings new jobs to the area, increases the tax base, and enhances the appeal of the community, many people benefit from the local government's action.

To other observers, the same action appears to be old-fashioned pluralism.[52] The business owners are likely to be primarily interested in profits and may have little or no interest in the community, especially if they have no previous roots in the area. Smart business owners and managers are also concerned about the reputations of their firms. Local officials are likely to be much more interested in the community generally and in the community's ability to finance basic services. People who need jobs are likely to be particularly interested in how many people will be hired, what skills they will need, and pay and benefits. People who live near the location of the new business may be concerned about traffic and environmental consequences of the new firm's operations.

The distribution of influence may also vary from one decision to another. The decision to close a manufacturing plant may be made by a group of business leaders hundreds or even thousands of miles away. An anti-crime initiative may be shaped by elected officials, the better-trained members of the police force and local prosecutors, and policy researchers at universities nearby. The conduct of an emergency rescue may be shaped by the firefighters and paramedics on the scene. The success of a policy to manage traffic may hinge on whether the driving public decides to cooperate with or ignore the policy.

Research on the influence of many different types of groups in many different communities and other settings found that more prosperous groups are indeed more influential, in part because they are more active, better organized, and larger. However, they also found that the influence of both relatively prosperous groups and relatively poor groups varied from one community to another.[53]

In sum, a rich variety of research has emerged in recent years seeking to explain the role of local government in the local political economy. Global capital theorists see local governments as virtually helpless in the face of world economic realities. Growth-machine theorists and regime theorists focus on a local, land-based elite and its relations with the local political system. Peterson's unitary interest theory focuses on the proper role for city government to play in handling urban problems and on the very real limits confronting those governments. And pluralists generally tend to reaffirm local government's independence in these conflicts, asserting that it is not simply a passive actor playing out a predetermined role.

Note, too, that the position of businesses and industries can fluctuate over time. During 2007 and 2008, the housing market declined in many parts of the country, and that decline set off problems in many lending institutions. The U.S. auto industry suffered a major slump that was partly due to the dramatic rise of fuel prices. Manufacturing employment fell considerably from 2000 to 2005, with some jobs moving overseas and others replaced by automation.[54] When companies are in financial trouble, their political power is likely to decline.

THE QUEST FOR LOCAL LEADERSHIP

Whatever the nature of the forces that are restructuring American localities today, local leaders must respond in ways that help the community prosper, although local politics is about more than just prosperity. The political leader who is best positioned to lead that response is usually the local chief executive—frequently the mayor.

The Changing Setting for Mayoral Leadership

Being mayor of a sizable city is one of America's impossible jobs.[55] It is "fun and exciting, but there's no future in it," said Boston's legendary mayor James Curley.[56] There is no future in it because, with a few notable exceptions (such as Pete Wilson of San Diego, Federico Peña of Denver, Henry Cisneros of San Antonio, or Richard Lugar of Indianapolis), most mayors do not move up to higher elective or appointive office. And it is an impossible job because the mayor is held responsible for solving the city's many problems while he or she is seldom given the resources to make a noticeable dent in those problems.

In large part, as a result of the Progressive Reform movement, the devices for accumulating political power have been weakened. The mayor's formal powers are sharply restricted by the state constitution, the legislature, and the city charter. Many of the most important governing functions in cities are carried out not by the city government but by other governments. Public health and welfare are usually administered by the counties; public transit, sewers, and airports are often under the control of metropolitan agencies; and schools are usually run by independent school districts. Even within the city government, the mayor often faces strong resistance from city council members who have their own agendas to push and are not too inclined to defer to the mayor.[57] Many council members would be happier with the chief executive's power vested in a city manager rather than a mayor.[58] The city manager by definition is supposed to implement the council's goals, but the mayor is likely to have goals of his or her own (Note: city managers often do, too). In addition to assertive city council members, there has been a growth in interest groups, neighborhood groups, ideological groups, and ethnic groups that all want a say in how the city conducts its business, as do many city employees.

TABLE 7.2

Preconditions for Mayoral Leadership

Governmental, or Formal, Preconditions

1. Sufficient financial resources with which a mayor can launch innovative social programs
2. City jurisdiction in the vital program areas of education, housing, redevelopment, and job training
3. Mayoral jurisdiction within the city government in those policy areas
4. A salary sufficiently high that the mayor can work full time at the office
5. Sufficient staff support for the mayor, such as policy planning, speech writing, intergovernmental relations, political work

Extragovernmental, or Informal, Preconditions

6. Ready vehicles for publicity, such as friendly newspapers and television stations
7. Politically oriented groups, including a political party, that the mayor can mobilize to help achieve particular goals

Source: Adapted from Jeffrey L. Pressman, "The Preconditions for Mayoral Leadership," *American Political Science Review* 66, no. 2 (June 1972): 512–513, 522.

In the face of these pressures on the mayor, two things must happen for mayors to exercise strong leadership. First, mayors must be given the legal and political resources to do their jobs.[59] Table 7.2 outlines seven such resources. The first five are legal or formal preconditions. Without sufficient jurisdiction, money, and staff, the mayor faces an uphill battle to implement his or her objectives. The last two items in Table 7.2 are informal or political preconditions.

Second, in addition to having the objective preconditions for power, an effective mayor must have a subjective vision of what needs to be done and how to do it. John P. Kotter and Paul R. Lawrence analyzed the subjective vision factor in terms of the mayor's ability to impose his or her own style on the city.[60] They analyzed the leadership styles of mayors in 20 different cities and isolated five variables that were critical to mayoral strength: setting a decision-making agenda, controlling the mayors' time, expanding their political alliances to attract new supporters, building a large staff to whom they could delegate appropriate responsibilities, and gaining political control over the city government.

If we juxtapose the objective preconditions with the subjective vision dimension, we derive four major types of leadership: the ceremonial mayor, the caretaker mayor, the crusader mayor, and the strong mayor or the program entrepreneur. These are shown in Figure 7.1. The dynamics at work here are also found for some other local executives, including elected county chief executives.

Types of Mayoral Leadership

The Ceremonial Mayor The person with little subjective vision who occupies an office that has few preconditions is very likely to follow the style that Kotter and Lawrence call the **ceremonial mayor**. These mayors make little effort to set a decision-making agenda for dealing with city problems. They have no broad goals to be accomplished; rather, they deal with problems individually. They have a modest staff and do not try to build new political alliances to contend with city problems; they rely instead on past friendships and

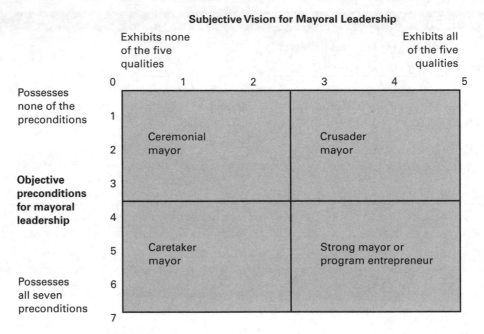

FIGURE 7.1

Styles of Mayoral Leadership

By juxtaposing the objective preconditions with the subjective vision for mayoral leadership, we can identify four major styles of mayoral leadership.

Sources: This figure was composed by juxtaposing criteria developed by Jeffrey L. Pressman in, "The Preconditions for Mayoral Leadership," *American Political Science Review* 66, no. 2 (June 1972): 511–524; John P. Kotter and Paul R. Lawrence, *Mayors in Action: Five Approaches to Urban Governance* (New York: Wiley, 1974), ch. 7; and Douglas Yates, *The Ungovernable City* (Cambridge, MA: M.I.T. Press, 1977), p. 165.

personal appeals. In coping with mayoral tasks, the ceremonial mayor attempts to tackle all the tasks individually rather than delegate authority to others.

The ceremonial mayor is content with presiding over dedications of bridges, buildings, harbor improvements, and other public facilities. Ceremonial mayors also try to be present for important private events, such as the opening of a new factory or shopping center, celebration of the anniversary of a prominent couple or business that has been in the community for many years, weddings, and funerals. An annual parade or the celebration of a major holiday will bring out ceremonial mayors, as will the arrivals of prominent people, whether they are entertainers, heroes, or elected officials.[61]

The Caretaker Mayor   The mayor with limited subjective vision who occupies an office that has several of the preconditions is likely to be a **caretaker mayor**. Like the ceremonial mayors, the caretaker mayors also do not set an agenda of goals to be accomplished. They, too, deal with problems individually. They do make more of an effort than the ceremonial mayors to build political alliances, to surround themselves with a loyal staff, and to delegate authority to others, especially to the established bureaucracies. The caretakers, however, do not seek to remake their communities; they are mainly interested in keeping the existing system working.

The prototype of a caretaker mayor was Ralph Locher of Cleveland (1962–1967). Locher dealt with city problems with an unsystematic approach. He let his own daily agenda be dictated by other people who placed demands on him and by regular office routines such as opening the mail and dictating letters. There is no evidence that Locher attempted to establish goals for some of Cleveland's broader social problems. He was simply a caretaker for the city.

Caretaker mayors generally focus on keeping current services and agencies running as smoothly as possible. They may make minor adjustments in response to citizen complaints or warnings from agency personnel that a problem is developing, but they do not usually take the initiative in recommending major policy changes. Some caretaker mayors believe that existing policies are reasonably good and that keeping the existing machinery of government running is laborious enough to consume all of their energy and skill. Moreover, failures in basic services may damage the local economy, harm the city's image, and anger the public.[62]

Citizens may sometimes prefer a mayor who lacks a broad vision and is willing to just focus on keeping established programs running and responding to citizen demands. A bold visionary may stir up conflict, upset many people, and build up expectations that are difficult to meet. Bold visions are also expensive, in many cases. A mayor may initially try to be a bold leader, but disappointments and criticism may eventually lead him or her to shift to a more modest approach, such as being a caretaker.[63]

The Crusader Mayor   The **crusader mayor** has the subjective vision for strong leadership to a high degree, but occupies an office that lacks several preconditions for strong leadership.[64] The crusader style emerges when the mayor's office is occupied by a very active, imaginative, and ambitious personality who has a very weak political power base. Douglas Yates points to former New York City mayor John Lindsay as a crusader. Lacking the political strength to control the city bureaucracies and dominate the government, Lindsay adopted a crusading, symbolic style of leadership. During the riots of the 1960s, he went into the streets in the riot-torn sections and urged people to return to their homes. He traveled often to Washington to testify before congressional committees and to serve as a spokesperson for the nation's urban problems. He engaged in political battles with New York State governor Nelson Rockefeller. Despite the battles, the conflicts, and the publicity, however, it is hard to identify Lindsay with very many significant accomplishments.

The Program Entrepreneur   The strong mayors or **program entrepreneurs** are the most ambitious of all the mayoralty types, and the offices they hold necessarily possess several of the objective preconditions. Their agendas are much more detailed. They have not only broad goals but even a list of objectives or priorities to be covered. Only a small portion of their daily work schedule is spent reacting to events. The rest is spent on activities tied to short- and long-range objectives. The program entrepreneurs skillfully build political alliances and surround themselves with a substantial staff.

Mayor Shirley Franklin of Atlanta is a good example of the program entrepreneur. She has worked with a wide variety of people, including Georgia's governor, Sonny Perdue, members of the state legislature, and Atlanta residents in order to develop a strategy for upgrading some major city utilities. She has worked with other local officials in order to deal with regional problems, such as traffic management and environmental protection. She also created task forces to develop proposals on a number of issues, from parking to the plight of the homeless.[65]

Mayor Franklin learned a great deal about local politics by serving in the administrations of two of her predecessors, Maynard Jackson and Andrew Young. She has reached out to a wide range of political figures, including some who appeared to be unfriendly at first. There is no guarantee that all of her efforts will bear fruit, but she is willing to explore many options and to seek assistance from many sources.

Another recent entrepreneurial mayor is Louisville's Jerry Abramson, who pushed through several redevelopment projects and the merger of Louisville and Jefferson County. Both brought a high level of energy, good negotiating skills, and a sense of direction to their office.[66]

The Prospects for Mayoral Leadership   Whatever the leadership type, few mayors today have enough formal authority and informal power to run their cities with a free hand, as, for example, Chicago's legendary mayor Richard J. Daley did (1957–1976). In contrast to Daley, most mayors today lack the powerful support that Daley enjoyed from business organizations, unions, and his political party. In addition, they face assertive city councils, cantankerous neighborhood organizations, and a smattering of ideological and single-issue groups that might not support the mayor's agenda. When the economy is struggling, mayors will often find that there is little or no money for new initiatives and there may not be enough money to maintain current programs.[67] State and federal government mandates also limit the options of mayors and other local officials, as does the difficulty of raising added revenues.

This type of environment puts a premium on mayors with a facilitative leadership style of compromising, keeping in touch with city council members, and courting a wide array of potential supporters. Philadelphia's Ed Rendell and Los Angeles's Richard Riordan have been pointed to as practitioners of the facilitator style of mayoral leadership. They were both adept at building cooperative working relationships rather than adversarial relationships with their city councils.[68] Note, however, that building cooperative working arrangements depends on much more than the mayor. If different members of the city council or different interest groups in a community are committed to fighting with one another as frequently as possible, even the most diplomatic mayors may find themselves fighting opposition more often than they would like.

The facilitative mayoral style also exists in some small communities where policy success requires the cooperation of people who may be providing voluntary help. Simply giving orders will be futile in that environment, and drawing on various ideas can help foster creative problem solving.[69]

One large-city mayor who often did not follow the facilitator approach was Rudolph Giuliani. During his tenure as mayor of New York City, his confrontational leadership style antagonized many people. On September 11, 2001, however, the attacks on the World Trade Center and its subsequent collapse created devastation in one of the most important parts of the city, killed and injured many people, and emotionally traumatized many more. People spent days looking for loved ones. Some businesses lost their offices and most of their employees. Many people were frightened and saddened by the event and wondered whether the city would ever recover.

Giuliani responded to the crisis much more effectively than many of his critics could have imagined. He was everywhere at once, offering encouragement and comfort, and pressing the state and federal governments to provide large amounts of help *quickly*. He bulldozed through various procedural obstacles to the recovery effort, and he gave New Yorkers assurance that in spite of the attack, the city would rebuild and recover. Some of the people who had previously been glad that he would soon leave office began to wonder if he might somehow be allowed to serve again. Under conditions of severe stress, his leadership helped move the recovery effort forward.[70]

MAYORS AND THE CHALLENGE OF SOCIAL CONFLICT

Mayors and other local officials are not immune to the great social conflicts that sweep through American society. Many cities are more racially diverse than they once were, and that includes many suburban communities. As recently as the 1960s, city politics in many areas was composed essentially of the clashes between different European nationalities. Today, the clash is not only between European nationalities but also between African Americans, Hispanics, American Indians, and Asians. Furthermore, none of these ethnic groupings is itself homogenous. The label *Hispanics,* for example, applies to the three largest groups—Mexicans, Puerto Ricans, and Cubans—but it also includes migrants from the five Central American nations plus the 14 South American nations. Asians are even more diverse than Hispanics, hailing from China, Japan, Korea, India, Vietnam, and dozens of other nations. As the people in each of these groupings become politically active, they contribute a new vibrancy and a new complexity to the tone of city politics. In addition, an increasing number of Americans are biracial or multiracial and do not want to be pigeonholed as a member of a single racial group.

The Minority Mayor

The growth of minority populations, changing social values, and increased voter participation by minorities have, quite naturally, made the minority mayor an increasingly common phenomenon. Minority mayors have included African Americans such as Wilson Goode (Philadelphia), Tom Bradley (Los Angeles), and Coleman Young (Detroit); Hispanics such as Federico Peña (Denver), Xavier Suarez (Miami), and Antonio Villaraigosa (Los Angeles); Asian Americans, such as Edwin Lee (San Francisco); and women such as Kathy Whitmire (Houston), Maureen O'Connor (San Diego), and Annette Strauss (Dallas). Minneapolis's former mayor Sharon Sayles Belton is both female and black, as is Atlanta mayor Shirley Franklin.

Minority mayors may confront problems and opportunities that white male mayors do not face. The minority mayor is much more likely than the white mayor to confront a problem of conflicting constituencies.[71] To get elected, the earliest African American mayors usually relied heavily upon an overwhelming vote from their neighborhoods plus a small minority of white liberals.[72] Providing these margins of victory, African American voters had some reason to expect favorable policies from the African American mayors they elected. However, to initiate the economic development activities that are needed to increase employment for the cities' minority populations, the African American mayors also have to cultivate a constituency of upper- and upper-middle-class whites who have the economic power to put economic development programs into action. The more that minority mayors cater to their minority election constituencies, the more problems they may create with their economic development constituencies, and vice versa. Some minority mayors have been able to build broader coalitions and thus might be less vulnerable to these conflicting constituencies. Sharon Sayles Belton, for example, won a majority of the Minneapolis white vote in her 1994 victory, and Cleveland's Michael White won a majority of the white vote in 1989 in a race that featured two African American candidates.[73]

If divided constituencies bring minority mayors special problems, these mayors also have special opportunities to increase employment and business prospects for the minority populations. Studies of African American mayors have shown that they indeed increased the number of African Americans employed by city government.[74] Similar studies of female mayors also found that they increased the number of women holding city jobs.[75]

The Bipolar City

Whatever the race or cultural background of the mayor, many central cities, especially many of the older ones, and some older suburbs face a growing *urban underclass* that is disproportionately African American, Hispanic, American Indian, and poor. There is a growing concern that for the first time in American history just such a permanent class of impoverished people, segregated within the confines of the central cities and older suburbs, is emerging, without realistic hope of achieving much, if any, upward social mobility. The average level of income and education for Hispanics and African Americans is far below that of the rest of the population, and many of them live far away from the areas of greatest job creation.

The concentration of impoverished people in central cities has several important political and economic consequences. Because of their impoverishment, they put a strain on many public services: public schools, public health agencies, social welfare agencies, and public housing agencies. Their neighborhoods attract a disproportionate share of drug peddling, prostitution, and violent crime, and this puts a strain most obviously on police services but, more importantly, on the social organizations of the neighborhoods themselves. Many impoverished rural areas face similar problems.

When individual residents of these neighborhoods, white or minority, take a good-paying job, they face difficult choices—the **exit option**, the **voice option**, or the **loyalty option**, to use Albert Hirschman's terms.[76] If they choose to exit the problems of the inner city or poor suburb and move to better neighborhoods or the suburbs, they take their spending power with them and this leaves the area slightly poorer as a result. To maintain homes, to pay for public services, and to support supermarkets and other amenities in the cities requires people with steady incomes. An alternative exit strategy for affluent people is to purchase services from private firms instead of working to improve local government services.

If they choose the voice option of staying in the older neighborhoods and fighting to improve them, they have a very constructive role to play. Poor neighborhoods rely heavily on residents who are just a little more affluent than the average, just a little better educated than the average, and just a little feistier than the average, to put pressure on the city to pay attention to neighborhood problems.[77] Similar forces are at work in poor rural areas, but with one difference: In some poor rural areas, there may be no good job opportunities in the area. Anyone who wants to move up the economic ladder may have to move away. Exactly that has been happening in many portions of the Great Plains for a considerable number of years.[78]

The third option, loyalty, involves staying in the community without necessarily fighting to eliminate or reduce its problems—at least, not on a consistent basis. Many people feel considerable fondness for the area where they grew up or where they have lived for a number of years. When those attractions are strong, they may lead people to stay in a community in spite of its problems. Even though people who primarily choose the loyalty option may not actively work in the political arena to help their communities, they usually help to maintain the social and economic fabric of the area. The small town of Cuba, Kansas, which was recently featured in an article in *National Geographic,* has survived in part because many people with deep roots in the town want it to survive and help in many ways to keep it going.[79] Their contributions range from being active in church to watching a local athletic team to competing in the town's lawnmower races (with the drivers wearing blindfolds!).

Unfortunately for poor cities and rural areas, the exit option is often the most attractive one for upwardly mobile people. This depletes the area's supply of families with sufficient spending power to pay for public services and to keep their own neighborhoods in good repair. When too many upwardly mobile people exert their exit option, a community becomes increasingly bifurcated between the very rich and the very poor. Poorer citizens often cannot afford to move to better neighborhoods, and non-white residents may find themselves excluded from some areas through a variety of informal mechanisms. The bipolar city emerges: A large underclass on the one hand and a small upper class on the other, without the stabilizing influence of the working and middle classes.[80] This is already the reality for some of America's oldest and most distressed cities, such as Atlantic City, New Jersey. And given present trends, it is the likely future for a great many other cities as well. In rural areas and small towns, the eventual result may be abandonment of the area by almost everyone.

For big-city mayors and other local officials, the central task confronting them in trying to forestall this bipolar situation is to create conditions under which upwardly mobile people will choose the voice or loyalty options rather than the exit option. There were traditionally two ways to do this. First, recognizing the interracial frictions that may underlie the exit option, the mayor must construct a political coalition that crosses racial and ethnic lines. Second, the mayor must promote economic development policies that create jobs in the area and provide taxes to support the badly needed public services. The dramatic rise in fuel prices in 2007–2008 brought a third method: The higher cost of commuting has led some more prosperous people to move closer to downtown areas.

Striving for Broad Coalitions

Local officials who hope for cooperation and harmony in their communities need to accommodate the concerns of a wide variety of people—different races, religions, ages, income groups, business leaders, and consumers. There are also differences of opinion and differing needs among people who have many other characteristics in common. Forging durable coalitions of people with many different interests is, however, often difficult, especially in communities with relatively few economic resources.

A number of analysts have explored the work of building and maintaining local coalitions that include people from a variety of different backgrounds and with different beliefs. The tasks of building and maintaining those coalitions are formidable. Poorer and less-educated whites are often reluctant to vote for African American candidates, especially in the South. Upper-middle-class whites are apparently more willing to support minority candidates than are poorer and less-educated whites. While building coalitions among different minority groups has sometimes been possible, some of those groups have a history of conflicts with one another in some areas of the country.[81] Nonetheless, the growing diversity of the country in future years[82] will make multiracial coalitions more and more necessary.

Part of the difficulty of building and maintaining broad coalitions is that people may be separated by a variety of differences that sometimes reinforce one another. People from one ethnic group may live in the northern part of a community, while another ethnic group is mainly found in the southern part. They may also tend to prefer different political parties. People of one nationality may be predominantly Catholic, while another nationality is mainly Protestant. People of different income levels may be working in different sectors of the economy. Even if two people have something in common, they may be divided by one or more other factors.

This does not mean that broad political coalitions are impossible. Particular mayors (or other local leaders, such as community organizers[83]) in specific circumstances will be able to forge such coalitions in their communities. Keeping them together over time, however, is likely to require considerable skill and effort, and in very diverse communities, some people are likely to be left on the outside. In addition, some local governments facing diverse political environments are sometimes unable to deal with major problems, a difficulty that has faced Dallas, Texas, in recent years.[84]

▶ YOU DECIDE

Should You Seek to Curb Immigration?

You are the chief speech writer for a mayor who is being pressured to take a position on federal legislation that would restrict immigration. Your city receives substantial immigration, as reflected by its ethnic composition: 45 percent white, 25 percent African American, 20 percent Mexican American, 8 percent Asian (mostly poor refugees from Southeast Asia), and 2 percent American Indian. Furthermore, your city has seen a significant outflow of jobs, and the city's unemployment rates are persistently above the national average.

On one side of the argument are powerful reasons to support an open-door policy on immigration:

- Your city has historically been a beacon for immigrants seeking upward mobility. Most of your white population are descendents from early twentieth-century immigrants.
- Church leaders argue that the city has a moral obligation to keep its doors open to immigrants.
- Hispanic and Asian leaders are vocal in their opposition to restricting immigration.
- Business leaders in the state complain that they need the immigrants to take the low-wage, physical jobs that unemployed and underemployed citizens will not take.
- Economists have demonstrated that immigrants put less of a burden on the city's welfare services than do the current residents of the city.
- If you come out strongly for restrictions, you will clearly be painted as a racist with no sympathies for immigrant cultures.

On the other side of the argument are some compelling reasons to support restrictions on immigration:

- Because of its limited economic prospects, new immigrants are unlikely to find lucrative job opportunities in your city.

- Because unemployment rates are high among your city's current residents, immigration will exacerbate the competition for already scarce jobs.
- There is a danger that the increased job competition brought on by immigration will spill over into interethnic conflicts that you would like to see the city avoid.
- In contrast to the rhetoric of Hispanic and Asian leaders, public opinion polls show that Hispanic and Asian residents are divided on the issue of curbing immigration.
- If you oppose restrictions, and the economic situation of your city worsens, the mayor will be blamed for not having taken a stand to reduce the competition for jobs when he or she could have done so (and you might get fired).

As the mayor's chief speech writer, your job is to draft his or her official statement on the proposed legislation restricting immigration. Do you:

A. Explicitly oppose the legislation?
B. Explicitly endorse the legislation?
C. Attempt to work out a compromise law that will put some curbs on immigration but not enough that will repel the opponents?
D. Prepare a statement that avoids taking an explicit position on the issue (for example, saying that the mayor will appoint an advisory commission to study the issue).

Explain the reasons for your choice. If your choice is C, what compromise would you endorse? ■

Social Conflict and Political Change

In summary, many communities have conflicts among different ethnic, racial, religious, partisan, and economic groupings. The key political leader is often the mayor, who must try to assemble and maintain a governing coalition among those numerous groups. When the local economy is in poor condition, the task of keeping very many people satisfied for very long is likely to be extremely difficult.

Minority mayors have sometimes been able to build coalitions from their own ethnic constituency plus a clustering of votes among other minorities and white liberals. When these mayors take office, however, they may be pulled between demands from members of their own ethnic or racial group, on one hand, and the rest of the community.

Where the chief local executive is a city manager, the leadership challenges are essentially the same.[85] However, the city manager normally serves at the pleasure of the city council and, therefore, is vulnerable to being pushed out when conflicts erupt. A city manager may also lack deep roots in the community and thus may be at a disadvantage relative to the typical mayor, who is likely to have established relationships with a variety of different groups and organizations in the community.

Some local problems can be dealt with by more localized groups, such as a neighborhood watch program or a volunteer group that repairs and renovates a local park. These smaller organizations may be able to address some problems, including substandard housing and creating small clusters of business development, without having a citywide coalition. The first people to respond to natural disasters are often residents of nearby homes and neighborhoods; those residents may help rescue people buried in rubble, marooned by floods, or bogged down in blizzards. The more localized activities may be sponsored by an existing organization, such as a church, or a newly formed group created specifically to address a specific problem.[86] Mayors and city managers can sometimes assist in the formation of those efforts.

The You Decide exercise on page 184 gives you a chance to wrestle with an important issue pertaining to social change.

MAYORAL LEADERSHIP AND THE URBAN POLITICAL ECONOMY

The name of the game for many local officials in recent years has been economic development, and their success has often been measured largely by whether the local economy improves, remains stable, or declines during their administrations. A number of development tools exist. Although these will be examined in detail in Chapter 17, we will briefly discuss them here. They can be categorized as either direct or indirect subsidies.

Direct Subsidies

Direct subsidies for economic development have been part of local government for many years in many parts of the country. Those subsidies have sometimes been encouraged by federal programs, beginning with the urban renewal programs of the 1950s, which provided federal funds for cities to clear blighted neighborhoods and to provide for new commercial and residential development projects in their place.

A critical change occurred with the Housing and Community Development Act of 1974, which established a Community Development Block Grant (CDBG) for urban redevelopment. This law permitted the mayor's office to take more direct charge of redevelopment activities.

Local officials used the CDBG grants as seed money to entice private developers into their communities. As a consequence, many cities have undergone a boom in the construction of downtown office buildings and retail shopping facilities. Many cities have also used their CDBG funds to redevelop local historic sites and attract middle- and upper-income people to some historic neighborhoods (a process known as "gentrification."). During the Reagan and first Bush presidencies (1981–1992), federal funds for urban development shriveled. However, they rebounded dramatically in the 1990s.

Indirect Subsidies

As federal funds for economic development dwindled in the 1980s and early 1990s, developers sometimes turned to tax subsidies that were made available by the states, localities, and/or the federal government. The most obvious tax subsidy is for a city or other local government to give a firm a property tax abatement (that is, forgive all or part of the tax) if the firm locates or expands within the city.

Another group of tax subsidies involves various types of tax deductions or tax credits. For example, allowing companies to depreciate investments more quickly gives them, in effect, a tax break for making that investment.

A popular credit subsidy is the IDRB, or Industrial Development Revenue Bond (see Chapter 12), under which a city, county, or other local government helps a company raise investment capital at lower interest rates by using the city's tax-exempt municipal bonding authority. Linked with the use of IDRBs are tax increment financing plans, under which the increased property taxes from a development project are used to pay off the city's investment rather than going into the city treasury. For example, a city might borrow money to prepare a site for a new business. Property taxes on those improvements will be used to repay the loan, so the company benefits fairly directly from the property taxes it is paying.

Note that the initiative in promoting direct or indirect subsidies does not always rest with the mayor or other local officials. Business leaders may press local officials for benefits of many kinds and may even take the step of trying to create new local governments (such as special districts) that will be easier for those business leaders to influence.[87]

CONCLUSION

Imaginative and aggressive mayors were sometimes able to centralize much of the planning for economic development activities in their own offices. This helped the mayor of the last 40 years acquire a stature that the office did not have in the 1950s and 1960s. Whether the mayor's new stature will continue, however, is unknown, but some threats are looming. Direct federal aid (adjusted for inflation) to many local governments has declined in the last 25 years, and revisions of the federal income tax code have reduced the attractiveness of IDRBs and real estate tax shelters. In addition, the diversity of interests and values in some communities sometimes produces more conflict than many mayors can manage.

In addition, some critics of the government-sponsored redevelopment activity of the last 40 years maintain that it did not really address the severe social and economic problems faced by many communities and the poorest residents of those communities.[88] We will examine these criticisms in Chapter 17.

The recent wave of efforts to encourage more secrecy in government in response to the September 11 attacks[89] may also affect patterns of local leadership. The less ordinary citizens know about what local governments are doing, the greater the influence of political insiders becomes. However, the need for pulling together all sorts of different skills and resources may also make larger numbers of people able to influence the overall strategies that result.

SUMMARY

1. Two competing theories of community power are the elitist, or stratificationist, theory and the pluralist theory. Elitist research contends that local power is often concentrated in the hands of a relatively small number of business leaders; the average person, in this view, has little influence. Pluralist research contends that power is dispersed among a variety of groups; competition among those groups gives many people a voice in important decisions. More recent research indicates that the business community's role in local politics is complex, has attributed greater importance to the concept of nondecisions, has shown that a variety of community power relationships exist, and has found that community power relationships can change over time. In the last 20 years, the community power debate has been enriched by neo-Marxist theory, growth-machine theory, unitary interest theory, systemic-power theory, and a pluralist counterattack.

2. The major office for providing focused leadership in local politics is often the mayor. Empowering mayors who are strong requires giving them the legal and political resources needed to do their jobs. Strong mayors have a subjective vision of what needs to be done in the city and how to do it—if and when the community desires that type of leadership. In some communities, professionally trained city managers are able to provide significant executive leadership, but only as long as they have adequate support from the city council.

3. The prospects of building and maintaining broad coalitions in our major metropolitan areas do not seem great. Some local officials have succeeded in doing so, at least for a time, but conflicts among groups are too severe in some communities to bring them together for very long.

4. Many local officials over the years have devoted considerable effort to economic development activities. Those efforts have produced mixed results, with some communities appearing to benefit while others do not.

STUDY QUESTIONS

1. According to the elitist theory of community, who controls local decision making? What does the pluralist theory say regarding who runs local politics? How would you account for the differences between the two perspectives?

2. How do mayors and other local officials try to lead their communities? Why are some local officials more successful than others in shaping the futures of their communities?

3. Why is building and maintaining a broad and diverse political coalition difficult much of the time? What does that difficulty imply for the debate between elitist and pluralist scholars?

4. Why have local officials been so interested in promoting economic development in their communities in recent years? What difficulties have they encountered?

KEY TERMS

Caretaker mayor   A mayor who has a primary focus on providing current services and keeping the community intact, but who fails to set a broad agenda of new goals to be accomplished.

Ceremonial mayor   A mayor who tackles problems individually and devotes much time and effort to ceremonial and symbolic acts.

Crusader mayor   An active and aggressive mayor, but one who lacks many of the preconditions for strong mayoral leadership and whose job is, therefore, frustrating.

Decision-making approach   The approach to analyzing community power that relies on identifying the people who participate in and influence local governmental decisions as the preferred method for determining who has power in the community.

Elitist theory   The theory of community power that sees communities as being dominated by a top elite composed principally of major business leaders.

Exit option   The option of exiting the community's problems by moving to another community or using the private marketplace to purchase services that are normally public services.

Loyalty option   The option of remaining in a community in spite of its problems, but doing relatively little in the political arena to solve those problems.

Nondecision   The exercise of power by keeping an issue off the decision-making agenda of a governmental body, out of the news, and out of public discussion generally.

Pluralist theory   The theory of community power that sees communities as being run through the competition of a variety of power centers.

Program entrepreneur   A dynamic mayor (or other official) who sets an agenda of goals to be accomplished, has a reasonable amount of governmental authority, and builds alliances with the interests needed to reach the goals.

Reputational approach   The approach to analyzing community power that relies on asking a panel of judges to indicate the most powerful people and institutions.

Stratificationist theory   See *Elitist theory.*

Voice option   The option of staying in the community and fighting to improve the quality of life there.

THE INTERNET CONNECTION

The National Civic League has been working to promote improvements in American local government for many years. Their *National Civic Review* includes articles on a variety of local governmental issues. You can contact the National Civic League at **www.ncl.org**. Find a large city newspaper on the Web; how well does it cover local governments in the area? Who appears to be playing a leadership role?

NOTES

1. Doug Goodnough, "Leading by Example," *American Profile,* April 16–22, 2006, pp. 1–3.

2. Robert S. Lynd and Helen M. Lynd, *Middletown in Transition* (New York: Harcourt, Brace, 1937), p. 74.

3. See Robert A. Dahl and Bruce Stinebrickner, *Modern Political Analysis,* 6th ed. (Upper Saddle River, NJ: Prentice-Hall, 2003), pp. 17–21, 32–34, 56–59; G. William Domhoff, *Who Rules America Now? A View for the Eighties* (New York: Touchstone, 1983); Thomas Dye, *Who's Running America?* (Englewood Cliffs, NJ: Prentice-Hall, 1990). Although much of Domhoff's and Dye's books focus on national politics, many of the same arguments apply locally.

4. See especially Gaetano Mosca, *The Ruling Class,* trans. Hannah Kahn (New York: McGraw-Hill, 1939); Roberto Michels, *Political Parties: A Sociological Study of the Oligarchical Tendencies of Modern Democracy,* trans. Eden Paul and Cedar Paul (New York: Free Press, 1962).

5. For a survey of these early studies, see Nelson Polsby, *Community Power and Political Theory* (New Haven, CT: Yale University Press, 1963).

6. Floyd Hunter, *Community Power Structure* (Chapel Hill: University of North Carolina Press, 1953).

7. Earlier editions of this book asserted that the power elite "vetoed" projects it disliked. But a recent analysis by Clarence Stone argues persuasively that elite control in Atlanta was really much more subtle. The word *veto* suggests a command-and-control form of influence. But, argues Stone, Hunter was really describing a preemptive form of influence by which elites controlled the decision-making agenda. See his "Toward An Urban-Regimes Paradigm," *Urban Politics and Urban Policy Section Newsletter* 1, no. 2 (Spring 1987): 7; and *Regime Politics: Governing Atlanta, 1946–1988* (Lawrence, KS: University Press of Kansas, 1989).

8. For overviews of power elite theories at all levels of government, see G. William Domhoff, *Who Rules America?*, 5th ed. (Boston: McGraw-Hill, 2006); Eva Etzioni-Halevy, *The Elite Connection* (Cambridge, UK: Polity Press, 1993).

9. See Polsby, *Community Power and Political Theory*; Herbert Kaufman and Victor Jones, "The Mystery of Power," *Administrative Science Quarterly* 14 (Summer 1954): 2–5; Raymond Wolfinger, "Reputation and Reality in the Study of Community Power," *American Sociological Review* 25 (October 1960): 636–644; Robert A. Dahl, "A Critique of the Ruling Elite Model," *American Political Science Review* 52 (June 1958): 463–469. Bear in mind that elite-oriented theories come in several different forms; criticisms that apply to one version may not apply to another.

10. See Polsby, *Community Power and Political Theory*, pp. 45–56. One of the most influential books on the American presidency contends that reputation is a key influence on a president's ability to get things done. See Richard Neustadt, *Presidential Power and the Modern Presidents* (New York: Free Press, 1990).

11. Robert Dahl, *Who Governs? Democracy and Power in an American City* (New Haven, CT: Yale University Press, 1966).

12. See Wallace S. Sayre and Herbert Kaufman, *Governing New York City* (New York: Russell Sage Foundation, 1960); Robert V. Presthus, *Men at the Top: A Study in Community Power* (Ithaca, NY: Cornell University Press, 1964); Aaron Wildavsky, *Leadership in a Small Town* (Totowa, NJ: Bedminster Press, 1964); Frank J. Munger, *Decisions in Syracuse* (Bloomington: Indiana University Press, 1961); Linton C. Freeman et al.,

Metropolitan Decision-Making (Syracuse, NY: Syracuse University Press, 1962).

13. See, for example, Delbert C. Miller, "Decision-Making Cliques in Community Power Structures: A Comparative Study of an American and an English City," *American Journal of Sociology* 64 (November 1958): 299–310; William H. Form and William V. D'Antonio, "Integration and Cleavage Among Community Influentials in Two Border Cities," *American Sociological Review* 24 (December 1959): 804–814; Robert E. Agger, Daniel Goldrich, and Bert Swanson, *The Rulers and the Ruled: Political Power and Impotence in American Communities* (New York: Wiley, 1964); John Walton, "Discipline, Method, and Community Power: A Note on the Sociology of Knowledge," *American Sociological Review* 31, no. 5 (October 1966): 684–689.

14. Lucius Beebe and C. M. Clegg, *Mixed Train Daily* (New York: E. P. Dutton, 1947), pp. 180–233.

15. Domhoff, *Who Rules*, pp. 77–78.

16. Ibid., pp. 82–85, 95–98.

17. Ibid., pp. 80–93.

18. Robert D. Schulze, "The Bifurcation of Power in a Satellite City," in Morris Janowitz, ed., *Community Political Systems* (New York: The Free Press, 1961).

19. Edward C. Banfield and James Q. Wilson, *City Politics* (New York: Vintage Books, 1963), pp. 261–276.

20. Robert Agranoff and Michael McGuire, *Collaborative Public Management* (Washington, DC: Georgetown University, 2003).

21. Peter Bachrach and Morton S. Baratz, "The Two Faces of Power," *American Political Science Review* 56, no. 4 (December 1962): 948; see also Thomas Dye, *Top Down Policymaking* (New York: Chatham House, 2001), pp. 31–34.

22. Clarence N. Stone, "Systemic Power in Community Decision Making: A Restatement of Stratification Theory," *American Political Science Review* 74, no. 4 (December 1980): 978–990.

23. Clarence N. Stone, "Social Stratification, Non-Decision-Making, and the Study of Community Power," *American Politics Quarterly* 10, no. 3 (July 1982): 293.

24. Larry Bartels, *Unequal Democracy* (New York: Russell Sage Foundation, 2008), pp. 259–277.

25. Domhoff, *Who Rules*, pp. 82–98; Dye, *Top Down*, ch. 3; Rob Gurwitt, "Are City Councils a Relic of the Past?" *Governing* 16, no. 7 (April 2003): 20–24.

26. Delbert C. Miller, "Industry and Community Power Structures," *American Sociological Review* 23 (February 1958): 9–15; Lawrence Herson and John Bolland, *The Urban Web* (Chicago: Nelson-Hall, 1998), pp. 183–184.

27. John Hill, "Receiver Acts Swiftly to Take Control of Central Falls, Demoting Mayor First," *Providence, RI, Journal,* July 20, 2010 (Web edition).

28. Julie Bykowicz, "Dixon Resigns," *Baltimore Sun,* January 7, 2010 (Web edition); Russell Lissau, "Ex-Kildeer Trustee Called New Hire the 'Last Straw,'" *Kildeer, IL, Daily Herald,* June 5, 2009 (Web edition); Justin Juozapavicius, "Leaders' Power Struggle Roils 'Most Livable' Tulsa," *Verizon Headlines* (Associated Press), January 30, 2011 (Web edition); Georgia Pabst, "Van Akkeren Defeats Ryan for Sheboygan Mayor," *Sheboygan Journal Sentinel,* February 21, 2012 (Web edition).

29. Well, at least the academic mind finds unexplainable facts hard to tolerate.

30. Richard Child Hill, "Fiscal Collapse and Political Struggle in Decaying Central Cities in the United States," in William K. Tabb and Larry Sawyers, eds., *Marxism and the Metropolis* (New York: Oxford University Press, 1978), pp. 213–240. Lynn Staeheli, Janet Kodras, and Colin Flint, eds., *State Devolution in America* (Thousand Oaks, CA: Sage, 1997).

31. See Richard Child Hill, "Crisis in the Motor City: The Politics of Economic Development in Detroit," in Susan Fainstein, et al., eds., *Restructuring the City: The Political Economy of Urban Redevelopment* (New York: Longman, 1983), pp. 98–102.

32. Elaine Sharp, "Culture Wars and City Politics," *Urban Affairs* 31, no. 6 (July 1996): 738–758.

33. Cable News Network broadcast, February 11, 2003.

34. Alex Veiga, "Voters in L. A. Suburb Reject Wal-Mart," *Moscow-Pullman Daily News,* April 8, 2004, p. 3A.

35. Paul Kantor and H. V. Savitch, "Can Politicians Bargain with Business? A Theoretical and Comparative Perspective on Urban Development," *Urban Affairs Quarterly,* 28 (December 1993): 230–255.

36. Carl Manning, "Modern Homesteading," *Moscow-Pullman Daily News,* March 27–28, 2003, p. 12A; Marti Attoun, "Where the Land Is Free," *American Profile,* April 30–May 6, 2006, pp. 6–9.

37. Harvey Molotch, "The City as a Growth Machine: Toward a Political Economy of Place," *American Journal of Sociology* 82 (September 1976): 309–332.

38. G. William Domhoff, "The Growth Machine and the Power Elite: A Challenge to Pluralists and Marxists Alike," in Robert J. Waste, ed., *Community Power: Directions for Future Research* (Beverly Hills, CA: Sage Publications, 1986), p. 57.

39. See Joel Rast, *Remaking Chicago: The Political Origins of Urban Industrial Change* (DeKalb, IL: Northern Illinois University Press, 1999); Alexander Reichl, *Reconstructing Times Square: Politics and Culture in Urban Development* (Lawrence, KS: University Press of Kansas, 1999).

40. Alan Finder, "Rural Colleges Seek New Edge and Urbanize," *New York Times* (electronic edition), February 7, 2007; Rob Gurwitt, "Eds, Meds, and Urban Revival," *Governing* 28, no. 8 (May 2008): 44–50.

41. William Fulton, "Refugee Renewal," *Governing* 18, no. 8 (May 2005): 32–41.

42. A. G. Sulzberger, "Hispanics Reviving Faded Towns on the Plains," *New York Times,* November 13, 2011 (Web edition).

43. Paul E. Peterson, *City Limits* (Chicago: University of Chicago Press, 1981).

44. See, for example, Domhoff, "The Growth Machine and the Power Elite," p. 70.

45. Dye, *Top Down,* pp. 25–33; *Statistical Abstract of the United States, 2003* (Washington DC: U.S. Government Printing Office, 2003), p. 459; *Statistical Abstract of the United States, 2008* (Washington, DC: U.S. Government Printing Office, 2008), p. 450.

46. Kirk Johnson, "Drilling in Fast-Growing Areas Ushers in New Era of Tension," *New York Times,* October 25, 2011 (Web edition); Sabrina Tavernise, "Rush for Gas Rights Plunges Towns into Battle for Control," *New York Times,* December 14, 2011 (Web edition); Mireya Navarro, "New York Judge Rules Town Can Ban Gas Hydrofracking," *New York Times,* February 21, 2012 (Web edition); Cable News Network reporting, January 13, 2012.

47. Clarence N. Stone, "Summing Up: Urban Regimes, Development Policy, and Political Arrangements," in Clarence N. Stone and Heywood Sanders, eds., *The Politics of Urban Development* (Lawrence, KS: University Press of Kansas, 1987).

48. Clarence N. Stone, "Systemic Power in Community Decision Making: A Restatement of Stratification

Theory," *American Political Science Review* 74, no. 4 (December 1980): 978–990.

49. Ibid., p. 987.

50. Alan Digaetano, "Urban Political Regime Formation: A Study in Contrast," *Journal of Urban Affairs* 11, no. 3 (1989): 269.

51. Paul D. Schumacher, *Critical Pluralism, Democratic Performance, and Community Power* (Lawrence, KS: University Press of Kansas, 1990).

52. Bryan D. Jones and Lynn W. Bachelor with Carter Wilson, *The Sustaining Hand: Community Leadership and Corporate Power* (Lawrence, KS: University Press of Kansas, 1986).

53. Zoltan Hajnal and Terry Nichols Clark, "The Local Interest-Group System: Who Governs and Why?" *Social Science Quarterly* 79 (1998): 227–241; see also the Symposium section of *PS: Political Science and Politics*, vol. XXXIX (January, 2006), pp. 19–65.

54. *Rural American at a Glance* (Washington, DC: U.S. Department of Agriculture Economic Information Bulletin no. 18), August 2006, pp. 4–5; Sharon Carty, "Automakers Seek Federal Help," *USA Today*, September 9, 2008, p. 1B; Jenny Anderson and Ben White, "Wall St.'s Fears on Lehman Bros. Batter Market," *New York Times*, September 10, 2008: A3.

55. James H. Svara, "Institutional Power and Mayoral Leadership," *State and Local Government Review* 27, no. 1 (Winter 1995): 71–83.

56. Robert S. Lorch, *State and Local Politics: The Great Entanglement* (Englewood Cliffs, NJ: Prentice-Hall, 1995), p. 275. Original source: John T. Galvin, *Twelve Mayors of Boston 1900–1970* (Boston: Boston Public Library, 1970).

57. Timothy Bledsoe, *Careers in City Politics* (Pittsburgh: University of Pittsburgh Press, 1993) and Alan Ehrenhalt, *The United States of Ambition* (New York: Random House, 1991). These two studies suggest that council members may be moving away from the belief in volunteerism (as described in Chapter 6) and toward a belief in the city council as a stepping stone to higher office.

58. Svara, "Institutional Power and Mayoral Leadership," pp. 77–78.

59. This was one of the conclusions of the so-called Winter Commission. National Commission on State and Local Public Services, *Hard Truths/ Tough Choices: An Agenda for State and Local Reform* (Albany: Nelson A. Rockefeller Institute of Government, State University of New York,

1993). See also James Svara, "Institutional Powers and Mayoral Leadership," *State and Local Government Review* 27 (1995): 71–83.

60. In addition to the three styles mentioned in the text, they identified two other styles: the personality individualist and the executive. For a discussion of these, see John P. Kotter and Paul R. Lawrence, *Mayors in Action: Five Approaches to Urban Governance* (New York: Wiley, 1974), ch. 7.

61. Ibid., p. 107.

62. Ibid., p. 111.

63. David Folz and P. Edward French, *Managing America's Small Communities* (Lanham, MD: Rowman and Littlefield, 2005), pp. 40–41.

64. Douglas Yates, *The Ungovernable City* (Cambridge, MA: M.I.T. Press, 1977), p. 165.

65. Rob Gurwitt, "Atlanta Reaches Out," *Governing* 17, no. 7 (April 2004): 22–27.

66. Alan Greenblatt, "Anatomy of a Merger," *Governing* 16, no. 3 (December 2002): 20–25; Rob Gurwitt, "In Recovery," *Governing* 14, no. 2 (November 2000): 25.

67. Michael Sauter, Ashley Allen, and Charles Stockdale, "5 American Cities Nearly Destroyed by the Recession," *Wall Street Journal*, January 25, 2012 (Web edition).

68. Svara, "Institutional Power and Mayoral Leadership," pp. 79–81.

69. Laurent Belsie, "Town Government...When There's not Much Town to Govern," in Bruce Stinebrickner, *State and Local Government*, 12th ed. (Dubuque, IA: McGraw Hill/Dushkin, 2005), pp. 156–157.

70. See Alan Ehrenhalt, "Hizzoner's Finest Hours," *Governing* 15, no. 3 (December 2001): 4, 6.

71. Peter K. Eisinger, "Black Mayors and the Politics of Racial Advancement," in William C. McReady, ed., *Culture, Ethnicity, and Identity* (New York: Academic Press, 1983), p. 106.

72. In Ernest N. Morial's first election as mayor of New Orleans, in 1977, he received only 19 percent of the white vote but 95 percent of the African American vote. In Richard Arrington's first election as mayor of Birmingham, in 1979, he won less than 15 percent of the white vote. Philadelphia's Wilson Goode won about 20 percent of the white vote in his 1983 victory. Chicago's Harold Washington won few white votes but an estimated 95 percent of the African American vote in his 1983 victory. In his 1987 reelection, Washington expanded his vote in white neighborhoods but still received only a small minority of white

votes. See John J. Harrigan, *Political Change in the Metropolis*, 4th ed. (Glenview, IL: Scott Foresman, 1989), p. 144.

73. Terrance D. Lumpkins, "From Stokes to White: Assessing a Lack of Political Power in Cleveland, 1965–1994," paper presented at the 1995 meeting of the American Political Science Association. Chicago, IL, September 1995.

74. Eisinger, "Black Mayors and the Politics of Racial Advancement," pp. 95–109.

75. Grace Hall Saltzstein, "Female Mayors and Women in Municipal Jobs," *American Journal of Political Science* 30, no. 1 (February 1986): 128–139.

76. Albert O. Hirschman, *Exit, Voice, and Loyalty: Responses to Decline in Firms, Organizations, and States* (Cambridge, MA: Harvard University Press, 1970).

77. See especially Matthew A. Crenson's *Neighborhood Politics* (Cambridge, MA: Harvard University Press, 1983).

78. John Mitchell and Jim Richardson, "The Late Great Plains," *National Geographic* 205, no. 5 (May 2004): 2–29.

79. Jim Richardson, "Cuba, Kansas," *National Geographic* 205, no. 5 (May 2004): 30–53. For more information about Cuba, see www.national-geographic.com/magazine/0405.

80. George Sternlieb and James W. Hughes, "The Uncertain Future of the Central City," *Urban Affairs Quarterly* 18, no. 4 (June 1983): 455–472.

81. Richard Murray and Arnold Vedlitz, "Racial Voting Patterns in the South: An Analysis of Major Elections from 1960 to 1977 in Five Cities," *Annals of the American Academy of Political and Social Science* 439 (September 1978): 29–39; Rufus P. Browning, Dale Rogers Marshall, and David H. Tabb, *Protest Is Not Enough: The Struggle of Blacks and Hispanics for Equality in Urban Politics* (Berkeley: University of California Press, 1984), pp. 46–53; Zoltan

Hajnal, "White Residents, Black Incumbents, and a Declining Racial Divide," *American Political Science Review* 95 (2001): 603–618; *The New York Times*, April 9, 1987, p. 11; Paul Green, "The Message from the 26th Ward," *Comparative State Politics Newsletter* 7, no. 4 (August 1986): 16; Joan Didion, "Miami: 'La Lucha,'" *The New York Review of Books* 34, no. 10 (June 11, 1987): 15; David Rieff, "The Second Havana," *The New Yorker* 63 (May 1987): 65–83; F. Chris Garcia and Rudolph O. de la Garza, *The Chicano Political Experience: Three Perspectives* (North Scituate, MA: Duxbury, 1977), pp. 36–37.

82. Statistical Abstract, 2006, pp. 15, 17.

83. Michael Brown, *Building Powerful Community Organizations* (Arlington, MA: Long Haul Press, 2006).

84. Rob Gurwitt, "Can Dallas Govern Itself?," *Governing* 19, no. 11 (August 2006): 42–47.

85. For a valuable overview of leadership by city managers, see Charldean Newell, ed., *The Effective Local Government Manager*, 2nd ed. (Washington, DC: International City/County Management Association, 1993).

86. Jim Diers, *Neighbor Power* (Seattle: University of Washington, 2004); Michael Gecan, *Going Public* (Boston: Beacon Press, 2002).

87. See Nancy Burns, *The Formation of American Local Governments* (New York: Oxford, 1994).

88. In defense of universalistic politics, see Theda Skocpol, "Sustainable Social Policy: Fighting Poverty without Poverty Programs," *The American Prospect*, no. 2 (Summer 1990): 58–70. In defense of race-based policies, see Donald L. De Marco and George C. Galster, "Pro-Integrative Policy: Theory and Practice," *Journal of Urban Affairs* 15, no. 2 (1993): 141–160.

89. Michele Mariani, "A Little Less Sunshine," *Governing* 17, no. 9 (June 2004): 38–41.

State Legislatures and Public Policy

CHAPTER PREVIEW

This chapter examines the role of state legislatures in establishing and overseeing public policy. We will discuss:

1 The five main functions performed by state legislatures.

2 The structure of state legislatures, with an eye to the impact of organizational patterns on policy making.

3 Legislative processes, including the bill-passing sequence.

4 The impact of legislative reform movements on state legislatures over the past four decades.

Introduction

State legislatures deal with many controversial issues, and tempers will sometimes flare even with the best of efforts to restrain them. Of course, not all legislators make the best of efforts. On a new member's first day in the Colorado legislature, he was apparently angry about being photographed by a journalist during a ceremonial prayer. The legislator responded by kicking the photographer in the knee. Unfortunately for the legislator, his actions were captured by a television camera.[1]

As the legislature considered disciplinary action against the member, he indignantly proclaimed his innocence and blamed the media for the entire incident. He also claimed that he had only nudged the photographer's knee. Ultimately the state House voted to censure[2] him, with only one dissenting vote.

The state legislatures are crucial bodies for setting public policies. Each regular session of each legislature enacts many policies that deeply affect our lives. Legislatures raise, do not raise, or reduce our taxes. They appropriate money for various purposes, such as higher education, highway maintenance, and public health. They pass laws that attempt to deal with various issues, such as crime, environmental protection, homeland security, and medical malpractice.

They oversee the operations of the executive and judicial branches and local governments. They some-times consult with other state legislatures around the country in hopes of finding better remedies for state problems. As they carry out these difficult responsibilities, they are often resoundingly criticized. James Bryce, the great English observer of American politics, once commented that "the state legislatures are not high-toned bodies."[3]

Many people today would agree with this understated criticism and perhaps express it even more vehemently.[4] Whether the state legislatures still deserve their disrepute is a topic we will examine in this chapter. We will do that by asking four broad questions. First, what do legislatures do? That is, what are their functions? Second, how are legislatures organized to carry out their functions? How are they structured? Third, what roles do individual legislators play in legislative policy making? What are the legislative processes? Fourth, can legislative performance be improved? Have the reforms of recent years been effective? Finally, when we ask these four questions of state legislatures, we must also ask what effects structure, process, and reform have on the kinds of public policies enacted.

LEGISLATIVE FUNCTIONS

Legislatures authorize the building of roads, set taxes and budgets, help constituents, and oversee state agencies, among many other things. In trying to categorize what legislatures do, five functions stand out: policy making, legislative oversight, representation, educating the public, and the judicial function.

Public Policy Making

One of the most important tasks of legislatures is to establish public policies. They do this in a variety of ways. When the state legislature appropriates money for the state budget, deter-mines which taxes will be used to raise money, or passes special educational programs that are mandatory for local school districts, it establishes a statewide policy that affects many people in numerous ways. In states where the constitution contains many policy provisions, the leg-islature may need to propose constitutional amendments in order to enact some new policies.

Legislatures also make policy through less formal means. Legislatures sometimes ask state agencies to do more work than the legislature will pay for. Agency personnel may then consult with legislators regarding which activities will be trimmed back to accommodate the funding shortfall. Administrators in charge of an established program may encounter a new problem and touch base with legislators regarding the best course of action to solve it.

Conventional wisdom holds that the governor initiates policy and the legislature reacts to the governor's agenda.[5] Governors certainly do submit proposals to their legislatures, but legislators have their own interests as well. Consequently, legislators are just as likely as the governor to try to set the state's policy-making agenda.[6] Legislative decision making is often more open to the public and the press than is decision making in most other state government arenas, although many citizens and journalists fail to take advantage of the openness.

Legislative Oversight

The legislature establishes policies and programs, but that does not necessarily mean that those programs will be implemented the way that the legislature intended. To take one example, most states have passed laws providing for the licensing of day-care establishments.

Frequently, such laws delegate to state welfare departments the jobs of formulating more specific rules and enforcing them. If the rules are too rigid, day-care providers will complain to their legislators, and the legislators will come under pressure to relax the rules. Or, if a child is badly maimed, abused, or even killed in one of these centers and the incident becomes widely publicized through television and other media, the legislators will feel pressure to tighten up the rules. An agency may be given money to do a task, but may use the money for something else. To deal with these types of situations, legislatures have adopted a variety of techniques for conducting **legislative oversight**, which involves checking on the bureaucracy's performance and assessing what sorts of changes might be needed.

Sunset Legislation One oversight technique is the **sunset law**, which confronts the problems that arise when some programs and agencies outlive their usefulness. To prevent this, legislatures establish a specific life span for an agency or policy (usually five to seven years). At the end of that period, the sun goes down on the agency or program, and it dies unless the legislature decides that it is still needed. The expiration date is expected to force the legislature to assess the program's accomplishments and whether they are worthwhile.[7]

Assessments of sunset legislation as an oversight mechanism have been mixed. The most comprehensive study of sunset laws found that more than 1,500 agencies in all sunset states had been reviewed over a five-year period (1976–1981), resulting in the termination of only 300 agencies and modifications in the procedures of 300 others. The vast majority were recreated without change.[8] Many legislators complain that the sunset review process is too time consuming, particularly for programs with such strong political support that they could not realistically be terminated. Thirty-six states adopted sunset review after it was begun in Colorado in 1976, but disillusionment with the process led 12 of those states to drop it or scale it back. Most states currently have sunset laws in one form or another, but most of the laws apply only to selected programs or regulations rather than to all state policies and agencies. Sunset reviews sometimes yield revisions of programs, but major cuts in programs rarely occur.[9]

Legislative Veto Another approach for overseeing situations like the administration of day-care licensing is the **legislative veto**, which allows one or both houses of the legislature to veto an agency rule within a specified period (usually 30 to 90 days) and prevent it from taking effect. Provisions vary considerably from state to state, but a large majority of the state legislatures have established some sort of process for reviewing administrative regulations.[10]

Unfortunately for the advocates of the legislative veto, however, it has run into trouble with the courts. The legislative veto was struck down in five states,[11] although one of them (Connecticut) reinstituted the legislative veto through a constitutional amendment.[12] Today, reliance on the legislative veto is on the decline,[13] and some states are replacing it with administrative commissions or committees that have the power to review proposed rules. The strongest legislative review powers enable the review committees to suspend rules that members dislike, but in a number of other states the review process is only advisory.[14] Bear in mind, however, that if agency personnel ignore "advice" from the legislature, future legislative relations may be more difficult.

Casework Casework, or constituency service, is the practice of individual legislators acting on constituent complaints regarding administrative agencies or asking for assistance. If there is a persistent pattern of complaints, casework can be an effective oversight tool for legislators to learn about the shortcomings of specific programs. Even a small number of inquiries from legislators who are on the committees dealing with the agency's duties may trigger a response.

By and large, however, casework as an oversight tool tends to be haphazard. Problems affecting politically active and vocal groups are more likely to receive casework attention than are problems affecting people who may suffer in silence. Casework is much more widely practiced in some states than in others; legislatures with more staff are able to handle more casework, and more experienced legislators receive more requests for help.[15] Depending on the state, the individual legislator receives anywhere from a few to 50 or more casework requests per week.[16] Some legislators view the handling of constituent complaints as a plus for their career aspirations and solicit casework by setting aside office hours when constituents can call in with their complaints. Other members may respond to requests for assistance but do not encourage constituents to ask for help.

Other Oversight Techniques   In addition to sunset legislation, review of administrative rules, and casework, legislatures also have other oversight mechanisms. Legislative committees review administrative agencies and can conduct investigations of administrators in special situations. If an agency requests additional money or new authority, legislators may inquire into the agency's current operations as part of the process of determining whether added funding or new authority is justified. Finally, there is the legislative audit (or postaudit) or program review (or performance review) under which a legislative body studies selected agencies to see how programs are working and whether the agencies are complying with legislative intent. Today, almost all of the states have some process for reviewing agency performance, and many of those provisions are linked to the budget process. Agencies may be required to submit information on their past performance as part of their budget requests for future funding.[17]

Representation

The third major legislative function—and the one causing considerable conflict much of the time—is representing the people in government. In America, this is done through the **apportionment** of seats in the legislature. Each legislature must be reapportioned (redrawing the boundaries of legislative districts) every 10 years, and the fundamental representation issue is this: Do we apportion our legislatures to represent individual citizens on the basis of one person, one vote? How should the boundaries of districts be determined? What should be the relationship between how people vote, on one hand, and the composition of the legislature, on the other? This question has faced legislatures repeatedly and promises to do so again whenever redistricting is needed.

One-Person, One-Vote (or Geographic) Representation   The legislatures are divided into geographic districts that are ideally supposed to be equal in population (one person, one vote), contiguous (no part of the district geographically separated from the rest), and compact. State legislatures began failing the one-person, one-vote test as the U.S. population shifted from a huge rural majority in the late 1800s to a huge urban majority later in the century. Several states stopped redistricting their legislatures to reflect population shifts and, by the 1960s, metropolitan areas were grossly underrepresented in every state except Wisconsin and Massachusetts.[18] The federal courts stayed on the sidelines as this was taking place.[19] Then, in the 1960s, the U.S. Supreme Court moved vigorously to enforce the principle of equal representation by forcing the states to reapportion their legislatures on the basis of one person, one vote.[20] The one-person, one-vote principle was subsequently applied to congressional districts and to general-purpose local governments.[21]

Looking back on these decisions 50 years later, it is clear that they had far-reaching consequences.[22] After reapportionment, legislatures became much more attentive to the problems of metropolitan areas,[23] and the states assumed more active roles in dealing with problems such as air pollution, housing, and sewage treatment.[24] Reapportionment also helped increase African American representation, and it led to the allocation of more state financial aid to local governments, especially those in metropolitan areas.[25] More generally, the distribution of state funds to county governments shifted along with the shifts in legislative representation: Counties that gained state legislative seats increased their shares of state aid, and counties that lost seats received smaller shares of state aid funds.[26]

Because suburbs were the fastest-growing part of the country, reapportionment in the 1960s increased suburban representation more than central-city representation. In a partisan sense, Democrats seemed to benefit most in the North, whereas Republicans made gains in the South.[27] The most long-standing impact of reapportionment may well have been that the influx of suburban, minority, younger, and more heterogeneous legislators led to important reforms of the legislatures themselves and made them more capable of confronting today's problems. Conversely, the political power of rural areas gradually declined as their share of state legislative seats declined.[28]

Partisan Gerrymandering   It is important to recognize that legislative seats can be perfectly apportioned on a one-person, one-vote basis and still leave groups of people feeling underrepresented. This can be accomplished through the **gerrymander,** the practice of mapping legislative boundaries into odd shapes so that one party's (or other group's) voters are heavily concentrated in a few districts, thus allowing the other party (or group) to win a majority of the legislative seats.

Charges of gerrymandering have surfaced in a number of states over the years. One of the most recent incidents occurred in Ohio in 2006, when a pro-Democratic tide swept across the state. Although the Democratic state legislative candidates received more votes, in the aggregate, than the Republican candidates, the Republicans remained in control of both houses of the legislature. How did that happen? A significant factor was the creative drawing of legislative district boundaries after the 2000 census.[29]

In 1986, the U.S. Supreme Court ruled that partisan gerrymandering cases should be considered justiciable, or subject to judicial review.[30] Despite this ruling, neither Indiana nor California[31] was ordered by the courts to undo their gerrymandered legislative districts. And the Supreme Court has subsequently seemed to lose its enthusiasm for venturing into issues of partisan redistricting.[32]

How extensive is partisan gerrymandering? It is probably not as extensive as commonly thought. Despite some exceptions, such as Texas, recent redistricting seems to have reduced the amount of partisan bias in representation.[33] Moreover, the limited party loyalty of voters in recent years and extensive split-ticket voting mean that the effects of gerrymandering tend to fade within a few years.[34] Nonetheless, the massive Republican gains in the 2010 elections led some observers to predict that the redistricting that follows the 2010 Census will yield many districting plans that benefit Republican candidates for the state legislatures and for Congress. Some states, however, assign redistricting to an independent commission that sometimes reduces partisan gerrymandering.[35] That strategy does not always succeed, though. Controversy erupted in Arizona in 2011 after Republicans in the legislature voted to remove a member of the state's redistricting commission for doing too little to draw district boundaries to assist Republican candidates for the U.S. House of Representatives.[36]

Racial Gerrymandering Gerrymandering can be used to strengthen or weaken a variety of different groups, and one of its most sensitive uses involves race. The Supreme Court has generally held that districts cannot be drawn deliberately to weaken minorities. One case involved Tuskegee, Alabama, which in the 1950s changed the city boundaries from a square to a 28-sided polygon that wove in and around African American neighborhoods, keeping enough of their residents out of the city that they could not elect a majority of the city council. This action was so flagrantly intended to dilute African American representation that the Supreme Court invalidated it in 1960.[37]

The Court was less venturesome, however, in striking down electoral arrangements that had a discriminatory impact even though they apparently had not been established with an intent to discriminate. At issue was the system of at-large elections of city council members, which was thought by many observers to dilute the voting strength of African Americans and Hispanics. Mobile, Alabama, for example, had never elected a single African American to its three-member, at-large city council, even though African Americans by the 1970s accounted for nearly 40 percent of the population. When this was challenged as discriminatory, the U.S. Supreme Court refused to strike down Mobile's at-large elections, because there was no evidence that the designers of the system in 1911 had intended it to dilute African American representation.[38]

This ruling infuriated Democrats in Congress, and they retaliated with the 1982 amendments to the Voting Rights Act. Under this legislation, an election system is illegal if it results in diluting minority representation, even when there was no proof of an intent to discriminate. In 1986, the Supreme Court relied on this law to strike down a multimember system for electing state legislators in North Carolina that had diluted African American representation.[39] The Court spelled out three principles for states to follow when conducting future reapportionments. A racial or language minority group must be given its own legislative or congressional district if:

- The minority population is large enough and localized enough to be a majority of the population within a district.
- It is a politically cohesive group.
- The surrounding majority of white voters vote often enough as a bloc that they can usually defeat minority candidates.

For the 1990 reapportionments, this decision obliged mapmakers to create a number of **majority-minority districts**. The results were some strange-looking districts (see Figure 8.1) that clearly violated the compactness principle and barely met the contiguity principle. The Supreme Court ordered lower federal courts to determine the legality of a bizarrely shaped North Carolina district,[40] and that action encouraged a flurry of suits challenging the legality of other majority-minority districts. Inconsistent Supreme Court rulings since then have left state officials uncertain regarding how much racial gerrymandering is allowed or required.[41]

What was the impact of majority-minority districting? As intended, its major impact was a dramatic increase in African American and Hispanic representation.[42] It also aided Republicans. By packing large numbers of minority Democrats into a majority-minority district and siphoning off white Democrats into surrounding suburban districts where they would be outnumbered by Republicans, race-based districting gave southern Republicans four additional

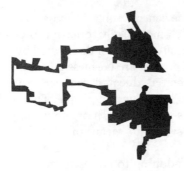

FIGURE 8.1

Gerrymanders: Illinois's 4th Congressional District

One result of the battles over reapportionment in the 1990s has been the creation of some legislative and congressional districts whose shapes are strikingly evocative of the original gerrymander. In 1992, Illinois's 4th Congressional District was designed to create a district for Chicago's Hispanic population. Puerto Ricans were heavily concentrated in its northern portion of the district and Mexican Americans in the southern portion.

Source: Chicago's 4th District, courtesy of U.S. Congress, Illinois 4th District Office.

seats in Congress in 1992 and made Republicans competitive in several other districts. Racial redistricting also cost the Democrats many state legislative seats all across the South.[43]

In recent years, however, the Supreme Court has been backing away from majority-minority districts if the minority population is geographically dispersed. The Court struck down two such congressional districts in Georgia in 1995, thus forcing a redrawing of that state's congressional districts. Despite the dissolution of the two majority-African American districts, their two African American representatives won reelection in 1996 in districts that were by then majority-white.

Social Change and Categorical Representation   The conflict over majority-minority districts opened up a Pandora's box of representational issues. Some reformers call for representing people by group categories in addition to, or perhaps even instead of, representation by geographic district on a one-person, one-vote basis.[44] If African Americans and Hispanics can have districts carved out for them, what other categories of people might be found to be grossly underrepresented in legislatures and thus deserving of special representative schemes?[45]

In terms of categorical representation, legislators are most representative of their constituents on the *birthright characteristics* of race, religion, and ethnicity and are becoming more so all the time. Nevertheless, some people have a smaller share of legislators than their percent of the population. Despite improvements in representation, only 8 percent of state legislators are African American (compared to about 12 percent of the overall population), another 3 percent are Hispanic (compared to 12 percent of the population), and about 22 percent are women. To some degree these diversity trends are related: African American and Hispanic state legislators are disproportionately female.[46]

Remember, however, that the composition of the legislatures varies considerably from state to state.

In general, legislators tend to be well grounded in their communities, having lived there longer than the average constituent and having been engaged in community life. They are more educated than the general population: Roughly 75 percent of state legislators have college degrees, in contrast with 28 percent of the general public.[47] In part because of the higher education level of state legislators, they are much more likely to have professional or managerial occupations. Contrary to popular beliefs, legislatures are not dominated by lawyers. Only about 16 percent of legislators are attorneys and 10 percent are business owners.[48]

Obviously, wealthier and better-educated Americans are much better represented in the legislatures than are poorer and less-educated people. This is less due to districting plans than to the tendency for upper-status people to be more active in politics and to the cost of running for office—a cost that is well beyond the means of most Americans.

Perceptual Representation In addition to representation by geographic district and by social category, representation can also refer to the *perceptions* legislators have about their representational role. The classic presentation of perceptual representation was made by Edmund Burke, the great British theorist, who distinguished between the trustee role and the delegate role. Burke advocated the **trustee** role, in which the legislators vote according to their own best judgment of the common good and not necessarily according to the wishes of their constituents. In the **delegate** role, by contrast, the legislators vote according to their constituents' wishes. Legislators sometimes balance the two roles, voting as a trustee on issues that generate little public interest or emotion but voting as a delegate on issues that enflame their constituents. Such legislators are said to play the **politico** role. Many legislators lean more toward following their own views, at least in the abstract, but members from smaller districts tended to be more sensitive to constituency opinion.[49]

Legislators who try to be delegates face the recurring problem of trying to determine what the public wants them to do. Many Americans do not pay much attention to many legislative issues, and public opinion rarely provides detailed guidance regarding specific proposals. Nevertheless, the broad drift of public opinion shapes many major decisions emerging from the state legislatures.[50]

Political Education

Another important legislative function is helping the public learn about important policy issues facing the state and what might be done about them.[51] Political education takes place during legislative campaigns, during committee hearings, when constituents read newsletters or other mail from their legislators, when college students serve as legislative interns, and when the news media cover legislative investigations or floor debates. Because the legislatures are more open to the public and the media than are the other major branches of government, they offer many opportunities for learning about state government and the issues facing state officials.

Critics complain that the state legislatures do not do a very effective job of educating the public about politics and policy issues, although that is not entirely the fault of the legislators. Many citizens pay little attention to state legislative activities, and media coverage of the legislatures is often spotty at best. Some research finds that media coverage of state legislatures has actually declined in recent years, particularly television coverage.[52] However, National Public Radio has received a grant to help local public radio stations to provide more coverage of state government, including the state legislators.[53]

The complexity of legislative organization and the large volume of proposals considered in a typical session will overwhelm all but the most interested citizens. Moreover, many state legislative campaigns are not particularly informative. Bear in mind that many legislators find the job of informing themselves to be very difficult, and sharing information with the public and media may produce criticism and conflict at times. Maintaining a low profile is sometimes safer.

Over the last few decades, legislative proceedings in most states have grown much more open to the public and the press. Moreover, an increasing amount of legislative information is now available through the Internet. Citizens in many states now have easy access to a wealth of legislative information, including (depending on the state) the texts of bills and proposed amendments, committee reports, legislative calendars (what activities are scheduled for the next several days), where various proposals are in the legislative process, and newsletters produced by individual members of the legislature.[54]

The Judicial Function

A traditionally unappealing legislative function involves investigating charges of misconduct and trying to resolve disputes between individuals.[55] Many of these cases involve members of the legislature, but judges and executive branch officials may also be the targets of inquiries from time to time. This function was traditionally unappealing because it rarely seemed to please anyone and often angered people—most commonly the targets of the investigation and their allies. Still, in the case of serious wrongdoing, legislators would often grit their teeth and investigate the matter. One fairly recent case involved Connecticut's governor John Rowland, who was the subject of a state legislative impeachment inquiry and a federal corruption investigation. His decision to resign his office brought a halt to the legislative inquiry, but the federal investigation ended his political career. He admitted receiving some gifts from state employees and contractors but denied giving them any special treatment in return.[56]

In recent years, the judicial function has gained popularity as a form of political combat.[57] If we cannot defeat a candidate for office in the election, perhaps we can accuse that person of some ethical violation or other misconduct. Even if the person is eventually vindicated, his or her reputation may be tarnished, perhaps permanently. These attacks may lead to retaliation and protracted infighting, which may seriously impair the legislature's ability to get much work done and which is hardly beneficial to the legislature's public image. The increasing polarization of the parties has probably encouraged legislators to attack members of the opposition party more than happened in less polarized eras, such as the 1950s.

LEGISLATIVE STRUCTURE: HOW ORGANIZATION AFFECTS POLICY MAKING

The 50 states are very similar in their legislative organization. All but Nebraska are bicameral, having two houses. All but Nebraska and, for many years, the one-party states of the South organize themselves around political party caucuses. In recent years, the growth of Republican strength in many southern legislatures has increased the role of party caucuses there. And all 50 states rely heavily on committees to do most of their work. Of these three structural features, bicameralism has the least effect on policy formulation, with one significant exception.

Bicameralism

Bicameralism developed during the colonial period, when the lower house was looked on as the body of the people and the senate, the upper house, as the body of the governor. After the Revolution in 1776, the state senates served mainly to represent wealthy people with property, who feared that the popularly dominated lower houses would redistribute their wealth. By the early nineteenth century, all the states were bicameral. Only Nebraska reverted to the unicameral form, doing so in 1934.

Unicameralism has worked well in Nebraska, and legislative reformers have urged it upon other states. Reformers argue that elimination of one of the two houses would make the legislature operate more efficiently and effectively (and cheaply). It would eliminate the need for conference committees (which are needed to iron out differences between house and senate versions of a bill) and might increase the prestige of the body.

In contrast, the supporters of bicameralism say that the two-house legislature helps preserve the traditional principle of checks and balances and impedes the hasty passage of poorly conceived bills by slowing down the legislative process. However, when the house is controlled by one party and the senate by the other party, legislative proposals of all sorts may fall victim to partisan quarreling. Bicameralism gives opponents of a bill more places in which to defeat it.

Whatever its merits, unicameralism is not popular with either legislators or the voters. When put on the ballot, unicameral proposals have been invariably voted down.

PARTIES AND POLICY MAKING: THE RESPONSIBLE-PARTY MODEL

The **responsible-party model** has been very popular with many reform-minded political scientists, who feel it is the best way to make the legislature accountable to the voters.[58] According to the responsible-party model, each party should adopt a clear, specific party program that is presented to the voters. All the party's candidates should support that program, and each voter should vote for the team of party candidates whose program seems best. The winning party should be cohesive enough to deliver on its promises. The losing party should monitor the actions of the party in power, alert the public in cases of failure or misconduct, and prepare constructive alternatives to the policies of the party in power.

Critics of the responsible-party model worry that it may escalate interparty conflict to a harmful level. They also doubt that either party in the larger, more diverse states can take clear stands on very many issues without causing the party to disintegrate. Moreover, as a practical matter, when a large majority of candidates are nominated in primaries, how can either party assure that all of its candidates will support the party program? Finally, although the responsible-party model tries to link the majority wishes of the public with public officials, most people do not vote in state legislative elections, especially when they are held in nonpresidential years.

In actual practice, the states vary widely on their degree of party strength and the ability of the parties to provide leadership and organization in the legislature.

Party Leadership

The key feature of party organization of the legislature is the attempt to provide for leadership through the *centralization of influence* in a few party leaders. The dominant party leader in the lower house is the **speaker of the house,** who is the presiding officer and is usually chosen from the majority party (or the majority coalition in one-party states). The speaker's powers vary from state to state, but speakers typically have the authority to assign bills to committee, to recognize house members who desire to speak on the floor, to influence committee assignments of the members, to determine the house calendars (which schedule legislative actions), and to control the ebb and flow of legislative business on the floor. In order to restrain the potential power of the speaker, 10 states limit how long any single person may serve in the office. In some cases (Florida, for example), speakers are limited to a single two-year term. In some other states, tradition holds that the office of speaker should rotate from one term to the next.[59]

Immediately subordinate to the speaker are the **majority leader** (or floor leader) and assistant majority leaders (or whips), who try to line up floor votes for the majority-party-supported bills and to monitor the sentiments of party members. The same job is performed for the minority party by the **minority leader** and the assistant minority leaders. From time to time, all the legislators of a party gather in a meeting called the party **caucus**, where they try to set goals and plan legislative strategies. At these meetings, the party determines who will hold the leadership positions, what bills (if any) will demand party discipline, and who will prevail in the recurring battles between opposing factions within the party.

It is up to the speakers and majority leaders to get their members to vote the party position (if there is one) on the most important bills. There are trends in place that both aid and hinder the leaders in this task.

Trends Supporting Stronger Party Leaders

A number of speakers have strengthened their leadership position by recruiting legislative candidates and raising campaign funds and distributing them to legislative candidates.[60] California's assembly speaker Willie Brown was so successful at raising campaign funds in the 1980s that he provided up to half the funding for Democrats running in open seat elections, and he regularly provided about one-third of the funds for Democrats running in marginal districts.[61] Ohio Speaker of the House Vernal Riffe doled out $2.7 million in 1990 legislative races.[62]

Party leaders also have other means to persuade fellow legislators to follow party discipline on crucial votes. They influence committee assignments, office space assignments, staff, and other perquisites that affect the job of a legislator. They can also use influence over legislative scheduling to reward their political allies—for example, by scheduling floor action on a bill when those allies and their supporters are ready for action.

Trends Hampering Party Leaders

There are countervailing factors, however, that may hamper the ability of legislative party leaders to influence their houses.[63] Most of these trends stem from developments in the political parties in general. There are very few states anymore where one political party consistently controls all three institutions of state government (the house, the senate, and the governorship). Party leaders may, therefore, have a difficult time delivering on some of the issues that their legislative colleagues favor. Incumbent state legislators are likely to raise the bulk of their campaign funds on their own, which may give them a feeling of independence from party leaders.

Strong leadership is also threatened by the movement to limit the number of terms that a legislator can hold office, in part because party leaders are often drawn from members with more legislative experience. Building long-term relationships with legislative colleagues is made more difficult when leaders and rank-and-file members leave the legislature more frequently.

Note, too, that leaders who are chosen by members of the legislature cannot afford to antagonize very many of their colleagues very often without triggering an uprising that may lead to the selection of new leaders. Aggressive leaders often antagonize members, so party leaders often try to rely on persuasion and negotiation rather than trying to issue orders. Party leadership can be especially difficult if a party is wracked by serious internal disagreements. In Kansas, the Republican Party has been plagued by a major dispute between moderates and conservatives, and conservative legislative candidates are challenging moderates in the party primaries in hopes of expanding conservative influence. Trying to lead both factions can be very time consuming and is sometimes impossible.[64]

Do Parties Make Any Difference?

In American political theory, competition between two well-organized parties should present alternative policy programs to the voters. As the two parties compete for votes, the competition forces the parties to be more responsive to the voters' wishes. In contrast, the absence of party competition is believed to lead to political factionalism built around personalities and temporary issues. The factions are not permanent and they fail to translate voter preferences into public policy.[65]

Do strong, competitive parties in fact affect state policies? Although the results of voluminous studies are not conclusive, several generalizations have emerged.

First, insofar as spending policies are concerned, states dominated by one party have lower state-local spending per capita than do the more competitive, two-party states (assessing competitiveness statewide). But the one-party states also tend to be poorer than the competitive states. And some studies find that it is their impoverishment, not their lack of interparty competitiveness, that leads these states to spend less money per capita.[66]

Second, there are, however, certain conditions under which party dynamics affect spending decisions. This is most likely to occur in states where competitiveness is highly volatile and the majority party has a realistic chance of losing control of state government, where competition reaches down into individual legislative races (as opposed to just statewide competition), and where the parties play a major role in legislative decision making and do a better job of mobilizing the electorate.[67]

Third, party politics seems to have more impact on nonexpenditure policies. Wayne Francis found that the competitive states were more likely to take action on issues before the legislature than were the noncompetitive states. More generally, the parties probably are freer to exert influence on policy decisions that do not cost money and, therefore, are not as limited by what the state can afford.[68]

Fourth, outside the South, when Democrats control the legislature, they often enact different kinds of policies than the Republicans enact when they have control. Civil rights laws, for example, were much more likely to be passed under Democratic control than under Republican control.[69]

Finally, state party ideologies affect many state policy decisions. Although Democrats and Republicans are found in all 50 states, some state parties are more conservative (or liberal) than other state parties bearing the same party label. In a state with many conservative Democrats, legislative decisions are likely to be different than the decisions made where the Democrats are more liberal, and the same tendency exists among Republicans.[70]

In sum, party competition, party strength, and party ideologies can make a difference in the kinds of policies a state adopts, but many other factors also influence policy choices. The parties have more impact on nonexpenditure policies than they do in spending decisions, however. Spending decisions are heavily influenced by the economy of the state; regardless of what legislators might want to do, their spending options will be limited by financial considerations. This dynamic came painfully to the attention of state legislators in the 2008 legislative sessions and beyond: An economic decline, produced in part by major increases in fuel prices and a downturn in the housing market, led to significant revenue shortfalls in most of the states. Legislators faced the unpleasant alternatives of cutting financial support for programs or raising additional revenue.

Committee Organization as a Decentralizing Force

In contrast to party organization, which may try to centralize political influence in the hands of party leaders, committee organization *decentralizes political influence* to the chairpersons and members of the various committees that study legislative proposals called bills. The typical legislature will consider 1,000 to 5,000 measures each biennium (New York considered more than 18,000 during its 2010 session).[71] In addition, the legislature must try to oversee the other branches, review existing programs, and explore ideas for improving state and local programs.

To provide a division of labor capable of processing this massive amount of work, legislatures have committees. Committees receive bills, conduct hearings, change the substance of bills, and vote to approve or disapprove them. There is usually a **standing committee** for each major area of legislation, such as finance, agriculture, education, or transportation.

In addition to standing committees, **select committees** are created on a relatively temporary basis to study important issues that do not fit readily into the workload of the standing committees. Another type of committee is the **joint committee**, which is composed of members of both houses. Connecticut, Maine, and Massachusetts rely heavily on joint standing committees.[72] The advantage of such an arrangement is that it precludes the necessity of a bill being examined separately by senate and house committees. A special type of joint committee is the **conference committee**, which is created to resolve the differences between house- and senate-passed versions of a bill. Finally, interim committees are sometimes used between legislative sessions to study complex issues and to develop proposals, especially in states with relatively short legislative sessions, and to monitor actions of the executive branch.

Committee influence in the state legislatures appears to be weaker than is committee influence in Congress. Many state legislative committees have only limited staff support, and high turnover among members in many states limits the development of expertise. Where the parties are especially strong, committees may be given relatively little leeway. Even so, considering the time pressures at work in most state legislatures, a large portion of committee work almost certainly escapes review by other members much of the time.

LEGISLATIVE PROCESS: HOW LEGISLATORS MAKE POLICY

Before an idea, no matter how brilliant, can be turned into public law, it must work its way through the legislative maze. Some of the procedures for doing this are very formal; others are very informal. Legislators play a variety of roles in this process, and they follow several unofficial and unwritten rules that govern legislative behavior.

Passing a Law

A simplified model of a bill's passage is shown in Figure 8.2. The bill may originally be conceived by a legislator, a lobbyist, a state agency, the governor's staff, a citizen group, or an interested citizen. But it can only be formally introduced by a house or senate member, who is called the bill's author. The bill's first reading* occurs when the clerk announces the bill's number and title to the full house or senate.

---

*It is called a reading because the clerks originally read the bills aloud to the full chamber. Although this requirement is still demanded by some state constitutions, bills are never read aloud anymore.

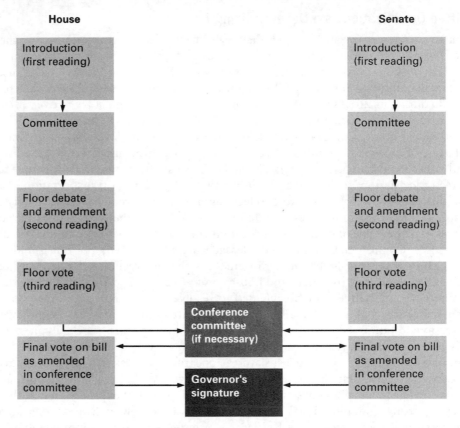

FIGURE 8.2
Steps in the Passage of a Bill

Before being enacted into law, a bill must go through several steps in the legislative maze. Probably 60 percent or more of bills are not enacted into law in a typical year.

After introduction, the bill is referred to a committee. If the author wants the bill to pass, he or she would hope it is referred to a friendly committee and will check on its status as the session proceeds. If it is referred to a hostile committee in a state with strong committees, it may be given an unfavorable recommendation or may simply be **pigeonholed** (that is, bottled up in committee). An important bill may be sent to a subcommittee that will conduct public hearings, invite all interested parties—or those likely to support the majority position—to testify, and possibly amend the bill. In states with effective **sunshine laws**, almost all official committee action is taken publicly in open meetings, records are kept of votes on amendments, and tape recordings of the debate are made available to reporters and the public. Note, however, that the sunshine laws may be undercut by private discussions that take place informally. Also, many of the sunshine laws contain various provisions allowing some meetings not open to the public.

After a bill is reported out of committee, it is put on a **calendar** to await its second reading and floor debate. Debate quite often occurs in a committee of the whole, which is simply the whole house meeting under the less formal committee rules. These allow a smaller **quorum** and make it easier to amend bills. Since the committee of the whole is where the full chamber often makes its most serious amendments, the votes in a committee of the whole may indicate a legislator's intent more than do the votes on final passage of bills.

Floor action on some bills is fairly harmonious, with almost all members agreeing on a preferred course of action. However, some proposals are highly controversial, and floor debate on those proposals may include accusations, denunciations, and heated denials, along with all sorts of conflicting evidence and arguments regarding the best course of action. Opponents of a bill may propose sending it back to committee for added work; approving that proposal often causes the bill to die.

Finally, after floor debate and amendment, the bill comes back for final consideration as amended. This is the third reading. Most states require roll call votes on the final passage of the bill and provide electronic voting devices that flash a green light for an *aye* vote and a red light for a *nay* vote, and automatically record the votes. When roll call votes are not needed or when unanimous consent is required, a voice vote may be used.

When the house-passed version of a bill differs from the senate-passed version, the first house to pass the bill will sometimes accept the amendments made by the second house. If not, a joint conference committee is appointed by the speaker of the house and the president of the senate to resolve the differences. The conference committee has an equal number of senators and representatives. The house and senate must approve or reject the conference committee report without amendment, although they may send it back to the conference committee for additional work.

Once the chambers pass a single version of a bill, it is printed in final form (called *enrollment*) and is sent to the governor for signature. At this stage, the governor has three choices. If the governor signs the bill, it becomes law. If the governor neither signs nor vetoes it, it becomes law in most states without his or her signature. If the governor vetoes the bill, it does not become law unless the veto is overridden by the legislature. This seldom happens, in part because some states require a two-thirds majority vote in each house to override a veto, and in part because many vetoes are made at the close of the legislative session, when the legislators are no longer present to conduct an override vote. To cope with this, more and more states are providing for special override sessions to give the house and senate a chance to override vetoes made after the regular session ends.

Finally, some states provide for a pocket veto. If a bill comes to a governor at the close of a session and it is not signed or vetoed within a specified number of days (usually 5 to 15), it does not become law, and the governor is said to have exercised a **pocket veto**.[73] Overall, there are many opportunities to block proposals in the legislative process; killing bills is much easier than passing them.

How Legislators Are Influenced to Vote

Perhaps the most important aspect of the informal legislative process concerns how legislators are influenced to vote on specific public policies. In some discussions of representation, people ask whether the legislator *should* be a trustee or a delegate. In reality, the pressures on legislators are much more complex than this. They consult and are influenced by a wide variety of sources, ranging from fellow legislators to individual constituents.

One survey asked state legislators to identify the sources they consulted most frequently when they decided how to vote. They tended to rely much more heavily on advice they got from fellow legislators than they did on advice from sources outside the legislature such as the governor or their constituents.[74] The only extralegislative sources that ranked high were lobbyists. Legislators rely on their colleagues for guidance because some of them are likely to be informed about the specific provisions of proposals and because legislative colleagues are available for guidance when decisions must be made quickly, particularly in the closing days of the session.

This finding about the influence of lobbyists was reinforced by a study of lobbyists registered in Iowa. It found that interest group lobbyists were more active than other actors concerned with the legislation. They took positions on 61 percent of the bills before the legislature, compared to 35 percent for the governor and only 26 percent for the house majority caucus. Further, on 84 percent of the bills, there was no conflict among lobbyists. When they came into conflict with the governor or the house majority caucus, however, the interest groups were more likely than the others to lose.[75]

Legislators are also affected by their own ideological beliefs. A study of voting in the Connecticut and North Carolina legislatures found that the liberal or conservative orientation of legislators had a greater impact on their votes than did their partisanship or the economic characteristics of the districts they represented.[76] The personal beliefs of legislators often affect which colleagues they choose when seeking guidance. Although many Americans believe that politicians have no principles and follow the prevailing political winds, this study and other evidence show that most legislators do stand for certain beliefs pretty consistently.

To varying degrees, the political parties also influence members' voting decisions. The personal beliefs of Republican legislators are often different from the beliefs of Democratic legislators, in large measure because party activists in the two parties have differing beliefs. Those activists affect which candidates are elected to office. Also, when looking to colleagues for guidance, Democrats often look to Democratic colleagues, while Republicans look to Republican colleagues.

LEGISLATIVE REFORM: IMPROVING LEGISLATIVE PERFORMANCE

As legislatures have gone about their tasks of making public policy, they have been heavily criticized for the way they conduct the public's business. The American Political Science Association's Committee on American Legislatures, for example, charged back in 1954 that "the state legislatures are poorly equipped to serve as policy-making agencies in . . . America."[77] Today, some five decades later, that charge no longer rings true. State legislatures are now a "leading source of policy innovations,"[78] at least when economic conditions are reasonably favorable. The legislatures have revamped themselves extensively over the years, but they still face numerous problems. We need to examine the agenda for legislative reform in the states, the accomplishment of reform, and the consequences of that reform.

The Agenda for Legislative Reform

Since the middle of the twentieth century, several prestigious organizations joined the call for reforming state legislatures.[79] The most ambitious calls came in a 1971 book, *The Sometimes Governments*,[80] that ranked the 50 states on an index of legislative reform and outlined dozens of specific steps that legislatures should take in order to make themselves more accountable to the voters and more responsible in carrying out their job. The goal of reform was to professionalize the legislatures, and professionalization was to be achieved through the following five-point agenda.

1. *Legislatures should meet full time and offer decent pay.* There should be more full-time legislatures capable of holding longer sessions in order to conduct the public business. Part-time legislatures, it was argued, inevitably make it harder for salary earners to give up their incomes in order to serve. Low salaries would perpetuate the dominance in legislatures of lawyers, farmers, and the small number of business owners who can afford to absent themselves from their primary occupations for two to four months at a time in order to serve in the legislatures.

   The growing responsibilities of state governments since 1900 has meant a growing workload for the legislatures, some of which met for only 30 to 90 days out of every two years in the early 1900s. Longer sessions were needed to cope with that heavier workload and with the increasing complexity of state issues.

2. *Legislatures should have better staff and research capabilities.* Without adequate staff and research capabilities, legislatures are unduly dependent on the information provided by interest groups, state agencies, and other interested parties. Legislative committees and individual legislators need staff assistance, especially to draft bills, analyze bills that legislators do not have time to read thoroughly, analyze the governor's budget proposals, and evaluate programs being administered by state agencies. As the responsibilities of state governments increased during the twentieth century and as state issues grew increasingly complex, the need for more and better information grew more pressing.

3. *Constitutional restrictions on state legislatures should be removed.* In particular, reformers seek to remove constitutional provisions that set legislative pay at very low levels, limit the length of sessions, and put restrictions on state budget-making powers. Of special concern are the many *earmarked funds* in state constitutions that hamper legislative flexibility to set spending policies for the state.

4. *Legislative ethics should be improved.* By its nature, campaign funding indebts some legislators to vested interests. Many legislators have hidden conflicts of interest. They receive benefits from organizations that in turn benefit from policies supported by those very legislators. Accordingly, reformers have called for extensive campaign finance reform that will disclose campaign contributors to public scrutiny, put limits on campaign contributions, provide public funds for legislative campaigns, and put tough restrictions on legislative lobbyists.

5. *Legislatures should be smaller in size.* Just how large a legislature should be cannot be determined precisely. Minnesota—with 67 members—has the largest state senate, and New Hampshire—with 400 members—has the largest house. The Committee for Economic Development recommends that state legislatures be no larger than 100 members. Reformers feel that a smaller legislature would enhance its prestige, make it possible to offer higher salaries, and enable more highly qualified people to run for office. Reducing the size would necessarily force the legislatures to restructure the committees and make it easier to pinpoint responsibility. However, a smaller legislature requires larger districts, which increase the cost of running for office.

Accomplishing Legislative Reform

Considerable progress has been made toward these reformist goals. All states adopted some of the reforms, and some states adopted a substantial majority of them. The most extensive progress has been made on the structural and procedural items spelled out in goals 1, 2, and 3. Less progress has come on goals 4 and 5.[81]

On goal 1, 8 legislatures have, for all practical purposes, become full-time bodies and another 36 meet annually. In addition to longer regular sessions in many states, special sessions are quite common; 22 states held one or more in 2007 alone.[82] As legislative sessions have lengthened, legislative pay has also gone up. Comparing legislative compensation across states is difficult due to the wide variety of compensation systems in use, but 17 states gave legislators compensation of at least $40,000 per year in 2005. Many legislatures also give members allowances for living expenses, and most state legislatures give extra compensation to at least some legislative leaders. Although no one will get rich on such incomes, legislative salaries are now high enough in some states that dedicated, frugal people can devote full time to their legislative tasks.[83] In other states, even part-time legislators are devoting more time to legislative work than in the past.

On goal 2, there has been a dramatic increase in legislative staff in the past 40 years. Today, the 50 state legislatures collectively employ roughly 28,000 full-time staffers during legislative sessions.[84] The state legislatures have also increased their information bases by using computers for a wide range of functions, from analyzing budgetary information to communicating with citizens and tracking legislative proposals.

The net impact of legislative reform has been to turn the most professionalized legislatures into dynamic institutions that now play a significant policy-making role.[85] The Oregon legislature, for example, took the lead in overhauling federally assisted health care programs; Wisconsin in 1996 restructured its welfare programs. Since some innovations lean in a liberal direction and others in a conservative direction, obviously no one is pleased with them all. What is beyond dispute, however, is the policy leadership exhibited by the state legislatures in recent years.

Consider, however, that the progress of legislative reform has varied considerably from state to state. As Table 8.1 indicates, the reformers have made more headway in the more populous, urban states, such as New York, Michigan, and California. The less populated, rural states have generally been less receptive to the reformers' proposals, in part because higher salaries and extensive staff support are expensive and in part because the legislature's workload in those states is lower, at least compared to the larger states (see also Table 8.2).

▶ TABLE 8.1

Highs and Lows in State Legislative Professionalism

The Most Professional Legislatures		The Least Professional Legislatures	
California	New York	Montana	Maine
Illinois	Ohio	North Dakota	Wyoming
Massachusetts	Pennsylvania	South Dakota	Utah
Michigan	Wisconsin	New Hampshire	
New Jersey			

Source: Keith Hamm and Gary Moncrief, "Legislative Politics in the States," in Virginia Gray and Russell Hanson, eds., *Politics in the American States*, 9th ed (Washington, DC: CQ Press, 2008), pp.155–156.

> ### TABLE 8.2
>
> **Legislative Salaries and Workloads**
>
> Legislative Salaries:
>
> | | |
> |---|---|
> | California | $95,291 |
> | New Hampshire | $200 |
>
> Additional Compensation for Presiding
> Officer of the Lower House:
>
> | | |
> |---|---|
> | New York | $133,639 |
> | Arizona (and several other states) | none |
>
> Bills Enacted in the 2010 Regular Sessions:
>
> | | |
> |---|---|
> | California | 1,039 |
> | Ohio | 41 |
>
> Source: *The Book of the States, 43* (Lexington, KY: Council of State Governments, 2011), pp. 88–91, 101–103, 110–111.

The Unintended Consequences of Legislative Reform

However innovative the legislatures have become, they are not getting much credit for their accomplishments. This is partly due to the cynicism of the press and the public, but may also be due to some unintended consequences that have accompanied reform.

First, legislative professionalization may have inhibited progress on the goal of improving legislative ethics. As legislatures spend increasing amounts of money on a wide range of public programs, they inevitably attract a larger number of interest groups and lobbyists who make campaign contributions, attend candidates' fund-raisers, and hold out the possibility of lucrative job opportunities.[86] Bear in mind, however, that in the unreformed, part-time legislatures, members earn most of their living doing some other job—banking, farming, and teaching, for example. Those legislators are likely to be sympathetic to the demands of groups representing their own occupational interests much of the time. Ethics problems are difficult to escape in both reformed and unreformed legislatures.

A second unintended consequence in the minds of some observers (one that is a point of dispute) is that legislative professionalism gives more political help to the Democrats than to the Republicans. According to this argument, as the legislatures become full-time jobs, they are less attractive to people with lucrative careers of their own than they are to people without well-paid careers. Since Republicans on average have better nonpolitical career opportunities than do the Democrats, highly qualified Republicans may be less likely to make careers out of the legislature. However, rising professionalism has not prevented Republican gains in Florida or Texas, nor did the reform legacy prevent major Republican gains in the 1994 elections or in 2010. On close inspection, the connection between professionalism and party success appears to be, at best, fairly inconsistent.[87]

If legislators who are students, retired, or housewives are included in the count, about one-fourth of all legislators are full time today. Increasing numbers of them are also staying in the job for longer periods. As recently as the 1960s, about 40 percent of all legislators would be serving their first term. That percentage has gradually dropped. In 1992, after a legislative redistricting that should have increased the number of first-timers, the number actually dropped to 30 percent.[88] However, during the period from 1987 to 1997, 72 percent of state senate seats and 79 percent of state house seats changed hands at least once.

If the legislature is someone's only career, he or she may become preoccupied with staying in office,[89] the important exception being members who find legislative work too difficult or stressful. The more that legislators become careerists with no outside occupation to fall back on, the more pressure they feel to preserve their seats in the state capitol. This might imply that greater professionalization leads to a greater incumbency advantage in state legislative elections. As with partisan consequences of professionalization, the impact of professionalization on incumbency advantage is difficult to assess. Researchers have found that, using one plausible measure of professionalization, more professionalized legislatures have higher reelection rates. However, when the researchers used a different measure of professionalism, they found the *opposite* tendency, with the less professional legislatures having higher reelection rates.[90]

The Term Limitation Movement

The trend toward legislative careerism has obviously not sat well with the public. By early 2002, 21 states had reacted to careerism by adopting legislative term limits, 19 of them through the initiative process described in Chapter 5. However, some of the term limit laws ran into legal or political problems and were sometimes overturned or trimmed back.[91] The most restrictive limits are in Arkansas, California, Michigan, and Oregon, which put a six-year limit on representatives and an eight-year limit on senators.

Is the idea of term limits a good one? On the positive side, proponents argue that term limits will ensure a constant infusion of new blood and new ideas into the legislatures, will reduce the advantages that incumbents have in elections, will create a healthy competition for other political offices, and will nip legislative careerism in the bud.[92]

Some scholars and practitioners, however, are negative. Their arguments fall into one of two camps. In the first camp are those who think that the fear of careerism has been overdone. They point out that most legislators voluntarily retire after a few terms even without term limits. One study of six states over an 18-year period found that less than 3 percent of legislators remained in office the entire 18 years.[93] Another study looked at all 50 states over 12 years and found that barely one-fourth of representatives and one-third of senators who were first elected in 1979 were still in office 12 years later in 1990.[94] A number of the states adopting term limits already had relatively high levels of turnover, which means term limits will not affect many legislative careers in those states.[95]

A third camp of observers, however, think that term limits will lead to some harmful unintended consequences. Term limits will impede the growth of leadership in legislatures. It takes a few years' experience for legislators to familiarize themselves with the goals and tactics of other political players such as lobbyists, legislative staff, and executive branch officials who have been around for a long time. Under California's six-year limit, just when these legislators reach the point where they have accumulated the experience and knowledge to become effective leaders, they will be forced to retire. Relatively inexperienced members will move into important leadership positions. This will necessarily increase the strength and influence of the bureaucracy, interest groups, paid legislative staff, and the governor.[96]

In addition, term limits deprive voters of the right to retain legislators who voters believe are doing a good job. This may help to explain why new legislators in term limit states place less emphasis on responding to the demands of their districts than do new members in states without term limits.[97]

Are these dire predictions about term limits coming to pass? We do not know for certain yet, since it was only in 1998 that the first class of legislators was forced out of office by term limits. However, early indications suggest that both the advocates and opponents of term limits can claim vindication. Proponents note that term limits have speeded up voluntary retirements and thus put a curb on careerism—although many legislative newcomers under term limits are veterans of local politics.[98] Opponents point to California as evidence that the negative predictions are starting to materialize. The speaker was forced from office in 1998, opening the probability of a leadership vacuum and a decline in party discipline.[99] And as the leadership began to lose influence over the legislature, lobbyists gained influence, writing speeches for legislators and, in some instances, even drafting legislation.[100]

The most exhaustive study of the impact of term limits so far also finds that term limited legislatures have less influence over budgetary decisions than do legislatures without term limits. In a similar vein, the term limited legislatures are less likely to adopt new policies than legislatures lacking term limits. In both cases, the common thread may be that more experienced members are needed for decision making (whether for budgeting or policy innovation), and term limits reduce the supply of experienced members.[101]

One other effect of term limits, which may or may not have been intended, is that it may have helped Republicans win more legislative seats.[102] If Republicans are less interested in building careers in legislative office, a term-limited legislature may be more attractive than one without limits. In addition, because term limits remove incumbents from office, they increase the importance of money in legislative elections. Historically, the Republican Party has usually been more successful at fund-raising than has the Democratic Party. However, term limits did not prevent major Democratic gains in the 2006 elections, just as legislative professionalism did not prevent Republican gains in the 1990s or in 2010.

ROLLING BACK REFORM: DEINSTITUTIONALIZATION?

Some observers, including Alan Rosenthal, the nation's leading authority on state legislatures, have speculated that we may be entering an era of eroding legislative capability.[103] Term limits will reduce the legislatures' ability to retain experienced, knowledgeable members (at least in states where turnover has recently been low). Voters in a number of states are increasingly turning to initiatives and referenda to make policy decisions without the legislature. Several states have frozen or cut legislative salaries and/or staff support in recent years. In addition, the purchasing power of legislative pay has been declining since 1972 in 20 states.[104] To the degree that state governments are being asked to shoulder more responsibilities, weakening legislatures may lead to serious difficulties when complex issues need attention.

Although term limits have been adopted in almost half of the states (although some later repealed them) and initiative and referendum activity have increased in a number of states, the other symptoms of **deinstitutionalization** are found in only a few states so far. It may be a bit early to declare this a national trend, but the developments are troubling to anyone who believes that strong, vigorous state legislatures are an important part of a representative democracy.

CONCLUSION

Despite its unintended consequences and its limited impact on the direction of public policy, legislative reform has been a positive development in some respects. Legislatures are generally much more capable institutions than they were 50 years ago and they have a much greater ability to cope with the increased complexity of state policy making. If from time to time they do not seem to measure up to their new capabilities, that is probably a reflection of the limitations of structural reform to deal with political divisions. As a political body, a legislature will necessarily mirror its state's political divisions. And the direction of public policy that flows from such a legislature is more likely to depend on which political interests are dominant in the state than on the elegance of the legislature's structural reform.

SUMMARY

1. The legislative functions discussed in this chapter are public policy making, legislative oversight, representation, political education, and the judicial function.

2. A major legislative representation conflict involves reapportionment. In the 1960s, the Supreme Court demanded apportionment according to the one-person, one-vote principle. The resulting changes made the legislatures more representative of their respective states in a geographic sense, but controversies regarding fair representation continue.

3. Several patterns were observed in the organization of state legislatures. All legislatures but one are bicameral. The two internal organizing devices are the political parties, which tend to centralize influence, and the committee systems, which tend to decentralize influence. Although state legislative committee systems have typically been much weaker than the congressional committee system, legislative parties are important organizations in many states. Many of them

have not yet developed the clear, public identities that the responsible-party model advocates, however.

4. The legislative process seems to put a premium on delay, caution, and checks so that powerful political minorities are able to block bills that threaten them. Prior to the 1960s, this phenomenon gave the state legislatures an unresponsive image in the face of pressing social changes. That image was accurate for some state legislatures, but not for others.

5. Partially in order to restore the vitality of state legislatures, the legislative reform movement accelerated in the late 1960s and the 1970s. Although the reforms improved the internal procedures of the legislatures, scholars have been able to find few consistent patterns in policies that resulted from legislative reform. The most recent move for legislative reform has been to impose limits on the number of terms that legislators may serve. Nearly half of the states have adopted some form of term limits.

STUDY QUESTIONS

1. What are the major functions that state legislatures try to perform? What difficulties do the legislatures sometimes encounter in trying to perform their various tasks?

2. Why is legislative districting controversial? How has the politics of districting changed over the years?

3. What are the major features of legislative organization? How do those features affect legislative operations?
4. What are the major aspects, both formal and informal, of the legislative process? How do those aspects affect legislative decisions?

5. How and why have reformers tried to change the state legislatures? How much of the reformers' agenda has been adopted, and how have reforms affected the legislatures?

KEY TERMS

Apportionment The allocation of legislative seats among the population. *Malapportionment* refers to a very unequal division of legislative seats. *Reapportionment* refers to the act of apportioning the seats once again to make their division more equal.

Calendar A list of bills that have been acted on by committee and are waiting for debate or final vote. There are specific types of calendars with a wide variety of names for the specific stages of floor consideration of bills.

Casework The practice of helping constituents handle their problems with government agencies (and sometimes with other organizations as well). So called because each constituent's problem becomes a "case" to be solved or processed.

Caucus A group of legislative members who meet jointly to push a legislative program. Usually refers to a party caucus such as the House Republican caucus or the Senate Democratic caucus.

Conference committee A temporary joint legislative committee created to work out a compromise when the house-passed version of a bill differs from the senate-passed version.

Deinstitutionalization A process of weakening legislatures as institutions. The adoption of term limits, the increasing use of initiatives and referenda to make policy outside of the legislature, and reductions in staff and salaries may be elements of that process.

Delegate The representational role in which legislators vote as their constituents wish rather than voting their own consciences.

Gerrymander The practice of drawing legislative district boundaries with the intent of reducing the political influence of a certain group of people.

Joint committee A committee composed of members of the house and senate.

Legislative oversight The legislature's responsibility to see that the executive branch implements laws as the legislature intended and to monitor the effectiveness of agency actions.

Legislative veto A device whereby the legislature can reverse an action of the governor or executive agencies by passing a resolution (the legislative veto) opposing the action within a short period after its announcement (usually 30 to 90 days).

Majority-minority district A legislative district deliberately created so that a majority of the people in it belong to a minority group. This may be done to encourage election of a minority representative or for other reasons.

Majority leader The majority-party leader responsible for managing legislation on the floor of the legislature and helping majority-party members accomplish their work.

Minority leader The minority-party leader responsible for managing legislation on the floor of the legislature and leading the minority party.

Pigeonholing The act of filing a bill for the record, but never taking it up for consideration or giving it only perfunctory consideration before discarding it.

Pocket veto The governor's act of killing a bill he or she has received after the close of a legislative session simply by not signing it within the required number of days (usually 5 to 15).

Politico The representational role in which legislators sometimes vote their consciences and other times vote as their constituents wish, depending on circumstances.

Quorum The number of members needed to be present for the legislature to conduct its business. A usual quorum is a majority of the members.

Responsible-party model A model of politics similar to that in Britain in which voters elect a party with a fairly clear program to power and the individual legislators are accountable to the party, which in turn is accountable to the voters. When voters become displeased with the party's performance, they can vote it out of power.

Select committee A temporary legislative committee that is responsible for an issue that has surfaced in a particular legislative session, but that is not expected to recur permanently.

Speaker of the house The key party leader, who presides over the lower house of the state legislatures.

Standing committee A permanent legislative committee that is responsible for legislation in each subject area that recurs in every legislative session, such as education or transportation.

Sunset law A law requiring programs to terminate in a given number of years unless they are reauthorized by the legislature. This forces the legislature to reevaluate the purposes and operations of the sunset agencies and programs.

Sunshine law Legislation requiring that all government business, including legislative business, be open to the public.

Trustee The representational role in which the legislators vote their consciences rather than as their constituents wish.

THE INTERNET CONNECTION

The National Conference of State Legislatures is a clearinghouse for many kinds of information about the state legislatures. Its magazine, *State Legislatures,* provides information on legislative leadership, staffing and organizational issues, and substantive policy questions facing the nation's legislatures. You can contact the Conference at **www.ncsl.org**. Look at the Web site for your state legislature. What kinds of information does it offer? Does it enable you to send messages to legislators? Does it have information on legislative internships?

NOTES

1. Dan Frosch, "Colorado Lawmaker Censured for Kicking," *New York Times,* January 25, 2008 (electronic edition).
2. A censure resolution is generally a formal statement of disapproval of a member's actions.
3. James Bryce, *The American Commonwealth*, vol. 2 (New York: Macmillan, 1906).
4. This extent of people's disapproval of state legislatures seems to vary from time to time. In a 1979 survey, the National Conference on State Legislatures found that only 31 percent of the people approved of their legislature. By 1989, this had gone up to 61 percent. Rich Jones, "The State Legislatures," in *The Book of the States: 1990–1991* (Lexington, KY: Council of State Governments, 1990), p. 115.
5. Sarah McCally Morehouse, for example, wrote that "few major state undertakings get off the ground without [the governor's] initiative." See her *State Politics, Parties and Policy* (New York: Holt, Rinehart & Winston, 1980), p. 243; see also Alan Rosenthal, *Heavy Lifting* (Washington, DC: CQ Press, 2004), especially ch. 8–9.
6. Alan Rosenthal, *Governors & Legislatures: Contending Powers* (Washington, DC: CQ Press, 1990), p. 119.
7. For a review of recent provisions, see *The Book of the States,* vol. 40 (Lexington, KY: Council of State Governments, 2008), pp. 152–154.
8. The Status of Sunset in the States: A Common Cause Report (Washington, DC: Common Cause, 1982).
9. *The Book of the States: 1990–1991* (Lexington, KY: Council of State Governments, 1990), p. 466. Six states repealed their sunset laws, and six others left the laws on the books, but ceased doing the review process. For recent provisions, which vary considerably from state to state, see *The Book of the States*, vol. 38 (Lexington, KY: Council of State Governments, 2006), pp. 132–134.
10. See *The Book of the States*, vol. 38 (Lexington, KY: Council of State Governments, 2006), pp. 125–131.
11. Alan Rosenthal, *Governors and Legislatures: Contending Powers* (Washington, DC: CQ Press, 1990), pp. 186–193.
12. Ibid., p. 184.
13. Ibid.
14. Lanny Proffer, "Legislative Veto Alternatives," *State Legislatures* 10, no. 1 (January 1984): 23–25; *The Book of the States* (2002), pp. 127–128.
15. Alan Rosenthal, "The Legislative Institution— In Transition and at Risk," *The State of the*

States, 2nd ed. (Washington, DC: CQ Press, 1993), p. 129; Rosenthal, *Heavy Lifting*, pp. 26–34; Richard Elling, "The Utility of State Legislative Casework as a Means of Oversight," *Legislative Studies Quarterly* 4, no. 3 (1979): 353–380.

16. Patricia K. Freeman and Lilliard E. Richardson, Jr., "Casework in State Legislatures," *State and Local Government Review* 26, no. 1 (Winter 1994): 21–26.

17. Alan Rosenthal, *The Decline of Representative Democracy* (Washington, DC: CQ Press, 1998), p. 320.

18. Gordon E. Baker, *The Reapportionment Revolution: Representation, Political Power and the Supreme Court* (New York: Random House, 1966).

19. *Colegrove v. Green*, 328 U.S. 549 (1946).

20. In *Baker v. Carr*, 369 U.S. 186 (1962), the Supreme Court agreed to hear reapportionment cases for lower houses of state legislatures, which eventually forced reapportionment upon the lower houses. In *Reynolds v. Sims*, 377 U.S. 533 (1964), the Supreme Court extended the one-person, one-vote principle to state senates.

21. *Wesberry v. Sanders*, 367 U.S. 1 (1964) was the congressional case.

22. The earliest research on reapportionment had not found a significant impact. Its effects became clear only as time went on. See Herbert Jacob, "The Consequences of Malapportionment: A Note of Caution," *Social Forces* 63 (1964): 261; Thomas R. Dye, *Politics, Economics, and the Public: Outcomes in the American States* (Chicago: Rand McNally, 1966), p. 273; David Derge, "Metropolitan and Outstate Alignments in the Illinois and Missouri Legislative Delegations," *American Political Science Review* 53 (1958): 1051–1065; Thomas A. Flinn, "The Outline of Ohio Politics," *Western Political Quarterly* 13 (September 1960): 712–721. On the delayed impact of reapportionment, see Yong Hyo Cho and H. George Frederickson, "The Effects of Reapportionment: Subtle, Selected, Limited," *National Civic Review* 63, no. 7 (July 1974): 357–362.

23. Michael C. Le May, "The States and Urban Areas: A Comparative Assessment," *National Civic Review* 61, no. 11 (December 1972): 542–548.

24. Ibid.

25. Paul N. Ylvisaker, "The Growing Role of State Governments in Local Affairs," *State Government* 51 (Summer 1968): 150–156.

26. Stephen Ansolabehere, Alan Gerber, and James Snyder, "Equal Votes, Equal Money: Court-Ordered Redistricting and Public Expenditures in the American States," *American Political Science Review* 96 (2002): 767–777.

27. See Timothy O'Rourke, *The Impact of Reapportionment* (New Brunswick, NJ: Transaction Books, 1980).

28. A. G. Sulzberger, "As Rural Areas Lose People, Legislators' Power Ebbs," *New York Times,* June 2, 2011 (Web edition).

29. Alan Ehrenhalt, "Party Lines," *Governing* 20, no. 4 (January 2007): 11–12.

30. *Davis v. Bandemer,* 106 S.Ct. 2797 (1986). Also see Malcolm E. Jewell, "What Hath *Baker v. Carr* Wrought?" *Comparative State Politics Newsletter* 9, no. 5 (October 1988): 3–15; and Robert X. Browning, "Partisan Gerrymandering: From *Baker v. Carr* to *Davis v. Bandemer,*" *Comparative State Politics Newsletter* 9, no. 5 (October 1988): 25–38.

31. *Badham v. Eu,* 109 S.Ct. 34 (1989).

32. Voinovich v. Quilter, S.Ct. (1993).

33. Andrew Gelman and Gary King, "Enhancing Democracy Through Legislative Redistricting," *American Political Science Review* 88, no. 3 (September 1994): 541–558.

34. Mark E. Rush, *Does Redistricting Make a Difference?: Partisan Representation and Electoral Behavior* (Baltimore, MD: Johns Hopkins University Press, 1993).

35. Josh Goodman, "Reform Collides with Power in Remap Process," *Stateline,* November 12, 2010 (Web edition); Louis Jacobson, "Forecasting the Redistricting Fight," *Governing,* October 25, 2010 (Web edition); Chris Cillizza, "Republicans' Allies Eye State Legislatures as Redistricting Nears," *Washington Post,* January 25, 2010, p. A2.

36. Alex Isenstadt, "Arizona Redistricting Chief Impeached," *Politico,* November 1, 2011 (Web edition).

37. *Gomillion v. Lightfoot,* 81 S.Ct. 125 (1960).

38. *City of Mobile v. Bolden,* 446 U.S. 55 (1980).

39. *Thornburg v. Gingles,* 106 S.Ct. 2752 (1986).

40. *Shaw v. Reno,* 113 S.Ct. 2816 (1993).

41. Alan Greenblat, "The Mapmaking Mess," *Governing* 14, no. 4 (January 2001), pp. 22–23.

42. African American representatives in Congress increased from 25 to 40, while Hispanic representatives increased from 11 to 17; African American representatives in state legislatures increased from 448 to 521, and Hispanic representatives increased from 140 to 182. U.S. Bureau of the Census, *Statistical Abstract of the United States, 1995* (Washington, DC: U.S. Government Printing Office, 1995), pp. 281, 287.

43. Kevin A. Hill, "Does the Creation of Majority Black Districts Aid Republicans? An Analysis of the 1992 Congressional Elections in Eight Southern States," *The Journal of Politics* 57, no. 2 (May 1995): 384–401; David Lubin and D. Stephen Voss, "Racial Redistricting and Realignment in Southern State Legislatures," *American Journal of Political Science* 44 (2000): 792–810.

44. See, for example, Lani Guinier, "Don't Scapegoat the Gerrymander," *The New York Times Magazine*, January 8, 1995, pp. 36–37 and *The Tyranny of the Majority: Fundamental Fairness in Representative Democracy* (New York: Free Press, 1994).

45. Tim Story, "2004 Legislative Elections," *The Book of the States*, vol. 37 (Lexington, KY: Council of State Governments, 2005), p. 110.

46. See Kathleen Bratton, Kerry Haynie, and Beth Reingold, "Gender, Race, Ethnicity, and Representation: The Changing Landscape of Legislative Diversity," *The Book of the States*, vol. 40 (Lexington, KY: Council of State Governments, 2008), pp. 73–79.

47. Winnie Hu, "Many State Legislators Lack College Degrees," *New York Times*, June 12, 2011 (Web edition).

48. Story, "2004 Legislative...;" Alan Rosenthal and Rich Jones, "Trends in State Legislatures," *The Book of the States* (Lexington, KY: Council of State Governments, 2002), p. 64; Gary Moncrief, Peverill Squire, and Malcolm Jewell, *Who Runs for the Legislature?* (Upper Saddle River, NJ: Prentice-Hall, 2001), p. 95.

49. Heinz Eulau, et al., "The Role of the Representative," *American Political Science Review* 53, no. 3 (September 1959): 742–756; see also Alan Rosenthal, Burdett Loomis, John Hibbing, and Karl Kurtz, *Republic on Trial* (Washington, DC: CQ Press, 2003), pp. 95–97; Rosenthal, *Heavy Lifting*, pp. 38–48; Michael Smith, *Bringing Representation Home* (Columbia, MO: University of Missouri, 2003).

50. David Nice, "Representation in the States: Policy Making and Ideology," *Social Science Quarterly* 64 (1983): 404–411; Gerald Wright, Robert Erikson, and John McIver, "Public Opinion and Policy Liberalism in the American States," *American Journal of Political Science* 31 (1987): 980–1001; Jeffrey Cohen, ed., *Public Opinion in State Politics* (Stanford, CA: Stanford University Press, 2006), especially chapters 10–13.

51. William Keefe and Morris Ogul, *The American Legislative Process*, 9th ed. (Upper Saddle River, NJ: Prentice-Hall, 1997), pp. 28–30.

52. Rosenthal, et al., *Republic on Trial*, pp. 162–163.

53. Elizabeth Jensen, "With Grant, NPR to Step Up State Government Reporting," *New York Times*, October 17, 2010 (Web edition).

54. For an exception to the openness trend, see Rob Gurwitt, "Yesterday's Legislature," *Governing* 13, no. 6 (March 2000): 26–29.

55. Keefe and Ogul, *The American Legislative Process*, p. 38.

56. Susan Haigh, "Connecticut Gov. John Rowland to Announce Resignation, Says Attorney," *Moscow-Pullman Daily News*, June 21, 2004, p. 5A.

57. Benjamin Ginsberg and Martin Shefter, *Politics by Other Means* (New York: Basic, 1990), pp. 26–35; Alan Rosenthal, *The Decline of Representative Democracy* (Washington, DC: CQ Press, 1998), pp. 92–93.

58. "Toward a More Responsible Two-Party System," *American Political Science Review* 44 (September 1950): supplement; for a recent discussion, see Marc Hetherington and William Keefe, *Parties, Politics, and Public Policy in America*, 10th ed. (Washington, DC: CQ Press, 2007), pp. 219–229.

59. Bill Moss, "Rotation: One Chance for the Brass Ring," *State Legislatures* 20, no. 7 (July 1994): 21; Thad Kousser, *Term Limits and the Dismantling of State Legislative Professionalism* (Cambridge, UK: Cambridge University, 2005), pp. 70–75.

60. Rosenthal, *Heavy Lifting*, p. 211.

61. Richard Clucas, "Legislative Leadership and Campaign Support in California," *Legislative Studies Quarterly* 17, no. 2 (May 1992): 276–277.

62. David C. Saffell, "Happy Birthday, Speaker Riffe," *Comparative State Politics* 12, no. 4 (August 1991): 16–18.

63. Alan Rosenthal, "Challenges to Legislative Leadership," *Journal of State Government* 60,

no. 6 (November–December 1987): 265–269. Also see his "A Vanishing Breed," *State Legislatures* 15, no. 10 (November–December 1989): 30–34.

64. Alen Greenblatt, "In Kansas, It's GOP vs. GOP," *Governing* 25, no. 4 (January 2012): 11.

65. See V. O. Key, *Southern Politics* (New York: Vintage Books, 1949), ch. 14.

66. Dye, *Politics, Economics, and the Public: Outcomes in the American States*, p. 258. In analyzing similar data somewhat differently, political scientist John H. Fenton came to the opposite conclusion. See John H. Fenton, "Two-Party Competition: Does It Make a Difference?" in John H. Fenton, ed., *People and Parties in Politics* (Glenview, IL: Scott Foresman, 1966). Also see John H. Fenton and Donald W. Chamberlayne, "The Literature Dealing with the Relationships Between Political Process, Socio Economic Conditions and Public Policies in the American States, A Bibliographic Essay," *Polity* 1, no. 3 (Spring 1969): 388–404. Finally, Virginia Gray analyzed competitiveness over time rather than at a single point in time as Dye had done. She discovered that party competition had a significant impact on changes in policy outcomes over time. Virginia Gray, "Models of Comparative State Politics: A Comparison of Cross-Sectional and Time Series Analyses," *American Journal of Political Science* 20, no. 2 (May 1976): 235–256.

67. Gray, "Models of Comparative State Politics"; Gerald C. Wright, Jr., "Interparty Competition and State Social Welfare Policy: When a Difference Makes a Difference," *Journal of Politics* 37, no. 3 (August 1975): 796–803; Thomas Holbrook and Emily Van Dunk, "Electoral Competition in the American States," *American Political Science Review* 87 (1993): 955–962; David Nice, "The Impact of Barriers to Party Government in the American States" (Ph.D. diss., University of Michigan, 1979).

68. See Wayne L. Francis, *Legislative Issues in the Fifty States: A Comparative Analysis* (Chicago: Rand McNally, 1967); Nice, "The Impact."

69. Robert S. Erikson, "Relationship Between Party Control and Civil Rights Legislation in the American States," *Western Political Quarterly* 24, no. 1 (March 1971): 178–182.

70. David Nice, "Party Ideology and Policy Outcomes in the American States," *Social Science Quarterly* 63 (1982): 556–565; David Nice, "State Party Ideology and Policy Making," *Policy Studies Journal* 13 (1985): 780–796.

71. *The Book of the States*, vol. 43 (Lexington, KY: Council of State Governments, 2011), p. 110–111.

72. George Goodwin, Jr., "State Legislatures of New England," in Josephine F. Milburn and Victoria Shuck, eds., *New England Politics* (Cambridge, MA: Schenkman, 1981), pp. 117–118.

73. For a listing of state veto provisions, see *The Book of the States* (Lexington, KY: Council of State Governments, 2002), pp. 104–105.

74. Eric Uslaner and Ronald Weber, *Patterns of Decision Making in State Legislatures* (New York: Praeger Publishers, 1977).

75. Charles W. Wiggins and William P. Browne, "Interest Groups and Public Policy Within a State Legislative Setting," *Polity* 14, no. 3 (Spring 1982): 548–558.

76. Robert M. Entman, "The Impact of Ideology on Legislative Behavior and Public Policy in the States," *Journal of Politics* 45, no. 1 (February 1983): 163–182.

77. Belle Zeller, ed., *American State Legislatures: Report of the Committee on American Legislatures of the American Political Science Association* (New York: Crowell, 1954), p. 2.

78. Jones, *The Book of the States: 1994–1995*, p. 99.

79. The most prestigious of these were the Advisory Commission on Intergovernmental Relations, the Council of State Governments, the Eagleton Institute of Rutgers University, the Committee for Economic Development, and the Citizens Conference on State Legislatures.

80. The Citizens Conference on State Legislatures, *The Sometimes Governments: A Critical Study of the 50 American Legislatures* (New York: Bantam Books, 1971); for a comparison of several measures of legislative professionalism, see Keith Hamm and Gary Moncrief, "Legislative Politics in the States," in Virginia Gray and Russell Hanson, eds. *Politics in the American States*, 9th ed. (Washington, DC: CQ Press, 2008), pp. 154–157.

81. Rosenthal, et al., *Republic on Trial*, pp. 177–178; Karl Kurtz, "75 Years of Institutional Change in State Legislatures," *The Book of the States*, vol. 42 (Lexington, KY: Council of State Governments, 2010), pp. 85–90.

82. Alan Rosenthal and Rich Jones, "Trends in State Legislatures," pp. 60–61; *The Book of the States* (2008), pp. 132–133; Kurtz, "75 Years...," pp. 85–86.

83. Ibid., pp. 71–72; Hamm and Moncrief, "Legislative Politics," pp. 154–155.

84. Kurtz, "75 Years...," p. 88.

85. See William T. Pound, "Legislatures: Our Dynamic Institutions," *State Legislatures* 19, no. 1 (January 1993): 22–25.

86. Ibid.

87. Morris P. Fiorina, "Divided Government in the American States: A Byproduct of Legislative Professionalism?" *American Political Science Review* 88, no. 2 (June 1994): 304–316. Jeffrey Stonecash and Anna Agathangelou, "Trends in the Partisan Composition of State Legislatures: A Response to Fiorina," *American Political Science Review* 91 (1997): 148–155; Morris Fiorina, "Professionalism, Realignment, and Representation," *American Political Science Review* 91 (1997): 156–162. Fiorina's own 1997 analysis indicates that his model linking professionalism and election outcomes does not work when all the state legislatures are included in the analysis.

88. Calculated from *The Book of the States: 1994–1995*, p. 115.

89. See especially Alan Rosenthal, "The Legislative Institution: Transformed and at Risk," in Carl E. Van Horn, ed., *The State of the States* (Washington, DC: CQ Press, 1989), pp. 69–101.

90. William Berry, Michael Berkman, and Stuart Schneiderman, "Legislative Professionalism and Incumbent Reelection: The Development of Institutional Boundaries," *American Political Science Review* 94 (2000): 859–874.

91. Jack Treadway, "Adoption of Term Limits for State Legislators: An Update," *Comparative State Politics* 16, no. 3 (June 1995): 1–3; Alan Rosenthal and Rich Jones, "Trends in...," (2002), p. 66; Rosenthal and Jones, "Trends in...," (2004), p. 75.

92. A good summary of the pros and cons of term limits is offered by Karl T. Kurtz, "Limiting Terms—What's in Store?" *State Legislatures* 18, no. 1 (January 1992): 32–34. For an excellent background on the term limitation movement, see Stuart Rothenberg, "How Term Limits Became a National Phenomenon," *State Legislatures* 18, no. 1 (January 1992): 35–40.

93. Norman R. Luttbeg, "Legislative Careers in Six States: Are Some Legislatures More Likely to Be Responsive?" *Legislative Studies Quarterly* 17, no. 1 (February 1992): 49–68.

94. Gary F. Moncrief, Joel A. Thompson, Michael Haddon, and Robert Hoyer, "For Whom the Bell Tolls: Term Limits and State Legislatures," *Legislative Studies Quarterly* 17, no. 1 (February 1992): 37–47.

95. Rosenthal, *The Decline,* pp. 73–75.

96. Cal Ledbetter, Jr., "Limiting Legislative Terms Is a Bad Idea," *National Civic Review* 80, no. 3 (Summer 1991): 243–247; Alan Greenblatt, "Crash Course," *Governing* 15, no. 2 (November 2001): 54–58; Rosenthal, et al., *Republic on Trial,* pp. 169–171; Senator Jake Flake, "Effects of Term Limits in Arizona: Irreparable Damage," in Kevin Smith, ed., *State and Local Government, 2007 Edition* (Washington, DC: CQ Press, 2007), pp. 64–66.

97. John Carey, Richard Niemi, and Lynda Powell, "The Effects of Term Limits on States Legislatures," *Legislative Studies Quarterly* 23 (1998): 271–300.

98. Claude R. Marx, "Limit Terms, and They Go Home," *Investors Business Daily*, March 13, 1996, p. 1; Greenblatt, "Crash Course," p. 56.

99. Chris Fastnow, "Willie Brown's Successor: or What Happens to Party Discipline After Term Limits?" Paper presented at the annual meeting of the Midwest Political Science Association, Chicago, IL, April 1996.

100. Douglas Foster, "The Lame-Duck State," *State Legislatures* 20, no. 7 (July 1994): 32–42.

101. Kousser, *Term Limits,* pp. 170–171.

102. Scott Meinke and Edward Hasecke, "Term Limits, Professionalization, and Partisan Control in U.S. State Legislatures," *Journal of Politics* 65 (2003): 898–908.

103. Paul Brace and Daniel Ward, "The Institutionalized Legislature and the Rise of the Antipolitics Era," in Ronald Weber and Paul Brace, eds. *American State and Local Politics* (New York: Chatham House, 1999), pp. 88–95; Rosenthal, *The Decline,* pp. 72–90; Rosenthal, et al., *Republic on Trial,* especially ch. 7–10.

104. Kurtz, "75 Years...," p. 88.

Governors and the Challenge of Executive Leadership

CHAPTER PREVIEW

This chapter examines the role of state governors in providing public policy leadership. We will discuss:

1 The demand for strong executive leadership.

2 The reformers' goal of increasing the formal powers of governors.

3 Governors' leadership styles.

4 Governors' careers.

5 Other state executives.

6 The impact of governors on public policy.

7 Governors and the political economy of states.

Introduction

In 2002, Rod Blagojevich was elected governor of Illinois. He had campaigned as a reformer in a state that has sometimes had problems with political corruption. However, federal officials eventually began to investigate the governor after reports of illegal campaign fund-raising and government favors being granted in return for money.[1]

According to published reports, investigators monitored telephone calls into and out of the governor's office. They allegedly heard the governor and other people discussing efforts to pressure the *Chicago Tribune* to fire personnel who had criticized the Blagojevich administration. In addition, the investigators heard the governor delaying funding for a charity hospital because its chief officer failed to give enough money to the governor.

When federal investigators heard Blagojevich trying to sell an appointment to the U.S. Senate, however, they felt that they needed to act. Authorities arrested the governor and his chief of staff for conspiracy to commit mail and wire fraud and solicitation of bribes. The state legislature began impeachment proceedings as well. A number of prominent politicians in Illinois called on the governor to resign. The Illinois House of Representatives voted to impeach Blagojevich, and the state senate voted unanimously to remove him from office. The state senate then voted to prohibit him from ever holding public office in Illinois.[2]

Following his removal from office, Blagojevich was tried and convicted on a number of criminal counts, including lying to the FBI, trying to "sell" an appointment to the U.S. Senate seat left vacant when Barack Obama became president of the United States, trying to pressure the chief executive of a hospital into giving him money, and trying to pressure a racetrack executive into giving him money.[3]

Most of the nation's governors are honest officials with high ethical standards. However, the Blagojevich case should alert us to the fact that governors may face numerous opportunities to take advantage of other people. Since the mid-1970s, governors in a number of states have left offices under a cloud of one sort or another.[4] In addition, several other governors have faced accusations of wrongdoing or questionable behavior.[5] Public alertness and a watchful news media are important in monitoring gubernatorial behavior. Moreover, voters need to be very careful when selecting governors (and other officials). Otherwise, official misconduct may tarnish a state's image for years and may damage any number of state programs.

Some governors come to office with a desire to do something about one or more problems facing the state, while others favor more drastic changes. Other governors are drawn to the office by its prestige and/ or its value as a stepping stone to higher offices. All types of governor discover that, without vigorous effort, their ideas may easily be ignored. However, they also discover that major efforts to change policies and programs will almost always antagonize some people. Conversely, governors who fail to attack major problems risk angering people who want action.

In most states, the governor is the most visible politician, and over the years governors have gone on to some of the most important leadership positions in American politics. Woodrow Wilson, Franklin Roosevelt, Jimmy Carter, Ronald Reagan, Bill Clinton, and George W. Bush used the governor's office as a springboard to the presidency. Many other governors have tried to win the White House but failed. A number of former governors have gone on to serve in Congress, as state or federal judges, or in national administrative positions.

Governors have a wide range of responsibilities. They have the opportunity to provide policy leadership in their states. They are often expected to make sure the state bureaucracy does its job responsibly, to cope with crises as they arise, and to preside over a strong state economy (or to fix the economy if it performs poorly). Governors may be involved in presidential election campaigns and in helping to recruit candidates for state offices. Governors also speak for their states in dealing with neighboring states, the national government, and even other countries.

This chapter examines executive power at the state level of government. It looks first at the effects of the political reform movement on the changing expectations about executive leadership. Second, it discusses leadership exercised by governors and other state executives. Third, it examines the importance of career patterns on gubernatorial leadership. Fourth, it asks whether strong executive leadership has any significant consequences for the public policies adopted and for the way in which public benefits are distributed. Finally, it explores the importance of the political economy (see Chapter 1) to governors today, as well as the role of governors in dealing with issues of that political economy and social conflict.

THE DEMAND FOR STRONG EXECUTIVES

Executive Representation

Our expectations of state and local executives have evolved through three historical stages. First, from the 1830s until about 1900 there was a demand for what Herbert Kaufman called **executive representation**.[6] This demand was based on the belief that the executive branch should represent people just as the legislature does. Its origins were in **Jacksonian democracy,** the concept of the **spoils system,** and the direct election of large numbers of administrative officials through the **long ballot,** so called because of its long list of elective executive offices. Voters choose not only governors and mayors but also other statewide administrators, clerks, and many local officials not engaged in broad policy making.

Philosophically, the case for executive representation was supported by three arguments. First, Andrew Jackson argued that the chief executive was chosen by a nationwide (in the case of presidents) or statewide (in the case of governors) constituency, in contrast to Congress and the state legislatures, whose members were chosen in districts (or states, in the U.S. Senate). Chief executives would, accordingly, have a broader perspective than individual legislators and could better stand up to the power of selfish interest groups (or so Jackson believed).

Second, some observers believed that the long ballot would make the bureaucracy conform to the wishes of the people. To a limited degree, the long ballot, when tied to the nineteenth-century political machines, may have helped accomplish this. As immigrants began to dominate some local electorates, they voted their fellow immigrants into office. These officeholders, in turn, hired their immigrant supporters to work in the public bureaucracies, including fire and police departments.

The third argument for executive representation was based on the separation of powers. Early American political philosophers—especially James Madison—taught that the concentration of power is dangerous.[7] They advocated dividing power among many hands. At the state and local levels, the number of elective executive offices was expanded. This change limited the power of governors and mayors to act as chief executives responsible for the overall direction of the executive branch and also provided some executive independence from the legislatures. The elected executives would each have a base of political support, which would give them some autonomy.

However, the system of executive representation and the machine politics that was closely associated with it soon led to widespread abuses—graft, corruption of law enforcement agencies, undemocratic politics, and inefficient government. These things soon came under attack by the Progressive political reformers of the late nineteenth and early twentieth centuries. As the scope of state and local governments grew, and as public policies gradually became more complex and expensive, the Progressive reformers gained support.

Neutral Competence: The Second Stage

As the nineteenth century ended, reformers demanded the removal of partisanship from public services. They wanted services to be performed competently and in a politically neutral fashion. The demand for **neutral competence** is reflected most obviously in the merit systems of employment. In 1883, the United States Civil Service System was established. In the same year, New York passed a civil service act, and Massachusetts passed one the following year. Today, almost all the states use some variation of a merit system for hiring, promoting, and firing many state employees, and the skill levels of state employees have risen considerably. (For greater elaboration, see Chapter 10.)

The administration of public services was another area in which reformers sought neutral competence. As the concept of neutral competence became popular, service delivery agencies were increasingly insulated from political interference by the governor or the legislators. This was particularly the case in public education. Requirements for teacher certification, systems of tenure for teachers, and state education boards composed of citizen members were instituted to protect the education delivery system from political interference. The governor's influence was increasingly restricted to the overall level of funding that the states would provide to local schools, at least for a time.

As demands for more government services grew during the twentieth century, the new services were increasingly provided by government institutions independent of governors, legislatures, mayors, and city councils. This led to a proliferation of independent agencies, special districts, licensing boards, and regulatory agencies, each of which had its own constituency and few of which were under the policy control of the governor and the legislature. As the concept of neutral competence was put into practice, critics complained that it led to a governmental structure characterized by weak governors, executive authority fragmented among a number of independent agencies, duplication of services, overlapping responsibilities, a lack of coordination, too little concern for overall state policy, and too little accountability to the voters.

Executive Leadership: The Third Stage

By mid-twentieth century, those deficiencies of neutral competence stimulated a demand for **executive leadership**. Critics wanted the chief executive's office to be strengthened so that it would exercise greater policy control over the delivery of services. These critics believed that meeting the service needs of the growing populations and establishing modern public policies to deal with these problems required strong governors and strong mayors who could control their bureaucracies. They wanted to counter the excessive fragmentation of authority that occurred as a result of both the executive-representation and neutral-competence philosophies. Control of administrative functions would be integrated and concentrated in the hands of a governor or mayor who would be chief executive in fact as well as in name.

As the movement for executive leadership picked up momentum, the governor's office grew in stature and began attracting higher-quality candidates. In the early twentieth century, the typical governor was more likely to be a "good-time Charlie" than a dynamic manager of government. The last several decades, in contrast, have seen the emergence of a "new breed" of governors who, in Larry Sabato's words, were "better educated than ever, and more thoroughly trained for the specific responsibilities of the governorship."[8]

EXECUTIVE LEADERSHIP AT THE STATE LEVEL: MAKING GOVERNORS STRONGER

From the preceding discussion, we see that the general trend in state government since the 1940s has been to strengthen the governor in order to provide effective leadership. Governors exercise this leadership most visibly by carrying out the roles outlined in Table 9.1. As chief legislator, chief administrator, leader of public opinion, and so on, the governor often provides leadership in the formulation, adoption, and execution of public policies in the state, although exercising leadership is not necessarily easy for governors, and it is not always rewarded.

The Governor's Role in Policy Making

Governors frequently try to influence the agenda for public-policy decision making, coordinate the formulating of policy proposals, and oversee implementation of programs.

TABLE 9.1

Governors' Roles

Chief of State

Performs ceremonial functions. Represents the state in Washington, DC, and in intergovernmental organizations such as the National Governors' Association. Note that these activities may be more than just ceremonial. Appears at dedications of public and private facilities.

Legislative Agenda Setting

Sends legislative proposals and budget proposals to the legislature. Gives an annual state-of-the-state message. Lobbies and bargains with legislators for or against passage of legislative proposals. Has veto power.

Chief Administrator

Appoints officials to many state agencies, regulatory commissions, and advisory boards. Requires state administrators to report on their activities. Prepares the state budget and issues executive orders.

Military Chief

Is commander-in-chief of the state National Guard. The Guard is often called out to maintain order during national disasters and civil disturbances. The Guard may also participate in search and rescue operations and help the state deal with emergencies of many types: sandbagging to limit flood damage, fighting fires, and so forth. National Guard units have been used for a variety of security purposes since the September 11 terrorist attacks, and some have been called into federal service in the Iraq war.

Chief of Party

In two-party states, the governor is usually the most prominent party leader, especially if the governor's party also controls the legislature. In one-party states, the governor usually leads only one of the major factions within the party. As chief of party, the governor can seldom control local nominations for the legislature or control state wide nominations. However, by judicious use of patronage and campaign assistance, by recruiting candidates, and by mobilizing activists who share the governor's policy beliefs, the governor can sometimes build support for the party and in turn get legislators to support his or her legislative program.

Leader of Public Opinion

Makes public appearances, holds interviews and press conferences, and corresponds with residents. Assigns some staff members to handle media relations. Tries to build support for the governor and his or her programs. Takes part in activities, such as planting trees on Arbor Day, that give symbolic support for causes the governor favors. Governors sometimes try to influence public opinion indirectly by having other people, including friendly journalists, make statements supporting the governor's position and respond to critics.

Ultimate Judge

Has power to grant pardons. May commute sentences. May grant paroles. May grant a reprieve that postpones the execution of a sentence. Has power of rendition that enables the governor to return a fugitive from justice to a state asking for the fugitive's return.

Crisis Manager

When a natural disaster occurs or some other crisis erupts, the governor is often expected to organize a state response and attack the problem. Most governors have emergency powers to help them cope with crisis situations. If a governor is perceived to be ineffective in handling a crisis or, even worse, appears to be uninterested in a crisis, the political consequences may be severe.

Setting the agenda for policy making is critical. Legislators can only pass bills that are put on their agenda, although many people try to influence that agenda. Ideas that are never drafted into bills or that fail to gain enough support to merit serious discussion in key committees do not get put on the decision-making agenda. Moreover, legislatures almost never have enough time or energy to consider all possible issues; particularly where legislative sessions are short, devoting more attention to one major issue may mean less attention is devoted to other issues. Agendas must also be set for the courts and in the executive branch. The governor can shape these various agendas by defining his or her own priorities, trying to bring issues to the attention of the public and the mass media, and sending proposals to the legislature, among other things.

The strong governor also tries to coordinate the formulation of policy proposals. The governor's support is sought for the legislative proposals that are made by state agencies, relevant interest groups, the governor's party, and the governor's staff. Since governors have several bargaining tools, such as the threat of a veto, usually their legislative requests are seriously considered by the legislators. This is especially true of budget requests. Because of their crucial position in the law-making process, strong governors can propose a legislative program and a budget and have a good chance of getting much of what they want enacted into law—especially if they consult with state legislators in the development of proposals and stay within the limits of what the public finds acceptable.

After the policies are established by the legislature, the courts, or through executive decision making, the strong governor is expected to oversee how well state agencies are carrying them out. If an agency falls under heavy public criticism for the way it implements the law, the governor is expected to bring that agency into line. The distinction between formulating policies and overseeing their implementation is not always very clear; by using executive orders, governors can both make policies and shape agency behavior.[9]

Some Governors Are Stronger Than Others   Despite the frequent expectations that the governor will play a strong policy role, not all governors' offices are equally equipped to provide that leadership. Thad Beyle constructed an index of the powers of governors.[10] The index has six measures of gubernatorial strength: (1) how many state executives are elected independently of the governor, (2) tenure potential (whether the governor can succeed himself or herself, and the length of the governor's term), (3) appointive powers (how many major policy-making state officials are appointed by the governor), (4) budget powers (how much influence the governor has over the state budget), (5) veto powers (the conditions under which he or she can veto bills), (6) party support (how strongly the governor's party controls the legislature). By these criteria, as Table 9.2 shows, the most powerful governors tend to be in heavily populated states (such as New York) and/or in the north-central or middle Atlantic states, whereas in the South and border states and in the less populous states of New England, governors are ranked among the weakest. Note that formal powers mean little without the willingness to use them, and clumsy use of powers can backfire at times.

Challenges to Gubernatorial Leadership

Leading the Legislature The success of contemporary governors is measured most visibly by how much of their agenda is passed by the legislature. Through their budget message, their state-of-the-state address, and other messages, the governors influence the agenda for legislative action. Their most dramatic legislative tool is probably the **veto**. All states give the governor the right to veto. Forty-three states additionally give the governor an **item veto** over appropriations bills; that is, they can veto specific spending items without vetoing the total package. Nine states allow governors to reduce the amounts appropriated. A number of states also give the governor an **amendatory veto**. Under this power, a governor can return a bill to the legislature with proposed revisions. If the legislature accepts the revisions, the bill becomes law. If the legislature does not accept the revisions, the bill is vetoed (although the legislature may try to override the veto).

TABLE 9.2

States Categorized by the Institutional Powers of Their Governors

Weakest	Moderately Weak	Moderately Strong	Strongest
Vermont	Arkansas	California	Massachusetts
Rhode Island	Indiana	Delaware	Alaska
Alabama	Louisiana	Florida	Maryland
Oklahoma	Missouri	Hawaii	New Jersey
Indiana	Nevada	Idaho	New York
Mississippi	New Hampshire	Iowa	West Virginia
North Carolina	Oklahoma	Kansas	Utah
	Oregon	Kentucky	
	South Carolina	Massachusetts	
	Texas	Michigan	
	Virginia	Mississippi	
	Washington	Montana	
	Wyoming	Nebraska	
		New Mexico	
		Pennsylvania	
		Wisconsin	

Source: Adapted from Thad Beyle, "The Governors," Politics in the American States, 8th ed., Virginia Gray and Russell Hanson, eds. (Washington, DC: CQ Press, 2004), pp. 212–213. The weakest governors have institutional powers rated as 2.5 to 2.9. The strongest governors are rated at 4.0 or higher.

There has been a great deal of interest in the item veto in recent years, primarily because Presidents Reagan, Bush, and Clinton sought an item veto on the grounds that it would enable them to impose fiscal restraint on the federal budget. Like governors with the item veto, presidents could then delete pork barrel items that legislators sneak into appropriations bills. Researchers who have studied the governor's use of the item veto, however, find that it has little, if any, impact on holding down state expenditures.[11] Most of the evidence suggests that governors employ the item veto primarily for the political purpose of gaining the upper hand over legislatures.[12]

One of the most striking uses of item vetoes was provided by Wisconsin Governor Tommy Thompson in 1987. Wisconsin law then went far beyond any other state's item veto by giving the governor a so-called partial veto that enables the governor not only to delete dollar amounts from appropriations but also to delete words, punctuation marks, and even individual letters from bills. In one of his partial vetoes, Governor Thompson crossed out selected letters and words of a juvenile detention bill to dramatically increase how long juveniles could be detained in county jails without charges. This action conflicted with the legislature's intent on the bill. The legislature sued, but the Wisconsin Supreme Court and the federal courts upheld the governor.[13] Wisconsin voters then reacted by approving a constitutional amendment that put a limit on the partial veto that would prevent the governor from scratching out specific letters.[14]

Few governors use the veto as aggressively as Governor Thompson did.[15] But when they do, the vetoes are rarely overridden. Overrides usually require a two-thirds vote in each house. Although overrides are becoming more frequent than in the past, they are still rare, happening less than 10 percent of the time.[16]

Because vetoes are so rarely overridden, the threat of a veto is a powerful tool that governors use to shape legislation, especially in the case of the amendatory veto.[17] Large numbers of vetoes may anger members of the legislature and other people interested in the vetoed proposals, however. In addition, for legislation that must be passed in some form (such as the state budget), the legislature may respond with a bill very similar to the bill that was vetoed.[18]

If the legislative session ends without passage of the governor's program, most governors have authority to call a special session of the legislature. They can usually control the agenda for these special sessions, and this gives them a powerful tool for coaxing action out of the legislature. However, the tactic can also backfire. Texas Governor James E. Ferguson called a special session in 1917 only to have the legislature impeach him and remove him from office. Less dramatically, a governor who calls a special session but is unable to pass his or her proposals may appear to be an ineffective leader. A considerable number of the special sessions held in 2010 passed no bills at all, and a number of other special sessions passed only one or two bills.[19]

Of all the weapons in the governor's political arsenal, probably none is more important than the backing of a strong political party that has a commanding majority in the legislature.[20] However, that support normally requires the governor to stay with policies acceptable to most people in the party. Too large a majority, however, can be too much of a good thing. When the majority goes beyond 70 percent, intraparty factionalism tends to erupt, partly because very large party coalitions often include a variety of different opinions on policies.[21] The Republican Party in Kansas far outnumbers the Democratic Party, and state Republicans have struggled with a major internal split for a number of years.[22] Nevertheless, control of the legislature by friendly partisans is usually key to the governor's ability to pass legislation, especially if the governor and fellow partisans in the legislature have similar policy views. Conversely, if the legislature is controlled by an opposition party with very different policy preferences than the governor's, relations are likely to be very difficult.

Despite their powerful tools for leadership, there is reason to believe that governors are losing ground to the legislatures in their perennial battles to influence state politics.[23] Governors' powers have increased over the past two decades, but so have legislatures' capacities to deal with the governor. The improved legislative staffs have especially helped to put the legislatures on a more even footing with the governor. Divided party control of state government, which has been fairly common in recent decades, growing party polarization in many states, and the proliferation of interest groups all create difficulties for governors trying to influence the legislature.

Moreover, when state revenues fall short of expectations, as they did in almost all of the states beginning in late 2008 and continuing since then, governors are less likely to propose tackling a wide range of issues in their state of the state addresses. In addition, the issues that receive attention are likely to revolve around financial concerns, such as economic development and revenue decisions and very costly programs, such as education.[24] When program costs outrun revenues, conflicts over how to allocate the pain of program cuts and/or higher taxes are likely to create strains between the governor and many legislators.

Running the Bureaucracy   As chief executive, governors are expected to run the state's administrative agencies. But they face several obstacles in this quest. First, they are confronted by several other state officers, such as the lieutenant governor, the attorney general, the treasurer, and the auditor, who in most states have been elected to office by the voters, some belonging to the governor's party and others belonging to the opposition (see Table 9.3). Some of those other executives may want to be the next governor, and some may have been in office longer than the current governor has.

TABLE 9.3

Statewide-Elected Executives

Office	Number of States in Which Position Is Elective
Governor	50
Lieutenant Governor	43
Attorney General	43
Treasurer	36
Secretary of State	35
Auditor	23

Source: The Book of the States, vol. 42 (Lexington, KY: Council of State Governments, 2010), pp. 213–214.

A second obstacle to strong administrative leadership is the autonomy of many individual departments. Some of the most important state departments are administered by a separately elected head or by an independent board or commission. Education is perhaps the most pertinent example. To be sure, the governor can also be a leading force for innovative educational programs, as exemplified by Governor John Engler of Michigan, who helped revamp the state's method for financing education[25] (see Chapter 14). But by and large, the governor has only limited influence over administrative matters such as personnel, curriculum, and the organization of public instruction, unless the legislature and governor can agree on a plan for change.

The third obstacle to strong administrative leadership is the relationship that exists between state agencies and private enterprise. All states have licensing boards that regulate various professions, administrative agencies that run programs, and regulatory agencies that oversee such functions as pollution control, health-care facilities, and utility rates. Critics charge that regulatory agencies often serve the interests of the industries they are supposed to regulate rather than serving the interests of the public.[26] And the licensing boards tend to be peopled by representatives from the sectors they are supposed to oversee. Many state agencies contract out some of their work to private companies, from engineering firms to privately owned prisons (see Chapter 10). In addition, nonprofit organizations are involved in tackling many problems, from improving education to providing health care and fighting poverty. The private groups may disagree with the governor's ideas and may use their political influence and program involvement to blunt or bog down gubernatorial ideas.

To strengthen the governor's administrative powers, reformers have sought to remove the three administrative obstacles just discussed, by:

1. Eliminating separately elected state executives.
2. Allowing the governor to appoint a cabinet of department heads.
3. Reducing the number of independent state agencies.
4. Centralizing the budget-making process in the governor's office.
5. Removing boards and commissions from direct administrative roles.

All of these reforms have been implemented in many states and some in all states. But the effect has *not* been to give the governor undisputed control over the executive. Glenn Abney and Thomas P. Lauth surveyed state agency heads and reported that a majority of them (53 percent) felt the legislature exerted more influence over them than did the governor.[27] For most governors, successful administrative leadership probably lies less in controlling administrative details than it does in carving out a limited number of policy initiatives, selecting competent agency heads who agree with those policy initiatives, securing a budget that reflects the policy priorities, and avoiding embarrassments in the few staff agencies directly under the governor's authority (such as Planning and Finance). Not all governors have much interest in administration, partly because much of the public and the news media lack an interest in it. However, if the governor cannot gain legislative approval for policy changes, administrative controls may help produce some policy changes.

Strengthening the Governor, in Practice

In practice, the governor has a number of sources of strength when attempting to exert policy leadership. Some of these (such as budgeting) result from increasing the governorship's formal powers, and some (such as public relations and political party) result from personal characteristics and political factors.

Budgeting as a Source of Strength   Budgeting helps the governor influence the state administration. (The budgeting process will be discussed in detail in Chapter 10.) The normal budgeting practice is for executive agencies to submit their budget requests to a budget office or a finance commissioner who works closely with the governor. The governor determines overall spending guidelines (often after consulting with numerous other people, including legislators) and tries to establish priorities on how funds are divided among the various programs and agencies. In addition, funding decisions may include policy guidelines that the agency must follow in using the money. The governor then submits the budget to the legislature, and is expected to fight for its passage there.

By establishing overall spending targets and by setting priorities, the governor can exert significant influence on policies and on the various agencies' procedures for implementing them. Most governors enjoy strong budget powers, but obviously they gain much more policy-making influence from these powers when there is a surplus of state revenues; this enables them to pump more new funds into their high-priority programs. Governors are likely to have a more difficult time when revenues are scarce and their programs can only gain funding by decreasing the funding of other programs or a tax increase. Either of those options is likely to create controversy. Moreover, much of the budget is tied up in long-standing programs, such as highways, that cannot realistically be cut very much without igniting a political firestorm.

The Governor's Staff as a Source of Strength   Choosing an effective staff is the governor's cardinal task.[28] Poorly chosen staff members can damage the governor's image, make poor suggestions on administrative appointments, alienate key legislators, and fail to accomplish important tasks. Governors' staffs have expanded dramatically in recent years, from an average of 4.6 persons in 1957 to 63 people in 2010.[29] Nearly 40 percent of staff members are women or minorities.[30] Staff members are needed to serve as media coordinators, administrative aides, personal secretaries, legislative liaisons, budget analysts, and policy analysts.

Public Relations as a Source of Strength   Governors have long recognized the importance of public relations as a source of gubernatorial strength. For one thing, the governor needs to project a positive public image if he or she hopes to be reelected.[31] Governors also use public relations to create popular support for their legislative programs, thus increasing chances of getting those programs passed by the legislature. So important are public relations that governors seldom pass up an opportunity to appear before the television cameras. Increased visibility may, however, bring dangers, including a greater risk of attracting blame when things go wrong and public expectations that are difficult to meet. Moreover, the public may not always respond to the governor's efforts to mold public opinion.

The Intergovernmental System as a Source of Strength   The governor's influence has also been enhanced by the growth of intergovernmental relations since the 1960s.[32] Governors now spend a fair share of their time lobbying for federal aid, overseeing much of the program planning that is required by federal programs,[33] and acting together with other governors in the National Governors Association (NGA) and regional governors' associations. Governors may also be drawn into helping individual localities or groups of localities cope with emergencies or to upgrade services. After the September 11 terrorist attacks, Governor George Pataki of New York helped to mobilize a variety of state agencies to assist New York City and the surrounding area in coping with the crisis. More recently, a number of governors called on the federal government to provide more financial assistance for state and local governments as the recession that began in 2007–2008 grew worse.[34] Many governors have taken their intergovernmental role a step further by leading trade missions to other countries to attract foreign investments in their states and to promote sales of major state products abroad.

Political Party as a Source of Strength   Finally, the political party is a potential source of strength for governors, although in some states it is an undependable asset. A survey of 15 governors who left office in the mid-1970s found that they made little use of the political party. They did not turn to the party as a source of either ideas for public policy or appointments to public office.[35] In many states, however, improvements in state party organizations since then have enhanced the parties' ability to help governors in campaigning and policy making.[36] As noted earlier in the chapter, governors are usually more successful if their political party controls the legislature. Governors are likely to feel that they can deal better with the federal government if their party controls the White House, and they must have party support to win renomination and reelection. Moreover, a governor who ignores her or his party may later have difficulties if an unfriendly political movement gains control of the party.[37]

EXERCISING LEADERSHIP: GOVERNORS' STYLES

In addition to formal powers, such as the veto power and the power of appointment, the successful governor needs effective leadership qualities. Without these, all the formal powers may still not produce a strong governor.[38] One scholar evaluated 312 governors in terms of their hard work, competence, dedication, and ability to meet the needs of their states.[39] He found that governors with stronger formal powers (see Table 9.2) were only slightly more likely to be outstanding than were governors with weaker formal powers (he also examined their education and experience and the degree of interparty competition in their states, among other things). The strongest relationship found was that the outstanding governors were usually younger than the less impressive governors. But youth as a factor may be "largely a proxy measure for personal dynamism and ambition."[40]

Bear in mind that different people may prefer very different types of governors. One person's effective governor may be another person's terrible failure. Particularly when people disagree over major public policies or have unrealistic expectations, governors are likely to find that they cannot satisfy large numbers of people.

In short, the leadership style of governors is just as important in determining their success as is the formal power of their office. Little has been written about the styles of governors' leadership. But at least four styles can be identified: the demagogue, the policy entrepreneur, the frustrated warrior, and the caretaker.

The Demagogue

The best-known **demagogue** was probably Huey ("the Kingfish") Long of Louisiana (1928–1931).[41] Long manipulated state judges so they would interpret the constitution to fit his political ambitions and policy views, siphoned state money into his political organization, and trampled unmercifully on opponents who dared to challenge him. His term did not lack substantive accomplishments, however. He provided free textbooks for the public schools for the first time in the state's history, broadened access to public higher education, established the state's basic highway structure, and engaged in well-publicized fights with the state utilities to lower their rates.

Huey Long's greatest success was in using public relations to please his lower-class supporters. He called for a nationwide "Share Our Wealth" plan that would prohibit anyone from earning more than $1 million a year. He appeared before news cameras at the sidelines of Louisiana State University football games. He showed his disdain for the upper class by greeting a foreign dignitary while dressed in his pajamas. The people of Louisiana repeatedly returned him and his political machine's candidates to power. Long moved on to the U.S. Senate; by then he enjoyed considerable national popularity. He was considering a 1936 presidential campaign when his career was ended by an assassin.

The Policy Entrepreneur

The **policy entrepreneur** works hard to bring about major changes in state policies and programs. A good recent example is Governor John Engler of Michigan, who managed to win adoption of a number of changes in the state tax code, in welfare and mental health programs, in education funding, and in state use of information technology. Some of those reforms have been controversial, but clearly Engler (working with many other people) succeeded in reshaping many policies.[42] The policy entrepreneur's style of leadership works best during times of economic expansion when there are growing revenues to fund new programs that seek to address a state's problems. Entrepreneurial leadership may also work well in times of crisis, as indicated by the many state policy changes adopted since the September 11 terrorist attacks.

Unfortunately for ambitious governors, surplus revenues are not always available. With revenue shortfalls in many states, many governors have had little choice but to trim back on many of the new policies they hoped to propose.[43] Some reformers believe that in this environment, entrepreneurial governors should try to create new policies without establishing new bureaucracies to carry them out.[44] States may be able to do this through public–private partnerships designed to achieve public goals without expanding the public sector itself.

Governors in both parties have used varying versions of this "governing paradigm." They have often emphasized greater government action than would traditional Republican conservatives. But they also seek less expansion of the government bureaucracy than would traditional Democratic liberals. One of the hallmarks of the new policy entrepreneurism is using the political arena to define public goals, but using the private sector as much as possible to implement those goals. Reinvention reformers emphasize focus on results rather than rules and regulations. They also prefer negotiation and cooperation in operating programs rather than orders and commands. They want government to prevent problems whenever possible, rather than waiting for a crisis and then responding. Some observers, however, have expressed doubts regarding the practicality of reinvention reforms, particularly if they are not backed up with adequate political and financial support.[45] And no reform proposal can replace regular monitoring of program performance and continuous efforts to improve that performance.[46]

Some governors have used the recession as a justification for a different style of policy entrepreneurship. Governor Rick Scott of Florida pushed through major cuts in taxes for businesses and property owners, significant cuts in education funding, and a halt to a major passenger rail project. However, as his public support eroded and he realized that he was angering a number of leaders of his own party, he dialed back on his efforts to make dramatic policy changes.[47]

The Frustrated Warrior

The frustrated warrior is, in essence, a governor who seeks to be a policy entrepreneur but who is unsuccessful. For many reasons, the frustrated warrior is unable to get his or her programs adopted. When Jesse Ventura became governor of Minnesota on the Reform Party ticket, he faced a legislature dominated by two different political parties, with a Democratic majority in the senate and a Republican majority in the house. After some initial policy successes, a disagreement over legislative restructuring caused him to give up trying to work with the legislature. Relations with the legislature were further strained when two legislative leaders began considering running for the governorship and Ventura's popularity simultaneously declined. His obvious disdain for the major parties and apparent unwillingness to help his own party further hampered his efforts.[48]

Governor Arnold Schwarzenegger also faced frustrations in trying to promote his policy agenda. The state legislature rejected a number of his proposals early in his tenure, and his efforts to bypass the legislature by appealing to the voters to adopt his policies via referenda were not successful. However, he later tried to adapt to California's complex political environment and achieved some successes.

The Caretaker

A fourth style of governor is the **caretaker**. Caretakers may be either Democrats or Republicans, but they are usually conservative or relatively cautious. They are not demagogues, nor do they push for major new programs. They see the job largely as one of maintaining current operations, but not using the state's power to pursue any new major social goals. Elected governors who become caretakers usually do so during times of governmental retrenchment, such as the 1980s, when a recession produced revenue shortages and cuts in many programs. If significant policy changes are adopted while a caretaker governor is in office, they will usually reflect the influence of other people, such as state legislators who took the initiative to enact the change.

When a caretaker or frustrated warrior occupies the governor's mansion, new problems may not be addressed effectively and may grow worse before the state takes action. However, many people sometimes prefer governors who don't launch major new initiatives, which can be expensive and carry the risk of unintended side effects.

Governors' Careers

What does it take to become governor? The formal guidelines (see Highlight below) tell only a little of the story. There seem to be two important informal criteria—developing the appropriate background and choosing the appropriate campaign strategy. To meet the background requirements, the most likely candidates are men between 40 and 45 years of age who share the dominant ethnic and religious backgrounds of their states. Asians do well in Hawaii, for example, Hispanics in Florida, Italians in New York, and Scandinavians in Minnesota. The most notable exception to this principle took place in 1989 when predominantly white Virginia elected Douglas Wilder, the nation's first African American governor since Reconstruction. Women are enjoying increasing success in their campaigns for the office, as the Highlight feature on the next page shows. In 2008, eight governors were women (including Jennifer Granholm of Michigan, Ruth Minner of Delaware, and Kathleen Sebelius of Kansas).[49]

Governors are usually more educated than the average citizen in their states and typically come from white-collar occupations. Many governors are lawyers.[50] And the successful

▶ HIGHLIGHT

Conditions of the Governor's Office

Legal Qualifications

The governor must be a citizen of the United States, and in some states must have been a citizen for a minimum number of years. Most states require the governor to have been a state resident for a minimum number of years. Most states also require a minimum age of 30, although 31 states have a minimum age of only 18.

Terms of Office

All states but two have a four-year term of office. Those two (New Hampshire and Vermont) have a two-year term of office, but put no limit on the number of terms a governor may serve. Twenty states have a four-year term with no limit on reelection. Twenty-six states have a four-year term with a limit of two consecutive terms.

Compensation

The range of governors' salaries is from $70,000 in Maine to $182,100 in Illinois. The median is about 135,000. Those salaries are far below the salaries of major executives in the private sector. All states provide the governor with access to an automobile, and most states cover transportation by air. Forty-five states also provide the governor with a mansion, and most states provide an expense allowance.

Succession

Forty-two states provide for a lieutenant governor to succeed to the office when it becomes vacant due to a governor's death or resignation. The others provide for either the secretary of state or the president of the senate to succeed.

Removal

All states but Oregon have an impeachment process, but only seven governors have been removed through impeachment since 1860. Four others resigned after being impeached. Several governors have been forced from office by criminal indictment and/or conviction. Thirteen states provide for a recall, but only two governors, Lynn J. Frazier of North Dakota (in 1921) and Gray Davis of California (in 2003), have been removed by recall. Few states have a well-developed system for removing governors in cases of physical or mental disability. ■

HIGHLIGHT

Minority and Female Governors in Recent Years

Women

Alaska: Sarah Palin (2007–2009)

Arizona: Rose Mofford (1987–1991); Jane Hull (1997–2003); Jan Brewer (2009–)

Connecticut: M. Jodi Rell (2004–2011)

Delaware: Ruth Minner (2001–2009)

Hawaii: Linda Lingle (2003–2010)

Kansas: Joan Finney (1991–1995); Kathleen Sebelius (2003–2011)

Louisiana: Kathleen Blanco (2004–2008)

Massachusetts: Jane Swift (2001–2003)

Michigan: Jennifer Granholm (2003–2011)

Montana: Judy Martz (2001–2005)

Nebraska: Kay Orr (1987–1991)

New Hampshire: Jeanne Shaheen (1997–2003)

New Jersey: Christine Todd Whitman (1993–2001)

New Mexico: Susana Martinez (2010–)

North Carolina: Beverly Perdue (2008–)

Oklahoma: Mary Fallin (2010–)

Oregon: Barbara Roberts (1991–1995)

South Carolina: Nikki Haley (2010–)

Texas: Ann Richards (1991–1995)

Utah: Olene Walker (2003–2005)

Vermont: Madeleine Kunin (1985–1991)

Washington: Christine Gregoire (2004–)

Minorities

Florida: Bob Martinez (1987–1991)

Hawaii: John Waihee III (1991–1995)

Louisiana: Bobby Jindal (2008–)

Massachusetts: Deval Patrick (2007–)

New York: David Paterson (2008–2011)

South Carolina: Nikki Haley (2010–)

Virginia: Douglas Wilder (1989–1993)

Washington: Gary Locke (2001–2005) ■

aspirant usually has a background of accomplishment in politics, business, civic affairs, or professional life. These accomplishments provide some degree of credibility for the candidate.

Although not essential, it helps one's quest for the governor's mansion to have held prior public office; more than 90 percent of governors held some other public office before being elected governor.[51] A very large majority has served in their state legislatures, and many have held statewide executive office, especially as lieutenant governor or attorney general. Roughly one-fourth have served in Congress.[52] However, it is possible to develop a campaign strategy that will bring a candidate enough public visibility and popular support to start at the top. Ronald Reagan, a retired movie star, succeeded in capturing the governorship of California (1967–1975) without prior political experience. More recently, Jesse Ventura capitalized on his fame as a professional wrestler and radio talk show host to win the 1998 gubernatorial election in Minnesota (although he did have some experience in local government prior to being elected governor). Arnold Schwarzenegger also jumped from show business to the governorship.

Finally, candidates who want to become governor need plenty of money. Gubernatorial campaign spending has risen dramatically in the last 25 years and exceeded one billion dollars during the 2001–2004 election cycle and again in the 2003–2006 period. However, total spending declined somewhat in the 2005–2008 season. Heavily populated states have especially costly campaigns (Michigan in 2006: $56 million; California in 2006: $137 million).[53] Campaigns in smaller states are usually less expensive, largely because advertising is less expensive, but multimillion dollar campaigns are far from rare even in modest-sized states.[54]

Even the most careful plans for becoming governor may be upset by circumstances beyond the candidate's control. National political tides may sweep through the state, as happened in the 2006 elections. As a result, the national division of governorships shifted from 28 Republicans and 22 Democrats to 28 Democrats and 22 Republicans.[55] Four years later, another tide shifted the governorships to 29 Republicans, 20 Democrats, and one Independent.[56] A state-level scandal or a new issue may shift the political terrain dramatically. Other candidates may enter the race unexpectedly and drain away campaign contributions, volunteer workers, and voters.

Governors' future career prospects are also important to their political influence. A governor eligible for reelection can often get more cooperation from recalcitrant legislators and bureaucrats than can a lame duck governor whose influence is going to disappear in a few months. The governor cannot seek reelection indefinitely, however, since 37 states put limits (usually two 4-year terms) on how long a governor can serve. Even lame duck governors can enhance their influence, however, if they have bright prospects for going on to the U.S. Senate, a future cabinet position, or the White House. "The lure of following a national leader to Washington can bring action out of legislators and administrators."[57]

Most governors, however, do not go on to the Senate or to cabinet positions. Many governors return to private sector occupations, in part because salaries for major private sector leaders are typically higher than are salaries for government office. In addition, governors typically have little privacy and little time for a private life. Leaving the governorship for the private sector produces more privacy and more time for family and friends. Many of those former governors remain active in politics, however.

In rare instances, governors are removed by impeachment or recall, or they resign under pressure, as the Highlight feature on the next page shows. Although highly publicized, impeachments are rare events. Out of more than 2,000 people who have ever served as governors, probably fewer than a dozen have been removed through impeachment or the threat of impeachment, the most recent example being Illinois' governor Rod Blagojevich.[58] Californians removed former governor Gray Davis through the recall process in 2003.

A few governors have found themselves imprisoned for breaking the law before, during, or after their terms of office. In 2006, former governor George Ryan of Illinois was sentenced to six years in prison following a corruption scandal, and former governor Rowland served 10 months behind bars. Ex-governor Don Siegelman of Alabama was convicted of corruption charges that year as well,[59] and Governor Blagojevich was also sentenced to prison after his conviction. Fortunately, these cases are quite rare. Most governors serve honorably and return to private business or to their former careers.

OTHER STATE EXECUTIVES

In their efforts to provide leadership, governors face competition from several other state-level executives, some of whom may have no allegiance to the governor, and some of whom are elected directly by the people. This is in sharp contrast to the federal government where all the top-ranked executive officials are appointed by the president, and therefore have at least

HIGHLIGHT

Some Major Stumbles by the Nation's Governors

On April 4, 1988, Governor Evan Mecham (R. Ariz.) became the fifth governor in the twentieth century to lose office through the impeachment process. Even before completing a single year in office, Mecham faced a grand jury criminal indictment that charged he failed to report a $350,000 campaign loan, and an impeachment movement to remove him was underway. In February 1988, the Arizona house of representatives voted to impeach the governor; shortly thereafter the senate voted to convict and remove him from office. Both houses were controlled by his own party. Mecham and his allies later mobilized opposition to a number of state legislators who supported the impeachment effort; 11 were defeated.

Other governors who faced major embarrassments include Guy Hunt, governor of Alabama, who was convicted of diverting $200,000 that was supposed to be used to cover inauguration expenses for his own personal use. He was automatically removed from office in 1993. That same year, Governor David Walters of Oklahoma pleaded guilty to a misdemeanor violation of a campaign finance law, a maneuver that enabled him to avoid prosecution on more serious charges. He was able to finish the remainder of his term. In 1997, Fife Symington of

Arizona resigned from office after being found guilty of fraud prior to becoming governor.

In 2003, Californians recalled Governor Gray Davis from office as the state struggled with a slumping economy. In 2004, Governor John Rowland of Connecticut resigned from office in the face of a possible impeachment proceeding and a federal corruption investigation. That same year, New Jersey governor James McGreevey resigned after admitting that he had an affair with another man. In 2008, Governor Eliot Spitzer of New York resigned after revelations of his repeated use of an escort service. The following year, Illinois' governor Rod Blagojevich was impeached and removed by the state legislature. He was later convicted on criminal charges. ■

Sources: Dan Harris, "The Arizona Impeachment," *State Legislature* 14, no. 6 (July 1988): 18–23; "Mecham's Revenge on Arizona Legislators," *State Legislatures* 14, no. 10 (November–December 1988): 13; Thad Beyle, *State and Local Government* (Washington, DC: CQ Press, 2001), p. 105; Mark Zarabak, "Schwarzenegger Digs In," *Moscow-Pullman Daily News,* October 9, 2003, p. 9A; Susan Haigh, "Connecticut Gov. John Rowland to Announce Resignation, Says Attorney," *Moscow-Pullman Daily News,* June 21, 2004, p. 5A; Daniel Vock, "Illinois Senate Removes Blagojevich," *Stateline,* January 29, 2009.

nominal loyalty to the president. Few governors enjoy this luxury. Most governors confront several statewide officials beyond the governors' appointive or dismissal powers, and this creates a high risk that some of those officials will be from the opposition political party or have incompatible political ideologies. The most important of these are the lieutenant governor, the attorney general, the secretary, of state, the auditor, the treasurer, and a number of independent executive boards and commissions.

Lieutenant Governor

The office of **lieutenant governor** exists in 45 states, but in only 23 are the governor and lieutenant governor elected jointly as a team. The lieutenant governor succeeds the governor if the office becomes vacant, may preside over the state senate, casts tie-breaking votes in 23 states, and in 30 states serves as acting governor while the governor is temporarily out of the state.

In addition, lieutenant governors in a number of states serve on state boards and/or commissions, with duties ranging from information technology to tourism to homeland security, and some lieutenant governors oversee the operation of some state agencies and/or programs that cut across a number of agencies.[60]

Like the vice presidency of the United States, lieutenant governors have been gradually gaining responsibilities in recent years. In addition, lieutenant governors often have ambitions for higher office and frequently run for governor or for Congress. As with governors, the lieutenant governors occasionally have problems regarding legal or ethical problems. South Carolina's lieutenant governor Ken Ard recently resigned because of a criminal investigation into possible use of campaign funds to cover personal expenses.[61]

Attorney General

In most states, the **attorney general** is the second most important statewide office. The attorney general is the official legal adviser to the state and the state's chief prosecutor. Before or after legislation is passed, legislators or administrators may ask the attorney general for a legal opinion on the wording of the law or its constitutionality. Although the attorney general's opinion is not necessarily legally binding and could be overturned by the courts, public officials normally will be reluctant to oppose the attorney general's ruling.

Besides giving legal opinions, the attorney general has considerable influence on policy. An attorney general who takes an interest in prosecuting consumer protection cases, for example, can make a significant impact on the lives of the average citizen. The same may be true of other areas of public concern such as nursing home facilities, health insurance provisions, corrections systems, and drug and other criminal prosecutions. Many states allow the attorney general to intervene in local prosecutions, and the attorney general's office typically has broad responsibilities in many administrative actions, from advising agencies on their rules to conducting litigation on behalf of, or against, individual agencies.[62] A number of state attorneys general banded together in the 1990s to sue tobacco companies for the health costs arising from the use of tobacco products.

More recently, a group of Republican attorneys general, joined by one Democrat, filed a lawsuit to block enforcement of the health insurance mandate provision of the 2010 national health care reforms. A more bipartisan group of state attorneys general has mobilized to fight some federal firearms regulations, and Virginia's attorney general, Ken Cuccinelli, has moved individually against federal regulations of greenhouse gases and new mileage standards for motor vehicles. State attorneys general have also worked through their nationwide organization, the National Association of Attorneys General, to lobby the federal government, exchange ideas, and coordinate their efforts on issues of common concern. Although conflicts often receive more attention, state attorneys general often work harmoniously with each other and with the national government.[63]

By using their prosecutorial powers aggressively, attorneys general are well positioned to create a popular image that can serve as a springboard to higher office. The two best-known historic examples of this are governors Robert M. La Follette of Wisconsin and Thomas E. Dewey of New York. Both prosecuted vice and organized crime to gain the prominence that eventually enabled them to be elected governor. More recently, Attorneys General Christine Gregoire of Washington and Eliot Spitzer of New York worked to protect consumers and punish business misconduct before becoming governors. However, activist attorneys general can also antagonize people and groups that are targets of investigations.

Eliot Spitzer found this out when, as governor, he was involved in a scandal and forced from office. A number of business groups have funneled large sums of money into campaigns against attorneys general who are regarded as too sympathetic to consumers and/or labor unions.[64] An analysis comparing attorneys general, lieutenant governors, state auditors, secretaries of state, and state treasurers who ran for governor from 1981 to 2001 found that the attorneys general were most likely to lose their bids for the governorship; more than 80 percent of them lost.[65]

Secretary of State

The third major statewide office is the **secretary of state**. This office is found in all states except Hawaii (where its duties are assigned to the lieutenant governor), and it is elective in 35 states. Typically, the secretary of state keeps the state archives, supervises elections, compiles election statistics, publishes a *Blue Book* on state government organization, and often serves on various state commissions and advisory boards. Some secretaries of state issue automobile and drivers' licenses, and certificates of incorporation. Many secretaries of state have been actively involved in efforts to promote Internet access to state government and greater use of electronic record keeping. Those efforts have, in turn, involved a number of secretaries of state in efforts to combat identity theft and protect privacy. In recent years, the office has sometimes been used as a springboard for a run at the governorship.[66]

Although much of the work of secretaries of state is fairly routine, they can sometimes exercise significant discretion. In the disputed 2000 presidential election in Florida, Secretary of State Katherine Harris, a co-chair of George Bush's campaign in Florida, issued a series of decisions, all of which sided with the Bush campaign.[67] More recently, California's secretary of state Kevin Shelley reviewed several studies and concluded that touch-screen voting machines, which some reformers had recommended after Florida's election problems, presented serious security and accuracy problems, with one brand being particularly troublesome.[68]

Auditor

Two tasks of auditing need to be accomplished in state government—a preaudit and a postaudit. The preaudit authorizes payment of state funds, ensures that funds for particular uses have been appropriated by the legislature, and makes certain that there is a sufficient balance in the appropriate state account. The preaudit is conducted by a person, technically called a comptroller, who certifies that funds are available before the state treasurer issues a check.

The postaudit occurs after the expenditure of funds and is made to ensure that the funds were spent in accord with the intent of state law. Because the postaudit provides considerable potential to investigate officials at both the state and local levels, public administration specialists normally think that an **auditor** should be accountable to the legislature rather than to the governor or the executive branch. In practice, the preaudit and postaudit functions are usually combined in the same office located in the executive branch. An activist auditor can play an important policy role by shedding light on how public policies are in fact carried out and by assessing the effectiveness of governmental programs. In addition, auditors in recent years have been heavily involved in disaster planning and preparation, and in promoting greater use of electronic record keeping.[69]

Treasurer

Treasurers are custodians of the state's funds. They determine which banks will be the depositories for the state monies, and they authorize the checks that pay for state obligations. They may also be responsible for overseeing the investment of state funds, including pension funds, which include enormous sums of money in some states. Treasurers may also guide borrowing funds by the state and by local governments in the state. Many state treasurers are also involved in overseeing state college savings programs, which help families raise the funds need to finance college costs.[70] Fifteen state treasurers also manage their states' rainy day funds, which are held in reserve for times when revenues slump.

Treasurers can have significant policy impact by, for example, refusing to deposit state money in banks that redline* or that fail to take part in central-city redevelopment. Seemingly minor savings on individual financial transactions can accumulate to considerable savings if those transactions are numerous. Careful investment of state funds may produce added revenues that help support programs without additional taxes; careless investment can mean financial losses. Thirty-six states have elected treasurers, but modern public administration theory suggests that appointed treasurers are preferable to elected ones, partly because many American voters have difficulty in assessing candidates' expertise in financial management.

Administrative Boards and Commissions

Finally, governors also face political competition from independent boards and commissions. Virtually every state, for example, has a state board of education that is responsible for setting (or helping to set) state educational policy. A forceful governor determined to reform state education can usually, but not always, convince the state board to support his or her efforts, especially if those efforts will give more money to the schools. But often the state board will resist excessive gubernatorial encroachment. The board was created in the first place to protect the schools from political influence by governors and legislators, and what may seem like sound policy to the governor can easily seem like political meddling to the board members. In 16 states, the boards of education are elective, which gives them even greater independence from the governor.

In addition to boards of education, states frequently have utilities commissions that determine how much citizens will pay for electricity and telephone usage, state regents who determine tuition and graduation requirements (for those attending a public university), insurance commissions that set automobile and health insurance rates, welfare boards that oversee welfare, and numerous boards in charge of regulating various professions, often including doctors, nurses, realtors, and barbers. How independent one wants these boards to be is in part a reflection of the demands for executive representation, neutral competence, or executive leadership discussed at the beginning of this chapter.

GOVERNORS AND PUBLIC CONFLICT

How do governors fit in with the two broad questions of public policy conflict—contemporary social change and the political economy—that we have been discussing? More than any other public official, the governor occupies the hot seat on both of these issues.

---

*Redlining in the financial industry is the practice of designating certain parts of a community as ineligible for mortgages or business loans, often on the basis of the area's poor economic health. The practice encourages further economic decline because people cannot get loans to make improvements. Many of these areas have large minority populations.

Governors and Social Conflict

American politics in recent years has included many controversies pitting various social groups against one another and involving disagreements over basic values. Florida's recent governor, Jeb Bush, illustrates a number of the ways in which governors become involved in social disputes. During his tenure as governor, Bush provoked controversy by pushing for race-neutral policies in fields such as higher education and state contracting. His efforts angered supporters of affirmative action, and the percentage of African American students at state universities subsequently declined. However, state contracts with minority contractors rose considerably.[71]

One of Jeb Bush's most dramatic actions as governor involved the case of Terry Schiavo, a woman who had suffered massive brain damage. When members of her family disagreed over whether to discontinue life-support measures, Bush intervened in an effort to continue them. His actions pleased many religious conservatives, but critics charged that his efforts contradicted his repeated calls for less governmental involvement in society. Regardless of the positions a governor takes, he or she is almost certain to be drawn into social conflicts of one sort or another.

Governors and Political Economy

If social conflict puts today's governors on the hot seat, so does the political economy. What happens in a state's economy is vitally important to the incumbent governor. If a significant part of the state's economy suffers from a prolonged recession, several repercussions are possible—none of them pleasant for the incumbent governor. Increasing unemployment caused by recession will reduce state tax collections, forcing the governor to call for budget cuts and tax increases. These actions do not necessarily cost governors a chance at reelection. But they risk losing votes when they raise taxes—especially for income tax and sales tax increases, and especially in the case of Republican governors.[72]

Governors also seem to pay a price for a general deterioration in the state's economy, even when tax increases are not needed. Recessions mean that more people file for unemployment compensation and welfare benefits. This may overload the state's capacity to provide those benefits, which will reflect poorly on the governor's leadership. Even if these things do not happen, many people demonstrate their economic frustrations and anxieties by voting against the incumbents, regardless of whether the incumbents have any real power to combat the economic conditions.[73] As the most visible of incumbents, the governors feel pressure to do something about their states' economies. Gray Davis reminded the nation's governors of that risk when he was recalled from office by California voters as the state struggled with a slumping economy and skyrocketing energy costs.

Governors find that dealing with the state economy is difficult because the American and world economies have changed considerably in recent decades. Older manufacturing sectors of the economy (especially those based in the Northeast and Midwest) had relatively slow economic growth or even declined since the 1970s and were badly damaged by foreign competition. Some of those states, however, have recently attracted firms in the technology sector and have experienced economic rebounds. The newer service sectors of the economy have led the nation's economic growth. This has been a boon to many parts of the South and Southwest. Energy-producing states of the West, after experiencing explosive growth in the 1970s, were decimated by the oil glut and falling energy prices in the mid-1980s. Most of them had at least partially recovered by the 1990s. By the winter of 2008–2009, however, almost all the states were facing revenue shortfalls due to a worldwide recession, and that problem has persisted in most states since then. In addition, some areas have lost jobs as more and more companies close production facilities in the United States and move the jobs overseas and as some companies replace people with more sophisticated automated equipment.

No state is untouched by these changes. Economic life today is characterized by intense competition among states to attract new economic development, to keep businesses they already have, and to position themselves for an increasingly global economy. At the political center of this competition is the governor. As the most visible state official, the governor is expected to take responsibility for the state's economic conditions. Even though the governor's actual influence over the economy is limited, a faltering economy can produce angry voters.

Instead of competing with each other, governors Jim Doyle of Wisconsin and Tim Pawlenty of Minnesota have decided to join forces by searching for opportunities to pool their resources and work together by joint purchasing of supplies, sharing equipment that is not always needed in one of the states, and having both states share some facilities, such as prisons, that have fluctuating workloads in both states. Both governors have urged state employees to repeatedly look for methods of cooperation that could save money or improve program performance.[74]

A Premium on Strong Leaders

In the final analysis, gubernatorial leadership makes a great deal of difference in how a state responds to social conflict and political economy. Strong governors have greater freedom to grapple with these issues than do weak governors. But even strong governors pay a cost if they stray too far from what public opinion or powerful state interest groups will tolerate.

Many observers believe that a strong governor is critical if the states are to meet the challenges they face today.[75] Since the federal government has often been unable or unwilling to launch major domestic initiatives since the 1980s—in large measure due to disagreements between presidents and Congress, in-fighting within Congress, and the massive budget deficits in most years since the 1980s—states sometimes stepped in to fill that void. The task has essentially been twofold: to foster economic growth in the state and to guide that growth so that the poor as well as the rich get some benefit from it (the latter idea being more controversial in some states). This is a daunting task because it often means reforming the revenue system and/or redistributing public funds from one set of programs to another.[76] It is to the governor, more than anyone else, that people look for leadership on these tasks. States with strong governors were in a much better position to confront the challenges of the 1990s and beyond than were the states with weak governors.

The poorer half of the population has the most to lose from weak governors because they are the people most in need of strong leadership in the area of social welfare policies. An ineffectual executive may make the passage of major new policies very difficult because there are more possible bases of opposition among the numerous elected executives.[77] At the same time, not all governors want to help the needy very much, and wealthier Americans tend to share that view. As we will see in Chapter 13, much of the thrust of welfare reform since 1996 has been in the direction of doing less to help the needy, and a number of governors have supported that change.

Note, too, that governors may not know what to do to improve the state economy overall or to provide better lives for poorer or wealthier people. National and international economic currents sweep through the states, and those currents often have far more influence than the governor.

CONCLUSION

To conclude this examination of governors and policy conflict, three generalizations are warranted. First, the formal powers of the governor do make a difference. It is easier for a person to be a dynamic governor if that position has been given substantial amounts of authority. Second, leadership qualities and other informal dynamics, such as popularity, also make a difference. Formal powers alone will not make a dynamic and forceful governor if the governor lacks the personal drive and skill to lead successfully. Finally, a strong governor may help produce greater responsiveness to people looking for action on an issue, but strong governors have fought for a variety of different political goals over the years. People who like the status quo may prefer a weaker governor.

SUMMARY

1. Although the substance of voters' demands on governors changes over time, a governor who appears uninterested in public sentiments or concerns is likely to suffer at the polls.
2. Views on executive leadership have evolved through three historical stages revolving around the Progressive reform movement.
3. The governors' main sources of leadership strength are legislative powers, administrative powers, budget powers, public relations powers, the capabilities and resources of their personal staffs, and influence that they derive from their roles as federal systems officers who lobby the federal government and interact with officials of other states.
4. The governor's ability to lead depends in part on the gubernatorial style he or she adopts. There are four main styles: the demagogue, the policy entrepreneur, the frustrated warrior, and the caretaker.
5. Governors' political influence is affected by their career record and prospects. Governors who win office with large victory margins carry more influence than governors who just squeak by. Governors with good prospects for reelection or moving on to higher office carry more influence than lame duck governors.
6. The governor's political influence may be challenged by other statewide-elected executives such as the lieutenant governor, attorney general, secretary of state, treasurer, auditor, and independent administrative boards.
7. Governors must often grapple with issues of social change and political economy. Governors with strong powers and strong political support are in a better position to deal with these issues than are weak governors.

STUDY QUESTIONS

1. How has the office of governor changed over the years? What reform movements have affected the governor's role in state politics?
2. What formal and informal powers influence a governor's ability to lead in state politics? How can a governor's approach to the office or leadership style affect his or her ability to lead?
3. What sorts of career paths do people commonly take to become governor? What career paths do people commonly take after they leave office? How can their career paths affect their ability to get things done?
4. What other state executives are commonly elected? How can they complicate the governor's job?

KEY TERMS

Amendatory veto Power of the governor in some states to return a bill to the legislature with proposed revisions. If the legislature accepts the revisions, the bill becomes law. If not, the bill is vetoed.

Attorney general The chief law enforcement officer of a state.

Auditor The state officer responsible for ascertaining that funds are spent properly and legally.

Caretaker A gubernatorial style in which the governor maintains the operations of the office, but rarely pushes for new legislation, new programs, or new authority.

Demagogue A political leader who builds his or her political support partly by enflaming people's passions over emotional political issues.

Executive leadership The belief that the chief executives in governmental jurisdictions (principally governors and mayors) should exercise considerable authority over other executives.

Executive representation The belief that people can be represented in the executive branch by elected executives just as they are represented in the legislative branch by elected legislators.

Item veto Power of the governor in some states to veto specific provisions of appropriations bills without vetoing the entire bill.

Jacksonian democracy A governing concept, attributed to the terms of President Andrew Jackson (1829–1837), that government should rule for the benefit of the common people and that the public should select many state and local officials.

Lieutenant governor A statewide officer who succeeds the governor if the governor leaves the governorship; lieutenant governors often have other responsibilities as well.

Long ballot An election ballot containing many offices to be filled by election.

Neutral competence The belief that public services should be provided competently and in a politically neutral fashion. Elected officials should make policy decisions, but the administrators responsible for carrying out those policies should be insulated from political influence.

Policy entrepreneur A dynamic governor or mayor who sets an agenda of goals to be accomplished and builds alliances with the interests needed to reach the goals.

Secretary of state A statewide office responsible for administering the state election system, publishing a legislative manual, caring for state records, and conducting various clerical duties.

Spoils system A patronage theory of public hiring in which the winning candidates in elections should be able to find jobs for their supporters in the public bureaucracies. "To the victors go the spoils" was the slogan of this theory.

Treasurer The state officer responsible for custody of state funds and for writing the checks that pay state obligations.

Veto Power of a governor to prevent a bill's passage by the legislature and block it from becoming law. Vetoes may be overridden by the state legislature, usually by a two-thirds majority in each house, but successful overrides are relatively rare.

THE INTERNET CONNECTION

The National Governors' Association serves as a clearinghouse for ideas about state politics and policies, and sometimes lobbies the national government on behalf of state interests (as defined by the governors). You can find the association's Web site at **www.nga.org**. Individual state government Web sites typically include a link to the governor's office as well. What can you learn about the governor of your state from the Web?

NOTES

1. See Douglas Belkin, Lauren Etter and Timothy Martin, "Governor Jailed in Alleged Graft Spree," *Wall Street Journal*, December 10, 2008, pp. A1, A16.
2. Daniel Vock, "Illinois Senate Removes Blagojevich," *Stateline*, January 29, 2009 (electronic edition);

"Senate Removes Blagojevich from Office," *Chicago Tribune*, January 29, 2009 (Web edition); "Blagojevich Banned from Public Office in Illinois," *Chicago Tribune*, January 29, 2009 (Web edition).
3. Natash Korecki, Lark Turner, and Abdon Pallasch, "'Stunned' Blagojevich Found Guilty on

17 Counts," *Chicago Sun-Times*, June 28, 2011 (Web edition).

4. Thad Beyle, "Gubernatorial Elections, Campaign Costs and Powers," in *Book of the States*, vol. 42 (Lexington, KY: Council of State Governments, 2010), p. 194.

5. See Jan Moller, "Gov. Bobby Jindal Defends His Wife's Charity," *New Orleans Times-Picayune*, March 3, 2011 (Web edition); Gromer Jeffers, "Exclusive: Perry Voter Turnout Project Signs up Felons," *Dallas Morning News*, January 24, 2010 (Web edition).

6. These three stages were articulated by Herbert Kaufman in "Emerging Conflicts in the Doctrines of Public Administration," *American Political Science Review* 50 (1956): 1057.

7. See especially *Federalist Papers* no. 10 and no. 51.

8. Larry Sabato, *Goodbye to Good-Time Charlie: The American Governor Transformed*, 2nd ed. (Washington, DC: CQ Press, 1983), p. 52; Nelson Dometrius, "Governors: Their Heritage and Future," in Ronald Weber and Paul Brace, eds. *American State and Local Politics* (New York: Chatham House, 1999), pp. 50–52.

9. For information on the governors' powers to issue executive orders, see *The Book of the States* (Lexington, KY: Council of State Governments, 2002), pp. 152–153.

10. For discussions of how to measure the governors' powers and some alternative measures, see Thad Beyle, "The Governors," in Virginia Gray and Russell Hanson, eds. *Politics in the American States*, 8th ed. (Washington, DC: CQ Press, 2004), pp. 210–218; Thad Beyle and Margaret Ferguson, "The Governors and the Executive Branch," in Virginia Gray and Russell Hanson, eds. *Politics in the American States*, 9th ed. (Washington, DC: CQ Press, 2008), pp. 203–214; Keith J. Mueller, "Explaining Variation and Change in Gubernatorial Powers, 1960–1982," *Western Political Quarterly* 38 (1985): 424–431; Nelson Dometrius, "Changing Gubernatorial Power: The Measure vs. Reality," *Western Political Quarterly* 40 (1987): 318–328; Robert Jay Dilger, "A Comparative Analysis of Gubernatorial Enabling Resources," *State and Local Government Review* 27, no. 2 (Spring 1995): 118–126. The index used for Table 9.2 has the advantages of being recent and including the political variable of party control in the legislature.

11. A study of the line item veto in Texas found that it did not give the governor any improvement in control over the budget. Pat Thompson and Steven R. Boyd, "Use of the Item Veto in Texas, 1940–1990," *State and Local Government Review* 26, no. 1 (Winter 1994): 38–45. This finding was consistent with earlier studies. See David C. Nice, "The Item Veto and Expenditures Restraint," *Journal of Politics* 50, no. 2 (May 1988): 482–502; B. Abrams and W. Dougan, "The Effects of Constitutional Restraints on Government Spending," *Public Choice* 49, no. 2 (1986): 101–116. One study, however, did find that the item veto produces a minor reduction in state expenditures when the governorship and legislatures are controlled by opposite parties. See James Alm and Mark Evers, "The Line Item Veto and State Expenditures," *Public Choice* 68 (1991): 1–15.

12. Glen Abney and Thomas P. Lauth, "The Line-Item Veto in the States," *Public Administration Review* 45, no. 3 (May–June 1985): 372–377. Abney and Lauth came to this conclusion after surveying the legislative budget officers in the 50 states.

13. See "Legislators Fight Item Veto in Wisconsin," *State Legislatures* 14, no. 8 (September 1988): 9. Also see Tony Hutchinson, "Legislating via Veto," *State Legislatures* 15, no. 1 (January 1989): 20–24.

14. Michael H. McCabe, "Wisconsin's 'Quirky' Veto Power," *State Government News* 34, no. 8 (August 1991): 11–14.

15. In the mid-1990s, governors in the 50 states vetoed about 3.7 percent of all bills and resolutions. See Thad Beyle, "The Governors," in Virginia Gray and Russell Hanson, eds. *Politics in the American States,* 8th ed. (Washington, DC: CQ Press, 2004), p. 216.

16. On the increasing frequency of overrides, see Charles W. Wiggins, "Executive Vetoes and Legislative Overrides in the American States," *Journal of Politics* 42, no. 4 (November 1986): 1110–1112. In California, the legislature failed to override even a single governor's veto from 1946 to 1974; in New York, from 1877 to 1976; in Texas, from 1941 to 1979. See Noel J. Stowe, *California Government: The Challenge of Change* (Beverly Hills, CA: Glencoe Press, 1975), p. 138; Eugene J. Gleason and Joseph Zimmerman, "The Strong Governorship: Status and Problems, New York," *Public Administration Review* 36, no. 1 (January–February 1976): 92–95; Clifton McCleskey et al., *The Government and Politics of Texas,* 7th ed.

(Boston: Little, Brown and Co., 1982), p. 176. In the 1990–1991 legislative sessions there were 206 overrides of 2,333 vetoes. *The Book of the States: 1992–93* (Lexington, KY: Council of State Governments, 1992), pp. 183–188; Thad Beyle, "The Governors," in Virginia Gray and Russell Hanson, eds. *Politics in the American States,* 8th ed. (Washington, DC: CQ Press, 2004), p. 216.

17. E. Lee Bernick, "Special Sessions: What Manner of Gubernatorial Power," *State and Local Government Review* 26, no. 2 (Spring 1994): 79–88.

18. For an example, see Alan Greenblatt, "States of Frustration," *Governing* 17, no. 4 (January 2004): 26.

19. On the executive amendment provision, see Coleman Ransone, Jr., *The Office of Governor in the United States* (Tuscaloosa: University of Alabama Press, 1956), pp. 182–184; for information on special sessions, see *The Book of the States*, vol. 43 (Lexington, KY: Council of State Governments, 2011), pp. 112–113.

20. Alan Rosenthal, "Legislative Oversight and the Balance of Power in State Government," *State Government* 56, no. 3 (1983): 90–98.

21. Thad Beyle, "Governors: The Middlemen and Women in Our Political System," in Virginia Gray and Henry Jacob, eds. *Politics in the American States: A Comparative Analysis,* 6th ed. (Washington, DC: CQ Press, 1996), p. 241.

22. Alan Greenblatt "In Kansas, It's GOP vs. GOP," *Governing* 25, no. 4, (January 2012): 11.

23. Rosenthal, "Legislative Oversight and the Balance of Power in State Government"; Glen Abney and Thomas Lauth, "The End of Executive Dominance in State Appropriations," *Public Administration Review* 58 (1998): 388–394; Wes Clarke, "Divided Government and Budget Conflict in the U.S. States," *Legislative Studies Quarterly* 23 (1998): 5–22.

24. Katherine Willoughby, "The State of the States: Governors Aggressively Chip Away," in *Book of the States*, vol. 43 (Lexington, KY: Council of State Governments, 2011), pp. 118–120.

25. Steven Williams, "Alexander's Master Teacher Program Fails in Tennessee," *Comparative State Politics Newsletter* 4, no. 3 (May 1983): 11–12; "Master Teacher Program Update," 4, no. 6 (December 1983): 21; and "The First Year of Merit Pay for Tennessee Teachers," 6, no. 5 (October 1985): 33; Jonathan Walter, "Full Speed Ahead," *Governing* 15, no. 2 (November 2001): 23.

26. See Louis M. Kohlmeier, Jr., *The Regulators: Watchdog Agencies and the Public Interest* (New York: Harper & Row, 1969).

27. Glenn Abney and Thomas P. Lauth, "The Governor as Chief Administrator," *Public Administration Review* 43, no. 1 (January–February 1983): 40–49. This was the same result as Deil S. Wright had found when he conducted a similar survey two decades earlier. See Deil S. Wright, "Executive Leadership in State Administration," *Midwest Journal of Political Science* 11, no. 1 (February 1967): 1–26.

28. Norton Long, "After the Voting Is Over," *Midwest Journal of Political Science* 6, no. 2 (May 1963): 183–200.

29. See Donald P. Sprengel, *Gubernatorial Staffs: Functional and Political Profiles* (Iowa City: Institute of Public Affairs, University of Iowa, 1969), pp. 34–52; *The Book of the States*, vol. 42 (Lexington, KY: Council of State Governments, 2010), p. 199.

30. Thad Beyle, "The Governors, 1988–89," in *The Book of the States: 1990–91* (Lexington, KY: Council of State Governments, 1990), p. 55.

31. James King, "Incumbent Popularity and Vote Choice in Gubernatorial Elections," *Journal of Politics* 63 (2001): 585–597; Patrick J. Kenney and Tom W. Rice, "Popularity and the Vote: The Gubernatorial Case," *American Politics Quarterly* 11, no. 2 (April 1983): 237–242. Kenney and Rice examined 19 gubernatorial elections in four states where polling organizations periodically track governors' popularity (California, Iowa, Minnesota, and New Jersey). In 15 of the 19 elections, the governors lost their reelection bids if their final preelection popularity ratings dropped below 48 percent.

32. See Deil S. Wright, "Governors, Grants, and the Intergovernmental System," in Thad Beyle and J. Oliver Williams, eds. *The American Governor in Behavioral Perspective* (New York: Harper & Row, 1972), pp. 187–193.

33. See Thad L. Beyle and Deil S. Wright, "The Governor, Planning, and Governmental Activity," in Beyle and Williams, eds., *The American Governor in Behavioral Perspective,* pp. 193–205.

34. Jeremy Peters, "Governors Call for Rescue Package for States," *New York Times*, October 30, 2008 (electronic edition).

35. Lynn Muchmore and Thad L. Beyle, "The Governor as Party Leader," *State Government* 53, no. 3 (Summer 1980): 121–124.

36. See John Bibby and Thomas Holbrook, "Parties and Elections," in Virginia Gray, Russell Hanson, and Herbert Jacob, eds. *Politics in the American States,* 7th ed. (Washington, DC: CQ Press, 1999), pp. 73–75, 79–83.

37. Sarah McCally Morehouse, "Money Versus Party Effort: Nominating for Governor," *American Journal of Political Science* 34, no. 3 (August 1990): 706–724. Morehouse conducted an elaborate statistical comparison of money spent in gubernatorial campaigns in states where the parties endorsed gubernatorial nominees (strong party states) and in states where parties do not endorse gubernatorial nominees (weak party states).

38. Lee Sigelman and Nelson C. Dometrius demonstrate that for the governor to exercise effective influence over state agencies, for example, the governor's formal powers need to be bolstered by informal sources of influence (especially the ability to win election by a substantial margin and the ability of the governor's party to control the legislature). See their "Governors as Chief Administrators: The Linkage Between Formal Powers and Informal Influence," *American Politics Quarterly* 16, no. 2 (April 1988): 157–171.

39. Larry Sabato, *Goodbye to Good-Time Charlie: The American Governor Transformed 1950–1975,* 1st ed. (Lexington, MA: Lexington Books, 1978), pp. 50–56.

40. Lee Sigelman and Roland Smith, "Personal, Office, and State Characteristics as Predictors of Gubernatorial Performance," *Journal of Politics* 43, no. 1 (February 1981): 169–180. Quote on p. 180.

41. The preeminent biography of Huey Long is T. Harry Williams's *Huey Long.* Also see Alan Sindler, *Huey Long's Louisiana: State Politics 1920–1952.* Also see Long's autobiography, *Every Man a King: The Autobiography of Huey Long* (New Orleans: National Book Co., 1933), and the political novel based on the life of Huey Long by Robert Penn Warren, *All the King's Men* (New York: Bantam Books, 1968).

42. Walter, "Full Speed Ahead," p. 23.

43. Pamela Prah, "Governors to Pare Back Agendas," *Stateline,* January 7, 2009 (electronic edition); Kathrine Willoughby, "The State of the States: Governors Aggressively Chip Away," in *Book of the States,* vol. 43 (Lexington, KY: Council of State Governments, 2011), pp. 117–126.

44. David E. Osborne, *Laboratories of Democracy* (Boston: Harvard Business School Press, 1988).

45. David E. Osborne and Ted Gaebler, *Reinventing Government: How the Entrepreneurial Spirit Is Transforming the Public Sector* (Reading, MA: Addison-Wesley, 1992); Charles Barrilleaux, "Statehouse Bureaucracy: Institutional Consistency in a Changing Environment," in Ronald Weber and Paul Brace, eds. *American State and Local Politics* (New York: Chatham House, 1999), pp. 110–113.

46. For a discussion of this theme and a critique of many administrative reforms in the public and private sectors, see John Macdonald, *Calling a Halt to Mindless Change* (New York: American Management Association International, 1998).

47. John Gramlich, "After a Contentious Political Year, Republicans May Moderate Their Approach," *Stateline,* January 9, 2012 (Web edition).

48. William Flanigan and Nancy Zingale, *Political Behavior of the American Electorate,* 12th, ed. (Washington, DC: CQ Press, 2010), pp. 8–13.

49. For a compilation of female governors over the years, see *Book of the States,* vol. 43, p. 134.

50. Sarah McCally Morehouse, "The Governor as Political Leader," in Herbert Jacob and Kenneth N. Vines, eds. *Politics in the American States: A Comparative Analysis,* 3rd ed. (Boston: Little, Brown and Co., 1977), p. 204. Of the 156 governors during the 1960s, 92 were attorneys and 32 were businesspersons.

51. Of 995 governors from 1870 to 1950, 90 percent had held prior public office. See Joseph A. Schlesinger, *How They Became Governors* (East Lansing: Michigan State University, Governmental Research Bureau, 1957), p. 11. That pattern has continued in more recent times. See Thad C. Beyle, "The Governors," *Politics in the American States* (Washington, DC: CQ Press, 2004), pp. 196–198.

52. Morgan Mundell, "Analysis: Governors and Past Elected Offices (1980–2006), National Lieutenant Governors Association, December 5, 2006, Web document (**nlga.us/web-content/Projects/Res_Anal_Gov_all_offcs.htm**).

53. Thad Beyle, "Gubernatorial Elections, Campaign Costs, and Powers," in *The Book of the States,* vol. 38 (Lexington, KY: Council of State Governments, 2006), pp. 146–149; Thad Beyle, "Gubernatorial Elections, Campaign Costs, and Powers," in *The Book of the States,* vol. 43 (Lexington, KY: Council of State Governments, 2011), pp. 127–137.

54. Beyle, "The Governors," p. 197; Anthony Gierzynski, *Money Rules* (Boulder, CO: Westview, 2000), p. 60; Beyle, "Gubernatorial Elections," p. 132.

55. Elizabeth Daigneau and Zach Patton, "The Governors: Democrats Sweep to a Majority," *Governing.com*, Web document, November 8, 2006 (www.governing.com/news/11govs.htm).

56. *Statistical Abstract of the United States* (Washington, DC: Bureau of the Census, 2012), p. 260

57. Morehouse, "The Governor as Political Leader," pp. 201–202.

58. Vock, "Illinois Senate"; Beyle, "Gubernatorial Elections," (2011), p. 194.

59. "Ex-Gov. Ryan Sentenced to Six Years in Prison," CNN, Web document, September 6, 2006 (www.cnn.com/2006/LAW/09/06/ryan.sentenced.ap/index.html); "Former Governor Released from Prison," *Moscow-Pullman Daily News*, February 10, 2006, p. 5A; Mike Linn, "Siegelman, Scrushy Denied New Trial, *Montgomery (Alabama) Advertiser*, Web document, December 14, 2006 (www.montgomeryadvertiser.com/apps/pbcs.dll/article?/Date=20061214&Category=...).

60. See Julia Hurst, "Lieutenant Governors: Significant and Visible," in *The Book of the States*, vol. 38 (Lexington, KY: Council of State Governments, 2006), pp. 181–183; Julia Hurst, "Office of Lieutenant Governor: Unheralded but Critical Leadership," in *The Book of the States*, vol. 42 (Lexington, KY: Council of State Governments, 2010, pp. 225–233.

61. Robbie Brown, "South Carolina Lt. Governor Resigns Amid Criminal Investigation," *New York Times*, March 9, 2012 (Web edition).

62. Angelita Plemmer, "Attorneys General: Trends and Issues," in *The Book of the States*, vol. 38 (Lexington, KY: Council of State Governments, 2006), pp. 198–201; *Book of the States*, vol. 42 (Lexington, KY: Council of State Governments, 2010), pp. 252–255.

63. Josh Goodman, "Rise of the Generals," *Governing*, June, 2010, pp. 31–34.

64. On La Follette, see Robert S. Maxwell, *La Follette and the Rise of the Progressives in Wisconsin* (Madison: State Historical Society of Wisconsin, 1956). On Dewey's use of the prosecution power to become governor, see Warren Moscow, *Politics in the Empire State* (New York: Knopf, 1948), pp. 29–32. Dewey, however, was not the attorney general; he was a special prosecutor appointed to prosecute organized crime figures. On recent developments, see Alan Greenblatt, "Where Campaign Money Flows," *Governing* 16, no. 2 (November 2002): 44–47.

65. Beyle, "The Governors," (2004), p. 198.

66. This was the case for California Governor Jerry Brown (1975–1983) and Oregon Governor Barbara Roberts (1991–1995). Arizona Governor Rose Mofford (1988–1991) ascended from secretary of state to the governorship when Governor Evan Mecham was impeached. Minnesota Secretary of State Joan Growe used the office as a launching pad for an unsuccessful bid for the U.S. Senate in 1986. Of the state secretaries of state who ran for governor from 1981 to 2001, only 30 percent were successful. See Beyle, "The Governors," (2004), pp. 197–198. On the duties of secretaries of state, see George Munro, "Secretaries of State: Trends and Issues," in *The Book of the States*, vol. 38 (Lexington, KY: Council of State Governments, 2006), pp. 189–192; Kay Stimson, "Secretaries of State: Focused on Redacting Social Security Numbers from Public Records in the Digital Age," in *Book of the States*, vol. 40 (Lexington, KY: Council of State Governments), pp. 218–222.

67. See Benjamin Ginsburg and Theodore Lowi, *Election 2000 Report* (New York: Norton, 2001), pp. 15–16.

68. Secretary of State Kevin Shelley, California, *Statewide Election Report*, March 2, 2004 (report appeared on the secretary of state's Web site).

69. Edward M. Wheat, "The Activist Auditor: A New Player in State and Local Politics," *Public Administration Review* 15, no. 5 (September–October 1991): 385–391; Nancy Kopp, "Faster, Cheaper, Better: Demands for Financial Reporting from State Government," in *The Book of the States*, vol. 43 (Lexington, KY: Council of State Government, 2011), pp. 183–190.

70. National Association of State Treasurers, "State Treasurers: Guardians of the Public Purse," in *The Book of the State*, vol. 38 (Lexington, KY: Council of State Governments, 2006), pp. 211–214; National Association of State Treasurers, "State Treasurers: Guardians of the Public Trust," in *Book of the States*, vol. 40 (Lexington, KY: Council of State Governments, 2008), pp. 241–243.

71. Alan Greenblatt, "Jebocracy," *Governing* 20, no. 3 (December 2006): 32–38.

72. Susan L. Kone and Richard F. Winters, "Taxes and Voting: Electoral Retribution in the American States," *The Journal of Politics* 55, no. 1 (February 1993): 22–40; Robert Lowry, James

Alt, and Karen Ferree, "Fiscal Policy Outcomes and Electoral Accountability in American States," *American Political Science Review* 92 (1998): 759–774.

73. The impact of economic conditions on the governor's reelection prospects is a contested issue. John Chubb analyzed this relationship for the years 1940 through 1982 and concluded that citizens do not hold their governors accountable for economic conditions. See his "Institutions, the Economy, and the Dynamics of State Elections," *American Political Science Review* 82, no. 1 (March 1988): 133–154. By contrast, analyses of gubernatorial elections from 1986 to 1990 found that governors lose votes when their states' voters perceive troubles in the state economy or in their personal finances. On the 1986 elections, see Richard G. Niemi, Harold W. Stanley, and Ronald J. Vogel, "State Economies and State Taxes: Do Voters Hold Governors Accountable?" *American Journal of Political Science* 39, no. 4 (November 1995): 936–957. On the 1990 elections, see Randall W. Partin, "Economic Conditions and Gubernatorial Elections: Is the State Executive Held Accountable?" *American Politics Quarterly* 23, no. 1 (January 1995): 81–95. See also Lonna Rae Atkeson and Randall Partin, "Economic and Referendum Voting: A Comparison of Gubernatorial and Senatorial Elections," *American Political Science Review* 89 (1995): 99–107; Lowry, Alt, and Ferree, "Fiscal Policy." Also, a survey of Louisiana voters in 1988 found that the state's economic conditions played a strong role in whether people approved or disapproved of the governor. See Susan E. Howell and James M. Vanderleeuw, "Economic Effects on State Governors," *American Politics Quarterly* 18, no. 2 (April 1990): 158–168.

74. Stacy Forster, "Doyle, Gov. Pawlenty of Minnesota Outline Collaboration Plan," *Milwaukee Journal Sentinel,* January 14, 2009.

75. This was the opinion of the National Commission on State and Local Public Service, popularly called the Winter Commission after its chair, former Mississippi Governor William Winter. For an assessment of the commission's recommendations, see Frank J. Thompson, "Executive Leadership as an Enduring Institutional Issue," *State and Local Government Review* 27, no. 1 (Winter 1995): 7–17.

76. See Thad Beyle, ed. *Governors and Hard Times* (Washington, DC: CQ Press, 1992), pp. 8–12.

77. Morehouse, "The Governor as Political Leader," p. 225.

Administrators and the Implementation of Policy

CHAPTER PREVIEW

This chapter examines the role of state and local administrators in carrying out the policies and implementing the programs established by political leaders. The main topics we will explore are:

1 Tensions between administrators and elected officials.

2 Public approaches to personnel practices.

3 Administrative reorganization as an approach to state government reform.

4 Budgeting and the attempts to reform budgeting as a device for improving executive management.

5 Reform alternatives for improving executive management.

6 The political economy and government productivity.

Introduction

Laura Chick spent eight years as the financial controller for the city of Los Angeles. She worked vigorously to monitor the use of city government funds in order to minimize wasteful spending and to increase the effectiveness of city programs. Her work led to major changes in the way that Los Angeles's airport authority selects and works with contractors and produced revelations that a private firm had greatly overcharged a city department.

When the national economy slipped into a recession in 2008, California, along with most other states, saw its expenses outpacing revenues. After the national government approved providing additional funds to state and local governments in order to help stimulate the economy, Chick shifted to being the state's inspector general to oversee the use of the federal fiscal stimulus funds.[1] A somewhat unusual feature of Chick's approach to financial monitoring is her practice of publicizing the results of audits, in part to increase the likelihood of corrective action. That publicity has sometimes angered officials who are cast in an unflattering light, but has also improved a number of programs. Especially when governments at all levels are short of funds, officials need to see that money is spent productively.

Criticizing public bureaucracies is a frequent American pastime. Many Americans believe that governmental bureaucrats arrive at work late, leave early, and don't accomplish much in between—except perhaps to develop complicated forms that citizens must fill out. When a program disappoints or angers people, elected officials are often quick to blame the bureaucracy, and many citizens often believe that explanation. However, if Americans are asked about their own actual experiences with public employees, the image looks considerably more positive. And few people who remember the September 11 terrorist attacks can forget the firefighters and police officers who lost their lives trying to help other people, or the city, state, and federal employees who worked around the clock during the rescue and recovery phases, trying to dig survivors out of the rubble, helping them cope with the physical injuries and emotional trauma that they suffered, or working to restore basic services. More recently, when an airliner crash-landed in the Hudson River, the combined skills of the pilot and crew and the quick responses of firefighters, the Coast Guard, police officers, a public ferry, and a pair of private ferries meant that not a single life was lost.[2]

This chapter looks at the major facets of public administration that are important to state and local governments. First, it examines a basic tension between elected officials and administrators that sometimes causes elected officials to clash with administrators, although relationships between them are often fairly cordial. The chapter then focuses on three traditional mechanisms that may enable elected executives and legislative policy makers to control or influence the administrators. These are personnel practices, reorganization, and budgeting. Next, the chapter will discuss a number of new management devices that have been tried since the mid-1960s. Finally, the chapter explores the political economy and its relation to government productivity.

TENSION BETWEEN ADMINISTRATORS AND ELECTED OFFICIALS

In theory, the legislators write the laws and the governors execute them. In practice, the legislators and governors combine to write the laws (with some involvement by judges at times), and the laws are implemented by numerous state and local government administrative agencies and by private organizations. (In the following discussion, we will use the word *executives* to mean the persons who are either elected or appointed through the political process to head public agencies. By *administrators* we mean the permanent, career employees of public agencies.) The job of the executive is to ensure that the administrative agencies implement the law in the way the governor and legislators intended (note: determining their true intentions can be difficult or even impossible). Governors and legislators, faced with electoral pressures, may demand changes in agency procedures or operations. Governors and legislators may make conflicting demands on agencies, and electoral pressures may lead governors and legislators to avoid taking clear positions on some issues.

Administrators sometimes defend or try to change their routines by actively trying to influence the formulation of policies. Conversely, administrators may call attention to problems that elected officials would rather not address or they may advocate program changes that the governor and/or legislators oppose. Administrators may also quietly resist the efforts of elected officials or act in ways not expected by them. The many services that are provided at least partly by private companies and/or nonprofit organizations add another layer of administrative complexity; people in those companies may have their own ideas regarding what should be done and how it should be done. Overall, the net result may be considerable tension and conflict between the elected officials and the public agency administrators.

This tension between executives and administrators is kept alive by several other factors.[3] First, the administrators are relatively permanent employees, whereas the executives are temporary. The average term of executives is only 5.6 years for big-city mayors and barely 4 years for governors. But top civil service employees often remain until they retire or resign, which gives them a longer-range perspective on the services provided by their agencies. If a governor's policy proposals challenge strongly held agency privileges or traditions, the civil servants can often stall the demanded changes until the governor is replaced. Stalling by agencies is also effective because governors, with a wide range of responsibilities, often have difficulty in sustaining a focus on any particular agency or issue for very long.

A second source of tension is that administrators are professionals in government, whereas the elected executives are not. The executives, who typically look on themselves as citizen-officials responsible for overseeing the activities of the professionals, are often skeptical of the supposedly professional expertise of the administrators.[4] Technical expertise is necessary in the case of highway engineering, for example. But decisions on the location of roads and freeway interchanges, the awarding of construction contracts, and the choice of urban neighborhoods to be torn up by freeways are primarily political decisions. In making such decisions, executives have to weigh the demands of professional standards against the vocal demands of various citizens.

A third source of tension is that the professional administrators have much more detailed knowledge about government programs than do most citizen-executives and legislators. Administrators are deeply embedded in a significant communications network involving other professionals at the federal, state, and local levels of government and in the private sector. In fact, the professional administrators often either initiate or review new policy ideas that the executives put forward to the public. Newly elected officials sometimes find that many governmental programs (and the problems they address) are much more complicated than they appeared during the campaign season.

A fourth major source of conflict that has received considerable attention in the wake of the 2010 elections is between Republicans and public employee unions, which a number of Republican officials regard as too friendly with the Democratic Party. The Republican officials in some states have tried to reduce the size and importance of the unions in hopes of promoting Republican prospects in future elections and pleasing some of their own political supporters. Those efforts have been bolstered by the revenue shortages that began in 2007–2008 and have continued since then. The unions and their political allies have tried to counterattack, with their largest success so far in Ohio, where voters overturned the Ohio legislation. The counterattack in Wisconsin has included an attempt to remove the governor and some state legislators from office.[5]

Relationships between career administrators and elected officials are not always or even primarily in conflict, however. Mayors and city council members generally agree with police that crime is a significant problem and needs to be addressed, although they may not agree regarding the best strategies to follow. Governors generally agree with transportation administrators that the state needs to have a good transportation system. Legislators and teachers agree that the state's children should receive an excellent education, even if they may disagree sometimes over what subjects should be emphasized and how students should be evaluated. Policies that involve major value conflicts, by contrast, are likely to produce more tension between elected officials and career administrators.

MANAGING PERSONNEL FOR BETTER POLICY IMPLEMENTATION

A major management problem lies in directing the daily activities of the 19.7 million people working for state and local governments (as of March, 2008).[6] Most of these employees, as shown in Table 10.1, work in education, health, law enforcement, the legal system, and the correctional system. Nearly three-fourths of them work at the local level. How are these many people to be hired, promoted, or fired? Should it be on the basis of political loyalties or technical skills? Should special preferences be given for racial minorities and females? Should salaries be determined by executive decision or by collective bargaining? What kind of pension systems, if any, should these employees have? And how should those pensions be financed and managed? These questions involve many billions of dollars in taxes and vital public services and go to the heart of the struggle over who should control state and local government.

The Patronage System of Employment

The **patronage** system, or the spoils system, is a recruitment method that gives government jobs to political supporters of the winning candidates. Traditional patronage was the main public employment system until late in the nineteenth century. Some of the best known patronage systems were in cities such as Chicago and New York, but patronage employment existed in many parts of the country, both urban and rural.[7] However, most elected executives today find traditional patronage difficult to manage. A new administration that fired large numbers of workers to make way for political appointees would, in most places, suffer a severe public relations setback and a wave of lawsuits. Former governor Robert Ehrlich of Maryland also found his administration under investigation by a state legislative committee on charges that party affiliations had too much influence on hiring and firing decisions. Three administration officials declined to answer numerous questions on their involvement in the controversy.[8]

The critical blows to patronage began with the passage of national, state, and local laws to limit political activity by public employees and to restrict hiring and firing based on political considerations.[9] The most dramatic restrictions on traditional patronage have come from the U.S. Supreme Court, which has ruled consistently since 1976 that politically motivated dismissals could only be made among policy-making officials and could not touch rank-and-file

TABLE 10.1

State and Local Government Employment by Function: 2008

Function	Percentage
Education	55
Health and hospitals	8
Police, corrections, judicial/legal	12
All other functions	25
Total	100

Source: Derived from *Statistical Abstract of the United States* (Washington, DC: U.S. Government Printing Office, 2008), p. 296.

employees.[10] The most recent and far-reaching case, *Rutan v. Republican Party of Illinois,*[11] involved former Illinois governor James R. Thompson, who had his personnel office review job and promotion applications to ensure that they were Republican supporters.

Patronage was further undercut by the need for greater expertise among public employees as the work of government became more complex and technical, including the growing use of computers. In addition, unionization of many state and local employees has made firing people because of their party affiliation much more difficult. Union contracts virtually never allow firing for political reasons. Informally, individual employees may be pushed out by a variety of methods (sometimes called "dehiring"), but those methods can rarely be employed to get rid of large numbers of employees at the same time. Nonetheless, the affiliations and contacts of people still sometimes affect hiring decisions. One Illinois community recently hired a village administrator who happened to be the mayor's brother-in-law even though his selection appeared to ignore the qualifications the village board had established in its original search for the administrator position.[12]

The Merit System of Employment

The **merit system,** or the **civil service system,** is a recruitment method that hires and promotes employees on the basis of their training and competence to perform specific jobs. Once employees are given civil service status, they are protected from arbitrary removal, but can be fired for inadequate performance.

One gets civil service status based on evidence of ability to do a particular job. A job description is drawn up for each civil service position. The position is classified at a specific level and assigned a pay range. Promotion to higher positions is achieved by competition, with the promotion ideally going to the candidate whose experience, qualifications, training, and/or test scores best fit the responsibilities of the job.

The first state civil service system was established in New York in 1883. Since then it has spread to virtually all states[13] and to many local governments, although coverage varies a good deal from place to place.[14] Most of these state and local civil service systems were established after 1939, in response to federal laws and court decisions that prohibited patronage systems in federally funded programs. One sign of the impact of merit systems is the fact that approximately 60 percent of all top administrators in the states have a graduate degree; another 15 percent have had some graduate study.[15]

Criticisms of Civil Service As merit systems of employment gradually replaced patronage systems, the quality of the state and local government workforce improved dramatically. But critics charge today that civil service systems are seriously outdated institutions that eventually led to severe management problems of their own.[16] For one thing, they conflict with the demand for executive leadership. High-ranking administrators with civil service protection sometimes drag their heels implementing policy changes sought by newly elected governors. From the administrators' viewpoint, many agency policies have worked well for years, and it would be chaotic and intrusive if each new governor were to overhaul them each time political winds blew in a new direction. Moreover, newly elected officials sometimes have unrealistic expectations regarding how quickly or cheaply something can be done. From the critics' viewpoint, however, the whole purpose of the democratic process is to keep administrators and policies in tune with political realities.

Some critics of civil service systems charge that they often mistake credentials for genuine ability to do the job. Applicants may be given points for having a certain college degree, for having five years of work experience, and for scoring a 93 on the civil service test. These characteristics are presumably related to the ability to do the actual work, but another candidate might have an equal ability without having a college degree (although most university professors would deny that). Assessing a person's actual abilities can be very difficult. And even if the initial assessment is correct, many employees will need periodic training to update their skills, especially if the nature of their work gradually changes. Especially when funding is tight, training budgets are often vulnerable to cuts.[17]

Critics also charge that civil service rules slow agency responses to changing conditions and make it difficult to fire incompetent workers. One study found that less than 2 percent of state and local employees are dismissed from their jobs each year, although the firing rates for public and private employment are roughly similar.[18] There is little doubt that cumbersome personnel rules sometimes hamper effective personnel management.

Another popular criticism of civil service is that it pays too well in comparison to the private sector. Critics note that public employees on average enjoy higher salaries than do private sector workers.[19] Such figures are often misleading, however, because the public workforce has a higher percentage of professional employees than does the private workforce. The best estimates are that the public employees at the lower levels enjoy higher pay than their private sector counterparts. But midlevel, professional, and upper-level employees do better in the private sector—sometimes much better.[20] Public employees with hard-to-find skills have some degree of bargaining power over salaries,[21] but even they are likely to receive better pay in the private sector. In recent years, state governments have been losing roughly 20 percent of their newly hired employees each year. Many employee departures are for higher salaries elsewhere.[22]

Civil Service Reform   Given these criticisms, it is not surprising that movements to reform civil service have emerged in recent decades. Two fairly common approaches to civil service reform can be identified. The more common approach is probably that pioneered by Wisconsin. Wisconsin's Civil Service Reform Law of 1977 increased the number of top-level political appointments that the governor can make and located the personnel management department directly in the governor's cabinet. The general goal was to enhance the governor's influence over state agencies, to increase the number of high-level political appointees, and to make it easier to dismiss poorly performing employees.[23]

A different approach to civil service reform is to set up a senior executive service tier of the civil service system. Under such a system, which now operates in a dozen states, several hundred of the top-ranking civil servants are given senior executive status, which allows the governor to move them around from agency to agency as needed. If they do not perform well, the governor can replace them with other senior executives.

In both of these approaches, the common goal is to make the bureaucracy more responsive to the democratic process. Both approaches seek to do this by making the top-ranking civil servants more accountable to the governor.

A few states have attacked civil service more drastically. Florida's new policy, which was strongly supported by Governor Jeb Bush, eliminates civil service protection for some state employees so that they can be fired more easily. It also gives top managers more flexibility regarding employee salaries and employee work assignments, as well as promotion. Critics complain that the new law makes agency employees vulnerable to pressure from politically influential groups. Some critics have also noted that the new system was supported by a number of business groups whose leaders hope to see large reductions in state government employment. How will work be done? The state will contract with private firms (including the businesses which supported the new law). That sounds a bit like old-fashioned patronage to critics. The fact that some state employee groups that endorsed the governor in 1998 were left with greater job security than many other state employees also sounds like patronage to the critics.[24] Texas and Georgia have also reduced civil service protection for many state employees, and managers now have more flexibility in many personnel decisions.[25]

Collective Bargaining

Another trend with considerable impact on state and local personnel practices is **collective bargaining**. This is the process by which a group of employees (called the bargaining unit) negotiates a master contract that stipulates conditions of employment, grievance procedures, salary schedules, fringe benefits, and seniority provisions. Collective bargaining among public employees made very little progress until the 1970s. During that decade, strikes by teachers, police officers, and other public employees led to state laws that permit employees to bargain collectively and, in many states, to strike under certain circumstances. Today, most states permit some form of collective bargaining for public employees, and some states even give them the right to strike. Forty-one percent of all government workers are represented by unions, with the greatest unionization occurring among firefighters, sanitation workers, and teachers. Union coverage in the public sector has declined slightly since the 1990s.[26]

The collective bargaining provision that causes the most conflict with civil service involves seniority. Civil service rules usually provide for advancement based on merit and performance, but collective bargaining contracts usually provide for advancement based mainly on seniority. If an engineering position becomes available, civil service rules usually call for a supervisor to hire from among the three or four most qualified applicants as judged by the civil service office. Collective bargaining rules often demand that the qualified person with the most seniority in the agency be given the position. In this example, two important principles are in conflict. Few people argue against promoting the most competent person to a position, at least in principle. But from the union's viewpoint, what looks like merit to the supervisor may look like cronyism or favoritism to other workers, especially if subjective judgments are part of the merit evaluations. Furthermore, the need to maintain morale and a high-quality workforce encourage officials to give some consideration to seniority, and many employees gain skills as they gain experience. A highly competent person who could not look forward to advancement after years of service in an agency might eventually look elsewhere for employment. Merit and seniority might not be incompatible in principle, but striking a proper balance between them is a tricky task.[27]

SOCIAL CONFLICT IN THE PUBLIC WORKFORCE

The public workforce has been a central arena for the social conflicts of the past two decades. Regardless of whether the personnel system was one of patronage, civil service, or collective bargaining, racial minorities and women historically did not fare well in the public bureaucracies. As minority and women's groups gained political clout, they demanded greater representation in the public workforce.

Pressure for a Representative Bureaucracy

The federal government has followed two policies that aimed to address these demands. The first, stemming from the Civil Rights Act of 1964, was to promote **equal employment opportunities**. Federal grants and loans for programs administered by state and local governments could be denied unless the recipient government hired its employees without regard to race, sex, religion, or country of origin. This equal employment opportunity principle was written into the 1970 Intergovernmental Personnel Act.

By itself, however, equal opportunity did not produce equality of results. The percentage of women and minorities in top government positions lagged far behind the percentage of men and whites, which led critics to complain of a "glass ceiling" that reserved top positions for white males.[28] To remedy this and gain equality of results, federal policy switched to emphasizing **affirmative action**. Each state and local agency receiving federal funds was required to have an affirmative action plan for increasing the employment of legally "protected classes" of people (mainly women and minorities) who had suffered from discrimination in the past. These affirmative action plans ranged from making diligent efforts to encourage more job applications from women and minorities to creating numerical quotas to guide hiring decisions.

How successful have the affirmative action programs been? Women now occupy nearly a third of the top-level state administrative positions, a figure far larger than their share of high-ranking positions in Fortune 500 companies.[29] In addition, women hold a majority of professional-level jobs from which future top administrators will be appointed.

Minorities are well represented at all levels except the top administrator and policy appointee levels, and their share of jobs at the middle and higher levels is increasing rapidly. African Americans have much greater presence in government employment than do Hispanics. Although white males occupy a majority of the top administrator positions, their share of these jobs will slowly erode over time since many of them are approaching retirement age, and they are not being recruited into these positions as fast as women and minorities. The biggest winners in this competition for jobs appear to be white females. The biggest losers are white males, at least in the sense that their share of top positions is declining, but they continue to be overrepresented in the top positions. Evidence does not show a systematic pattern of promoting minorities and women over better qualified white males,[30] but many white males charge that affirmative action has become "reverse discrimination" designed to reduce their numbers in the public workforce. Federal enforcement of equal employment opportunity laws and affirmative action policies has fluctuated over the years, depending on the political beliefs of the president, members of Congress, and members of the Supreme Court.[31]

Underlying the concern over the success of women and minorities in state government employment is the concept of **representative bureaucracy**. This is an old concept that surfaced during the period of Jacksonian Democracy (1829–1837) and was a component of machine politics (1870–1930), when European immigrants demanded that they have representatives in the public bureaucracies as well as in the state legislatures and city councils. As executive representation under the political machines degenerated into political favoritism and patronage, civil service practices and merit systems of employment were promoted to create a fairer system of hiring and dismissing public employees. The contemporary move to affirmative action is in some ways reminiscent of the motives of European immigrants a century ago. Immigrants then and minorities and women today wanted jobs and hoped that getting some of their own people into public employment would ensure them better treatment by the bureaucracies.

However, research on the impact of making agency personnel more representative of the general public has reached mixed conclusions. Some studies have found instances when the personal characteristics of administrators are related to their actions and decisions, but other studies find little or no relationship.[32]

Affirmative Action Under Fire

Affirmative action efforts sometimes conflict with two other important approaches to personnel management today (merit and collective bargaining). At least in principle, affirmative action's goal of promoting people with some consideration for gender and/or ethnic origin may conflict with the civil service notion of promoting people on the basis of merit—although some affirmative action cases have revealed that some "merit" systems would not hire women or minorities regardless of their abilities. Additional conflicts have arisen between affirmative action and collective bargaining. Usually these conflicts center on the concept of seniority rights, which, as we saw, is a hallowed principle in collective bargaining. Seniority provides loyal workers with employment stability and protects them from arbitrary dismissals as they move up the pay scale and reach a point where employers could save some money by firing these highly paid senior workers and replacing them with newer workers who are paid less. Of course, as the female and minority members of the public workforce gain tenure, seniority provisions will work in their favor. But in the fiscally stringent environment of the 1980s and 1990s, the last-hired, first-fired principle of seniority distinctly threatened to undermine affirmative action attempts to increase minority employment in government.

In the 1980s, the U.S. Supreme Court sent mixed signals regarding affirmative action programs. In one case it upheld affirmative action, but in cases involving Memphis, Tennessee,[33] and Birmingham, Alabama,[34] the Court seemed to back away from affirmative action programs.

The net impact of these decisions and some related cases involving the business world was to require proof from employees that they had been individually subjected to racial discrimination.[35] In 1991, Congress amended the Civil Rights Act so that the burden of proof would henceforth be on employers to show that any racial imbalances in their workforce did not result from discrimination. In 1994, Republicans gained control of the U.S. Congress and threatened to dismantle much of the affirmative action legal edifice, but to date they have not done so. President George W. Bush, however, recently criticized an affirmative action plan at the University of Michigan, and his administration filed a legal brief in favor of striking down the plan. A number of legal scholars concluded that the administration's position casts a shadow over all types of affirmative action programs. The Supreme Court upheld Michigan's affirmative action plan for the law school but struck down the university's less flexible program for undergraduates.[36] It has remained skeptical of affirmative action since then.

Sexual Harassment

Another major personnel issue is that of sexual harassment. As women workers gained in numbers and influence, they became much better positioned to challenge long-standing practices of sexual harassment on the job. Sexual harassment includes, among other things, unwanted sexual advances, sexually offensive jokes, demeaning comments about women, or any other behavior that reduces a person's stature solely because of gender. Although sexual harassment is illegal under the 1964 Civil Rights Act, it is nevertheless common.

Most states and communities have adopted policies that both define and prohibit sexual harassment. Most state and local governments have also instituted training programs to bring an end to sexually harassing behaviors.

RECONCILING WORK AND FAMILY CONCERNS

In both the public and private sectors, a major concern for many employers and employees is making the workplace more compatible with family responsibilities. This concern has gained attention in state and local governments, in part, because of the growing numbers of women working in them. In addition, the growing number of single-parent families has meant that many workers cannot rely on a spouse to help meet child care responsibilities. Many workers must also help to care for aging parents, spouses with serious health problems, or grandchildren. The conflicting demands of work and family can mean exhaustion, low morale, excessive absenteeism, and the loss of skilled workers. Making the workplace more compatible with family responsibilities will be increasingly critical as large numbers of state and local employees retire in the next 5 years—an estimated 27 percent of the entire state–local workforce.[37]

States and localities have tried many different techniques for reducing conflicts between work and family. More flexible work schedules can enable workers to do their jobs, but also be able to take children to medical appointments, meet with teachers, and prepare meals for aging relatives. Part-time jobs and job sharing (in which two or more employees split what traditionally would have been a single, full-time position) can enable skilled workers to stay on the job when their family responsibilities do not enable them to work full time. Being more flexible regarding where work is done (for example, permitting employees to do some work at home by telecommuting) may enable workers to care for small children or a sick relative while still fulfilling job responsibilities.

Some localities, for example, have adopted more flexible benefit policies to enable families with a major health problem to trade away vacation benefits for more extensive health insurance or sick leave. Family leave policies permit workers to take time off after the birth of a child or to care for a sick relative without losing their jobs. Providing help with child care can greatly reduce the problems faced by single parents with young children and by two-parent families when one parent is ill or when both parents are busy with work. Flexible work schedules, telecommuting, and job sharing programs are now very common in state agencies all over the country, although not all types of work are equally suitable for these practices.[38]

REORGANIZING AND REENGINEERING BUREAUCRACY TO IMPROVE PERFORMANCE

There is a strong feeling that political executives at both the state and local levels could do a better job of managing the public bureaucracies and implementing public policies if the bureaucracies were better organized. "Reinventing government" became a popular phrase in the 1990s[39] as political reformers sought innovative ways to make government more effective in an era of significant distrust of the public sector.

The Administrative Reorganization Movement

The reinventing government movement is one of the latest in a long history of administrative reforms. As early as 1910, President William Howard Taft established the Commission on Economy and Efficiency to recommend improvements in the federal government. The first major state reorganization occurred in 1917 in Illinois under Governor Frank D. Lowden, who consolidated more than a hundred independent agencies, boards, and commissions into nine departments. Following the lead of Illinois, more than a dozen states made some effort at reorganization over the next decade.

A second stimulus to state reorganization was the publication in 1949 of the report of the National Commission on the Organization of the Executive Branch of the Government, known as the Hoover Commission, after its chairman, Herbert Hoover. In the next few years, 35 states formed so-called **Little Hoover Commissions** to study reorganization. These commissions generally argued for a hierarchical form of state government structure to be built on the following six principles:[40]

1. Concentrate authority and responsibility in the governor.
2. Consolidate the many separate agencies into a small number of departments so that all agencies working in similar service areas will be grouped under the same functional department.
3. Eliminate boards for purely administrative work.
4. Coordinate staff and other administrative services.
5. Provide an independent audit.
6. Provide a governor's cabinet.

The immediate response to these recommendations was mixed, but they grew increasingly popular as time went on. Between 1965 and 1991, 26 states underwent major administrative reorganizations that incorporated one or more of these six principles.[41] In the early 1990s, the well-publicized Winter Commission endorsed continued administrative reform at the state level with particular emphasis on reorganizations that would strengthen the governor's authority over the bureaucracy.[42]

Assessing Reorganization: Some Caveats

Reorganization advocates assume that more public services can be delivered at a lower per capita cost if state administrative activities are coordinated so that all independent agencies performing related activities are consolidated into one large department.[43] In practice, the cost savings are usually small, if they result at all, and lumping many small agencies into one super-agency sometimes simply creates a large agency that is internally unmanageable because it is wracked by internal conflict, and because many employees may continue to operate as they did before the reorganization.[44] Reorganized states do not necessarily provide equal services for fewer dollars than do unreorganized states.[45]

Another study compared the performance of departments headed by a single executive (favored by reformers) with departments headed by boards or commissions (not favored by reformers). The study failed to find that single-head departments consistently outperformed multihead departments, but also found that the multihead departments had some advantages that were lacking in the single-head departments. Multihead commissions improve representation in the bureaucratic process, and they absorb public criticisms when things go poorly in the department.[46]

The traditional reform approach in state politics also runs afoul of the fact that the state legislatures and state courts also have considerable authority over state agencies and expect those agencies to pay attention to their concerns. Moreover, many agencies receive funds from the federal government and need to follow federal guidelines to some degree, and federal courts may also review state agency actions. Note, too, that many state programs are implemented to varying degrees by local governments and by private actors; state influence over those actors is at best modest.[47]

Nevertheless, administrative reform efforts continue in various states, spurred in part by the waves of financial problems that have affected state governments (and the rest of American society) since the mid-1970s. Advisory commissions search for ways to revamp agencies, departments, and programs in hopes of saving money and improving performance. Benefits may not be guaranteed, but they seem to result often enough to encourage other officials to try more reforms.[48]

Other Approaches for Improving Administrative Performance

In addition to executive reorganization, administrative reformers have introduced a number of other devices to improve administrative performance.

Program Evaluation   One approach to improving administrative performance is **program evaluation**. Governments cannot make rational policy choices unless they can evaluate whether their programs attain their objectives. Without evaluation, they cannot know which programs are successful, which administrative practices work, and even which groups of employees are competent.[49] By the mid-1980s, 43 states had adopted some formalized form of program evaluation,[50] and all states and localities conduct evaluations from time to time. The methods of program evaluation run the gamut from highly sophisticated cost-benefit analyses to public opinion surveys to unsystematic anecdotal descriptions.

Accurate evaluations of program impact are difficult for a variety of reasons. Many programs try to accomplish several things at the same time, and people may disagree regarding what they want a program to do. In addition, untangling the effects due to the program from effects due to other factors is often difficult. Cleaner air might be the result of a new environmental program or the result of polluting factories closing for reasons unrelated to the program.

One of the most interesting evaluation projects was a national survey of the population, called *Bureaucratic Encounters,* that sought to measure how well people evaluated public bureaucracies. Based on a national sample, the study found that people tended to give higher evaluations to the agencies they encountered than to government agencies in general. For example, 71 percent of the people said that the agency they contacted had solved their personal problem satisfactorily, and 79 percent felt that they had been treated fairly. When the same people were asked to evaluate government offices generally, however, only 30 percent thought that the agencies could take care of problems, and only 42 percent thought that government offices treated people fairly. Research on the public schools finds a similar pattern: Nationwide, people tend to evaluate the schools they know about more positively than the public schools in general.[51]

Management by Objectives (MBO)   Under **management by objectives (MBO)**, each agency director stipulates his or her objectives for the upcoming year.[52] Once the agency head's objectives are defined, the bureau chiefs propose their objectives, which will be consistent with the director's. The subordinates of the bureau chiefs then define their objectives for the year in relation to those of the bureau chief. Theoretically, all the employees of a given department work to attain a common set of objectives for the department as a whole. Throughout the year, supervisors evaluate their subordinates' progress toward the objectives. In systems that provide merit pay, MBO can be tied to pay increases for employees so that employees who exceed their objectives get the best pay raises. Although MBO rarely works this neatly in practice, evaluation studies suggest that MBO does bring productivity gains when implemented properly.[53] Note, however, that giving managers some flexibility in goal setting may anger governors and legislators, who often believe that *they* should establish goals for agencies.

Total Quality Management (TQM)   One of the latest reform movements is total quality management (TQM). Like many other public management innovations, TQM is borrowed from private industry, and seeks to instill a performance-based culture in government. Just as a private business should focus on performance that meets the needs of its customers in order to be profitable, TQM argues that public agencies must treat the public as customers and satisfy their customers' needs if they hope to gain and keep the public's confidence. Thus, focusing on the public as a customer is the key to TQM, and accomplishing this goal requires the following adjustments in public agencies:[54]

- Empowering employees to participate in decentralized agency teams that make important decisions about the planning and implementation of agency services
- Utilizing modern information technologies, base agency decisions on the systematic analysis of data and facts about the public's needs, agency services, and how those services are provided
- Seeking continual improvement in the quality of services as the agency's customers evaluate that quality, and encouraging the public to participate in developing agency plans and performance standards

By 1994, some components of TQM had been adopted in 40 states.[55] After that, interest in TQM declined somewhat, partly due to budgetary pressures and partly due to government's greater emphasis on services, with many workers dealing with the public directly, rather than production (as in manufacturing automobiles). Even so, it remains influential.[56]

BUDGETING AS A DEVICE FOR IMPROVING EXECUTIVE MANAGEMENT

Budgeting is one of the most important tools that governors and legislatures (as well as local officials) have for imposing policy control over their administrators. To the extent that they influence the budget, elected officials can influence the overall level of expenditures, the allocation of funding across programs, and various rules and regulations that accompany the use of the funds. The ease of using this leverage, however, depends on the extent to which a state has moved from traditional budgeting practices to newer approaches such as program budgeting and performance budgeting.[57] Budgetary flexibility is also affected by a number of other factors that are not easy to change by reforms.

Traditional Budgeting

Incrementalism Traditional budget making is an incremental process.[58] An *increment* is simply a small step, and an *incremental process* is a process that moves in small steps over time. Budgeting is an incremental process because most agencies get a budgetary change each year that makes the budget slightly larger or smaller than that of the previous year's. Only under extraordinary circumstances, such as a major crisis, the creation of a new agency, or the introduction of a new federal program, is an agency or department's budget changed drastically. **Incrementalism** produces stability in the budgeting system. Since each agency knows it will normally get small changes each year, its personnel know that they will not be able to make drastic changes in their allocation of funds.

Common Steps in Budgeting State agency heads often make initial budget requests that exceed what they expect are their actual needs. This allows the governor, the budget director, and the legislature to cut the requests without harming the agency's programs very much (assuming that the cuts are proportionally modest). The governor leaves the total requests high enough so that the legislature can make more cuts without damaging the governor's priorities. Finally, the legislature often makes cuts that leave the agency with an amount slightly larger than its previous year's budget.[59]

In this process, both the governor and the legislature can tell tax-conscious citizens how much money they cut. And the program administrators can count on getting just about as much money as they really had expected, assuming that they have correctly assessed the behavior of the governor and legislature. However, when revenues fall below expectation, many agencies find their budgets declining rather than growing. When revenues are scarce, as in the 2008 to 2012 legislative sessions in many states,[60] budgetary conflicts often escalate.

Line-Item Budgeting **Line-item budgeting** (sometimes called object-of-expenditure budgeting) refers to the way that budgetary information is organized; that is, by what an agency buys or how it otherwise spends its funds. For example, the budget for a bureau of vocational rehabilitation might authorize expenditures for the line items of salaries, postage, mailing expenses, supplies, telephone expenses, travel, in-service training for employees, and contracted services (such as hiring a company to perform janitorial services). An assumption in this budgetary format is that we want to prevent agencies from spending money on unnecessary or extravagant things, so we need detailed information on those purchases.

Although these line items enable officials to keep track of the bureau's expenditures, they do not show them how the bureau's money is being divided among its various programs. The object-of-expenditure budget also tells officials little regarding agency activities or accomplishments. Since many services are delivered by more than one agency, the budget review process is, to a considerable extent, divorced from the actual operation of programs.

Earmarking Revenues **Earmarked revenues,** as noted in Chapter 2, are revenues dedicated to a specific state program. Earmarking became extremely popular with the expansion of lotteries in the 1980s, with a large share of lottery revenues typically earmarked for education or some other specific purpose. Motor fuel taxes are often earmarked for road and highway programs. The argument for earmarking is that it provides some continuity in funding for specific programs and limits the ability of the governor or legislators to shift money out of those programs for their pet short-term projects.[61] From the budgeter's point of view, however, earmarking is a nuisance. It increases the difficulty that governors and legislators have in responding to the changing needs of changing times.

Budgeting Innovations

Because of these limitations on traditional budgeting, reformers began seeking ways to make budgeting more "rational" and more responsive to policy makers. The most important of the resulting innovations are program budgeting and performance budgeting (bear in mind that different authors may define those terms in different ways).

Program Budgeting   In the early 1960s, the U.S. Department of Defense introduced a new concept called **planning program budgeting (PPB)**. The concept quickly spread to other departments and then to states and localities. PPB was a complicated budgeting device that attempted to eliminate the separation between program planning and budget planning that was inherent to the line-item budget. Instead of organizing the budget by traditional line items, PPB organized a budget by programs, such as improving public health or environmental protection.

With PPB, agencies were to define each activity's objectives and to indicate how the budget amounts related to the objectives, how to accomplish the objectives in alternative ways, and whether the objectives were being accomplished. This procedure involved a **cost-benefit analysis** of programs. If five different programs operated by three different agencies dealt with vocational-technical education, PPB enabled the policy makers to compare the results of these programs in terms of the costs involved and the benefits received. In theory, at least, policy makers could then choose the program that brought the most benefits to the largest number of people at the lowest cost.

Program budgeting produced large amounts of analytical information, which many officials found difficult to understand. In addition, discussion of program goals sometimes produced major conflict. As a result, the federal government eventually abandoned PPB and in most states and localities the elaborate PPB process never got off the ground.[62] Less elaborate attempts to institute cost-benefit analysis and to draw up budgets in a program format did take hold, however. Since the mid-1980s, most states have been using some elements of program budgeting, although not all of them call it by that name.[63]

Performance Budgeting   A less ambitious budgetary reform is *performance budgeting*, a term that unfortunately refers to two somewhat different approaches to budgeting. In current usage, performance budgeting gives budget increases to agencies that perform well and small increases or even decreases to agencies that perform poorly. In principle, this is a sound idea. In practice, however, it has some inherent problems. One of the problems is coming up with one or more relatively objective measures of performance. If agency performance is evaluated based on only a few aspects of its work, agency personnel may start to neglect other activities that are also important but more difficult to measure.

Another problem concerns what to do about an underperforming agency if that agency happens to be a critical one. If a city's fire department performed poorly last year, could the mayor and city council realistically cut its budget for the following year and run the risk of major property damage and loss of life when the department's ability to respond deteriorates further? Probably not. Note, too, that an agency may perform poorly because it is not adequately funded in the first place. Cutting its budget is likely to make things worse. If performance standards are chosen carefully, however, performance budgeting may encourage administrators to try to increase productivity.

Coping with Declines in Revenue   From time to time in our country's history, the revenues of various states and localities have declined. Sometimes the declines are relatively modest, but some declines are more dramatic. In addition, some declines are brief, but others may last for a number of years. When revenues fall, state and local officials may try a variety of methods for coping with that decline.

Many states and localities have rainy day funds that have been set aside for emergencies, and officials may withdraw cash from those funds to make up for some of the revenue short-fall.[64] However, most of the rainy day funds are not large enough to compensate for major revenue declines or for revenue slumps that last for several years.

A second coping strategy is borrowing. Because most state and local governments are usually considered good credit risks, they can often borrow at relatively low interest rates. In addition, the spending funded by borrowing can help to stimulate the state or community's economy. Unfortunately, the result can be a debt burden that must be repaid at some future date, and too much debt can lead to a reduced credit rating.[65]

Another frequent coping device involves the system of intergovernmental grants. States may respond to a revenue slump by reducing state aid to local governments and pressing the national government to provide more aid to the states. Local officials are likely to try to persuade state and national officials to provide additional grants funds. The conflicting pressures may produce intense wrangling between levels of government, between the political parties, between different regions of the country or a state, and among supporters of individual programs.[66]

Officials may reduce maintenance and postpone the replacement of aging facilities and equipment. If the revenue shortfall extends for very long, agencies may not be able to replace employees who leave and may even be forced to lay off some employees. Public services will also be reduced.[67]

If officials are feeling sufficiently brave, they may propose raising taxes or fees to make up for some of the revenue shortage. If they are only moderately brave, they may propose a public vote on the fee or tax hike. There are also extreme cases when local governments have filed for bankruptcy or at least discussed the possibility. That discussion may sometimes lead creditors to negotiate new payment terms for the locality but may also trigger a lower credit rating, which will make subsequent borrowing more expensive.[68]

Unfortunately, these coping methods may eventually reduce employee morale as they struggle with personnel shortages, aging equipment, a lack of supplies, cutbacks in programs they believe are important, and a feeling of hopelessness as the difficult environment persists. Some employees may leave the agency and take valuable skills and experience with them. The combined effects of all the coping methods may mean a loss of governmental capability that may take years to restore.[69]

Regulatory Policy

Many state and local government agencies are involved in regulating various aspects of our lives.[70] Some agencies regulate individual professions, such as doctors, nurses, realtors, and accountants. Those agencies develop and try to enforce guidelines regarding access to the profession and standards of professional conduct. A number of agencies, including some in the offices of state attorneys general, investigate consumer complaints and try to resolve them.[71]

Another important regulatory issue involves the finance industry. Although not all analysts agree, part of the housing bubble and subsequent decline in the housing market resulted from looser regulation of the finance industry. When some financial institutions extended mortgages to people who were not likely to be able to maintain the required level of payments, that practice helped boost housing prices in the short run but eventually led to foreclosures on a large scale. Placing large numbers of homes on the market at the same time in some areas led to declining home values.

Environmental protection is another important regulatory arena. It sometimes produces clashes between business interests whose leaders want to be free to conduct business in any way they want and citizens and some other businesses who want to protect the environment, in part to encourage visitors to keep coming to visit their respective states or communities. We will explore environmental issues in more detail in Chapter 16.

A recent and sensitive regulatory issue involves information security. The Internet has helped businesses and government agencies exchange enormous amounts of information on almost all Americans. This information may include your age, where you shop, what kinds of products you buy, what Web sites you visit, what groups you have joined, how many children you have, and many other things. Critics note that more personal information, such as what over-the-counter medicines people take, can also be accessed. In addition, many agency records are stored in electronic format, and control systems for public utilities and many other public services are computerized. Agencies that work with private contractors often communicate with them electronically. Officials responsible for the security of these systems must deal with the threats of deliberate intrusion, accidental disclosure of sensitive information, recreational hackers, and disgruntled staffers.[72]

Enthusiasm for regulation appears to go in cycles. The 1970s and 1980s were a time of loud complaints regarding regulations that made products and services more expensive and discouraged innovation. As a result, many regulations were weakened or eliminated. The recent waves of corporate scandals, fears of terrorist attacks, bank failures, and concerns regarding global warming, however, have convinced many people that more regulation is needed. Precisely what sort of regulation would be best remains controversial, however.

POLITICAL ECONOMY AND REENGINEERING FOR GREATER PRODUCTIVITY

As public resources remain tight and as public confidence in government stays low (according to some measures, at least), there is considerable demand for increasing the productivity of public employees and agencies. This demand is reflected in most of the reform measures examined earlier. In the 1990s, a new twist was put on the productivity demand with David Osborne's notion that we can reengineer government so that it does the "steering" of the ship of state instead of the "rowing."[73] By this the advocates of governmental reengineering mean that government should set the policy goals for society, but should spin off the implementation of these goals to the private sector. To some analysts, the lynchpin of reengineering is privatization.

Privatization of Public Services

One of the hottest concepts in state and local administrations since 1980 has been **privatization,** or the use of private organizations to produce certain public services. This is not actually a new idea; governments have relied on private firms to do many tasks for centuries, but the idea has been more popular in recent years. Government agencies often contract with private companies or nonprofit organizations to help perform agency work. The government then becomes an overseer of the service, at least in part, rather than a producer of it, although some jurisdictions allow public organizations to compete with private ones for government contracts. In some versions, the government withdraws from responsibility entirely, leaving individual people to deal with private firms directly for services such as trash collection.

Advocates of privatization make several arguments on its behalf. First, they contend that it will be cheaper than providing services through governmental agencies. Second, privatization may enable governments to draw on skills in the private sector that some state or local governments lack in their workforces. Third, greater use of private contractors may bypass bureaucratic red tape and provide greater flexibility in the operation of some programs.[74]

Privatization received a substantial boost from a body of research that compared the cost of public service delivery with private delivery of similar services. Several studies found evidence of private organizations doing work at a lower cost than did public agencies, although the cost differences varied considerably from place to place and program to program. To the extent that public services generally could be produced more cheaply by private companies, governments had a tremendous incentive to contract out as many services as feasible, other things being equal.

Privatization is not always cheaper than government production of public services.[75] In the early 1980s, Phoenix, Arizona, began a competitive bidding procedure for handling garbage collection. At first, the private contractors underbid the city's sanitation department. Within a few years, however, the sanitation department reduced its costs by one-third and began recapturing some of the contracts it had lost.[76]

Privatization can sometimes be more expensive than having public employees perform work themselves, especially if officials negotiating a contract are not careful. One major example of this phenomenon emerged in the war with Iraq. When the Haliburton Corporation was placed in charge of importing gasoline from Kuwait to Iraq, the fuel cost $2.68 per gallon. When a Department of Defense office took charge of fuel imports, the gasoline cost $1.57 per gallon, a savings of just over 40 percent. Critics charge that officials overseeing contracts may be swayed by the possibility of future employment with one of the private firms providing the services.[77] Moreover, privatization can trigger legal disputes regarding whether or when the contract can be terminated or extended.[78]

In a related vein, the huge sums of money at stake in privatization can lead to corruption problems and questionable ties between contractors and state or local officials. Those problems have cropped up all over the country, from Florida and Connecticut to Wisconsin and Los Angeles.[79] They have even cropped up outside the United States, as in the case of a company that provided quasi-military services in the second Iraq War. Its chief executive and his family had been major contributors to then-President George W. Bush's campaigns over the year.[80] Contractors may try to sway the judgment of public officials with campaign contributions, gifts, and/or promises of future jobs. Unethical officials may pressure potential contractors to provide favors in exchange for lucrative contracts. These considerations are most likely to be influential when contracts are let without competitive bidding and when the process receives little public or media attention. Influential contractors may continue to receive new contracts even after they have helped to create a major problem.[81]

Even when privatization is cheaper, is it better than government-produced public services? Not necessarily, depending on your values. Much of the advantage that private contractors have over public agencies is simply the cost of the labor force. The private contractors often pay workers less, give them less vacation time, and often offer no health insurance or other fringe benefits.[82] One factor contributing to the September 11 terrorist attacks was the private airport security guards, many of whom were poorly paid, poorly trained, and subject to high rates of turnover.

One of the most controversial areas of privatization today is that of corrections. Seventeen states have laws that permit some of their jails, prisons, and other corrections facilities to be run by private companies. However, less than 2 percent of all inmates are held in private facilities.[83] If this number can be expanded, it will provide a lucrative business opportunity for corrections entrepreneurs. Proponents claim that they can save taxpayers up to 15 percent of the cost of housing prisoners. But critics counter that the private prisons are usually given the healthiest and easiest (and least dangerous) prisoners to manage, so their costs are unrealistically low. A recent study of private versus public prisons in Arizona found that the private facilities were actually more expensive than are public facilities.[84] Critics also bristle at the idea of the state contracting out the authority to punish and detain people to profit-making entrepreneurs, in part because those entrepreneurs have an economic incentive to support keeping more people in prison.[85]

Whether privatization is *better* than government production of services in these circumstances depends in great measure on what value one ascribes to maintaining a stable labor force and what value one places on the idea of paying a livable wage to workers who provide public services. Because privatization touches so specifically on this question of moral values, much of the debate over privatization is highly polemical. Many of its strongest supporters are not only antiunion, with little concern for ordinary workers, but they are also antigovernment, viewing privatization primarily as a means to reduce the role of government in modern society.[86] Its strongest opponents are the labor unions, which take a very uncompromising attitude toward it.[87]

For the citizens trying to make up their own minds about privatization, it is useful to separate the polemics from the reasonable arguments. Some public services, such as garbage collection and water-meter reading, might be produced better by private companies under some circumstances than by government agencies. For some other public services, such as prison administration and licensing of day-care centers, the reverse is probably true. A survey of 82 cities in 1995 found that food services, janitorial services, and major construction projects were the activities most frequently contracted out, whereas street sweeping, jail food service, and bill collection were the least likely to be contracted out.[88]

In deciding whether to privatize a service, public officials should resist making short-run cost saving the sole criterion. Charles T. Goodsell recommends a number of other criteria as well. In privatizing a service, government agencies should not give up control over the service. They should not let their own permanent workforce be undermined by privatization; otherwise they may be unable to respond if a contractor fails to perform as expected or withdraws from the market. The desire to produce services more cheaply should not lead officials to compromise the goals of the services themselves. They should not privatize so many functions that the government itself loses its vital force for achieving public goals. And they should be careful about awarding contracts to entrepreneurs with strong political connections or without track records in providing that particular type of service.[89] Successful privatization requires a carefully negotiated contract and diligent enforcement in order to assure that its provisions are met. Officials must be willing and able to punish contractors who fail to perform as the contract requires.[90]

The most recent controversy over privatization involves outsourcing work to firms outside the United States. In a time when many Americans need good jobs, they have been angry to learn that some state and local governmental work is now being done by workers in other countries. Officials in most of the states have been discussing whether that practice should be restricted or even eliminated in order to keep more jobs in the United States. Critics worry, however, that eliminating foreign firms from privatization opportunities may lead to higher costs and may also conflict with free trade laws.[91]

Even under the best of circumstances, privatization may create additional problems of accountability when something goes wrong. Public officials will often blame the contractor, who in turn will blame the officials. Even so, privatization is sometimes a helpful way to reduce the cost of providing public services and may give a government access to specialized skills that none of its employees possess.

The Information Revolution Comes to State and Local Government

One of the most striking developments in state and local administration in the past 40 years is the increasing use of computers for all sorts of purposes, from record keeping to program evaluation and improving access to governmental agencies and services. As Internet access has become more widely available to the public, reformers have pressed states and localities to make services and information available over the Web. The first response to that pressure was often making information and forms available online. More recently, many agencies allow people to conduct agency business online as well. People may be able to pay taxes and fees, purchase licenses, apply for jobs, and enter bids on government contract opportunities. Moreover, some agency Web sites give people the opportunity to rate the service they have received. However, options for conducting agency business online vary considerably from one state to another and, within some states, from one agency to another.[92]

The growing Internet accessibility of state and local agencies is making them much more available to the public and enables some agency employees to do more work from home as their schedules and supervisors permit. That access is certain to expand in the coming years, with additional impetus provided by efforts to improve homeland security. Law enforcement, public health, and emergency response agencies are all working to speed up information flows to increase their abilities to prevent terrorist attacks and improve responses to incidents. However, analysts are also very concerned that Internet accessibility may make all sorts of agencies vulnerable to hacker incursions and possibly sabotage by terrorists. A variety of efforts are currently underway to minimize those risks, but the concerns remain.[93]

The Courts and Administration

Another important development in state and local administration is the growing role of the courts. Since the 1950s, court challenges to state and local government agencies have grown increasingly common. An agency may be challenged in state court for failing to follow a state law's requirements and/or challenged in federal court for violating a federal law. The challenges have ranged from agencies infringing on someone's civil rights to whether an environmental protection rule has been followed to disputes over hiring, promotion, and firing public employees.[94]

State and local administrators sometimes find the legal challenges highly stressful, and legal challenges may delay a project for years. In addition, administrators may become very timid in their work from their fear of court challenges. The costs of protracted legal wrangling may also take money away from agency operations.

Crisis Management

Since the September 11 terrorist attacks, and with renewed interest since Hurricane Katrina, state and local officials have been assessing their preparedness for dealing with major emergencies. Some parts of the country began the process much earlier, primarily due to concerns about natural disasters, such as earthquakes, hurricanes, tornadoes, and floods, but terrorism has made emergency preparedness a more urgent matter. Crisis and emergency management have many facets, but several of the most important deserve mention.[95]

First, officials need to assess what types of crises they are most likely to face and what types of problems would result. Next, they need to prepare a plan of response and assess what the state or community would need to respond to the crisis. If the community or state does not have some of the resources it would need to respond effectively, officials must try to correct those deficiencies as much as possible. They may also try to minimize future harm with public policies devoted to damage limitation; San Francisco's building codes require new buildings to have designs and materials to withstand earthquakes, for example.

As the September 11 attacks demonstrated, officials and the public may be hit with a crisis that virtually no one expected. Even if some preparations have been made, they may be overwhelmed by an emergency that is worse than anticipated. Agencies must be prepared to improvise and to reach out in all directions for assistance—to other levels of government, to surrounding governments at the same level, and to private organizations. Flexibility and adaptability appear to be vitally important if a locality is to recover in a reasonable period of time.[96] Moreover, businesses, families, and individuals need to make their own emergency plans and need to prepare their own emergency supplies.

Unfortunately, state and local officials and the public may not know in advance what sorts of emergencies they might face in the homeland security arena. Preparation is, therefore, fraught with uncertainty. Some preparations are also expensive, and many local governments are hard-pressed to generate funds for traditional services. Setting aside funds to prepare for possible future crises is, therefore, very difficult. Communications systems are still inadequate in many areas, and large-scale emergencies that would call for mass evacuations would be difficult to manage in some parts of the country.[97]

CONCLUSION

It has become imperative for state and local governments to improve their productivity. There is more at stake than simply reducing the cost of public services, however. The effective delivery of public services makes a significant difference in the quality of our lives and the ability of private-sector institutions to function. If the potholes in our streets are not filled, our vehicles are damaged. If the police do not respond to our calls, our lives are less secure. How do public managers today ensure that the most appropriate agencies deliver the right services most effectively to people in need on time? And how do they meet the demands of cost-conscious groups that all these services be delivered at the lowest possible cost per unit of service?

Although efforts to improve bureaucratic performance are clearly worthwhile, bear in mind that public agencies have accomplished a good deal over the years. The drinking water in virtually all communities is much safer than it was in the late 1800s. The highway accident fatality rate has declined dramatically since the 1950s. The proportion of elderly people living in poverty has fallen dramatically since World War II. Some pollutants are less widespread than they once were. These and many other improvements are due, in large measure, to the efforts of government agencies.

SUMMARY

1. A basic tension exists between career administrators and policy-level executives, such as governors and their appointed department heads.

2. With 19 million state and local employees, personnel management is a vital governmental task. Traditional patronage systems of recruitment have given way to more modern civil service personnel management practices, with greater emphasis on employee skills and expertise.

3. State and local governments have traditionally been organized in a fragmented manner. In order to modernize their governments, many states have reorganized their bureaucracies. The goals of these reorganizations are to concentrate more authority in the governor, to create a hierarchical form of organization, and to consolidate hundreds of scattered agencies into a limited number of departments that are directly accountable to the governor.

4. A major tool for improving the governor or the mayor's ability to manage administrative departments is the budget. Budgeting at the state level has become the task of a budget director, who is usually tied closely to the governor. At the local level, budgeting is less centralized. It is most centralized in city-manager and strong-mayor systems and least centralized in weak-mayor, commission, and traditional county governments. The desire to use budgeting to control the executive branch and improve productivity has led to a series of budget innovations such as program budgeting and performance budgeting.

5. In the 1990s, the movement for reengineering government provided support for privatization as a means of increasing the productivity of public employees. That movement continues today.

6. The courts have become increasingly involved in many administrative issues. At best, court involvement can help people protect their rights and promote compliance with legal and constitutional guidelines. At worst, court involvement can delay public programs and consume significant sums of money from agency budgets.

7. Since September 11, 2001, state and local administrators have paid considerable attention to homeland security and emergency management. Many officials remain uncertain regarding which threats deserve the most attention, however, and funding has been limited.

STUDY QUESTIONS

1. Why do conflicts sometimes erupt between elected officials and agency personnel? Are those conflicts necessarily bad? How can they be resolved?
2. What are the various reform movements that have swept through state and local bureaucracies over the years? How have the goals of reformers varied in the different movements? What have they accomplished?
3. What strategies have been employed in hopes of improving bureaucratic performance, whether in terms of organization, personnel, budgeting, or other arenas? What difficulties have the reforms encountered?

KEY TERMS

Affirmative action   The principle that special efforts should be made to encourage the hiring of minorities and women for public jobs. The objective of affirmative action is to make up for past discrimination against minorities and women.

Civil service system   A form of recruitment for government jobs in which people are hired on the basis of their performance on competitive examinations and/or training and work experience.

Collective bargaining   The process of workers banding together and bargaining as a unit with their employer over wages and job conditions.

Cost-benefit analysis   A budgeting procedure that weighs the costs of different programs against the benefits to be derived from them so that officials can select the programs that achieve agency goals at the lowest cost-benefit ratio.

Earmarked revenues   Revenues raised from specific sources (such as gasoline taxes) that can be spent only for related purposes (such as transportation).

Equal employment opportunity   The practice of giving equal opportunity to all job applicants, regardless of race or religion.

Incrementalism   A budgeting process in which budgets change in proportionally small amounts from one year to the next.

Line-item budgeting   A form of budgeting in which budgets are organized by specific items that agencies buy or expend money for, such as motor vehicles, office supplies, and employee salaries.

Little Hoover Commission   A type of commission appointed in the 1950s to study the organization of state government and make recommendations for improvement. About 35 states formed such commissions.

Management by objectives (MBO)   A procedure in which managers and supervisors set annual objectives that are consistent with agency goals. Managers' performance is then measured by their ability to attain their objectives.

Merit system (employment)   A recruitment method for government that hires and promotes people on the basis of their training and competence to perform specific jobs. See *Civil service system*.

Patronage   A recruitment method for government jobs in which people are hired as a reward for their political support of the winning candidates.

Planning program budgeting   A form of budgeting organized around programs rather than line items and planned out two or three years into the future. Budgeters try to compare different activities devoted to a common goal, such as environmental protection, and target money to the activities that seem most efficient.

Privatization   The practice of governmental contracting with private firms to provide public services.

Program evaluation   A procedure for determining if programs meet their objectives. Program evaluations seek to determine how much a program is accomplishing relative to its costs.

Representative bureaucracy   The concept that different ethnic and categorical groups should be represented in the public bureaucracy in proportion to their percentage of the overall population.

Total quality management (TQM)   A management reform that involves continually gathering information on the quality of public services (including the public's views of the services), using modern information technologies to gather and analyze evidence about agency performance, and involving agency employees and the public in developing plans of action.

THE INTERNET CONNECTION

The United States Government Accountability Office (GAO) does research and analysis on the activities of government agencies at the national, state, and local levels. The GAO's reports contain a wealth of information on all major administrative issues. You can access the GAO at **www.gao.gov**. Select a state or local government agency and see what you can learn about it from the Web. What types of business can you conduct with it over the Internet? How would you compare it with private business Web sites with which you are familiar?

NOTES

1. Rob Gurwitt, "Laura Chick Is Watching," *Governing,* (July 2009): 22–29.
2. William Prochnau and Laura Parker, *Miracle on the Hudson* (New York: Ballantine, 2009).
3. For additional sources of friction, see Donald Kettl, *The Politics of the Administrative Process,* 5th ed. (Los Angeles: Sage/CQ Press, 2012), pp. 143–155; B. Guy Peters, *The Politics of Bureaucracy,* 6th ed. (London: Routledge, 2010), pp. 211–227.
4. Ira Sharkansky, "State Administrators in the Policy Process," in Herbert Jacob and Kenneth N. Vines, eds., *Politics in the American States: A Comparative Analysis,* 2nd ed. (Boston: Little, Brown and Co., 1971), p. 238.
5. Steven Greenhouse, "Strained States Turning to Laws to Curb Labor Unions," *New York Times,* January 3, 2011 (Web edition); James Hoffa, "Citizens United Decision at Root of War on Public Union Workers," *Detroit News,* March 9, 2011 (Web edition); M. J. Lee, "Ohio Poll: Repeal Anti-Union Law," *Politico,* October 25, 2011 (Web edition); "Their Real Agenda," *New York Times,* February 6, 2011 (Web edition); Daniel Vock, "In Wisconsin, Assessing a New Labor Law's Impact," *Stateline,* February 13, 2012 (Web edition).
6. *Statistical Abstract, 2011–2012* (New York: Skyhorse, 2011), p. 300.
7. Martin Tolchin and Susan Tolchin, *To the Victor: Political Patronage from the Clubhouse to the White House* (New York: Vintage Books, 1972), chs. 2 and 4.
8. Jennifer Skalka, "Firings under Ehrlich Violated Rights and Md. Law, Panel Says," *Baltimore Sun,* Web document, October 10, 2006 (www.baltimoresun.com/news/local/bal-te.md.personnel10oct10,0,7436836story).
9. See *Oklahoma v. U.S. Civil Service Commission,* 330 U.S. 127 (1947).
10. *Elrod v. Burns,* 427 U.S. 347 (1976). In subsequent cases, the Supreme Court upheld the principle established in this case but allowed some exceptions. In *Branti v. Finkel* (1980), the Court allowed a public employee to be fired for political reasons if the employer could demonstrate that the employee's political beliefs in fact interfered with the performance of his or her duties. In *Connick v. Myers* (1983), the Court allowed governments to fire public employees who complained about their supervisors and their working conditions. But in 1990, the Court outlawed patronage employment in the state of Illinois. *Rutan v. Republican Party of Illinois,* 110 S.Ct. 2729 (1990).
11. *Rutan v. Republican Party of Illinois,* 110 S.Ct. 2729 (1990).
12. Russell Lissau, "Ex-Kildeer Trustee Called New Hire the Last Straw," *Daily Herald,* June 5, 2009.
13. *The Book of the States: 1982–83* (Lexington, KY: Council of State Governments, 1982), pp. 312–313.
14. An official of the Bureau of Intergovernmental Personnel Program of the United States Civil Service Commission cites a survey that indicates that 95 percent of all local employees are covered by some form of merit system. Whether all those systems are free of political influence, however, is debatable. See Andrew W. Boesel, "Local Personnel Management: Organized Problems and Operating Practices," *Municipal Yearbook: 1974* (Washington, DC: International City Management Association, 1974), pp. 92–93.
15. Deil Wright, Chung-Lae Cho, and Yoo-Sung Choi, "Top-Level State Administrators: Changing Characteristics and Qualities," in *The Book of the States* (Lexington, KY: Council of State

Governments, 2002), p. 371; for an overview of the various ways in which personnel powers are distributed, see *Book of the States*, vol. 38 (Lexington, KY: Council of State Governments, 2006), pp. 423–429.

16. This was the testimony of David Osborne before the Winter Commission on State Government Organization. See Steven D. Gold, "The Compensation Conundrum," *State Legislatures* 18, no. 9 (September 1992): 21.

17. Katherine Barrett and Richard Greene, "Resume Follies," *Governing* 14, no. 2 (November 2000): 96; "Training Wheels," *Governing* 14, no. 4 (January 2001): 57.

18. Richard C. Elling, "Bureaucracy: Maligned Yet Essential," in Virginia Gray and Herbert Jacob, eds. *Politics in the American States: A Comparative Analysis,* 6th ed. (Washington, DC: CQ Press, 1995), p. 300; O. Glenn Stahl, *Public Personnel Administration,* 8th ed. (New York: Harper and Row, 1983), pp. 304–305.

19. According to U.S. government data, average annual wages and salaries for private workers totaled $29,367 in 1993, compared to a median salary of $30,800 for state and local employees. *Statistical Abstract of the United States, 1995* (Washington, DC: U.S. Government Printing Office, 1995), pp. 323, 431.

20. Elling, "Bureaucracy: Maligned Yet Essential," p. 300.

21. See Jonathan Walters, "Worth the Money?," *Governing* 17, no. 10 (July 2004): 34–37.

22. Will Wilson, "Hold That Hire," *Governing,* (July 2009): 55–56.

23. Dennis L. Dresang, "The Politics of Civil Service Reform: Lessons from Wisconsin," A paper presented at the 1978 meeting of the Midwest Political Science Association, Chicago, April 1978.

24. Jonathan Walters, "Civil Service Tsunami," *Governing* 16, no. 8 (May 2003): 34–41; Alan Greenblatt, "Jebocracy," *Governing* 20, no. 3 (December 2006): 32.

25. Kettl, *The Politics of the Administrative Process,* pp. 284–285.

26. *Statistical Abstract of the United States, 2011–2012* (New York: Skyhorse, 2011), p. 429; *Statistical Abstract of the United States, 1995* (Washington, DC: U.S. Government Printing Office, 1995), p. 443; *Statistical Abstract of the United States, 2001* (Washington, DC: U.S. Government Printing Office, 2001), p. 637; *Statistical Abstract of the United States, 2006* (Washington, DC: U.S.

Government Printing Office, 2005), p. 436. For a good overview of collective bargaining, see Lloyd Nigro and Felix Nigro, *The New Public Personnel Administration,* 5th ed. (Itasca, IL: Peacock, 2000), ch. 7.

27. Joel Douglas, "State Civil Service and Collective Bargaining: Systems in Conflict," *Public Administration Review* 52, no. 1 (January–February 1992): 162–169.

28. Mary E. Guy, "Three Steps Forward, Two Steps Backward: The States and Women's Integration into Public Management," *Public Administration Review* 53, no. 4 (July–August 1993): 285–291.

29. Christine Kelleher, Cynthia Bowling, Jennifer Jones, and Deil Wright, "Women in State Government: Trends and Issues," in *The Book of the States,* vol. 38 (Lexington, KY: Council of State Governments, 2006), p. 417; Susan Carroll, "Women in State Government: Past, Present, Future," in *Book of the States,* vol. 43 (Lexington, KY: Council of State Government, 2011), p. 346.

30. Angela Bullard and Deil Wright, "Circumventing the Glass Ceiling: Women Executives in American State Governments," *Public Administration Review* 53 (1993): 189–220; Norma Riccucci and Judith Saidel, "The Representativeness of State-Level Bureaucratic Leaders: A Missing Piece of the Representative Bureaucracy Puzzle," *Public Administration Review* 57 (1997): 423–430.

31. See Joseph Stewart, "Between 'Yes' and 'But': Presidents and the Politics of Civil Rights Policy-Making," in Richard Waterman, ed., *The Presidency Reconsidered* (Itasca, IL: Peacock, 1993), pp. 327–346.

32. Peters, *The Politics of Bureaucracy,* p. 87.

33. *Memphis v. Stotts,* 467 U.S. 561 (1984).

34. *Martin v. Wilks,* 109 S.Ct. 2180 (1989).

35. *Ward's Cove Packing Co., Inc. v. Antonio*, 109 S.Ct. 2115 (1989).

36. Amy Goldstein and Dana Milbank, "'Divisive' Diversity," *Washington Post National Weekly Edition* (January 20–26, 2003), p. 13; Sue Davis and J.W. Peltason, *Understanding the Constitution,* 16th ed. (Belmont, CA: Wadsworth, 2004), pp. 425–426.

37. Leslie Scott, "States Anticipate Talent Shortage," in *Book of the States,* vol. 40 (Lexington, KY: Council of State Governments, 2008), pp. 455–457.

38. Lloyd Nigro and Felix Nigro, *The New Public Personnel Administration,* 5th ed. (Itasca, IL: Peacock, 2000), ch. 11; Jonathan Walters, "The

Employee Exodus," *Governing* 13, no. 6 (March 2000): 36–38; *The Book of the States*, vol. 38 (2006), pp. 436–437.

39. David Osborne and Ted Gaebler, *Reinventing Government: How the Entrepreneurial Spirit Is Transforming the Public Sector* (New York: Penguin Books, 1993).

40. The original outlining of these six principles is usually attributed to A.E. Buck, *The Reorganization of State Governments in the United States* (New York: Columbia University Press, 1938), pp. 14–28. These provisions were also reiterated in an influential document of the Committee for Economic Development, *Modernizing State Government* (New York: Committee for Economic Development, 1967), pp. 49–60.

41. Karl A. Bosworth, "The Politics of Management Improvement in the States," *American Political Science Review* 47, no. 1 (March 1953): 84–99. James Conant "Executive Branch Reorganization in the States, 1965–1991," in *The Book of the States* (Lexington, KY: Council of State Governments, 1992–1993).

42. Frank J. Thompson, "Executive Leadership as an Enduring Institutional Issue," *State and Local Government Review* 27, no. 1 (Winter 1995): 7–17.

43. York Willbern, "Administrative Organization," in James W. Fesler, ed., *The 50 States and Their Local Governments* (New York: Knopf, 1967), pp. 341–342.

44. Elling, "Bureaucracy: Maligned Yet Essential," p. 294.

45. See Kenneth J. Meier, "Executive Reorganization of Government: Impact on Employment and Expenditures," *American Journal of Political Science* 24, no. 3 (August 1980): 396–412.

46. Charles T. Goodsell, "Collegial State Administration: Design for Today?" *Western Political Quarterly* 34, no. 3 (September 1981): 447–466.

47. For a discussion of these and other complications, see Donald Kettl and James Fesler, *The Politics of the Administrative Process,* 3rd ed. (Washington, DC: CQ Press, 2005), pp. 396–398.

48. Jonathan Walters, "By the Board," *Governing* (February 2011): 42–43.

49. See Richard Bingham and Claire Felbinger, *Evaluation in Practice* (New York: Chatham House, 2002); Dipak Gupta, *Analyzing Public Policy* (Washington, DC: CQ Press, 2001).

50. Stanley B. Botner, "The Use of Budgeting/Management Tools by State Governments," *Public Administration Review* 45, no. 2 (September–October 1985): 618.

51. Daniel Katz, et al., *Bureaucratic Encounters: A Pilot Study in the Evaluation of Government Services* (Ann Arbor, MI: Institute for Social Research, 1975), pp. 120, 182; *Gallup Report* (September 1985), pp. 19–21.

52. On MBO, see Jong Jun, "Introduction: Management by Objectives in the Public Sector," *Public Administration Review* 36, no. 1 (January–February 1976): 1–4; Frank Sherwood and William Page, "MBO and Public Management," *Public Administration Review* 36, no. 1 (January–February 1976): 5–11.

53. Robert Rodgers and John E. Hunter, "A Foundation of Good Management Practice in Government: Management by Objectives," *Public Administration Review* 52, no. 1 (January–February 1992): 27–37.

54. Evan Berman, "Implementing TQM in State Governments: A Survey of Recent Progress," *State and Local Government Review* 26, no. 1 (Winter 1994): 46–53; George Beam, *Quality Public Management* (Chicago: Burnham, 2001).

55. "TQM Rings Cash Registers for States," *State Trends,* A publication of the Council of State Governments 1, no. 2 (February–March 1995): 2.

56. David Rosenbloom and Robert Kravchuk, *Public Administration* (New York: McGraw-Hill, 2005), pp. 175–177.

57. Robert Lee, Ronald Johnson, and Philip Joyce, *Public Budgeting Systems,* 7th ed. (Sudbury, MA: Jones and Bartlett, 2004), pp. 110–118; Janet Kelly and William Rivenbark, *Performance Budgeting for State and Local Government* (Armonk, NY: M. E. Sharp, 2003).

58. There are two different versions of incrementalism. The *rational incremental* version argues that the largest increments go to the agencies that run programs consistent with the short-term political interests of the legislators who approve the budget. See Charles E. Lindblom, "Decision Making in Taxation Expenditures," in National Bureau of Economic Research, *Public Finances: Needs, Sources and Utilization* (Princeton, NJ: Princeton University Press, 1961), pp. 295–329. In contrast, the *role-constrained* model of incrementalism argues that the budget increments get determined by individual actors playing out predetermined roles. It is essentially this model that is described in the text. See Thomas J. Anton, "Roles and Symbols in the Determination of State Expenditures," *Midwest*

Journal of Political Science 11, no. 1 (February 1967): 27–43; David Nice, *Public Budgeting* (Belmont, CA: Wadsworth, 2002), ch. 1.

59. Anton, "Roles and Symbols," pp. 27–40. Anton's model was derived from a study of the budgeting process in Illinois.

60. Pamelah Prah, "Economic Crisis Overshadows Policy Goals, Results," in *State of the States* (Washington, DC: Pew Center on the States, 2009), pp. 10–14; "Recessions and the States," in *State of the States* (Washington, DC: Pew Center on the States, 2009), pp. 18–19; *State and Local Government's Fiscal Outlook* (Washington, DC: United States Government Accountability Office, 2010).

61. Jim Rosepepe and Christopher Zimmerman, "The Case for Earmarking," *State Legislatures* 17, no. 9 (September 1991): 22–24.

62. Aaron Wildavsky says of PPB, "I have not been able to find a single example of successful implementation of PPB," and he makes specific reference to attempts at zero-base budgeting in the U.S. Department of Agriculture. See Wildavsky, *The Politics of the Budgetary Process,* 2nd ed. (Boston: Little, Brown, 1974), pp. 195, 200. Also see John A. Worthley, "PPB: Dead or Alive?," *Public Administration Review* 34, no. 4 (July–August 1974): 393.

63. Stanley B. Botner, "The Use of Budgeting/Management Tools by State Governments," *Public Administration Review* 45, no. 2 (September–October 1985): 618.

64. Rob Silverblatt, "States Draw Down Rainy Day Funds," *Stateline,* August 27, 2009.

65. Dennis Cauchon, "States and Cities Borrow Big," *USA Today,* May 4, 2009 (Web edition).

66. Tony Romm, "Cities, States Wrangle Over Cuts to Local Aid," *Stateline,* August 26, 2009 (Web edition).

67. Michael Cooper, "Governments Go to Extremes as the Downturn Wears On," *New York Times,* August 6, 2010 (Web edition); Leslie Eaton, Ryan Knutson, and Philip Shishkin, "States Shut Down to Save Cash," *Wall Street Journal,* September 4, 2009.

68. Dennis Cauchon, "Hundreds of Tax Issues on Ballots This Year," *USA Today,* October 17, 2010; Richard Dujardin, "Central Falls Seeks Ability to File for Bankruptcy," *Providence, RI, Journal,* April 23, 2010.

69. John Gramlich, "Weekly Wrap: Reports Spell Deep Trouble," *Stateline,* November 19, 2009 (Web edition); Fernanda Santos, "Teacher Survey Shows Morale Is at a Low Point," *New York Times,* March 7, 2012 (Web edition).

70. For a valuable overview of regulation at all levels of government, see Kenneth Meier, *Regulation* (New York: St. Martin's, 1985).

71. For information on some aspects of state regulatory authority, see *The Book of the States*, vol. 38 2006), pp. 207–208, 461–464.

72. Doug Robinson, "Trends and Issues for State Chief Information Officers," in *Book of the States*, vol. 40 (Lexington, KY: Council of State Governments, 2008), pp. 450–454; Christopher Conte, "Getting to Know You," *Governing* 15, no. 8 (May 2002): 46–51.

73. David E. Osborne and Ted Gaebler, *Reinventing Government: How the Entrepreneurial Spirit Is Transforming the Public Sector* (Reading, MA: Addison-Wesley, 1992).

74. Kettl and Fesler, *The Politics of the Administrative Process,* pp. 315–316.

75. Ron Nixon, "Government Pays More in Contracts," *New York Times,* September 12, 2011 (Web edition).

76. *The New York Times*, April 26, 1988, p. 34A.

77. Larry Margasak, "Democratic Report Alleges Halliburton Overcharges for Fuel Deliveries to Iraq," *Moscow-Pullman Daily News,* July 22, 2004, p. 9A; Vera White, "They're Acting with Blatant Self-interest," *Moscow-Pullman Daily News,* July 17–18, 2004, p. 6D.

78. Steve Bousquet, "Florida Judge Rules Prison Privatization Procedure Unconstitutional," *St. Petersburg Times*, September 30, 2011 (Web edition); Mark Naymik, "GTECH Loses Court Bid to Block Ohio Lottery Commission form Choosing New Operator Intralot," *Cleveland Plain Dealer*, March 12, 2009 (Web edition); Motoko Rich, "A Hidden Toll as States Shift to Contract Workers," *New York Times*, November 6, 2011 (Web edition).

79. Alan Greenblatt, "Sweetheart Deals," *Governing* 18, no. 3 (December 2004): 20–25.

80. Jeremy Scahill, *Blackwater* (New York: Nation Books, 2007), ch. 1.

81. Robert Garrett, "Exclusive: State Privatization Champion Gets Contract to Help Clear up Welfare Mess," *Dallas Morning News*, March 13, 2010 (Web edition).

82. *The New York Times,* April 26, 1988, p. 34A; Eileen Brettler Berenyi and Barbara J. Stevens, "Does Privatization Work? A Study of the Delivery of Eight Local Services," *State and Local Government Review* 20, no. 1 (Winter 1988): 11–20.

83. Donna Hunzeker, "Private Cells, Public Prisoners," *State Legislatures* 17, no. 11 (November 1991): 24–26.

84. Rich, "A Hidden Toll."

85. Ibid.

86. See especially, E. S. Savas, *Privatizing the Public Sector* (Chatham, NJ: Chatham House Publishers, 1982).

87. Linda Lampkin, "Contracting Out: Public Employees' Group Contends the Practice Has Serious Shortcomings," *American City & County* 99, no. 2 (February 1984): 49–50.

88. *The New York Times*, March 2, 1995, p. A-8.

89. Charles T. Goodsell, "Perspective on 'Privatization': In Defense of Bureaucracy," *State Government News* 29, no. 6 (July 1986): 20–21. See also Donald Kettl, *Sharing Power* (Washington, DC: Brookings, 1993); Alan Ehrenhalt, "Mental Adjustment," *Governing* 13, no. 6 (March 2000), p. 84; *Privatization: Questions State and Local Decision Makers Used When Considering Privatization Options,* Report GAO/GGD-98-87 (Washington, DC: General Accounting Office, 1998); Larry Terry, "The Thinning of Administrative Institutions in the Hollow State," *Administration and Society* 37, no. 4 (2005): 426–444; Jeffrey Brudney, et al., "Exploring and Explaining Contracting Out: Patterns Among the American States," *Journal of Public Administration Research and Theory* 15 (2005): 393–419.

90. See Kettl and Fesler, *The Politics of the Administrative Process*, pp. 317–320; Kimball Payne, "McDonnell Wants Probe of Computer Breakdown," *Newport News, VA, Daily Press*, August 31, 2010 (Web edition).

91. Robert Tanner, "States Take a Hard Look at Outsourcing," *Moscow-Pullman Daily News*, April 24–25, 2004, pp. 1C, 6C; Alan Greenblatt, "Offshoring Hits Home," *Governing* 17, no. 8 (May 2004): 54.

92. Doug Robinson, "Trends and Issues for State Chief Information Officers," in *Book of the States*, vol. 40 (Lexington, KY: Council of State Governments, 2008), pp. 450–454; Ed Janairo, "The Digital Transformation of State Government," in *The Book of the States* (Lexington, KY: Council of State Governments, 2002), pp. 400–405, 406–409.

93. Ellen Perlman, "Digital Nightmare," *Governing* 15, no. 7 (April 2002): 20–25.

94. For a valuable overview of the major issues involving courts and administration, see David Rosenbloom, James Carroll, and Jonathan Carroll, *Constitutional Competence for Public Managers*, (Itasca, IL: Peacock, 2000).

95. See Arnold Howitt and Herman Leonard, eds., *Managing Crises* (Washington, DC: CQ Press, 2009); Irwin Redlener, *Americans at Risk* (New York: Knopf, 2006); Steven Stehr, "Community Recovery and Reconstruction Following Disasters," in Ali Farazmand, ed., *Handbook of Crisis and Emergency Management* (New York: Marcel Dekker, 2001), pp. 419–432.

96. See Stehr, "Community Recovery," pp. 419–432.

97. Donald Kettl, *System Under Stress* (Washington, DC: CQ Press, 2004), ch. 4; Beverly Bell, "State Emergency Management and Homeland Security: More Changes Ahead after Hurricane Katrina," in *The Book of the States*, vol. 38 (Lexington, KY: Council of State Governments, 2006), pp. 467–473.

Courts, Crime, and Corrections in American States

CHAPTER PREVIEW

One of the most important concerns of state and local government is the courts and their handling of crime and other disputes. In this chapter, we will survey this topic by examining:

1 How the courts play important roles establishing and implementing public policy.

2 The structure of court organization and court procedures.

3 How politics is inherently embedded in the judicial process in American states.

4 How crime and the means of dealing with it put state courts

at the forefront of this aspect of social conflict.

5 The importance of political values in setting and carrying out criminal justice policies.

6 The challenges faced by state and local law enforcement and court systems in the wake of the September 11 terrorist attacks.

Introduction

In 1983, Calvin Burdine was suspected of stabbing another man to death. Burdine eventually confessed to the killing, but later recanted his confession. The following year he was convicted and sentenced to death, a relatively common event in the state courts of Texas. After several unsuccessful efforts at appeals at the state level, he was able to bring the case to federal court. Burdine claimed that he did not receive adequate legal representation because his attorney repeatedly fell asleep during the trial! The court clerk and several jurors who were involved in the case confirmed the attorney's tendency to doze off at times.

The first federal court to hear the case agreed with Burdine's argument, but that decision was later reversed by a federal appeals court in 2000. Apparently the judges felt that a sleeping attorney could still provide adequate legal representation. After a storm of protest, the full appeals court heard the case again and ruled that Burdine had *not* received adequate counsel during his original trial. The state of Texas appealed that decision to the U.S. Supreme Court, which declined to hear the case in 2002. As a result, Burdine won the opportunity for a new trial.

The Burdine case illustrates a number of major points about the legal system at work. First, note that almost 20 years passed between the original conviction and the appeal that reached the U.S. Supreme Court. Second, access to skilled legal representation is very unevenly distributed in the American judicial system; some people and organizations can afford to spend considerable sums preparing their cases, but others cannot.[1] Third, the treatment you receive from the legal system depends on where you are. From 1977 through 2009, 1,188 prisoners across the country were put to death. Texas alone accounted for 447 of those executions, and all but a handful of the others occurred in other southern or border states.[2] Variations in the treatment given to criminal suspects and concerns about unequal access to legal representation raise serious questions about the fairness of the criminal court system.

In addition to the questions about the ability of courts to render justice in criminal cases, state and local courts have been attacked for their handling of some highly publicized civil cases. These cases include a tort award of nearly a million dollars for being burned by a spilled cup of coffee, generous malpractice awards against physicians that united the medical and insurance industries in an effort to put a cap on such judgments, and court involvement in the administrative affairs of schools and prisons. In addition, there were politically divisive decisions on issues such as abortion and school desegregation, and court decisions in New Jersey forcing the state to adopt an income tax in order to reduce the funding disparities among the state's school districts.*

Whatever one thinks of the merits of these decisions, it is clear that state and local courts today are in the forefront of the great social conflicts that confront the nation. The judicial branch is no longer the "least dangerous" branch of government, as Alexander Hamilton called it more than 200 years ago.[3] In this chapter, we will discuss six major facets of state court systems: (1) public policy and the courts, (2) the organization of court systems, (3) the role of politics in American courts, (4) crime and the legal system in America, (5) political values as they affect the criminal justice system, and (6) the problem of terrorism and the issues it has created for the legal system. Although we will focus heavily on crime and criminal justice to illustrate the courts at work, it is important to note that the legal system also devotes considerable effort to handling civil cases, which can affect our lives in many ways.

PUBLIC POLICY AND THE COURTS

State and local courts play three major roles in the creation and implementation of public policy. First, the courts try to resolve legal disputes. Second, they help set many public policies. And third, they become intimately involved in the administration of some of these policies.

Resolving Legal Disputes and Administering Justice

The primary role of the courts is to resolve legal disputes. These may be disputes of **civil law** or of **criminal law**. In civil cases, one individual or group sues another, and the court's job is to settle the dispute and determine whether damages will be awarded. In some civil cases, a person or group may ask a court to prevent an action, such as destruction of an historic landmark or some wildlife habitat. Typical civil cases involve divorce, settlement of estates, malpractice suits, and business

---

*The New Jersey case challenged the state's system of financing schools, primarily because districts with prosperous economies could afford to spend much more per student than could poorer districts.

disputes. In criminal cases, the government prosecutes an individual for violating a law. The court is called on to determine whether the accused person is guilty and, if guilty, to apply a jail sentence, fine, or other punishment prescribed by state law. A serious crime such as murder, arson, or theft of large amounts of money is called a **felony**. A lesser crime is called a **misdemeanor**. Although criminal cases usually get more media attention than civil ones, the overwhelming majority of cases handled in court are civil cases.

Setting Public Policy

As they go about their primary business of resolving disputes, state courts often establish public policies. They do this mainly by interpreting the law and by determining whether a law is constitutional (**judicial review**). When a state supreme court declares a law unconstitutional, that law becomes unenforceable, and the court may establish a new policy. Action by the state legislature and/or governor may be needed to replace the policy that has been struck down. The power of judicial review in the states is enhanced by the practice of writing state and local policy provisions in the state constitution. Whenever a new policy appears inconsistent with those provisions, legal challenges are likely to follow. State courts also provide for judicial review of local government actions; in those cases, the court is likely to assess whether a local action is consistent with the state constitution, ordinary state statutes, and/or the authority granted to that local government by the state or by the locality's own citizens. Some of the most notable judicial review cases in recent years have involved budgetary decisions made in response to the recession. Courts have overturned state actions to reduce spending or raise more revenue, primarily when the actions conflict with the state constitution or with ordinary state statutes.[4]

When judges engage in extensive policy making that strikes down the existing policies of legislatures or governors, the judges are sometimes said to be practicing **judicial activism**; and when they limit themselves to narrow interpretations of the law that do not challenge legislative or gubernatorial policy, they are said to exercise **judicial restraint**. Whether judges should exercise activism or restraint is a highly controversial issue that is seldom separated from the purposes for which judicial activism is used. Conservatives object when judicial activism is used for liberal purposes, but not when it is used for conservative purposes. Liberals object to conservative judicial activism, but not to liberal activism.

The judicial review role of state courts is carried out primarily by the state supreme courts. The lower courts are usually limited to applying the law. Most cases are simply applications of statutory guidelines and previous decisions, referred to as *precedents*. Lower state courts can, nevertheless, make an impact on public policy by issuing declaratory judgments, injunctions, and cease-and-desist orders and through the use of discretion. A **declaratory judgment** is a legally binding court order, and anyone who disobeys it is liable for a fine or a jail sentence. The **injunction** and the **cease-and-desist order** are court orders to stop some particular action. Such court orders can be used to set public policy. For example, courts that consistently use these powers to stop strikes or to permit nonunion workers to fill the jobs of striking workers are clearly setting a legal policy that is pro-management and antiunion. When judges have discretion in deciding penalties, one judge may consistently prefer to award longer sentences than another judge hearing similar cases.

Even the decision to hear a case can be important, for a legal case can produce delays, expenses, and embarrassing publicity, regardless of the official outcome. Many interest groups use the legal system in an attempt to modify policies adopted by the executive and legislative branches. Groups with sufficient funds or legal talent may also use the courts to delay action on a matter until the arrival of a new governor or a new crop of state legislators.

Distributive or Redistributive Policies?   The most frequent conflict between liberal values and conservative values in court occurs when judges must choose between a **distributive policy** and a **redistributive policy**. Throughout most of American history, state and local court policies have been distributive; that is, they have followed a conservative pattern of reinforcing the existing distribution of wealth and influence. However, redistributive policies sometimes emerge; when most state attorneys general banded together to sue the tobacco industry, the industry was required to pay considerable sums to the states to help cover the health costs created by tobacco products.

Perhaps nowhere have recent redistributive decisions of state courts been more controversial than in those cases in which the courts have sympathized with plaintiffs against doctors in malpractice suits, against manufacturing corporations in product liability suits, and against insurance companies in a variety of personal injury and liability suits. These types of suits for damages fall under a category of common law called *torts*. In the wake of some highly publicized tort cases in which juries awarded extremely lucrative settlements to the plaintiffs, insurance companies raised malpractice rates and liability rates. Physicians, in particular, reacted by threatening to withhold services because they did not want to pay the high malpractice insurance rates.

As a result of complaints from businesses, insurance companies, and physicians, many states have seen protracted battles between trial lawyers, doctors, insurance companies, hospitals, and manufacturers, as state legislatures sought to limit the amount of damages that courts could award to plaintiffs in such tort cases. President Bush joined the calls for limiting malpractice awards in a speech before the American Medical Association in 2003. The doctors in the audience applauded.[5]

Some critics of these efforts contend that the actual harm caused by the lawsuits is greatly overblown, in part because punitive damage awards (given to the plaintiff to punish the defendant beyond the cost of medical treatment and so forth) are relatively rare, and that limiting access to the courts may leave people who are seriously hurt unable to obtain reasonable compensation from the companies or individuals who are responsible. Moreover, large financial sums awarded by juries are often reduced by the trial judge or on appeal to a higher court, or the plaintiff agrees to a less expensive settlement rather than go through an appeal, which risks delays and the possibility that the earlier decision may be overturned altogether.[6]

Administration of Public Services

Another controversial area of judicial activism has been court administration of public services. This has sometimes happened when a court found a public service to be operating in violation of constitutional principles, particularly if the problem persists in spite of repeated legal action. The Alabama prison system, for example, was found by federal courts to be so overcrowded and so brutal in its living conditions that the court took over the entire prison system in the 1980s and held control of it until a series of prison reforms were adopted.

Courts rarely take such direct control of agencies, but judges have become increasingly willing to hear challenges to administrative actions. That development has led many agencies to devote more attention to whether actions can be defended in court in the event of a legal challenge.[7]

COURT ORGANIZATION AND PROCEDURE

A dual court system exists in the United States—the federal court system and the state court systems. But there is a fair amount of overlap in their jurisdictions, for crimes such as kidnapping, sale of illegal narcotics, and robbery of federally insured banks violate both state and federal laws. Moreover, if someone violates a state law and then flees the state to avoid prosecution, that is a federal offense. The judgment of the state courts is final and cannot be appealed to the U.S. Supreme Court unless the case involves a *federal question*—a possible violation of either federal law or the U.S. Constitution.

Court Organization

In Figure 11.1 the organization of a typical state court system is shown in its hierarchical structure. At the top is the court of last resort, usually called a supreme court.* It hears appeals from the lower trial courts. Forty states have created intermediate appellate courts under the supreme court to reduce the work loads of the supreme courts. Like the U.S. Supreme Court, these intermediate courts primarily hear appeals only to determine if proper judicial procedures

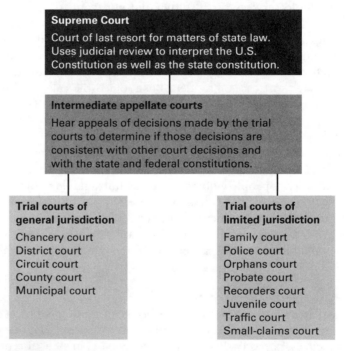

FIGURE 11.1
Structure of a Typical Court System

---

*Two states—Maryland and New York—simply call the court of last resort the *court of appeals*. Confusing matters somewhat, New York uses the term *supreme court* to refer to its trial courts of general jurisdiction. Texas and Oklahoma have two supreme courts, one for civil cases and the other for criminal cases.

were followed in the trial court or to make an interpretation of the law or the constitution. With the task for making such decisions removed from the supreme courts, the supreme courts can generally do a more thorough job of focusing on the most important constitutional and legal problems.[8]

At the bottom of the organization chart are the trial courts, where the parties present their testimony, facts are investigated, and a judicial decision is made. For trial courts of general jurisdiction, the state is divided into districts, and thus these courts are usually called district courts, county courts, municipal courts, or sometimes circuit courts or chancery courts. All major state criminal and civil cases are tried in these courts.

For minor criminal cases such as misdemeanors, for civil cases involving relatively small sums of money, or for specialized problems such as traffic tickets and divorces, courts of limited jurisdiction are used. Small-claims courts, for example, deal with civil cases in which the amount of damages is usually no more than a few thousand dollars and the parties can present their testimony in person without the expense of hiring a lawyer.[9] Another option for resolving civil disputes is alternative dispute resolution under which a relatively neutral third party meets with the disputants and helps mediate a solution to their disagreement. Many states and localities are experimenting with alternative dispute resolution as a faster and less expensive alternative to a formal court hearing. Maryland is one of the national leaders in alternative dispute resolution; it has a state office to oversee those processes, regional advisory boards, and has made a series of efforts to bring the process to a wide variety of cases.[10]

Keeping Judges Honest

Public faith in the court system depends as much as anything on ensuring that judges act ethically and competently, and adhere to professional standards. Sadly enough, not all judges have behaved in that fashion. In the famous "Greylord" scandal, four Chicago judges and a court clerk were convicted of bribery and corruption for fixing cases.[11] A Rhode Island chief justice resigned in 1986 under threat of impeachment for his ties with organized crime. A series of public opinion surveys conducted from 1978 through 1999 revealed that many Americans are skeptical about the fairness of the courts and have concerns about political pressures, especially campaign contributions, influencing court cases.[12]

But impeachment, recall, and criminal prosecution are not necessarily reliable ways of holding judges accountable. To provide systematic restraints, all the states have created judicial performance commissions to investigate charges of judicial impropriety. These commissions allow any citizen to make a complaint about improper judicial behavior. Most of these complaints focus not on corruption or bribery, but on slow decisions or inappropriate courtroom behavior, such as appearing in court smelling of alcohol or using abusive, sexist, or racist language. Some states also give the state supreme court supervisory powers over judges on the lower state courts; sometimes those powers are shared with the judicial performance commission.[13]

POLITICS IN AMERICAN COURTS

Politics can enter the judicial process in various ways, three of which are of specific importance. First, the selection of judges is itself a political act. Second, judicial decisions are influenced by the political and socioeconomic backgrounds of the judges. Last, the courts have become the focus of interest group activity, especially in recent years.

Selecting Judges

Five selection methods exist, as Table 11.1 shows, and all five have political dynamics. Political party interests benefit most from partisan elections of judges or from direct appointments by the governor or the legislature. Under these methods, party supporters and contributors with many years' service to the party, legislators, or the governor can be rewarded with nominations or appointments to the bench. Not surprisingly, judges with political party connections in those states using party selection resist proposals for a merit plan of selection.[14] Most judges, however, prefer a merit plan of selection or, as a second choice, election on a nonpartisan ballot.[15]

Judicial reformers strive for nonpartisan elections or, better yet from their viewpoint, **merit plans** of selection. Since the first merit plan was put into practice in Missouri in 1930, such plans are often known as **Missouri Plans**. Under such plans a nominating commission usually suggests a list of three judicial nominees to the governor, who must select the judge from among those three. The nominating commission typically includes one or more citizens (often appointed by the governor), one or more judges, and representatives of the bar association. The bar association is a formal organization of lawyers in each state that sets standards for admitting lawyers to practice and ethical codes that govern the lawyers' conduct. Under the merit plan, bar associations usually control the selection of nominees sent to the governor. After appointment by the governor, the judge stays in office for a specified time period and then must stand unopposed in a retention election on the merits of his or her record in office. Needless to say, very few judges lose their elections for retention.[16] Unlike federal judges who hold their positions for life, most state judges serve terms of six to ten years.

Does Merit Selection Make Any Difference?   Notwithstanding its advantages, the merit plan does not remove politics from the judicial selection process. Missouri, the birthplace of the merit plan, was rocked by a scandal in 1985 that involved overt partisan manipulation of its merit plan of selection. One supreme court appointment went to an allegedly unqualified governor's aide, and two other supreme court appointments were apparently engineered by the Republican state party chairperson.[17]

The most controversial example of the inherent political nature of judicial selection was that of California Chief Justice Rose Bird. In her 1986 reelection bid, she faced a $7 million

---

TABLE 11.1

Methods of Selecting Judges for Appellate and Major Trial Courts, with Examples

Much Party Influence and Little Bar Influence		Little Party Influence and Much Bar Influence	
Partisan Election	Appointment	Nonpartisan Election	Merit Plan
Alabama	*By governor*	Georgia	Colorado
Illinois	Maine	Michigan	Missouri
Texas	New Jersey	Oregon	New York
	By legislature		
	South Carolina		

Source: The Book of the States, vol. 43 (Lexington, KY: Council of State Governments, 2011), pp. 211–212. Some states use more than one method of selection, and some selection systems do not fit perfectly into the categories.

conservative Republican campaign to unseat her because of her opposition to the death penalty. Two other supreme court justices went down to defeat with Bird in November 1986, thus enabling Governor George Deukmejian, an outspoken Bird foe, to appoint a new, conservative majority to the court.[18] Whereas the court under Bird's chief justiceship upheld only 4 out of 68 death penalty cases it reviewed, in the next four years the court upheld 84 out of the 109 death penalties it reviewed.

Across the country, interest groups are increasingly active in the judicial selection process, with groups working to add judges favorable to their viewpoints and rid the bench of judges that do not support the groups' views.[19] Judges are especially likely to face challenges in partisan election systems and are at greater risk of being removed from office (in contrast to nonpartisan elections and retention elections).[20] Some critics worry that greater political controversy over judicial selection and retention has increased the cost of judicial elections. As a result, judges may be increasingly at the mercy of campaign contributors, many of whom have interests in cases the courts must later address. Conversely, people who may appear before a judge in the future may be vulnerable to pressures from unscrupulous judicial candidates to make contributions or risk an unfriendly reception in court later. A number of states now have looser fund-raising rules for judges (often as a result of lawsuits), a development that may make this problem more common.[21]

Not only did the merit plan fail to remove politics from judicial selection, but it also failed to meet reformers' expectations that it would produce judges with greater expertise. One study of state supreme court justices from the 50 states found that the merit plan had no advantage over other selection methods in getting judges from prestigious law schools or judges with relevant legal experience. The study did find, however, that merit plans had some biases of their own. The states with merit plans systematically had fewer Catholics or Jews on their supreme courts than did states with other selection methods.[22] African Americans, by contrast, fared better when their initial move to a judgeship was by appointment rather than by election.[23] Judges are often elected from multijudge districts that can put African American candidates at a disadvantage just as at-large city council districts often put African American candidates at a disadvantage. These types of judicial elections have been increasingly struck down by federal courts.[24] State court systems in recent years have developed a considerable amount of racial and gender diversity.[25]

Reformers also expected that since appointed judges do not have to gain popular support, merit plan judges would be more likely than elected judges to support upper-class economic interests and be tougher on criminal defendants. However, a study of the highest appellate courts in the 50 states found that the method of selecting judges had no significant impact on the kinds of decisions made. Elected judges were just as likely as appointed judges to espouse upper-class economic interests or to favor the prosecution rather than the criminal defendant.[26] Judges are not immune to electoral considerations, however. Researchers have found that elected justices were sometimes swayed by constituent opinion in death penalty cases and in the severity of punishment in other cases if it looked as if the justices faced a tough reelection battle.[27]

One reason why different selection systems often produce similar mixes of judges is that many governors have the authority to appoint new judges to fill vacancies when a judge retires or dies during his or her term. In addition, merit plans, partisan election systems, and nonpartisan elections all require judges to face voters directly, and governors who are interested in reelection or a chance to win higher office need to consider voter reaction to their judicial appointments. The informal political currents may then help reduce the apparent differences in formal selection systems.[28]

The Policy Influence of Judges' Backgrounds

Studies of judicial decisions have consistently found a relationship between the backgrounds of judges and the kinds of decisions they make. In workers' compensation cases, for example, Catholic or Democratic judges are much more likely than are Protestant or Republican judges to hand down decisions that favor workers over employers. In criminal cases, Catholic or Democratic judges are much more likely than Protestant or Republican judges to rule in favor of defendants rather than plaintiffs.[29]

Although the patterns vary from state to state,[30] significant partisan differences were found in 15 different kinds of cases, ranging from unemployment compensation to the governmental regulation of business. You are much better off in front of a Democratic or Catholic judge if you are a tenant being sued by a landlord, a consumer seeking damages for shoddy merchandise bought as a result of misleading sales tactics, a person injured in an automobile accident, or a government tax lawyer seeking to collect more taxes from a taxpayer. Conversely, you are much better off in front of a Republican or Protestant judge if you are the landlord, the merchant being sued for unfair sales tactics, the insurance company being sued in the automobile case, or the taxpayer being sued for more taxes by the government.

Prior work experience is also related to judicial decisions. Judges who have previously served as prosecutors appear to be tougher on criminal defendants and are more sympathetic to prosecutors.[31]

Do the racial and gender backgrounds of judges also make a difference in their decisions? Apparently so. But not always in the direction that one would expect. A study of judicial decisions over a ten-year period in a major metropolitan area found that African American judges were more likely than white ones to send defendants to prison, but they also tended to hand out shorter sentences than did the white judges. Moreover, African American judges sent African American and white defendants to prison in about equal proportions, whereas white judges sent a higher percentage of African American defendants to prison than white defendants.[32] Another study found that female judges in one metropolitan area were more likely than male judges to send women defendants to prison.[33]

These relationships between judges' backgrounds and court decisions do not mean that justice is impossible to achieve and that judges are arbitrary. But the relationships do demonstrate quite clearly that judges are human and that their decisions reflect the values they have acquired over a lifetime, in part as a result of their religious, political, occupational, and racial backgrounds.

Pressure on the Courts

Pressure group activities are usually more subtle in the judicial arena than in the legislature or administrative agencies. Groups can contribute to judges' reelection campaigns and run "independent" campaigns attacking judicial candidates that they dislike.[34] In 2008, interest groups and political parties paid for most of the $20 million in television advertisements run in elections for state supreme court justices.[35] Groups sometimes lobby the governor and legislature in states where the governor and legislators participate in the selection process. However, interest groups cannot use business luncheons, cocktail parties, or other entertainments to influence judicial opinions. They also have to be more restrained and formal in presenting information they hope will sway judges' opinions. They have traditionally relied on two major tactics: initiating or supporting litigation and presenting **amicus curiae** (or "friend of the court") briefs in cases filed by other parties.

One of the most important influences on state and local courts is the state attorney general (AG), who typically has very broad powers in state and local legal systems. Attorneys general typically have the authority to participate in local cases (possibly subject to some restrictions), initiate legal action on behalf of consumers, oversee prosecution in state criminal courts, and participate in court cases involving state agencies. AGs win about two-thirds of the cases they litigate before their supreme courts. This is a much higher batting average than any other category of litigant.[36]

State AGs have become much more visible in recent years as they have tackled some major cases and controversies. Many of the state AGs joined in a lawsuit against some major tobacco companies and won a large financial settlement from those firms. A number of AGs also launched an antitrust investigation of Microsoft and have pursued numerous cases addressing major business scandals that have occurred in recent years. These efforts have triggered significant complaints from conservative interest groups, who prefer that state AGs be less active in cases against businesses.[37] As noted in Chapter 10, a number of state attorneys general, primarily Republicans, have launched a legal challenge to the national, 2010 health care reform law.

An interest group tactic for influencing the courts indirectly is **court stripping**, which involves passing legislation or a constitutional amendment to prohibit the courts from hearing cases on particular issues. Proposals for court stripping often reflect anger over previous court rulings and/or fears regarding possible future court decisions. Congress and a number of state legislatures have considered court-stripping bills in recent years, but few have passed so far.[38]

COURTS AND SOCIAL CONFLICT: COPING WITH CRIME

Courts, like other governing institutions, are obliged to deal with the great social conflicts of our time. One of the most important arenas of social conflicts for the court system is crime. To explore the courts' handling of crime and the social conflicts surrounding it, we need to examine (1) the different kinds of crime and trends in crime, (2) how the courts process criminal cases, and (3) how different political values influence law enforcement and correctional policies.

Crime

Because different kinds of crime have different degrees of impact on society, it is useful to detail the important distinctions among them.

Index Crime   **Index crime** refers to the crimes listed annually in the Uniform Crime Reports of the Federal Bureau of Investigation (FBI). These are based on crimes reported each year by police departments. They are divided into two major categories—crimes against property (larceny of $50 or more, burglary, auto theft) and crimes against persons (assault, rape, robbery, murder). *Assault*, *auto theft*, *rape*, and *murder* are self-explanatory. *Robbery* is stealing someone's property through the threat or use of force. *Burglary* is the act of entering a building unlawfully to commit a felony or a theft. Roughly 11 million index crimes are reported by the police annually in recent years—a significant reduction from the nearly 15 million reported in 1991.[39]

Because index crime refers only to reported crimes, the Uniform Crime Reports index has been subjected to considerable criticism.[40] Since much crime goes unreported,[41] the Uniform Crime Reports index greatly understates the amount of actual crime, especially rapes and assaults. Surveys of the public find approximately twice as much crime as the Uniform Crime Reports indicate.[42] Many crimes are not reported for a variety of reasons: some people don't believe reporting will achieve anything, some victims are afraid to talk to the police, and the perpetrator of the crime may be a family member or a friend. Police departments sometimes distort their reports for political purposes—to get a bigger budget, to respond to newspaper criticisms, or to cover up administrative problems.[43] For all these reasons, the FBI has been studying ways to improve the Uniform Crime Reports.[44] One major improvement is regular surveys of the public to assess the frequency of crimes in their lives.

White-collar crimes (embezzlement, fraud, and commercial theft, for example) are not included in the FBI index. The President's Commission on Law Enforcement and the Administration of Justice argued that white-collar crime was just as costly to society, if not more so, than index crime.[45] Concerns over white-collar crime rose dramatically in 2002–2009 with a series of corporate scandals featuring top executives who apparently siphoned off immense sums of money from their companies; these businesses subsequently ran into serious financial problems and stockholders lost their investments. In addition, a prominent financier swindled a number of investment clients out of billions of dollars. One feature of the troubled housing market in recent years has been the dramatic rise in mortgage fraud.[46]

Organized Crime The FBI crime index also does not provide a sufficient accounting of *organized crime*. The index does not show how much crime is attributable to organized criminal elements and how much of it is done by isolated individuals or gangs.

U.S. government reports during the 1960s argued that in the United States a national confederation existed of 24 criminal organizations or families called La Cosa Nostra or the Mafia.[47] They controlled prostitution, narcotics, and gambling activities—especially gambling on major league sports such as football and horse racing.[48] The traditional structure of organized crime was seriously disrupted by a number of successful trials in the 1980s that sent the leaders of many of the crime families to prison.

The more modern version of organized crime in recent years involves gangs, many of which are involved in illegal drugs—especially crack and cocaine. The widespread use of drugs is disastrous for the social fabric of many communities, leading to violent street crime and serious health problems such as HIV and AIDS among drug users. Researchers report that one-half to four-fifths of men arrested for serious offenses tested positive for drugs in their blood.[49] Despite a succession of "drug czars" at the Drug Enforcement Administration in Washington and a dramatic stiffening of penalties for drug use and drug trafficking, criminal justice experts do not at this point see any realistic way either to reduce drug use or to neutralize the new organized crime groups responsible for drug smuggling and distribution that are becoming so powerful. One strategy, nicknamed "broken windows," involves more attention to relatively minor crimes and careful screening of people apprehended for minor offenses; a considerable proportion of them are likely to be involved in more serious drug offenses.[50]

Crime Trends As Figure 11.2 shows, the growth of crime was explosive in the 1970s but had slowed dramatically by the 1990s. Nationwide, the crime rate (the number of index crimes per 100,000 people) fell by 37 percent between 1990 and 2008. Even more dramatically, the

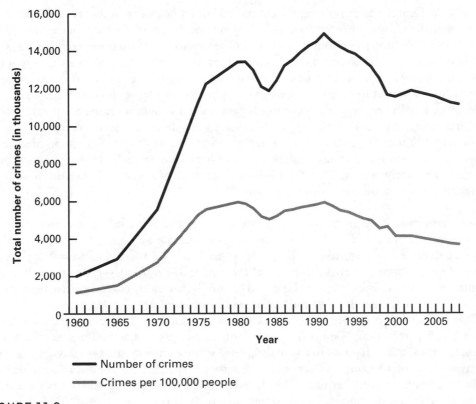

FIGURE 11.2

How Much Crime?

Note: The total number of crimes is in thousands; the crime rate is the number of crimes per 100,000 population.

Sources: Bureau of the Census, *Statistical Abstract of the United States, 1972* (Washington, DC: U.S. Government Printing Office, 1972), p. 143; *Statistical Abstract, 1977*, p. 168; *Statistical Abstract, 1992*, p. 180; *Statistical Abstract, 1996*, p. 201; *Statistical Abstract, 2003*, p. 199; World Almanac (New York: World Almanac Education Group, 2005), p. 162; Statistical Abstract, 2008, p. 192.

rate of murder and nonnegligent manslaughter fell by 43 percent. Even the total number (not adjusted for population) of index crimes began a gradual decline in 1992. Surveys of the public, which show considerably more crime than the FBI's index, also reveal substantial declines in crime after 1993.[51] Much of the trend's decline was due to the aging of the baby boomer generation that was born between 1945 and 1964. Even with the reduced amounts of crime in recent years, the total number of crime victimizations in 2008 still exceeded 21 million,[52] and many Americans feel unsafe in their own neighborhoods.

Bear in mind that the severity and composition of the crime problem varies considerably from place to place. The violent crime rate, for example, is particularly high in a number of southern and border states, along with California, Illinois, and Nevada. Violent crime rates are far lower in some of the states of the upper Midwest and Northeast, especially the less urban ones; the violent crime rate in South Carolina in 2008 was more than six times as high as in Maine. Crime rates are considerably higher in urban areas than in rural areas, although crime rates in large cities vary a great deal from one city to another.[53]

Crime and the Courts   In examining the courts' role in crime policy, it is very important to keep in mind that the criminal justice process is only one of the many factors that influence crime, and the courts do not have control over the other factors. Demographic change is a prime variable over which the courts have no control, as are inequalities in wealth, psychological problems, laws passed by legislatures, and implementation of those laws by administrators. If a crime is not reported to police or not treated by police or prosecutors as a crime, the courts can do little. Finally, courts do not control society's values toward crime. Some criminologists argue that crime exploded in the 1970s because society became more tolerant of criminally deviant behavior than it was a generation earlier. More recently, an examination of state death penalty decisions reveals that although many states have death penalty laws, the courts in some of those states rarely sentence anyone to death. The bulk of the actual executions since 1977 have taken place in southern and border states.[54]

The Jury System   There are two types of juries—the grand jury and the trial jury. The **grand jury** is an official panel of citizens who investigate a crime and determine whether there is enough evidence to warrant filing charges. If a grand jury finds sufficient evidence, it reports a *true bill,* or indictment. Few states require indictment by grand jury. Prosecutors file most of the criminal charges. They rely on the grand jury only for cases that are extremely sensitive, such as those involving public officials or organized crime.

   Trial juries can be used in either civil cases or criminal cases. In civil cases, the trial jury decides which party (if any) deserves to be awarded damages and sometimes sets the amounts. In criminal cases, the trial jury's role is to determine whether a defendant is guilty. Traditionally, conviction requires a unanimous verdict of 12 jurors persuaded "beyond a reasonable doubt" that the defendant is guilty. Because of this standard, it often is very difficult to obtain unanimity among the 12 jurors. In reaction, some states have relaxed this requirement. Louisiana permits convictions on a vote of only 9 of the 12 jurors. Florida now permits six-member juries instead of the traditional 12. As jury size gets smaller, the chances of a hung jury decrease. Relying on this experience, the Supreme Court in 1978 refused to approve five-person juries.[55]

   Courts in a number of states have experienced increasing difficulty in getting people to serve on juries. As a result, several states are cutting back exemptions from jury service usually given to professionals.[56] The hope is that these reforms will help produce juries better qualified to weigh evidence and follow complicated legal arguments.

   Note that many cases are not heard by a jury. People may prefer a trial decided by a judge, in part because they may receive a hearing more quickly than if they had to wait until a time slot is available for a jury trial. A trial before a judge may also be attractive if a case primarily involves different interpretations of the law (rather than a case emphasizing factual issues, such as whether the defendant is the one who fired a gun). As we will see shortly, many cases are settled without a trial of any kind.

Money and Criminal Justice   An important component of America's legal system is money. A complicated trial can easily involve court fees, lawyers' fees, fees for investigators and court recorders, costs for getting witnesses to testify, and expenses for specialists such as accountants, psychiatrists, scientists, and jury selection consultants. If a person cannot afford a lawyer, the state is obliged to provide one (usually called a public defender),[57] but the quality of these court-appointed lawyers varies from state to state.[58] Moreover, public defenders often have only a small budget for preparing a defense and have many cases waiting to be argued, so some defendants may not receive much of a defense.[59] In civil cases, the federal government established the Legal Services Corporation to provide lawyers for poor people.[60] Conservatives have periodically called for abolishing the Legal Services Corporation, in part because it sometimes represents poor people who are involved in disputes with businesses.

Bail is a sum of money an accused person must deposit with the court to ensure that he or she will show up for trial. People without much money must borrow from a bail bondsperson at a very high interest rate or stay in jail until their case comes to trial. For persons acquitted of the charges against them, the time spent in jail awaiting trial amounts to a punishment without a conviction. A study in Baltimore found that 38 percent of felony defendants were kept in jail right up to the moment of their trial,[61] greatly compounding their difficulty in finding witnesses and taking other actions that might help their defense. As a consequence of experiences like this, the 1970s and 1980s saw a number of programs to release suspects without bail—on their own recognizance—if the suspects were reputable people with a job and stable residential history. Kentucky's experience with this and other pretrial release programs was so successful that it abolished all commercial bail bondspersons.[62]

By the 1990s, criticism was being raised about pretrial release programs in the conservative press. One such criticism cited a U.S. Justice Department study in the 75 largest counties that found that one-third of defendants in serious felony cases were released without bail. About one-fourth of these failed to turn up for their trials, and about one-tenth of them committed another felony while out on pretrial release. Defendants who had been released on bail were much more likely to show up for their trial and much less likely to commit crimes while out on bail.[63]

Overall, money affects legal outcomes; thoroughly preparing a case is expensive, and many skilled attorneys charge very high fees. Appealing a decision is also expensive, as is making a generous campaign contribution to a judicial candidate or candidate for prosecuting attorney. One consequence of the current recession is an increase in the number of people who represent themselves in court. Because many people are not very familiar with the law, people without lawyers are unlikely to do very well in court.[64] Relatively few reformers seem to be working to reduce the influence of money in our legal system.

Plea Bargaining   A third target of criticism is the practice of **plea bargaining**. The prosecutor may have several possible charges on which to prosecute the defendant, but the evidence on some charges may not be strong enough to win a conviction. So the prosecutor may offer to drop one or more charges if the defendant will plead guilty to the other charges. The prosecutor is likely to have many other cases waiting and does not have time for lengthy trials for all of them. The prosecutor may also reduce the severity of the charge (from first degree murder to manslaughter, for example) in exchange for a guilty plea on the lesser charge. Another variant is that the prosecutor may let the charge stand, but promise a relatively light punishment (rather than the maximum penalty) in exchange for a guilty plea.

From the defendant's point of view, the certainty of a milder penalty might be preferable to risking a conviction and a possibly harsher penalty. From the prosecutor's standpoint, getting a guilty plea on some charge is often preferable to running the risk that the defendant might be acquitted altogether in a trial. The defense attorney and the prosecutor thus bargain with each other until they reach an agreement about the plea that the defendant will make and the penalty that will result—hence the term *plea bargaining*. Plea bargaining is so popular that it is used in the vast majority of criminal cases each year.[65]

Plea bargaining has both its opponents and its defenders. Opponents of plea bargaining view the compromises made as inherently contrary to the ideal of impartial justice. The bargaining inevitably leads to different punishment levels for the same crime (although note that going to trial may also produce differing sentences). Some critics also complain that the practice of dropping some charges or reducing their severity means that defendants are not held fully accountable for what they have done.[66] Some prosecutors appear to compensate for that concern by charging defendants with an especially large number of crimes or starting with more serious charges to compensate for later bargaining. If a defendant receives poor legal advice, he may be pressured into pleading guilty without understanding the full consequences.

Defenders of plea bargaining point out that criminal courts would be intolerably overloaded with cases if plea bargaining were eliminated. In this view, the overloaded courts and the long delays in getting to trial would provoke much more injustice than does plea bargaining. Alternatively, we might vastly increase the number of courts, judges, and lawyers in America to handle the increased workload, but that would be expensive. These arguments appear to be persuasive to state legislators, who have generally chosen not to abolish plea bargaining, and to the American Bar Association, which would prefer to see the practice refined and improved.[67] The U.S. Supreme Court recently ruled that defendants have a right to effective legal representation during plea bargaining and that higher courts need to be more willing to review cases resolved by plea bargaining.[68]

Bargaining is also very common in civil cases and sometimes takes place even when a trial is in progress—or even after a trial. A large corporation that loses a major lawsuit to a consumer may threaten to appeal the decision, perhaps repeatedly, unless the consumer agrees to accept a smaller settlement.

Minimum Standards of Justice   Attaining a high quality of justice also depends on the substantive decisions that judges make and the tactics that police use to get evidence. The idea of justice would be a sham, for example, if court standards regarding the rights of suspects were so lax that police were permitted to torture their suspects in order to gain confessions or if court standards were so rigid that nobody ever got convicted.

Between these extremes has been a wide variety of minimum standards of justice in the 50 states and among different communities in the same state. Although some disparities may be acceptable, the U.S. Supreme Court has ruled that most of the provisions of the Fourth, Fifth, Sixth, and Fourteenth Amendments to the U.S. Constitution should be applied with consistency in all the states. The application of these federal provisions to the states is called the *incorporation* of the **Bill of Rights**.

Although the Supreme Court never stated that the establishment of minimum standards of justice was its goal, its decisions have accomplished this to some degree. Table 11.2 outlines the major Supreme Court cases addressing the question of minimum standards of justice. Probably the most controversial cases have been those involving the exclusionary rule, the Miranda rule, and the death penalty. Some recent decisions regarding homeland security and the war on terrorism are also noteworthy.

The **exclusionary rule** states that evidence obtained illegally may not be used against a defendant in a trial. The rule was first applied to the states in *Mapp v. Ohio* and involved evidence obtained during a search of Mapp's home without, the Supreme Court ruled, an appropriate search warrant.[69]

The **Miranda rule** was established in *Miranda v. Arizona*. In that case, the Supreme Court ruled that police must advise a suspect of the right to speak to a lawyer before interrogation and the right to remain silent until legal representation is provided. The Supreme Court

TABLE 11.2

Setting Minimum Standards of Justice: Incorporating the Bill of Rights into State Criminal Law

Expanding the Minimum Standards

1957	If a suspect is not taken before a judge as soon as possible after arrest, any unnecessary delay will make it impossible to admit into court any confession made prior to being brought before the judge. *Mallory v. United States*
1961	If a person's constitutional rights have been violated by a police officer, that person may sue the police officer in federal court. *Monroe v. Pape*
1961	Evidence collected in an "unreasonable" search and seizure may not be used against a person in court. Established guidelines for obtaining evidence and conducting searches. *Mapp v. Ohio*
1963	Free legal counsel must be provided in felony cases for defendants who cannot afford to hire a lawyer. *Gideon v. Wainwright*
1964	A person is not required to testify against himself or herself. *Mallory v. Hogan*
1964	If police obtain a confession from a suspect before letting him or her see an attorney, that confession cannot be used in court. *Escobedo v. Illinois*
1966	A suspect must be warned of the rights to be represented by a lawyer and to remain silent. If such warning is not given, no information provided by the suspect may be used against the suspect in court. *Miranda v. Arizona*
1967	The right to free counsel is guaranteed to juveniles being tried in juvenile court. *In Re Gault*
1972	In any case for which a jail sentence might be imposed, free legal counsel must be provided for defendants who cannot afford to hire a lawyer. *Argersinger v. Hamlin*
1972	The death penalty was struck down as unconstitutional because it was applied capriciously and arbitrarily. *Furman v. Georgia*
2004	People designated as "enemy combatants," whether U.S. citizens or not, have access to American courts in order to determine whether they are being held legally. *Hamdi v. Rumsfeld, Rasul v. Bush,* and *Al Odah v. United States*
2012	Police must have a warrant before placing a Global Positioning device on a suspect's car without his or her knowledge. *Antoine Jones v. Washington, DC*
2012	Criminal defendants have a right to effective legal representation in plea bargaining, even if the ineffective lawyer's advice is to reject a plea bargain. *Missouri v. Frye* and *Lafler v. Coper.*

Relaxing the Minimum Standards

1971	If a suspect, during a legal interrogation, contradicts any voluntary statements made prior to seeing a lawyer, those prior statements may be used as a basis for further questioning. *Harris v. New York*
1972	A unanimous jury verdict is not necessarily required for a guilty verdict in felony cases. Nine of twelve jurors is sufficient if permitted by state law. *Johnson v. Louisiana*
1976	The death penalty *may* be imposed if the legislation establishing it and the judicial sentencing procedures provide safeguards against arbitrariness and capriciousness. *Gregg v. Georgia*

(continues)

(continued)

1976	States may not impose a mandatory death penalty. *Woodson v. North Carolina*
1980	Exclusionary rule relaxed in a case where a prisoner may have been tricked into providing incriminating evidence without benefit of a lawyer. Being transported in a patrol car past a school for handicapped children, Thomas Innis overheard a police officer express hope that the murder weapon would not be found by one of the children. Innis led the officer to the spot where he had left the weapon, and it was used as evidence against him. *Rhode Island v. Innis*
1984	Good-faith exception to the exclusionary rule permitted. Police who try to respect rights of suspects but unintentionally stray from proper procedures may be able to use evidence that results. *United States v. Leon* and *Massachusetts v. Sheppard*
1987	Death penalty expanded so it could apply to accomplices in murder cases even though they did not kill or plan to kill. *Tison v. Arizona*
1987	Death penalty expanded by rejection of the contention that the death penalty is racially discriminatory because of the statistical fact that blacks who murder whites get the death sentence more often than blacks who murder blacks. *McCleskey v. Kemp*
2003	The Supreme Court refused to hear legal challenge to antiterrorism efforts, particularly broader use of electronic surveillance.

Note: The USA Patriot Act passed in 2001 limited a number of procedural safeguards for people and groups suspected of involvement in terrorist activities.

overturned Ernesto Miranda's conviction, which gave him the right to a new trial. Some critics of the Miranda decision have complained that it hampers law enforcement, but other critics charge that it still leaves the police free to deceive and manipulate suspects after the required Miranda statement is read.[70]

Relaxing the Minimum Standards   In recent years, the exclusionary rule and the Miranda rule have been relaxed somewhat. In 1980, the Supreme Court upheld the conviction of a man who had given police incriminating evidence before he had a chance to see his attorney.[71]

In the 1980s, the Supreme Court permitted a "good-faith exception" that would allow illegally seized evidence to be used in court if the police officer involved believed in good faith that the seizure was legal. The relaxing of federal standards for criminal investigations is consistent with a broader tendency, especially since the mid-1980s, for the U.S. Supreme Court to give the states somewhat more freedom to deal with some of these issues rather than having a single, national policy.

Minimum standards of justice were further relaxed in 2001 by the Patriot Act that broadened governmental authority to conduct surveillance, including monitoring people's telephone calls and electronic mail. The standards were relaxed even more in 2001 by antiterrorism legislation that broadened governmental authority to conduct surveillance, including monitoring people's telephone calls and electronic mail. Critics were also alarmed by the Bush administration's refusal to allow the Red Cross to visit the secret prisons.[72]

However, the Supreme Court veered in the opposite direction in 2004, when it rejected the Bush administration's claim that the executive branch had unchecked authority in dealing with people suspected of being involved in terrorism. The Court ruled that some-one detained as a possible terrorist had the right to know why he or she was being held, the right to legal counsel, and the right to dispute any accusations in court or in some other legal arena.[73] The Supreme Court subsequently struck down the use of military commissions for trying suspected terrorists without clear congressional authorization; that ruling also raised further doubts about the legality of the Bush administration's decision to permit monitoring of some communications without a warrant. The combined effects of court rulings and political pressures eventually led President Bush to change course on several policies: he approved applying the protections of the Geneva Convention to all U.S. detainees (after refusing to for several years), he agreed to seek warrants for eavesdropping on U.S. citizens in the United States, and he agreed to seek more explicit congressional authority for military tribunals.[74]

The Supreme Court also expanded minimum legal rights involving Global Positioning technology. Criminal investigators in a number of communities have placed tracking devices on the cars of criminal suspects in order to monitor their movements. For some years this was done without a court warrant, but the Supreme Court ruled in 2012 that GPS units could only be placed on a suspect's vehicle if the police obtained a proper warrant.[75]

A third area where the establishment of minimum standards has generated controversial court decisions involves the death penalty. In 1972, the Supreme Court struck down the death penalty as arbitrary and capricious punishment.[76] In reaction to that decision, many states rewrote their death penalty laws in order to make them less arbitrary, and most of these have been upheld. Thirty-seven states now have death penalty laws, but two-thirds of the executions since the reintroduction of the death penalty in 1976 took place in just four states (Florida, Georgia, Louisiana, and Texas).[77]

About three-fourths of the American public support the death penalty, although attitudes appear to shift somewhat if people begin thinking about various aspects of the death penalty, such as the possibility of an innocent person's execution.[78] According to one analysis, 123 people who were sentenced to death were subsequently exonerated in the period from 1973 to 2006. Many factors contributed to the exonerations, including discoveries of mistaken witnesses, inadequate legal representation, and faulty scientific evidence. Florida led the nation with 22 death row inmates being subsequently cleared.[79] Given the finality of executions, many observers worry about legal errors that could lead to the death of an innocent person.

In January of 2000, Governor George Ryan of Illinois stopped all executions in his state, at least temporarily, and ordered a sweeping review of the state's death penalty system after new evidence revealed that a number of inmates on death row were apparently innocent. After Ryan's proposed reforms of the state's death penalty system died in the Illinois legislature, he commuted the death sentences of all prisoners on death row, an action that produced a storm of criticism. Also in 2002, the governor of Maryland ordered a moratorium on executions in light of evidence that death penalty sentences appeared to be affected by racial biases.[80] More recently, Governor Jeb Bush of Florida suspended all executions in Florida after a bungled execution by lethal injection caused an unusually protracted death for an inmate. At about the same time, a federal judge in California extended a delay for all executions in that state based on evidence that the state's method of execution (by lethal injection) constituted cruel and unusual punishment. A federal judge in Missouri reached similar conclusions for that state.[81]

The death penalty encountered an additional problem in the recession that began in 2007–2008. The death penalty is a relatively expensive policy to use; defendants who know they could receive the death penalty may be more likely to demand a jury trial or to conduct more protracted plea bargaining. Defendants who are sentenced to death may try to launch numerous appeals to avoid being executed.[82]

POLITICAL VALUES AND CONFLICTS OVER CRIMINAL JUSTICE POLICY

How we deal with social problems depends in great measure on how we think about them, what we think causes them, and how we think they might best be solved (if, indeed, we think they can be solved). This is as true of crime as of all social problems.

Approaches to Coping with Crime

As we noted in Chapter 1, political ideologies can be visualized along a liberal–conservative, left–right spectrum. Although the percentage of people at either extreme is fairly small, it is useful to describe the ideologies' positions on crime and punishment in their extreme versions, for this gives us criteria for evaluating what political leaders tell us. It also enables us to examine our own attitudes about crime in connection with ideological positions. Are our beliefs consistent with our underlying set of values about society? Once we draw these connections between our beliefs and values and ideological positions, we are in a good position to evaluate the campaign promises of candidates and the anticrime bills put before the legislatures. The liberal and conservative ideological positions on crime and punishment are summarized in Table 11.3.

TABLE 11.3

Overview of Theories of Crime and Punishment

	Liberal	Conservative
Major cause of crime	Social injustice	Individual defects
View of the criminal offender	Can be rehabilitated (probably)	Probably cannot be rehabilitated
View of punishment	No useful function	Deters others from committing crime
View of prisons	Reduce to the minimum needed to incarcerate dangerous criminals; prefer community corrections	Prisons preferred over community corrections; prisons protect general public while offenders are in prison
View of police	Skeptical	Positive, usually
Preferred policy solutions	Make educational, employment, and social reforms to reduce the stimuli to crime	Make punishment more severe and increase the likelihood of getting caught and being punished

Conservatives—The Criminal Is Depraved   The traditional conservative views crime as a moral or psychic defect in the individual person. Crime is an irrational deviation from social norms that exhort us not to kill, steal, rape, and so on. The criminal is personally defective, and there is not much hope for improvement. This conservative view has a strong concern for social order and emphasizes the government's role in preserving social order and preventing violence. In reaction to the Supreme Court decisions protecting the rights of criminal suspects, such as *Miranda v. Arizona* (see p. 294), a typical conservative might point out that society also has the right to be protected from violent crimes.

The traditional conservative policy for crime logically follows. If crime is a moral defect, the criminal must be punished for the transgression. Most criminals cannot be rehabilitated; thus, the punishment must be both harsh (long jail or prison terms) and certain to keep the offender off the streets and to deter others from committing the same crimes. Consistent with their concern for social order, conservatives usually view the police favorably as the keepers of order—although a number of conservatives have criticized instances of police misconduct. They favor increasing the size of police forces; giving the police sophisticated hardware such as helicopters, computers, thermal monitoring equipment, and lethal weapons; and experimenting with crime-prevention tactics. They see a need for prisons to house habitual criminals who are too dangerous to be returned to society, where they can prey on innocent victims. The worst criminals should be executed. Conservatives are likely to oppose gun control laws.[83]

Liberals—Crime Is Rooted in Social Problems   In contrast to conservatives who think crime is caused by defects in the individual person, liberals trace the causes of crime to social problems. Most index crimes are committed by poor people against other poor people living in poor neighborhoods. The liberal views this as evidence that poverty, economic deprivation, and lower-class social conditions are the main causes of crime. These conditions alienate criminally disposed persons from society and make them unreceptive to middle-class social values. Moreover, we often give stiffer penalties to people convicted of "blue-collar crime," such as burglary, than we give to people convicted of white-collar crimes, even though the latter crimes may involve far more money.

Just as the conservative policy responses of force and punishment are consistent with conservative beliefs on the causes of crime, so are liberal policy responses consistent with liberal beliefs. Liberals aim at two things—rehabilitating the criminal offender and improving the social conditions that breed crime.

Liberals view the police more negatively than do conservatives. Liberals note that police officers have frequently been hostile toward racial minorities and poor white communities. Rather than giving the police more lethal weapons to deal with criminals, liberals seek to sensitize the police to these communities' needs, improve police–community relations, and to increase the number of minority police officers.

Liberals also support reform efforts to overhaul the criminal justice system. This includes professionalizing police departments and implementing court reforms such as modernizing bail systems and providing better legal representation to poor defendants. Liberal reforms also emphasize rehabilitation programs that train offenders in marketable job skills and reorient their value systems so they can function better in society.[84]

Correctional Policy 1: Rehabilitation   Nowhere is the impact of these diverse viewpoints seen more dramatically than in recent trends in corrections philosophy. Until the 1930s, the dominant views of corrections were primarily punishment and deterrence. Most felt that criminals could not be rehabilitated. From the 1930s to the 1970s, the concept of rehabilitation came into greater favor. With the tools of modern psychology, counseling, and the teaching of marketable skills in prison, it was hoped that prisoners could be rehabilitated and rejoin society in a productive capacity.

As time went on, however, it became apparent that correctional institutions did not rehabilitate many criminals. Many released inmates ended up back in prison once again. This is called **recidivism**. About two-thirds of all persons arrested for felonies had previously served time in prison.[85] To some observers, these high rates of recidivism suggested that the prisons were training young offenders to become better criminals instead of rehabilitating them.

In most instances, rehabilitation was not taken seriously. Only a fifth of all corrections personnel worked in rehabilitation or in treatment.[86] Many vocational programs taught skills that are unmarketable. For example, many vocational programs taught barbering; yet in most communities, felons usually did not become barbers because they could not obtain the necessary professional licenses.[87]

Nobody really knew for certain which rehabilitation programs might cut down recidivism. Robert Martinson surveyed 231 experimental studies of juvenile and adult offenders of both sexes. The experiments included vocational training, individual counseling, transforming the atmosphere of the prison to be less custodial and more rehabilitative, the use of drugs and surgery, manipulating the length of the sentence, and moving the inmates to community-based facilities. In each study, the experimental group in the rehabilitation program was compared to a control group in a regular prison population. After this intensely thorough review of all these experiments, Martinson came to the conclusion that "with few and isolated exceptions, the rehabilitative efforts that have been reported so far have no appreciable effect on recidivism."[88] Some isolated programs seemed to hold some promise, but Martinson's overall conclusion was pessimistic.

Correctional Policy 2: Getting Tough Although later research put some qualifications on Martinson's findings,[89] the overall impact of his pessimistic conclusions was to support those who wanted to scrap rehabilitation approaches in favor of "get tough" approaches.[90] Getting tough is exemplified by two popular ideas in the 1980s and 1990s—determinate or mandatory sentences and a three-strikes-and-you're-out approach to sentencing.

Determinate or mandatory sentencing was a reaction to indeterminate sentencing under which a judge might sentence a felon to a term of from 5 to 20 years. Felons who took part in rehabilitation programs and convinced their parole boards that they were good risks sometimes won release after only a few years of their sentence. Other offenders committing similar crimes might be kept in prison much longer. Under **determinate sentencing**, the judge had to give a sentence for a fixed number of years, regardless of the inmate's participation in rehabilitation programs. Furthermore, in giving their sentences, the judges usually had to adhere to a set of sentencing guidelines based on severity of the crime and the conviction history of the felon. The theory behind this approach was that mandatory punishment and determinate sentencing would influence criminals to commit fewer felonies,[91] perhaps by a combination of deterrence and incapacitation. This latter, pessimistic view held that at least while the criminals were locked up, they could not commit crimes against the public.

The result was a general trend toward increasing the length of prison sentences, making parole more difficult to get, and setting minimum sentences for certain crimes, such as those involving drugs. However, prosecutors and judges can sometimes weaken or undercut the required sentences by reducing the charges against a defendant or using exceptions to the required sentences.[92]

The 1990s saw a sharp growth in the prison population. The total number of persons in prison across the country rose from 176,000 in 1970 to 1.6 million in 2008. If we add in the people in local jails and those on parole or probation, the total number of people in the corrections system reached 7.3 million by 2008.[93]

The growing incarceration rates also stimulated a boom in new prison construction. At an estimated construction cost of $125,000 per cell and an annual operating cost of $20,000 per inmate, the politics of getting tough was not cheap. According to the American Bar Association, state and federal spending on jails and prisons rose from about nine billion dollars in 1982 to $49 billion in 1999.[94]

In the sluggish economy of 2002–2003 and the recession that began in 2008, state officials grew so concerned by the costs that they began to release inmates who appeared to be less dangerous to other people and to use alternatives to prison for people committing nonviolent offenses.[95] By the summer of 2004, two-thirds of the states had reduced prison sentences for some offenses and/or adopted alternatives to prison. Steering nonviolent drug offenders into drug treatment programs is much cheaper than prison and may be more effective than prison for some offenders. Many states are also experimenting with community-based corrections systems, such as placing some offenders under house arrest; they may be fitted with an electronic bracelet that will signal the authorities if the person leaves home. Mental health treatment for some offenders may also be more effective than prison.[96] In addition, people getting out of prison may need transitional assistance (such as drug treatment or half-way houses) to help them avoid a return to old habits.[97]

The U.S. Supreme Court raised questions about the constitutionality of mandatory sentencing guidelines in 2004 and again in 2005, when it ruled that they might interfere with the right to a jury trial (the justices did not agree on whether or why that was the case). The result was to weaken the influence of sentencing guidelines somewhat, although many courts continue to follow the guidelines anyway.[98]

Correctional Policy: An Assessment   Have the new get-tough policies worked? Rehabilitationists charge that they have been counterproductive, have not reduced crime, and have put many people into prison who were no real threat to society.[99] Defenders of the get-tough policy, by contrast, maintain that the new policies are working. They point to high recidivism rates as evidence that most prisoners are in fact repeat offenders who threaten society, and the crime rate clearly has declined.[100] And studies of New Jersey and Wisconsin inmates in the 1990s found that the average inmate had participated in an average of 12 crimes in the year preceding his or her incarceration. Even including the enormous expenses of prisons, the cost of keeping these people locked up for a year was less to society than the cost of the crimes they had committed while on the streets for a year.[101] The authors of the study concluded that prison works for probably three-fourths of all offenders, but the other one-fourth could be more appropriately sentenced to a nonprison supervised facility.

In addition to mandatory sentencing, several states adopted a three-strikes-and-you're-out law in the early 1990s. California's version, for example, called for a minimum 25-year sentence for a third conviction for a violent or serious crime. This led to a number of anomalies such as the man who received a 25-year sentence because his third felony was stealing a slice of pizza; another defendant was sentenced to 50 years to life with a third offense of stealing several video tapes. According to one estimate, approximately half the people sentenced under the three-strikes law were convicted of misdemeanors or victimless crimes. In 1994, the California Supreme Court overturned the three-strikes law. Nine years later, legal wrangling over a revised three-strikes law was still underway. The U.S. Supreme Court upheld the revised law, but California's budget problems present another threat to the law.[102]

The get-tough policies have produced a result that many Americans apparently did not expect, although they should have: a considerable increase in the elderly prison population. A number of states have designated some prisons for elderly inmates, and some others have special units for the elderly as part of larger facilities. Although older inmates are less likely to engage in disruptive or violent behavior behind bars, they are subject to health problems that can make caring for them fairly expensive. Their ranks will grow over the next two decades.[103]

Policing as a Crime Control Approach

Scholars have recently produced evidence that improved policing practices reduce crime. Professor John Dilulio, who has studied the crime problem for many years, calls for more community policing patrols. This is an approach that gets police officers out of their squad cars and into neighborhoods, where they can help mobilize the citizens against crime. The hope here is to turn policing from a confrontational cops-and-robbers game to a cooperative cops-and-citizens game.[104] New York City also attributed much of its 1990s' crime drop to better policing strategies. These put a heavy emphasis on quality-of-life offenses such as low-level drug dealing and street prostitution, with the assumption that tolerance of low-level crimes such as these leads to the fear and disorder that create the atmosphere for major crime. New York City also increased pay for police officers, attacked crime strategically, strove for

▶ YOU DECIDE

Public Policy for Crime

Assume that you have just been hired as the chief criminal justice adviser to the mayor of your city. The mayor wants to make a serious attempt to reduce crime and has called on you to outline policy alternatives. To do this, you must use your general knowledge about crime and corrections and create practical policy proposals. As you go through this exercise for the mayor, several things become apparent.

First, you must determine whether the mayor seriously wants to reduce crime or whether the real goal is to make symbolic gestures that will gain newspaper publicity and voter support. If the goal is symbolic gestures, then the mayor will respond favorably to proposals for crackdowns on vice or juggling police crime reports to show crime reductions on paper. The mayor will give speeches with police officers in the background.

Second, as you try to assess the practical consequences of the liberal and conservative philosophical positions, you will note that both positions help us understand crime, but neither has a monopoly on the truth. At least two generalizations seem warranted by empirical social science research. First, research by Robert Martinson and other scholars provides impressive (although inconclusive) evidence that liberals have emphasized rehabilitation too much and have not paid enough attention to the possibility that some crime does pay and to the suffering that crime causes poorer people (who are more likely to live in high-crime areas). At the same time, other research findings, that most of the index crimes are committed by people low on the socio-economic ladder, suggest that the conservative position does not pay enough attention to the impact that social and economic inequality have on crime rates.

(continued)

Unfortunately, the mayor does not exert much influence over either of these things. Questions of punishment and determinate versus indeterminate sentencing are in the hands of legislators, not mayors. Sentences, convictions, paroles, and rehabilitation programs are the domain of the courts and corrections departments, neither of which are under the mayor's control. Finally, issues of social justice and providing a livable income for all the city's residents are not controlled by the mayor either, although mayors can sometimes influence both.

What the mayor can do, however, is to use the visibility of the mayor's office to lobby for appropriate legislation and to drum up public opinion on behalf of his or her criminal justice goals. The mayor may also help formulate economic development strategies to help attack the social conditions that are associated with some crimes.

Third, you can recommend utilizing the mayor's ability to propose law enforcement strategies to the city's police department. Even if the mayor does not immediately oversee the police, the police may respond to political pressures created by the mayor. A local criminal justice crime-reduction commission can survey law enforcement strategies that have been successful in other cities and investigate their appropriateness for your city. Crime attack strategies, community service strategies, or police deployment strategies may be appropriate in your city. Once these are identified, the mayor is in an influential position to get the police department to adopt some of them. Bear in mind, however, that some improvements in policy operations are expensive. Evaluations of crime laboratories across the country indicate that many technicians are poorly trained, and the quality of work is sometimes low. Improving crime labs is costly.[114]

Fourth, the mayor can urge reforms in the state and county corrections agencies. It may take courageous intervention by the mayor to get certain neighborhoods to accept community-based facilities. The mayor's support for reforms in sentencing, parole boards, juvenile justice, and the administration of state prisons may be instrumental in getting such reforms adopted by the legislature.

Fifth, the mayor must take a strong role in raising money for these experiments and reforms. The mayor's staff clearly needs a grants person who can get federal funds for projects. An active mayor testifying before the legislative appropriations committees will get more funds for the projects than a passive mayor who neglects to testify.

In taking this swift look at what a mayoral aide might suggest that the mayor do about crime and corrections, three broad generalizations are evident. First, the strategies the mayor adopts will reflect the mayor's personal philosophical perspectives on crime and his or her assessment of the prevailing attitudes among the city's voters. Second, since responsibilities for dealing with crime are spread out among all levels and agencies of government, any comprehensive attack on crime is obviously an intergovernmental enterprise. Third, because crime is disproportionately concentrated in urban areas, the mayor has an opportunity to exercise leadership and influence to solve problems.

What crime control strategies would you recommend? Why? ■

accountability, and decentralized authority to precinct commanders.[105] Houston saw a big drop in crime rates in the 1990s, but credited it not to community-based policing but to an expansion of the police force, better pay, and a get-tough policy on crime.[106] Developing strategies for combating crime will remain a major issue in many states and localities (see the You Decide exercise on pp. 300–301).

Political Economy and the Privatization of Prisons

If determinate sentencing was the corrections fad of the 1970s, the contemporary fad is privatization. This can take various forms, the most controversial of which is the contracting out of the actual operation of prisons. In fact, the contracting out of prison operations was a common practice in America in the nineteenth century. Contracting firms would make a profit by hiring out convicts to work in mines, on farms, and in other labor-intensive industries. There were so many scandals, abuses, and slavery-like conditions, however, that these systems were gradually abandoned in the twentieth century. Today's privately run prisons are a far cry from these nineteenth-century enterprises. The largest firm, Corrections Corporation of America, is an institution well respected within the correctional community and has all its facilities accredited by the American Correctional Association. By 1989, it was running 11 correctional facilities in four states and for the Immigration and Naturalization Service.[107]

Supporters of privatizing prisons argue that it might be cheaper and that many state prisons are so inhumane and incapable of rehabilitating inmates that private industry ought to be given an opportunity to see if it can do better. On the negative side, many in the legal profession argue that privatization of prisons would necessarily create a strong interest group lobbying for more frequent and longer prison sentences (because more money could be made that way). Privatization of prisons raises a fundamental issue about constitutional governance. Under a constitutional democracy, only the state has the authority to deprive people of their liberty and to run their lives while they are incarcerated. How much of this authority can be legitimately delegated to private corporations without violating this fundamental principle of government and without rupturing the bonds of constitutional accountability?[108] Also, the private prison firms typically want only nonviolent and easy-to-manage prisoners and leave the more difficult cases to public prisons. When private prisons have more dangerous inmates, the less transparent dynamics of private organizations may hide a very troubled environment. Surveillance tapes from a privately run prison recently revealed that for some time the guards allowed and even encouraged violence between inmates and denied them medical care to prevent the attacks being detected.[109]

COURTS AND CORRECTIONS IN THE AFTERMATH OF SEPTEMBER 11

Soon after the September 11, 2001, terrorist attacks, the Bush administration proposed establishing new policies for combating terrorism. The resulting law, commonly known as the USA Patriot Act, contains a number of complex provisions, but several deserve mention. First, the law created a new class of crime, domestic terrorism. Second, the law allows federal agents to search the homes and businesses of suspects without informing them of the searches until weeks afterwards. People who are suspected of involvement in terrorism can be locked up for extended periods without a trial. The law provides more lenient rules for exchanging information among law enforcement and intelligence agencies, as well as easing restrictions on electronic surveillance.[110]

The Patriot Act has generated considerable criticism from a wide variety of critics, many of whom complain that the law has unnecessarily reduced personal freedoms and given the government too much power to intrude into the lives of law-abiding citizens and to detain people without a trial. A report from five U.S. government inspectors general concluded that the warrantless wiretaps received too little legal review and were of uncertain value.[111] Critics have also denounced the use of interrogation techniques that amount to torture; their concerns were heightened by the revelation that the Central Intelligence Agency had destroyed nearly 100 videotapes of interrogations.[112]

A number of states have also passed new antiterrorism laws, created agencies and/or task forces to explore various terrorism issues, or used executive orders to improve security. Many states and localities are also developing plans and policies for fending off or coping with terrorist attacks of many types, from biological warfare to computer sabotage. More attention is being paid to managing emergencies of all types, including floods, hurricanes, and epidemics. Some of these efforts have been hampered by the tightness of state and local budgets and by federal funding that is too small to enable many localities to cover the cost of frequent terror alerts, much less invest in costly facilities to reduce major terror threats. Funding problems have also produced a common response: different communities quarreling with one another regarding the distribution of state and federal funds. Some basic problems, including inadequate communications systems, have not yet been resolved.[113] While we cannot yet assess the effectiveness of state and local efforts, there is little doubt that many state and local officials are genuinely concerned about the terrorism issue. Many of them also feel unsure regarding what would be the best response.

One other important lesson from the major emergencies of the past several years is that many private groups and individuals need to do more to prepare for emergencies. People may need to evacuate an area for an extended period. Immediately following a disaster, whether caused by nature or human beings, the first rescuers at many locations will be neighbors, friends, and relatives. Their level of preparedness may affect their neighbors' chances of survival. See the "Where Do I Fit In?" box for some suggestions.

▶ WHERE DO I FIT IN?

A number of sources provide ideas and guidance for families and businesses to prepare for emergencies. Here are some suggestions:

1. Decide on a meeting place where family members can gather if their home is inaccessible or destroyed.
2. Prepare a kit of emergency supplies that can be carried with you or quickly transferred to your car or truck.
3. Make copies of vital records and store those copies in a safe place outside of your home community.
4. Learn some basic first aid.
5. If one or more family members have special needs (prescription medication, hearing aids, and so forth), consider having extra supplies available in case regular replacements are difficult to obtain.

6. If you need to evacuate the area where you live or work, devote some thought to where you might go and learn the major routes you might use.
7. Include one or more items that will help to boost your morale (a favorite book, for example). If you have children, include one or more morale boosters for them, too.

For more detailed ideas, see *Disaster Preparation Handbook* (Olympia, WA: Washington Military Department, 2004); *Your Family Disaster Supplies Kit* (Washington, DC: Federal Emergency Management Agency, undated); Dr. Bob Arnot and Mark Cohen, *Your Survival* (New York: Hatherleigh, 2006); Lt. Gen. Russel Honore, and Ron Martz, *Survival* (New York: Atria, 2009); on the Web, see www.fema.gov and www.redcross.org. ■

SUMMARY

1. Courts in America resolve legal disputes, help set many public policies, and become intimately involved in the administration of some of those policies.

2. A dual court system exists in the United States: a single federal court system and 50 separate state systems. State and local judicial systems handle a large majority of the court cases heard each year.

3. Politics enter the judicial process in several ways: through the selection of judges, the political nature of some judicial decisions, the socioeconomic backgrounds of judges, and the activities of interest groups.

4. Crime presents an important example of courts confronting today's social conflicts. Crime rates mushroomed between 1960 and 1980, and then declined. Experts have not reached a consensus on how crime can best be combated. Conservatives attribute crime to defects in the individual and look to prison as a means of punishment and deterrence. Liberals attribute much crime to social injustices and look to prisons as a place where

criminals should be rehabilitated, although that view is less popular than it once was.

5. Empirical social research does not provide unequivocal support for either of these two orientations. Punitive approaches adopted in the 1980s led to problems of their own, principally dramatic growth in the prison population and rising costs.

6. Courts play a major role in dealing with crime. Considerable criticism has been aimed in recent years at the jury system, the role of money in the justice system, plea bargaining, and the attempts of some courts to establish minimum standards of justice.

7. Since September 11, 2001, state and local officials have struggled with the terrorism issue. They are attempting to work with one another and the federal government to fend off future attacks. Many local officials complain that they cannot afford to do all that they should to promote homeland security, and many officials at all levels feel unsure regarding the best approaches to fighting terrorism.

STUDY QUESTIONS

1. What roles do the courts play in state and local policy making? Why is judicial involvement in policy making sometimes controversial?

2. How are state court systems organized? Where are most of the cases heard?

3. What political forces influence the operation of state courts? How and where are those forces applied?

4. How has the crime rate changed in recent years? What difficulties do we encounter in trying to determine the actual extent of crime?

5. Why are some critics concerned about the role of money in the legal process, the use of plea bargaining, and efforts to establish (or weaken) minimum standards of justice?

6. How do political values influence strategies for dealing with crime? What have we learned from trying different strategies?

7. One feature of the war on terrorism is the relaxation of some legal guidelines designed to protect people's rights. Might those changes ultimately weaken protections outside of the arena of terrorism?

KEY TERMS

Amicus curiae   Friend of the court. Refers to a third party permitted to file a brief arguing on behalf of one of the two parties involved in a legal dispute.

Bill of Rights   The first ten amendments to the Constitution of the United States.

Cease-and-desist order   A court order to a person to stop carrying out a particular act.

Civil law   That portion of law that deals with conflicts between individuals and groups rather than with crimes (though some cases involve both civil and criminal aspects).

Court stripping Passing legislation that prevents the courts from hearing cases involving certain issues.

Criminal law Law that deals with the violation of legislative statutes that prohibit various behavior, such as murder, kidnapping, and robbery.

Declaratory judgment A legally binding court order.

Determinate sentencing The practice of sentencing inmates to very specific prison terms rather than giving a sentence with a wide range of possible time in prison, and adjusted to the inmate's behavior in prison.

Distributive policy A policy that allocates benefits to citizens, but does not upset the prevailing distributions of wealth and influence. Also called *distributive services*.

Exclusionary rule The rule that prohibits illegally obtained evidence from being used in a trial.

Felony A major crime.

Grand jury A group of citizens impaneled to examine a particular situation and determine whether enough evidence exists to indict somebody for a crime.

Index crime The seven types of crime listed annually in the FBI's Uniform Crime Reports.

Injunction A court order prohibiting a person from carrying out a particular act.

Judicial activism Judges' practice of using judicial review to impose their own beliefs on the law and to overrule policies set by legislators and executives; the term is typically used by people who disagree with a particular court decision.

Judicial restraint Judges' practice of making limited use of judicial review and generally restraining from overruling the policies set by legislators and/or executives.

Judicial review The power of courts to determine the constitutionality of acts of other government officials.

Merit plan A plan for judicial selection on the basis of qualification for office. A common version begins with a nominating committee that selects a list of qualified judicial candidates; the governor then appoints one of those candidates to office; after a set period of time, the voters have the chance to decide whether to keep or remove the judge from office. See *Missouri Plan*.

Miranda rule The rule that police officers must warn suspects of their constitutional rights to remain silent and to be represented by an attorney before they are questioned.

Misdemeanor A lesser crime, which usually brings a limited fine or short jail sentence.

Missouri plan A merit plan for judicial selection under which a nominating commission suggests a list of three nominees to the governor, who makes the appointment from that list. See *merit plan*.

Plea bargaining A bargaining process between a prosecutor and defense attorney; the prosecutor offers a reduction in charges or a milder penalty in exchange for a guilty plea from the defendant.

Recidivism Describes the problem of convicts who, after serving their terms, commit new crimes when they are released.

Redistributive policy A policy that takes wealth or income from one class of citizens and gives it to another class.

Trial jury A group of citizens selected to determine the innocence or guilt of a person being tried.

White-collar crime Crimes such as embezzlement, fraud, and commercial theft, usually committed by professionals (people in "white collar" jobs).

THE INTERNET CONNECTION

The National Criminal Justice Reference Service gathers and distributes information on a wide range of legal issues. You can find this resource at **www.ncjrs.org**.

NOTES

1. Amy Bach, *Ordinary Justice* (New York: Holt, 2009); David Cole, *No Equal Justice* (New York: The New Press, 1999).

2. *Statistical Abstract of the United States, 2011–2012* (New York: Skyhorse, 2011), p. 217.

3. Hamilton was talking about the federal courts, not the state courts. See *Federalist 84*.

4. Michael Cooper, "Courts Upend Budgets as States Look for Savings," *New York Times,* June 6, 2011 (Web edition).

5. News broadcast, *CNN Headline News*, March 4, 2003.

6. Lawrence Baum, "State Supreme Courts: Activism and Accountability," in Carl E. Van Horn, ed. *The State of the States* (Washington, DC: CQ Press, 1989), pp. 116–121; William Glaberson, "When the Verdict Is Just a Fantasy," in Bruce Stinebrickner, ed. *Annual Editions: State and Local Government*, 10th ed. (Guilford, CT: McGraw-Hill/Dushkin, 2000), pp. 118–119; Henry Glick, "Courts: Politics and the Judicial Process," in Virginia Gray, Russell Hanson, and Herbert Jacob, eds. *Politics in the American States*, 7th ed. (Washington, DC: CQ Press, 1999), pp. 251–253.

7. Larry W. Yackle, *Reform and Regret: The Story of Federal Judicial Involvement in the Alabama Prison System* (New York: Oxford University Press, 1989); James Fesler and Donald Kettl, *The Politics of the Administrative Process*, 2nd ed., (Chatham, NJ: Chatham House, 1996), pp. 360–363.

8. Herbert Jacob, "Courts," in Virginia Gray, Herbert Jacob, and Kenneth N. Vines, eds. *Politics in the American States*, 4th ed. (Boston: Little, Brown and Co., 1983), p. 226.

9. See Alfred Steinberg, "The Small Claims Court. A Consumer's Forgotten Forum," *National Civic Review* 63 (June 1974): 289; John H. Weiss, "Justice Without Lawyers: Transforming Small Claims Courts," *Working Papers for a New Society* 2, no. 3 (Fall 1974): 45–54.

10. See Mary Hune, "Trends in the State Justice System: Improving Public Trust and Confidence," in *The Book of the States* (Lexington, KY: Council of State Governments, 2002), pp. 194–195.

11. See *The New York Times*, December 19, 1984, p. 10A; May 31, 1984, p. 11A; March 16, 1984, p. 8B; December 15, 1983, p. 1A. Also see James Tuohy and Rob Warren, *Greylord: Justice Chicago Style* (New York: Putnam, 1989).

12. See Hune, "Trends in the State," pp. 193–194; *The New York Times*, May 29, 1986, p. 7A.

13. For an overview of the various state provisions, see *The Book of the States*, vol. 43 (Lexington, KY: Council of State Governments, 2011), pp. 221–223.

14. On New York, see *The New York Times*, October 23, 1985, p. 22A; on Pennsylvania, see *The New York Times*, January 4, 1984, p. 8B.

15. A survey of 562 judges in 49 states found that 48.7 percent of trial court judges preferred the merit plan and 24.3 percent preferred nonpartisan elections. Only 10.7 percent preferred partisan elections and 7.8 percent preferred appointment by the governor. The comparable percentages for appellate judges were 56.2, 16, 9.2, and 11. John M. Sheb II, "State Appellate Judges' Attitudes Toward Court Reform: Results of a National Survey," *State and Local Government Review* 22, no. 1 (Winter 1990): 18.

16. See Melinda Hall, "State Courts: Politics and the Judicial Process," in Virginia Gray and Russell Hanson eds. *Politics in the American States*, 9th ed., (Washington, DC: CQ Press, 2008), pp. 247–249; Melinda Hall, "State Supreme Courts in American Democracy: Probing the Myths of Judicial Reform," *American Political Science Review* 95 (2000): 315–330. A few states with merit plans use other systems to review judicial performance. A special commission may review performance periodically; in Vermont, the state legislature has the reviewing and retention function. A few states have a multistage review process; one version has a special commission review the judge's performance and make a recommendation to the governor, who may (or may not) reappoint the judge, possibly with the legislature's approval. See *The Book of the States* (Lexington, KY: Council of State Governments, 2003), pp. 247–251.

17. Kenyon D. Bunch and Gregory Casey, "Political Controversy on Missouri's Supreme Court: The Case of Merit vs. Politics," *State and Local Government Review* 22, no. 1 (Winter 1990): 5–16.

18. See *The New York Times*, March 20, 1985, p. 10A; January 17, 1986, p. 23B; *Washington Post National Weekly Edition*, November 11, 1985, p. 12; *Minneapolis Star and Tribune*, November 6, 1986, p. 15A.

19. Lawrence Baum, *American Courts* (Boston: Houghton Mifflin, 2008), pp. 109–110.

20. Glick, "Courts: Politics and the Judicial Process," pp. 242–244; Hall, "State Supreme Courts."

21. Alexander Wohl, "Justice for Rent," *The American Prospect*, May 22, 2000, pp. 34–37; reprinted in Bruce Stinebrickner, ed. *State and Local Government*, 11th ed., (Guilford, CT: McGraw-Hill/Dushkin, 2003), pp. 48–51; David Rottman, "The State Courts in 2005: A Year

of Living Dangerously," in *The Book of the States*, vol. 38 (Lexington, KY: Council of State Governments, 2006), pp. 237–238.

22. Craig F. Emmert and Henry R. Glick, "The Selection of State Supreme Court Justices," *American Politics Quarterly* 16, no. 4 (October 1988): 445–465. The inability of merit plans to produce judges from prestigious law schools and judges with the most relevant legal experience was also found in earlier studies of California, Iowa, and Missouri. See Richard A. Watson and Rondal G. Downing, *The Politics of Bench and Bar: Judicial Selection Under the Missouri Non-Partisan Court Plan* (New York: Wiley, 1969), pp. 338–339. For research on California and Iowa, see Larry L. Berg et al., "The Consequences of Judicial Reform," *Western Political Quarterly* 28, no. 2 (June 1975): 263–280. See also Lawrence Baum, *American Courts*, 5th ed. (Boston: Houghton Mifflin, 2001), pp. 119–123.

23. Barbara Luck Graham, "Do Judicial Selection Systems Matter? A Study of Black Representation on State Courts," *American Politics Quarterly* 18, no. 3 (July 1990): 316–336.

24. Ibid., p. 331.

25. Hall, "State Courts," pp. 244–245.

26. Burton M. Atkins and Henry R. Glick, "Formal Judicial Recruitment and State Supreme Court Decisions," *American Politics Quarterly* 2, no. 4 (October 1974): 427–429.

27. Paul Brace and Brent Boyea, "State Public Opinion, the Death Penalty, and the Practice of Electing Judges," *American Journal of Political Science* 52 (April 2008): 360–372.

28. See Baum, *American Courts*, pp. 120–121.

29. See Stuart Nagel, "Political Party Affiliation and Judge's Decisions," *American Political Science Review* 55, no. 4 (December 1961): 851–943; Nagel, "Ethnic Affiliation and Judicial Propensities," *Journal of Politics* 24 (1962): 92–110; Sidney Ulmer, "The Political Variable in the Michigan Supreme Court," *Journal of Political Law* 11 (1963): 552–562.

30. In the Wisconsin Supreme Court, political party background did not have an independent effect on justices' voting records. David W. Adamy, "The Party Variable in Judges' Voting: Conceptual Notes and a Case Study," *American Political Science Review* 63, no. 1 (March 1969): 57–73. But a study of Michigan justices found that when party background is consistent with other background factors, such as religious denomination and social status, there is a cumulative effect on justices' voting behavior. Malcolm M. Feeley, "Another Look at the Party Variable in Judicial Decision Making: An Analysis of the Michigan Supreme Court," *Polity* 4, no. 1 (Autumn 1971): 91–104.

31. Melinda Hall, "Justices as Representatives: Elections and Judicial Politics in the American States," *American Politics Quarterly* 23 (1995): 485–503.

32. Susan Welch, Michael Combs, and John Gruhl, "Do Black Judges Make a Difference?" *American Journal of Political Science* 32, no. 1 (February 1988): 126–136.

33. John Gruhl, Cassia Spohn, and Susan Welch, "Women as Policymakers: The Case of Trial Judges," *American Journal of Political Science* 25, no. 2 (May 1981): 308–322.

34. Baum, *American Courts*, p. 109.

35. David Rottman, "Decimated Budgets, Judges as Conveners, and Bloody Judicial Elections: The State Courts in 2008," in *Book of the States*, vol. 41 (Lexington, KY: Council of State Government, 2009), pp. 71–76.

36. This was the conclusion of James Brent who analyzed the litigation of attorneys general in 12 states in the 1980s. See his "State Attorneys General Before Their State Courts of Last Resort: A Research Note," *Comparative State Politics* 17, no. 2 (March 1996): 16–30. For an overview of the powers of attorneys general, see *The Book of the States* (2002), pp. 185–188.

37. See Alan Greenblatt, "The Avengers General," *Governing* 16, no. 8 (May 2003): 52–57; Alan Greenblatt, "Super-Activist," *Governing* 16, no. 2 (November 2002): 22; Angelita Plemmer, "Attorneys General: Trends and Issues," *The Book of the States*, vol. 38 (Lexington, KY: council of State Governments, 2006), pp. 198–201.

38. Rottman, "The State Courts," pp. 237–240.

39. *Statistical Abstract of the United States, 2008* (Washington, DC: U.S. Government Printing Office, 2008), p. 192; *Statistical Abstract 2011–2012* (New York: Skyhorse, 2011), p. 194.

40. See Wesley G. Skogan, "The Validity of Official Crime Statistics: An Empirical Investigation," *Social Science Quarterly* 55 (June 1974): 25–38. Skogan compared reported crime in ten cities with crime discovered through survey research.

Although reported crime apparently understated the actual level of crime, Skogan found a high correlation between the two methods of measuring crime rates. He concluded that reported crime rates do have valid uses.

41. A Department of Justice study in the mid-1980s concluded that two-thirds of crimes go unreported. *Minneapolis Star and Tribune*, December 2, 1985, p. 13A.

42. *Statistical Abstract 2011–2012*, pp. 194,199.

43. Arthur Niederhoffer, *Behind the Shield: The Police in Urban Society* (Garden City, NY: Anchor Books, 1967), pp. 14–16.

44. *The New York Times*, November 19, 1984, p. 13A.

45. President's Commission on Law Enforcement and the Administration of Justice, *The Challenge of Crime in a Free Society: A Report* (Washington, DC: U.S. Government Printing Office, 1967), pp. 155–159.

46. For statistics on a number of white collar crimes, see *Statistical Abstract 2011–2012*, pp. 210–211; see also the Federal Bureau of Investigation Web site.

47. The governmental viewpoint was fairly well summarized in two documents by the President's Commission on Law Enforcement and the Administration of Justice, *The Challenge of Crime in a Free Society*, Ch. 7; the Commission's Task Force on Organized Crime, *Task Force Report: Organized Crime* (Washington, DC: U.S. Government Printing Office, 1967). The testimony of former FBI Director J. Edgar Hoover was widely used in promoting the notion of the dominance of the Mafia over all organized crime in this country. See Hoover's testimony in U.S. Congress, Senate, Permanent Subcommittee on Investigation of the Senate Committee on Governmental Operations, *Organized Crime and Illicit Traffic in Narcotics*, 89th Cong., 1st sess., 1965, S. Rep. 72. See also U.S. Congress, House, Appropriations Subcommittee of the House Committee on Appropriations, testimony of J. Edgar Hoover, *Hearings Before the Subcommittee of Departments of State, Justice, and Commerce, the Judiciary and Related Agencies*, 89th Cong., 2nd sess., 1966, H. Rep. 273.

48. Ralph Salerno and John S. M. Tompkins, *The Civic Confederation: Cosa Nostra and Allied Operations in Organized Crime* (Garden City, NY: Doubleday, 1969), p. 89.

49. *Statistical Abstract 2008* (Washington, DC: U.S. Government Printing Office, 2008), p. 203; *The New York Times*, January 22, 1988, p. 1A.

50. See Jerome H. Skolnick, "Seven Crack Dilemmas in Search of an Answer," *The New York Times*, May 22, 1989, p. 21A; John Buntin, "Gangbuster," *Governing* 17, no. 3 (December 2003): 20–25.

51. *Statistical Abstract 2011–2012*, pp. 194, 199; *Statistical Abstract, 2006*, pp. 194, 202.

52. *Statistical Abstract 2011–2012*, p. 199.

53. Ibid., pp. 195–196.

54. James Wilson, *Thinking About Crime*, 2nd ed. (New York, Basic: 1984); *Statistical Abstract 2011–2012*, p. 217.

55. The Supreme Court cases that upheld these developments were *Johnson v. Louisiana*, 406 U.S. 356 (1972); *Williams v. Florida*, 399 U.S. 78 (1970); *Ballew v. Georgia*, 435 U.S. 223 (1978).

56. *The New York Times*, November 4, 1995, p. 7A.

57. *Argersinger v. Hamlin*, 407 U.S. 25 (1972).

58. See Christopher E. Smith, *Courts and the Poor* (Chicago: Nelson-Hall Publishers, 1991), p. 29.

59. See David Cole, *No Equal Justice* (New York: The New Press, 1999); Bach, *Ordinary Injustice*, ch. 1.

60. See Susan E. Lawrence, *The Poor in Court: The Legal Services Program and Supreme Court Decision Making* (Princeton, NJ: Princeton University Press, 1990).

61. Smith, *Courts and the Poor*, p. 24.

62. Ibid., p. 25; also see Julian M. Carroll, "Pretrial Release: The Kentucky Program," *State Government* 49, no. 3 (Summer 1976): 187–189.

63. See *The Wall Street Journal*, July 9, 1996, p. 15.

64. Jonathan Glater, "In a Downturn, More Act as Their Own Lawyers," *New York Times*, April 10, 2009 (Web edition).

65. H. Ted Rubin, *The Courts: Fulcrum of the Justice System* (Pacific Palisades, CA: Goodyear, 1976), pp. 26, 37; Baum, *American Courts*, pp. 168–180.

66. Baum, *American Courts*, p. 173–174.

67. See Herbert Jacob, *Justice in America: Courts, Lawyers, and the Judicial Process*, 2nd ed., (Boston: Little, Brown and Co., 1972), pp. 171–172. On the American Bar Association, see Rubin, *The Courts: Fulcrum of the Justice System*, p. 26. On legislators' attitudes, see Mike Kennensohn and Winifred

Lyday, "Legislators and Criminal Justice Reform," *State Government* 48, no. 2 (Spring 1975): 122–127.

68. Adam Liptak, "Justices' Ruling Expands Rights of Accused in Plea Bargains," *New York Times*, March 21, 2012 (Web edition).

69. *Mapp v. Ohio*, 367 U.S. 643 (1961).

70. *Miranda v. Arizona*, 384 U.S. 436 (1966); Anne Coughlin, "Why Miranda Is Suspect," *Washington Post National Weekly Edition*, December 20–27, 1999, p. 23.

71. *Rhode Island v. Innis*, 446 U.S. 291 (1980).

72. *United States v. Leon*, 104 S.Ct. 3405 (1984) permitted searches with an invalid search warrant. *Massachusetts v. Sheppard*, 104 S.Ct. 3424 (1984) permitted the use of a warrant that did not specify the materials to be seized; Glick, "Courts: Politics and the Judicial Process," pp. 260–263; Kenneth Palmer and Edward Laverty, "The Impact of *United States v. Lopez* on Intergovernmental Relations: A Preliminary Assessment," *Publius* 26 (1996): 109–126; Anne Gearan, "High Court Rejects Attempt to Appeal Cases Testing Scope of Secret Spy Court," *Moscow-Pullman Daily News*, March 24, 2003, p. 7A; Jennifer Loven, "Bush Defends Spying to Fellow Republicans," *Moscow-Pullman Daily News*, February 11–12, 2006, p. 9A; Dan Eggen, "Bush OK's Domestic Spying," *Daily News*, December 16, 2005, p. 11A; Matt Apuzzo, "Retired Judges Say Detainee Law Unconstitutional," *Daily News*, November 2, 2006, p. 7A; "Red Cross Chief Deplores U.S. Bar to Secret Prisons," *Daily News*, May 12, 2006, p. 5A; Sam Cage, "U.S. Should Close Guantanamo Bay Detention Facility, U.N. Panel Says," *Daily News*, May 19, 2006, p. 11A.

73. Anne Gearan, "Supreme Court Delivers Setback to Bush Terrorism Detention Policies," *Moscow-Pullman Daily News*, June 28, 2004, p. 5A; Linda Greenhouse, "Justices Affirm Legal Rights of 'Enemy Combatants,'" *The New York Times*, June 29, 2004, pp. 1A, 24A.

74. Pete Yost, "Court Ruling Weakens Foundation for Domestic Spying Program," *Moscow-Pullman Daily News*, July 1–2, 2006, p. 7A; Anne Flaherty, "Administration Decides All U.S. Detainees Entitled to Geneva Conventions Protections," *Daily News*, July 11, 2006, pp. 1A, 10A.

75. Adam Liptak, "Justices Say GPS Tracker Violated Privacy Rights," *New York Times*, January 23, 2012 (Web edition).

76. *Furman v. Georgia*, 408 U.S. 238 (1972).

77. *Statistical Abstract 2011–2012*, p. 217; A Gallup Poll in 1985 found 72 percent favoring the death penalty. See *Gallup Report*, nos. 232 and 233 (January–February 1985): 4.

78. Gregg Murray, "Raising Considerations: Public Opinion and the Fair Application of the Death Penalty," *Social Science Quarterly* 84 (2003): 753–770.

79. *Time Almanac 2007* (Boston: Pearson Education, 2006), p. 369. The statistics are from the Death Penalty Information Center.

80. "Illinois Executions Put on Hold," *The Daily Evergreen* (Pullman, Washington), February 1, 2000, p. 6; Tom Stuckey, "Maryland Bans Executions Pending State Study of Racial Bias in Punishment," *Moscow-Pullman Daily News*, May 10, 2002, p. 4A; Lee Hockstader, "Rage and Remembrance," *Washington Post National Weekly Edition*, January 20–26, 2003, p. 31.

81. Ron Word, "Fla. Governor Suspends Executions; Calif. Judge Declares Injection Method Unconstitutional," *Moscow-Pullman Daily News*, December 16–17, 2006, p. 4C.

82. Ian Urbina, "Citing Cost, States Consider End to Death Penalty," *New York Times*, February 25, 2009.

83. See David M. Gordon, ed. *Problems in Political Economy: An Urban Perspective*, 2nd ed. (Lexington, MA: D.C. Heath, 1977), p. 356.

84. Ibid.

85. The U.S. Department of Justice studied the criminal records of 16,000 persons released from prison in 11 states in 1983. Within three years, 62 percent of them were arrested once again on felony or serious misdemeanor charges. Reported in *St. Paul Pioneer Press and Dispatch*, April 3, 1989, p. B-1.

86. Alan E. Bent and Ralph A. Rossum, *Police, Criminal Justice, and the Community* (New York: Harper & Row, 1976), p. 156.

87. Ibid.

88. Robert Martinson, "What Works? Questions and Answers About Prison Reform," *Public Interest*, no. 35 (Spring 1974): 25.

89. James Q. Wilson, "'What Works?' Revisited: New Findings in Criminal Rehabilitation," *Public Interest* no. 61 (Fall 1980): 3–18. These later studies

showed that some offenders were indeed amenable to rehabilitation, whereas others were not, and they suggested that different approaches should be taken to the two different types of offenders. Also, studies in Utah and Illinois showed that strict supervision of youthful offenders decreased the frequency with which they were subsequently rearrested.

90. Ibid.; Gordon Tullock, "Does Punishment Deter Crime?" *The Public Interest*, 61 (Summer, 1974): 103–111.

91. On determinate and indeterminate sentencing, see Suzanne de Lesseps, "Reappraisal of Prison Policy," *Editorial Research Reports*, March 12, 1976, p. 189.

92. See Baum, *American Courts*, pp. 189–191; *The New York Times*, December 13, 1985, p. 1A.

93. James Austin, "Too Many Prisoners," *State Legislatures* 12, no. 5 (May–June 1986): 12–19; *One in 31: The Long Reach of American Corrections* (Washington, DC: Pew Center on the States, 2009); *Statistical Abstract 2011–2012*, pp. 215–216.

94. Julie Lays, "The Complex Case of Costly Corrections," *State Legislatures* 12, no. 5 (May–June 1986): 20–24; Anne Gearan, "American Bar Association Report: Abolish Mandatory Minimum Prison Terms," *Moscow-Pullman Daily News*, June 23, 2004, p. 6A.

95. Fox Butterfield, "States Easing Stringent Laws on Prison Time," in Bruce Stinebrickner, ed. *State and Local Government*, 11th ed. (Guilford, CT: McGraw-Hill/Dushkin, 2003), pp. 209–210 (reprinted from *The New York Times*, September 2, 2001); Lance Gay, "Mandatory Jail Time Losing Battle with Budget Deficits," *Moscow-Pullman Daily News*, January 7, 2003, pp. 1A, 8A; Christopher Swope, "Taking Aim at Correction Costs," *Governing* 15, no. 7 (April 2002): 54.

96. Christopher Swope, "Revising Sentences," *Governing* 17, no. 10 (July 2004): 38–41.

97. John Buntin, "Mean Streets Revisited," *Governing* 16, no. 7 (April 2003): 30–36.

98. Baum, *American Courts*, p. 192.

99. See, for example, Lois G. Forer, *A Rage to Punish: The Unintended Consequences of Mandatory Sentencing* (New York: W. W. Norton, 1994).

100. Michael K. Block and Steve J. Twist, "Lessons from the Eighties: Incarceration Works," *Commonsense: A Republican Journal of Thought* 1, no. 2 (Spring 1994): 73–83.

101. Anne Morrison Piehl and John J. Dilulio, Jr., "'Does Prison Pay?' Revisited: Returning to the Crime Scene," *The Brookings Review* 13, no. 1 (Winter 1995): 21–25.

102. *Los Angeles Times*, June 21, 1996, p. 1; Rene Sanchez, "California's Three-Strikes Debate Revived," *Washington Post National Weekly Edition*, May 13–19, 2002, p. 30; "Tough Sentencing Law in California Upheld by Nation's Highest Court," *Moscow-Pullman Daily News*, March 6, 2003, p. 7A.

103. Bob Johnson, "Graying Cons," *Moscow-Pullman Daily News*, October 6–7, 2001, p. 9A.

104. John J. Dilulio, Jr., "A Limited War on Crime That We Can Win," *The Brookings Review* 10, no. 4 (Fall 1992): 6–11.

105. William J. Bratton, "How to Win the War Against Crime," *The New York Times*, April 5, 1996, p. 15A. Bratton was the New York City police commissioner who was credited with much of the city's crime reduction. See also, John Buntin, "Gangbuster," *Governing* 17, no. 3 (December 2003): 20–25.

106. *St. Paul Pioneer Press and Dispatch*, June 1, 1994, p. 4.

107. *The New York Times*, March 17, 1989.

108. See John J. Dilulio, Jr., "What's Wrong with Private Prisons," *Public Interest*, no. 92 (Summer 1988): 66–83.

109. "AP Enterprise: Guards Shown Watching Inmate Attack," *New York Times*, November 30, 2010 (Web edition).

110. See Peverill Squire, "The Pendulum Swings: Civil Liberties after September 11," in James Lindsay, ed. *American Politics after September 11* (Cincinnati: Atomic Dog Publishing, 2003), pp. 19–24.

111. James Risen and Eric Lichtblau, "Report Says Wiretaps Got Too Little Legal Review," *New York Time*, July 11, 2009 (Web document); Curt Anderson, "Justice Details Uses of Patriot Act for Lawmakers," *Moscow-Pullman Daily News*, July 13, 2004, p. 5A; Camille Penix, "Moscow's Trail Pushes for Unity Against Provisions of the Patriot Act," *Moscow-Pullman Daily News*, February 18, 2004, p. 3A.

112. Charlie Savage and Neil Lewis, "Release of Memos Fuels Push for Inquiry into Bush's Terror-Fighting Policies," *New York Times* (March 4, 2009) (Web document).

113. Ellen Pearlman, "IT in the Ruins," *Governing* 15, no. 2 (November 2001): 38–41; Ellen Pearlman, "Digital Nightmare," *Governing* 15, no. 7 (April 2002): 20–24; Peverill Squire, "Not Washington's Job Alone: American States and the Terrorist Threat," in *American Politics after September 11* (Cincinnati: Atomic Dog Publishing, 2003): 83–88; Donald Kettl, *System under Stress* (Washington, DC: CQ Press, 2004), ch. 4; Devlin Barrett, "Big Cities, Small Towns Spar Over Homeland Security Dollars," *Moscow-Pullman Daily News*, June 10, 2004, p. 9A; Anya Sostek, "Orange Crush," *Governing* 16, no. 11 (August 2003): 18–23; Beverly Bell, "State Emergency Management and Homeland Security: More Changes Ahead after Hurricane Katrina," in *The Book of the States*, vol. 38 (Lexington, KY: Council of State Governments, 2006), pp. 467–473.

114. Solomon Moore, "Science Found Wanting in Nation's Crime Labs," *New York Times*, February 5, 2009 (Web edition).

Financing State and Local Governments

CHAPTER PREVIEW

Chapter 12 examines the financing of state and local governments. State and local fiscal policies affect state and local economic conditions and vice versa. The overall economic trend in a region sharply affects how much money states and communities can spend on public services. And at the same time, state and community fiscal policies may also affect how vibrant their economies are. We will examine these relationships in this chapter by asking:

1 For what purposes do state and local governments spend your money?

2 How do state and community governments raise their revenues?

3 What major financial conflicts and issues concern states and communities?

4 What is the importance of the political economy in state and community finances?

Introduction

The financing of government presents us with many difficulties. Most Americans have high expectations regarding public services—they want good roads, good schools, a clean environment, safe streets and homes, good health care, and so forth—and they also have high expectations regarding their private lives—they want nice homes, nice motor vehicles, suitable clothing, modern appliances, and other amenities. Unfortunately, we don't often have enough money to pay for all of these things. When the economy is performing poorly, as occurred after the September 11, 2001, attacks, or when the costs of some programs rise dramatically, state and local officials find themselves scrambling to find politically feasible sources of more revenue and cost savings that will produce minimum political backlash.

The recession that began in 2008 has caused a considerable decline in revenues for many state and local governments. John McGlennon, a county board member in Maryland, is one of thousands of local officials who are scrambling to find revenues to enable the country to continue providing necessary services. One option for the county is to increase the fees that it charges for all sorts of county services. Fee increases have been a popular revenue source for many state and local governments in the last 30 years, with fees covering everything from building permits and dog licenses to downtown parking and various school activities. In fact, fees and charges now generate roughly the same amount of local government revenue as do property taxes.[1]

Unfortunately, fee increases can create financial hardship for families of modest means, especially if the fees take repeated slices of a family's income. In addition, the repeated fee increases in earlier years may trigger some resentment of additional fee hikes. Moreover, some fees may anger citizens if they believe that certain services should be provided without added charges. In one community that began charging the drivers responsible for accidents for the costs of the accident investigations, many people simply refused to pay the fees. Even if fees and charges are often politically less controversial than tax increases, some fee increases may still anger the public.

Making sense of state and local finance requires us to grapple with a number of questions, none of which is easy to answer.

1. What sort of state/community/nation/world do we want? How important is health? Privacy? Wealth? Attractive scenery? Safety? Knowledge? Creativity? Fairness? Freedom?
2. What role should governments play in helping to achieve what we want? For present purposes, what roles should state and local governments play? What services should state and local governments offer (or help to offer)? That is, for what purposes should these governments spend their money?
3. Where should government money come from? The property tax? Sales tax? Income tax? Entrepreneurial activities? Other sources?
4. What is meant by various technical terms—such as *assessed valuation, market value, property tax relief, circuit breaker, tax burden, tax effort,* and others—used in discussing government finances?
5. How should the burden of financing government be distributed? For example, if a state lets most of its services be provided by local governments and paid for by local property taxes, who should pay the biggest share of the taxes? The rich? The poor? Businesspeople? The elderly? The young? Or you?

HOW STATE AND LOCAL GOVERNMENTS SPEND YOUR MONEY

In absolute terms, state and local governments spend a lot of money. We saw in Chapter 1 (Figure 1.1, p. 3) that state and local government spending since mid-twentieth century rose faster than either federal government expenditures or the economy as a whole. The major index of national economic growth is the gross domestic product (GDP). State and local government spending in 2007 was roughly 19 times its 1970 level, while the GDP rose at a substantial but noticeably lower rate. (NOTE TO STUDENTS: For a number of reasons, different financial sources give significantly different figures for many aspects of governmental finance. We will try to highlight some of the major reasons for these differences as we go).

During the twentieth century, growth has been much more dramatic at the state level than locally. In 1902, local governments were raising more than four times as much revenue as were state governments. By the end of the 1990s, the states were raising considerably more money than were local governments, a pattern that has continued since then (see Table 12.1).

TABLE 12.1			
State and Local Revenue Growth			
	1902	2007	
		Own-Source	Total
State	$.2 billion	$1,570 billion	$2,000 billion
Local	$.9 billion	$1,035 billion	$1,539 billion

Note: Own-source revenues exclude grants-in-aid. Total revenues include grants.

Sources: Frederick Mosher and Orville Poland, *The Costs of American Governments* (New York: Dodd, Mead, 1964), p. 163; *Statistical Abstract of the United States,* 2008 (Washington, DC: U.S. Government Printing Office, 2008), pp. 282, 288–289.

Why Costs Have Gone Up

There are several explanations for these rapid increases in state and local expenditures. The first explanation is inflation. In the period from 1960 to 2000, the purchasing power of the dollar declined to 22 cents.[2] Rising government expenses may anger many people; but in practical terms, a significant amount of the rise in government spending in some areas has resulted simply from maintaining the same level of services when the dollar value doesn't go as far as it once did.

However, citizens and interest groups are not content with simply maintaining the same level of services; this trend is a second explanation for the rise of government spending. During the entire post–World War II period, Americans demanded more services in education, health care, transportation, law enforcement, housing, and other areas. Increases in services usually mean an increase in dollars spent and employees hired. The number of state and local employees has approximately doubled since the mid-1960s, compared to an increase of less than 20 percent in federal employment. Most of this increase in employment occurred at the local level. The growth in the number of government employees also helped stimulate government spending, as those employees in turn became a growing source of demands for more funding.[3]

Population growth has also increased the workload of state and local governments. Population growth means more children in school, more cars on the roads, more people needing law enforcement protection, and so forth, which produces higher costs, at least in absolute terms.

Where Your Money Goes

Half the money spent by state and local governments goes for just three services: public education, public welfare, and health care. But Figure 12.1 shows that states spend their money slightly differently than do local governments. For states, the single biggest expenditure is for education (mostly in grants to local school districts), welfare (including health care for the poor), followed by insurance trust spending (much of it for pension programs), health and hospitals, and highways and transportation. A large portion of state spending ($460 billion in 2007) is devoted to grants to local governments, particularly school districts.

For local governments, the single largest expenditure is for public education, followed by utilities, public safety, health and hospitals, highways and transportation, and welfare.

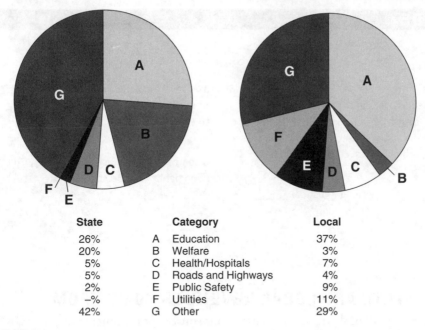

State	Category		Local
26%	A	Education	37%
20%	B	Welfare	3%
5%	C	Health/Hospitals	7%
5%	D	Roads and Highways	4%
2%	E	Public Safety	9%
–%	F	Utilities	11%
42%	G	Other	29%

FIGURE 12.1

Where State and Local Governments Spend Your Money: Expenditures, 2007

Note: Expenditure figures include spending financed by aid from other levels of government.

Source: Statistical Abstract 2011–2012 (New York: Skyhorse, 2011), pp. 274, 286.

Conflict over Expenditures

Political controversies regarding governmental expenditures largely fall into two broad categories, which sometimes overlap. First, generations of critics have complained that government expenditures are too high. They contend that state and local (and federal) budgets include considerable fat and waste, and could easily be cut back.

The level of government spending is a key issue in the conflict between the parties and between liberals and conservatives. Republicans and conservatives are usually more inclined than Democrats and liberals to favor cutting government expenditures, at least in the abstract.[4]

Public sentiments on taxes and spending appear to shift over time. Note, too, that people may feel one way regarding spending in general and quite differently regarding spending for specific programs. It is not uncommon to encounter people who demand lower spending in one breath and costly improvements in roads or schools or health care in the next.[5]

If the level of spending is the first key conflict between the parties and between liberals and conservatives, the second is over the purposes for which money should be spent. Continually faced with limited resources, state and local leaders must regularly set priorities among their programs. This is especially difficult when revenues fall below expectations and officials must decide where spending cuts must be made. The problem also arises when the costs of some major programs rise faster than do revenues. Many state and local officials find that one of the most worrisome examples of rising costs is Medicaid.[6] The following "You Decide" exercise asks you to take a shot at setting priorities among competing public purposes.

Cutting Budgets

Suppose the budgets of your state and local governments have to be curtailed. Which of these programs
would you cut most severely? Put a number 6 by that
program. Then rank the rest of the programs in priority, from 1 (the one with the fewest cuts) to 5 (the one
with the most cuts).

Public safety (fire, police, criminal justice) _____
Public schools (kindergarten through
   twelfth grade) _____

Tax-supported colleges and universities _____
Aid to the needy _____
Streets and highways _____
Parks and recreation _____

To compare your choices with those of the
American public, see Table 12.2. ∎

WHERE STATE AND LOCAL REVENUES COME FROM

In general, state and local governments have four sources of revenue: taxes, intergovernmental
aid, charges on services or enterprises they operate, and borrowing. Figure 12.2 shows that
the revenue sources for state governments differ significantly from those for local governments. Local governments rely heavily on state and federal aid, property taxes, and charges
levied on services (such as parking meters and sewer fees). Most state governments place little
or no reliance on property taxes. They rely most heavily on aid from the federal government,
insurance trust revenues, income taxes, sales taxes, and charges and fees.

Conflict over Revenue Sources

The revenue sources of a government strongly affect the distribution of the tax burden. **Tax
burden** is the total amount of taxes paid as a percentage of a person's income (we can also
include here the various fees that are particularly important in many local governments). A
progressive tax system places a relatively large tax burden on upper-income people and a
relatively small tax burden on lower-income people. A **regressive tax** system places a relatively
large tax burden on lower-income people and a relatively small tax burden on upper-income
people. A **proportional tax** system takes the same percentage of each person's income, regardless of whether the income is high, medium, or low. Some states have progressive tax systems,
and others have very regressive ones, as will be shown at the end of this chapter.

Note that many taxes and fees are not officially linked to a person's income. The motor
fuel tax you must pay when purchasing gallons of unleaded gasoline is the same whether you
earn $16,000 a year or $16 million. In addition, a tax may be officially paid by one person, but
that person may be able to shift some or all of the tax to other people. One example is a sales
tax that is officially paid by the merchant; under some conditions, the merchant may be able to
pass the cost of the tax along to the customers. Some people may be able to avoid paying a tax,
too. They may fail to report cash income on their income taxes, for example, or they may shop
at out-of-state businesses to avoid paying sales taxes. Determining whether a tax is regressive
or progressive takes careful research.

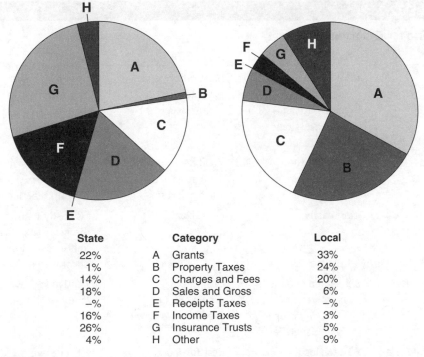

State		Category	Local
22%	A	Grants	33%
1%	B	Property Taxes	24%
14%	C	Charges and Fees	20%
18%	D	Sales and Gross	6%
–%	E	Receipts Taxes	–%
16%	F	Income Taxes	3%
26%	G	Insurance Trusts	5%
4%	H	Other	9%

FIGURE 12.2

Where State and Local Governments Get Their Revenues: 2007

Note: Figures are for own-source revenues (that is, revenues that are directly raised by the level of government that will spend them) plus intergovernmental grants.

Source: Statistical Abstract (New York: Skyhorse, 2011), pp. 274, 286.

Taxation as a Revenue Source

Few of us like to pay taxes, but we dislike some taxes more than others. For much of the last 40 years, the most unpopular taxes have been the federal income tax and the local property tax. However, their relative unpopularity has shifted considerably over the years.[7]

Evaluating the Major Taxes In order to evaluate taxes, we need to consider a variety of possible concerns. Table 12.2 provides six criteria for evaluating taxes—equity, yield, certainty, administrative convenience, economic effect, and appropriateness. *Equity* has various meanings* but it will be used here to mean taxation based on the ability to pay. *Yield* means how much money a tax will raise; closely akin to the concept of yield is the *certainty* that the tax can be counted on to yield a relatively predictable amount of money. *Administrative convenience* refers to how difficult it is to collect and pay the tax. *Economic effect* refers to

*Economists distinguish between vertical equity, horizontal equity, and equity in relation to benefits received from the tax. *Vertical* equity refers to whether the tax is based on the ability to pay. *Horizontal* equity refers to levying the same tax rate on all persons within the same taxable class. For example, if identical houses on the same block have different property taxes, that violates horizontal equity. Equity *in relation to benefits received* refers to whether the value of benefits a person receives from paying a tax equals the amount of the tax paid.

TABLE 12.2

Criteria for Evaluating Taxes

Criterion	Property Tax	Income Tax	Sales Tax
Equity	Most regressive (according to some critics), but regressivity can be reduced	Most progressive (depending on rate structure)	Regressive, but regressivity can be reduced
Yield and certainty	High yield; the most certain	Yield depends on other variables; least certain	High yield; less certain than property tax, more certain than income tax
Administrative convenience	Most costly	Least costly	Less costly than property tax; possibly more costly than income tax
Economic effect	Associated with no incentives for improving property; fiscal disparities	Useful for controlling economy's growth	Incentive for saving and investing
Appropriateness	Best for local	Best for federal and state	Best for state, acceptable for local level

the consequences the tax can have on the economy that surrounds the government levying it. Finally, *appropriateness* refers to the level of government that gets the best use out of the tax.

Property Tax　A person's **property tax** is based on two factors—the assessed value of the property subject to the tax and the tax rate, which local governments levy on property. The assessed value is determined periodically by an assessor. Your house, for example, may have a taxable assessed value of $100,000. If the tax rate is 2 percent, then your property tax will be $2,000 ($100,000 × 2% = $2,000). If your home's value and the tax rate each go up by only 10 percent this year, your total taxes will go up by 21 percent ($110,000 × 2.2% = $2,420). When property values rise dramatically, property taxes will rise dramatically, too, unless officials reduce the tax rate.

Property taxes receive their heaviest criticism on the criteria of equity, administrative convenience, and economic effect. The property tax is not dependably based on the ability to pay, although wealthier people tend to live in more valuable homes. You must pay that $2,420 next year whether you get a big salary increase or lose your job. Most states have taken steps to make the tax more equitable or to shift the tax burden off certain kinds of property. One device is the **circuit breaker**, which limits how much of your income can be taken in property taxes. If the state sets a 4 percent limit, then your property taxes should not exceed 4 percent of your income. If they do exceed that amount, the circuit breaker protects you by giving you a tax deduction or credit to reimburse you for part of the excess amount.

In addition to the circuit breaker, most states have *homestead* and *senior citizens' credits.* Your taxes will be lower for a building that you make your home than for a building in which you operate a business. Many states have adopted a special credit for senior citizens that freezes their property taxes once they retire.

States also grant *exemptions* to certain property, such as nonincome-producing church property or property used for charitable purposes. Finally, states shift the property tax burden by creating different property tax *classifications.* Farmland usually is classified in a lower bracket than land in a city.

Although the property tax has historically been considered regressive, circuit breakers, credits, and exemptions have made the property tax much more equitable than it was 20 or 30 years ago. Economists and tax experts are consequently beginning to view the property tax more positively.[8]

The other criteria on which property taxes are heavily criticized are administrative convenience and economic effect. The need to hire assessors, create boards of appeal, process complaints about assessments, and make fair assessments of different kinds of property can make the property tax difficult and costly to administer. Moreover, politically powerful individuals and groups may pressure assessors into giving them unrealistically low assessments. And, as will be shown in the special case of schools, property taxes breed fiscal disparities between communities. The same $100,000 house might have taxes that are twice as high in one municipality as in a neighboring community. Moreover, a community with many valuable properties can produce substantial revenues through property taxes, but a community with few valuable properties will yield low revenues.

Property taxes score reasonably high on the criteria of yield and certainty. This is because the property tax is among the most certain of all the taxes; it will normally produce about as much revenue as the assessor projects. Property taxes not paid this year must be paid next year, and if you go too long without paying them, the government will sell your property for the amount of back taxes you owe. During periods of declining property values, however, the property tax is somewhat less dependable. The major slump in home values beginning in 2007–2008 produced a major drop in local property tax revenues in many parts of the country.[9]

During the Great Depression, many local governments seized property for back taxes, only to find that no one would buy it. Large businesses may pressure local officials for formal or informal property tax breaks that erode revenues. Finally, the property tax appears to be most appropriate at the local level. It provides a fairly stable source of revenue for funding basic local services such as schools, police protection, street maintenance, and building code enforcement, among others.[10] When states relied more heavily on property taxes, they often had problems with local officials (who helped administer the tax) giving informal tax breaks to people in their communities.

Income Taxes The vast majority of states levy personal income taxes. State income taxes score highest on the criteria of equity, administrative convenience, and economic effect. They have the greatest chance of taxing people on their ability to pay, especially in states that use a graduated income tax. In these states, the rate goes from a very small percentage for low-income residents to higher percentages for people with higher incomes. The income tax is easy to administer since much of it is collected automatically by employers. However, some administrative costs are incurred in auditing returns and in trying to discourage tax evasion. Income taxes have some value as tools for influencing the overall economy since tax rates can be manipulated to stimulate or retard growth rates. However, this works much more successfully at the federal level than at the state level because the economic effects of individual state actions may be diluted or offset by the actions of other states. Raising income taxes can also anger the voters.

On the questionable side, the yield from state income taxes is unstable because it depends on several factors—the rate of inflation, the rate of unemployment, income levels, the tax rates, and the amount of tax money lost because of credits, deductions, exemptions, and loopholes. The income tax is, therefore, one of the least certain of all taxes. During years of economic boom, income tax revenues often exceed estimates, giving the state treasuries a surplus. When the economy experiences a recession, however, income tax revenues lag behind forecasts, as occurred in 2002–2003 and again since 2007.[11]

The income tax works best at the federal and state levels. Some large cities (New York City, for example) impose a small income tax on people who live or work there. However, cities that impose an income tax risk driving residents and employers out of the city and into suburbs that do not levy such a tax.

In addition to the personal income tax, 47 states levy a corporate income tax, a business activities tax, or a franchise tax, which in many respects is even more controversial than the personal income tax. Critics complain that the corporate tax can create an unfriendly environment for business and that it is simply a personal tax in disguise since corporations may be able to pass the tax on to their customers or their employees. Supporters of the corporate income tax argue that corporations should pay their share of the cost of government just as citizens do. Corporations certainly use many types of governmental services.

Over the years, corporate income taxes have declined as a percentage of state revenue. Moreover, corporations pay only about half of the apparent state corporate income tax liability. This partly reflects all sorts of tax breaks granted to various companies to attract them to the state or keep them in the state. Companies also use various accounting techniques to shift their apparent income to states with low or no corporate income taxes.[12]

Sales Tax　Forty-five states levy a general **sales tax.*** According to critics, sales taxes score negatively on the criterion of equity. Mississippi, for example, has a 7 percent sales tax on all retail items except prescription drugs. This tax is traditionally considered regressive because it usually takes a higher percentage of the incomes of poor people than it takes from rich people. Poor people generally spend all of their incomes, but wealthy people typically save some money. Savings and investments pay no sales taxes. In addition, wealthier people are likely to spend significant sums on professional services and purchases from out-of-state businesses. Both types of spending are likely to escape paying sales taxes.

Some states seek to reduce the regressivity of sales taxes by granting tax credits and exempting certain categories of purchases, such as food, clothing, medicines, and textbooks. Since the poor spend a greater percentage of their income on food and clothing than do the wealthy, these exemptions help shift the tax burden from the poor onto the higher-income groups in those states. Some analysts, however, argue that progressivity could be best achieved if no exemptions were granted and a circuit-breaker income tax credit (for sales taxes paid) were given to poor people, instead. Getting that provision adopted has not proven easy, however.

On all the other criteria, the sales tax scores high. It generally produces a high yield, although this yield is reduced if the state grants many exemptions in order to make it less

---

*The states without a general sales tax are Alaska, Delaware, Montana, New Hampshire, and Oregon.

regressive. Sales tax revenues are less certain than those from the property tax, but more certain than those from the income tax. Sales tax revenues fluctuate with changes in the national economy, but not nearly as much as revenue from income taxes. The sales tax is easy and inexpensive to administer since it is collected by retailers who send their tax receipts to the state tax office.

One administrative difficulty, however, involves the taxation of interstate sales. Shoppers may avoid sales taxes by shopping from mail-order companies in other states. In many cases, those companies will not charge sales taxes even though they and the customers are located in states with sales taxes. While some states have adopted agreements with other states to correct this situation, many have not. The growing importance of Internet commerce has increased concern in many state capitals over interstate sales escaping sales taxation. By 2002, the sales tax revenue that would have been generated by applying state and local sales taxes to Internet commerce was estimated at $18.9 billion and projected to grow dramatically in coming years.

Local merchants who must collect sales taxes complain that they are placed at an unfair disadvantage, but many businesses that sell to out-of-state customers resist efforts to tax their operations. Even so, in the slumping economy of 2002–2003, state and local officials continued to explore ways to collect sales taxes on Internet sales.[13] Economic improvements since then[14] reduced the urgency of those explorations, but the recession that began in 2007 raised the issue again. When several states proposed requiring Amazon to collect sales taxes on sales in their states, Amazon severed its ties with businesses in those states and refused to pay. Eventually, California faced up to Amazon in spite of numerous threats, and Amazon eventually agreed to collect sales taxes on California sales and to pay them to the state government.[15] The agreement between Amazon and California may serve as a model for other agreements.

In theory, sales taxes encourage people to save and invest since the tax bears on consumption. However, many of the lower-income families that pay considerable portions of the sales taxes cannot afford to save very much in any case.

Finally, sales taxes seem to work well at the state level. Many local governments do impose local sales taxes. However, if these are too high or too inconvenient, shoppers go to neighboring communities to shop. Politically speaking, sales taxes also allow the shifting of some of the tax burden to people from other states. In areas that are popular vacation destinations, a considerable amount of sales tax revenue is generated by tourists from other states and even other countries.

Other Tax Sources In addition to the three major taxes, state and local governments rely on a number of others (see Figure 12.2). Major among these other taxes are motor fuel taxes, alcohol and tobacco taxes, and severance taxes. About three-fifths of the states levy **severance taxes** on industries that extract (that is, "sever") natural resources such as timber, ore, coal, and natural gas. But few states rely on severance taxes for more than 10 percent of their tax revenue.

The beauty of severance taxes is that they *export* much of the tax burden to people in other states who buy the natural resources. One state's beauty, however, is another state's beast, as Louisiana and Montana discovered when other states protested bitterly in the late 1970s when Louisiana raised its severance tax on natural gas and Montana raised its tax on coal. The U.S. Supreme Court struck down Louisiana's tax because it exempted Louisianans.[16] The Court upheld Montana's 30 percent coal tax, however, because the tax had to be paid by Montanans as well as by others.[17] In these two cases, the Court seemed to be saying that it would not interfere with a state's severance taxes unless that state was blatantly using such taxes to export the tax burden to other states; this is just what Louisiana was doing when it exempted its residents from its new gas tax.

Tax-Base Breadth   One final concern today is **tax-base breadth**. If too many people are exempted from the tax base (through property tax classification, income tax loopholes, sales tax exemptions, or untaxed so-called underground transactions such as getting paid in cash to paint your neighbor's house and paying no income tax on that income), then the tax base is narrow, which has a number of consequences. Principally, states relying on a narrow tax base tend to have a much more volatile flow of tax revenue than do states with a broader tax base, and states with narrow tax bases also need to have higher tax rates on the smaller number of people and businesses that pay the taxes. The traditional reason for narrowing the tax base has been to achieve progressivity or some other *social good* (see below), such as attracting a major company to the state by granting the company a tax break. But some analysts assert that progressivity could be obtained just as easily by broadening the tax base and providing income tax credits for low-income people. Whether proposals of that sort could pass in some of the state legislatures is far from certain.

Entrepreneurial Sources of Revenue

In addition to taxes, state and local governments operate enterprises that generate revenue. At the state level, about one-fourth of all own-source revenue (that is, revenue raised by the state itself rather than from federal grants) is typically raised from insurance and quasi-insurance programs. These include workers' compensation, unemployment compensation, and public employee retirement funds. The monies contributed to these programs by workers and employers are kept in large trust funds run by the state. The interest from these funds is earmarked for the benefits of the programs.

States collect another one-fifth of their own-source revenue from state-owned liquor stores and from charges for college tuition, highway tolls, public hospitals and health facilities, professional licenses, and many other things. As some of you know, tuition and fees at many universities have risen dramatically in recent years, and so have fees of many other types of services. However, some groups are beginning to complain that too many fees have been raised too often; there may be greater opposition to fee hikes in coming years.[18]

At the local level, the major entrepreneurial sources of revenue are public utilities (such as transit systems, power plants, and water supply companies). Local governments also earn substantial revenues from fees for sewer service, garbage collection, parking facilities, building permits, franchises, and the use of publicly owned facilities, such as golf courses, tennis courts, and swimming pools. Municipalities also have licensing powers and can tax commercial establishments such as movie theaters, bars, restaurants, sports arenas, and hotels. In the tight budget environment that has prevailed since the early 1970s, many communities have doubled and tripled the fees and charges they collect in order to cover revenue shortfalls.

If local governments can raise money by charging fees and running profit-making enterprises, and if state governments can run lotteries at a profit (see the Highlight feature on pp. 323–324), we might ask why they do not run more and more enterprises until their profits are such that they do not need to levy taxes at all. The answer seems to be that in our society, governments traditionally run only certain kinds of enterprises. Economists distinguish between private goods to be distributed by private companies and public goods to be distributed by governments. One of three criteria can be used to make this distinction.[19]

First, some public goods are **social goods**, which are goods (such as clean air) that nobody can be excluded from and that cannot be divided up among the users so that what is used by one person is unavailable to be used by another. In contrast, a dinner at your favorite restaurant is a private good. People unwilling to pay the price are excluded, and the portion consumed by one customer is no longer available to be used by another. Thus, social goods are nonexclusive and nondivisible, in contrast to private goods, which are exclusive and divisible.

A second criterion for distinguishing public from private goods is that of merit. **Merit goods** are those (such as minimal public health care and free public education) that society judges all citizens should have, whether or not they can personally afford them. People can and do disagree regarding which goods should be considered merit goods.

Finally, the criterion of **externalities** can be used to distinguish between public and private goods. Private economic activities sometimes produce certain external costs that are not reflected in the purchase price of the good and affect people who are not parties to the transaction. The construction of a major shopping center, for instance, requires police protection, streets, and storm sewers, costs that may not be borne by the shopping center owners or passed on to the consumers. Although the costs are external to the shopping center, they are nevertheless real and somebody must pay them. They are paid for by local governments in the area (and their taxpayers), unless a policy is adopted to require the shopping center and its customers to pay for the costs they are generating.

Following these criteria, economists argue that governments normally engage in entrepreneurial activity only when that activity involves a good that cannot or will not be produced by

HIGHLIGHT

Legalized Gambling as a Way to Reduce Direct Taxes on Citizens

With the fiscal stress of recent years, it is not surprising that states have increasingly looked to legalized gambling as a revenue source. Nevada is the most extensive user of gambling taxes, collecting almost 20 percent of its tax revenue from them. Only two states prohibit all gambling.

Lotteries have become the most widespread form of state-sanctioned gambling since New Hampshire started its lottery in the 1960s. Thirty-seven states currently have lotteries, which raise over $23 billion per year in state revenues, about 3 percent of all state revenues.

Casino gambling has also been spreading, with casinos of one type or another existing in 20 states. Whereas the main argument for lotteries is tax revenue, casino gambling is usually promoted as a tool for economic development and job growth. This was the case in New Jersey, where casino gambling was sold in the mid-1970s as a surefire means to revitalize the decaying Atlantic City. In fact, Atlantic

City has gained very little from the casinos despite the creation of 42,000 jobs there. Most of the jobs went to suburban commuters, and Atlantic City itself has continued to deteriorate. Property values escalated along the beach where the casinos are located, but the rest of the city shared very little in the growth of casino gambling.

In contrast to Atlantic City, where casino gambling did little for overall economic development, there is reason to think that gains from Indian reservation casinos may be more widespread. Under federal statutes, if state law permits any form of gambling within its borders, then it cannot prohibit Indian tribes from opening gambling houses on their reservations. By 2007, these activities were bringing $26 billion in gross revenue into the impoverished reservations. This provided jobs for many Indians, significant cash distributions to tribal members, and some investment in other development enterprises on the reservations.

(continues)

(continued)

In addition to lotteries and casinos, many other forms of gambling can also raise state revenue. Bingo is permitted in all but five states. The next most popular form of legalized gambling is horse racing. Other forms of legalized betting include numbers games, sports betting, off-track betting, dog racing, and jai alai. If all states were to adopt all these forms of gambling, then—some people project—state gambling revenues would rise sharply. To keep this projection in perspective, however, we must also recognize the possibility that expansion to all types of legalized gambling could simply increase the competition between the types for existing customers, in which case the take would fall short of projections.

By the mid-1990s, a backlash was starting to emerge against the rapid spread of gambling. With huge amounts of money at stake, gambling had become a very big business. Lobbyists were beginning to show up in state capitols in efforts to legalize further gambling opportunities. And political action committees with gambling ties made large contributions to campaigns for gambling referendums. The potential for corruption between the gaming industry and state licensing officials bothers an increasing number of critics, who noted that gambling issues played a major role in the national scandal involving lobbyist Jack Abramoff and his political friends. In addition, slumping lottery

profits in a number of states since 2007 have added to the other financial headaches facing state officials.

Nonetheless, many states continue to explore various ways to increase gambling revenues, from legalizing casinos and taxing them, having state lotteries, and racetracks with gambling. Moreover, a number of states are considering sports betting as another way to boost gambling revenues. Although gambling revenues form only a small share of total state revenues, when funds are difficult to come by, even small sums can attract interest. ■

Sources: George Sternlieb and James Hughes, *Atlantic City Gamble* (Cambridge, MA: Harvard University Press, 1984); Charles Clotfelter and Philip Cook, *Selling Hope* (Cambridge, MA: Harvard University Press, 1989); Henry C. Cashen and John C. Dill, "The Real Truth About Indian Gaming and the States," *State Legislatures* 18, no. 3 (March 1992): 23–26; Pam Greenberg, "Not Quite the Pot of Gold," *State Legislatures* 18, no. 12 (December 1992): 24–27; Steven D. Gold, "If It's Not a Miracle, It's a Mirage," *State Legislatures* 20, no. 2 (February 1994): 30; *The New York Times*, December 18, 1995, p. A-8; *Washington Post National Weekly*, March 11–18, 1996, p. 6; Ellen Perlman, "Losing Numbers," *Governing* 14, no. 12 (September 2001): 46–47; William Eadington, "The Impact of Permitted Gambling on States," in *Book of the States*, vol. 41 (Lexington, KY: Council of State Governments, 2009), pp. 405–409; Pamela Prah, "States Ponder Sports Betting as Source of New Revenue," *Stateline*, November 3, 2011 (Web edition); Pamela Prah, "States' Casino Tax Revenue Tops $7 Billion," *Stateline*, May 5, 2011 (Web edition).

private entrepreneurs at a level that the public judges to be adequate. The goods that cannot be produced profitably by private entrepreneurs (at levels acceptable for the public) are the social goods, merit goods, and goods that generate externalities.

Intergovernmental Aid as a Revenue Source

As was shown in Figure 12.2, intergovernmental aid is the single largest source of revenue for both state and local governments. In recent years, the federal government has provided from $350 billion to $500 billion in aid to the states and localities. As a percentage of state and local revenue, federal aid peaked in 1978, declined during the 1980s, rose gradually until 2004, and then declined slightly.[20]

Federal Aid Federal aid has a number of important financial consequences. First, it was one of the major reasons for the rapid increase in state and local expenditures over the years.[21]

Second, much federal aid has been channeled into human services programs, and this has encouraged state and local budgets to provide more money for programs such as Medicaid, TANF,* and other social services. Third, since much federal aid is deliberately used to get state and local governments to carry out federal objectives, federal aid has significant influence on how state and local governments will spend their money (although probably not as much as many federal officials would like).[22] Finally, when federal aid was cut back during the 1980s, many states and communities found themselves severely strapped to meet the obligations they had taken on. The economic growth of the 1990s encouraged states to expand a number of programs, but an erratic economy after that produced revenue shortfalls all over the country—especially with the recession that began in 2007.[23] Some state officials and some members of Congress have been discussing a possible expansion in federal aid, and much of the economic stimulus package adopted in 2009 was devoted to aiding state and local government.

State Aid to Local Governments   State aid to local governments follows the same pattern as federal aid. Some aids are **categorical aids**. Others are similar to revenue sharing in that they simply support local budgets and give local governments great discretion in spending the money. In the education sector, for example, states finance public schools primarily through categorical aids and foundation aids. The foundation aids are based on a per-pupil amount that the state contributes to each local school district. In contrast to the overall budget support provided by the foundation aids, educational categorical aids are aimed at specific program objectives, such as transportation, aiding children with learning disabilities, and providing special assistance to children from low-income backgrounds.

The biggest complaint local officials have about state aid is probably over mandating. Many state programs are *mandated* (required) by state law, and some have matching-fund provisions. This pressures local governments to adopt the program, but does not provide all the finances for it. The local governments thus must either raise local taxes or, if that is impossible, cut other programs to pay for the state-mandated programs. Because local governments may not cut programs mandated by the federal or state government (at least, not officially), mandating has contributed to the declining autonomy of local governments discussed in Chapter 3.

Local officials also complain that when the economy is performing poorly, state officials facing revenue shortages will sometimes freeze or even cut state aid to local governments. When state revenues slump, however, local revenues are also likely to fall. Reductions in state aid will make local financial problems even worse.[24]

Borrowing as a Revenue Source

If state and local governments had to finance every operation on a pay-as-you-go basis, it would become impossible for them to function in today's world. They need to borrow money to build school buildings, universities, and prisons or to install sewer systems or water

---

*Medicaid is a program that provides health care to poor people. TANF (Temporary Assistance to Needy Families) provides cash payments for the care of dependent children in low-income, mostly single-parent families. Temporary Assistance to Needy Families replaced Aid to Families with Dependent Children (AFDC) under legislation adopted in 1996.

purification projects. All these large construction projects are referred to as **capital expenditures** and are often financed by long-term debt, just as many families use a mortgage to finance the purchase of a house. State and local governments also borrow money on a short-term basis to meet immediate payroll or other obligations when they have not yet received the taxes levied to pay for those obligations. This short-term borrowing is accomplished through **revenue-anticipation notes** or **tax-anticipation notes**.

Long-term borrowing is accomplished by selling bonds. The person who buys a $5,000 municipal bond actually lends the city $5,000. The city pledges to repay the $5,000 and to pay a fixed amount of interest.

A **general-obligation bond** puts the full faith and credit of the issuing agency behind it. The issuing government guarantees that it will use its taxing powers to pay off the bonds. These bonds become, in effect, a charge against all the taxpayers in the jurisdiction. For this reason, general-obligation bonds often require approval by a voter referendum. Because these bonds are backed by the taxing power of the government, they are very safe investments; and because their interest is exempt from federal income taxes, they usually pay fairly low interest rates.

Distinct from general-obligation bonds are **revenue bonds**. These are not guaranteed by the taxing power of the issuing government. Rather, they are paid off from the revenue earned by the facility or project for which they were issued. Toll bridges, toll roads, convention centers, industrial parks, and municipally owned athletic stadiums are common examples of projects financed by revenue bonds. Interest on these bonds is usually exempt from federal income taxes. Since the bonds are slightly riskier than general-obligation bonds, they carry a slightly higher interest rate. A special type of revenue bond is the **Industrial Development Revenue Bond (IDRB)**, through which a city uses its tax-exempt status to raise money for commercial development projects (although federal law now limits the amount of tax-free funds that can be raised in that manner). IDRBs will be discussed more fully in Chapter 17.

Most state and local government borrowing is now done through nonguaranteed bonds, which account for most of the dramatic growth in state and local government borrowing since World War II. A considerable number of states and localities have borrowed funds as one way to cope with the recession that began in 2007. According to one recent estimate, the total debt of state governments, including pension obligations that are not yet funded, exceeds four trillion dollars.[25]

CONFLICTS AND ISSUES IN STATE AND LOCAL FINANCE

As should be apparent from the discussion up to this point, state and local finances are highly politicized. If there is a major shift in the expenditure or revenue patterns of these governments, some people win and others lose. These conflicts are probably most apparent in four specific issues facing state and local finance in recent years: (1) the special problem of property taxes and the public schools, (2) the regressivity or progressivity of the tax burden, (3) attempts to reform state tax structures, and (4) the management of state investments, especially pension funds.

The Special Problem of Property Taxes and Public Schools

The biggest portion of most people's property tax bill supports public schools. The amount of money the typical local school district can raise is based directly on the assessed valuation of property within its boundaries. Assume that school districts A and B have the same number of pupils. School district A has a large shopping center, a number of commercial and manufacturing establishments, and many expensive homes. District B, in contrast, has no large shopping center or commercial or manufacturing establishments. It has only small supermarkets and gas stations, and it has few expensive homes. School district B has a much lower total assessed valuation than does district A. To provide the same level of educational services as those provided in district A, the residents in district B will have to pay a much higher property tax rate. If the district B homeowners are less affluent than the district A homeowners, which is likely since they live in cheaper houses, they may be unable to pay higher taxes. In that case, their children will get fewer educational services. This will mean larger classes, older textbooks and buildings, fewer extracurricular activities, fewer course offerings, and less access to computers and the Internet in district B compared with district A. The term given to this situation is **fiscal disparities**.

Critics look to the states to alleviate fiscal disparities. One obvious way to do this is to shift some of the financial burden from the local property tax to the state income and sales taxes. By financing schools more heavily from the state level, the burden is borne throughout the state, and the fiscal disparities can be evened out. In recent years, the states have assumed increasing shares of the cost of public education. In addition, states can improve equality in education funding by targeting aid to poorer districts rather than giving all districts approximately the same amount of money per student.[26]

Reformers who have been unhappy with unequal education funding have sometimes turned to the courts if governors and legislatures refused to act. California provided a high-profile case in point. In 1971, its supreme court, in *Serrano v. Priest*, ruled that financing public education through local property taxes violated both the California and the federal constitutions. Despite this decision, the California legislature moved slowly to equalize funding.

Another important conflict over fiscal disparities took place in Texas, where people challenged fiscal disparities in federal court. However, in *Rodriguez v. San Antonio School District*, the U.S. Supreme Court decided that the U.S. Constitution did not preclude property taxes as the method for funding local schools. The Supreme Court did agree that fiscal disparities in public education should be eliminated, but felt that this action should come from the states. In 1989, the Texas Supreme Court ruled that the fiscal disparities among school districts violated the state constitution and ordered the Texas legislature to find an equitable system of finance.[27] A tax sharing plan was adopted in 1993.

One of the most dramatic reforms of school financing in recent years occurred in Michigan, which totally revamped its school funding system. In 1993, the Michigan legislature scrapped its traditional use of property taxes to fund the public schools, thus giving homeowners a huge property tax reduction. To compensate for this multibillion-dollar loss of revenue, the legislature called a referendum for a constitutional amendment that forced voters to choose between two options. One would replace the lost property tax revenue by boosting the state income tax from 4.6 to 6 percent, and the other would make a comparable increase in the state sales tax from 4 to 6 percent. In 1994, the voters resoundingly voted for the sales tax option and thus made Michigan the only state to move from heavy reliance on property taxes in funding schools to the total elimination of property taxes in the funding system. Since the mid-1960s, there have been a considerable number of lawsuits over education funding. A number of those suits led the courts to strike down various funding systems. In addition, some states have revamped their systems of education funding because of concerns about possible lawsuits.[28]

Shifting the Tax Burden

The hottest tax controversy, not surprisingly, is over the distribution of the tax burden. How heavy will it be, and who will bear the brunt of it? Fairness is, of course, a matter of personal values, and tax burdens apparently paid by one person may sometimes be shifted to someone else, as when a landlord facing a property tax increase on an apartment building raises people's rent to cover the added expense.

A recent effort to assess the fairness of state tax systems considered a number of factors, including regressivity, the use of loopholes that may produce different tax burdens for people or businesses that are similar to one another, and the distribution of those loopholes. The study concluded that Hawaii's tax system was the most fair; the least fair tax systems were mainly found in the South (Alabama, Florida, Tennessee, and Texas) but also in Illinois and Nevada. In the average state, the tax burden of the poor is higher than the tax burden of the wealthy.[29]

The most direct way to shift the tax burden in a progressive manner is to adopt a graduated income tax. But imposing or even increasing the income tax often draws strong opposition from upper-middle-income earners, as the case of New Jersey's 1990 income tax increase. These taxpayers get hit the hardest by graduated income taxes, and they also tend to be the most active and influential participants in state politics. Even when graduated income taxes are adopted, it is difficult to keep their graduations meaningful. Through a process called **bracket creep**, inflation pushes people into higher tax brackets, so that eventually middle-income earners pay the same rate as high-income earners. To avoid this, some states adopted **indexation** of their income taxes so that tax brackets go up to match inflation.

In no small measure, the **tax or expenditure limitation (TEL) movements** that have emerged in the last 35 years have been based, in part, on a conflict between the haves and the have nots.[30] Combined with the federal grant-in-aid reductions of the early Reagan years, the TELs sought to shift the tax burden from upper-income and upper-middle-income people to lower-middle-income and lower-income people. They sought to do this by putting a lid on government expenditures for social welfare purposes, increasing reliance on user fees for public services, and reducing the ability of states to export their tax burdens to the federal treasury through the use of grants-in-aid.

Looking back on those events, however, it appears that the revolt of the haves against the have nots was only partially successful. Although reliance on federal aid dropped markedly (but only temporarily), so did reliance on regressive property taxes. And this was accompanied by an increased reliance on the more progressive personal income tax as well as on severance taxes.[31] Also, federal aid to states and localities eventually began to grow again.

State Tax Reform

The last 35 years have witnessed considerable turmoil in state and local tax systems due to the tax limitation movements, the recession of 1980–1982 and the milder recession of 1990–1991, the slumping economy of 2002–2003, the recession that began in 2007, shifting federal aid, significant tax changes at the federal level, and interstate competition to reduce taxes in order to create a more attractive business climate. Moreover, the growth of Internet commerce has increased worries that many purchases avoid paying state sales taxes. Many states and localities raised taxes to make up for revenue shortfalls caused by the recessions of 1980 to 1982 and the federal grant-in-aid cutbacks. Then, as the economy rebounded in the mid-1980s, most states reduced taxes. Throwing another ingredient into the pot, Congress in 1986 dramatically cut the federal income tax rates, eliminated the federal deductibility of state sales taxes, and sharply restricted the use of tax-favored economic-development tools. These actions by Congress forced the states once again to reform their tax structures anew.

These reforms were dominated by two major concerns: (1) reducing reliance on the personal income tax and (2) broadening the tax base.[32] States wanted to reduce reliance on the personal income tax because it made revenue collection vulnerable to economic slowdowns. And by broadening the tax base, tax reformers meant to eliminate a number of tax exemptions and deductions that had been built into state tax structures in order to ease the tax burden on certain groups of people and make revenue flows more stable.

After years of wrangling, considerable discussion of the "taxpayers' revolt," and adoption of various reforms to make raising taxes more difficult, a surprising result emerged. In 1970, state and local government revenues amounted to $11.30 per $100 of personal income. By 2007, after TELs, fiscal restraint, initiatives, and referendums, that figure stood at $21.90. per $100 of personal income.[33]

How could the TELs, the federal cutbacks, the fiscal restraint, and the voter initiatives against government growth over such a long period have had so little effect? Scholars have spent considerable energy studying this question, and two answers seem to predominate. First, despite citizen disapproval of government growth in the abstract, virtually every major public service has citizen groups that want to protect it and see it grow. In this kind of environment, the mark of a successful politician is to preserve the service quite openly, but to hide the tax increases necessary to pay for it. That strategy is particularly easy because the public in a number of states has used the initiative process to require higher spending for some programs. When that occurred, officials could emphasize that they were trying to fulfill the voters' demands.

Second, politicians are able to raise more revenues because the revenue structures are so diverse and so complicated that citizens cannot keep track of every move to escalate some revenues (user fees, for example) to make up for tax reductions in other areas (the property tax reductions of Proposition 13 in California, for example).[34] When all else fails, officials may create quasi-independent organizations with their own financial powers that are separate from the state budget or the budgets of existing local governments.

Management of Invested Funds, Including Pension Funds

For many years, state and local officials have invested funds on hand that were not needed for immediate use. These investments rarely attracted much public attention until recent years. Unfortunately, much of the increased attention is due to problems of one type or another.

One of the most spectacular problems occurred in Orange County, California, and produced the largest municipal bankruptcy in American history. For some time, Orange County managed an investment fund that included the county's surplus funds as well as the funds of a number of other local governments. Aggressive management of the fund, including some rather risky investments, had produced dramatic gains for the local governments who participated. However, when the investment market shifted in a way the fund manager did not expect, the fund lost $1.7 billion and eventually plunged Orange County into bankruptcy. Nor was Orange County alone; a number of other states and localities lost large sums at about the same time.[35]

More recently, the decline in the value of many high technology stocks and the wave of corporate scandals and financial losses, including firms such as Enron and Worldcom, have cost many state and local investment funds a great deal of money. The losses from Enron's collapse alone reached an estimated $1.5 billion. New York City's investment funds lost $9 billion when a number of its investments slumped in 2001. Nationwide, public pension funds lost an estimated $120 billion that year.[36] More recently, a number of communities in Tennessee invested considerable sums in risky investments. When the market did not perform as they expected, the 38 cities and counties faced considerable financial losses.[37]

Furious state officials have responded with investigations of corporate misdeeds, lawsuits, and efforts to establish new ground rules among investment fund managers, corporations in which funds are invested, and the companies that provide financial advice to those managers. Those new ground rules include having fund managers play a larger role in the governing of the corporations in which funds are invested, stricter conflict of interest guidelines for firms providing investment advice, and more complete disclosure of corporate financial operations. While not all business leaders are happy with those new ground rules, the huge sums of money in state and local investment accounts can make disregarding those ground rules a potentially expensive proposition.[38]

STATE-COMMUNITY FINANCE AND THE POLITICAL ECONOMY

The ability of states and communities to finance their public services is tightly interwoven with the overall economy within which they operate. Revenue raising is easiest, obviously, when the economy is booming, most people have jobs, and tax collection is relatively simple. Holding down expenditures is easier in low-inflation periods than in periods of high inflation because the cost of government purchases and payrolls will not escalate so rapidly. We will use the term *political economy* to refer to this reciprocal relationship between government and the economy.

The Impact of Economic Trends

Since 1990, national economic dynamics are both a plus and a minus for state and local fiscal systems. On the plus side has been the low inflation of recent years. On the minus side is the simple fact that economic growth has been erratic. The economy grew fairly slowly in the early 1990s, grew somewhat more rapidly in the late 1990s, slumped in 2002–2003, gradually rebounded, and then slumped again beginning in 2007. As a result, revenue growth has sometimes been slower than the rising demand for some services, such as health care.[39]

Regional Economic Dislocations

In addition to inconsistent economic growth nationwide, the national economy sometimes affects different regions of the country differently. In the 1970s, the industrial economies of the Northeast and Midwest were devastated by escalating energy prices and a rising tide of good-quality, cheaply priced, imported manufactured goods. During the same period, the Southwest prospered from the energy boom and, not being dependent on heavy manufacturing, was only marginally affected by foreign competition in manufactured products.

In the 1980s, these situations partially reversed. Energy-producing states of the Southwest, such as Texas and Oklahoma, were badly hit by the petroleum glut and the 50 percent drop in oil prices in 1986.[40] The Northeast, in the meantime, staged a vibrant recovery. The Midwest, still staggering from its industrial losses, fell into the worst agricultural depression in 50 years. By the mid-1990s, these patterns seemed staged for another reversal. The Northeast had gone through a deep recession, while Midwestern agriculture and manufacturing were booming. California, meanwhile, was badly hit by the end of the Cold War and resulting cutbacks in defense industries. The state lost an estimated 750,000 jobs between 1990 and 1992. This loss of jobs brought a sharp reduction in state tax collections, and a bitter conflict broke out in 1992 between the Republican governor and Democratic legislature on how to make up for this shortfall of state revenues. For two months, the state was unable to issue checks to pay its bills, and state workers received their pay in the form of warrants or IOUs. When the budget conflict was finally resolved, there were substantial cuts in welfare services and state aid to local government, combined with significant increases in college tuitions and fees for other public services.[41]

More recently, state and local officials have struggled to cope with the recession using a variety of methods, from drawing down financial reserve funds and borrowing money to raising additional revenues through higher fees and/or taxes and laying off employees. Some states and localities postponed paying some bills to comply with various legal and economic demands. Some state and local budgets assumed financial improvements (such as "cutting fat and waste") may not actually take place. Some states and localities have laid off personnel and/or declined to hire replacements for workers who leave. Unfortunately, the layoffs in turn have delayed the processing of financial assistance for the unemployed and for people with disabilities, as well as various other state and local services.[42]

The Impact of International Economic Forces

These domestic and regional economic trends are more closely tied to the international economy than they were in the past. Consider, for example, the economic fate of oil states and states based on heavy manufacturing. During the 1970s, state governments in the oil patch saw their revenues skyrocket as oil prices rose. Then in the mid-1980s, their revenues plummeted as oil prices dropped. In great measure, their revenues were driven not by their state economies but by the success or failure of OPEC (Organization of Petroleum Exporting Countries) in controlling the price of oil. And the governors of Oklahoma and Alaska recognized this fact in 1988 when they traveled to an OPEC meeting in Europe to urge that organization to stabilize oil production and prices.[43] The tax revenues of the industrial states were also affected by the exchange rate of the dollar. When the value of the dollar falls, as it does periodically, those states see their revenues increase, because American industrial production soars when the dollar falls. The cheaper dollar makes it easier to export American manufactured goods.

Federal Budget Pressures

Federal grants to states and local governments have increased substantially since the mid-1980s, although state and local officials have sometimes complained that the increases have not kept pace with rising program needs. The state and local revenue shortfalls triggered by the slumping economy during 2002–2003, coupled with the need to increase spending for homeland security programs and rising Medicaid and prison costs, left many state and local governments under severe financial pressure. The results were painful cuts in a number of programs, efforts to raise additional revenues without upsetting too many people, and some requests for additional federal assistance. The same things have occurred since 2007.

Because of the erratic performance of the U.S. economy since the 1970s, some experts have warned that officials should do more to prepare for future budgetary problems. Among other things, they should build up financial reserves (sometimes called "rainy-day funds") to help their state or community cope with the next major period of revenue shortfalls. In addition, officials should avoid going overboard during prosperous periods; a major increase in funding for highways (or other programs) or a major tax cut may seem appealing when the economy is doing very well, but may leave the state or local government in financial difficulty when the next recession occurs. Moreover, officials need accurate information regarding future costs of current programs and future revenues. If previous predictions have been inaccurate, officials need to determine why and take corrective action.[44]

Interstate and Interlocal Tax Competition

There is today intense competition among states and localities to maintain an attractive tax climate in order to attract high-income in-migrants and to foster business expansion. Many state and local leaders fear their areas will not attract new businesses or even keep existing businesses if their tax rates are much higher than those of neighboring areas. The bottom line is that states and especially localities feel powerful pressures to make tax concessions to large corporations and major athletic teams in order to keep them from moving away.[45] Whether these efforts actually succeed in stimulating economic development is a question we will address in Chapter 17.

SUMMARY

1. Officials and citizens confront many complex issues in financing state and local governments. What services should state and local governments offer? On what sources of revenue should these governments rely? How should the tax burden be distributed? How can needed tax relief best be implemented?

2. Since 1950, state and local government expenditures and employment have risen faster than the gross national product or federal government expenditures.

3. The major state government expenditures are for insurance trust benefits, education, welfare, highways, and aid to local governments. The major local government expenditures are for education, health, public safety, utilities, and environmental programs (natural resources, sewerage, solid waste management, and parks and recreation).

4. State governments get over half their revenues from federal aid, sales taxes, and income taxes. Local governments get about three-fourths of their revenues from state and federal aid, property taxes, and charges and fees.

5. Six criteria for evaluating taxes are equity, yield, certainty, administrative convenience, economic effect, and appropriateness.

6. In deciding what kinds of entrepreneurial activities are proper for governments, economists have presented the criteria of social goods, merit goods, and externalities.

7. In borrowing money, states and local governments rely on general obligation bonds and revenue (nonguaranteed) bonds, especially the latter.

8. Key problems for state and local finance in recent years include property taxes and public schools, shifting the tax burden, tax reform, the controversies surrounding state and local government investment activity, and the interplay between public fiscal policy and economic development.

STUDY QUESTIONS

1. Why have state and local revenues and spending increased so dramatically since the 1950s? What sources provide most state and local government revenue, and what programs account for most of the spending? How does your state revenue system compare with other states? What are the major differences between state and local revenue systems?

2. How do different state and local revenue sources perform according to the various criteria used to evaluate revenue sources?

3. What roles do intergovernmental grants and borrowing play in state and local government finance?

4. Why are many people concerned about unequal funding for education? Why has it produced so much conflict? What have been the major components of tax reforms in recent years?

KEY TERMS

Bracket creep The phenomenon of a person being boosted into a higher income tax bracket by inflation.

Capital expenditure Expenditure for buildings and other durable equipment.

Categorical aid A grant-in-aid for a specific purpose. Also called *categorical grant.*

Circuit breaker A device that limits the amount of a person's income that can be taken in property taxes.

Externalities Costs that are not borne directly by the buyers or sellers of a particular product; for example, cleanup costs of air pollution produced by automobiles are not included in the price of cars.

Fiscal disparities The situation in which neighboring governmental jurisdictions vary widely in their ability to raise revenue. One jurisdiction may have a substantial property tax base, whereas a neighboring one has a meager tax base.

General-obligation bond A government bond that is backed by the taxing authority of the issuing government.

Indexation The practice of adjusting income tax brackets to rise with the cost of living. Also refers to the practice of making benefit levels in certain programs adjustable for inflation.

Industrial Development Revenue Bond (IDRB) A revenue bond issued by a government to enable a particular company or a collection of companies to raise funds to develop a site by selling bonds with the tax and interest rate advantages of government bonds.

Merit goods Goods that society judges all citizens should have as a matter of right.

Progressive tax A tax that takes a higher percentage of the income of upper-income people than it does of lower-income people.

Property tax A tax levied on real estate.

Proportional tax A tax that takes the same percentage of each person's income, regardless of whether the income is high, medium, or low.

Regressive tax A tax that takes a higher percentage of the income of lower-income people than it does of upper-income people.

Revenue-anticipation note A short-term note a government uses to borrow money to make payments that will come due before a next revenue payment comes in. The note is paid off from the proceeds of the next revenue payment.

Revenue bond A public bond that is paid off from revenue earned by the facility that was built with the bond's proceeds.

Sales tax A tax levied on retail sales.

Severance tax A tax levied on natural resources extracted from the earth.

Social goods Goods whose benefits are nondivisible and nonexclusive. Their enjoyment by one person does not prevent their enjoyment by others, and if the good is made available, people have the chance to enjoy it without regard to whether they have paid for it. Clean air is a social good.

Tax-anticipation note A short-term note a government uses to borrow money to make payments that will come due before a next tax payment comes in.

The note is paid off from the proceeds of the next tax payment.

Tax-base breadth The broadness or narrowness of the base on which a tax is levied.

Tax burden The total amount of taxes paid as a percentage of a person's income.

Tax or expenditure limitation (TEL) movement The movement, especially strong in the late 1970s and early 1980s, to put legal or constitutional limits on the amount of money a government can raise or the amount of money it can spend.

THE INTERNET CONNECTION

The U.S. Bureau of the Census gathers information on many aspects of state and local government finance (along with a wide variety of other topics). On their Web site, **www.census.gov**, you can find out about the major revenue sources of your home state and its local governments, and their spending decisions. How do they compare with other states? How much information can you find on your state government Web sites regarding the state financial activities? How much does the information tell you about what your state government does?

NOTES

1. Penelope Lemov, "Find Me the Money," *Governing* (May 2009): 55–56; *Statistical Abstract 2011–2012* (New York: Skyhorse, 2011), pp. 292–293.
2. Derived from United States Bureau of the Census, *Statistical Abstract of the United States, 2001* (Washington, DC: U.S. Government Printing Office, 2001), p. 417.
3. Advisory Commission on Intergovernmental Relations, *Significant Features of Fiscal Federalism: 1994, Vol. 2 Revenues and Expenditures* (Washington, DC: Advisory Commission on Intergovernmental Relations, 1994), M 190-II, p. 11. James C. Garand tested five possible explanations for government growth in the 50 states. In 38 of the 50, he found that the extent of government employment had a larger impact on government spending than the other four variables (party control, intergovernmental aid, reliance on corporate taxes and withholding taxes, and Wagner's law that traces government growth to industrialization). The second most important variable was the extent of intergovernmental aid. See Garand's "Explaining Government Growth in the U.S. States," *American Political Science Review* 82, no. 3 (September 1988): 837–849.
4. William Flanigan and Nancy Zingale, *Political Behavior of the American Electorate*, 10th ed. (Washington, DC: CQ Press, 2002), p. 123.
5. David Broder, "Voters' Mixed Messages," *Washington Post National Weekly Edition* 16, no. 49 (October 4, 1999): 4; Everett Ladd, *Where Have All the Voters Gone?*, 2nd ed. (New York: Norton, 1982), pp. 30–34; William Flanigan and Nancy Zingale, *Political Behavior of the American Electorate*, 10th ed. (Washington, DC: Congressional Quarterly, 2002), pp. 120–124; Robert Erikson and Kent Tedin, *American Public Opinion*, 6th ed. (New York: Longman, 2001), pp. 86–87.
6. Kevin Sack and Katie Zezima, "Growing Need for Medicaid Strains States," *New York Times*, January 22, 2009 (Web edition).
7. See Advisory Commission on Intergovernmental Relations, *Changing Public Attitudes on Government and Taxes: A Commission Survey*, Report S-23 (Washington, DC: U.S. Government Printing Office, 1994), p. 1.
8. See Henry J. Aaron, *Who Pays the Property Tax? A New View* (Washington, DC: Brookings Institution, 1975); James A. Maxwell and J. Richard Aronson, *Financing State and Local Government*, 3rd ed. (Washington, DC: Brookings Institution, 1977).

9. Amy Merrick, "Housing Slump Strains Budgets of States, Cities," *Wall Street Journal*, September 5, 2007, p. A1; Marisol Bello, "Cities Cut Back, Expecting Shortfalls," *USA Today*, December 2, 2008 (Web edition).

10. Ronald K. Snell, "The Tax the Public Loves to Hate," *State Legislatures* 17, no. 12 (December 1991).

11. Daniel Vock, "Sour Economy Limits States' Options in '08," *Stateline*, July 8, 2008 (Web edition); Pamela Prah, "Governors to Pare Back Agendas," *Stateline*, January 21, 2009 (Web edition).

12. Penelope Lemov, "Losing Out on Corporate Taxes," *Governing* (January 18, 2012) (Web edition).

13. See Penelope Lemov, "The Untaxables," *Governing* 15, no. 10 (July 2002): 36–37; Christopher Swope, "E-conomics Problem," *Governing* 13, no. 6 (March 2000): 20–23.

14. Don Boyd, "State Finances: Solid Recovery But Challenges Ahead," in *The Book of the States*, vol. 38 (Lexington, KY: Council of State Governments, 2006), pp. 333–334.

15. Josh Goodman, "Amazon Deal with California May Set Precedent for Online Tax Collection," *Stateline*, September 29, 2011 (Web edition).

16. *Maryland v. Louisiana*, 451 U.S. 725 (1981).

17. *Commonwealth Edison v. Montana*, 453 U.S. 609 (1981).

18. Maggie Clark, "A Backlash Against Rising State Fees," *Stateline*, October 11, 2011 (Web edition).

19. These arguments are taken from Richard Musgrave, *Fiscal Systems* (New Haven, CT: Yale University Press, 1969), Ch. 1.

20. *Statistical Abstract of the United States, 1984* (Washington, DC: U.S. Government Printing Office, 1984), p. 278; *Statistical Almanac of the United States 1995* (Washington, DC: U.S. Government Printing Office, 1995), p. 302; *Statistical Almanac of the United States 2001* (Washington, DC: U.S. Government Printing Office, 2001), p. 262; *Statistical Abstract of the United States 2008* (Washington, DC: U.S. Government Printing Office, 2008), p. 265.

21. Susan B. Hansen, "Extraction: The Politics of State Taxation," in Virginia Gray, Herbert Jacob, and Kenneth N. Vines, eds. *Politics in the American States: A Comparative Analysis*, 4th ed. (Boston: Little, Brown and Co., 1983), p. 433.

22. On the consequences of federal grants, see David C. Nice, *Federalism: The Politics of Intergovernmental Relations* (New York: St. Martin's Press, 1987), pp. 57–60.

23. See Penelope Lemov, "Deficit Deluge," *Governing* 15, no. 8 (May 2002): 20–25; T. R. Reid, "In the Pink, But Not Quite Rosy," *Washington Post National Weekly Edition*, May 17–23, 2004, p. 30; Daniel Vock, "Sour Economy."

24. Tony Romm, "Cities, States Wrangle Over Cuts to Local Aid," *Stateline*, August 26, 2009 (Web edition); Alan Greenblatt, "Enemies of the State," *Governing* 15, no. 9 (June 2002): 26–31.

25. Dennis Cauchon, "States and Cities Borrow Big," *USA Today*, May 4, 2009 (Web edition); Lisa Lambert, "Debts of States over $4 Trillion: Budget Group," *Reuters*, October 24, 2011 (Web edition).

26. School Finance: State Efforts to Reduce Funding Gaps Between Poor and Wealthy Districts (Washington, DC: General Accounting Office, 1997).

27. *Serrano v. Priest*, 5 Cal. 3d 584 (1971) *Rodriguez v. San Antonio School District*, 411 U.S. 59 (1973). On the 1989 Texas Supreme Court ruling, see *The New York Times*, October 3, 1989, p. 1A.

28. Kenneth Wong, "The Politics of Education," in Virginia Gray and Russell Hanson, eds. *Politics in the American States*, 9th ed. (Washington, DC: CQ Press, 2008), pp. 360–363; William Celis III, "Michigan Votes for Revolution in Financing Its Public Schools," *The New York Times*, March 17, 1994, p. A-1; "Centralizing Educational Responsibility in Michigan and Other States," *National Tax Journal* (September 1995): 417–428; Dennis Farney, "Insufficient Funds," *Governing* 18, no. 3 (December 2004): 26–29.

29. See Katherine Barrett, Richard Greene, Michele Mariani, and Anya Sostek, "The Way We Tax," *Governing* 16, no. 5 (February 2003): 20–97; see also, Kendra Hovey and Harold Hovey, *CQ's State Fact Finder 2003* (Washington, DC: CQ Press, 2003), p. 161.

30. Robert Kuttner, *Revolt of the Haves* (New York: Simon and Schuster, 1980).

31. David Lowery, "After the Tax Revolt: Some Positive If Unintended Consequences," *Social Science Quarterly* 67, no. 4 (December 1986): 736–766. Lowery made this discovery in comparing the mixtures of state and local revenue sources in 1976–1977 to those of 1981–1982.

32. Ronald K. Snell, "Our Outmoded Tax Systems," *State Legislatures* 20, no. 6 (August 1994): 17–22.

33. Steven D. Gold, "Tax Revenues Soar and Tumble," *State Legislatures* 15, no. 4 (May–June

1989): 30; *Statistical Abstract of the United State,* *2011–2012,* pp. 274, 286, 292.

34. David Nice, *Introduction to Public Budgeting* (New York: Wadsworth, 2002), ch. 11. For empirical tests of fiscal illusion theory, see David Lowery, "Electoral Strength and Revenue Structures in the American States: Searching for the Elusive Fiscal Illusions," *American Politics Quarterly* 15, no. 1 (January 1987): 5–46; and Elaine B. Sharp and David Elkins, "The Impact of Fiscal Limitations: A Tale of Seven Cities," *Public Administration Review* 47, no. 4 (September–October 1987): 385–392.

35. Philippe Jorion and Robert Roper, *Big Bets Gone Bad* (San Diego: Academic Press, 1995).

36. John Peterson, "Searching for Security," *Governing* 15, no. 9 (June 2002): 64–70; Jonathan Walters, "Pension Fund Follies," *Governing* 13, no. 11 (August 2000): 54–56; John Peterson, "Can Enron Happen Here?," *Governing* 15, no. 7 (April 2002): 64.

37. Don Van Natta, "Tennessee Failed to Protect Cities in Bond Deals, Governor Says," *New York Times,* April 10, 2009 (Web edition).

38. Penelope Lemov, "The Pension Offensive," *Governing* 15, no. 12 (September 2002): 24–26; John Peterson, "States and the Markets," *Governing* 15, no. 11 (August 2002): 58.

39. *Statistical Abstract of the United States,* 1995, p. 451; *Statistical Abstract,* 2001, pp. 417–419.

40. For an assessment of the impact of falling oil prices on the Texas budget, see *The New York Times,* January 4, 1983, p. 9. On oil-producing states generally, see *The New York Times,* April 8, 1986, p. 1.

41. *Washington Post National Weekly,* September 7–13, 1992, p. 33.

42. Melissa Maynard, "Short-Staffed and Budget-Bare, Overwhelmed State Agencies are Unable to Keep Up," *Stateline,* December 13, 2011 (Web edition); Dennis Cauchon, "States and Cities Borrow Big," *USA Today,* May 3, 2009 (electronic edition); Jason DeParle, "Jobless Checks for Millions Delayed as States Struggle," *New York Times* July 23, 2009 (electronic edition); Robert Pear, "State Cuts Delay U.S. Benefits, Official Says," *New York Times,* April 13, 2009 (electronic edition); Pamela Prah, "State Budget Gaps Top $200 Billion," *Stateline,"* April 24, 2009 (electronic edition); Rob Silverblatt, "States Draw Down Rainy Day Funds," *Stateline,* August 27, 2009 (electronic edition).

43. See David Davis, *Energy Politics,* 4th ed (New York: St. Martin's, 1993), pp. 119–120.

44. See Jeffrey Chapman, ed., *Long-Term Financial Planning* (Washington, DC: International City Management Association, 1987), especially Part 4; Nick Samuels, "Long-Term Budget Stability Amidst Fiscal Crisis: What Can States Do to Better Navigate the Next One?," in *The Book of the States,* vol. 36 (Lexington, KY: Council of State Governments, 2004), pp. 330–332.

45. Monica Davey, "Budget Worries Push Governments to Same Mind-Set," *New York Times,* January 17, 2011 (Web edition).

Poverty and Social Welfare Policies

CHAPTER PREVIEW

Few phenomena are more of a challenge to the widely held American value of upward social mobility than the continued existence of widespread poverty. And few public policy areas evoke as much emotion as trying to determine what to do about poverty in America. This chapter explores these issues by examining:

1 Poverty as a social problem.

2 The importance of conservative, liberal, and other values to understanding poverty policy.

3 The roles of federal, state, and local governments in carrying out social welfare policy.

4 The major social welfare programs.

5 Health care policies.

6 The attempts to reform social welfare policy since the 1960s.

7 The interrelationship between social welfare policy, social conflict, and political economy of states.

Introduction

America, we are taught, is the land of opportunity. Immigrants arrived, worked hard, saved their money, and saw their children move up a rung on the social ladder. **Horatio Alger** grew rich writing stories about boys who climbed to the top of the social ladder in a single lifetime. This message was so popular that his books sold more than 20 million copies.[1] And there were plenty of real-life examples to sustain this Horatio Alger theme. The ingenious Thomas Edison rose from telegraph boy to become the nation's foremost inventor. Andrew Carnegie, an impoverished immigrant, became the nation's foremost steel magnate. Even in our own day, the dynamic American economy has provided many opportunities for upward mobility.[2]

Not everyone prospers, however. When Barbara Ehrenreich wanted to understand the lives of people working in low-wage jobs in America, she decided to live and work as they did. She held several different jobs, including working as a waitress, a maid, and an aide in a nursing home.[3]

Even with no children to support, she found that making ends meet was difficult. In one community, she had to work seven days a week. In another location, she had only 22 dollars left at the end of one month (after paying for food, rent, and other necessities). A major illness or accident, a brief bout of unemployment, or major problems with her car would have left her in a very difficult position. She found many people who worked hard but did not prosper. They struggled just to make ends meet, and many of them had lost hope that they would ever rise to the ranks of the middle class.

As Figure 13.1 shows, the percent of people in poverty goes up during periods of recession and down in times of economic expansion. But the total number of people in poverty in recent years—38 million in 2005—is 13 million more than in 1970. After an extended period of economic growth through much of the 1990s and a modest recession after that, 13.3 percent of the population remained in poverty—*before* the 2008–10 recession began. The persistence of poverty is a challenge to the Horatio Alger myth for contemporary America and raises several questions. What is poverty? Why does it exist? Who is poor? Do different kinds of poverty require different kinds of public policies?

In 1996, the federal government devolved a significant share of its poverty and welfare policies to the states. How effectively have states dealt with poverty and welfare policies since then? And how will

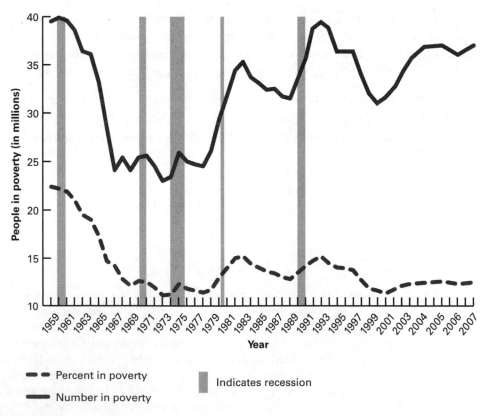

FIGURE 13.1

Number and Percent of People in Poverty

Sources: United States Bureau of the Census, *Statistical Abstract of the United States, 1971,* p. 322; *1984,* p.471; *1996,* p. 472; *World Almanac,* 1999, p. 393; World Almanac (2003), p. 409; *Statistical Abstract, 2003,* p. 465; *World Almanac, 2009:* p. 88.

the states deal with their new responsibilities in the health care system with the adoption of the Obama administration's health care reforms?

These questions will occupy this chapter. We will first examine poverty as a social problem. Second, we will look at conflicting views on the causes of poverty and ways to deal with it. Third, we will differentiate between the roles played by the federal, state, and local levels of government in setting and implementing social welfare policies. Fourth, we will outline the major welfare programs that operate at the state and local levels. Fifth, because health care programs are a vital and expensive area of social welfare policy, we will examine them in some detail. Sixth, we will discuss attempts over the last 40 years to reform social welfare programs. Finally, we will look at the relationship between social welfare policy, social conflict, and the political economy.

POVERTY AS A SOCIAL PROBLEM

What Is Poverty?

Poverty can be defined in two ways. The first definition is **absolute deprivation** and the second is **relative deprivation**. Both of these definitions are somewhat arbitrary and judgmental. And as will become apparent, one's definition of poverty affects the policies one favors. Calling poverty absolute deprivation leads to one policy approach; calling it relative deprivation often leads to other policy approaches.

Poverty as Absolute Deprivation   In absolute terms, poverty can be defined as the minimum subsistence income needed to survive without deprivation. Anybody below that income level is judged to live in poverty. Based on the assumption that poor families spend one-third of their income on food, the U.S. Social Security Administration sets an official **poverty line** at three times the amount of income needed to eat according to a modest food plan.[*] Researchers find that millions of American families are at least occasionally hungry because they cannot afford enough food, and millions more worry that they may be unable to obtain enough food.[4]

The official poverty level is adjusted each year to compensate for inflation. Table 13.1 lists the official poverty-level income by family size and by year. Because the poverty line is one of the criteria used to determine eligibility for federal programs, it is important that this line be set at a realistic level. However, some critics argue that the level is too low, especially in areas where housing costs tend to be high. Other critics argue that the assumptions behind the poverty line are no longer valid.[5] One economist argues that the poverty line ought to be set at four times the economy food plan instead of three times.[6] Other analysts complain that many of America's poor people are actually prosperous compared with people in many other countries.[7]

At whatever level the poverty line is set, compensating for special circumstances of each and every family is impossible. Obviously, $19,971 will cause less deprivation for a family that owns its house than for a family still making rent or mortgage payments. It will cause less deprivation for a family in subsidized housing than for a family in nonsubsidized housing. If all

---

[*]This modest food plan is actually the economy food plan prepared by the U.S. Department of Agriculture. The Department of Agriculture annually estimates the cost of buying food on an economy plan, a low-cost plan, a moderate plan, and a liberal plan. For a description of how the poverty line is calculated, see *Social Security Bulletin, Annual Statistical Supplement: 1991* (Washington, DC: U.S. Government Printing Office, 1991), pp. 321–323.

TABLE 13.1			
The Poverty Level: 2005 and Previous Years			
The 2005 Poverty Level for Nonfarm Families by Size		The Poverty Level in Selected Years for a Four-Person, Nonfarm Family	
Size of Family	Average Poverty Line	Year	Average Poverty Line
1 person	$ 9,973	2005	$19,971
2 persons	12,755	2000	17,604
3 persons	15,577	1995	15,569

Source: *Statistical Abstract of the United States, 2008* (Washington, DC: U.S. Government Printing Office, 2008), p. 458.

government assistance programs, such as public housing, food stamps, and medical assistance, were counted in determining poverty status, the number of people considered to be living in poverty would be sharply reduced.[8] This fact obviously complicates the task of defining poverty, and its implications for government policy have stimulated considerable debate among social welfare policy specialists.

Poverty as Relative Deprivation Partly because of the difficulty in making an absolute deprivation definition of poverty, some critics prefer to define poverty relative to society's overall standard of living. According to this view, as the standard of living goes up, the poverty level should also rise. A majority of poor people today have conveniences that only a generation or two ago would have been considered luxuries—a television set, a refrigerator or freezer, an oven, hot water, access to a telephone, a private bath, and a flush toilet.[9]

At the same time, many low-income people feel poor because they see, both in person and through the mass media, other Americans who have luxurious homes in nice neighborhoods, fancy cars, expensive clothes, recreational vehicles, home computers, and many other amenities of life that are far beyond the reach of the poorest families. When a person's social position is significantly influenced by what he or she owns, those who have less feel (and may be encouraged to feel) poor and inferior.

A recent study of child poverty in 15 different countries used a relative deprivation threshold, which was one-half of the median family income[10] in each country. The researchers found that children are more likely to be in poverty in the United States than in the other 14 countries (mainly western European countries, along with Australia and Canada). Moreover, America's disadvantaged children appear to be poorer than their counterparts in a number of other countries.[11]

Discussions of relative deprivation alert us to the fact that determining the extent of poverty is not a simple task and that poverty is partially a function of social and individual judgments regarding what is a suitable standard of living. Saint Francis or Henry David Thoreau might have been perfectly content to live in what most people would regard as poverty, and a millionaire might feel acutely inferior to Microsoft founder Bill Gates, with his estimated fortune of at least $40 billion. Defining poverty as relative deprivation presents a complex and difficult task.[12]

The U.S. government continues to use its official definition based on a principle of absolute deprivation. That definition is important for determining eligibility for several federal social programs and for allotting several federal grants-in-aid to states and communities. Because of these reasons, this chapter will primarily rely on the official poverty definition in discussing trends in poverty.

Who Is Poor?

The incidence of poverty is deeply affected by two broad factors—birthright character-istics and behavioral characteristics (see Table 13.2). Birthright characteristics are the ones you are born with and over which you have no control. These include your gender, your ethnic background, and the cultural-class-religious milieu in which you grow up. Behavioral characteristics are the ones over which you do have some control. Although you do not have complete control over these things, your behavior greatly influences whether you become a high school dropout or a college graduate, an unemployed person or a full-time worker.

Studies of poverty consistently find that birthright characteristics are strongly related to poverty. Poverty rates are higher among minorities than whites, higher among women than men, and higher among children than adults. However, poverty rates also vary with different behavioral traits, even for people with the same birthright characteristics. Children in families with both parents present, for example, are much less likely to be poor than are children in female-headed families. For all groups, higher levels of education reduce the likelihood of being poor. In 2005, the average income of full-time workers with less than a ninth grade education was almost identical to the poverty level for a family of six. The median income for male workers with a bachelor's degree was more than three times as high as for workers with less than a ninth grade education. People who work full time are less likely to be poor than are people who work part time or not at all.[13]

None of us controls everything in our lives, and while the path to a high school degree and full-time work is harder for many minorities than it is for most whites, the message is clear. Economic disaster is least likely among those people who develop the personal behaviors than

TABLE 13.2	
People Likely to Be Poor	
Characteristics	Percentage Below the Poverty Line, 2005
All	9.9
White	8.0
African American	22.1
Hispanic	19.7
Family status	
Female-headed households	28.7
Children	17.1
Work experience	
Worked full-time year-round	2.8
Did not work	21.8

Source: Statistical Abstract, 2008, pp. 458–460.

enable them to complete as much formal education as possible, work full time, and attract a marriage partner who exhibits similar behaviors. However, circumstances beyond individuals' control and circumstances they can control may become heavily entangled with one another over time, with the result that we may be unable to separate the influence of different causes of poverty.[14]

The most disturbing statistics in Table 13.2 are those showing poverty among children. Recent decades have seen an explosion in divorce rates and in the percentage of children born to unmarried mothers. By 2005, 37 percent of all births were to unmarried mothers, a dramatic increase from 11 percent in 1970.[15] Poverty rates are especially high for children in female-headed households and minority households.[16]

Children raised in poverty confront a wall of disadvantage that becomes increasingly difficult to scale as each year passes. Children born into poverty are more likely than others to be sickly at birth and to spend their infancies suffering from malnutrition and the physical and developmental deficiencies caused by malnutrition.[17] They receive less health care. They do worse in school. As they grow older, they experience more unemployment, have more problems with drugs and alcohol, and spend more time in jail. Finally, poor children are more likely than others to become teenage parents, with all the attendant risks that they will raise another generation of children in poverty.

Kinds of Poverty

Permanently vs. Marginally Poor In trying to decide what, if anything, should be done about poverty, it is important to distinguish between the *permanently poor* and the *temporarily* or *marginally poor*. One family may fall into poverty for a two- or three-year (or even less) period immediately following a divorce, job loss, or a major illness or accident, for example, but subsequently recover. During that two- or three-year period, members of the family may need job training, placement counseling, and direct financial assistance. Poverty, in this case, is a temporary status.

The Survey Research Center traced the economic fortunes of more than 5,000 families for a nine-year period and found that only about 3 percent had lived in poverty all nine years.[18] This suggests that only about seven million people live below the poverty line all the time. Another study spanning 24 months found that 21 percent of the population fell into poverty for two or more months. Many of the people who are poor for lengthy periods have one or more family members with chronic health problems that make getting and keeping a good-paying job very difficult and bring major health care costs.[19]

However, the Survey Research Center study also found that poverty is much more widespread than suggested by the Census Bureau. Nearly a third of all American families fell into poverty at least once in the nine years. This means that as many as 90 million people live in a fairly precarious situation. Normally, they earn enough money to manage reasonably well, but they fall into poverty during various stages of their lives—when they are laid off work because of a recession, when they are divorced and have to divide their incomes between two homes, when they are fired or widowed or face a medical or financial disaster, like the one that wiped out the retirement investments of many of Enron's employees when the company collapsed in 2002.

People who live in poverty or on the fringes of poverty do not get a proportionate share of the national income. They do not accumulate much savings. They have few assets other than their houses, and many do not own their homes. The majority work as regularly as possible, but they are extremely vulnerable to technological change, social developments, and other events over which they have no control.

The Working Poor and the Nonworking Poor   Another important distinction is between the *working poor* and the *nonworking poor*. More than half of all poverty families are headed by somebody with a job.[20] However, their jobs are often part time and/or do not pay enough to keep them above the poverty level. One of the ironies of the 1996 welfare reforms (to be discussed shortly in the chapter) is that many of the people who left the welfare roles remained in poverty and often need continuing governmental assistance.[21]

As Figure 13.2 shows, the plight of people with average or below average incomes is getting worse today, relatively speaking. The poorest two-fifths of Americans saw their share of the national income steadily grow from 12.5 percent in 1929 to 17.6 percent in 1970 and then decline slightly in 1980. Since then, it has fallen considerably to 12 percent. During the same period, the richest two-fifths of Americans saw their share of the national income decline until about 1970 and then rise until today, when it is higher than it has been since the 1930s. The 5 percent of households with the highest incomes take home nearly twice as much money as the bottom two-fifths of households.

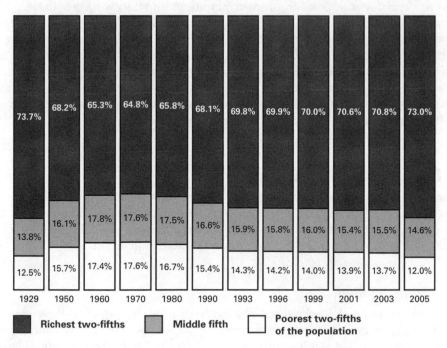

FIGURE 13.2

Trends in Income Inequality: Percentage of the National Income
Earned by Each of Three Income Groups

Sources: For 1970 through 1988, Bureau of the Census, *Current Population Reports: Trends in Income by Selected Characteristics: 1947 to 1988* (Washington, DC: U.S. Government Printing Office, 1990), p. 9. For earlier data, *Statistical Abstract of the United States* (Washington, DC: U.S. Government Printing Office, various years). For 1990, *Statistical Abstract, 1992,* p. 450; *Statistical Abstract, 1995,* p. 475; *Statistical Abstract, 1998,* p. 473; *Statistical Abstract, 2001,* p. 438; *Statistical Abstract, 2006,* p. 464; *Statistical Abstract, 2008,* p. 450.

Figure 13.2 clearly illustrates that income inequality in America is growing, with income shifting away from the 60 percent majority of Americans to the 40 percent who make the highest incomes. One group that has been affected by the income inequality is children. In 1970, 14.9 percent of all children lived in poverty. Childhood poverty rates rose to 21.8 percent of all children in 1983, dipped slightly, and then rose to 22 percent in 1993. A noticeable decline in childhood poverty rates followed, but by 2005, poverty rates among children were still higher than they were in 1970.[22] A way of viewing the same trend from a perspective closer to that of a middle-class college student would be to compare the average income of a well-paid corporation president to that of a typical middle-income professional person, a school teacher. In 1960, the average corporation chief executive earned 38 times as much as the average school teacher. In 1995, the CEOs of America's 100 largest corporations earned an average of $2.8 million, or 76 times as much as the average school teacher.[23]

Why is this happening? There are many explanations, but analysts point to three overriding reasons. First, the transformation of the American economy from one based on manufacturing to one based on services eliminated 11.5 million well-paying manufacturing jobs from 1979 to 1984. Only 60 percent of those workers found new jobs during that period.[24] At least that many new jobs were created in the same period, but these were primarily lower-paying service jobs in such enterprises as restaurants, hotels, and hospitals.

A second reason for the growing inequalities stems from international competition. American workers now compete for jobs with ambitious and hardworking contemporaries all over the world. Most low-skilled production jobs today can be done just as competently and much more cheaply by someone in Mexico or Brazil or Indonesia or just about any country bent on boosting its economic growth.

A third reason for growing inequality in incomes can be traced to the changes in national tax and welfare policies since the early 1980s. As will be discussed later in this chapter, these policies had the effect of further reducing the incomes of low-income families while increasing the take-home pay of upper- and upper-middle-income families.

POLITICAL VALUES AND POVERTY

Many perceptions exist about the causes of poverty and how it can best be dealt with. Some of these perceptions (but not all) can be placed along the leftist–rightist continuum. On the right side of the spectrum, conservatives look at the poverty data in Table 13.2 and draw one conclusion; liberals look at the same data and draw a different conclusion.

The View from the Right

Conservatives focus on the behavioral characteristics of the poor. In their view, people are poor because of their individual shortcomings. They believe the dynamic, capitalistic American economy provides millions of opportunities for self-advancement. They see the individual as master of his or her fate: If the individual is too lazy, too dumb, or too irresponsible to work, or if an individual makes imprudent choices, then that is the individual's own fault. Those people trapped in poverty are trapped there, according to one conservative analyst, "because they usually do not work." Only 11 percent of poor adults worked full time all year in 2005. Most people "responded to stagnant wages by working *more*; only the poor have worked less."[25]

Conservatives tend to view poverty not only as an individual matter, but also as inevitable. Life circumstances will always put some people into poverty, but the people with initiative will overcome their poverty. For this reason, the conservative is likely to attribute great significance to the difference between temporary and permanent poverty. Many people are temporarily thrown into poverty by external circumstances such as a divorce, accident, or illness, but those people usually climb out of poverty eventually.

More disturbing to the conservative, however, is the long-term poverty of what has come to be called the underclass. Some social critics argue that a **culture of poverty** exists among the underclass. These people become cynical about the social system. They fail not only to develop marketable job skills, but also to develop positive attitudes that would enable them to work eight hours daily and cause no trouble to their supervisors.

In its most extreme form, during the late nineteenth and early twentieth centuries, the classic conservative explanation for poverty was **Social Darwinism**. Charles Darwin argued that natural evolution occurred through the survival of the fittest. Social Darwinists, such as Herbert Spencer,[26] applied that argument to the evolution of society. Poverty is a mechanism for the survival of the fittest in the social sphere. It weeds out the weakest members of the species and the overall result is a healthier society.

The extreme conservative would carry this argument to its logical conclusion and deny that the government has any responsibility to combat poverty. Indeed, Charles Murray argues that government welfare programs have only made problems worse by sapping poor people of their initiative and making them dependent on the welfare system.[27] He further argues that technological change will make the poor even worse off in future years because he thinks that the poor lack the basic intelligence needed to function in the coming high-tech world.[28] The classic conservative believes that the best antipoverty policy is one of **laissez-faire**, a policy by which the government leaves the marketplace alone and does not intervene.

More moderate conservatives do favor some intervention in the marketplace and some programs to help people who have fallen into poverty. If the government must intervene, however, the conservative would usually prefer that the government give financial incentives to private industry to carry out government objectives or to couple assistance with strong requirements that people who receive aid should work or prepare to enter or reenter the workforce by learning better job skills. Assistance, in most cases, should be temporary rather than a long-term substitute for work.

Some conservatives emphasize the distinction between absolute poverty and relative deprivation. Edward C. Banfield, for example, argues that most poverty today is little more than a gap between poor people's limited capabilities and their inflated aspirations for an upper-middle-class lifestyle.[29]

The View from the Left

In contrast to the conservative emphasis on individualism, liberal theories stress that much poverty is rooted in the structures of the economy and society and would still exist if everybody had a future-oriented value system.[30] Moreover, much poverty is rooted in factors that poor people cannot control, such as major illnesses, accidents, and the loss of jobs. Tracing their views back to the Great Depression of the 1930s and President Franklin Roosevelt's New Deal response to it, liberals point out that private enterprise cannot by itself consistently produce enough jobs for everybody. Even during the high tide of one of the greatest economic booms in history in the late 1960s, the unemployment rate usually remained above 4 percent.

The liberal policy approach for dealing with poverty reflects this belief in the structural causes of poverty. Government spending should stimulate economic growth so that full employment can be maintained. Specific government programs such as unemployment compensation and welfare should strive to protect people from recessions that occur in the business cycle and, in the process, help to stabilize the economy. The conservative is pessimistic about individuals, but the liberal is optimistic. The liberal supports education programs, retraining programs, and job placement programs that give individuals an opportunity to take advantage of structural changes in the economy.

Liberals do not deny the importance of individual traits for **social mobility**. Some gifted and ambitious people can work their way from the bottom to the top of the social ladder. Liberals, however, contend that not all people have an equal chance of succeeding. Most poor people have parents who are poor, and 25 years from now most poor people will be the sons and daughters of today's poor people. Many rich people, interestingly, do not seem to have come from rich parents. A survey of the country's wealthiest 1 percent of the population found that only 10 percent said they inherited their wealth.[31] However, some families are able to remain quite wealthy from generation to generation.

In truth, there is evidence for both the conservative and the liberal views of poverty. The conservative's emphasis on individual behavior is supported by the fact that within various population subgroups, poverty rates are lowest among those people who succeed in finding full-time jobs and those who get married and stay married. Poverty rates are also lowest among people who complete high school, achieve some post high school education or training, and behave in ways that make them attractive to employers. It is impossible to reject completely the conservative's belief that individual behavior has an effect on one's economic success or failure.

However, the evidence also provides some support for the liberal's contention that poverty is caused by social structures and other uncontrollable factors. Within any of the marital or employment categories, poverty rates always end up being higher among African Americans, Hispanics, and Native Americans, and the lowest among whites and Asian Americans. Having a full-time job is very likely to keep you out of poverty, but a fundamental problem in recent years is that increasing numbers of employers have cut back on their full-time workforce and rely more heavily on part-time and temporary employees, whose jobs are less likely to come with fringe benefits such as health insurance and retirement programs. Furthermore, many of the people in poverty (more than 12 million in 2005) are children under the age of 18 who have no control over the marital or employment status of their parents.

To cope effectively with poverty, public policy must take into account both the behavioral and the structural factors that lead to poverty. There is a need both for educating poor children about behaviors that maximize their chances of escaping the poverty trap and also for public policies that provide economic opportunities.

STATE, LOCAL, AND FEDERAL ROLES IN SOCIAL WELFARE POLICY

These theories of poverty have had a profound influence on the social welfare system that evolved in the United States. Prior to the Depression of the 1930s, classic laissez-faire conservatism was the dominant theory of social welfare, and the government intervened minimally in the economy. The Depression was such a monumental catastrophe, however, that laissez-faire was no longer a viable policy. The economy's total output of goods and services (the **gross national product,** or **GNP**) dropped 45 percent between 1929 and 1933, and did not get back to its 1929 level until 1941. By 1932, a quarter of the workforce was unemployed. Traditional systems of welfare, or relief, as they were called in those days, were overloaded with requests for help. These traditional relief systems were run and financed by local governments and private organizations, but they were overwhelmed by the Depression.

In response to the disaster of the Great Depression, a social welfare system gradually emerged that intricately involved all three levels of government. The federal role initially attempted to provide financial support for local governments to give traditional relief.

Federal Roles

In time, a completely new intergovernmental welfare system evolved. The federal government's role in this system now embraces four elements. First, through the grant-in-aid system, the federal government provides financial incentives to the states to run a variety of social welfare programs that will be described shortly.

Second, the federal government established minimum levels of payments and services for some of the programs run by the states. Third, because the federal government provides financial incentives, it often plays a key role in deciding which poverty problems will be tackled and what programs will tackle them. Fourth, in addition to setting up and financing programs for the states to run, the federal government directly operates a number of programs itself. Medicare and Social Security, for example, are handled exclusively by the federal government.

State Roles

Whereas the federal government exerts considerable influence on the structure of social welfare programs, the states implement most programs and set the policies that govern eligibility for many programs and the ultimate benefit levels. The states also provide a considerable amount of funding for some programs. One important component of this intergovernmental approach to social policy was a relatively small federal program called **Aid for Families with Dependent Children (AFDC)**, which was substantially revamped in 1996 and renamed Temporary Assistance to Needy Families (TANF). Congress wrote the program into the **Social Security Act of 1935** to provide financial relief for widows with dependent children. The federal government provided a minimal AFDC payment level. The state legislatures supplemented this amount and made decisions about eligibility, which led to wide differences in benefit levels and access to benefits since some states are more generous than others.

After a state's legislature and governor establish policy for the benefit levels and various regulations regarding the program, implementation was turned over to the state and local departments of human services. During the 1990s, a number of states experimented with modified versions of AFDC. Starting in 1997, the state role in welfare policy was expanded when Congress replaced AFDC with a block grant that gave states much greater leeway on how they spent their federal welfare grant monies, although the new law also placed new restrictions on the state programs.

The states are also important players in a number of other social welfare programs. Some programs give the states relatively limited discretion, but others, such as General Assistance (to be discussed shortly) are funded entirely by state and local governments and are, therefore, relatively free of federal influence.

Local Roles

Local departments of human services, which are usually found at the county level of government, are most often the agencies that run the welfare programs. People apply for welfare assistance at the local level. Local officials determine whether the applicant is eligible and what level of benefits the applicant will receive; many of these decisions will follow state guidelines to varying degrees. If the applicant is female and has children, the local welfare officials may try to find the father of the children and force him to make child support payments. After going through all the steps to ensure the applicant's eligibility and to boost her outside sources of income, the local department begins to send monthly checks. Sometimes welfare officials find it difficult to set eligibility rules that are fair and equitable. The causes of poverty are numerous and complex, and some poor families are struggling with two or more different causes of poverty at the same time. Moreover, people who are eligible for assistance may not apply for it.

Why Welfare Policies Differ Among the States

States differ greatly in the generosity of their welfare benefits. In 2003, average monthly benefits for TANF, the program that replaced AFDC, in Alaska were four times as high as the benefits in South Carolina.[32] In 2006, the average weekly benefit for unemployment insurance ranged from $184 in Alabama to $366 in Massachusetts.[33] Why do states differ so much in their benefits for the needy?

Affluence as an Explanation   One explanation for the disparities seems to be the level of affluence of the state. Benefit levels tend to be higher in wealthier states, in part because raising revenues to finance higher benefits is easier in wealthier states. However, affluence alone does not explain all of the variation in benefit levels. Some states that are similar in terms of prosperity have differing benefits, and the disparities in benefit levels for some programs are much larger, proportionally, than the differences in state wealth.

Politics as an Explanation   One popular **hypothesis** among political scientists has been that welfare benefits will be highest in the states where strongly organized, issue-oriented political parties compete for power and where voter turnout, especially among the poor, is high. The assumption behind this hypothesis is that the voters will choose the party that gives them the most benefits, causing the two parties to outbid each other. The higher the turnout, the greater the competitiveness, and the better organized the parties are, the more incentive the parties have to bid against each other for voter support. In states with little competition and low voter turnout, the dominant party has little fear of losing office and thus has no incentive to give the voters high benefit levels.

Moreover, a lack of competition will cause the dominant party to become factionalized and disorganized, conditions that would be harmful to the party's chances of winning in a competitive setting and that make action on controversial issues difficult. This hypothesis has fared unevenly, however, with some studies finding that competition has little independent influence once we take into account other state characteristics such as affluence, education, and urbanization. Other research, however, finds that some combination of party competition, high voter turnout, and party strength in the policy-making process, leads to more generous welfare policies.[34]

In addition to two-party competition and high voter turnout, in some states, blue-collar workers and poorer people have politically influential interest groups, vote regularly, and encounter both political parties and a broader climate of opinion receptive to their concerns, which shapes social welfare policies. The strength and influence of labor unions appears to have a significant impact on social welfare benefits. The political culture of states also helps explain the differences in welfare benefits. Generally speaking, governmental intervention in the economy is favored much more in moralistic political cultures than it is in traditionalistic or individualistic cultures. Welfare programs tend to be more generous in states with liberal electorates and liberal political parties, moralistic political cultures, and relatively high voter turnout by poorer people.

In sum, state and local governments play a vital role not only in administering federal welfare programs, but also in determining the generosity of the benefit levels. Affluence and the political values of politically active people, at least to the point of voting, appear to be important predictors of welfare policies. In general, programs tend to be most generous in states with wealth, strong labor unions, high turnout by poor people, and liberal political beliefs or cultures. The generous states are found disproportionately in the Northeast, Midwest, and Pacific regions, and the least generous states tend to be in the South, Southwest, and Rocky Mountain regions.[35]

THE MAJOR SOCIAL WELFARE PROGRAMS

There is no agreement on what programs are included under the term *welfare*. Most of the debate over welfare reform in the 1990s focused on AFDC (which became Temporary Assistance to Needy Families, or TANF, in 1997) and food stamps, but those two programs account for a very small share of the money that governments spend on assistance to individuals.[36] As Table 13.3 shows, social welfare programs provide three types of assistance: (1) social insurance transfer payments, (2) cash transfer payments that are not social insurance, and (3) in-kind assistance.

Social Insurance Transfer Payments

A **transfer payment** is a direct payment of money by the government to individuals. It is not a payment for purchasing goods or services, as are federal expenditures. Nor is it a payment to run a program, as are the services listed in the third section of Table 13.3. It is called a transfer payment because its net effect is simply to transfer money from the people who pay taxes to the people who receive the cash. Some transfer payments, such as **Old Age, Survivors, Disability, and Health Insurance (OASDHI;** what is commonly called Social Security), are **social insurance.** That is, individuals make payments into a social insurance trust fund much as they would make payments into a private insurance policy. Later on, they receive benefit payments when they become eligible. The three major social insurance programs—OASDHI, Medicare, and Unemployment Compensation—were established by the Social Security Act of 1935 and its later amendments (Medicare was added in 1965).

Note that individuals do not have to be poor to receive social insurance benefits. Most Social Security and Medicare benefits go to people who are middle class or upper class and who, consequently, are often active in politics. As a result, these programs are politically strong.

TABLE 13.3

Approaches to Social Welfare Policy

Approach and Program	Major Recipients of the Assistance	Level of Government That Writes the Checks or Administers the Delivery of the Service
1. *Social insurance transfer payments*		
a. OASDHI ("Social Security")	Retired people and/or the survivors of workers who died; many nonworkers; all income categories	Federal
b. Medicare	The aged; all income categories; both the working and the nonworking poor	Federal
c. Unemployment compensation	Mostly the bottom 40 percent of the income workers who are temporarily unemployed	State
2. *Nonsocial insurance cash transfer payments*		
a. Family support (mainly TANF)	The nonworking poor; the bottom 20 percent of the income recipients; mostly single, divorced, or widowed mothers and their children	State and county
b. Food stamps	The bottom 40 percent of the income recipients; both the working and the nonworking poor	Federal and county
c. Supplemental Security Income (SSI)	The aged, the blind, and the disabled; the nonworking poor; the bottom 20 percent of the income recipients	Federal (and state in some states)
d. General public assistance (excluding TANF and SSI)	The nonworking poor; the bottom 20 percent of the income earners; mostly destitute and homeless people who do not qualify for TANF, SSI, or unemployment compensation	State and county
e. Earned Income Tax Credit	Lower-income workers	Federal tax credit
3. *In-kind assistance*		
a. Housing programs	Mostly the bottom 40 percent of the income recipients; both the working and the nonworking poor	Municipal or county housing authorities
b. Medicaid	The bottom 40 percent of the income recipients; both the working and the nonworking poor	State and county welfare departments
c. State Children's Health insurance program	Provides health care coverage for children of low-income families not eligible for Medicaid	State and county welfare departments

	TABLE 13.3 *(continued)*		
Approach and Program	Major Recipients of the Assistance	Level of Government That Writes the Checks or Administers the Delivery of the Service
d. 2010 Health care reforms	Provides multiple components to enhance health care access, especially for low-income workers and people with chronic health problems	Federal, state, and local governments
e. Employment programs	Middle 40 percent of the income recipients; the working poor who are unemployed	Federal, state, county, and municipal
f. Other social services (e.g., child day care, foster care, planning, family services for the mentally retarded)	The bottom 40 percent of the income recipients; both the working and the nonworking poor; people with special needs and special problems	State, county, and municipal

Old Age, Survivors, Disability, and Health Insurance (OASDHI)   OASDHI is one of the most important federal social welfare programs. It is also the most expensive—more than $581 billion in 2007. While working, you make regular payroll contributions to the Social Security trust funds. When you retire, become disabled, or die, you or your beneficiaries receive a monthly payment just as would happen under a pension program or a life insurance plan. This is why it is called social insurance, although your benefits are not limited to the funds you have paid in.

Social Security probably does more than any other program to reduce poverty in America. A 1988 Census Bureau study calculated that 15 million people were lifted above the poverty line by their Social Security benefits. Without such benefits, the poverty rate would likely be six percentage points higher than it is. The impact on the poverty rate of the elderly is much greater.[37]

Social Security is currently undergoing a great debate that will affect your well-being enormously. The elderly population is growing much faster than the working population, which provides the revenues for the system. Although the Social Security trust fund currently has assets of many hundreds of billions of dollars, recent projections have indicated a future decline in the trust fund's reserves, which might be depleted by approximately 2042 (although the system could continue to pay benefits, at a reduced level, from current revenues). This forecast has led to a variety of proposals to change or even abolish the Social Security System[38] as well as fears among younger people that the system will collapse before they retire.

However, some analysts have concluded that the fears are greatly exaggerated. They note that long-term forecasting is far from precise and that the Social Security System trustees' more optimistic forecasts, which have received almost no news coverage, indicate that no crisis is impending. Even using the more pessimistic forecast, if relatively modest changes are adopted soon, the system will be able to continue functioning for the foreseeable future.[39]

Calls for a radical reform of Social Security with greater reliance on stock market and/ or other private investments ran into a major snag with a series of problems in the business world. From 2000 to July of 2002, the Nasdaq index, which includes many of the high-technology stocks that had been rising in value, declined by almost 75 percent, leaving many investors with huge financial losses. Since then, a number of businesses have been rocked by revelations of misleading financial reports, destruction of financial records, and executives who walked away with huge sums of money, leaving bankrupt firms and empty-handed investors and employees behind them.[40] The housing market, which had seemed a good investment while it was rising in many parts of the country, began a major decline in most areas. A wave of foreclosures as people fell behind in their mortgage payments pushed prices even lower.[41] The stock market subsequently declined, along with many other parts of the U.S. economy, which is still in recession as of this writing. The relatively cautious investment practices of the Social Security System began to look more sensible than they had a few years earlier.

Medicare   Persons over age 65 are eligible for Medicare, along with other individuals in some situations. Part A of Medicare primarily pays for hospital care. Part B of Medicare is optional; for an additional premium, Part B will help to pay for doctors' bills and a number of medical procedures not covered by Part A. Recent legislation added optional prescription drug coverage to the program; recipients can select from a number of different plans but must pay premiums and a share of the costs of their prescriptions. Medicare does not pay for long-term nursing home care. Like other social welfare programs, Medicare spending has risen dramatically over the years.

Unemployment Compensation   Unemployment compensation is a social insurance program. While you work, your employer makes regular contributions to an unemployment compensation trust fund; if you become unemployed, you can draw benefit checks for up to 26 weeks. Congress and the president sometimes provide funds for longer time periods when recessions occur. Federal involvement in unemployment compensation was initiated by the Social Security Act of 1935. It is financed jointly by employers, the states, and the federal government, but it is administered by the individual states, which also have authority to set benefit levels.

Transfer Payments That Are Not Social Insurance

In contrast to the social insurance programs, some other transfer payment programs, such as TANF (formerly AFDC), are not social insurance. People can receive assistance from those programs when they meet the eligibility requirements and if they can pass a **means test**; that is, if their income or assets fall below a certain level. The main cash transfer payments of this type are TANF, food stamps, SSI, and General Public Assistance (GPA).

Temporary Assistance to Needy Families (TANF)/Aid for Families with Dependent Children (AFDC)   Until its demise in 1996, AFDC was the most controversial transfer payment. TANF, which succeeded it, remains controversial. It provides a direct monthly payment to poor, usually single, parents with dependent children. In 2006, TANF payments ranged from $326 to $2,620 per family per month. Roughly 1.7 million people received TANF in 2008.[42] TANF costs only about 6 percent as much money as OASDHI.[43]

The TANF program is controversial not only because of the sums of money involved, but also because of a very negative stereotype ascribed to TANF recipients. According to this stereotype, the typical recipient misspends welfare checks on alcohol, gambling, and frivolities. Nevertheless, rigorous research has shown that program recipients spend more of their income on food and housing and less on frivolities than do other people.[44] Another stereotype is that the recipient is able-bodied enough to work, but is simply ripping off the system by drawing welfare checks. Federal investigations found that only a small minority of welfare recipients are truly ineligible; most parents on TANF have some combination of physical and/or mental disabilities, limited education, and limited work experience. They have a particularly difficult time competing for jobs during recessions.[45]

The overwhelming majority of people on the TANF rolls are young children, and most of the rest are single or divorced women. Moreover, almost half of all TANF families include at least one person with some degree of physical or mental impairment.[46] Another stereotype is that the typical TANF/AFDC mother becomes permanently dependent on welfare. The fact is that 50 percent of recipients receive this benefit for four years or less. Thirty percent received AFDC for eight or more years,[47] but most TANF recipients can only receive its benefits for five years over the course of a lifetime.

Food Stamps   Another controversial measure has been the **food stamps program,** which was started in 1961 as a pilot project and then established on a permanent basis in 1964. Its adoption grew from a growing awareness that many American families could not afford an adequate supply of food. The food stamps program is totally funded by the federal government, but is administered by the federal Department of Agriculture, Food, and Nutrition jointly with state and county departments of welfare.

Food stamps serve both the working and the nonworking poor. To qualify, the family income must be below a certain cutoff level. Eligible households receive a monthly allotment that is tied to the amount of money needed for the Agriculture Department's "thrifty food plan." In the welfare reforms of 1996, Congress tightened eligibility requirements for food stamps, and the number of recipients gradually declined for several years. An upward trend began in 2000, and recipients totaled 27 million by 2006.[48] The recession that began in late 2007 pushed food stamp caseloads even higher. The U.S. Department of Agriculture, Food, and Nutrition has forecast that more than 40 million Americans are likely to receive food stamps for a least part of 2010.[49]

According to recent research, over half of the families eligible for food stamps don't receive them, sometimes because they don't know they are eligible. In addition, although hunger in cities receives considerable news coverage, rural areas also have serious hunger problems.[50] Moreover, if a large number of people apply for food stamps at the same time, the system may be overwhelmed, with the result that many people must wait weeks or even months for assistance.[51] A large majority of the households receiving food stamps have children at home, have one or more elderly members, or have one or more family members with disabilities.

Private organizations in many parts of the country provide additional food assistance to the needy by operating food banks, which are primarily supported by donations and often staffed by unpaid volunteers. They provide help for many needy people who do not qualify for food stamps. According to recent estimates, at least 13 million Americans live in households where one or more family members at least occasionally are hungry due to an inability to obtain food; that number does not include homeless people, many of whom also have trouble obtaining food.[52]

Supplemental Security Income (SSI)   Supplemental Security Income (SSI) is a federal-state program that provides aid to the aged, the blind, and the permanently or totally disabled. The Social Security Administration sends a monthly SSI check to each recipient, and each state is permitted to supplement the federal payment. Many states do that, but some published tables of benefit levels in each state only include state supplements that are administered by the federal government and omit any supplements sent directly by states to the recipients. SSI is clearly a relief program, not a social insurance program. However, it is much less controversial than TANF, largely because many people perceive SSI recipients as the "deserving poor." Nonetheless, SSI is considerably more expensive than TANF.

General Public Assistance (GPA)   The final transfer payment program is general public assistance (GPA), or general relief. This is administered and financed exclusively by state and local governments. Homeless and destitute persons who do not qualify for other public assistance programs can sometimes get general relief from their state and county welfare departments, although the amounts are very restricted in many states. In some states, general assistance is restricted to certain categories of persons, such as people with disabilities or families with children, and nine states do not have a state general assistance program of any kind.[53]

Earned Income Tax Credit (EITC)   Started in 1975 as a minor program to provide tax relief for the working poor, this program escalated to $38 billion by 2007. A family with two children is eligible for a maximum of about $3,800, depending on the family's income. At a yearly income of about $12,000, the family would receive the entire $3,370. The amount received goes down as the family's earned income goes up, until the credit phases out entirely at about $27,000. If the family's income is so low that they do not owe any federal income tax, they receive the tax credit as a cash payment on top of any other refund to which they are entitled. The EITC is not an easy benefit to receive. Not only must you file an income tax return, but you also must understand that the program exists and you must fill out the required tax forms. Despite these difficulties, 22 million families participate in the program, which raises several million people (who do participate) above the poverty level.[54]

In-Kind Assistance Programs

In addition to transfer payments, the federal, state, and local governments have a wide range of specific services for the poorer members of the population. These are sometimes called **in-kind assistance,** because they provide assistance that has a cash value, even though it is not received in cash. Five of the most prominent social services are outlined in Table 13.3: public housing, Medicaid, the State Children's Health Insurance Program (SCHIP), employment services, and general social services. Housing and health will be discussed later, so only the last two will be addressed here. In-kind assistance helps to reduce concerns about poor people wasting their benefits (compared to giving them money) and may create a nonpoor group of supporters for the program—such as the health care industry which makes a great deal of money from Medicaid.

Employment Programs   All states provide employment services through which they help people find jobs. In addition, a number of federal, state, and local programs have existed over the years to provide training, job location services, and public jobs for teenagers. A recent addition to the employment programs is connected with the TANF program, which includes work requirements and job training programs for many recipients.

Other Social Services   In addition to the programs just discussed in the chapter, state and local governments provide a wide variety of other social services, such as child day-care licensing, adoption, homemaker services for the elderly, and child-protection services. Federal involvement in these programs is traced to the 1975 Title XX amendment to the Social Security Act, which established a social services block grant.

HEALTH CARE POLICIES: THE INTERGOVERNMENTAL SYSTEM IN PRACTICE

State and local governments have traditionally maintained public health departments to curb communicable diseases and to promote the general public health. Additionally, cities and counties in many parts of the country have maintained large public hospitals where needy persons could go for emergency care.

These traditional programs often attracted only limited public attention for years unless a major, localized problem developed. However, in the wake of the September 11 terrorist attacks, public health programs across the country have mobilized in order to develop better systems for detecting patterns of symptoms indicating exposure to chemical or biological weapons and to prepare responses to the health problems those weapons (or any others) would produce. Public health officials have also been developing plans and preparing for dealing with deadly epidemics, particularly due to recent concerns over bird influenza. Some experts believe that if the bird influenza virus mutates into a form that can be transmitted from person to person, it could be as serious as the 1918 flu epidemic, which killed approximately 500,000 Americans.[55]

Growing State and Local Government Roles

In recent years, state and local government roles in health care have expanded far beyond traditional roles. In many instances, the state and local expansion occurred as a response to new federal programs. One of the first was the Hill-Burton Act of 1946, which provided funds for hospital construction. Later amendments to this act provided federal funds for rehabilitation facilities and nursing homes. Federal funds went to both public and private facilities.

As public and private health care facilities expanded, the states saw themselves forced into a much stronger regulatory role. A major consequence of the Hill-Burton Act, for example, was the overbuilding of hospital capacity and bed space, thus contributing to the inflation of health care costs. In order to gain better control over hospital construction costs, most states have passed certificate-of-need laws. These require any organization to get state certification that the new construction is actually needed before it can add to its hospital, nursing home, or clinic, or before it can buy expensive diagnostic equipment.

State and local governments are also heavily involved in the financing of health care services to the poor. This role expanded dramatically after the passage of the Medicaid Act in 1965. Medicaid must not be confused with its partner, Medicare; the two are very different. **Medicare** is a health insurance program for elderly people of all income levels. **Medicaid** provides medical services for people who cannot afford health care on their own. All public assistance recipients (AFDC, SSI, and GPA) are eligible for Medicaid, as are the aged who cannot afford the Medicare premiums.

Medicaid is based on some federal policies and some state policies, and state discretion has increased in recent years. A cost-sharing formula is scaled to the state's per capita income. More than 55 million people received some Medicaid benefits in 2004, and it now pays about 43 percent of all nursing home receipts in the United States. Medicaid costs have risen considerably over the years, with most Medicaid outlays going to help elderly and/or disabled Americans.[56]

In the 1990s, the federal government enacted the SCHIP in order to expand health care coverage for poor children. The program combines federal and state funds to fill gaps in the Medicaid system, with the result that more than 80 percent of poor children are eligible for one form of coverage or the other. However, eligibility does not necessarily mean actual coverage. Confusion about eligibility and, in some states, a sluggish state response to the program have limited the program's impact. However, a number of states are working to broaden access to the program.[57]

Continuing Issues for Health Care

As more and more government funds have gone to health care, a number of issues have surfaced that will plague Americans and their governments at all levels for the foreseeable future. First, the U.S. health care system is extremely expensive. Health care costs exceeded $2 trillion by 2006, about 16 percent of the gross domestic product, up from only 7.4 percent in 1970.[58]

Although the United States spends an unusually large amount of money on health care, relative to the population or to the economy, some measures show that our country is less healthy than are some other countries (see Table 13.4). Deaths in the first year of life are proportionately more common in the United States than in a number of other countries, and infant death rates actually increased from 2001 to 2002. The death rate for toddlers (ages one to four years old) also increased from 2000 to 2001.[59] Infant death rates are particularly high in states with proportionally more people living in poverty.

TABLE 13.4

Health in the United States and Other Western Democracies, 2004

	Life Expectancy	Infant Mortality Rate
United States	77.4	6.6
Australia	80.3	4.8
Canada	80.0	4.8
France	79.4	4.3
Germany	78.5	4.2
Japan	81.0	3.3
Netherlands	78.7	5.1
Spain	79.4	4.5

Source: Statistical Abstract, 2006 (Washington, DC: U.S. Government Printing Office, 2005), pp. 868–871. Life expectancy is in years; infant mortality rates are deaths of children under one year old per 1,000 live births. The United States spends more per person on health care than does any of the other countries in this table.

Second, an estimated 45 million people currently lack health insurance coverage, and 82 million Americans were uninsured at some point during 2002–2003. Even worse, 108 million Americans have no dental coverage. The state of Washington recently provided a striking example of the consequences of inadequate dental coverage: Approximately 30 percent of the National Guard members called to active duty in Washington in 2004 needed dental work before they were fit for duty.[60] Most of the people who lack health care coverage are working people who earn too much money to qualify for Medicaid, but whose jobs do not provide health insurance. Research indicates that people who lack insurance receive less health care and lower quality health care. Health insurance coverage varies considerably from state to state: In 2005, Texas led the nation with 24 percent of its population lacking health insurance. Only eight percent of the population of Minnesota, by contrast, lacked insurance.[61]

Third, the difficulty of getting health insurance is also cited as one of the major factors keeping single mothers on welfare. Until 1997, AFDC recipients automatically qualified for Medicaid. But if they left AFDC to work in a job without health insurance, they found themselves and their children without either health insurance or Medicaid.

Another controversial area in which states are being forced to act is to determine who will have access to health care in a fiscal environment where not every person or every health problem can be covered. Today, access is primarily determined by ability to pay. The more money you have and the more insurance you have, the more health care you can buy. Health insurance companies have moved many people to a concept called managed care, which tries to hold down medical costs by forgoing some expensive procedures and limiting access to others. This is accomplished by having primary care physicians and insurance company gatekeepers screen patients for specialized treatments. If your insurance company will not pay for a procedure you want, you will have to foot the bill or go without.

Obviously, the less money you have, the more restrictive your care. Managed care has lost some of its luster in recent years; a number of health maintenance organizations (HMOs) are now in financial difficulty, in part because they came under a barrage of complaints from patients, doctors, and hospitals for late payments and refusal to pay for care. Many patients and physicians complained that HMO staff with little or no medical training were, in effect, making health care decisions. State officials have responded with tougher regulations, and some states passed new laws to permit lawsuits against HMOs. However, in June of 2004, the U.S. Supreme Court ruled that people cannot sue HMOs in state court for refusing to pay for health treatment.[62] Roughly two-thirds of the nation's HMOs are currently in financial difficulties, and several have collapsed.[63]

One aspect of rising health care costs that has greatly concerned state officials is the increasing cost of Medicaid. Medicaid has many more recipients than does TANF and it costs a great deal more, especially in recent years. Almost all of the states have responded by moving many of their Medicaid recipients into managed care programs. This movement was encouraged by a new federal law in 1997 that enabled states to move recipients into managed care without obtaining federal approval first. Although not all states have moved with equal speed, the typical state now has 61 percent of its Medicaid recipients in managed care.[64] Efforts to restrain the growth of Medicaid costs have angered many doctors, pharmacists, and directors of hospitals and nursing homes. If a state Medicaid program pays considerably less than the usual fee to a medical vendor, many vendors will refuse to treat Medicaid patients or place limits on the number that they will serve at one time. That is happening in a number of states. The 2007–2010 recession has simultaneously increased the number of people in need of Medicaid coverage and reduced the state revenues needed to finance that coverage.[65]

A National Health Insurance Plan?

Given the magnitude of these issues and the widely varying abilities of individual states to cope with them, should we have a national health insurance plan that would ensure everyone's right to some minimal level of health care? President Bill Clinton thought so and in 1993 proposed an ambitious overhaul of the nation's health services system. Clinton's plan aimed to reduce the number of people without health insurance and to expand the role of both the federal government and the states in providing a national system of managed care. The plan was narrowly defeated by Congress in 1994. And when conservative Republicans gained control of Congress later that year, national health insurance was quietly laid to rest.

However, President Obama and Congress adopted a broad package of health care reforms in 2010. Although the legislation is complex, it has several important features:

1. All Americans must obtain some type of health insurance coverage; people who cannot afford private insurance on their own may receive governmental aid. Small businesses will receive federal tax credits to help them offer insurance coverage to their employees.
2. Health insurance companies can no longer deny coverage to people with pre-existing health problems, such as cancer or heart disease. Annual and lifetime benefit limits in health insurance policies will no longer be allowed. State governments will help to enforce those rules. The national government has also created a pool for high-risk patients who would face very high insurance premiums in the private insurance market.
3. Medicaid coverage will be expanded, and payment schedules will cover a larger share of customary charges from medical vendors.
4. States can also create new public health insurance programs (most states already had some sort of health insurance pool before the federal law was passed).[66]

The health care reform legislation has been attacked by Republicans, who regard it as too expensive and too intrusive. A number of state attorneys general have filed lawsuits challenging the constitutionality of the new law. Even so, most states are preparing to help implement the new policies.[67]

REFORMING SOCIAL WELFARE

The American public exhibits a schizophrenic view of social welfare programs. National surveys find broad support for government aid to helpless people, but the word *welfare* is greeted with considerable hostility. A recent poll found the public almost equally divided between those who felt welfare recipients truly need help and those who did not. The public is also divided on the issue of whether poor people do enough to help themselves, and on whether more spending on antipoverty programs would help reduce poverty. However, large majorities of Americans supported increased spending on medical care for the needy, on jobs programs, and on housing and food assistance.[68]

But there is more to welfare's poor image than simple confusion about the labels. For one thing, there is a perception of widespread "welfare cheating" that tarnishes the image of welfare recipients. When asked in 1994 whether most welfare recipients are genuinely needy or just taking advantage of the system, 69 percent of whites and 63 percent of African Americans said that most people were taking advantage of the system.[69] In contrast to this perception, federal investigations reveal that only 5–8 percent of AFDC recipients have taken benefits to which they were not legally entitled. Whatever the reality of welfare cheating, welfare recipients are an easy target for public officials currying popular support. Moreover, whites with negative attitudes regarding African American welfare recipients are particularly likely to be critical of welfare programs. White attitudes regarding white welfare recipients are not as strongly related to attitudes regarding welfare.[70]

Whatever the reasons for welfare's unpopular image, the fact of its unpopularity has provided continuing support over the years for reform of the system. Four important approaches to welfare reform have been attempted since the 1950s.

The 1960s: War on Poverty

The Lyndon Johnson administration (1963–1969) did not really have a welfare reform plan; instead, Johnson proposed an approach called the **War on Poverty**. Called the **Great Society**, the Johnson program brought about a major expansion of social service funding and several new programs such as Medicare, Medicaid, and the legal services program. The keystone of the War on Poverty was the **Economic Opportunity Act of 1965**, which created the Office of Economic Opportunity to conduct experiments in social services and to coordinate all the poverty-related efforts of the agencies of the federal government. In 1966, the Model Cities program was created to concentrate and coordinate federal programs in specific neighborhoods of 150 selected major cities. However, neither the Model Cities nor the economic opportunity programs were consistently successful in coordinating the poverty efforts at either the federal or the local level.[71]

Perhaps the most significant impact was their requirement that the people affected by the programs participate in drawing up the program plans. In each locality receiving War-on-Poverty funds, a community action agency (CAA) was created to draft a community action plan for that community. The net effect was to stimulate community organizing efforts in poor neighborhoods. In particular, the CAAs developed community leadership in African American neighborhoods, provided jobs for poor and middle-class African Americans, and organized residents of those neighborhoods to battle for better services from the city government, to vote, to combat slum landlords, and to become politically active.

These social programs of the War on Poverty are under heavy criticism even today, especially by some conservatives, who point out that poverty has not been eliminated and who argue that welfare efforts have trapped people in poverty by making them dependent on government aid.[72] Most analysts, however, while recognizing the failure to end poverty, credit the social programs of the 1960s with some important successes.[73] They put more economic resources into the hands of many poor people, and they were a major factor (along with a booming economy) in cutting in half the percentage of people living in poverty.

The 1970s: Aborted Attempts at Income Maintenance

The second approach to welfare reform was **income maintenance,** the attempt to ensure that everybody in the country had a cash income above the subsistence level. This was the approach of Presidents Richard Nixon (1969–1974) and Jimmy Carter (1977–1981). Nixon called his proposal the **Family Assistance Plan (FAP)**. A four-person family with no income would receive $1,600. For each dollar the family earned, the government's payment would decrease by 50 cents. When the family's earnings reached $3,920, the government benefits would be phased out completely.

Although this was a truly revolutionary approach to welfare reform, it never became law. Liberals, who had previously pushed for income maintenance as the ideal tool for income redistribution, feared that FAP would phase out other major programs, such as food stamps.[74] They complained that Nixon's proposed benefit levels were too low and would reduce overall welfare benefit levels in most states.[75] Conservatives objected that FAP would reward poor families for not working. Social work professionals had no incentive to support FAP since it would reduce the need for AFDC caseworkers. Finally, there was no broad public support for the concept of income maintenance. A *New York Times*/CBS poll in 1977 found that 50 percent of the people opposed a guaranteed minimum income, and only 44 percent supported it.[76]

Unable to build the political support needed for his plan, Nixon himself grew cool to it. A version of it twice passed the House of Representatives, but died in the Senate. During the Nixon years, however, the national government did assume a larger role in providing for needy people who were blind, disabled, or elderly by replacing older programs with the SSI program.

When Jimmy Carter became president in 1977, he proposed a similar income maintenance plan to replace the existing AFDC, SSI, and food stamps programs. Carter's plan provided a mandatory work requirement for adults classified as able to work. To ensure an adequate supply of employment opportunities, he proposed an extensive expansion of public service jobs at the minimum wage. And to help out the working poor, he proposed a cash payment to supplement their wages. Under this plan, a family of four would receive a cash payment of $2,300 as long as its earned income was less than $3,800. For each dollar earned above that amount, the cash supplement would be reduced by 50 cents until it was completely phased out at $8,400. Thus, every four-person family in the country would be guaranteed a minimum income of $6,100, and there were strong work requirements in the program.

Carter's plan quickly ran into the same kind of opposition that had killed Nixon's FAP earlier in the decade. The benefit levels were attacked as too high by the chairpersons of the House and Senate tax committees and too low by both the AFL-CIO and the Congressional Black Caucus.[77] The mandatory work provisions were criticized. The public service jobs at the minimum wage, it was said, would displace working people from jobs that would otherwise pay twice that amount for the same work. Labor leaders feared that this would give local governments an incentive to fire their regular employees and hire them back at the minimum wage with federal funds. Faced with this opposition, Congress again aborted the income maintenance approach and instead expanded the food stamps program.

The 1980s: From Welfare to Workfare

Following the failure of guaranteed income plans in the 1970s, welfare reform in the 1980s shifted toward the goals of reducing the welfare rolls and making welfare recipients work to earn their grants, if possible. This shift took place in three stages, culminating with a major change in AFDC regulations in 1988.

The Reagan Approach to Welfare Cuts Picking up on the themes of conservative critics[78] (see pp. 344), President Ronald Reagan (1981–1989) charged that welfare programs sapped people of their will to become self-supporting.[79] He also believed that plenty of jobs were available for people who truly wanted to work. Following on these beliefs, his approach to welfare was to force welfare recipients into the job market by reducing expenditures for most social service programs and by tightening up eligibility requirements for the programs. By these measures, less money would be available for welfare and fewer people would qualify for it. The tightening of federal funds, coupled with developments at the state level, including more criticism of welfare programs, contributed to a 30 percent decline in the purchasing power of AFDC benefits between 1977 and 1995. Reagan also pushed Congress to enact lucrative income tax cuts for upper- and middle-income people, and Congress, on its own initiative in 1986, removed the lowest-income people from any income tax liability whatsoever.[80]

The hope of all this macroeconomic activity was, of course, that a reduction in tax burdens combined with a booming economy would lift most people out of poverty and make welfare unnecessary. Unfortunately, economic growth in the 1980s did not bring many people out of poverty. As Figure 13.1 shows, there were more people in poverty at the end of Reagan's administration than there had been when he was elected (31.9 million in 1988 versus 29.3 million in 1980). When he left office in 1989, the percentage of people in poverty was still higher than it had been 20 years earlier.

State Initiatives in Workfare   While the federal government sought to reduce federal welfare benefits in the 1980s, states began to experiment with a number of approaches to moving people off of AFDC and into the workforce. What made these experiments different from previous attempts to force AFDC recipients into the job market was the recognition that welfare mothers can only be successful in the job market if certain conditions are met: There must be jobs available for them, they must have the skills and attitudes to win the jobs, they must have reliable day-care help (which is rather expensive in many parts of the country), and they must have medical insurance to make up for their being taken off Medicaid.

The pioneers in seeking to meet these conditions were California's GAIN (Greater Avenues to Independence) plan and Massachusetts' ET (Employment and Training) plan. GAIN was passed in California through a fascinating political compromise between liberal Democrats (who agreed to the conservative demand for a mandatory work requirement) and conservative Republicans (who agreed to the liberal demand for putting up money for training and child-care expenses). The result was an elaborate program begun in 1985 that screened participants into appropriate training programs, created "job clubs" to teach them how to find jobs, and gave them money for child care while they were in training and for their first year on the job.[81]

Analyses of the 1980s reforms were cautiously optimistic about the ability to move welfare recipients into decent-paying jobs under the proper conditions. In its first two and one-half years, Massachusetts' ET program claimed to have made a significant reduction in the state's welfare caseload and to have moved a significant number of recipients into the workforce.[82] A San Diego workfare plan reported that its participants not only were more likely to get off welfare than were comparable nonworkfare recipients, but when they found jobs, those jobs also paid higher wages than did jobs found by the nonworkfare recipients.[83]

Federal Workfare   Reflecting the growing belief that welfare recipients should be working toward the goal of making themselves self-sufficient, Congress, on its own initiative in 1988, passed an AFDC reform law that obliged the states to draw up training and employability plans for welfare recipients, required the states to improve collection of child support payments from noncustodial parents, and provided for up to one year of transitional Medicaid benefits while the welfare mother was moving into the workforce.

The 1990s and Beyond: Behavior Modification

Despite the far-reaching nature of the 1988 reform act, it did not go far enough for welfare critics who focused increasingly on the responsibility of welfare recipients to develop attitudes and behaviors that would lead them out of welfare dependency. The problem of welfare dependency, according to conservative analyst Lawrence Mead, is not the lack of economic opportunities; the problem is the lack of will to seize the opportunities that exist.[84]

Changing Public Opinion   The growing conservative attack on welfare was accompanied by public opinion that seemed increasingly receptive to conservative-oriented welfare reforms. The Gallup Poll in 1995 found that 58 percent of the people favored moving mothers off welfare after two years, 62 percent favored a five-year time limit on welfare, and 78 percent favored no increased benefits if a mother had a child while on welfare.[85] When asked by a *Wall Street Journal*/NBC poll whether the welfare system did more good than harm or vice versa, 72 percent of whites and 57 percent of African Americans said that it did more harm.[86]

State Initiatives   With a public opinion increasingly receptive to forcing welfare recipients to modify their attitudes and behavior, it is not surprising that the states began to act. One of the first states to use its welfare policies to modify the attitudes and behavior of welfare recipients was Wisconsin. The Wisconsin reforms cut welfare grants for parents whose children missed too many school days, denied increased grants to AFDC mothers who had another child while on welfare, encouraged teenage welfare mothers to get married, and reduced benefits to welfare recipients who moved into the state.[87] Wisconsin required mothers with young children to find work. And if they could not find private sector jobs, Wisconsin demanded that they work in subsidized community service jobs.

Several other states passed similar legislation designed to make qualification of welfare assistance dependent upon the behavior of the welfare recipients. By 1996, 14 states had adopted some form of time limit for welfare recipients, 23 had adopted a work requirement, and 19 had adopted a family cap that forbade increasing welfare benefits if another child was born to a mother already on welfare. Thirty-three states had adopted at least one of these three measures.[88]

Federal Reform: 1996   In 1996, these piecemeal steps toward welfare reform culminated in the federal **Personal Responsibility and Assistance Act**, which produced the most dramatic changes in federal welfare policy since the 1960s. This act:

- Replaced AFDC with a block grant program that would enable each state to design its own assistance plan for the poor.
- Limited to two years the amount of time a family could stay on welfare at any one time.

- Put a five-year lifetime limit on welfare for any one person.
- Prohibited benefits to minor mothers unless they lived with an adult and were attending school.
- Provided extra funds for states that reduced births to unmarried women.
- Enacted stricter eligibility standards for SSI and food stamps.
- Prohibited SSI and food stamp benefits to legal immigrants until they become citizens or work in the country for ten years.

WELFARE REFORM, SOCIAL CONFLICT, AND THE POLITICAL ECONOMY

What can we conclude about the welfare reforms of the 1990s? Are conservatives correct that the reforms would lead to financial independence for people previously trapped in a system of welfare dependency? Or are liberals correct that these reforms would throw millions of women and children into the streets and turn the nation's back on the plight of the needy? We can gain insight into the questions by looking at the relationships of welfare reform to our two theoretical concerns in this book—social conflict and political economy.

Welfare Reform and Social Conflict

The welfare reforms of 1996 are a great experiment in managing the dramatic social changes of our time. These include rising divorce rates, huge jumps in the number of children being raised in poverty, and a dramatic worsening of the job prospects of the bottom half of the population. By replacing the keystone welfare program for single mothers (AFDC) with the Temporary Assistance of Needy Families block grant, the federal government permitted a major wave of state and local experimentation. Some aspects of the experiments have pleased neither liberals nor conservatives. Liberal critics charge that the federal government has turned its back on the nation's poor by terminating a 60-year federal guarantee of assistance to needy single mothers and their children. Conservatives fear that the reforms left so many hardship exemptions that some welfare recipients will avoid the two-year and five-year limits and fail to work even though they probably could.[89]

Clearly, welfare caseloads have fallen dramatically (by more than 60 percent) since AFDC was converted to TANF; the decline varies from state to state, however. In Idaho, Wisconsin, and Wyoming, caseloads have fallen by more than 80 percent, but caseloads declined by less than 40 percent in Minnesota and Rhode Island. The purchasing power of benefits has continued to decline. The proportion of poor children receiving food stamps fell from 88 percent in 1995 to 70 percent in 1998. The average income of the poorest 20 percent of female-headed families declined between 1995 and 1997, and many families leaving the welfare rolls report continuing problems in paying for food, housing, and utilities. Many who have found jobs continue to live in poverty. Families with one or more family members suffering from physical or mental impairment have had an especially difficult time. Overall poverty rates increased every year during the period from 2000 to 2004, declined slightly in 2006, and then began to rise again. Poverty rates for children also increased, with some fluctuations.[90] All of these developments are consistent with the concerns expressed by liberal critics.

On the other hand, many of the former welfare recipients have been able to find jobs, in part due to new program incentives and in part due to the economic growth of the middle and late 1990s, a finding consistent with the views of conservative critics of welfare over the years. Even if recipients initially land low-paying jobs, if they develop a strong work record, they may eventually move to better paying jobs. In addition, a considerable number of the welfare recipients who left the welfare rolls since 1995 later returned to welfare, a development that echoes conservative fears that even the new incentives and regulations may not be strict enough.[91]

Welfare Reform and Political Economy

The success of the welfare reforms will depend greatly on the political economy. Each state will be pressured to have lower welfare benefits than neighboring states for fear that high benefits might attract a flood of poor migrants. Critics fear that this will provoke a "race to the bottom" as each state seeks to become the one with the lowest benefit levels and the fewest people receiving assistance. Researchers disagree on the likelihood of this phenomenon; clearly benefits for AFDC/TANF and General Assistance have declined on average over the years, but the pattern appears to vary considerably from state to state.[92] Officials in the state of Washington were recently embarrassed by revelations that the Department of Social and Health Services actually held contests to see how many people could be kicked off the welfare rolls and how many needy people could be denied assistance.[93]

Another concern lies in the nature of the economic cycle. When the economy enters one of its periodic recessions, finding jobs for welfare recipients becomes more difficult. Moreover, critics noted that the reformed system's stricter eligibility rules and procedures has weakened its ability to respond to major recessions. When the recession beginning in 2008 worsened, welfare rolls in a number of states *declined* even as more people were falling into poverty. Time limits on benefits also meant that families were losing welfare benefits even when jobs were increasingly difficult to find. A number of states also found themselves running low on funds for unemployment insurance[94]

Even when the economy is not in a recession, it has undergone profound changes over the past quarter century that limit the number of well-paying jobs, especially for people with limited education. As noted in previous chapters, the major changes are twofold. First is the shift from an economy based on heavy, so-called smokestack industries (such as automobiles, steel, and rubber) to one based on services, communications, and high technology. The heavy industries required a huge unskilled labor force that became a formidable economic force once it unionized. But unskilled workers are at a severe disadvantage in the newer service- and technology-oriented economy.

A second change impinging on the political economy is the growing challenge of foreign competition with American manufacturing. This challenge has been most dramatic, perhaps, in the automobile industry, where foreign competition rose from a minimal share of the American automobile market to a considerable share of it today. During the 1980s, these two developments provoked high unemployment in the Northeast and Midwest, where much of America's heavy industry was located. In the early 1980s, the value of U.S. manufactured exports exceeded the value of our manufactured imports. Since then, the value of manufactured imports has exceeded the value of manufactured exports, with the gap exceeding $700 billion annually in 2005 through 2007.[95]

One other point of concern regarding recent and proposed changes in the social safety net: Recall that the federal government's involvement in most antipoverty programs began during the Great Depression. Those federal programs were both an effort to provide for individuals in need and an effort to create systems that would help to stabilize the economy in future recessions.[96] The declining purchasing power of welfare benefits, the greater difficulty of qualifying for benefits, the limits on the length of time that people can receive TANF benefits, and the cap on federal aid for TANF have all reduced the welfare system's ability to help cushion the economy in major recessions. If the past is any guide, Congress and the president would very probably add additional funding for TANF in a major recession, but the national government has often been unable to move quickly on financial decisions since the late 1960s, largely due to conflicts between the White House and Congress and conflicts within Congress. Proposals to privatize Social Security and/or invest much of its funds in the stock market present a similar risk; a major recession, accompanied by a major drop in the stock market, would greatly undercut the system's ability to provide income support.

Some reformers, including President George W. Bush, have called for shifting more of the responsibility for helping the needy from government to private charities. However, a variety of evidence indicates that private charities cannot do much more than they are doing now, in part because the areas with the greatest need for assistance often have the most difficulty raising donations to fund that assistance.[97]

SUMMARY

1. The official U.S. poverty income line is based on the amount of money needed to purchase food on a modest food plan. The percentage of people below the poverty line declined from nearly 25 percent in 1960 to about 12 percent in the early 1970s. In recent years, the poverty rate has usually ranged from 11 to 15 percent. Poverty rates for children are higher.

2. Liberals and conservatives present conflicting views on the causes of poverty and the ways that government should deal with poverty. These value conflicts, coupled with the complexity of poverty, have produced repeated efforts to reform antipoverty programs over the years.

3. The implementation of welfare policies is done on an intergovernmental basis, with complicated interactions among federal, state, and local governments, along with private sector groups. This decentralized process of implementation has led to differing benefit levels from one state to another and has made the rational and efficient administration of welfare policies very difficult.

4. Welfare benefit levels vary from state to state, in part because of differences in affluence and levels of political competition, the political activity of blue-collar workers and the poor, and differences in political cultures.

5. The major social welfare programs can be grouped under three general headings: (1) social insurance transfer payments, (2) cash transfer payments that are not social insurance, and (3) in-kind assistance programs.

6. The most costly social welfare policies are Social Security and health care programs. A number of volatile health care issues face state governments, and the federal government is trying to broaden access to health care.

7. Ongoing controversies over welfare programs have produced several waves of reform efforts since the mid-1960s. In 1996, AFDC was replaced with a welfare block grant, TANF, and states were given more flexibility regarding some aspects of antipoverty programs, but less flexibility regarding other aspects in the mid- to late 1990s. TANF caseloads have fallen dramatically since 1996, but poverty rates only declined slightly and then rose during the 2001–2002 recession and again as the 2008–2010 recession deepened.

STUDY QUESTIONS

1. What is poverty? What difficulties have we encountered in trying to define and measure poverty?
2. Why are antipoverty programs often controversial? Why are some more controversial than others? What value disagreements underlie some of the controversies?
3. What are the major antipoverty programs? Which ones are most expensive? Are the most expensive programs the most controversial ones?
4. Why do welfare policies vary from state to state? What sort of state would you prefer to live in if you were poor (assuming that you had a choice of location)?
5. How have antipoverty programs varied over the years? What considerations have led to reform efforts? What consequences have the reforms produced?

KEY TERMS

Absolute deprivation A definition of poverty that says that one is deprived of the necessities of life if one falls below a specific income line.

Aid for Families with Dependent Children (AFDC) A federal program from 1935 to 1997 that provided cash assistance primarily for single parents without income, but with dependent children.

Culture of poverty A term used to describe a combination of psychological traits among many people who are permanently poor. These traits include cynicism toward the social system, lack of hope for escape from their plight, inability to defer gratification, and inability to plan for the future.

Economic Opportunity Act of 1965 The fundamental legislation of President Johnson's War on Poverty. It created the Office of Economic Opportunity to conduct experiments in social services and to coordinate all the poverty-related efforts of the agencies of the federal government.

Family Assistance Plan (FAP) An income maintenance proposal of the Nixon administration that did not pass Congress.

Food stamps program A program that provides vouchers to low-income people to help them buy food.

Great Society See *War on Poverty*.

Gross national product (GNP) A nation's total output of goods and services.

Horatio Alger An author who grew rich writing stories about boys who climbed to the top of the social ladder. The "Horatio Alger myth" is synonymous with upward social mobility.

Hypothesis A scientific term that refers to an educated guess or tentative assessment about the factors that explain some phenomenon.

Income maintenance An approach to social welfare that seeks to provide cash assistance that will maintain people's income above the poverty line.

In-kind assistance Social programs, such as medical aid, that provide help that has a cash value, even though the help is not received in the form of cash.

Laissez-faire The concept that government should leave the economy to the forces of the marketplace and should not seek to regulate the economy.

Means test A test that makes eligibility for benefits dependent on a person's ability to show need, usually by showing an income that falls under a specified level.

Medicaid A program that provides medical assistance for people who cannot afford their own health care.

Medicare A government-run health insurance program for elderly people of all income levels.

Old Age, Survivors, Disability, and Health Insurance (OASDHI) The fundamental social insurance programs for retirement, disability, and Medicare set up under the Social Security Act.

Personal Responsibility and Assistance Act The 1996 welfare reform law that replaced AFDC with a block grant.

Poverty line The federal government's official definition of poverty, based on the assumption that having less than three times the income needed to buy food on a modest food plan constitutes poverty.

Relative deprivation A definition of poverty that says that a person can be considered poor only in relation to the rest of the people in a society.

Social Darwinism A reference to the social sphere of Darwin's theory of natural selection and survival of the fittest. Accordingly, Social Darwinists oppose social welfare policies.

Social insurance A societal program in which one pays money into a government-sponsored trust fund and draws benefits from that fund later, when one becomes eligible.

Social mobility Movement upward or downward in society's class structure.

Social Security Act of 1935 The original legislative authority for much of the social welfare programs existing today.

Transfer payment A direct payment of government money to individuals.

War on Poverty President Lyndon Johnson's Great Society approach to poverty. Johnson vastly expanded social service programs in the hopes of eliminating poverty.

THE INTERNET CONNECTION

The Urban Institute has published a large number of reports on various developments in antipoverty programs in recent years. Many of its reports discuss variations in programs from state to state. You can find the Urban Institute at **www.urban.org**. The Social Security Administration also has considerable information on the social welfare programs that involve the federal government, including variations among state programs receiving federal funds. You can find it at **www.ssa.gov**.

NOTES

1. Robert E. Spiller et al., eds., *Literary History of the United States: Bibliography* (New York: Macmillan, 1974), p. 226.

2. Bureau of the Census, *Statistical Abstract of the United States, 1982–83* (Washington, DC: U.S. Government Printing Office, 1982), p. 256.

3. See Barbara Ehrenreich, *Nickel and Dimed: On Not Getting by in America* (New York: Holt, 2001). See also David Shipler, *The Working Poor* (New York: Vintage, 2004).

4. Emily Gersema, "Number of Hungry Families Is Increasing," *Moscow-Pullman Daily News*, November 1–2, 2003, p. 8A.

5. Sar Levitan, Garth Mangum, Stephen Mangum, and Andrew Sum, in *Programs in Aid of the Poor*, 8th ed. (Baltimore: Johns Hopkins University, 2003), pp. 1–7.

6. For critiques of the methods of drawing the poverty line, see Lee Rainwater, "Economic Inequality and the Credit Income Tax," *Working Papers for a New Society* 1, no. 1 (Spring 1973): 50–61; Michael Harrington, "The Betrayal of the Poor," *Atlantic* (January 1970): 71–72; Martin Rein, "Problems in the Definition and Measurement of Poverty," in Louis Ferman et al., eds. *Poverty in America*, rev. ed. (Ann Arbor: University of Michigan Press, 1968), pp. 123–125; Daniel M. Gordon, ed. "Trends in Poverty," in *Problems in Political Economy: An Urban Perspective*, 2nd ed. (Lexington, MA: D.C. Heath, 1977), pp. 297–298. Also see Alan Haber, "Poverty Budgets: How Much Is Enough?" *Poverty and Human Resources Abstracts* 1, no. 3 (1966): 6.

7. Robert Rector and Kirk Johnson, "Understanding Poverty in America," *The Insider*, no. 314 (February 2004): 3–6.

8. Timothy M. Smeeding, *Alternative Methods for Valuing Selected In-Kind Transfer Benefits and*

Measuring Their Effects on Poverty (Washington, DC: U.S. Bureau of the Census, 1982).

9. Thomas R. Dye, *Politics in States and Communities*, 3rd ed. (Englewood Cliffs, NJ: Prentice-Hall, 1977), p. 439.

10. The median family income is the income level that half of the families in the country earn more than and half of the families earn less than.

11. Lee Rainwater and Timothy Smeeding, *Poor Kids in a Rich Country* (New York: Russell Sage Foundation, 2003); Duncan Lindsey, *The Welfare of Children* (New York: Oxford University Press, 2004), pp. 230–238.

12. Thomas Dye, *Understanding Public Policy*, 7th ed. (Englewood Cliffs, NJ: Prentice-Hall, 1992), pp. 119–120.

13. *American Almanac* (Austin, TX: Hoover's, 1996), pp. 472–475; *Investment in Education: Private and Public Returns* (Washington, DC: Joint Economic Committee, 2000); *World Almanac* (New York: World Almanac Education Group, 2003), pp. 147, 408; *Statistical Abstract of the United States, 2006* (Washington, DC: U.S. Government Printing Office, 2005), pp. 467–473.

14. See Shipler, *The Working Poor*, especially ch. 11.

15. *Time Almanac* (Boston: Information Please, 1997), p. 840; *Statistical Abstract*, 127th ed. (Washington, DC: U.S. Government Printing Office, 2008), pp. 64, 66.

16. See "Number of Black Children in Poverty Up Sharply, Report Finds," *Moscow-Pullman Daily News*, April 30, 2003, p. 6A.; *Statistical Abstract*, 127th ed., p. 459.

17. Loretta Schwartz-Nobel, *Growing Up Empty* (New York: Perennial, 2003).

18. James N. Morgan et al., *Five Thousand American Families: Patterns of Economic Progress* (Ann Arbor: University of Michigan, Institute for Social Research, 1974); Sar Levitan, Garth Mangum, Stephen Mangum, and Andrew Sum, *Programs in Aid of the Poor*, 8th ed. (Baltimore: Johns Hopkins, 2003), p. 26.

19. See *Welfare Reform: Outcomes for TANF Recipients with Impairments* (Washington, DC: General Accounting Office, 2002), report no. GAO-02-884.

20. Bureau of the Census, *Current Population Reports: Characteristics of the Population Below the Poverty Level: 1977*, Series P-60, no. 119 (Washington, DC: U.S. Government Printing Office, 1979), p. 4; *Statistical Abstract, 2008*, p. 460.

21. Jonathan Walters, "The Flip Side of Welfare Reform," *Governing* 15, no. 6 (March 2002): 16–21.

22. *Statistical Abstract, 2008*, p. 459; Genaro Armas, "Ranks of Poverty, Uninsured Rose in 2003," *Moscow-Pullman Daily News*, August 26, 2004, p. 5A.

23. *American Almanac, 1996*, p. 163; Andrew Hacker, *Money* (New York: Scribner's, 1997), p. 115.

24. From a study by the Congressional Office of Technology Assessment. See *The New York Times*, February 7, 1986, p. 1; see also Hacker, *Money*; Robert Frank and Philip Cook, *The Winner-Take-All Society* (New York: Penguin, 1995).

25. Lawrence M. Mead, "The New Politics of the New Poverty," *Public Interest*, no. 105 (Spring 1991): 107; Laura Egendorf, ed., *Poverty: Opposing Viewpoints* (San Diego: Greenhaven Press, 1999), ch. 2, selections 1, 3, 6, and ch. 3, selections 2, 5; *Statistical Abstract, 2008*, p. 460. The 11 percent figure excludes workers under 16 years old.

26. See Herbert Spencer, *Social Statics* (London: John Chapman, 1951).

27. Charles Murray, *Losing Ground* (New York: Basic Books, 1984), p. 9.

28. Charles Murray and Richard J. Herrnstein, *The Bell Curve: Intelligence and Class Struggle in American Life* (New York: The Free Press, 1994).

29. Edward Banfield, *The Unheavenly City* (Boston: Little, Brown, 1968), p. 118; see also Rector and Johnson, "Understanding Poverty."

30. A summary of ideological orientations to poverty is presented by David M. Gordon in his *Problems in Political Economy: An Urban Perspective*, 2nd ed. (Lexington, MA: D.C. Heath, 1977), pp. 272–281; see also Laura Egendorff, *Poverty* (San Diego: Greenhaven, 1999), ch. 2, selections 2, 4, 5, and 7, and ch. 3, selections 1 and 6.

31. A survey conducted by U.S. Trust of people with greater than $200,000 in income or $3 million in assets. Reported in Gary Belsky, "Why Most of the Rich Will Get Richer," *Money* (May 1995): 135.

32. Mark Rom, "State Health and Welfare Programs," in Virginia Gray and Russell Hanson, eds. *Politics in the American States*, 9th ed. (Washington, DC: CQ Press, 2008), pp. 327–329.

33. *Statistical Abstract, 2008*, p. 356.

34. See especially Thomas R. Dye, *Politics, Economics and the Public* (Chicago: Rand McNally, 1966); Richard E. Dawson and James A. Robinson, "Interpreting Competition, Economic Variables and Welfare Policies in the American States," *Journal of Politics* 25, no. 2 (May 1963): 265–289; Gary L. Tompkins, "A Causal Model of State Welfare Expenditures," *Journal of Politics* 37, no. 2 (May 1975): 392–416; Samuel Eldersveld, *Political Parties in American Society* (New York: Basic, 1982), pp. 381–382; Thomas Holbrook and Emily Van Dunk, "Electoral Competition in the American States," *American Political Science Review* 87 (1993): 955–962.

35. An excellent review of the relative influence of economic and political variables on public policy is Jack Treadway, *Public Policy-Making in the American States* (New York: Praeger, 1985), pp. 131–176; see also Kim Hill and Jan Leighley, "The Policy Consequences of Class Bias in State Electorates," *American Journal of Political Science* 36 (1992): 351–365; David Nice, "State Party Ideology and Policy Making," *Policy Studies Journal* 13 (1985): 780–796; Gerald Wright, Robert Erikson, and John McIver, "Public Opinion and Policy Liberalism in the American States," *American Journal of Political Science* 31 (1987): 980–1001.

36. For an excellent summary of the major social welfare programs, see "Social Security Programs in the United States," *Social Security Bulletin* 49, no. 1 (January 1986): 5–61.

37. Based on 1986 data, the Bureau of the Census calculated that the percentage of people in poverty would have been 21.2 percent instead of the 14.9 percent that prevailed at the time. Reported in the *Minneapolis Star Tribune*, December 28, 1988, p. 3N; for a user-friendly introduction to the Social Security System, see *Social Security: Understanding the Benefits* (Washington, DC: Social Security Administration, 1999); Levitan, Mangum, Mangum, and Sum, *Programs in Aid*, pp. 48–49.

38. For an articulate statement of this viewpoint, see Laurence J. Kotlikoff and Jeffery Sachs, "Privatizing Social Security: It's High Time to Privatize," *The Brookings Review* 15, no. 3 (Summer 1997): 16–22. For critiques of this view, see Theodore Marmor, Jerry Mashaw, and Philip Harvey, *America's Misunderstood Welfare State* (New York: Basic, 1990), ch. 5;

Max Skidmore, *Social Security and Its Enemies* (Boulder, CO: Westview, 1999); Michael Hiltzik, *The Plot Against Social Security* (New York: HarperCollins, 2005).

39. Henry J. Aaron, "Privatizing Social Security: A Bad Idea Whose Time Will Never Come," *The Brookings Review* 15, no. 3 (Summer 1997): 17–23; Marmor, Mashaw, and Harvey, *America's Misunderstood Welfare State*, ch. 5; Skidmore, *Social Security*. On the difficulties of budgetary forecasting, see *The Economic and Budget Outlook: Fiscal Years 2000–2009* (Washington, DC: Congressional Budget Office, 1999), ch. 5; David Nice, *Introduction to Public Budgeting* (Belmont, CA: Wadsworth, 2002), ch. 5.

40. *World Almanac* (New York: World Almanac Education Group, 2003), pp. 33–34, 196.

41. Amy Merrick, "Housing Slump Strains Budgets of States, Cities," *The Wall Street Journal*, September 5, 2007, p. A1.

42. *The Book of the States*, 2009, p. 484; *Statistical Abstract*, 2008, p. 359; *World Almanac* (Pleasantville, NY: Reader's Digest, 2009), 417.

43. *Statistical Abstract*, 2006, pp. 363, 373.

44. Teh-Wei Hu and Norman Knaub, "Effects of Cash and In Kind Welfare Payments on Family Expenditures," *Policy Analysis* 2, no. 1 (Winter 1976): 81–82.

45. Sheila, Zedlewski, "State Safety Net Programs," in *Book of the States*, vol. 41 (Lexington, KY: Council of State Governments, 2009), p. 483; Office of Management and Budget, *Budget of the Government of the United States for FY 1978* (Washington, DC: U.S. Government Printing Office, 1977), p. 172. A 1987 study found that about 8 percent of AFDC funds were spent either on people who were ineligible or on overpayments. *The New York Times*, December 7, 1987, p. 17A.

46. *Welfare Reform: Outcomes for TANF Recipients with Impairments* (Washington, DC: General Accounting Office, 2002), report no. GAO-02-884; Sheila Zedlewski and Meghan Williamson, "Trends in Welfare Programs," in *The Book of the States*, vol. 38 (Lexington, KY: Council of States Governments, 2006), pp. 539–544.

47. Kenneth T. Jost, "Welfare Reform," *CQ Researcher* 2, no. 14 (April 10, 1992): 320. Data from the House Ways and Means Committee.

48. *Statistical Abstract*, 2008, 361.

49. "ID Food Stamp Use Rise Doubles National Average," *Moscow, ID/Pullman Daily News*, July 5, 2010, p. 3A.

50. *Statistical Abstract, 2001*, p. 356; Rebecca Cook, "'Immoral Irony': Hunger Rates Highest in Rural West," *Moscow-Pullman Daily News*, December 7–8, 2002, p. 5A; *Statistical Abstract, 2003*, pp. 374–375.

51. Michelle Roberts and Justin Juozapavicius, "Millions of Americans Forced to Wait for Food Stamp Benefits," *Moscow, Id/Pullman Daily News*, June 10, 2010, p. 6A.

52. *Statistical Abstract*, 2006, p. 134; *Statistical Abstract*, 2008, p. 133. See also Loretta Schwartz-Nobel, *Growing Up Empty* (New York: Harper Collins, 2002).

53. Cori Uccello and L. Jerome Gallagher, *General Assistance Programs: The State-Based Part of the Safety Net* (Washington, DC: Urban Institute, 1997).

54. Christopher Howard, "Happy Returns: How the Working Poor Get Tax Relief," *The American Prospect*, no. 17 (Spring 1994): 46–52; Ronald Sider, *Just Generosity* (Grand Rapids, MI: Baker Books, 1999), pp. 103–106; *Statistical Abstract, 2006*, p. 325; *Budget of the United States for FY 2009: Historical Tables* (Washington, DC: U.S. Government Printing Office, 2008), p. 143.

55. Lauran Neergaard, "Preparing for an Outbreak," *Daily News*, December 16–17, 2006, pp. 5C, 7C.

56. Henry J. Aaron, "End of an Era: The New Debate Over Health Care Financing," *Brookings Review* 14, no. 1 (Winter 1996): 350–357; Diane Rowland, "Medicaid: A Future Challenge for the States," in *The Book of the States* (Lexington, KY: Council of State Governments, 2002), pp. 432–439; Kaiser Family Foundation Web site (State Health Facts Online), August 11, 2004; *Statistical Abstract, 2008*, pp. 104–105. The average number of Medicaid beneficiaries at any given time was about 37 million.

57. Rowland, "Medicaid," pp. 433–435; *Statistical Abstract, 2006*, p. 107.

58. *Statistical Abstract of the United States, 1996*, p. 109; World Almanac (New York: World Almanac Education Group Reference, 2003), pp. 82, 107; *Statistical Abstract*, 2003, pp. 104, 848; *Statistical Abstract*, 2008, pp. 96, 429.

59. *Statistical Abstract, 2003*, pp. 87, 847–848; Siobhan McConough, "Report Finds Children Making Strides in Health, Education," *Moscow-Pullman*

Daily News, July 16, 2004, p. 2A; Forum on Child and Family Statistics (www.childstats.gov, 2004); *Statistical Abstract, 2006*, p. 98.

60. "Dental Problems Take Bite Out of Deployment for Washington Guard," *Daily News*, May 23, 2005, p. 4A.

61. See Genaro Armas, "Census: Number of Uninsured Up; Employment-Based Coverage Down," *Moscow-Pullman Daily News*, September 30, 2002, pp. 1A, 8A; Diana Mason, "Covering the Uninsured," *American Journal of Nursing* 103, no. 3 (March 2003): 11; Laura Meckler, "75 Million People in United States Uninsured for Part of 2001–2002," *Moscow-Pullman Daily News*, March 6, 2003, p. 18A; Randolph Schmid, "Report: Insurance Crucial for Health," *Moscow-Pullman Daily News*, May 22, 2002, p. 12A; Mark Sherman, "82 Million People in U.S. Uninsured for Part of 2002–2003," *Moscow-Pullman Daily News*, June 16, 2004, p. 2A; "Millions Without Dental Coverage," *Moscow-Pullman Daily News*, July 20, 2004, p. 3A; *Statistical Abstract, 2008,* p. 107.

62. CNN broadcast, June 21, 2004.

63. Penelope Lemov, "The HMO Laid Low," *Governing* 13, no. 9 (June 2000): 32–36.

64. Mark Rom, "Transforming State Health and Welfare Programs," in Virginia Gray, Russell Hanson, and Herbert Jacob, eds. *Politics in the American States*, 7th ed. (Washington, DC: CQ Press, 1999), pp. 361–374; *Statistical Abstract, 2003*, p. 113.

65. Kevin Sack, "Medicaid Cut Places States in Budget Bind," *New York Times*, June 7, 2010 (electronic edition).

66. See *Landmark* (Washington, DC: Washington Post, 2010) and Kate Tormey and Debra Miller, "Health Care Reform: Six Ways It Will Affect States," in *Book of the States*, vol. 42 (Lexington, KY: Council of State Governments, 2010), pp. 517–523, for additional information.

67. Jake Grovum, "With Health Care Lawsuits, States Hope for Victory But Plan for Defeat," *Stateline*, June 14, 2010 (electronic edition).

68. Richard Morin, "A Welfare Tug of War," *Washington Post National Weekly Edition*, May 14–20, 2001, p. 34.

69. *The Gallup Poll: Public Opinion, 1994* (Wilmington, DE: Scholarly Resources, Inc., 1995), p. 85.

70. In 1977, the federal government estimated that 5.5 percent of AFDC recipients were ineligible. See Office of Management and Budget, *FY 1978*

Budget, p. 172. A decade later, a federal study estimated the number to be about 8 percent. See The New York Times, December 7, 1987, p. 17B. See also Martin Gilens, "'Race Coding' and White Opposition to Welfare," American Political Science Review 90 (1996): 593–604.

71. See James E. Anderson, "Coordinating the War on Poverty," Policy Studies Journal 2, no. 3 (Spring 1974): 174–178; and James L. Sundquist, Making Federalism Work: A Study of Program Coordination at the Community Level (Washington, DC: Brookings Institution, 1969).

72. See especially Stuart Butler and Anna Kondratas, Out of the Poverty Trap (New York: Free Press, 1987); Murray, Losing Ground.

73. See John E. Schwarz, America's Hidden Success: A Reassessment of Twenty Years of Public Policy (New York: Norton, 1983), especially pp. 57–59. Also see Sar A. Levitan and Robert Taggart, "Great Society Did Succeed," Political Science Quarterly 91 (Winter 1976–1977): 601–618.

74. Ellen Kelman, "Welfare Reform," Dissent 24 (Spring 1977): 126–128.

75. Lester C. Thurow, "The Political Economy of Income Redistribution Policies," Annals of the American Academy of Political and Social Science 409 (September 1973): 146–155.

76. The New York Times, August 3, 1977, p. 1A.

77. See President Jimmy Carter's welfare reform message in The New York Times, August 7, 1977, pp. 1A, 40A. Also see The New York Times, September 16, 1977, pp. 4B, 13B; The New York Times, December 11, 1977, p. 43A.

78. See especially Butler and Kondratas, Out of the Poverty Trap; Murray, Losing Ground.

79. In his weekly radio address of February 15, 1986, Reagan blamed welfare programs for teenage pregnancies, family breakups, worsening poverty, and the creation of a permanent state of dependency among the poor. See The New York Times, February 16, 1986, p. 27A.

80. The Omnibus Tax Act of 1981 provided a 25 percent reduction in income tax rates staged over the next three years. The 1986 Tax Act reduced the number of rates to three: 15 percent on incomes under $29,750 (for married couples filing jointly), 28 percent on incomes from $29,751 to $71,900, and 33 percent on incomes from $71,900 to $149,250. Incomes over $149,250 were taxable at the 28 percent rate. This act effectively eliminated the income tax liability for any married couple with income under $6,200 and for any single person with an income under $3,750. See also Rom, "Transforming State," pp. 361–362.

81. David L. Kirk, "The California Work/Welfare Scheme," Public Interest, no. 83 (Spring 1986): 34–48.

82. Michael Wiseman, "Workfare and Welfare Reform," in Harrell R. Rodgers, Jr., ed., Beyond Welfare: New Approaches to the Problem of Poverty in America (Armonk, NY: M. E. Sharpe, 1988), p. 30.

83. Judith M. Gueron, "State Welfare Employment Initiatives: Lessons from the 1980s," Focus (a newsletter of the University of Wisconsin Institute for Research on Poverty), 11, no. 1 (Spring 1988): 17–23; See also, Rebecca Cook, "Work First Study: Job Training Helps, but Problems Persist," Moscow-Pullman Daily News, November 23–24, 2000, p. 6A.

84. Lawrence M. Mead, "Jobs Programs and Other Bromides," The New York Times, May 19, 1992, p. 18.

85. The Gallup Poll: Public Opinion, 1995 (Wilmington, DE: Scholarly Resources, Inc., 1996), pp. 28–32, 203–206.

86. Public Perspective 6, no. 4 (June–July 1995): 25.

87. Julie Kosterlitz, "Behavior Modification," National Journal, February 1, 1992, pp. 271–275.

88. Washington Post National Weekly, February 12–18, 1996, p. 29. Time limits were adopted by WA, MT, AZ, ND, SD, NE, MO, WI, IL, IN, FL, VA, DE, CT. Work requirements were adopted by OR, MT, WY, VT, CO, ND, SD, NE, OK, IA, MO, WI, IL, IN, MS, LA, SC, VA, MD, DE, CT, VT, HI. Family caps were adopted by CA, AZ, NE, KS, OK, AR, WI, IL, IN, MS, FL, GA, SC, NC, VA, MD, DE, NJ, MA.

89. See Investors Business Daily, August 22, 1996, p. B-1.

90. Welfare Reform (Washington, DC: General Accounting Office, 2002), report no. GAO-02-884; Walter Trattner, From Poor Law to Welfare State, 6th ed. (New York: Free Press, 1999); Time Almanac (Needham, MA: Pearson Education, 2004), p. 630; Sheila Zedlewski, "Trends and Issues in Welfare Reform," in The Book of the States (Lexington, KY: Council of State Governments, 2004), pp. 586–591; Statistical Abstract, 2008, pp. 458–489; C. Alan Joyce, ed., World Almanac 2009 (World Almanac Books: Pleasantville, NY, 2009), p. 88.

91. Pamela Loprest, How Families That Left Welfare Are Doing: A National Picture (Washington, DC: Urban Institute, 1999); Kathy Sawyer, "The Poorest Get Poorer," Washington Post National Weekly

Edition, August 30, 1999, p. 34; Jonathan Walters, "The Flip Side of Welfare Reform," *Governing* 15, no. 6 (March 2000): 16–21; *Governing State and Local Source Book* (a supplement to *Governing* magazine: 2002): p. 88; *Welfare Reform: Outcomes* (GAO); Amy Goldstein and Jonathan Weisman, "The Present's War on Poverty," *Washington Post National Weekly Edition*, February 17–23, 2003, pp. 11–12; Zedlewski, "Trends and Issues," pp. 586–591.

92. Rom, "Transforming State," p. 360.

93. Rebecca Cook, "Aggressive Tactics for Reducing Welfare Rolls Decried," *Moscow-Pullman Daily News*, August 24, 2004, p. 2A.

94. Jason Deparle, "Welfare Aid Isn't Growing as Economy Drops Off," *New York Times*, February 2, 2009 (electronic edition); Robert Pear, "In a Tough Economy, Old Limits on Welfare," *New York Times*, April 10, 2010 (electronic edition); Dan Murphy, "A Tattered Safety Net for U.S. Unemployed," *Christian Science Monitor*, December 11, 2008.

95. *World Almanac, 2009*, p. 116.

96. Martin Bronfenbrenner, Werner Sichel, and Wayland Gardner, *Macroeconomics* (Boston: Houghton Mifflin, 1990), pp. 235–236.

97. Julian Wolpert, *Patterns of Generosity in America* (New York: Twentieth Century Fund, 1993).

Education

CHAPTER PREVIEW

In Texas, the public school districts must use textbooks that follow the state board of education's curriculum guidelines or else pay for the textbooks themselves. Because the state's textbook market is so large, it has traditionally influenced the features of textbooks marketed all across the country. The 2010 revisions to those guidelines in social studies triggered a storm of criticism, with critics complaining that the state board was injecting political ideology into the schools and replacing substantive factual information with political opinion.[1]

One change involved reducing coverage of Thomas Jefferson because some board members disliked his emphasis on separation of church and state. Another change was adding the claim that the U.S. government was significantly infiltrated by communists during the Joseph McCarthy era. The new guidelines also called for more criticism of the War on Poverty and affirmative action and for replacing the term "capitalism" with "free enterprise system" (the latter term apparently sounding more positive than the former). Historians complained that the changes were based more on political correctness than careful historical analysis. Textbook manufacturers tried to cope with the controversy by noting that newer digital technology enables them to produce multiple versions of the same book, a development that will probably reduce Texas' influence on the national textbook market.

One of the most important services provided by state and local governments is public education. This service generally consumes more tax dollars and employs more people than any other state or local policy area. In recent years, much of education politics has focused on improving the quality of education, and controversies regarding what the education system should emphasize. We will examine this phenomenon in this chapter by studying:

1 How state, local, and federal governments work together (not always harmoniously) in providing public education.

2 How political values affect the roles people think education should play in society.

3 How state and local governments cope with major educational problems today.

4 How state and local governments have responded to the demands for educational reform.

5 How education is linked to the political economies of states and communities.

Introduction

Public education in the United States has traditionally been viewed as the means by which people can learn skills and attitudes that will make them employable, enrich their lives, and/or help them move up socially. And there can be little doubt that education has accomplished some of these goals for the average person. One group of researchers tried to assess the effects of education by studying the life earnings of identical twins. The researchers concluded that each year of schooling adds 16 percent to a person's earnings over a lifetime.[2] Education also confers other benefits. Well-educated people tend to have better health habits than poorly educated people. They tend to know more about the world around them, and they tend to enjoy a wider variety of leisure activities. As we saw earlier in the book, they are also more active in politics.

Despite the importance of education for an individual's lifetime opportunities, a large number of critics question whether the quality of American education is as good as it once was or whether it is good enough for America to keep up in an increasingly competitive and high-technology world. Knowledge of science is critical to high technology, but an international science test for eighth graders found that while American youngsters were outscored by children in seven other countries, they still scored above the average for all of the countries included in the study. However, American students in the final year of secondary school science performed less impressively, falling below the international average and below the average scores of 15 of the 19 other countries examined.[3]

Eighth grade mathematics scores for American students were approximately at the international average, but below the average scores of students in 14 other countries. American students in their final high school mathematics course scored below the average scores of students in 17 of the 19 other countries.[4] Earlier studies of math and science proficiency found similar results.[5] However, a test of reading abilities found that the American youngsters did somewhat better, scoring fifth out of 11 countries studied.[6] In addition, the United States has lost its traditional lead in the proportion of its young adults who have a college degree.[7]

These results are not encouraging for America's future, and they have stimulated a succession of national reports on the state of education in America. The first and most seminal of these reports was *A Nation at Risk*, issued in 1983 by the **National Commission on Excellence in Education**. This report charged that, for the first time in American history, the average high school graduate is less well educated than the average graduate a generation earlier, and that American students performed poorly in comparison to the students of other industrialized nations.[8] As a consequence of this report, education suddenly became an issue, both at the national and state levels.

Critics of this perspective, however, charge that the education "crisis" is greatly overblown and, in some respects, misunderstood. In *The Manufactured Crisis*, David Berliner and Bruce Biddle carefully analyze the evidence used in *A Nation at Risk* and in other reports denouncing America's schools.[9] Berliner and Biddle find that much of the evidence used to condemn the educational system is faulty and that some of it has been misinterpreted. (Anyone interested in education should read their book.)

In this chapter, we will examine these educational concerns. We will first examine the eroding tradition of local control over education and the conflicts growing out of the increasing state and federal responsibilities. Second, education will be viewed from the liberal and conservative philosophical perspectives. Third, the way governments cope with the main problems of education will be examined in detail. Fourth, we will explore developments in educational reform since the 1983 publication of *A Nation at Risk*. Finally, we will discuss the role of education in our dual concerns of social conflict and the political economy.

STATE, LOCAL, AND FEDERAL ROLES IN EDUCATION

Local Roles

The basic unit governing public education at the primary and secondary level in most parts of the country is the local, **independent school district**. The main exceptions to this are in Alaska, Hawaii, and Maine, where all the schools (Hawaii) or some (Alaska and Maine) are run by the state. In a dozen states, some school systems are subordinated to local governments such as counties (Virginia and North Carolina, for example) or to cities (New York City and Chicago, for example). But 90 percent of all public school systems are independent school districts governed by locally elected **boards of education** that are officially independent of counties, cities, and other units of local government (although there may be informal relationships between school districts and other local governments). The local school boards establish local school district policies, set the budget, and decide how much money to raise in property taxes.

In practice, the initiative in these matters usually is taken by the local superintendent of schools, not the school boards. The superintendent proposes policies and budgets to the board, sets the school board meeting agendas, and presents the board with a limited number of options. The board members often lack the educational expertise to become effective policy leaders. Moreover, school board members usually have personal responsibilities (jobs, families, and so forth) that leave only limited time to devote to major educational issues. Instead, board members tend to involve themselves in small details of school operations and to lose their focus on the board's primary task—setting educational policy.[10]

At the same time, in the event of a major problem, the school board may become more involved, even to the point of replacing the superintendent. Community sentiments informally influence local schools in countless ways, from the values that students bring to school to whether the local community votes for or against providing additional funds for education. Local public opinion has, therefore, considerable impact on local educational spending and other features of local education policy, such as disciplinary actions.[11]

The Trend Toward Greater State Centralization

The existence of independent school districts provides some degree of local control over schools. In fact, however, local control has eroded steadily over the past 40 years as the state and federal governments have gained influence in setting education policy. This trend is reflected in the decreasing role of local governments in financing public schools (see Table 14.1) and the declining number of local school districts themselves—from more than 127,000 in 1932 to 13,506 in 2002. Small, rural districts with only a few dozen high school students lacked the resources to finance modern laboratories, more specialized teachers, elaborate extracurricular activities, and the other expensive features of modern schools. Consequently, legislatures forced many small districts to consolidate, although the process was very controversial in some areas.

TABLE 14.1

Centralization of Public School Finance

Percentage of Public School Expenditures Financed

Level of Government	1960	1970	1980	1990	2002	2005
Federal	4%	7%	9%	6%	7%	9%
State	39%	41%	49%	4%	50%	48%
Local	56%	52%	42%	45%	43%	43%

Sources: Calculated from the Bureau of the Census, *Statistical Abstract of the United States, 1982–83* (Washington, DC: U.S. Government Printing Office, 1982), p. 154; *Statistical Abstract, 1991*, p. 149; *Statistical Abstract, 2003*, p. 160; *Statistical Abstract, 2006*, p. 155, *Statistical Abstract* (online edition).

The traditional keystone of state educational policy making is the **state education agency (SEA)**. The SEA is usually composed of a state board of education, a chief state school officer who is often called a **commissioner** or **superintendent of schools**, and a department of education. The state board of education adopts many of the overall educational policies for the state. It sets minimum high school graduation requirements; it legitimizes decisions made by the state department of education; it insulates the department from the governor (to varying degrees); and, in almost half the states, it appoints the chief state school officer. Sixty percent of the state boards of education are appointed directly by the governor.

Although the SEAs historically exercised limited influence on local school districts, their influence has grown in recent years. The local school districts, the governor, and the legislature often look to the SEA to provide educational leadership—to initiate new ideas, to ask for money, to see that local districts carry out state and national policies, and to maintain a positive public image for public education. The SEA distributes state educational funds to local school districts, approves requests for categorical grants, and provides basic research and information to legislative committees that must deal with school problems. SEAs also provide a number of services to local school districts, from coping with specific problems to conducting analyses to help local school officials assess their schools' performance. The more that other political figures look to the SEAs for educational leadership and services, the more important the SEAs become.[12]

Since the early 1980s, governors and legislatures have assumed increasing influence over educational policy, in part due to public concerns over educational system performance. As we will see later in the chapter, some of the most visible reforms in some states, such as testing teachers and tightening graduation requirements, have been forced on local school districts by governors and legislatures over the initial objections of teacher organizations and other educator groups. Greater involvement by governors, legislators, and SEAs is also due, in part, to recent federal initiatives in education.

Federal Roles

Historically, the federal government played a small role in public education, although limited aid programs date back to the 1780s. It was not until 1965 that Congress passed a broad program of aid to all public school districts (see Table 14.2), but even today the federal government provides only 9 percent of all public school funding.

TABLE 14.2

Federal Aid to Education Landmarks

1787	Northwest Ordinance. Reserved one section of each township in the Northwest Territory for the endowment of schools.
1862	The Morrill Act. Provided grants of federal land to set up land-grant colleges for agriculture and mechanical arts.
1917	The Smith-Hughes Act. Provided federal grants for vocational education at the precollegiate level.
1944	The Servicemen's Readjustment Act (GI Bill of Rights). Provided educational benefits to World War II veterans. Later expanded to include Korean, Cold War, and Vietnam veterans.
1946	National school lunch and milk programs. Provided for lunches and milk to be served in public and private schools.
1950	National Science Foundation (NSF) established. The NSF encouraged scientific research and the education of scientists.
1958	National Defense Education Act (NDEA). Provided grants for equipment, loans for college students, and fellowships for graduate students.
1965	Elementary and Secondary Education Act (ESEA). This act, plus its later amendments, set the framework for contemporary aid to education, including funds for compensatory education for children in poverty areas.
1965	Head Start Program. Provided federal aid to support preschool education, health care, nutrition, and social services for poor children.
1965	National Endowments for the Arts and Humanities (NEA and NEH) established. Created to stimulate the arts and humanities; similar to the stimulus that NSF provided for science.
1965	Higher Education Act. This act, plus its later amendments, set the basic framework for federal aid to higher education, including student financial assistance such as Upward Bound, scholarships, loans, and cooperative education.
1972	Basic Educational Opportunity Grant (later called Pell Grant) program started. Initiated federal assistance programs for college students.
1997	Initiated tax credits to finance part of the tuition for college.
2001	No Child Left Behind Act. This law mandated creating state accountability systems to monitor school performance. Local education authorities were to take corrective action in failing schools or permit students to transfer to another school within their school district, and some federal aid money could be used to finance that transfer. School systems were given somewhat increased flexibility in using federal education funds and the law also emphasized improving reading skills.

The federal government's impact on public education, however, goes beyond the small share of schooling that it funds. The federal influence comes largely from the federal mandates that we studied in Chapter 3. Through congressional and judicial mandates, the federal government has played a major role in public school desegregation, in seeking parity for male and female athletic programs, and in prodding local schools to offer **compensatory education** for disadvantaged children. The main instruments for this have been the 1965 **Elementary and Secondary Education Act** and the Head Start program, which was designed to give culturally deprived children some preschool preparation for the first grade. According to some studies, these and other federal programs have been effective in improving the education of poor children.[13] In 1981, several educational grants were consolidated into a block grant under the **Education Consolidation and Improvement Act,** which reduced the amount of federal funds involved, but increased the authority of states over how the funds would be spent.[14]

More recently, the **No Child Left Behind Act** of 2001 (which was a reauthorization of the Elementary and Secondary Education Act) offered a number of new policies that, in some respects, increased state and local discretion, but did the opposite in other respects. The law required states to have statewide accountability systems to monitor the performance of individual schools and of various subgroups of students within each school. If a school failed to meet the standards, the school system must take corrective action. If the problems were not resolved within five years, state officials must take corrective actions. The new law gave state and local school authorities more flexibility in their use of federal education aid (which is, however, a relatively small share of total education funding). The law required the states to ensure that teachers are well trained in the subjects they teach, although the states have significant leeway in deciding how that should be assessed. The law also placed increased emphasis on reading skills and provides funds for upgrading teacher training. A growing chorus of critics complained that the law had too many rules and regulations, put too much emphasis on testing, and failed to provide enough funding or assistance for schools that need to improve.[15]

Criticism of the No Child Left Behind law came from all shades of the political spectrum, from conservative states (Virginia, Utah) and liberal states (Hawaii, Vermont). As a result, the Bush administration eventually agreed to give the states more flexibility in implementing the law. At the same time, all of the states have made significant efforts to comply with at least some features of the law.[16]

The Obama administration retained many features of No Child Left Behind, especially its emphasis on systematically evaluating the performance of schools, teachers, and students. However, the administration also created a competitive grant program, "Race to the Top," to support innovative, new educational programs; virtually all of the states that reached the second stage of the grant process included some form of added payments for teachers and principals who were especially successful. The administration also pushed for greater support for early childhood education and more financial aid for college students.[17] Officials in some states have continued to oppose efforts to develop nationwide standards for assessing school performance,[18] even though most of the work to develop nationwide standards has been done by state and local education officials.

Although federal influence in some areas of education policy making is significant, the federal role is relatively limited in scope. Some of the most fundamental educational policy decisions, such as what courses a student must complete in order to graduate from high school or what training a teacher must receive, are primarily up to states and localities to decide.

Postsecondary Public Education

At the postsecondary level, the most significant public institutions are the state universities, the state college systems, the community college systems, and the postsecondary vocational schools. In addition, private colleges, universities, and technical schools serve many students every year. There is a clear pecking order among the public institutions. At the top of the pecking order are the central campuses of the state universities, which get the biggest share (per student) of the state higher education budget. They have the most affluent undergraduates.

They generally pay their faculty higher salaries than are paid by other public higher education facilities. They tend to be research-oriented institutions, but teaching is still taken seriously. And they get most of the grants awarded to higher education in the state for research, experimentation, and program implementation.

Less prestigious than the major campus of the state university is the state college system. These colleges often started as teachers' colleges early in the twentieth century, but were expanded into extensive university systems to accommodate the boom of students during the 1950s and 1960s and to increase the supply of highly educated professionals in a variety of fields.

At the bottom of the pecking order are the two-year community colleges and the *postsecondary vocational schools*. On the average, they get the least money per student, have the poorest libraries, and give their instructors the heaviest teaching loads. A Brookings Institution study in 1981 charged that the community colleges have diluted academic rigor in their attempts to increase their budgets and enrollments. Only 10 percent of community college students graduated from the two-year programs, and fewer yet transferred to four-year programs at colleges and universities,[19] although not all of that pattern may be due to inadequacy. Some students take particular courses because they are interested in the topic, for mental stimulation, or to improve their job skills rather than to pursue a degree. This seems to be particularly true for people who are already college graduates and for older students, millions of whom take adult education courses[20] (not all are taught by community colleges, but many are). Some students also terminate their studies due to financial problems.

Critics have called attention to the fact that the United States has lost its lead in the proportion of young adults with college degrees. The latest statistics put the United States in twelfth place in college degree rates.[21] However, the proportion of young people with an associate's degree or higher varies greatly from state to state. Massachusetts led the nation in 2006, with roughly half of all young adults having a degree. That is within a few percentage points of the world leaders. At the other extreme, just over one-fourth of the young people in Arkansas and Nevada held an associate's degree or higher.[22]

As many of you know, one reason why the United States has not kept pace with the world leaders in college graduation rates is the dramatic increase in the costs of going to college. From 1985 to 2008, tuition and fees at public, four-year colleges and universities more than quadrupled.[23] Tuition at private colleges and universities rose only slightly more slowly. Growth at both types of institutions far exceeded the growth rate of family income in the same period. A major reason for the rising tuition and fees at public universities is the gradual decline of state funding for higher education (relative to the cost of running the universities). Not surprisingly, therefore, young people from wealthy families are much more likely to attend college than are young people from poor families. Students and their families are also borrowing more money to finance college.[24]

Due in part to economic disparities, African American and Hispanic students are less likely to go on to college than are whites. Another part of the college enrollment issue is the new gender gap. For many years, males were much more likely to attend college than were females. However, since the 1970s, female high school graduates have been more likely to attend college than have males. The differences have not been very large in most years, but college enrollment nationwide has consistently shown a larger female contingent than male contingent.[25] Increasing college graduation rates will probably require overcoming the financial obstacles to higher education, encouraging more minority students to attend college, and increasing male enrollment.

Another issue in higher education is the rise of for-profit colleges, many of which offer much of their instruction over the Internet. They have proliferated in recent years, and a recent study found that some for-profit colleges encouraged students to lie on their financial aid applications to qualify for more federal financial help.[26] Critics have also charged that some of the for-profit colleges have very low academic standards and fail to give students a decent education.

POLITICAL VALUES AND PUBLIC EDUCATION

The View from the Right

Conservatives view public education as a force for promoting upward social mobility and developing the human capital (skills, knowledge, attitudes) that will improve overall economic productivity. For the hundreds of thousands of young people who become high school dropouts and remain functional illiterates, however, public and private education programs have failed.

Conservatives view these failures as partly the fault of the individuals and partly the fault of the schools. Edward Banfield, a national authority on urban politics, once asserted that some students were not mentally capable of doing high school work.[27] Some observers contend that these individuals tend to be concentrated in the lower classes and the racial minorities, many of whom share a culture of poverty, which inhibits the desire for achievement and self-improvement, and the ability to defer gratification.[28] In this view, lower-class students will often fail to make use of available education opportunities.[29] Other writers have tried to relate poor educational achievement to genetic factors.[30] Some people have more talent than others, and some people are more willing to work hard to make the most of their talents. Some writers predict a hardening and widening of socioeconomic divisions as people with low IQs fail to acquire the knowledge and skills needed to function in a high-tech world.[31]

Conservatives also blame America's school problems on liberal educational philosophies traced to John Dewey. In this view, educational permissiveness has let the schools drift away from the basics of education, which focus on reading, writing, and mathematical skills. However, some conservative critics also want the schools to give students a greater appreciation of American culture and values. Some conservatives call for more rigid discipline; in some instances they favor giving schools greater flexibility to suspend or expel students identified as troublemakers. In sum, conservatives are very concerned about the ability of the educational system to provide a competent workforce for American business.

The View from the Left

Many liberals agree with the conservatives on the premise that education should provide economic opportunity, assure upward social mobility, and produce skilled workers for the economy.[32] The liberal, having an optimistic view of human nature, also views education as a force for human development, the expansion of minds. Unlike the conservative, the liberal views our educational shortcomings as largely failures of the school system, not the individual— although most liberals recognize that some students fail to make use of educational opportunities. Many liberals believe that the basic problems lie in segregated schools, unequal education funding, and in poor people's lack of control over their educational environment.

According to this perspective, our problems could be reduced if we would just spend enough money (for the right things), eliminate the inequalities in school finance, and do a better job of motivating students. Many liberals also believe that, with the exception of the severely mentally retarded, everyone has the potential to acquire knowledge and develop employable skills, although not necessarily to the same degree. What prevents this development is that the school systems have never reformed themselves enough to cope with a broad range of students' backgrounds, interests, and needs. That range is strongly influenced by home environments. Children from poorer families and with less educated parents are less likely to participate in literacy activities (such as being read to) at home during their preschool years or to have access to a computer or the Internet at home.[33]

Many liberals advocate more reforms and more experimentation, and often reject the conservative emphasis on basic skills, rigid discipline, and rote learning, all of which may bore and alienate students. Much liberal support goes to such school reforms as open schools, programs that allow greater individual flexibility in the classroom, and programs to keep disruptive youngsters in the classroom (possibly a separate classroom or alternative schools) rather than expelling them. Many liberals also support bilingual education and multicultural education, as we shall discuss shortly.

STRUGGLES OVER VALUES

Not all educational conflicts fit neatly in the liberal–conservative spectrum. For example, what role, if any, should religion play in public education? If some religions do not agree with some scientific theories, should that conflict be part of the science curriculum?[34] If schools should promote good citizenship, what is a good citizen? Should the schools encourage obedience or political involvement? Should schools teach students to trust public officials or view them skeptically? Should schools emphasize individualism or cooperation and living harmoniously with other people? What moral values, if any, should the schools teach?

At the heart of these differences over educational practice are conflicts over fundamental social values themselves. A survey of state educational policy leaders found that four fundamental values predominated.[35] These were: (1) quality, as exemplified by conflicts over making graduation requirements more strict or lengthening the school year; (2) equity, as exemplified by conflicts over attempts to provide special programs for handicapped and disadvantaged youngsters; (3) efficiency, as exemplified by conflicts over holding down school costs in the face of potentially expensive reform measures; and (4) choice, as exemplified by conflicts over decentralization, giving local schools more flexibility in providing educational services, and using a **voucher plan** to give parents more freedom to choose which public or private school their children will attend. **Charter schools**, which are exempt from many regulations and have more operational flexibility, also fit into the decentralization view.

There are important inconsistencies in these values. Liberals and conservatives would agree, for example, on the value of quality education, but they might well part company on the trade-offs between quality education and some of the other values. Liberals are likely to charge that the conservative emphasis on efficiency will reduce the quality of education. Conservatives, in turn, are likely to charge that the liberal emphasis on equity will divert resources from the goal of quality education and make it more difficult to attain. Political moderates sometimes worry that wrangling between liberals and conservatives may divert attention from the daily tasks of studying and learning.

EDUCATION AND SOCIAL CONFLICT

The social conflicts of recent years have not left public education untouched. Three areas in particular have felt the brunt of these conflicts—racial desegregation, equalization of school finance (or not), and politicization of the curriculum.

Desegregation

De Jure Segregation   In 1954, the Supreme Court struck down public school segregation as a violation of the Equal Protection Clause of the U.S. Constitution. The clause states that no state may deny any person the equal protection of the law. In a famous case in 1896, the Supreme Court set down the legal justification for segregation (initially for transportation services, but the principle gradually spread). The Court approved separate public facilities for African Americans and whites as long as the separate facilities were equal. This was the famous **separate-but-equal doctrine**. Several states used this ruling to justify the establishment (or continuation) of separate school systems for whites and minorities, and in 1927 the Supreme Court specifically approved this practice.[36] By the mid-twentieth century, 17 states plus the District of Columbia legally required segregated schools, and another four states permitted segregation at the local level.

Segregation consisted of a dual school system—one for white children and an entirely separate system for minority children. Because this system was established by law, it is referred to as *de jure* **segregation**. The school system for minorities was almost never given as many resources as the white system, thus making a mockery of the provision that the separate systems be *equal*.

African American civil rights leaders, working through the National Association for the Advancement of Colored People (NAACP), spent the first half of the twentieth century attempting to have these dual systems declared unconstitutional. Their first victory came in 1938 in Missouri. The University of Missouri Law School refused to admit African Americans even though the state had no separate law school for them. It attempted to meet the separate-but-equal requirement by offering scholarships to send African Americans to out-of-state law schools. The U.S. Supreme Court struck this down as unconstitutional.[37]

Ten years later, the University of Oklahoma was obliged to admit African Americans to its law school.[38] The university discriminated against these newly admitted students, however. They were not allowed to use the cafeteria at the same time as the white students or to use the regular desks in the reading room of the library, and they were required to sit for classes in an anteroom adjoining the classroom, where they could not see the professor. The Supreme Court also struck down this practice as unconstitutional.[39] Texas attempted to meet the separate-but-equal requirement by building a separate law school for African Americans, but the Supreme Court ruled that no such segregated school could possibly be equal to the University of Texas at Austin with its excellent library, its top-notch faculty, and its prestige.[40]

All these developments came to a climax in the famous 1954 *Brown v. Board of Education* decision, in which the Supreme Court unanimously struck down the dual school systems as violating the **Equal Protection Clause** of the U.S. Constitution.[41] The schools were ordered to desegregate with all deliberate speed. However, desegregation made little progress in its first ten years.[42] In succeeding years, however, the pace of integration increased, and by the 1990s considerable progress had been made in desegregating the once legally segregated school systems of the South, at least as far as the public schools were concerned.

Outside the South, there were usually no laws requiring racial segregation in schools. Rather, the schools were segregated in fact because minorities lived in one part of the city while whites lived in another. This has been called *de facto* **segregation**.

Coping with *de facto* segregation is much harder than coping with *de jure* segregation. Although a variety of techniques have been attempted in the *de facto*-segregated cities to put African American and white children into the same classrooms (such as magnet schools, voluntary transfers, open enrollment plans, and paired schools), the most direct tactic was the involuntary busing of both African American and white children to integrated schools. In *Swann v. Charlotte-Mecklenburg Board of Education* (1971),[43] the U.S. Supreme Court ruled that federal district courts may require busing to desegregate if there is evidence that the segregation results from legal measures to alter school boundaries or to impose residential segregation.

Busing and White Flight   The Court's busing decisions were extremely unpopular. Court-ordered busing was greeted with open resentment in several major cities. Since the school-age populations of many big cities were disproportionately composed of minorities, however, there were limits as to how much desegregation could be achieved by busing within the central cities. By 1980, only three of the nation's 25 largest school districts had more white students than minority students.[44]

According to critics of busing, the movement from segregation to desegregation to resegregation stemmed in large part from **white flight**. White parents with enough money could flee the whole problem of desegregation. If they did not want to flee by actually moving to the suburbs, they could send their children to private academies or parochial schools.

The critics noted that between 1973, when forced busing started in Boston, and 1975, the city lost more than a third of its white pupils, while its minority population increased.[45] In Atlanta, busing went into effect in 1972. By 1975, the African American share of school enrollment increased from 56 to 87 percent. In Memphis, busing started in 1973 and by 1976, the African American share of enrollment increased from 50 to 70 percent.[46]

Not all white flight from central-city schools can be attributed to mandatory busing, since white enrollment also dropped off in cities that did not have compulsory busing programs.[47] But white flight was much greater in places with the mandatory busing plans. According to one respected pair of researchers, white enrollment dropped an average of 25 percent between 1968 and 1991 in districts with mandatory busing plans, compared to a drop of only 3 percent in districts without such plans.[48]

Desegregation and Alternatives to Busing   Mandatory busing, of course, is not the only way to achieve desegregation, and evidence suggests that some other alternatives are more effective. An analysis of desegregation in more than 600 school districts found that the most effective approach is a voluntary desegregation plan based on alternatives such as magnet schools and majority-to-minority transfer programs. These transfer programs permit students to transfer from a school in which their race is a majority to a different school where they will be a minority. Voluntary plans such as these produced less white flight on average than did the mandatory busing plans, and they produced more interracial exposure, as measured by the percentage of white enrollment in the average African American child's school. The least successful desegregation tactics were controlled choice plans in which parents had some choices in where to send their children, but the choices were limited to those that would increase rather than reduce racial balance in the schools. Controlled choice plans produced almost as much white flight as mandatory busing and accomplished less interracial exposure than the voluntary plans.[49]

Desegregation and the Suburbs   In retrospect, white flight was not anticipated very well by the advocates of mandatory busing, and it has led to problems that we as a nation have failed to cope with successfully.[50] It has left most large central cities such as Washington, DC, Chicago, New York, and Atlanta with white school populations so small as to make meaningful central-city desegregation impossible.

Is it possible to enlist the suburbs of these and other central cities in the quest to desegregate the schools? The record to date is not very encouraging, at least not very encouraging for mandatory enlistment. The only places where mandatory desegregation could easily include the suburbs are those places where the school district boundaries follow county lines. And this phenomenon is limited primarily to the South and the border states.

In most instances, suburbs were exempted from forced busing. The Supreme Court, in the 1974 case *Millikin v. Bradley*, refused to extend busing to the Detroit suburbs because it could not be shown that the suburban school district boundaries had been drawn deliberately to exclude African Americans.[51] In the absence of a clear suburban intent to segregate their schools, the Supreme Court seemed to be saying that racial homogeneity in the suburbs was an example of *de facto* segregation and beyond the Court's authority to remedy.

Critics of the Court and its refusal to require cross-district busing reject this distinction between *de jure* segregation that the Court can remedy and *de facto* segregation that is beyond the Court's reach. In the critics' view, the concentration of racial minorities in the big cities is in reality *de jure* segregation because governments at all levels consistently support racial segregation in housing. Federal loan programs guaranteed many suburban mortgages. Federal and state highway programs built the transportation network that enabled suburbia to be built. And the states sanctioned many exclusionary zoning and planning devices that protected suburbia from racial integration. These critics of the Court's unwillingness to require cross-district school integration charged that the application of the intent-to-segregate principle should have been broadened to include a whole range of government actions whose effect has been to concentrate minorities in the central-city schools. From this viewpoint, there is no distinction between *de jure* and *de facto* segregation.

Some state courts have expressed sympathy with this view of the critics,[52] but the federal courts have consistently upheld the distinction between *de facto* and *de jure* segregation.[53] Where segregation appears to have resulted from *de facto* housing and demographic trends, however, the federal courts have not intervened. In a 1992 case, the Supreme Court said, "Racial balance is not to be achieved for its own sake...the school district is under no duty to remedy the imbalance that is caused by demographic factors."[54]

Successful Suburban Experiments   Where cross-district busing has been achieved, it has usually involved special circumstances. In Louisville, Kentucky, the central city and Jefferson County merged their two separate school systems in 1975 and initiated a countywide desegregation program. Although greeted by considerable white protest, this project was carried out successfully. [55]

In Delaware, the city of Wilmington was excluded from a 1968 statewide school district consolidation plan that changed the boundaries of all other school districts. Ruling that this exclusion had the effect of legally concentrating African American students in the Wilmington school district, thus constituting *de jure* segregation, the federal courts ordered busing between the suburban and central-city schools.[56]

Judicial Backtracking   In recent years, the federal courts have backed away from pressuring school systems into making desegregation agreements. In 1986, the Supreme Court allowed Norfolk, Virginia, to end its court-ordered busing plan even though that meant an increase in the number of children attending all-African American schools.[57] The following year, federal courts returned control over Boston schools to the local school board. From 1973 to 1987, the Boston schools had been overseen by U.S. district court judge W. Arthur Garrity. He reacted to

Boston's foot-dragging on desegregation by literally taking over the schools, imposing a busing plan, and overseeing day-to-day school operations down to the point of assigning teachers and approving specific budget items. After Garrity withdrew his control in 1987, the school board, on a racially divided vote, drew up a new attendance plan that would give both white and African American parents unprecedented flexibility in choosing the schools for their children.[58]

Four years later, in 1991, the Supreme Court backed even further away from forced desegregation. It permitted Oklahoma City to end a court-ordered busing plan that had been in force since 1972.[59] A federal court had previously recognized the district as having put an end to its segregation, but the 1972 desegregation order nevertheless remained in force. Challenging the court order, the district cut back on cross-town busing in 1985 and made more use of neighborhood schools. Parents of African American children sued, and a federal district court ordered that the school system continue operating under the original desegregation order. In 1991, the Supreme Court overturned that judgment and freed the Oklahoma City schools from the court-imposed desegregation plan. Central to the Court's ruling was Oklahoma City's claim that its previously segregated school system had been made *unitary*. To be considered unitary, a school district had to meet three tests. First, it had to show that it had continuously complied with the court desegregation decree in good faith. Second, it had to have abandoned any intentional act of segregation. And third, it had to eliminate the vestiges of prior discriminatory conduct.

One year later, in 1992, on similar grounds, the Supreme Court also allowed the De Kalb County, Georgia, school system (suburban Atlanta) to end its desegregation plans.[60] These two cases are viewed as ominous by advocates of court-ordered desegregation. With Oklahoma City and De Kalb County as precedents, there might be many other school systems around the country that would seek to overturn desegregation court orders by claiming that they too had been made unitary. In 1995, the Supreme Court ruled that enough progress had been made on desegregation goals in Kansas City that it permitted the state of Missouri to reduce its expenditures for magnet schools and other expenses associated with the Kansas City desegregation efforts.[61]

The most dramatic judicial backtracking occurred in 2007 when the U.S. Supreme Court ruled that Louisville, Kentucky's desegregation system was unconstitutional because it considered the races of students in deciding which students went to which schools.[62] The divided nature of the decision left many schools officials uncertain regarding what courses of action might or might not be legally permitted.

How Schools Are Financed

Funding the schools has been a recurring source of controversy over the years. One of the most sensitive financial aspects of school funding is the contrast of some schools that can afford virtually anything that parents and teachers desire with other schools that lack the money needed to meet more basic needs. This imbalance in fiscal resources can be traced to the way in which public education is financed.

Table 14.1 shows that about 43 percent of the money for public schools comes from local governments, almost exclusively from the property tax, the traditional means for financing public education. In order to supplement local property taxes, the states have historically offered a **foundation aid program** that gives each school district a certain number of dollars for each pupil in the schools. The foundation aids frequently have an equalization formula so that more money goes to districts with many poor students and a small property-tax base.

Fiscal Disparities in School Finance   In places where a majority of school money comes from local property taxes, a small school district with an electric power plant, a large shopping center, or an industrial park will have abundant tax resources for public schools, whereas a neighboring district without these developments will be short on tax resources. The term for this uneven distribution of property tax resources is **fiscal disparities**. In some states, the disparities from one district to another lead to extreme differences in educational spending. In the late 1980s, the 100 poorest districts in Texas were able to spend barely 40 percent as much per child (less than $3,000 per year) as the 100 richest districts (over $7,000 per year). A more recent analysis found that wealthier districts (measured by personal income) had more generously funded schools in roughly three-fourths of the states. The wealthiest public schools in the United States spend ten times as much per student as do the poorest schools.[63]

The result, according to Jonathan Kozol, is a pervasive pattern of inequalities that trap the poorest and most disadvantaged children in the school districts that lack resources to provide them with effective schooling.[64] Although experts disagree on the impact of financial resources on school performance, some research finds that schools with better technological resources and better physical conditions have higher student achievement.[65] Schools that are poorly funded also risk losing their best teachers to schools offering higher pay and more generous benefits.

Attempts at Finance Equalization   The problem of fiscal disparities came to a head in 1971 in the California court case of *Serrano v. Priest*.[66] Serrano lived in a school district that lacked substantial property tax resources and consequently found it hard to spend as much on schools as nearby districts that had a larger property tax base. Serrano sued the state of California for not providing equal educational opportunity for all children and all school districts in the state. The California Supreme Court agreed that the fiscal disparities inherent in the property tax financing of public education violated the state constitution and ordered California to find an alternative financing method.

No sooner had the California Supreme Court made this decision than parents in other states sought to get the principle applied nationwide under the Equal Protection Clause of the U.S. Constitution. A San Antonio, Texas, case came before the Supreme Court for decision in 1973. However, in *San Antonio School District v. Rodriguez*, the U.S. Supreme Court refused to apply the *Serrano* principle under federal law. The Court agreed that the states relied too heavily on the property tax. However, the court held that there is no federally guaranteed right to equal education.[67]

Since the *Rodriguez* case foreclosed the federal courts as an avenue for equalizing school finance, the battle shifted to state politics. Several general approaches emerged. One approach to finance equalization was to increase state funding for schools and allow local school districts to levy additional local property taxes to augment the state funds. The most explosive battle over this approach started in New Jersey in 1973 when the state's supreme court ordered the legislature to come up with a state income tax to equalize school finances.[68] The legislature, however, repeatedly refused to follow those directions, and in the summer of 1976, the supreme court reacted by closing all New Jersey public schools on the grounds that they were operating in violation of the state constitution. Faced with the prospect of schools not being able to start the next September, the legislature relented and passed a state income tax that enabled the state to absorb a major share of school funding.

As a consequence of this new funding law, the state portion of school finances rose from 23.6 percent in 1975 to 33.8 percent in 1980. This helped reduce disparities in tax rates between school districts, but over the next ten years the gap began to widen again.[69] In the light of this development, the New Jersey Supreme Court in 1990 ordered the state to bring the spending level of impoverished districts up to the level of the average suburb. New Jersey's Democratic Governor, Jim Florio, proposed raising the income tax by $2.8 billion, with $1.1 billion for the schools. Voter disenchantment with this solution was swift and harsh. The voters dealt a resounding defeat to the Democrats by returning the Republicans to a majority in the legislature, and in 1993 Governor Florio was himself unseated by Republican challenger Christine Whitman, who pledged to roll back the tax increases. Under Whitman, the $1.1 billion earmarked for schools was pared to $800 million. In 1994, the state supreme court once again ruled that the state needed to do more to reduce the disparities.[70]

New Jersey's wealthiest school districts hampered the state's efforts to equalize education funding by allotting local dollars that, when combined with state aid, still exceeded total funds available in poorer districts. The wealthiest districts continued their high level of local property taxes after receiving their state aid. The poorer districts, however, tended to reduce their property taxes after receiving the state funds. Even though their overall funding went up, it continued to fall behind that of the rich districts.[71] Disparities have declined somewhat.

The second approach to equalization relies solely on state funds. Hawaii has done this since achieving statehood, but Michigan presents the only example of a state moving to this method after having previously relied on property taxes for school funding. In 1990, Republican John Engler won the governorship in part by promising to reduce property taxes. In 1993, the Democratic-controlled legislature passed a bill that eliminated property taxes as a funding mechanism for schools, but they did not provide an alternative source of funds to make up for the loss of property tax revenues. They hoped to draw a governor's veto that would embarrass Engler by making it look as though he had reneged on his property-tax-cut pledge. Instead, Engler signed the bill into law, which threatened to leave the state's schools without any money. This self-inflicted crisis prodded the legislature to submit two funding proposals to Michigan voters in a referendum. The first option would increase the sales tax from 4 to 6 percent, and the second would make a comparable increase in the income tax. The voters chose the sales tax method, and in 1995–1996, Michigan schools were completely freed from their previous dependence on local property taxes.[72]

The third approach to reducing fiscal disparities occurred in Texas, which kept the property tax system but forced wealthy districts to share their property tax wealth with poor districts. In 1989, the Texas Supreme Court ordered the state to reduce the fiscal disparities in school finance. The legislature failed to act, and the court subsequently ordered all Texas public schools to close on June 1, 1993, if a new funding scheme was not in place by that date. Just a month before the deadline, voters rejected a funding proposal and thereby threw the state into a major crisis. To keep the schools open, the state now had to find a new funding scheme that would be acceptable to the state supreme court and still gain a majority vote among legislators whose constituents had just spoken loudly against equalization. The legislature accomplished this difficult feat just days before the deadline with a plan that would guarantee each school district $280,000 in property tax wealth per student. Wealthy school districts with more property tax wealth than this would have to give away some of their excess tax base so that it could be used to increase the tax base of poorer school districts.[73]

A fourth, hybrid approach emerged in Kentucky after a court ruling struck down Kentucky's school funding system. Inequalities in school financing and relatively low levels of educational attainment had triggered worries that the state's economy would suffer in competition with other states for new industries and investment. State and local officials assembled a complex package of reforms, including a foundation of state aid to all districts, additional state aid to districts that have higher tax effort for schools, performance standards for children and schools, and a preschool program for all four-year-old children.[74]

It is impossible to predict which of these approaches to finance equalization will produce the best long-term results. Important philosophical positions underlie each approach. And it is difficult to gain universal support for equalization, in part because of controversies regarding whether equal funding in the absence of other reforms will make dramatic improvements in educational quality or student performance.[75] In addition, residents of wealthier areas often resist paying additional taxes for improving the financial support of schools in poorer areas of the state. Moreover, some recent research suggests that certain school systems use creative accounting methods in order to conceal the fact that they are more generously funded than others.[76]

The push for more equal education funding has been hampered by the recent recession, which has triggered cuts in state aid to education and declining local revenues in many school districts.[77] In addition, the recession has reduced voter support for higher school taxes and school bond proposals.[78] The recession has also led to controversies in some states as governors, primarily Republicans, have tried to eliminate some or all collective bargaining rights for school teachers.

A parallel funding issue is the rising cost of higher education in many parts of the country. Between the mid-1970s and 2008–2009, average in-state tuition and related fees at the nation's public colleges and universities rose more than tenfold, and tuition at the private, four-year colleges and universities rose almost as rapidly. Room and board rates also rose dramatically, but at a somewhat slower rate than tuition and related fees. Partly as a result, many students graduate with thousands of dollars of debt—tens of thousands of dollars in the case of students earning doctoral or professional degrees.[79] Rising costs present the risk that many students with the ability to do well in college may not be able to afford to attend. Those rising costs have helped the United States to lose its lead over other countries in the percentage of U.S. students attending college.[80]

Politicizing the Curriculum   A recurring issue in education centers on whether public schools should try to teach students moral and ethical principles, and, if so, which principles. In a related vein, conflicts have erupted over whether religious or ideological values should influence the content of various courses. In recent years a number of groups, liberal and conservative, secular and religious, have called on the schools to teach moral precepts, and these issues have sometimes cropped up in private schools as well, particularly in higher education. To the extent that schools have taught citizenship, democracy, and support for free enterprise, they have never been politically neutral in the broad sense of the term *politics*. But the last three decades have seen a number of controversies over what types of values, political or otherwise, the schools should foster.

First in the 1980s came the objection of fundamentalist Christians to the teaching of evolutionary theory in biology classes, an effort that echoed similar controversies in the early twentieth century. Responding to these objections, the Arkansas and Louisiana legislatures passed laws requiring that equal time in biology classes be given to teaching creationist theories of the origins of human life. However, federal courts struck down this law as a violation of the constitutional separation of church and state.[81]

By the mid-1980s, fundamentalist Christians were making a broad assault on a variety of textbooks and other teaching materials that they claimed promoted "secular humanism,"[82] a vague concept that could be applied to many things. A group in Tennessee initially persuaded federal courts to exempt their children from public school reading classes that featured books the parents opposed on religious grounds. In particular, the parents had objected to *The Diary of Anne Frank* because Anne Frank asserted that all religions were equal. A federal appeals court, however, overturned this ruling. In 1999, state officials in Kansas eliminated the teaching of evolution from state guidelines for science instruction, although local districts apparently retained the option of including it. The board later backtracked and returned evolution to the science curriculum, but held hearings regarding the science guidelines. Voters subsequently intervened and elected a new state board with most of its members favoring the teaching of evolution.

Some religious groups call for teaching the theory of *intelligent design*, which holds that many aspects of the universe strongly indicate the influence of a guiding intellect in creating and organizing the natural world. In 2004, the local school board of Dover, Pennsylvania, adopted a policy requiring science teachers to read a disclaimer indicating that evolution was unproven and referring them to an intelligent design textbook. A number of families filed a lawsuit, claiming that the policy amounted to an endorsement of creationism and, therefore, violated the principle of separation of church and state. A federal judge agreed with their arguments and struck down the policy. Many voters apparently agreed as well, for they voted out the school board members that had adopted the intelligent design policy and elected a new board willing to remove intelligent design from the science curriculum.[83] The issue is not likely to be resolved finally for some time.[84]

Another religious and educational controversy involves complaints that the schools have given too little attention to the role that religion has played in American history, politics, and society over the years. Critics have complained that, as a point of factual accuracy, the schools need to place more emphasis on religious institutions, forces, and ideas.[85] Increasing that emphasis risks conflict because different religious traditions have sometimes pulled in very different directions.[86]

A second area of curricular conflict stems from the demographic and sociological forces that are reshaping American society. America has been a great stewpot of many different subcultures, most of which have never fully melted into the common culture. Indeed, the common culture itself continually evolves as each group makes its unique contribution. However, many women, African Americans, and other minorities argue, with considerable justification, that their contributions to the development of American culture have been traditionally ignored by the public school curriculum.

To the extent that these critics want the social studies curriculum to include the historical accomplishments of African Americans, Latin Americans, American Indians, other ethnic minorities, and women, they represent an emphasis on **cultural pluralism** that most scholars view as legitimate. Distinguished from cultural pluralism is what educational historian Diane Ravitch calls **ethnic particularism**.[87] This is the attempt of ethnic groups to use ethnic history, ethnic mathematics, and ethnic science to boost the self-esteem of children from these ethnic groups. The ethnic particularists condemn the idea of a common American culture as a racist "Eurocentrism" and seek instead to replace it with a curriculum that is organized around the achievements of a specific group.

Of course, it is possible for a curriculum to be responsive to cultural pluralism without a loss of factual accuracy—indeed, many cultural pluralists complain that the failure to cover the experiences and contributions of various ethnic groups to American life, history, and literature is itself inaccurate. But it is also impossible to deny that the public school curriculum has become highly politicized as it seeks to grapple with the wide variety of peoples that constitute America today.

At issue in the schools, as in society at large, is our vision of ourselves as a nation. To pose this issue in the extreme, will the prevailing vision be that of cultural pluralists who view the different subcultures as natural resources that contribute positively to the evolution of a common culture and a common society? Or will it be that of the ethnic particularists, some of whom reject any common ground among the various subcultures? Is there some common ground among the various groups that will enable us to live and work together?

A second area where multicultural issues affect education is in affirmative action—although the conflicts here have been more pronounced at the postsecondary level than at the elementary and secondary school level. The University of California at Berkeley presents an example of these conflicts at work. One of the nation's most prestigious campuses, Berkeley sought to admit more racial minorities and set up a *de facto* two-track admission process. This brought about an overrepresentation of African Americans and Hispanics in comparison to whites and Asians. In the 1988–1989 school year, whites made up 70 percent of the eligible applicants, but only about 40 percent of those accepted. African Americans made up 3 percent of the applicants, but 11 percent of the admittees, and Hispanics made up 7 percent of the applicants, but 19 percent of the admittees. More than 70 percent of eligible African American applicants were admitted versus only about 25 to 30 percent of whites and Asians.[88]

Critics looked at these data and concluded that Berkeley's affirmative action program was unfair. Defenders pointed out that 85 percent of affirmative action admittees met Berkeley's minimum admission standards. Further, there is a pressing social need for a diverse state like California to ensure that all categories of people have access to the state's flagship campus.[89]

In 1996, California Governor Pete Wilson persuaded the University of California Board of Trustees to end the school's affirmative action program. However, California, Texas, and Florida have recently been experimenting with geographic-based admission systems, which give automatic admission to the top graduates of each high school in the state. Because many high schools are predominantly white or African American or Hispanic, geographic-based admission, in effect, works like an affirmative action program for undergraduate admissions, but does not seem to generate as much controversy—at least not so far.[90]

Conflicts over affirmative action continue to develop; one recent case involved the University of Michigan. Its admissions system awarded points for students' grades, test scores, and other qualities, including being a member of a racial minority group or disadvantaged group. President George W. Bush, after some internal fighting in his administration, condemned the university's admissions system, and his administration filed a legal brief against the university in 2003.[91]

Although Bush said he supported diversity, he claimed that the university was using, in effect, a quota system. The university's president replied that Bush did not appear to understand the university's admissions policy, and denied it was a quota. Some observers wondered whether the administration's action, coming a month after Senate Republican leader Trent Lott was forced to step down from his leadership position after remarks he made that appeared to endorse racial segregation, might weaken the Republican Party's efforts to reach out to minority groups. Subsequently, the U.S. Supreme Court upheld the university's admissions system for the law school but struck down the undergraduate admissions system. The court seemed to approve taking racial or other qualities into account to some degree, but most of the justices felt that the undergraduate admissions system placed too much emphasis on race relative to other applicant characteristics.[92]

REFORMING PUBLIC EDUCATION

The combination of conflict among various groups and complaints that schools were failing or losing quality[93] have produced tremendous pressures for school reform—although defenders of the schools point out that some indicators of education performance show no sign of decline, or declined briefly and then rebounded. For example, between 1970 and 2004, ACT scores for science reasoning remained very stable. Scores for mathematics, English, and reading all increased noticeably from 1980 to more recent times. Mathematics scores on the SAT declined from 1967 to 1980 and then rose again to a level somewhat higher than in 1967. Verbal scores on the SAT, however, have shown only slight improvement from their 1980 level. Scores on the National Assessment of Educational Progress (NAEP) tests for primary and secondary schools students were generally stable or gradually improved in recent years. NAEP scores for fourth graders rose noticeably between 1998 and 2007, and scores for eighth graders were very stable. Moreover, student achievement seems to vary considerably from state to state.[94]

Reformers, nonetheless, called for less free time in schools, more homework, more time spent in the classroom, more rigid graduation requirements, and higher preparation standards for teachers. The school reform movement received a very prestigious boost in 1983 when the National Commission on Excellence in Education proposed several measures to improve the schools—raising teachers' salaries, creating a cadre of master teachers, lengthening the school year, and raising requirements for graduation. Within a year, a half-dozen other prestigious commissions presented similar proposals.[95] The get-tough philosophy had struck the public schools.

School Reform and Its Implementation

Some of the proposed reforms proved easier to implement than others. Within two years of the 1983 publication of *A Nation at Risk*, 47 states had raised or proposed raising graduation requirements, 44 had done so for testing students in minimum academic competencies, 49 had done so for raising teacher preparation standards, and 34 had done so for increasing the amount of instructional time.[96] By the end of the decade, every state had adopted at least one of the measures.

Some reform efforts were reinforced by the No Child Left Behind Act of 2001. The law directed states to adopt student performance standards and to assess student performance relative to those standards. In addition, the states must have timetables for improving student performance, both overall and for various subgroups of students, where it fails to meet the standards. Further, the states must assure that "highly qualified" teachers cover the core academic subjects.[97]

After 2001, efforts to adopt new reforms seemed to decline a bit, with more attention turning to implementing existing reforms and assessing how they worked. State after state adopted guidelines for assessing educational performance, although the guidelines varied considerably from state to state. Common assessment criteria included standardized testing, attendance and/or truancy records, and graduation or completion rates. State requirements for high school graduation were widespread, with a particular emphasis on English and language skills, social studies, mathematics, and science.[98]

However, even these seemingly straightforward reforms have encountered some difficulties. Higher teacher certification requirements coupled with relatively low teacher salaries have led to shortages of qualified teachers in some districts, particularly in science and mathematics. Student testing requirements have led to several embarrassing incidents when scores were incorrectly tabulated; in one case, several thousand students were required to take remedial summer coursework or repeat a grade after a private testing company mistakenly gave them failing scores. Moreover, state standards appear to vary a good deal from state to state. In one study, only 18 percent of Mississippi fourth graders achieved a "proficient" or higher score on the National Assessment of Educational Progress test of reading proficiency, but 88 percent of the fourth graders rated "proficient" or above on the state assessment. Eighty percent of Texas fourth graders reached or exceeded the state's math proficiency standard, but only 40 percent did as well on the National Assessment of Education Progress.[99]

Students, teachers, and school administrators sometimes respond to a greater emphasis on standardized testing in unfortunate ways. Reports in several states indicate that some teachers have tried to boost test scores by coaching their students on specific questions from the exams and even allowing the students to correct wrong answers. Critics complain that the law encourages teachers to focus on coaching students on the narrow range of material covered by the tests at the expense of everything else. Recent reports also indicate that some teachers and administrators may have changed student answers in order to improve the average performance of classes and schools.[100]

State and local opposition led the Bush administration to compromise on a number of points, including relaxing the standards for teachers in rural areas and small towns (where a teacher often must teach a wider variety of courses). The administration also eased requirements for student attendance on days when standardized testing is done.[101]

The Obama administration retained most of No Child Left Behind but added a new initiative, Race to the Top, which offers additional funds to enhance education performance. Although the new policies are just getting underway, they currently emphasize linking teacher compensation to the performance of students. Race to the Top also includes efforts to improve high school graduation rates, early childhood education, and increased use of charter schools.[102]

When local school districts perform especially poorly, state officials or, in some cases, mayors, may have authority to step in and take corrective action. Some of those interventions have been triggered by corruption or financial mismanagement, but others have grown out of poor academic performance. Some of the takeovers have combined state intervention with the continued presence of local authorities; complete state takeovers may cause local complaints of state intrusion and may also yield political problems for state officials if conditions do not improve.[103]

One important development, which is partially separate from other reforms, is the increasing use of computers and modern information technology in schools at all levels. Computers, Internet access, and other high-tech components have become much more widespread in schools in recent years.[104] This technological revolution has proceeded more rapidly in public schools than in private schools, although many private schools are gradually narrowing the gap. With computer skills increasingly necessary for jobs of many kinds, schools have placed more emphasis on computer literacy.

The Case of Adult Education

The many changes in all fields of knowledge and the changing structure of the economy, along with increasing life expectancy, have produced a strong demand for adult education in recent years. Motives for seeking more education vary from person to person and by age group. Younger and middle-aged adults hope to improve their opportunities for promotion or advancement in their jobs, but older adults (especially those 65 or older) take courses because of interest in a subject or the desire to interact more with other people.[105] Many adult learners cannot easily move their families near a university, so they need educational opportunities that are available where they live. The community colleges serve many of those students, and a number of colleges and universities have established branch campuses and satellite programs to make education more available.

Distance learning programs offer another strategy for making education more available to potential students who cannot easily relocate. A recent study found that more than 4,000 institutions offered distance learning programs, which involve computer-based instruction, television, and video and audio tapes for instruction. More than 2.8 million students are now participating in distance learning programs, which are offered by most large universities and some smaller institutions as well.[106] However, a recent Colorado audit of online education programs found that they often showed poor student performance, sloppy accounting, and inadequate state oversight.[107]

Assessing Educational Reform

Has all this commitment of money and energy to educational reform produced significant improvements in student achievement? Judging from the NAEP tests, which are probably the best available measure of student achievement, the results present a complex pattern. From 1977 through 1999, mathematics scores improved for 9-year-olds, 13-year-olds, and 17-year-olds. Science and writing test scores improved slightly for younger students, but reading scores did not improve noticeably. Even worse, from 1998 through 2003, the scores of high school students declined slightly.[108]

As noted earlier in the chapter, studies comparing the performance of U.S. schools with schools in other countries often find that U.S. performance is only average (or slightly worse, depending on the countries in the comparison group). The one indicator where the United States once held a dominant position, the percentage of young people attending college, has shown a considerable decline in the U.S. position.

Although research on educational performance has produced conflicting findings, many studies find that socioeconomic factors, especially the education levels of parents, are a powerful influence on student performance. However, a number of studies also find that school improvements can also help boost student performance. A recent study of prekindergarten education in Tulsa, Oklahoma, found that it significantly improved student performance, even when other influences on student performance were taken into account.[109] Unfortunately, schools with many students from poor families tend to be poorly financed, a situation that limits what those schools can do.[110]

For those who doubt the ability of public schools to improve their performance significantly, school choice (particularly giving parents greater freedom to send their children to private schools or to public schools outside of their neighborhoods) seems an attractive option. A number of proposals along these lines have surfaced in recent years. However, research on why people select private schools and their role in improving educational performance has produced conflicting results, with some studies finding beneficial effects and others finding none.[111] The benefits of school choice and voucher programs are limited, in part, because many schools, both public and private, will not admit students from low-income schools or low-income families.[112] Moreover, although the public has slightly higher confidence in private schools and universities than in public ones, the differences are rather small.[113]

School choice programs face a number of practical problems as well. Many poorer families simply cannot afford to send their children to private schools without considerable financial help. In addition, information regarding how a particular child might benefit from attending a specific school is not readily available.

The public also has mixed feelings about voucher plans, which give a student's family financial help in shifting from one school to another. Although many people support voucher programs in general, they are less supportive if the voucher programs will take money away from the public schools, as they certainly would if many students went to private schools instead. Many Americans believe that if private schools accept vouchers, they have an obligation to admit all students who apply to them, an expectation that would not be met by a number of private schools.[114] In addition, an analysis of Milwaukee's school voucher program found virtually no significant differences between the achievement of students who used the program to change to private schools and the achievement of students who remained in the public schools.[115]

Historically, education has occupied a critical place in the American political economy. Through the public and private school systems, people were educated to play a variety of roles in an industrial and highly sophisticated society. Children received the educational basics they needed to become skilled workers, technicians, engineers, accountants, and professionals. Furthermore, education was assumed to play a great equalizing role in American democracy. So many millions of people enjoyed upward social mobility, partially as a result of skills, knowledge, and credentials acquired at school, that it became easy to believe that education was the answer to many social problems.

In recent years, many critics have complained that the schools are not preparing children well enough for the high-technology economy of the future. As a result, many business leaders have supported education reforms of one sort or another. Most of today's students will work for business corporations tomorrow, which gives those corporations an important interest in seeing that their recruits have the vital skills and the ability to adapt to a changing economy. Business needs exist on at least two levels. First, keeping America competitive with the rest of the world requires highly skilled engineers, scientists, researchers, and technicians who can function comfortably in today's high-tech world. Hence, many business leaders have voiced concerns about reading skills, writing skills, and the quality of scientific learning. In all probability, however, the number of very lucrative high-tech jobs is somewhat limited.

Second, a great many of the jobs created since 1980 have been very low-tech jobs—in restaurants, hotels, and other service establishments. What is needed for these jobs is not a highly skilled workforce, but large numbers of people willing to work at repetitive tasks for long hours, day in and day out. They also need the ability to cope with unexpected problems, such as a dirty hotel room, or an unhappy customer at a fast food restaurant. Hence, many corporations are working closely with local school districts to train teenagers for this kind of job environment.

Perhaps the most obvious link between public education and the political economy occurs with higher education. The link is especially strong between business corporations and the large research-oriented universities. Corporations benefit from the technical research done at those universities. And universities benefit from equipment donations, consulting contracts, and friendly ties with the corporations. From the point of view of state government, a well-functioning university system is a definite asset in attracting more industry.

SUMMARY

1. Local school districts have historically been the dominant unit of school governance. However, educational problems such as desegregation and financing could not be solved by small districts; thus, in recent years, policy making and financing have been increasingly centralized at the state level, and the federal government has become more and more involved in public education. The federal government's greatest impact has been in the desegregation of public schools.

2. Conservatives view educational problems as both failures of individual students and failures of the public school systems. They attribute the difficulties of the school systems to liberal educational philosophies that have led to permissiveness in the classroom, open schools, and poor discipline. Liberals attribute the difficulties of the school systems to inadequate funding of schools in poor neighborhoods and a failure to reach out to students from different backgrounds.

3. The impetus for desegregation came mostly from the federal courts. The Supreme Court first struck down *de jure* segregation as unconstitutional. The courts have had less success in ending *de facto* segregation. One of the most volatile desegregation controversies has been over the use of forced busing to desegregate schools. By 1990, the federal government had retreated from requiring busing to bring about desegregation.

4. The main school finance problems stem from fiscal disparities in the distribution of property-tax resources; districts with a valuable property tax base can raise more money than can districts in poor areas. State governments supplement local school resources with foundation aids and categorical grants. There have been three approaches to equalizing school funding. The New Jersey approach was to increase the state share of funding while permitting local districts to gain revenue from a local property tax in addition to the state funds. The Michigan approach was to move to an exclusively state-funded system paid for by the state sales tax. And the Texas approach was to distribute some of the property tax base of the more affluent districts to the less affluent districts.

5. The culture wars of recent years have provoked intense conflict over the public school curriculum and over affirmative action admissions at the university level.

6. Critics of America's schools have called for a variety of reforms in education, and the states have enacted numerous reform measures in recent years. But it is not clear whether these reforms will bring about very dramatic improvements in student learning.

STUDY QUESTIONS

1. How have the roles of state, local, and national governments in education policy making changed over the years? Why have they changed?

2. Why are political values an important part of the conflicts over education policies? How do the concerns expressed by conservatives and liberals in the education arena differ?

3. What has the federal government done to try to eliminate racial segregation in schools? Why has that effort been so difficult?

4. How have the states tried to deal with disputes regarding unequal funding of schools? Why has equalizing financial resources across school districts been so difficult?

5. What cultural values are involved in conflicts over affirmative action and curricula, such as whether or how to study evolution or people from different cultures or backgrounds? Why do these issues arouse such strong feelings?

6. What are the major reforms that have been adopted in recent years in order to improve educational performance?

KEY TERMS

Board of education The governing board of a local school district.

Charter schools Schools, whether public or private, that are exempt from many or even most of the rules and regulations applied to most public schools. They are greater flexibility with regard to hiring personnel, choosing curriculum, and when students are ready for promotion.

Commissioner of education See *Superintendent of schools*.

Compensatory education The tenet that disadvantaged children suffer from poor preparation for school and must be given special educational help to compensate for their backgrounds. See *Elementary and Secondary Education Act of 1965*.

Cultural pluralism An educational emphasis on including instruction about many cultural groups in American society. Does not reject the ideal of a mainstream, overall American culture.

De facto **segregation** Segregation that arises because of residential practices rather than because of laws requiring segregation. See *de jure segregation*.

De jure **segregation** Segregation that is imposed by law rather than by informal residential practices. See *de facto segregation*.

Education Consolidation and Improvement Act of 1981 A law that consolidated several educational categorical grant programs into a block grant, reduced the total funding for the programs involved, and increased state discretion in dispensing the funds.

Elementary and Secondary Education Act of 1965 The first extensive form of federal aid to public schools. Famous for its Title I compensatory-education provisions. See also *Compensatory education*.

Equal Protection Clause The provision of the Fourteenth Amendment that forbids any state to deny persons in its jurisdiction the equal protection of the laws.

Ethnic particularism A form of cultural pluralism that rejects the idea of a mainstream American culture as oppressively Eurocentric.

Fiscal disparities The situation in which neighboring governmental jurisdictions vary widely in their ability to raise revenue. One jurisdiction may have a substantial tax base, while a neighboring one has a meager tax base.

Foundation aid program A program of state aid for public schools in which the state provides a specific amount of money to each school district for each full-time pupil enrolled in that district.

Independent school district The basic governing unit for public schools.

National Commission on Excellence in Education A commission that reported in 1983 that the nation's school systems were failing to provide children with the quality of education they need in the contemporary world.

No Child Left Behind Act A federal law adapted in 2001. It requires creation of statewide school performance measures, improvement of failing schools, and allowance for low-income children in persistently failing schools to use some federal aid funds to transfer to other schools.

Separate-but-equal doctrine The principle established in *Plessy v. Ferguson* (1896) that segregated facilities do not violate the Equal Protection Clause as long as the separate facilities are equal.

State education agency (SEA) State educational policy maker, composed of the state board of education, the chief state school officer, and the department of education.

Superintendent of schools The chief executive officer for public schools. May be either a local or state superintendent. The state superintendent is sometimes called the *commissioner of education*.

Voucher plan A proposal that gives parents vouchers to pay the cost of sending their children to the public or private school of their choice.

White flight The theory that middle-class whites have, in large numbers, withdrawn their children from the central-city public schools in order to avoid school desegregation.

THE INTERNET CONNECTION

The U.S. Department of Education includes many officials who are interested in improving the performance of America's educational system. They have compiled a variety of resources on educational reform, which you can find at **www.ed.gov**. What educational institutions offer post-high school (or postsecondary) education in your area? What kinds of courses do they offer? What do their Web sites say about them?

NOTES

1. Michael Birnbaum, *The Washington Post*, "Historians Speak Out Against Proposed Texas Textbook Changes," March 18, 2010, p. A3; (electronic edition) James McKinley, *New York Times*, March 12, 2010 (electronic edition); Rick Casey, "Don't Sweat Curriculum (Un)civil War," *Houston Chronicle*, May 24, 2010 (electronic edition).

2. The study was conducted by Princeton economists Orley Ashenfelter and Alan Kreuger and was reported in *The New York Times*, August 19, 1992, p. 1A.

3. *Time Almanac* (Boston: Family Education Company, 1999), p. 881; more recent evidence points to the same conclusion. See *Educate to Innovate* (Washington, DC: The White House Web site, 2010).

4. *Time Almanac* (1999), p. 881.

5. *Newsweek*, February 17, 1992, p. 57; *The Minneapolis Star Tribune*, December 2, 1993, p. 26A; *The New York Times*, December 2, 1993, p. 26A.

6. Ibid.

7. Tamar Lewin, "Once a Leader, U.S. Lags in College Degrees," *New York Times*, July 23, 2010 (electronic edition).

8. National Commission on Excellence in Education, *A Nation at Risk: The Imperative for Educational Reform* (Washington, DC: U.S. Government Printing Office, 1983).

9. David Berliner and Bruce Biddle, *The Manufactured Crisis* (Cambridge, MA: Perseus, 1995). For a critique of using many standardized tests for assessing school performance, see W. James Popham, *America's "Failing" Schools* (New York: Routledge Falmer, 2004).

10. This was a major conclusion of a study by the Institute for Educational Leadership, "Governing Public Schools: New Times, New Requirements." Reported in *The New York Times*, October 28, 1992, p. 12A.

11. Michael Berkman and Eric Plutzer, *Ten Thousand Democracies* (Washington, DC: Georgetown University, 2005), p. 57.

12. See Burton Dean Friedman, *State Government and Education Management in the State Education Agency* (Chicago: Public Administration Service, 1971).

13. M. W. Kirst and R. Jung, "The Utility of a Longitudinal Approach in Assessing Implementation: A Thirteen-Year View of Title I, ESEA," *Educational Evaluation and Policy Analysis* 2 (1980): 17–34; E. Garces, et al., *Longer Term Effects of Head Start* (Washington, DC: National Bureau of Economic Research, 2000).

14. Russell Vlaanderen, John Augenblick, and Chris Pipho, *The Book of the States: 1982–83* (Lexington, KY: Council of State Governments, 1982), p. 432.

15. "Education Reform: The No Child Left Behind Act of 2001," in *The Book of the States* (Lexington, KY: Council of State Governments, 2002), pp. 472–474; Dewayne Matthews, "No Child Left Behind: The Challenge of Implementation," in *The Book of the States* (Lexington, KY: Council of State Governments, 2004), pp. 493–496; Deborah Meier and George Wood, eds., *Many Children Left Behind* (Boston: Beacon Press, 2004); Alan Greenblatt, "The Left Behind Syndrome," *Governing* 17, no. 12 (September 2004), pp. 38–43; Jennifer Hochschild and Nathan Scovronick, *The American Dream and the Public Schools* (New York: Oxford, 2003).

16. Paul Foy, "States Are Rebelling Against New Federal Education Rules," *Daily News*, February 18, 2004, p. 9A; Ben Feller, "State Lawmakers Call for Major Changes to No Child Left Behind Law," *Daily News*, February 24, 2005, p. 5A; Ben Feller, "Spellings Gives States Leeway on Law," *Daily News*, January 19, 2006, p. 7A; Ben Feller, "No States Meet Teacher Quality Goal, But Most Do Enough to Avoid Penalties," *Daily News*, May 13–14, 2006, p. 9A; Ben Feller, "Unreliable Data Hampers Education Law," *Daily News*, October 2–3, 2004, p. 5A; Frederick Hess, "No Child Left Behind: Trends and Issues," in *The Book of the States*, vol. 38 (Lexington, KY: Council of State Governments, 2006), pp. 474–477.

17. Stephanie Rose, *Pay for Performance Proposals in Race to the Top Round II Applications* (Denver: Education Commission of the States, 2010); *Education* (Washington, DC: White House Web document, 2010).

18. Steven Pearlstein, "Virginia's Latest Attempt to Secede from the United States," *Washington Post*, Friday, July 23, 2010, p. A14 (electronic edition).

19. Cited in *St. Paul Pioneer Press*, December 6, 1981, p. 16.

20. See *Statistical Abstract, 2001* (Washington, DC: U.S. Government Printing Office, 2001), p. 178; *Statistical Abstract 2006* (Washington, DC: U.S. Government Printing Office, 2005), p. 189.

21. Tamar Lewin, "Once a Leader, U.S. Lags in College Degrees," *New York Times* July 23, 2010 (electronic edition).

22. *International Comparisons* (Information Center for Higher Education Policymaking and Analysis, 2010) web document.

23. *Statistical Abstract of the United States: 2008* (Washington, DC: U.S. Bureau of the Census, 2007), p. 183; Jonathan Glater, "As Support Lags, Colleges Tack on Student Fees," *New York Times*, September 4, 2007 (electronic edition).

24. Patrick Callan, *The 2008 National Report Card: Modest Improvements, Persistent Disparities, Eroding Global Competitiveness* (National Center for Public Policy and Higher Education, 2008), Web document.

25. *Statistical Abstract of the United States: 2008* (Washington, DC: U.S. Census Bureau, 2007), pp. 172, 178–179.

26. Tamar Lewin, "Senator to Review Accreditation of For-Profit Colleges," *New York Times*, August 4, 2010 (electronic edition).

27. Edward C. Banfield, *The Unheavenly City* (Boston: Little, Brown, 1970), p. 134.

28. This was especially the theme of Oscar Lewis. See his *La Vida* (New York: Random House, 1965). Also see Barbara E. Coward, Joe R. Feagin, and J. Allen Williams, Jr., "The Culture of Poverty Debate: Some Additional Data," *Social Problems* 21, no. 5 (June 1974): 621–633.

29. Banfield, *The Unheavenly City*, p. 139.

30. The proponents of this view are Arthur Jensen and William Shockley. See H. J. Eysenck, *The I.Q. Argument* (New York: Library Press, 1971). For a contemporary statement of it, see Michael Levin, "Implications of Race and Sex Differences for Contemporary Affirmative Action and the Concept of Discrimination," *The Journal of Social, Political and Economic Studies* 15, no. 2 (Summer 1990): 175–212. Subsequent research has largely undercut Shockley's work.

31. See Charles Murray and Richard J. Herrnstein, *The Bell Curve: Intelligence and Class Structure in American Life* (New York: The Free Press, 1994).

32. See David M. Gordon, *Problems in Political Economy: An Urban Perspective*, 2nd ed. (Lexington, MA: D. C. Heath, 1977), pp. 108–112.

33. See *Statistical Abstract, 2008*, p. 700.

34. Alan Geyer, *Ideology in America: Challenges to Faith* (Louisville, KY: Westminster John Knox Press, 1997).

35. D. Mitchell, C. Marshall, and Frederick M. Wirt, *Culture and Education Policy in the American States* (New York: Falmer), ch. 4.

36. *Plessy v. Ferguson*, 163 U.S. 537 (1896); *Gong Lum v. Rice*, 275 U.S. 78 (1927).

37. *Missouri ex rel. Gaines v. Canada*, 305 U.S. 337 (1938).

38. *Sipuel v. Oklahoma*, 332 U.S. 631 (1948).

39. *McLaurin v. Oklahoma State Regents*, 339 U.S. 637 (1950).

40. *Sweatt v. Painter*, 339 U.S. 629 (1950).

41. *Brown v. Board of Education*, 347 U.S. 483 (1954).

42. Charles S. Bullock III and Harrell R. Rodgers, Jr., "Coercion to Compliance: Southern School Districts and School Desegregation Guidelines," *Journal of Politics* 38, no. 4 (November 1976): 987–1013.

43. *Swann v. Charlotte-Mecklenberg Board of Education*, 402 U.S. 1 (1971).

44. Gary Orfield, *Public School Desegregation in the United States: 1968–1980* (Washington, DC: Joint Center for Political Studies, 1983), p. 26.

45. Diane Ravitch, "The 'White Flight' Controversy," *Public Interest*, no. 51 (Spring 1978): 142.

46. Mary Costello, "Busing Reappraisal," *Editorial Research Reports*, December 26, 1975, pp. 945–964.

47. Christine H. Rossell, "School Desegregation and White Flight," *Political Science Quarterly* 90, no. 4 (Winter 1975–1976): 692. This was a very controversial article. It was criticized for its methods and policy suggestions by Diane Ravitch in her article, "The 'White Flight' Controversy," pp. 135–150. See also the exchange of views by Christine H. Rossell, Diane Ravitch, and David J. Armor, "Busing and 'White Flight,'" *Public Interest*, no. 53 (Fall 1978): 109–115.

48. See Christine H. Rossell and David J. Armor, "The Effectiveness of School Desegregation Plans, 1968–1991," *American Politics Quarterly* 24, no. 3 (July 1996): 289. Rossell and Armor have been two of the major researchers of desegregation efforts for the past two decades. This

article is somewhat inconsistent with Rossell's earlier article "School Desegregation and White Flight" cited in endnote 38. It appears that the accumulation of evidence from her research over a 20-year period has led her to a less benign view of mandatory busing today than she expressed in the earlier article.

49. Ibid., pp. 267–302.
50. Charles S. Bullock III, "School Desegregation After a Quarter Century," *Urban Affairs Quarterly* 18, no. 2 (December 1982): 295–296.
51. *Millikin v. Bradley*, 418 U.S. 717 (1974).
52. In 1996, the Connecticut Supreme Court obliterated the distinction between *de jure* and *de facto* segregation when it ordered the state to eliminate racial imbalances between the Hartford school systems, whose schools were 94 percent minority, and the surrounding suburban schools, which were overwhelmingly white; *The New York Times* July 10, 1996, p. 13A. Twenty-one years earlier, the California Supreme Court had made a similar ruling, but it was overturned by an amendment to the California constitution that prohibited busing plans in excess of principles established by federal courts.
53. *Columbus Board of Education v. Penick*, 443 U.S. 449 (1979); *Dayton Board of Education v. Brinkman*, 443 U.S. 526 (1979).
54. *Freeman v. Pitts*, 498 U.S. 1081 (1992).
55. John B. McConahay, "Self-Interest Versus Racial Attitudes as Correlates of Anti-Busing Attitudes in Louisville: Is It the Buses or the Blacks?" *Journal of Politics* 44, no. 3 (August 1982): 692–720.
56. *The New York Times*, July 20, 1977, p. 10A.
57. For background, see *The New York Times*, November 4, 1986, p. 1B; *Newsweek*, November 17, 1986, p. 60.
58. *The New York Times*, December 28, 1988, p. 1A; March 1, 1989, p. 8B; *Minneapolis Star Tribune*, June 21, 1989, p. 6A.
59. *Board of Education of Oklahoma City v. Dowell*, 498 U.S. 237 (1991).
60. *Freeman v. Pitts*, 498 U.S. 1081 (1992).
61. *Missouri v. Jenkins*, 115 S.Ct. 2038 (1995).
62. Robert Barnes, "Three Years after Landmark Court Decision, Louisville Still Struggles with School Desegregation," *Washington Post*, September 20, 2010 (electronic edition).
63. *The New York Times*, October 3, 1989, p. 9B. *School Finance: State Efforts to Reduce Funding Gaps Between Poor and Wealthy Districts* (Washington, DC: General Accounting Office, 1997); Linda Darling-Hammond, "From 'Separate But Equal' to 'No Child Left Behind:' The Collision of New Standards and Old Inequalities," in Meier and Wood, eds. *Many Children...*, p. 6.
64. Jonathan Kozol, *Savage Inequalities: Children in American Schools* (New York: Harper Perennial, 1992).
65. Berliner and Biddle, *The Manufactured Crisis*, pp. 75–78; *Statistical Abstract, 2001*, pp. 157–159; George Walter, "For Want of a Modem and a Comfortable Chair: A Research Note," *American Journal of Political Science* 42 (1998): 705–708.
66. *Serrano v. Priest*, 3d 384 Calif. (1971).
67. *San Antonio School District v. Rodriguez*, 411 U.S. 1 (1973).
68. *Robinson v. Cahill*, 355 A.2d 129, 69 N.J. 1449 (1975). For an excellent background on the history of this case, see Richard Lehne, *The Quest for Justice: The Politics of School Finance Reform* (New York: Longman, 1978).
69. Michael Minton, "Why Efforts to Equalize School Funding Have Failed: A Political Economy Perspective," A paper presented to the Midwest Political Science Association, April 1–11, 1992, p. 30.
70. *The New York Times*, October 12, 1994, p. 15C.
71. Minton, "Why Efforts to Equalize School Funding Have Failed."
72. *Time*, March 28, 1994, p. 38.
73. *The New York Times*, May 28, 1993, p. 7A; June 1, 1993, p. 8C; June 2, 1993, p. 9A.
74. Hochschild and Scovronick, *The American Dream*, pp. 73–75.
75. Some studies have found that resources make a difference in some aspects of education performance. For example, see George Waller, "For Want of a Modem and a Comfortable Chair: A Research Note," *American Journal of Political Science* 42 (1998): 705–708.
76. Erin Van Bronkhorst, "Study Shows District Accounting Hides Wealthy Schools' Teacher Advantage," *Moscow-Pullman Daily News*, May 30, 2003, p. 4A.
77. Winnie Hu, "Court Backs New Jersey Aid Revision: Less Focus on Poorest Schools," *New York Times*, May 29, 2009 (electronic edition).
78. For example, see "N. J. Voters Reject School Budgets in Heated Elections." *New Jersey Real-Time News*, April 21, 2010.

79. See *The New York Times 2010 Almanac* (New York: Penguin, 2009), p. 372.

80. Tamar Lewin, "Once a Leader, U.S. Lags in College Degrees," *New York Times*, July 23, 2010 (electronic edition).

81. *The New York Times*, January 6, 1982, p. 1B; June 20, 1987, p. 4A.

82. John Hanna, "Kansas Board of Education Begins Hearings on Evolution," *Daily News*, May 6, 2005, p. 5A; *CNN Headline News*, August 2, 2006.

83. Martha Raffaele, "Federal Judge: No Room for Intelligent Design in Biology Classes," *Moscow-Pullman Daily News*, December 20, 2005, p. 1A.

84. On the Tennessee case, see *The New York Times*, February 28, 1986, p. 11C; October 25, 1986, p. 1B; August 25, 1987, p. 1C; for an analysis of state actions regarding evolution in the schools, see M. Troy Gibson, "Culture Wars in State Education Policy: A Look at the Relative Treatment of Evolutionary Theory in State Science Standards," *Social Science Quarterly* 85 (2004): 1129–1149.

85. For a valuable overview of the role of religion in U.S. history, see Edwin Gaustad and Leigh Schmidt, *The Religious History of America*, rev. ed. (New York: HarperCollins, 2002). See also Stephen Webb, *Taking Religion to School* (Grand Rapids, MI: Brazos Press, 2000).

86. Geyer, *Ideology in America*.

87. Diane Ravitch, "Multiculturalism: E Pluribus Plures," *The American Scholar* 59, no. 3 (Summer 1990): 337–354.

88. These data are taken from Lewis R. Jones, "Affirmative Action at Berkeley," *The American Prospect*, no. 12 (Winter 1993): 154; and Jerome Karabel, "Berkeley and Beyond," *The American Prospect*, no. 12 (Winter 1993): 157. Jones presents his data in a fairly anti-affirmative action manner, whereas Karabel presents his in a pro-affirmative action manner. Where the two differed on a piece of data, the text here leaned in the direction of using Karabel's data so as not to overstate the reverse discrimination aspects of the argument.

89. Jones, "Affirmative Action at Berkeley," p. 155; Karen Paget, "Diversity at Berkeley: Demogoguery or Demography?" *The American Prospect*, no. 8 (Spring 1992): 157; Jerome Karabel, "Berkeley and Beyond," *The American Prospect*, no. 12 (Winter 1993): 156–160.

90. "Affirmative Geography," *Washington Post National Weekly Edition*, December 6, 1999, p. 25.

91. Amy Goldstein and Dana Milbank, "'Divisive' Diversity," *Washington Post National Weekly Edition*, January 20–26, 2003, p. 13.

92. Anne Gearan, "Court Preserves Narrow Use of Affirmative Action in College Admissions," *Moscow-Pullman Daily News*, June 23, 2003, p. 5A.

93. For example, on a cross-national science test, American 13-year-olds ranked behind those in 12 other societies, including Scotland, Slovenia, and the USSR. *Newsweek*, February 17, 1992, p. 57. Another cross-national survey in 1992 found American school children ranked last in a comparison of nine nations in math, eighth out of nine in science, and fifth out of nine in geography. *The New York Times*, October 1, 1992, p. 10A.

94. For a powerful argument that many of the complaints about school performance are overstated and/or based on faulty evidence, see Berliner and Biddle, *The Manufactured Crisis*. For recent test scores, see *World Almanac* (New York: Infobase Publishing, 2010), pp. 388–399; *Statistical Abstract, 2008* (U.S. Census Bureau, 2007), pp. 168–169.

95. See Diane Ravitch, *The Troubled Crusade: American Education 1945–1980* (New York: Basic Books, 1983). Also see Deborah Meier's excellent critique in "Getting Tough in the Schools," *Dissent* (Winter 1984): 61–70. See also Task Force on Education for Economic Growth, *Action for Excellence: A Comprehensive Plan to Improve Our Nation's Schools*, Education Commission of the States, June 1983; The National Science Board, Educating Americans for the 21st Century, 1983; The Twentieth Century Fund Task Force on Federal Elementary and Secondary Education Policy, *Making the Grade*, 1983; John I. Goodland, *A Place Called School: Prospects for the Future* (New York: McGraw-Hill, 1983); Ernest L. Boyer, *High School: A Report on Secondary Education in America* (New York: Harper & Row, 1983); Theodore R. Sizer, *Horace's Compromise—The Dilemma of the American High School* (Boston: Houghton Mifflin, 1984).

96. D. Doyle and T. Hartle, *Excellence in Education* (Washington, DC: American Enterprise Institute,

1985), p. 18. Figures include the District of Columbia as though it were a state.

97. See Dewayne Matthews, "No Child Left Behind: The Challenge of Implementation," in *The Book of the States* (Lexington, KY: Council of State Governments, 2004), pp. 493–496.

98. *The Book of the States* (2002), pp. 475–485.

99. "Scoring Error Holds Kids Back," *Daily Evergreen* (Pullman, Washington), September 16, 1999, p. 10; Martha Mendoza, "Testing Company Has Botched Scores Around the Nation," *Moscow-Pullman Daily News*, September 18–19, 1999, p. 6B; *Book of the States*, vol. 40 (Lexington, KY: Council of State Governments, 2008), p. 480; "SAT-takers Got Wrong Scores Mailed to Them," *Daily News*, March 8, 2006, p. 5A.

100. Trip Gabriel, "Under Pressure, Teachers Tamper with Test Scores," *New York Times*, June 10, 2010 (Web edition); Ken Miller, "The Second Body," *Governing*, July 6, 2011 (Web edition); Irregular Results Surface on WASL," *Moscow-Pullman Daily News*, May 31, 2004, pp. 1A, 8A; Meier and Wood, *Many Children.*

101. Ben Feller, "No Parent Left Behind?," *Moscow-Pullman Daily News*, March 3, 2004, p. 10A.

102. Ibid.

103. Kenneth Wong, "The Politics of Education," in Virginia Gray and Russell Hanson, eds. *Politics in the American States*, 9th ed. (Washington, DC: CQ Press, 2008), pp. 373–375.

104. *Statistical Abstract, 2008*, pp. 164–166.

105. *Statistical Abstract, 2001*, p. 178.

106. See Trip Gabriel, "More Pupils Are Learning Online, Fueling Debate on Quality," *New York Times*, April 4, 2011 (online edition); David Harrison, "Virtual Education Boom Hits the States," *Stateline*, March 4, 2011 (online edition); *Statistical Abstract, 2006*, p. 181.

107. Karen Rouse and Jennifer Brown, "Online Schools Flunk Audit," *Denver Post*, December 11, 2006 (Web document: www.denverpost.com/portlet/ article/html/fragments/print_article.jsp? articleId=482).

108. *Statistical Abstract, 2003*, pp. 174–175; "Writing Scores Rise; More Work to Be Done," *Moscow-Pullman Daily News*, July 10, 2003, p. 5A.

109. William Gormley and Deborah Phillips, "The Effects of Universal Pre-K in Oklahoma: Research Highlights and Policy Implications," *Policy Studies Journal* 33, no. 1 (2005): 65–87.

110. For a careful review of much of that research, see Berliner and Biddle, *The Manufactured Crisis.*

111. See John Chubb and Terry Moe, *Politics, Markets, and America's Schools* (Washington, DC: Brookings, 1990); Christopher Simon, *Public Schools as 'Coping' Organizations* (Ph.D. dissertation, Washington State University, 1997); Kevin Smith and Kenneth Meier, *The Case Against School Choice* (Armonk, NY: M.E. Sharpe, 1995); Robert Wrinkle, Joseph Stewart, and J.L. Polinard, "Public School Quality, Private Schools, and Race," *American Journal of Political Science* 43 (1999): 1248–1253; John Witte, *The Smarter Approach to Education: An Analysis of America's First Voucher Program* (Princeton, NJ: Princeton University Press, 2000).

112. Hochschild and Scovronick, *The American Dream*, pp. 130–132.

113. See *Statistical Abstract, 2001*, p. 249.

114. David Broder, "Lines Dividing Vouchers," *Washington Post National Weekly Edition*, July 15–21, p. 4; Will Lester, "AP Poll Finds Enthusiasm for Vouchers Fades When People Hear That Public Schools Could Lose Money," *Moscow-Pullman Daily News*, August 8, 2002, p. 9A; James Ryan and Michael Heise, "Taking School Choice to the Suburbs," *Washington Post National Weekly Edition*, July 15–21, 2002, p. 25.

115. John Witte, *The Market Approach to Education: An Analysis of America's First Voucher Program* (Princeton, NJ: Princeton University Press, 2000).

Infrastructure Policies: Transportation, Housing, and Community Development

CHAPTER PREVIEW

One of the most important roles of state and local governments is building and maintaining the physical infrastructure of modern society. In this chapter, we will examine three areas of infrastructure policy and analyze them from the perspective of political values and their social consequences. We will discuss:

1 Transportation policy.

2 Housing policy.

3 Community development policy.

4 Political values and the social consequences of infrastructure policy.

Introduction

One of the most critical functions played by state and local governments is building, maintaining, and overseeing the physical infrastructure that makes our modern society possible. This chapter examines that part of the physical **infrastructure** that includes roads, transportation systems, housing, and community development projects. Some of this infrastructure, such as roads, is often built by governments, although they may hire private contractors to do much of the actual construction. Some infrastructure, such as housing, is usually built by private companies, but is regulated and subsidized by governments. Still other infrastructure, such as water mains and sewer lines, may be built by a complex web of public and private organizations. A city or county government may build some sewer lines, but a real estate developer may install other lines as part of a new residential subdivision or shopping mall.

Some aspects of infrastructure policy produce relatively little conflict most of the time, but controversies do erupt occasionally. When President Obama took office in 2009, he proposed a multiyear commitment to establishing a high-speed rail network connecting a number of densely populated areas of the United States. The system would be based on national, state, and local government and private-sector negotiations, with state governments applying for federal funds to finance improvements on selected routes. The result would be a number of good-paying jobs (needed during a major recession) and a more modern transportation system, eventually.[1]

President Obama's proposal was based in part on improvements that were already underway in a number of states and reflected a more cautious approach than the National Association of Railroad Passengers recommended in 2007.[2] Although the high-speed rail improvements were fairly popular with the public and with many state officials, some significant snags developed when the newly elected Republican governors of three states that had been approved for high-speed rail grants backed away from the program. In part they were concerned about possible costs that their states would have to bear. In addition, they had ideological objections to the effort, as well as a possible desire to make the (Democratic) Obama administration appear ineffective.[3]

The U.S. Department of Transportation responded by distributing the refused funds to other states and to Amtrak. Circumstances became even more complex when one of the three governors began to shift away from his position, in part due to complaints from other Republican officials in the state and perhaps in part due to public complaints.[4]

In this chapter, we will examine the issues associated with some of the physical structures that are important in most people's lives. On the face of it, transportation, housing, and infrastructure generally might seem to be technical matters better left to the engineers and city planners. In fact, however, these policies have sparked bitter conflicts across the nation over freeway location, airport noise, housing prices, downtown reconstruction, inner-city neighborhood deterioration, and suburban sprawl. In addition, the slump in the housing market since 2007 has created many problems, including large numbers of families losing their homes, increased homelessness, strains on financial institutions, and declining state and local government revenues.[5] How much should governments assist homeowners who cannot keep up with their mortgage payments? How much should governments aid financial institutions that hold large numbers of troubled mortgages?

At the heart of these conflicts over infrastructure policy are conflicting values about the role of government, its costs, and its benefits. If neighborhoods have to be torn up for government projects, is the burden borne equally by all ethnic groups and social classes? Or do only certain ones pay the cost? Who benefits from infrastructure policies? Most infrastructure projects, without doubt, provide a public good. Everybody, for example, benefits from well-maintained streets. But do some groups of people benefit more than others? Finally, what impacts do infrastructure policies have on the social problems we examined in the two previous chapters? Is *de facto* racial and economic segregation in most metropolises truly just a by-product of the choices people make privately about where they want to live? Or did transportation, housing, and community development policies play a role in establishing the segregated metropolis?

We cannot answer all these questions in this chapter, but we will touch on many of them and try to provide a factual base for you to make your own judgments. We will examine transportation policy first, since the building of roads and transportation networks greatly influences where people are able to live and which communities will prosper. Second, we will examine housing and then community development policies. Finally, we will examine the role of political values in these areas.

TRANSPORTATION

Since the mid-twentieth century, the American transportation system has been dominated by streets and highways and the automobiles and trucks that travel on them. Typically, most Americans get around by car. The widespread use and popularity of automobiles, coupled with our extensive system of roads and highways, has given most Americans more mobility than even very wealthy people had in 1910. This phenomenon has produced a number of positive results, from providing many people with greater flexibility in choosing homes and jobs to giving many families enjoyable vacations. A large fleet of trucks and an extensive road and highway system also enables businesses to move merchandise with considerable flexibility.

The extent of our reliance on automobiles and trucks, however, has also led to some problems in the transportation system and a variety of social costs. Perhaps a third of the population is too old, too young, too disabled, or too poor to own and/or drive an automobile. Approximately a tenth of all households do not have private transportation, and about the same amount do not have a reliable vehicle. This 20 percent of the population is unable to take advantage of the extensive mobility offered by automobiles, roads, and freeways unless they can afford to be driven by someone else or can obtain a ride from friends, relatives, or neighbors. America's heavy reliance on automobiles and trucks has also produced traffic congestion, pollution, growing dependence on imported oil, more than 6,000,000 motor vehicle accidents per year, and thousands of traffic deaths annually.[6]

These transportation issues pose several important questions for state and local governments. First, how did automobiles, trucks, and highways become dominant in the transportation system? Why were railroads and mass-transit commuter systems allowed to deteriorate? Second, what prospects exist for public transportation today? Third, what respective roles can states, communities, and the federal government, as well as the private sector, play in improving our transportation system?

THE GROWING ROLE OF THE HIGHWAY SYSTEM

During the early twentieth century, the highway system and the railroad system competed to be the dominant means of transporting people around the country. As the road system grew more extensive and cars became more comfortable and reliable, the shortcomings of railroad passenger service became increasingly apparent. The railroads either would not or could not improve passenger service to the level of most European nations, in part because much of the United States was more sparsely populated than most of Europe in those days. As a result, the U.S. railroads carried only a small fraction of the people carried by European railroads.[7] Although the United States had excellent passenger rail service in some areas of the country, other areas, especially in the western states, had more limited service— sometimes provided by only one company. In addition, travelers had to adjust their travel plans to meet the railroad's schedules.

As the railroads began trimming passenger service in response to financial losses, more and more people began to travel by automobile once cars became reasonably priced (and more dependable) and paved highways covered more and more of the country. Especially in rural areas, cars met an economic need not fulfilled by any other system of transport. Highway improvements also helped trucking companies gain a growing share of the freight market.[8]

The Federal Role in Highway Development

The federal government played an important role in the creation of the highway system. In 1916, Congress created the Bureau of Public Roads, which was authorized to provide federal highway funds to the states on a 50-50 matching grant basis for highways on selected routes. To get federal funds, the states had to create state highway agencies that would draw up highway construction plans and submit them to the Bureau of Public Roads for approval. To ensure that the state-built roads would tie together into a national system, the Bureau of Public Roads was empowered to establish construction standards and to see that the routes joined at state boundary lines.

In 1944, Congress passed a law calling for a new system of multilane highways, although money for the new system was not provided until the **Federal Highway Act of 1956**. This act earmarked the revenues from a new 4-cents-per-gallon gasoline tax (increased to 14 cents by 1991) for the highway trust fund that was used to construct the **interstate highway system**. With a generous 90-10 matching formula, each state received $90 million in federal funds for each $10 million it contributed. Today, the federal government gives more than $34 billion per year to the states for construction and maintenance of our nation's highway system.[9]

Along with these generous matching grants have come a dozen so-called crossover mandates or sanctions, by which the national government tries to influence states. One of the best known of these mandates was the 1984 requirement that each state raise its drinking age to 21 if it wanted to continue receiving its full share of federal highway aid. Also, along with the huge amounts of money invested in highways came the growth of the so-called highway lobby, which has been a potent political force at all levels of government. The highway lobby includes the automobile manufacturers, the trucking companies, the oil companies, the firms that do much of the actual highway construction and repair, and the many businesses that ship merchandise by truck or serve traveling motorists, along with the employees in all of these firms.

The State Role in Highway Development

State governments have the main responsibility for actually constructing and maintaining the intercity highways, either directly or by hiring private contractors or assisting local governments. In addition to federal funds, the states primarily rely on motor fuel taxes for this task. To ensure that those taxes would be earmarked for transportation purposes, most states enacted **antidiversion legislation** that prevented motor fuel taxes from going into the general treasury. A number of states put that requirement in their constitutions.[10]

The most common purposes for which fuel taxes were earmarked were highways, airports, state police, water transport, and boating. Few states designated fuel tax revenue for public transit purposes or intercity rail transportation. In recent years, state and local government spending for highways and roads has exceeded $140 billion annually.[11]

The Consequences of Heavy Reliance on Roads and Highways   These developments in the highway system have had several important consequences for the lives of most Americans. First, because of the unprecedented mobility it gave people, the highway system helped connect the metropolis to the countryside. The highways and the electronic communications systems of telephone, television, radio, satellite systems, fax machines, and computer modems now link the small town intimately to the metropolis. Because of these communications links, many corporations increasingly construct new facilities in small towns beyond the fringes of the metropolis rather than in the heart of it.

This unprecedented mobility has permitted, paradoxically, both a *decentralization* and a *recentralization* of social activities. Until the 1920s, cities developed along streetcar and railroad lines,[12] but the combination of excellent roads and mass-produced automobiles permitted real estate developers to build subdivisions in suburban areas not served by streetcars or buses. Retail merchants began to abandon the congested central business districts for attractive new suburban shopping centers that had plenty of parking space. In this way, the road network decentralized and dispersed the metropolis. At the same time, the rise of the automobile brought more small towns and rural areas within the reach of metropolitan areas, with people commuting long distances to work and driving to the city to shop and enjoy a wider range of social and cultural activities. In effect, society was recentralizing.

A second consequence of the automobile age becomes apparent every time there is a petroleum shortage, a threat to our oil sources, or an upsurge in oil prices. The United States imports roughly 67 percent of the petroleum that Americans use each year, and dependence on imports has been rising. In addition, the United States' proven petroleum reserves fell by 28 percent between 1980 and 2004.[13] This makes the new diffuse lifestyle increasingly vulnerable to an interruption in foreign oil supplies. In 1991, the United States fought the first Persian Gulf War to protect oil sources in Kuwait from falling under the control of a hostile regime in Iraq, and in March of 2003, a second war with Iraq began and is still in progress with some insurgent groups. The second war was initiated by other concerns besides oil, at least officially, but those concerns were undoubtedly heightened by the importance of Iraq's oil supplies and the oil reserves of other Middle Eastern countries. The war, combined with growing petroleum demand from growing economies in other countries and some production problems, led to higher fuel prices and to increased costs for road building and maintenance,[14] as well as contributing to the recession that began in 2007.

A number of efforts to reduce the oil dependence of the automobile system are underway. Among these are automobiles that can use alternative fuels, such as alcohol or biodiesel, hybrid vehicles, and electric cars. A major problem with electric vehicles is their limited range before they need recharging, which is unavailable in many places. However, a number of cities have attacked this problem by creating charging stations in a variety of locations; Knoxville, Tennessee, for example, will soon have over 300 charging stations.[15]

A third consequence of the automobile age was the decline of the central cities of the Northeast and Midwest.[16] The freeways enabled retailers to abandon the central business district for the shopping centers in the suburbs, making it unnecessary for most people to venture into the old business districts except for an occasional excursion. Other businesses also relocated away from the central city to have better highway access. The freeways built in the central cities destroyed large numbers of residential buildings, split up neighborhoods, and wiped out numerous small businesses. In some cities, such as Los Angeles, Chicago, Denver, and Phoenix, heavy volumes of motor vehicles produced serious smog and air pollution. The third of the population that was too old, young, disabled, or poor to drive was increasingly compressed into the central cities, where they had access only to bus or subway lines. Growing reliance on road and highway transportation did not by itself cause all this, but the increasing use of highways after 1945 was one important factor in the decline of the central cities.

A fourth area of significant concern is the cost of maintaining the road system. The federal highway trust fund, for many years, only paid for constructing the highways; maintenance costs were left to the states. In addition, state and local spending for maintenance has often lagged behind the costs of adequate care. As a consequence, the road systems have deteriorated in many places, especially when and where budgets are tight.[17] Maintenance is an acute problem on the interstate highway system, which now allows heavy trucks weighing up to 80,000 pounds. One transportation study estimated that it would take 9,600 automobiles to do the amount of road damage caused by one 80,000-pound truck,[18] and the Congressional Budget Office and the Governmental Accountability Office have estimated that taxes on large trucks in this size range paid for only a fraction of the wear and tear they added to the roadways.[19] To alleviate these problems, Congress in 1982, 1983, and 1991 increased the road taxes on trucks and increased the federal gasoline tax to 14 cents per gallon. Several states also raised their gasoline taxes. These measures are beginning to slow down the deterioration of the nation's roads, but many miles of highways and roads still need replacement or major repair. In addition, roughly 150,000 road and highway bridges in the country (almost 25 percent of all the bridges) are structurally deficient, functionally obsolete, or both.[20]

One other important consequence of America's heavy reliance on automobiles and trucks is that motor vehicle accidents kill tens of thousands of Americans and cause millions of injuries every year. In 2008 alone, roughly 37,000 people died in traffic accidents, and millions were injured. According to one estimate, the total cost of all motor vehicle accidents in 2005 was approximately $248 *billion,* including lost workplace productivity, property damage, medical costs, and travel delays.[21] The accident rates of commercial airplanes and passenger trains are far lower than the accident rate for automobiles.

The heavy toll of motor vehicle accidents has led to a number of efforts to improve traffic safety, and many of those efforts have succeeded. Fatality rates for road and highway travel have declined dramatically, falling by over 60 percent between 1980 and 2008. Much of the improvement is due to better highway designs, better lighting, improvements in car design, and increased use of seat belts. According to one estimate, seat belts alone prevent roughly 15,000 fatalities and 350,000 serious injuries each year. Declining alcohol consumption has also helped increase traffic safety. State and local officials have been exploring many other ideas for promoting traffic safety, from computerized mapping programs to identify dangerous intersections and stretches of road, to graduated licensing, which permits new drivers to acquire their initial driving experience under supervision on a limited license and gradually move to having a full-fledged license.[22]

In spite of those improvements, a great deal remains to be done. Fatality rates vary considerably from state to state and from one road to another. In 2008, the traffic death rates in Louisiana and Montana were more than twice as high as the death rates in Connecticut, Massachusetts, Minnesota, New Jersey, and Rhode Island. Rural roads tend to be particularly dangerous, because people tend to drive fast on these roads that often were not originally designed for high speeds. Although seat belt use has risen over the years, the United States still lags behind many other Western democracies in seat belt use. Significant numbers of children are killed or injured each year, in part because they are not using seat belts or appropriate safety seats.[23]

America's state legislatures have been in the forefront of efforts to promote transportation safety. One major facet of that effort focuses on drunk driving, which is involved in more than one-third of all traffic fatalities each year. Some recent efforts to reduce drunk driving have focused on people who repeatedly drive while intoxicated. The National Highway Traffic Safety Administration has developed a set of 11 proposals to combat repetitive drunk driving, and most states have adopted at least some of the proposals.[24] Conversely, Illinois and several other states are trying to crack down on first-time drunk drivers. Responding to pressure from Mothers Against Drunk Driving, Illinois now promotes the use of alcohol interlock devices in response to the first drunk driving incidents in an effort to change behavior patterns earlier.[25]

Many experts believe that significant improvements in traffic safety are possible, but some proposals trigger complaints that they intrude too much into people's lives and/or cause inconvenience to travelers.[26] For example, when highway speed limits were reduced in the 1970s to conserve fuel (and also saved lives), many motorists and the trucking industry complained about longer drive times, especially in more sparsely populated states. When a number of states later raised their speed limits, they often had increasing numbers of traffic deaths.[27]

One other sensitive safety issue involves elderly drivers. Old age often brings a variety of health problems, including poorer vision, poorer hearing, slower reactions, and orthopedic problems, that affect older Americans' abilities to drive. Those health problems, coupled with greater difficulty in recovering from injuries, cause fatality rates to rise considerably as drivers go beyond age 70. Many older drivers are, however, reluctant to give up driving, partly because they fear a loss of independence and partly because public transportation systems in some areas are very limited or even nonexistent. A number of states now have special procedures for license renewals for older drivers, and other states have been discussing possible changes. As the population ages, the problem will become increasingly serious.[28]

The dramatic changes in communications technology in recent years have brought a new safety hazard to roads and highways: drivers who are distracted by talking on their cell phones, exchanging text messages, and surfing the Internet. Although early research on the safety effects of cell phone use produced mixed conclusions, eventually most analysts concluded that using cell phones and especially texting while driving significantly increase the risks of accidents. State and local government officials all over the country have discussed a variety of proposals to limit or prohibit driver use of cell phones and other communications technologies; the issues are far from settled. Many drivers apparently do not regard the distractions as presenting a major safety hazard, and many businesses rely on those in-car communications systems to contact employees and customers.[29] That does not present a congenial environment for strong actions against distracted driving, although some states have tried to discourage driving while using a cell phone or texting.

The Uncertain World of Public Transportation

While automobile usage continues to climb, the use of public transit declined steadily from the 1940s until 1972. It then rose for more than ten years and peaked in the mid-1980s at levels it had not seen since 1960. Ridership declined until the mid-1990s, then rebounded to levels well above the 1980s' levels by 2000 and beyond. This renaissance in public transit in the 1970s and 1980s and growth in ridership since was due in no small measure to five factors: disenchantment with freeway construction in the early 1970s, serious traffic congestion, new federal incentives for public transportation, a new state government interest in public transit, and unhappiness with higher fuel prices.

Disenchantment with Freeways Part of the public transit renaissance in the 1970s was due to a growing disenchantment with urban freeway systems. Whereas the state highway departments successfully overrode neighborhood objections to the metropolitan freeways during the 1950s and 1960s,[30] by the 1970s legal and political infighting had altered or terminated new freeway projects in Memphis,[31] Washington, DC, Boston,[32] New York City, and several other cities.

Freeway construction in built-up areas is normally very expensive due to the cost of acquiring a right of way for the freeway. Displaced homeowners and businesses must be paid for their properties, and some will fight against that in court. Governments can use the power of eminent domain to compel people to sell property needed for a freeway, but legal challenges to that effort may delay the project for years. Assessments of environmental consequences may present further difficulty, with probable increases in exhaust fumes, noise, and dust where the freeway is located. Moreover, building more freeways may encourage more people to drive farther each day, which yields more exhaust fumes, noise, and dust.

Traffic Congestion Most Americans travel to and from work by car, and the typical car used for commuting has only the driver in it. In 2008, just over three-fourths of commuters drove alone to and from work. Many Americans also drive alone when going shopping and for a wide variety of other activities. As the population of an area increases, the practice of one person-one car produces more and more traffic congestion, a problem that is compounded as truck traffic increases. The average American worker now spends nearly 40 minutes per day commuting, although travel times vary greatly from place to place. Traffic congestion in recent years has grown increasingly serious in moderately large metropolitan areas as well as the very large ones.[33]

When cars and trucks creep along due to traffic jams, fuel is wasted, pollution increases, and commuters take longer to reach their jobs and homes. Emergency vehicles may have difficulties in reaching the scenes of accidents, crimes, and fires. Nationwide, traffic congestion costs the country billions of dollars each year. Many Americans do not regard congestion as a serious problem, however, in part because they live in areas where congestion is not terribly severe, and partly because traffic congestion typically increases very gradually (except in the case of major construction projects that close roads). Experts predict that congestion problems will grow significantly in future years.[34]

Federal Incentives for Public Transit Equally important for the renaissance of public transit was a series of financial incentives starting in the 1960s and continuing into the 1970s. The first incentives were federal grants-in-aid for transit planning. In the **Urban Mass Transit Act of 1974**, Congress authorized an annual expenditure of roughly $2.2 billion through the end of the decade. Renewed in the 1980s and in 1991, this act led to a total of about $89 billion in federal public transit spending through the mid-1990s.[35] Annual federal aid for mass transit systems increased to more than 11 billion dollars by 2009, although federal highway aid far exceeded the mass transit funds.[36]

Federal aid has helped subsidize operating expenses of transit systems as well as capital expenditures for construction and equipment. Also significant in this legislative history was the **Surface Transit Assistance Act of 1982** that earmarked, for the first time, some of the federal gasoline tax for public mass transit. It was primarily these earmarked funds that enabled mass transit to obtain federal funding during the 1980s when the Reagan and the first Bush administrations repeatedly proposed reducing mass transit subsidies and eliminating completely the subsidies for the operating expenses of Amtrak, the national railroad passenger system.

Despite the large sums of money, subsidies for public transportation are highly controversial. Opponents complain that local transit systems and Amtrak (which operates a number of transit systems) generate recurring financial losses.[37] Proponents reply that all transportation modes receive public subsidies and note that public transportation can help the nation cope with traffic congestion that is gradually growing worse in densely populated areas, and can help reduce environmental damage in the process. A number of states, from New York and

California to North Carolina and Oklahoma, help to finance Amtrak service, and officials in many parts of the country are studying proposals to upgrade passenger rail service, with a particular emphasis on higher-speed operations. Modern technologies and other improvements have helped to provide faster, more comfortable, and more reliable service, and further improvements are being explored. Those improvements, which have helped to increase rail passenger travel, have taken on greater importance as America's oil supplies continue to decline and the population ages.[38]

Europeans have consistently invested in modernizing train and transit facilities even though their passenger rail service also requires extensive government subsidies. The result is an elaborate system of intercity and intracity transit that is clean, fast, convenient, impressively punctual, and widely patronized by tens of millions of riders. With extensive public ridership, the Europeans save themselves a fortune in the cost of imported oil, and they make a major impact on holding down air pollution.

To utilize these advantages of public transit, however, it probably is not possible for public transit systems to run at a profit. Less than half of public transit revenues come from fares, transit taxes, and advertising. The rest comes from state, federal, and local government subsidies.[39] Even at the peak of public transit ridership in the early twentieth century, transit operations lost money. In Boston, early transit operators built their streetcar systems primarily to transport people to real estate they were developing on the fringes of the city. They not only lost money on their transit operations, but they also had to use their real estate profits to subsidize transit operations. Once the real estate was sold, they had no more incentives to subsidize the transit operations, and at that point they appealed to the city for financial aid. This occurred several times in Boston's history and the pattern was repeated throughout the United States.[40]

An Increasing State Role   State and local governments have also been forced to consider expanding their roles in the transportation system, although not all of them have responded in the same way. On one extreme, transit systems in Chicago and Boston were so plagued with financial difficulties that they cut service, raised fares, and saw their riderships decline. At the other extreme, San Diego relied exclusively on state and local funds to build its famous light rail system, the Tijuana Trolley, and Dallas voters increased the sales tax to build a rapid rail system in their area. The Texas state legislature recently approved a bill to enable suburban counties to create their own mass transit systems. A considerable number of states and localities have become involved in efforts to preserve and even expand rail freight service, often in response to possible abandonment of rail lines. These preservation efforts range from tax relief and financial subsidies to public ownership of railroad lines.[41] Those freight lines may eventually serve as commuter train routes, too.

Fuel Prices and the 2008 Recession   One other factor encouraging transit use in recent years is the combination of high gasoline prices and a recession that has squeezed many family budgets. An analysis by the American Public Transit Association (which advocates for public transit improvements) found that in the 20 communities with the highest volume of transit ridership in 2010, transit riders saved an average of $800 per month compared to people who commuted alone in their cars or other personal vehicles.[42]

Transit Options   In planning for effective public transit, each community must select the combination of transit vehicles and structures that are most appropriate for its particular transit problems. Five major vehicle systems form the bulk of the U.S. transit options—bus service, light rail systems, heavy rail systems, multimodal bus rapid transit, and commuter railroads.

Bus Service   Buses carry the largest number of passengers of any public transit mode and will remain the core of most transit systems for the foreseeable future. The greatest advantage of the bus is its flexibility. It can be driven on many streets, and it can be used in a variety of ways. As traffic patterns shift, bus routes can readily change. Many metropolitan areas now reserve special lanes on freeways for buses so that the buses can move faster than the automobile traffic. Some larger cities have buses that are powered by electricity from overhead wires to reduce exhaust fumes in high-traffic areas. *Para transit* refers to small vans that cruise fixed routes and pick up and drop off passengers at any point.

Minibuses or *stop-and-ride* buses have been used for shuttle purposes between central business shopping areas and outlying parking lots. *Dial-a-ride* is a system of small buses: When residents telephone, a minivan cruising in the neighborhood is dispatched to residents' homes to transport them to some point within the area serviced by the dial-a-ride system.

In addition to flexibility, bus service has the lowest capital costs of any existing public transit system. *Capital costs* refer to the cost of building or purchasing a facility or vehicles, and they are distinguished from *operating* or *maintenance costs*, which are the costs of running the facility once it is built. Buses have relatively low operating costs because they primarily use existing streets and highways shared with other vehicles.

One disadvantage of buses involves operating costs. Each bus, van, minibus, or other vehicle must have a driver. Drivers sometimes unionize. They bargain for higher wages, which increases the costs of operation. Bus operating expenses are also high for bus routes that do not attract enough passengers to pay for themselves. In addition, buses that operate on city streets are delayed by traffic congestion just as are cars unless there are specially designated routes for buses only.[43]

Light Rail Systems   The light rail system is an updated version of the old streetcar. Streetcars are usually large vehicles, often electric powered, that ride on tracks in the street or sometimes in median strips adjacent to the streets. Most streetcar systems disappeared in the 1940s, when the transit companies changed to buses and paved over the streetcar rails. Between 1935 and 1970, the number of streetcar track miles declined from 25,000 to 762. In Los Angeles, which had an extensive streetcar system, the public transit company was purchased by a consortium owned by General Motors, Firestone, and Standard Oil, that tore up the tracks and replaced the streetcars with buses.[44]

In the 1980s, **light rail transit (LRT)** gained popularity. Light rail systems do not pollute the air as much as do automobiles, and electrified light rail systems can operate without petroleum fuels. Some systems differ from the old-fashioned streetcars in that they can carry many more passengers (up to 500 in three linked cars) and they are more likely to run on separate railways than they are to run down the middle of busy streets, as did the old streetcars. The first new LRT system began operating in 1981 when San Diego opened its Tijuana Trolley, and New Orleans opened a new line a few years later. Memphis recently opened the first portion of a new streetcar system, and the modern system of Portland, Oregon, is very successful. A number of other communities are also exploring the option.[45]

Most of these LRT systems have been quite expensive to build and some have not met their builders' goals of getting very large numbers of automobile commuters to abandon their cars in favor of LRT. Two major exceptions to the general disappointment of LRT have been

San Diego's Tijuana Trolley system and Portland's, which recently added a new line from the downtown area to the city's major airport.[46] The recent improvements in the New Orleans trolley system have also been praised by a number of observers.[47]

Heavy Rail Systems   Heavy rail systems use conventional passenger train equipment and usually operate on existing rail lines. In densely populated areas, heavy rail systems can move large numbers of people in a brief period of time. The trains can be operated by a local government authority or by a contractor hired by the authority. Amtrak, for example, operates commuter service in a number of communities across the country and carries millions of commuters each year.[48]

HIGHLIGHT

PRT in Morgantown

Morgantown, home of West Virginia University, was the scene of a daily traffic jam between the university's three campuses and the city's central business district. To relieve this congestion, the university requested a $13.5-million grant from the federal Department of Transportation (DOT) to construct a 3.6-mile, $18-million PRT system with six stops that would connect the university's parking lots, its three campuses, and downtown Morgantown. The 45 proposed vehicles would be 6 feet wide by 15 feet long, would seat 8 and take another 12 standing commuters. The chauffeurless cars would be electrically driven at 30 miles per hour by a computer. The system would run on an elevated concrete guideway that, on completion, would extend 5.4 miles. The riders would signal for a car by placing their fare cards in a slot and pressing a designation button. This would signal the computer to dispatch a car to the riders' station to take them to their destinations.

Early in the planning, Morgantown's PRT got caught in national politics. DOT decided it wanted to dedicate the Morgantown PRT guideway before the 1972 presidential election, but it did not yet know how heavy the cars would be. To accommodate the heaviest possible car, it built a much heavier and thus much costlier structure than the one originally anticipated. Planning and construction were rushed, the project manager was changed, designs were altered,

inflation hit double digits, and the cost of the project quickly overran the original estimates.

When the first phase was completed, costs had reached $59.8 million. Rather than a 5.4-mile system reaching all three university campuses, it was only 2.2 miles long and reached only two campuses. Rather than six stations, the system had only three. At one point, when the development of vehicles was delayed, the university ran golf carts along the guideway.

The university complained that this abbreviated system did not meet its needs and threatened to tear it down at a cost to DOT of $7 million if DOT did not move into phase II, which would complete the original plans. Phase II was projected at the time to cost another $53.8 million. This would bring the total cost for the system to $113.6 million, nearly $100 million more than the original estimate of $18 million. DOT agreed to finish phase II, which would add two more stations and complete the 5.4 miles of guideways.

Despite its high start-up costs and the glitches surrounding its construction, Morgantown's PRT has run successfully since its maiden trip in 1975. It carries 16,000 riders a day and has generally operated free of serious problems. Despite running its cars at headways of only 15 seconds at times, the system has never suffered a collision. ∎

Sources: "Trouble in Mass Transit," *Consumer Reports* 40, no. 3 (March 1975): 190–195; *St. Paul Pioneer Press*, July 22, 1990, p. 179.

Rapid Transit The fifth option for urban transportation is the traditional **rapid transit**—electrically driven trains that run in subways, on the ground, or on elevated guideways. Such systems currently exist in a number of U.S. cities. The major advantage of rapid transit is that it can move large numbers of passengers in a brief period of time. In addition, rapid transit systems, with their own exclusive rights of way, can move quickly when street traffic is snarled in traffic jams.

Rapid rail transit works best in areas with large populations, high densities, and large numbers of people commuting into the central business district (CBD) each day.[49] Unfortunately for rapid-rail boosters, few metropolises meet these criteria. In the 25 largest urban areas in the 1980s, only 8.5 percent of workers commuted to jobs in the CBD. Nearly half (45.7 percent) commuted from homes in the suburbs to jobs in the suburbs.[50] And sprawling suburbs with low-density populations are not conducive to rapid rail transit.

Even in places with large numbers of people commuting to the CBD, such as San Francisco and Washington, DC, rapid rail has had a number of problems. San Francisco's BART (Bay Area Rapid Transit), which opened in 1972, was the first rapid rail system to be built since the early 1900s. It has been heavily criticized for its initial cost overruns, its inability to run at a profit, and its failure to reduce traffic congestion in the San Francisco area.[51] However, the system has gradually won over many travelers who use the system at least occasionally. In the smaller metropolitan areas, new rapid rail experiences have been even more disappointing. Miami's metrorail has suffered from insufficient ridership—only one-fifth of original projections.[52]

Given all these considerations, it appears as though the smartest cities were the ones that resisted the temptation to use federal grants to build rapid rail or LRT. But it is possible that history may judge otherwise. Few of the new systems have been operating for more than 20 years, and this may well be too short a time in which to evaluate such an expensive undertaking as an LRT. Conceivably, both New York and Chicago could have shown disappointing results only a few years after their subways first opened. Yet today those subway systems are invaluable, and in 40 years, Atlantans, Miamians, and residents of the District of Columbia may well be grateful for their rail systems.

Because rapid transit systems are often electric powered, they do not consume as much oil as does commuting by car. In view of the continuing conflicts in the Middle East, that advantage may become increasingly important in future years.

Multimodal Bus Rapid Transit Finally, buses can be used on fixed guideways to gain the speed and passenger volume of an LRT. Unlike an LRT, however, these same vehicles can leave the fixed guideways to run as regular buses on city streets. Variations of this multimodal rapid transit have been used successfully in England, Germany, Brazil, and Australia. Because the fixed guideways are only needed for portions of the routes (the remainder being on city streets) and because the buses are cheaper to purchase than rail vehicles, a multimodal bus rapid transit can be built at a lower cost than LRT.

The most elaborate system is probably the so-called O-Bahn in Adelaide, Australia, a city of about one million people with a low-density population similar to most American cities. Express buses on separate, fixed guideways connect the city of Adelaide to its suburbs. Once they enter the city, the buses leave the fixed guideway and cruise the city streets like regular buses. This gives the O-Bahn the high-speed, high-occupancy characteristics of LRT on the guideways combined with the flexibility of an ordinary bus on city streets. Although more expensive to build than simply adding more buses, the O-Bahn was built for one-half the cost of an LRT system, and it has proved immensely popular. Because its vehicles can cruise the city streets to pick up passengers as well as speed along the fixed guideways, O-Bahn has reduced the need for transfers between buses and for park-and-ride facilities. This has dramatically decreased travel time compared to automobile commuters.

The Uncertain Future of Mass Transit

It is not clear whether mass transit can eventually attract enough riders to provide very much help with traffic congestion. Furthermore, the cause of mass transit has sometimes been hurt by inflated projections of the benefits that would flow from transit improvements. When the benefits fell short of these rosy predictions, public mass transit itself came under powerful attack by critics who sought to turn opinion against it.[53] Some recent systems, which began with more modest traffic projections, have been more successful in meeting initial expectations. The second war in Iraq, coupled with rising gasoline prices, growing concern about global warming, and increased traffic congestion, helped bolster voter approval of major transportation ballot measures in a number of states in the 2006 elections. Voters in California, Georgia, Louisiana, Minnesota, New Jersey, and Rhode Island all approved measures dealing with a range of transportation policies, including revenue increases, safety-related projects, public transit, roads, and bridges.[54]

Overall, efforts to cope with metropolitan traffic congestion have met with limited success at best. Many commuters complain about traffic congestion, but many are also unwilling to give up the convenience and flexibility of driving alone for public transportation or even carpooling. As the nation's dependence on imported oil gradually rises, however, and as the population ages and traffic congestion slowly worsens in our larger communities, citizens and officials will continue to struggle with the age-old task of getting people and merchandise from place to place.[55]

A number of communities have experimented with various methods for attacking congestion. Some employers provide workers with free or discounted transit passes. Some highway lanes have been designated for buses and cars with two or more people in them to encourage using the buses or carpooling. New Jersey Turnpike officials are trying somewhat higher tolls during peak traffic periods. Public officials who try to reduce congestion must proceed carefully, however, for remedies that are very costly or that inconvenience people who refuse to carpool or use public transportation are likely to trigger public opposition.[56]

In 1991, the national government gave the states somewhat more flexibility in federal highway aid by adopting the Intermodal Surface Transportation Efficiency Act (ISTEA). The law allowed states to reallocate some funds from one highway program to another and to some nonhighway transportation programs, such as mass transit. However, most states made little use of the flexibility, in part because of the ongoing costs of highway programs and, perhaps, in part because of the strength of the highway lobby, which did not favor shifting funds to nonhighway uses. In 1998, ISTEA was succeeded by the Transportation Equity Act (TEA-21), which retained some state flexibility, but also gave Congress more influence regarding individual highway projects.[57]

HOUSING AND COMMUNITY DEVELOPMENT

A second area of infrastructure policy involves the framework for housing people and activities. In discussing these policy areas we will examine: (1) the basic problems associated with housing and physical deterioration; (2) the roles that states, communities, and the federal government play in housing and redevelopment policies; and (3) alternatives to present-day housing and community development programs.

The Basic Problems of Housing

The Homeless   The most visible housing problem is that of the homeless. Their numbers are estimated to be somewhere between 350,000 and 3 million, with the most likely number being somewhere between half a million and one million. Why such a large number of homeless should exist today seems traceable to three explanations. First is the argument that there simply is not enough low-income housing and this forces some low-income people into homelessness. Advocates of the homeless point out that the Reagan years saw a sharp dropoff in the number of public housing units built each year. The net result was that the national supply of low-income, public housing remained roughly constant from 1980 through 1992, even as the population was growing and more families were having trouble affording housing.[58] As we will see shortly, housing prices have risen dramatically in recent years, at least until the recession arrived.

Some analysts offer a second explanation for homelessness. In 1990 roughly nine million housing units were vacant all year; that number swelled to more than 14 million by 2008.[59] From this perspective, homelessness stems not from a lack in housing units but from the behavioral characteristics of the homeless people themselves.[60] A survey of California homeless, for example, found that 69 percent were abusers of either drugs or alcohol, and 77 percent suffered from either mental illness or substance abuse.[61] Note, however, that the existence of vacant housing does not mean that it is fit to live in and/or affordable for people with low incomes. Even many occupied homes have significant problems, from inadequate police protection and high neighborhood crime rates to mice, holes in floors or walls, and water leakage.[62] Also, vacancy rates vary considerably from state to state and from one metropolitan area to another.

A third reason for the growth of homelessness is traced to deinstitutionalization. Mental institutions housed half a million patients in 1963. By 1992, that number had dropped to about 125,000.[63] By these calculations, more than 300,000 previously institutionalized people had to find a place to live. For years, many of the people released from mental institutions drifted into single-room occupancy (SRO) hotels, but the gentrification process of the 1970s saw many SRO hotels torn down for condominiums and commercial buildings.[64]

Beginning in the 1990s, many people began to lose patience with the large numbers of homeless people, particularly those who were begging or detracting from the appearance of parks or businesses. A number of communities adopted new ordinances against aggressive panhandling, begging in specific locations, or sleeping in public places. Other communities began to enforce older laws against vagrancy in order to encourage homeless people to go somewhere else.[65]

What to do about the homeless is not self-evident. There is a growing belief that the problem requires more than just increasing the number of shelters. The McKinney Act of 1987 set up a number of programs that sought to provide medical care, mental health care, education, and job training for the homeless. Nevertheless, homelessness persists and is likely to persist unless the nation addresses the twin issues of "housing that is too expensive and incomes that are too low" to afford housing.[66] That assessment has been underscored by the recession and wave of home foreclosures that began in 2007, particularly with the growth in the ranks of homeless families.[67]

Housing for Low- and Moderate-Income People   If the first basic housing problem is the homeless, the second is alleviating the difficulties facing low- and moderate-income people whose incomes are so low that they could easily become homeless without some form of public assistance. In 2003, households in poverty usually paid more than half of their income for shelter.[68] One study concluded that a full-time worker earning the federal minimum wage in 2004 could only afford the rent and utilities in a one-bedroom apartment in four of the America's 3,066 counties.[69] Many people working in low-wage jobs can only afford housing if they avoid unexpected expenses, such as a major illness; even then they cannot afford to live in many communities unless they have more than one source of income. The sad reality is that roughly 20 percent of all U.S. jobs pay a wage that leaves a full-time worker with a family of four below the poverty line. Roughly 50 local governments in the United States have adopted "living wage" ordinances, which require many firms doing business with the local government to pay their workers at least the minimum wage needed to provide the typical family with a decent living standard.[70]

For moderate-income families, whose goal most often is to own their home rather than to rent it, the perennial problem is cost. On the face of it, these people do not seem to be priced out of today's housing market. About two-thirds of American families own their own homes today, up from 44 percent in 1940.[71] However, many young, middle- and working-class families are able to afford the down payment and monthly mortgage payments only if both spouses work. As Figure 15.1 shows, the cost of houses has risen dramatically since 1970, although prices slumped noticeably with the collapse of the housing bubble in 2007.

There are several reasons for the escalation of new home prices prior to the recession. New single-family homes are seldom designed for the moderate-income household. They are designed for a much more upscale buyer than was the case 40 years ago.[72] In 1970, the average new house had 1,500 square feet of living space, only 34 percent of new houses had central air conditioning, and only 35 percent had a fireplace. By 2009, the average square footage had grown to more than 2,400, 88 percent of new houses had central air conditioning, 55 percent had more than two bathrooms, and 51 percent had at least one fireplace.[73]

Although the moderate-income family has largely been priced out of the market for new single-family homes, they have a much better shot at getting a used home. Figure 15.1 shows that existing homes are noticeably less expensive than are new homes. Home mortgage rates have also fallen considerably since the early 1980s, which significantly reduces the cost of a mortgage loan. These rates averaged 14 percent in the early 1980s,[74] but dropped to 5.1 percent by 2009.[75] On a 30-year fixed-rate mortgage, a drop of only 2 percentage points in the interest rate on a $75,000 mortgage reduced the monthly payment by $110. As mortgage rates dropped in the early 1990s and again during the 2000–2002 and the 2007 recession, it was not only easier for first-time home buyers to make the purchase, but those who had bought homes at the high 12–14 percent mortgage rates of the early 1980s could also refinance.

Another option for families with modest incomes is a manufactured or mobile home, which typically costs less than one-third of the price of a new house built on the site and only slightly more than one-third the price of an existing house.[76] Some communities prohibit manufactured and mobile homes, and many others restrict where they can be located. Nonetheless, many families find them to be an attractive option as a first home.

Racial Separation in Housing   Racial minorities find more obstacles in their search for decent housing than do whites of similar income levels. Only in 1948 did the Supreme

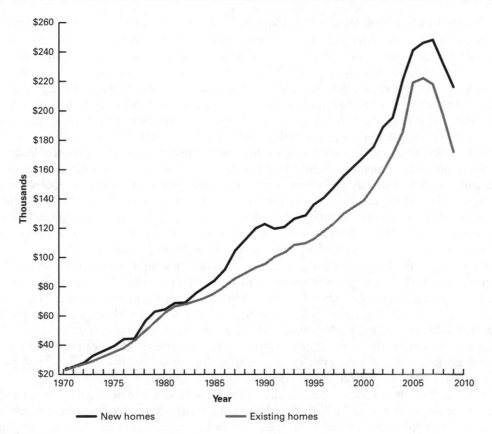

FIGURE 15.1

Median Cost of Single-Family Homes Sold

Sources: Bureau of the Census, *Statistical Abstract of the United States, 1995* (Washington, DC: U.S. Government Printing Office, 1992), pp. 492, 730; *Statistical Abstract, 1996*, pp. 716–717; *Statistical Abstract, 2003*, pp. 612–613; *Statistical Abstract, 2006*, pp. 622, 624; *Statistical Abstract, 2011–2012*, pp. 610–611.

Court hold that deed covenants that prohibited the sale of property to non-Caucasians were unenforceable in the courts. Federal Housing Administration (FHA) loans to non-whites were prohibited as late as 1962. The Housing Act of 1968 made discrimination in the sale and rental of housing illegal. This legislation expanded housing opportunities for many middle-income racial and cultural minorities. And racial separation is measurably less today than it was 40 years ago.[77] Nevertheless, separation and discrimination continue to exist.

In the face of national legislation against racial discrimination in housing, how can it be that racial separation in housing is still the predominant pattern throughout the nation? Part of the racial separation can be attributed no doubt to whites freely choosing not to live among African Americans and African Americans freely choosing not to live among whites. But much of it also is due to exclusionary zoning practices in the richest suburbs. **Exclusionary zoning** exists when a suburb requires each house in it to have expensive amenities, such as a large lot, a garage for two or more cars, many square feet of floor space, a paved driveway, and other costly **building code** demands, and prohibits low-rent apartment buildings. The more such requirements, the more expensive it is to build housing in a community. An elite suburb can easily exclude low-income people this way. Since racial minorities disproportionately earn lower incomes, minorities are considerably affected by exclusionary zoning. The motivation behind exclusionary zoning is often class based rather than race based, but the practice has racial consequences. By keeping out low-income people, a community can effectively keep out many African Americans and other minorities. If a single developer or small group of developers build an entire community of expensive homes, the result is the same.

Perhaps the most visible example of exclusionary housing takes place in **gated communities**. These are developments of high-priced homes surrounded by walls with gates at each of the entries. Security measures at the gates ensure that unauthorized people cannot drive or walk into the gated development. The residents may hire their own security forces, send their children to private schools, utilize private recreational facilities, and oppose spending programs on these same services for the rest of their towns; they can literally wall themselves off from many of the problems that face society—until they leave the gated community to go to work or shop.

According to the Census Bureau, roughly ten million households now live in "secured communities," in which public access is restricted by gates, fences and/or walls, or private security forces. In addition, many multiunit buildings, whether of apartments or condominiums, have some restrictions on public access.[78] If present trends continue, this will be a growing option for many doctors, lawyers, businesspersons, and other people in the upper-middle-income range. Nobody knows what the consequences would be for the social fabric of society if its most dynamic professional and business classes were to wall themselves off from the rest of society. But it is hard to believe that the consequences would be positive.

In 1975, New Jersey initiated a practice called **inclusionary zoning**. In that year, the New Jersey Supreme Court refused to allow the Mount Laurel township to zone out low-income housing. Instead, it required every town to "include" low-income housing in their development plans—hence the term *inclusionary zoning*. Implementation of inclusionary zoning has been plagued with

HIGHLIGHT

Keeping Minorities Out of Birmingham

Birmingham, Michigan, is an upper-income Detroit suburb with few African Americans or other racial minorities among its 26,000 residents.

In the fall of 1977, Michigan's Housing Development Authority agreed to finance a 150-unit apartment complex for the elderly if Birmingham would in turn rehabilitate 50 existing houses for rental to low- and moderate-income families. Assuming that the low- and moderate-income families would be poor African Americans, 4,600 Birmingham voters signed a petition urging the Birmingham Commission (the city council) to turn down this bargain.

When the city commission voted to approve the bargain, opponents began a petition drive to recall the six city commissioners who had voted for the plan. In April 1978, three of those city commissioners stood for reelection and were defeated by candidates who opposed the housing plan. Also on the ballot was a referendum on the housing plan itself. It was resoundingly defeated. ■

Source: The New York Times, April 12, 1978, p. 1A.

difficulties and, in 1983, the court reaffirmed its decision that all communities must include low-income housing. In 1985, the New Jersey state legislature created a Council on Affordable Housing to determine how the principle would apply in each town and each development project.[79]

Minnesota tried to deal with exclusionary housing in 1995 by passing a Livable Communities Act. This law requires that some of the tax base created by expensive homes in the Minneapolis–St. Paul suburbs be used to construct low- and moderate-income housing. Suburbs that refuse to construct this type of housing lose their excess tax base to other communities that take steps to provide housing for low- and moderate-income people.[80]

Deterioration of Central-City Neighborhoods (and Some of the Older Suburbs) As wealthier people and businesses moved away from downtown areas, many central-city neighborhoods deteriorated. One of the worst examples was the South Bronx section of New York City from the mid-1970s to the mid-1980s, when 100,000 dwelling units were destroyed through arson, vandalism, and abandonment. What 50 years earlier had been a working-class, predominantly Jewish community became, by the 1980s, a burned-out shell of a neighborhood dominated by crime, vandals, and gangs.[81]

Many cities face the problem of deteriorating neighborhoods as middle-class residents move out to the suburbs and are replaced by people with less spending power, less ability to pay taxes, and less ability to maintain their residences. Similar problems exist in many older suburbs, smaller towns, and rural areas that have lost jobs and population over the years.

The problem of declining neighborhoods is exacerbated by the practice called **redlining**. Banks and insurance companies supposedly draw a red line around deteriorating neighborhoods and communities, where it is a risky investment to make a mortgage loan or to insure a building. In fact, there is evidence to suggest that race is an important motive in redlining. A study of commercial homeowners insurance by zip code in Milwaukee found that the single strongest variable explaining the extent of commercially available homeowners insurance was race. The zip codes with the most African American residents had the lowest incidence of homeowners insurance.[82]

When apartment owners are unable to get loans to improve their buildings, the more affluent tenants eventually move out and are replaced by the less affluent. Homeowners where buyers are lucky enough to qualify for financing can sell their homes and purchase new ones in better neighborhoods. The redlining practice accelerates the flight of the middle class to the suburbs. The low-income people who replace the middle class have more financial and social problems, and the inevitable result is that those neighborhoods denied mortgage funds and homeowners insurance continue to deteriorate. Because of these debilitating effects of redlining, several states as well as Congress have passed laws seeking to discourage the practice.

Gentrification Paradoxically, while some central-city neighborhoods are in decline and find it difficult to attract mortgage money, other neighborhoods have experienced **gentrification**. This has been characterized by upper-middle-income and professional people moving into old neighborhoods, refurbishing the houses there, and turning aged apartment or commercial buildings into condominiums or upscale apartments. In most cities, the gentrified neighborhoods are usually near the downtown area, are blessed with houses or other buildings that have distinctive aesthetic qualities, and are often large enough to be converted into two- or three-unit condominiums. On the positive side, gentrification has led to neighborhood restoration, added to the urban tax base, and attracted an upper-middle-income population. This, in turn, provides an economic base for restaurants, cultural activities, and shopping facilities. In addition, some of the new arrivals may live closer to their jobs and therefore reduce traffic and commuting problems.

However, gentrification may also cause problems. It may result in the **displacement** of lower-income people, who are driven out of the houses and apartments that are being gentrified (although some gentrification has used idle business properties rather than existing homes and apartments).[83] Displacement occurs because gentrification increases property values to the point where landlords can no longer charge cheap rents. As low-income people are displaced from their former homes, they are forced to rent newer ones in adjacent neighborhoods, often at higher prices.

The Intergovernmental Connection in Coping with Housing Problems

Governmental initiatives to deal with these housing and community development problems began in the late nineteenth century at the local level. Social reformers attacked the spread of urban slum housing by enacting building codes that established minimum requirements for space, electricity, plumbing, and health matters such as garbage disposal. The first building codes were adopted in New York City in the 1860s after a cholera epidemic had spread through slum neighborhoods. By the early twentieth century, most cities and states had adopted some form of housing regulations.[84]

In addition to building codes, cities also began enacting zoning codes, which divide a community into zones restricted to specific uses. The **zoning codes** were largely designed to keep residential, middle-class, single-family-home neighborhoods free from low-income apartments, industrial establishments, and other developments that were considered undesirable. Business interests, however, were often able to obtain changes in zoning regulations to allow new business development.

Finally, in response to the Great Depression of the 1930s, the federal government set up programs that the state and local governments were charged with implementing. This intergovernmental approach still characterizes housing and community development policy making.

Helping Out the Middle and Upper Classes—Mortgage Protection and Tax Expenditures

The Federal Role   The Great Depression of the 1930s effectively destroyed the existing system of financing home purchases. The most common method to finance a home then had been the so-called **balloon mortgage**. This required a down payment of 35–40 percent, and the life of the loan extended for 10–15 years. During those years, the home buyer made only interest payments and was required to pay off the entire principal with a single, so-called balloon payment at the end of the period. If the home buyer had not accumulated enough savings to make the final payment, the lending institution foreclosed on the mortgage, sold the house, and used the proceeds of the sale to pay the balance of the loan and other bank charges.

The Great Depression set off a vicious cycle of events that destroyed this system. By 1932, nearly 25 percent of the workforce was unemployed. Many employed workers saw their incomes fall as their employers faced declining business activities. Those workers were unable to make their mortgage payments, thus depriving financial institutions of needed income. Because there was no national system of insured savings accounts when the Depression struck, this declining income made it impossible for banks to pay their depositors. In order to generate income, the banks regularly foreclosed on mortgages that fell behind in interest payments. The supply of foreclosed homes vastly exceeded the demand for them, and home values dropped sharply. Unable to sell their foreclosed houses at a profit, unable to attract new depositors, and unable to pay existing depositors, many banks simply closed their doors. In 1930, 150,000 homes were foreclosed on, and in 1933 more than 4,000 banks failed.[85]

The federal government responded by creating programs to insure mortgages and to insure people's savings deposits. By insuring mortgages against default, the federal government gave financial institutions confidence to make more loans. And by insuring people's savings accounts, the government boosted their confidence in the banking industry. The federal government also introduced the low down payment, long-term mortgage that helped average families secure home ownership.

The federal government has also assisted middle- and upper-income families by providing income tax deductions for home mortgage interest costs, and property taxes on homes, as well as a generous exclusion of capital gains from home sales from paying capital gains taxes. These tax breaks, which reached $135 billion in 2010, far exceed the entire budget of the federal Department of Housing and Urban Development.[86]

State and Local Roles These programs giving help for middle- and upper-class housing have been partly a transaction between federal government agencies and private lending institutions. State and local governments play a regulatory role. They charter and regulate the lending institutions. They establish the building codes and zoning regulations to which the newly built FHA and VA homes must conform. Many states have active programs of their own to generate housing opportunities for middle- and moderate-income people. Finally, many states have adopted property tax relief programs to reduce the tax burdens of homeowners and, in some cases, renters or businesses.

Housing Programs for the Poor—Public Housing

The Federal Role The Housing Act of 1937 provided for the Public Housing Administration (since 1965, a division of HUD) to contract with a local housing authority (LHA) to build apartment units that would be rented to low-income tenants at a subsidized rate. In 2008, more than ten million low-income families received some form of federal housing assistance, either by living in publicly owned housing or in private housing with federal rent subsidies.[87] Many communities have waiting lists of people applying for federally funded housing assistance.

Public housing was originally designed to provide housing assistance for middle- and working-class people who had been temporarily driven out of decent housing by the Depression. Because very little housing was constructed from 1929 until the end of World War II, by 1945 an enormous housing shortage existed. During the next 30 years, a housing construction boom took place largely in the suburbs and in the fast-growing cities of the South and Southwest. By the early 1960s, the supply of middle-class housing had caught up with the demand. Upwardly mobile tenants abandoned the public housing projects in the 1950s and 1960s. They were replaced by poorer families.

State and Local Roles Although initiated and overseen by the federal government, public housing is typically implemented by a local government agency, the LHA (Local Housing Authority). The local city council established the LHA and approved its contract with the Public Housing Administration to build low-income apartments. Early in the program, most

LHAs were formed in the large central cities,[88] although LHAs eventually existed in many medium-sized and smaller communities, too. Once created, the LHA sold tax-exempt municipal bonds to raise the funds needed to buy land and build the projects. The LHA administered the project and retired the debt through the rent it collected from tenants. Since these rents were never high enough to let the project break even, the Public Housing Administration subsidized the LHA for each low-income family in the project.

If success is measured by the demand for a product, then public housing has been very successful. Long waiting lists exist for most projects. Nevertheless, public housing has its problems and has been bitterly criticized. In some places, public housing was used deliberately to relocate African Americans from scattered locations throughout the cities to a few large ghettoes.[89] Some public housing projects concentrated large numbers of people with extensive social problems into the same residential area, leading to unsatisfactory living conditions for the majority of the residents of those projects. One of the worst of these was the Pruitt-Igoe project in St. Louis, which finally had to be closed.

Pruitt-Igoe was not typical of all public housing projects. Other cities followed different site patterns. In Dade County, Florida, public housing was located on 100 sites scattered throughout the county. In New York, Chicago, and St. Louis, it was commonly located in high-rise apartments, at least in part because many neighborhoods bitterly opposed low-income housing in their areas of town.

Many of the public housing defects were attributed to the program's tendency to concentrate racial minorities, broken families, families subsisting on welfare, and recent migrants into the big cities. Concentrating people with several social problems together into large, high-rise buildings without supportive social services probably made social disorganization in the public housing projects inevitable. These problems were compounded by poor maintenance at some projects and by placing the large projects in very poor areas of town. Those areas were least able to resist having projects, but they also provided few opportunities for decent jobs.

One innovative effort to provide better living conditions for the poor involves requiring developers to build some modestly-priced housing in new upscale subdivisions. Some of the low-priced homes are sold, but others are acquired by local housing authorities and rented to poor people. The result is that poorer people are included in a variety of neighborhoods rather than clustered in a small place. Some of the programs appear to be working smoothly, but others have produced opposition from developers and the wealthier residents of the new subdivisions.[90]

Other local housing authorities have tried to rely on relatively small projects, which often generate less resistance than often occurs with large projects. The smaller projects are often easier to manage and can sometimes place poor residents closer to where there are jobs. Housing authorities have also tried providing rent subsidies to low-income families so that they can afford (sometimes) to select their own housing, which may be privately or publicly owned. A problem with this approach in some areas is that there may be no housing available that poor families can afford, even with rent subsidies.

Urban Renewal and Other Efforts to Combat Economic Decline

Distinct from federally sponsored housing programs was the **urban renewal** program, which was created by a 1949 amendment to the Housing Act of 1937 and which allowed part of the housing money to be used for commercial development. The resulting program was called urban renewal.

The primary objective of urban renewal was to clear blighted areas and redevelop them with a mixture of commercial and residential establishments that would truly renew the old neighborhoods. Urban renewal was thus distinguished from public housing in that it focused on commercial redevelopment. Also, in contrast to public housing, urban renewal developments were turned over to private entrepreneurs rather than being owned by a government body, the local housing authority.

To qualify for urban renewal funds, a city had to create a local public agency (LPA), which was sometimes the same as the local housing authority. The LPA designated the land to be cleared with urban renewal funds and submitted to the federal urban renewal agency a *workable program* for redevelopment.

When the local plan was approved, the federal urban renewal agency provided funds for the LPA to acquire the land, clear it, and reinstall public facilities such as sewer and water lines. After this was completed, the LPA offered the land to redevelopers, who bought it at a much reduced price and erected new buildings on it. The federal government typically paid two-thirds of the LPA's net cost (acquisition, clearance, and upgrading costs less the price paid by the redeveloper), and the rest was made up through local bonds, cash, or other funds.

The residents and former merchants in the redevelopment area had to relocate to new areas. The LPA was obliged to give relocation assistance to the residents. But in fact this aid was seldom adequate,[91] and displacement of these residents became one of the biggest complaints against urban renewal.

In sum, the major impact of urban renewal was to redevelop the CBDs and other commercial areas of the major cities. Although urban renewal was instrumental in rebuilding many CBDs, it was resoundingly criticized from a variety of fronts. Community activists and architectural critics objected to it for destroying functioning communities.[92] Black leaders referred to urban renewal as "Negro removal." Conservatives criticized it for using governmental authority to take property from one group of private citizens (the private homeowners, landlords, and merchants) and turning it over to another (the redevelopers).[93]

Restructuring Housing and Renewal Programs

The Housing and Community Development Act of 1974

By the early 1970s, federal housing and urban renewal programs had come under considerable criticism. These criticisms came to a head under the presidency of Republican Richard Nixon (1969–1974) who wanted a program that would be cheaper and simpler to administer. After several years of political battles, Congress finally passed the **Housing and Community Development Act of 1974**, which established the structure of housing and community development programs that still exists today.

The community development provisions consolidated seven categorical grant programs, including urban renewal, into a community development block grant (CDBG) of $8.4 billion annually from 1975 to 1977. Successive renewals have kept it alive, with some variations in funding, for community development and area and regional development.[94] Cities may use their community development funds for urban renewal purposes, more public housing, or other activities ranging from building code enforcement to improving certain public services. Under a complicated formula, each community of over 50,000 is automatically entitled to a specific sum.

The housing portion of the Housing and Community Development Act of 1974 created a rent supplement program called **Section 8**. Under Section 8, the local housing authority

(HRA) provides rent assistance for tenants whose total family income is less than 80 percent of the median for the area. Tenants pay 30 percent of their income to the landlord. The LHA uses federal funds to pay the landlord the difference between that amount and a maximum allowable rent established by HUD.

Was the 1974 restructuring successful? The answer seems to be both yes and no. On the positive side, the new programs clearly strengthened mayors in their dealings with the LPAs and LHAs.[95] They also gave cities a great deal of flexibility in adapting the CDBG block grants to local needs. In St. Paul, Minnesota, a strong mayor exerted considerable influence to promote several large redevelopment projects and industrial parks. In four New England cities, by contrast, the mayors exerted very little influence, and CDBG funds were disbursed to neighborhood projects throughout the cities.[96] In much of the South, as civil rights groups complained, compliance with CDBG requirements for citizen participation mostly ignored activists in poor communities.[97] But in Austin, Texas, poor neighborhoods were well represented.[98] The intended effects of greater influence by local, elected officials and greater citizen participation were only partly realized.

The Section 8 rent supplement program also had its successes. By guaranteeing landlords a fair rent, Section 8 encouraged many developers to build apartments in the low- to moderate-income rental range. Section 8 rent supplements also made it possible to spread subsidized housing into white, middle-class neighborhoods where job opportunities were relatively close by. Although these neighborhoods had historically been willing to accept subsidized housing for the elderly, they usually balked at providing such units for poor families, and previous attempts at scattered-site public housing had failed in some communities. The Section 8 program was more successful than previous public housing programs at spreading subsidized housing into the suburbs. Neighborhood reaction varied from place to place, however, and opposition to the presence of even small numbers of poor people erupted in some neighborhoods.[99]

Though Section 8 has simplified federal housing programs and has usually run fairly smoothly, other problems have emerged in some areas.[100] For example, since Section 8 subsidizes the difference between actual rent and 30 percent of a tenant's income, this means that in reality local housing markets determine how much of a subsidy is paid under Section 8 and they also determine the range of choices open to the poor. In high-cost housing markets such as New York and San Francisco, this makes Section 8 a very expensive program.[101] Conversely, as noted earlier, if local officials in a community with high-cost housing provide only limited assistance, low-income families may not be able to find decent housing. In traditional public housing projects, the rental subsidies are not driven up so readily by the private housing market. Recent proposals to cut back the Section 8 program have created fears among many families that they will soon be unable to afford decent housing.[102]

Housing programs for poorer people often provoke conflict between the political parties. Democrats have tended to push for a **direct-production strategy** under which programs like Section 8 are used to construct new rental units for the poor. Republicans, on the other hand, tend to favor a **filter-down strategy** that lets the free market construct new housing for the affluent. As affluent people move into the new housing, this sets off a chain reaction in which middle-income people buy the homes vacated by the affluent, and the lower-middle-income people buy the homes vacated by the middle-income people. As these lower-middle-income people move up, their units become available for rent to the poor. Republicans have also pushed fairly consistently for a **housing voucher plan** that gives eligible people a voucher to pay for a portion of their rent on any unit in the private market, rather than having publicly owned housing.[103]

Because of these perennial conflicts between Democrats and Republicans, national housing policy has fluctuated back and forth depending upon which party had the upper hand in Washington. With conservative Republican Ronald Reagan in the White House in the 1980s, Section 8 and CDBG funds suffered severe budget cuts. These were somewhat undone by the 1990 National Affordable Housing Act, which mollified congressional Democrats with an increase in Section 8 funding and mollified Republicans by creating a new program that encouraged the sale of public housing units to their tenants. When the Republicans took control of Congress in 1995, however, they pushed their approach by slicing HUD's budget by 25 percent, with the bulk of the cuts coming in Section 8. Federal spending on housing assistance reached a plateau between 2004 and 2008 but has since increased somewhat since then.[104]

POLITICAL VALUES AND THE SOCIAL CONSEQUENCES OF INFRASTRUCTURE POLICY

Infrastructure policies do not exist in a vacuum. They reflect the political values of society at large. And they have important social consequences.

Political Values and Infrastructure Policy

The importance of political values to infrastructure policy is very clearly seen in relation to housing policies. The conservative perspective[105] seeks to minimize public-sector involvement in direct subsidy of low-income housing as much as possible. Thus, conservatives opposed the original Public Housing Act in 1937, and in 1949 they used their influence to involve the private sector in the Urban Renewal amendments to the Housing Act. They favor income tax deductions to help middle- and upper-class people pay for their homes. The Reagan administration briefly considered ending income tax deductions for second homes and vacation homes, but the proposal rapidly fell victim from opposition by realtors, real estate developers, and owners of second homes and vacation homes (the latter group tend to be relatively prosperous and, therefore, somewhat influential).

Conservatives are reluctant to provide housing assistance to the poor for the same reasons that they are reluctant, in general, to provide welfare assistance to the poor. Poverty is seen as an individual defect rather than a product of the social structure. To the extent that conservatives support housing assistance to the poor, they tend to favor housing allowances or vouchers, as proposed by the Reagan and first Bush administrations. From a philosophical point of view, vouchers have a decided advantage over public housing programs because they maximize freedom of choice. Vouchers are most effective, however, where there is a reasonable supply of modestly priced housing. Where inexpensive housing in decent condition is scarce or nonexistent, vouchers are of little value.

In contrast to the conservative perspective, liberals prefer housing aid as in-kind assistance through direct-production strategies. Thus, they are more favorable to the rental-housing construction and rehabilitation components of Section 8 than they are to housing vouchers. Liberals fear that widespread use of housing vouchers will only drive up rents and effectively negate the impact of the aid. Liberals usually face an uphill battle for housing aid (as with other welfare aids) against majority political forces that want to provide only minimal welfare or housing assistance, if any. This puts liberals in the position of having to make compromises that undermine the very programs they are trying to create.[106]

In relation to transportation policy, liberal–conservative differences are not as marked as they are in housing and social welfare areas. Nonetheless, differences exist. Conservatives are more receptive to highway aid than they are to public transit aid. Road and highway transportation is more consistent with their philosophy of freedom of choice. Public transit can take you only where the transit lines run, but automobiles can take you virtually anyplace you want to go (if you have access to a car and are able to drive). In addition, many businesses rely heavily on trucking to deliver supplies and products, and conservatives tend to support business interests. Conservatives also favor privatization of public transit systems by divesting them of services that could be run profitably by private companies.

However, conservatives are sometimes willing to support active governmental involvement to assist the transportation system when failure to act could mean harm to the economy. Governmental aid to the airline industry after the September 11 attacks is probably the most conspicuous recent example. Long before September 11, public subsidies helped to build the nation's major airports, and many medium-sized communities would not have regular airline service without public subsidies.[107] Less conspicuous are governmental efforts to preserve or even expand rail freight service. Conservatives have supported a number of those efforts.

Liberals, since they also drive automobiles, do not reject highway aid, but they are much more sympathetic to public transit aid than are conservatives. Liberal ideology is also much more sympathetic to the notion that metropolitan development should be planned and coordinated. And liberals favor the use of public transit planning as a means to shape metropolitan growth. Pointing out that many people cannot get around without public transportation, liberals would much prefer that all services be centralized in a metropolitan or areawide transit commission in hopes of developing a system that can reach all parts of an area. Recent concerns regarding global warming have given liberals another reason to support transit systems: They are generally more energy efficient than are automobiles carrying one person each.

The Social Consequences of Infrastructure Policy

If infrastructure policy reflects ideological differences, it also has important consequences for the social services discussed in Chapter 13. First, as seen from our review of transportation and housing policies, these policies played important roles in creating residential segregation by income and by race. The great central cities, for example, might have kept expanding and never been ringed by independent suburban municipalities had it not been for a number of government policies and practices: federal highway aid and subsidies for home ownership, which helped build the suburbs; lax state municipal incorporation laws, which permitted suburban governments to form; and rigid annexation laws, which prevented central cities from expanding through annexation. Added to these were policies that enabled many suburbs to segregate: restrictive covenant clauses in deeds that prohibited the sale of such houses to minorities and that were not struck down until 1948;[108] FHA regulations that financed much of suburbia, but that prohibited mortgage loans to minorities until 1962; local exclusionary zoning ordinances, which drove up the price of homes to the point where few minorities could afford them; deliberate attempts by some housing authorities to keep minorities out of housing projects in white neighborhoods or white suburbs; and deliberate attempts to keep public housing out of specific suburbs.

A second way in which infrastructure policies have social consequences is that they may impede upward social mobility for the very poor. The housing displacement that results from urban renewal and highway construction usually forces the affected people into more

> ## ▶ WHERE DO I FIT IN?
>
> Anyone who is concerned about the problems created by large volumes of traffic can help matters in many ways:
>
> | | |
> |---|---|
> | Carpool or vanpool | Try to schedule trips during periods of lower traffic |
> | Use public transportation (if available) | volume when possible |
> | Travel on foot or by bicycle | Do some work from home if possible ■ |
> | Combine two or more trips into one when possible | |

expensive homes that take a larger share of their income, to inexpensive housing somewhere else, or into homelessness. Redevelopment projects that replace mom-and-pop stores with shiny office buildings reduce entrepreneurial opportunities in poor neighborhoods. Policies promoting suburban sprawl move the most dynamic economic areas many miles from poor residential neighborhoods. And policies that permitted the decline of public transit make it harder for poor people to get to locations where jobs are growing at the most rapid rate.

Of course, not all physical development policies hinder upward mobility. Public housing programs help poor people meet their housing costs. Public transportation systems give a degree of mobility to people who cannot afford their own cars, and some communities and states have clearly worked to improve transit services in recent years. However, the lion's share of transportation funding since 1910 has been devoted to road and highway transportation, and the largest housing subsidies have been given to middle- and upper-income families.

America's heavy reliance on automobile and truck transportation has given most people remarkable mobility but has also produced a variety of environmental problems and helped foster growing American dependence on imported oil. Many metropolitan areas are struggling with serious traffic congestion and the pollution generated by cars and trucks, and efforts to encourage motorists to carpool or use public transportation have not been very successful in many areas.

SUMMARY

1. According to critics, a basic transportation problem in America is the lack of balance. Heavy reliance on the highway system has left a substantial minority of the population without mobility, has made our transportation dependent on foreign supplies of fuel, and has created a maintenance problem that may be more costly than the original highway construction. However, our extensive road and highway system has given most Americans extraordinary mobility and helped businesses move supplies and merchandise efficiently.

2. The 1970s saw what appeared to be a renaissance in public transit. Public transit ridership began to increase for the first time in a generation, and substantial federal aid was earmarked for transit purposes for the first time. By the 1980s, however, public transit ridership was no longer rising, and federal transit expenditures were no longer growing. States were forced to assume greater responsibility for financing public transit. Many transit systems have experienced growing ridership due to the current recession.

3. Urban transit options are most often discussed in terms of the kind of *vehicle* that should be used. The major options are expanded bus service, light rail systems, people, heavy rail systems, and the rapid rail

systems. Multimodal use of buses as rapid transit has worked successfully in Australia, Brazil, and Europe.

4. Housing problems have led to the evolution of housing and community development programs that are intergovernmental in scope. Federal housing programs are implemented by local public housing authorities. Until 1974, urban renewal programs were administered by local public agencies, which had considerable autonomy from local mayors and city councils.

5. The Housing and Community Development Act of 1974 restructured housing and renewal programs. It consolidated ten categorical grants into a single community development block grant. It gave the city councils greater control over the LPAs and LHAs. It gave local governments more discretion over the use of housing and community development funds. It required citizen participation in planning the use of community development funds. And it put the emphasis on rent supplements rather than on construction of more public housing projects.

6. After several years of housing-policy stalemate during the Reagan presidency, Congress and President George H. W. Bush enacted the 1990 National Affordable Housing Act. This act increased funding for traditional housing programs such as Section 8, and it initiated a Bush proposal to begin selling off public housing units to the tenants.

STUDY QUESTIONS

1. How have public policies encouraged the United States' heavy reliance on road and highway transportation? What are the consequences of that reliance?

2. How have state and local governments tried to encourage greater use of public transportation since the early 1970s? What difficulties have those efforts encountered?

3. Why have governments become involved in the housing market since 1900? What difficulties have people encountered in trying to find affordable housing? What strategies have been tried by national, state, and local government officials in grappling with the country's various housing problems? How successful have those efforts been?

4. Who has benefited most from infrastructure policies in recent decades? Why have some infrastructure policies been more controversial than others?

KEY TERMS

Antidiversion legislation   State laws that prohibit gasoline taxes and highway-use funds from being used for purposes not related to highways and automobiles or trucks.

Balloon mortgage   A mortgage plan in which one makes interest payments over the life of the mortgage, but does not make any repayment of principal until the end of the mortgage, when the entire principal is due in a single, so-called balloon payment.

Building code   A municipal ordinance that establishes minimum requirements for space, electricity, plumbing, and health issues for residential buildings.

Direct-production strategy   The housing production strategy that focuses on providing housing assistance directly to low-income people.

Displacement   The phenomenon whereby low-income people are forced to move out of their homes by urban renewal agencies, the gentrification process, or freeway construction.

Exclusionary zoning   The practice by a municipality of putting expensive construction requirements in the local zoning plan and building code. This drives up the cost of new housing and thus excludes low-income people.

Federal Aid Highway Act of 1956   The act that established the federal gasoline tax and provided revenue earmarked for construction of the interstate highway system.

Filter-down strategy   A housing production strategy that focuses on constructing new housing for upper-middle-income people on the assumption that their old housing will "filter down" to poor- and moderate-income people.

Gated communities   Exclusive upper-income housing developments surrounded by walls. Entrances are limited to a small number of security gates which can be used to keep out unauthorized people.

Gentrification   The process whereby upper-middle-income people move into inner-city neighborhoods and rehabilitate the homes there (or move into homes rehabilitated by developers).

Housing and Community Development Act of 1974   The federal legislation that established the Section 8 housing program and the Community Development Block Grant program.

Housing voucher plan   A proposal of the Reagan administration to replace existing housing programs with a voucher plan in which poor people could receive government vouchers that would be redeemable for rent payments much in the same way that food stamps are redeemable for groceries.

Inclusionary zoning   The practice, as adopted in New Jersey, of requiring municipalities to include in their housing plans provisions for low-income people.

Infrastructure   The roads, buildings, sewers, water supply systems, and similar structures essential for an economy to operate.

Interstate highway system   The system of more than 40,000 miles of divided, limited-access highways that crisscross the United States.

Light rail transit (LRT)   A modern-day version of the streetcar. A large vehicle that's powered by overhead electric cables, runs on tracks in city streets, and is capable of carrying up to 200 passengers.

Rapid transit   The traditional big-city subway or elevated train systems that run large, electrically driven trains along fixed guideways that may be at ground level, elevated, or underground.

Redlining   The practice of mortgage lenders and insurance firms not providing mortgages or home insurance in risky areas of cities. So called because the lending associations have supposedly drawn a red line around the affected areas.

Section 8   A housing program initiated by the Housing and Community Development Act of 1974. It provides for leased public housing by authorizing a local housing authority to pay a portion of poor people's rent directly to the landlord.

Surface Transit Assistance Act of 1982   A federal law that earmarked, through 1988, 1 cent of federal gasoline tax revenues for public transit.

Urban Mass Transit Act of 1974   The act that authorized the first extensive federal funding of mass transportation, including operating expenses as well as capital expenses.

Urban renewal   This program has traditionally relied on local governments to acquire and clear parcels of land in run-down areas. The land is sold to developers to use for new buildings.

Zoning code   A municipal ordinance that divides the city into different zones, with each zone being limited to specific kinds of structures. Some zones permit only single-family residences, others permit retail commercial buildings, and others permit heavy industry.

THE INTERNET CONNECTION

The American Association of State Highway and Transportation Officials works to help improve the nation's transportation system. It has published a wide range of studies of many transportation issues. You can contact this association at **www.aashto.org**. For more information about Amtrak, contact **www.amtrak .com**. For information on highway safety issues, see the National Highway Traffic Safety Administration at **www.nhtsa.gov**.

NOTES

1. *President Obama, Vice President Biden to Announce $8 Billion for High-Speed Rail Projects across the Country* (Washington, DC: U.S. Department of Transportation press release DOT 18-10), January 28, 2010; Joseph Rosenthal, "U.S. High-Speed Rail's Ship Finally Comes in," *Washington Post*, April 25, 2010, p. F05; *Intercity Passenger Rail* (Washington, DC: American Association of State Highway and Transportation Officials, 2009).

2. *NARP Unveils Proposal for More Extensive Passenger and Freight Rail Network* (Washington, DC: National Association of Railroad Passengers, 2007), Web document.

3. "American Shouts a Collective 'Yes' for High-Speed Rail," (Washington, DC: Official Blog of the U.S. Secretary of Transportation, 2010), February 1, 2010; "Poll: Half of U.S. Backs High-Speed Rail," (Washington, DC: United Press International, April 6, 2010), Web document.

4. "15 States and Amtrak Receive $2 Billion in Grants Given up by Florida," *AASHTO Journal*, May 13, 2011 (Web document).

5. Andrea Fuller, "Homeless Families Increasing, U.S. Finds," *New York Times*, July 10, 2009 (electronic edition); Amy Merrick, "Housing Slump Strains Budgets of States, Cities," *Wall Street Journal*, September 5, 2007, p. A1; Zach Patton, "Stemming the Tide of Homelessness," *Governing* (February 2010): 32–33; Sephen Fehr, "Tracking the Recession: States Boost Foreclosure Programs," *Stateline*, March 9, 2009 (electronic edition).

6. *Statistical Abstract, 2006* (Washington, DC: U.S. Government Printing Office, 2006), pp. 582–584, 713, 715–721.

7. K.H. Schaeffer and Elliott Sclar write: "Even in their heydays around 1920 the U.S. railroads on a per-capita basis carried only a third of the passengers of the British and German railroads, or a fifth of the passengers of the Swiss system." *Access for All, Transportation and Urban Growth* (Baltimore: Penguin, 1975), pp. 41, 44.

8. David Nice, *Amtrak* (Boulder, CO: Lynne Rienner, 1998), ch. 1.

9. James J. Gosling, "Changing U.S. Transportation Policy and the States," *State and Local Government Review* 20, no. 2 (Spring 1988): 86; *Statistical Abstract, 2006* (Washington, DC: U.S. Government Printing Office, 2005), p. 278.

10. Advisory Commission on Intergovernmental Relations, *Toward More Balanced Transportation: New Intergovernmental Proposals*, Report A-49 (Washington, DC: U.S. Government Printing Office, 1974), p. 218.

11. *Statistical Abstract 2011–2012*: 274.

12. See Sam Bass Warner, Jr.'s analysis of Boston's growth in his *Streetcar Suburbs: The Process of Growth in Boston, 1870–1900* (Cambridge, MA: Harvard University Press, 1962).

13. *Statistical Abstract 2008* (Washington, DC: U.S. Government Printing Office, 2007), p. 564.

14. See David Gram, "Another Effect of Oil Prices: The Rising Paving Costs," *Moscow-Pullman Daily News*, June 15, 2005, p. 10A.

15. Andy Kim, "16 Cities to Create Electric Car Charging Stations," *Governing*, October 1, 2010 (electronic edition).

16. On the costs of central-city expressways to the city's residents, see Anthony Downs, *Urban Problems and Prospects* (Chicago: Markham, 1970), ch. 8.

17. *Top Five Transportation Headaches and Remedies Identified*. Washington, DC: American Association of State Highway and Transportation Officials, January 14, 2009; Ashley Halsey III. "Decaying Infrastructure Costs U.S. Billions Each Year, Report Says," *Washington Post*, July 27, 2011 (electronic edition); David Hartgen, Ravi Karanam, M. Gregory Fields, and Travis Kerscher, 19th *Annual Report on the Performance of State Highway Systems (1984–2008)*. Adrian Moore, Project Director. Washington, DC: Reason Foundation, 2010, pp. 2–3, 96–97, 99.

18. Gosling, "Changing U.S. Transportation Policy and the States," p. 90. Also see *The New York Times*, February 4, 1983, p. 27A.

19. For a recent analysis, see *Surface Freight Transportation: A Comparison of the Costs of Road, Rail, and Waterways Freight Shipments That Are Not Passed on to Consumers* (Washington, DC: Governmental Accountability Office, 2011), Report No. GAO-11-134.

20. Jeremy Herb, "150,000 U.S. Bridges Are Still Rated 'Deficient.'" *Star Tribune* (Minneapolis), July 21, 2010 (electronic edition). See also *Statistical Abstract 2011–2012*, p. 685. Structurally deficient bridges are those restricted to lightweight vehicles, in need of immediate work in order to remain open, or that have been closed. Functionally obsolete bridges are those that have deck geometry, load capacity, or alignment with the road that is not appropriate for current use of the bridge. For more information, see the Federal Highway Administration, Office of Bridge Technology, at www.fhwa.dot.gov/bridge/.

21. *Statistical Abstract, 2008*, pp. 125, 686; *Statistical Abstract 2011–2012*, p. 693; "U.S. Secretary of Transportation Mary E. Peters Announces New Data Showing Record Low Highway Fatalities; Americans Safer Than Ever on the Nation's Roads, Rails, and in the Skies," U.S. Department of Transportation press release, December 12, 2008.

22. Anthony Downs, "Safe-Driving Lesson," *Governing* 15, no. 12 (September 2002): 73; Susan Pikrallidas, "Making the Case for Graduated

Driver Licensing," *State Government News* (April 1999): 28–30; p. 895; Dee-Ann Durbin, "Deaths, Injuries on U.S. Highways Drop," *Moscow-Pullman Daily News,* August 11, 2004, p. 9A; Ken Thomas, "Nearly Everyone's Buckling Up," *Daily News,* August 1–2, 2005, p. 14A; Ken Thomas, "Seat Belt Use Climbs in 34 States in 2005," *Daily News,* December 17–18, 2005, p. 10A; Ken Thomas, "Study: Laws Restricting Teenage Drivers Can Reduce Fatalities for 16-Year-Olds," *Daily News,* July 3, 2006, p. 5A.

23. Richard Powelson, "Coalition Wants Feds to Press Issue of Seat-belt Use," *Moscow-Pullman Daily News,* January 2, 2003, p. 3A; Jonathan Salant, "More Deaths on Two-lane Highways," *Moscow-Pullman Daily News,* August 16, 2001, p. 10A; Melissa Savage, "Walking Away—Safe," in Bruce Stinebrickner, ed. *State and Local Government,* 11th ed. (Guilford, CT: McGraw-Hill/Dushkin, 2003), pp. 211–214; *Highway Safety: Federal and State Efforts to Address Rural Road Safety Challenges* (Washington, DC: General Accounting Office, 2004), Report No. GAO-04-663; *Statistical Abstract 2011–12,* p. 693.

24. "Most Wanted Transportation Safety Improvements: State Issues: Eliminate Hard Core Drinking Driving." National Transportation Safety Board, press release (Web document; December 15, 2010). The proposals range from having sobriety checkpoints and vehicle sanctions (such as ignition interlocks that test for alcohol before the vehicle will start) to administrative proceedings to suspend drivers' licenses and checking for previous offense looking back ten years.

25. Heather Kerrigan, "Problem Solver: A Paradigm Shift on First-Time Drunk Drivers." *Governing.* January 2011, pp. 40–41.

26. Savage, "Walking Away—Safe," pp. 211–214.

27. "Study: More Highway Speed, More Deaths," *USA Today,* November 25, 2003, p. 3A.

28. Leslie Miller, "There's No Easy Way to Tell When Someone Is Too Old to Drive," *Moscow-Pullman Daily News,* July 18, 2003, p. 10A; "Proceed with Caution," *USAA Magazine* 31, no. 4 (August/September 2000): 15–17; Larry Copeland, "Groups Seek National Standards on Older Drivers," *USA Today,* April 19, 2006, p. 3A.

29. See Matt Sundeen, *Cell Phones and Highway Safety: 2005 State Legislative Update* (Denver: National Conference of State Legislators,

2005); Matt Richtel, "Dismissing the Risks of a Deadly Habit," *New York Times,* July 19, 2009, pp. 1, 20.

30. See Alan Altshuler, *The City Planning Process: A Political Analysis* (Ithaca, NY: Cornell University Press, 1965).

31. *Citizens to Preserve Overton Park, Inc. v. Volpe,* 401 U.S. 402 (1971).

32. See Alan Lupo, Frank Colcord, and Edmund Fowler, *Rites of Way* (Boston: Little, Brown, 1971).

33. *Statistical Abstract, 2011,* pp. 690–691.

34. Genaro Armas, "Census: When Commuters Hit the Road to Work, Most Go It Alone," *Moscow-Pullman Daily News,* August 21, 2002, p. 5A; Anthony Downs, "Overrating the Rush Hour," *Governing* 15, no. 10 (July 2002): 66; *Statistical Abstract, 2003,* p. 699.

35. *Congressional Quarterly Almanac* (Washington, DC: CQ Press, 1991), p. 137.

36. *Statistical Abstract, 2003,* p. 280.

37. Paul N. Tramontozzi and Kenneth W. Chilton, *The Federal Free Ride: The Economics and Politics of U.S. Transit Policy* (St. Louis: Washington University Center for the Study of American Business, 1987), pp. 15–16.

38. *Amtrak National Timetable* (Washington, DC: National Railroad Passenger Corporation, Spring/Summer 2010); David Luberoff, "Reinventing Transit," *Governing* 11 (May 1998): 78; David Nice, *Amtrak,* chs. 2, 6–8; *Amtrak: An American Story* (Washington, DC: National Railroad Passenger Corporation, 2011); *High Speed Rail: Learning from Service Start-ups, Prospects for Increased Industry Investment, and Federal Oversight Plans* (Washington, DC: Government Accountability Office, 2010); *Surface Infrastructure* (Washington, DC: General Accounting Office, 1999); *Intercity Passenger Rail Transportation* (Washington, DC: American Association of State Highway and Transportation Officials, 2002).

39. Robert Beneson, "Mass Transit's Uncertain Future," *Editorial Research Reports* (June 21, 1985): 464; *Statistical Abstract* (Washington, DC: Skyhorse, 2010), p. 699–701.

40. Schaeffer and Sclar, *Access for All,* pp. 30, 39, 61–79, 97.

41. David Nice, "Public Ownership of Railroads in the United States," *Transportation Quarterly* 51 (1997): 23–30; *Transportation: Invest in America, Freight-Rail Bottom Line Report*

(Washington, DC: American Association of State Highway and Transportation Officials, 2002).

42. *Statistical Abstract* (2010), p. 699. Because of the Association's potential biases, the figures should be treated with some caution.

43. Anthony Down, "Fast-Track Commutes," *Governing* 16, no. 2 (November 2002): 76.

44. See Jonathan Kwitny, "The Great Transportation Conspiracy," *Harper's* (February 1981): 14–21. Also see Schaeffer and Sclar, *Access for All*, p. 45; and Arnold W. Reitze, Jr., and Glenn L. Reitze, "Lau: Deus Ex Machina," *Environment* 16 (June 1974): 3–5. On streetcar track mileage, see *Transit Fact Book: 1970–71* (Washington, DC: American Public Transit Association, 1971), p. 12.

45. Mary Foster, "Renewed Interest in Streetcars in New Orleans, Other Cities," *Moscow-Pullman Daily News*, July 15, 2004, p. 3A.

46. Eliza Carney, "A Desire Named Streetcar," *Governing* 7 (February 1994): 36–39.

47. Mary Foster, "Renewed Interest in Streetcars in New Orleans, Other Cities," *Moscow-Pullman Daily News*, July 15, 2004, p. 15A.

48. *Commuter Rail* (Washington, DC: U.S. Government Accountability Office, 2006), Report GAO-06-470.

49. See Advisory Commission on Intergovernmental Relations, *Toward More Balanced Transportation*, pp. 45–48.

50. Peter Gordon and Harry Richardson, "The Failure of Urban Mass Transit," *Public Interest*, no. 94 (Winter 1989): 77–86.

51. See Melvin M. Webber, "The BART Experience— What Have We Learned?" *Public Interest*, no. 45 (Fall 1976): 79–108; and "Trouble in Mass Transit," *Consumer Reports* 40, no. 3 (March 1975): 190–195.

52. Miami Metrorail planners projected 117,000 to 202,000 daily trips. But when the first phase opened in 1986, ridership averaged only 33,000 trips daily. Tramontozzi and Chilton, *The Federal Free Ride*, pp. 15–16.

53. See especially Gordon and Richardson, "The Failure of Urban Mass Transit"; Tramontozzi and Chilton, *The Federal Free Ride*; and Webber, "The BART Experience."

54. "Voters Back All Major Transportation-Related Ballot Issues Nationwide," *AASHTO News* (Washington, DC: American Association of State Highway and Transportation Officials, November 8, 2006), press release.

55. Anthony Downs, *Stuck in Traffic* (Washington, DC: Brookings/Lincoln, 1992); James Dunn, *Driving Forces* (Washington, DC: Brookings, 1998).

56. Melissa Conradi, "Voters Bring Traffic to a Halt," *Governing* 16, no. 3 (December 2002): Anthony Downs, "Some Like It HOT," *Governing* 15, no. 8 (May 2002): 68; "N.J. Rides the E-Z Road to Value Pricing," *Governing* 14, no. 3 (December 2000): 59; Patrick Fisher, Johnathan Gerber, and David Nice, "Toll Roads in America," in Jeremy Plante, ed. *Handbook of Transportation Policy and Administration* (New York: Taylor and Francis, 2007), pp. 107–120.

57. *Department of Transportation: Flexible Funding Within Federal Highway Programs* (Washington, DC: General Accounting Office, 1997); Martin Saiz and Susan Clarke, "Economic Development and Infrastructure Policy," in Virginia Gray, Russell Hanson, and Herbert Jacob, eds. *Politics in the American States*, 7th ed. (Washington, DC: CQ Press, 1999), pp. 482–483; Patrick Fisher and David Nice, "Variations in the Use of Grant Discretion: The Case of ISTEA," *Publius* 32, no. 1 (Winter 2002): 131–142.

58. The high estimate of three million was produced by homeless advocate Mitch Snyder's Communities for Creative Non-Violence. The low estimate of 250,000–350,000 was made in 1984 by the Department of Housing and Urban Development. Robert C. Ellickson, "The Homelessness Muddle," *Public Interest* no. 99 (Spring 1990): 52. The Census Bureau counted 459,209 homeless people on the night of March 20, 1990. Eileen Quigley, "The Homeless," *CQ Reporter* 2, no. 29 (August 7, 1992): 669. Several mayors and homeless advocacy groups criticized the Census Bureau over this count, claiming that it grossly undercounted the number of homeless. *The New York Times*, October 9, 1992, p. 13A. Bureau of the Census, *Statistical Abstract of the United States, 1989* (Washington, DC: U.S. Government Printing Office, 1989), p. 713; *Statistical Abstract, 2003*, p. 630; Sar Levitan, Garth Mangum, Stephen Mangum, and Andrew Sum, *Programs in Aid of the Poor*, 8th ed. (Baltimore: Johns Hopkins, 2003), pp. 112–114; *American Almanac 1996– 1997* (Austin, TX: Hoover's, 1996).

59. Irving Welfeld, "Our Nonexistent Housing Crisis," *Public Interest*, no. 101 (Fall 1990): 56; *Statistical Abstract, 2011–12*, pp. 613–615.

60. Welfeld, "Our Nonexistent Housing Crisis," p. 57.
61. Ellickson, "The Homelessness Muddle," p. 58; Levitan, et al., *Programs in Aid*, p. 112.
62. *Statistical Abstract, 2011–2012*, pp. 625–626.
63. Quigley, "The Homeless," p. 672.
64. Ibid., p. 670.
65. Ibid., p. 671; Elaine Sharp, "Policy Change in American Cities and Counties," in Ronald Weber and Paul Brace, eds. *American State and Local Politics* (New York: Chatham House, 1999), pp. 311–313.
66. Gordon Berlin and William McAllister, "Homelessness: Why Nothing Has Worked—And What Will," *The Brookings Review* 10, no. 4 (Fall 1992): 12–17.
67. Patton, "Stemming the Tide," pp. 32–33.
68. Levitan et al., *Programs in Aid*, pp. 102–104, 252–253; *Statistical Abstract, 2006*, p. 632.
69. Genaro Armas, "Report Finds Only Four Counties Where a Minimum Wage Earner Can Afford Cost of One-Bedroom Rental," *Moscow-Pullman Daily News*, December 21, 2004, p. 9A. The report assumed that a family could afford to spend no more than 30 percent of its income for housing.
70. Barbara Ehrenreich, *Nickel and Dimed* (New York: Metropolitan, 2001), pp. 197–201; Genaro Armas, "39 Million Americans Live in Working Poor Families, Study Finds," *Moscow-Pullman Daily News*, October 12, 2004, p. 9A.
71. *Statistical Abstract of the United States, 2011–2012*, p. 625; *American Almanac* (1996), p. 721.
72. Welfeld, "Our Nonexistent Housing Crisis," p. 58.
73. *Statistical Abstract, 2001*, pp. 597, 721; *Statistical Abstract, 2011–2012*, p. 608.
74. Ibid., p. 508.
75. *Statistical Abstract 2011–2012*, p. 742.
76. *Statistical Abstract 2011–2012*, pp. 610–611. John Steinbeck noted the appeal of mobile homes for working-class families in *Travels with Charlie in Search of America* (New York: Penguin, 1962).
77. John E. Farley analyzed 1988 census data on St. Louis and concluded that a modest decrease in racial segregation had occurred since 1980. See his "Black-White Housing Segregation in the City of St. Louis, A 1988 Update," *Urban Affairs Quarterly* 26, no. 3 (March 1991): 442–450. Karl Taeuber calculated a segregation index for 28 central cities and found a 9 percent decrease in racial separation between 1970 and 1980. See Karl Taeuber, *Racial Residential Segregation, 28 Cities, 1970–1980*, Working Paper 83–12 (Madison, WI: Center for Demography and Ecology, University of Wisconsin, March 1983). A similar calculation for metropolitan areas rather than central cities found an 8 percent decrease in racial separation between 1960 and 1970. See Thomas L. Van Valey, Wade Clark Roof, and Jerome E. Wilcox, "Trends in Residential Segregation, 1960–1970," *American Journal of Sociology* 82, no. 14 (January 1977): 836; Thomas Hargrove, "Segregation Declines Since MLK's Days," *Moscow-Pullman Daily News* (January 20, 2003).
78. *Statistical Abstract, 2011–2012*, p. 625.
79. *The New York Times*, February 21, 1986, p. 35B; February 24, 1986, p. 13A. For background on Mount Laurel, see Alan Mallach, *Inclusionary Housing Programs: Policies and Practices* (New Brunswick, NJ: Rutgers University Center for Urban Policy Research, 1984).
80. *Minnesota Journal*, April 18, 1995, p. 6.
81. Nathan Glazer, "The South-Bronx Story: An Extreme Case of Neighborhood Decline," *Policy Studies Journal* 16, no. 2 (Winter 1987): 269–276.
82. Gregory D. Squires and William Velez, "Insurance Redlining and the Transformation of an Urban Metropolis," *Urban Affairs Quarterly* 23, no. 1 (September 1987): 63–83.
83. See Chester Hartman, Dennis Keating, and Richard L. Gates, with Steve Turner, *Displacement: How to Fight It* (Berkeley, CA: National Housing Project, 1982).
84. For a summary of these early developments, see Marian Lief Palley and Howard A. Palley, *Urban America and Public Policies* (Lexington, MA: DC Heath, 1977), pp. 161–164.
85. Even during the banking and real estate crisis of the 1980s, the largest number of foreclosures in a year was 100,000, the largest number of banks closed was 221, and the largest number of savings and loans turned over to the Resolution Trust Corporation was 318. *Statistical Abstract of the United States, 1991*, pp. 502, 505.
86. *Statistical Abstract, 2011–2012*, pp. 311–315.
87. Ibid., p. 354.
88. Larry Sawyers and Howard M. Wachtel, "Who Benefits from Federal Housing Policies?" in

David M. Gordon, ed. *Problems in Political Economy: An Urban Perspective*, 2nd ed. (Lexington, MA: DC Heath, 1977), p. 484.

89. Theodore J. Lowi, *The End of Liberalism: Ideology, Policy and the Crisis of Public Authority* (New York: Norton, 1969), pp. 251–266.

90. Christopher Swope, "Little House in the Suburbs," *Governing* 13, no. 7 (April 2000): 18–22.

91. See Chester W. Hartman, "A Rejoinder: Omissions in Evaluating Relocation Effectiveness Cited," *Journal of Housing* 23, no. 2 (February 1966): 88–89. Also see Herbert Gans, "The Failure of Urban Renewal: A Critique and Some Proposals," *Commentary* (April 1965): 29–37.

92. This in particular is the lament of Jane Jacobs, *The Death and Life of Great American Cities* (New York: Vintage Books, 1961).

93. See Martin Anderson, *The Federal Bulldozer* (Cambridge, MA: M.I.T. Press, 1964).

94. See *Statistical Abstract, 2011–2012*, p. 312.

95. Raymond A. Rosenfeld, "Implementation of the Community Development Block Grant Program: Decentralization of Decision-making and Centralization of Responsibility," A paper presented at the 1977 meeting of the Midwest Political Science Association, Chicago, April 1977.

96. Donald F. Kettl, "Can Cities Be Trusted? The Community Development Experience," *Political Science Quarterly* 94, no. 3 (Fall 1979): 437–452.

97. Raymond Brown with Ann Coil and Carol Rose, *A Time for Accounting: The Housing and Community Development Act in the South* (Atlanta: Southern Regional Council, 1976).

98. Ibid., pp. 86–87.

99. Swope, "Little House in the Suburbs," pp. 18–22.

100. For criticisms of Section 8, see Irving Welfeld, "American Housing Policy: Perverse Programs by Prudent People," *Public Interest*, no. 48 (Summer 1977): 128–144.

101. Edgar O. Olsen, "Housing Programs and the Forgotten Taxpayers," *Public Interest*, no. 66 (Winter 1982): 97–109.

102. Ron Marose, "Rent Subsidy Can Provide a Better Life," *Moscow-Pullman Daily News*, June 2, 2004, pp. 1A, 3A.

103. Housing vouchers are discussed favorably from several perspectives in Joseph Friedman and Daniel H. Weinberg, eds. *The Great Housing Experiment*, Urban Affairs Annual Reviews, 24 (Beverly Hills, CA: SAGE Publications, 1983). See especially the chapter by Ira S. Lowry, "The Supply Experiment." Also see Bernard J. Frieden, "Housing Allowances: An Experiment that Worked," *Public Interest*, no. 59 (Spring 1980): 15–35.

104. *Statistical Abstract, 2011–2012*, p. 312.

105. An excellent overview of ideology and policy can be found in R. Allen Hays, "Ideological Context of Housing Policy," in *The Federal Government and Urban Housing*, 2nd ed. (Albany: State University of New York Press, 1995).

106. Ibid., p. 33.

107. Elizabeth Olson, "Small Cities Pay to Keep Air Travel," August 18, 2009 (electronic edition); Jeff Baily, "Subsidies Keep Airlines Flying to Small Towns," *New York Times*, October 6, 2006 (electronic edition).

108. *Shelley v. Kramer*, 334 U.S. 1 (1948).

Regulating
the Environment

CHAPTER PREVIEW

*In this chapter, we will explore the roles of state and local governments
in protecting the environment. We will examine:*

1 Pollution control and regulation of the environment.

2 Social conflicts associated with environmental protection.

3 The reciprocal relationship between state and local

governments and environmental protection on the one hand, and the political economy of states on the other.

4 A cost-benefit approach to assessing environmental policies.

Introduction

One of the most important environmental controversies in recent years involves global climate change and the related concern that releasing some types of gases (sometimes called greenhouse gases) into the atmosphere may gradually increase temperatures around the world. Until recently, the U.S. government has been reluctant to act on global warming, and major actions have been blocked by wrangling over how much global warming is actually occurring, how much of that warming (if any) is due to human activity, and what would be the best methods (if any) for dealing with the problem. In addition, there have been major conflicts regarding how the cost of reducing greenhouse gases should be distributed across the various nations of the world and within individual countries.[1]

America produces an enormous amount of greenhouse gases each year, as do many other countries, and many analysts contend that reducing those gases will produce significant benefits for the entire world.[2] Concern for global warming has grown as more evidence indicates that it is happening and that much of it is due to human actions.

One scientist who criticized the claims about global warming for years just recently concluded that global warming has indeed been occurring. The long-term consequences could include widespread flooding as ocean levels rise, drought, and thirst.[3] Although some critics have charged that coping with global warming could be unreasonably expensive, other analysts have concluded that the costs would be manageable.

In part due to a lack of action at the national level, state and local governments have launched a number of efforts to reduce emissions of greenhouse gases. One of the more important efforts involves ten states in the northeastern and middle Atlantic regions of the country. In 2008 their Regional Greenhouse Gas Initiative (RGGI) adopted a cap-and-trade system on major power plants in five states in the area. Plants that reduce their greenhouse gas emissions more than the policy required could sell their additional gas savings (in effect) to other plants that found making their own reductions too difficult and expensive. A properly crafted cap-and-trade system can reduce greenhouse gas emissions more economically than would requiring all plants to make the same reduction without regard to differences in the costs and difficulty of making reductions from one plant to another.

The states involved in the plan agreed to sell permits for the release of greenhouse gases, partly to encourage utilities to reduce greenhouse gases and partly to raise modest revenues. Companies could buy and sell the permits among themselves as they gained more precise information regarding the costs and difficulties of reducing greenhouse gases. In addition, they could save permits for future use if they didn't need them at the moment to meet future state standards. The participating states also agreed to put almost all of the revenue generated by permit sales into projects to enhance energy efficiency, environmental research, renewable energy projects, and financial help for utility customers whose bills might rise due to the new efforts.[4]

Many other states and even more local governments have also taken steps to reduce greenhouse gases. In some cases the efforts have been supported by local Chambers of Commerce, in part because the efforts may stimulate the development of new industries and new technologies. The U.S. Conference of Mayors has also tried to encourage local efforts to reduce greenhouse gases, and more than 1,000 mayors have endorsed the idea. A school district in Alaska has asked its students to develop and assess proposals to protect the environment or enhance the area's ability to cope with a natural disaster. Several of the students' ideas have been enacted into law. A number of state and local officials have found that some projects to curb greenhouse gases can save their jurisdictions money. Although many of the individual state and local efforts may seem proportionally small, the combined effects could be substantial. Their examples may also encourage others to act as well.[5]

Not all states and localities have been pressing forward on dealing with environmental protection. Some have no established goals for energy savings, and some are behind schedule in meeting their goals. Some officials are not very enthusiastic regarding environmental protection: The New Mexico Supreme Court recently ruled that Governor Susana Martinez's delaying of publication of environmental protection rules was unconstitutional. Still, most of the states are making some progress toward greater energy efficiency and renewable energy.[6]

State and local governments play major regulatory roles in our lives today. Among other things, legislation requires us to have our pets inoculated, send our children to certified schools, purchase automobile insurance if we want to drive, and, in many states, submit our cars for annual or periodic inspections. In addition to restricting the behavior of individuals, state and local regulators impose a host of restrictions on business corporations. Regulators stipulate many provisions of health and life insurance coverage, determine the conditions under which alcoholic beverages can be sold, and decide which corporations will be granted exclusive franchises to market electricity, cable television, and natural gas. States also regulate, license, and certify a wide range of professionals, from accountants to funeral directors to dentists, nurses, and physicians.

Why do governments intervene in our lives in these ways? Governments intervene when they are called on to correct for failures in the marketplace. In the mixed, public–private, capitalistic type of economy that exists in the United States, most major goods and services are sold by private companies competing with each other in a market economy. According to most traditional free-market theories, this competition ensures that goods and services will exist over a wide range of quality and prices. In theory, the public good is served through unrestrained competition in the marketplace. In the real world, however, the market-directed economy sometimes fails to serve the public good, and government is called upon to correct for these market failures.

What kinds of market failures could justify governmental intervention and regulation? Economists have identified three types of market failures. First are those involving **externalities**—that is, costs that are not borne directly by the buyers or sellers of a particular product. A large feedlot for cattle or hogs will greatly affect the smell of the air and may pollute water in the area at times.[7] People who live in the area will be affected by the air and water pollution, whether they purchase meat produced from those animals or not. If they want the problem corrected, they need to give government an environmental regulatory role.

A second type of market failure involves **social goods**. Clean air and clean water are social goods; to a lesser degree, public recreational areas and parks are social goods. Their benefits are indivisible and non-exclusive because everybody in the community can enjoy them without depriving anyone else of their use—even though water supplies may sometimes run short and park facilities may become overcrowded at times. Because private companies are in business to make profits, they have a very limited ability or inclination to provide free parks or other social goods for the general public. A community that wants a well-developed park system will necessarily have to purchase the park land publicly and create a public agency to develop and maintain the facilities (or pay a private firm to maintain them).

A third type of market failure involves **merit goods**. Merit goods are those that society deems everyone deserves. In America today, merit goods include public education, medical care (except for the people who don't have health care coverage) by doctors and dentists who must meet minimal professional standards, and the right to assume that foods and medicines sold in the marketplace are safe. To ensure that the public receives these merit goods, governments either provide them directly (as in the case of schools) or regulate their provision by private entrepreneurs (as in the cases of most medical care and food inspection).

Historically, government's regulatory role in the environmental field was much less extensive than it is today. State and local governments were the primary regulators, and the federal government played a relatively small role. State and local governments traditionally tried to protect the environment in a number of ways. Although licensing and regulating hunting and fishing, protecting wildlife habitat, and preserving park and forest lands for public use all served to protect the environment somewhat, many states and localities permitted the dumping of raw sewage into waterways, destruction of forests and wildlife habitat, and release of harmful substances into the air, water, and the ground.

Starting in the 1960s and 1970s, however, the sheer volume of regulation expanded gradually, and the federal government saw its regulatory responsibilities increase. As the federal government began playing a role in areas such as environmental protection that had previously been considered state responsibilities, and as the substance of policies changed, the whole topic of regulation itself came into question. Since the early 1980s, there have been a number of proposals to limit the federal government's efforts to protect the environment and, in some cases, to give the states a larger voice in environmental issues. Some of the calls for a smaller federal role are actually calls for less environmental protection at all levels of government. As we will see later in the chapter, the state role has expanded significantly.

This chapter will examine the issue of environmental protection and the related conflicts it has sometimes produced between governments and businesses. We will also examine some aspects of other regulatory activities that may affect the environment. In examining these issues and conflicts, we will pay particular attention to the intergovernmental politics involved, the question of cost–benefit analysis, and the implications for state and local political economies.

ENVIRONMENTAL REGULATION

In the Love Canal neighborhood of Niagara Falls, New York, the air was so foul in 1978 that the mail carrier began wearing a gas mask. Miscarriages were exceedingly high in 1978, and during that summer five children were born with congenital defects.[8] Love Canal had been the dumping site for 21,800 tons of 200 different waste chemical compounds (11 of which cause cancer) from 1947 to 1952. After the dumping ceased, the toxic wastes were covered with earth. Several years later, a real estate subdivision was built along the canal. In 1978, a season of heavy rains brought the buried toxic chemicals to the surface. Complaints from neighborhood residents led government officials to measure the air quality in local basements. The readings in many homes showed highly dangerous concentrations of 11 toxic chemicals, including two that were carcinogenic (that is, cancer causing).

So dangerous was the environment along Love Canal that New York State provided money to help relocate 37 families with children under the age of two. The local elementary school was closed for health reasons. Further research found other people endangered, and a complicated program of federal and state funding was set up to enable New York State to buy up the contaminated homes. Two hundred thirty-seven homes and the elementary school were eventually bought, bulldozed, and the debris removed to special lined landfills. Ten years after the incident, 1,000 families had moved out.

Some critics believed that the dangers of Love Canal had been overblown. And in 1990, the Love Canal Revitalization Agency began selling the Love Canal houses that still existed to new buyers who believed that the hazardous wastes in the canal were by then safely contained.[9]

Health hazards from toxic materials and environmental pollution are major concerns today. State and local governments have the primary responsibility for managing the environment, although traditionally states and localities were not highly active in environmental protection. It was not until 1970 that the federal government became heavily involved in environmental management, although the national government had long been involved in some environmental activities, such as the national park system. Federal intervention brought greater financial resources and an ability to set national environmental standards that were to be enforced at the state and local levels. The political conflicts involving ecological management have sometimes been very intense, with disagreements over political values, priorities, and costs.

Since 1970, the result of all these developments is a wide range of public policy areas that interconnect: air and water pollution, solid and hazardous waste disposal, litter, the exhaustion of natural resources, dwindling water supplies, and nuclear energy, to name a few. In order to present a sufficiently detailed discussion, this chapter is limited to three aspects of environmental management—air and water pollution control, hazardous waste management, and energy regulation. In this examination, several questions arise. What steps have been taken at all levels of government to protect the environment? How does the intergovernmental system work? What policies have been established? How are they implemented? Have the policies and their implementation been effective? And, of course, are things getting better or worse? What are the trends?

A National Environmental Policy: New Tools for Environmental Management

The evolution of pollution-control policy making has dramatically changed the traditional relationship between the states and the national government. Historically, the states had primary responsibility for pollution control, although many of the states were not usually very aggressive in fighting pollution. During the 1950s and 1960s, however, the federal government became increasingly involved, and the intergovernmental mechanism began to resemble cooperative federalism rather than the traditional dual federalism model. A partnership existed between the state and federal governments in which the federal government assisted the states in defining their own policies and priorities. This system did not work effectively, however, in part due to state officials' fears that strong efforts to protect the environment would drive away businesses and jobs and, consequently, harm their state's economy. By the 1970s, the mechanism had changed to more closely resemble centrally directed federalism, at least to some degree.

A key step in this direction was the **Environmental Protection Act of 1970.**[10] This act declared "a broad national policy for environmental protection."[11] It created the Environmental Protection Agency (EPA) to coordinate and oversee the federal government's wide-ranging activities in the field of environmental protection. It also established the Council on Environmental Quality (CEQ) within the Executive Office of the President to monitor progress in environmental quality and to make annual recommendations to the president for improving it.

The National Environmental Protection Act also created the **Environmental Impact Statement (EIS).** Each federal agency (as well as each state and local agency) is required to file with the CEQ a statement outlining the environmental impacts of any major construction project it plans to undertake. The EIS must outline adverse environmental effects of the project, alternatives to them, and the project's relation to maintaining and enhancing the long-term protection of the environment.[12]

Water Pollution Management

At the Federal Level: Setting National Policy Today's water pollution management is traced to the **Water Pollution Control Act of 1972** (also called the **Clean Water Act**). This act and its amendments of 1977, 1987, and 1996 set the overall framework for water pollution management that still exists. Central to this system of management is a distinction the act drew between point-source and nonpoint-source pollution.

Point-source pollution refers to pollution that can be traced to a specific point of introduction into the water—hazardous wastes dumped in a river by a chemical company, for example, or untreated human waste discharged into a river by a city's sewers.

The Clean Water Act had two major provisions to deal with point-source pollution. First, it established the National Pollution Discharge Elimination System (NPDES). The NPDES required any organization that discharged waste products (called effluents) into a waterway to obtain a permit. National standards for discharges were established, and any discharge that exceeded those standards was not permitted. Second, the act also obliged municipal sewer systems to install secondary sewage treatment facilities. The EPA was responsible for administering the act, but it delegated much of its authority to the states. If a state or local government failed to set up a permit system or if its water-quality standards did not meet EPA criteria, the EPA could take over. Most states did act, and only a small minority preferred to have the EPA administer the program for them. To assist the state and local governments in costly planning and sewer system construction, federal law provided billions of dollars in matching grants.

Nonpoint-source pollution in waterways is more difficult to manage because it comes from a variety of sources and cannot be traced to a single, specific point of entry. The most prominent example would be pesticides and fertilizers, which wash into lakes, streams, and underground aquifers when it rains and which come from many sources. Northern states that salt their roads to prevent ice in the winter find that the salt flows into the waterways and pollutes them during the spring thaw. Rain washes drips of oil and tiny fragments of tires from roads and highways into waterways. Acid rain occurs when rain washes certain air pollutants into streams and lakes miles away from where the pollutants were released. Thus, automobiles, roads parking lots, lawns, and fields are nonpoint sources of water pollution.

Section 208 of the 1972 act provided funds for setting up agencies to develop environmental management systems. These so-called Section 208 agencies were established throughout the country[13] and were responsible for developing regional plans to cope with all the varied nonpoint sources of pollution. Nationwide, clear progress has been made in reducing several types of air pollution, but the progress has been rather uneven. Pollution in some communities remains distressingly high.[14]

Whereas the 1972 Clean Water Act created the basic framework, subsequent legislation and amendments fine-tuned the system of water-quality control. The Safe Drinking Water Act of 1974 and its later amendments directed the EPA to set maximum allowable levels for certain chemical and microbial pollutants in the nation's water systems. The 1987 Water Quality Act sought to improve the ability of states to cope with nonpoint-source pollution and groundwater pollution.[15]

Today, this water-quality-control system is at a crossroads. Tens of billions of dollars in federal and state funds have been spent since 1972 in constructing public sewer systems and waste-treatment plants.[16] The steps taken to date have halted the deterioration of the nation's water quality, but the budgetary squeeze on all levels of government raises questions about public willingness to continue high levels of investment in water-quality control. Three studies estimate that state environmental spending falls at least one billion dollars below what the states need to enforce federal environmental policies.[17] Environmental officials at the state, local, and national levels are not always very active in enforcing regulations, in part due to fears of angering business groups and in part because not all officials want vigorous enforcement due to their ideological leanings.[18] Finally, most pollution-control efforts have focused on surface water (lakes and streams), much of which remains polluted to varying degrees.

Communities that rely on that surface water have sometimes had problems with contaminants in their drinking water, even after the water is treated. Roughly ten percent of all Americans consume or are exposed to drinking water with some sort of contaminant, and millions of people become sick each year from contaminated water, whether from surfaces or from underground sources. As a result, some of those communities are working to curb upstream pollution of those surface water supplies. New York City is paying some upstream communities to improve their sewage treatment systems, rather than the city having to pay far more to purify the water after it is contaminated. A number of other communities, including Boston and Philadelphia, are involved in similar efforts. Some of the efforts have been hampered by rural residents who fear that regulations may limit their abilities to make money from their land.[19]

Half of the nation's drinking water comes from groundwater, which in many regions is endangered by toxic wastes that seep into underground water sources. Some pollutants come from leaking underground fuel and chemical tanks; agricultural chemicals and mining provide additional contamination. Inadequately maintained or outmoded septic tank systems are also a source of pollutants—700 million gallons of raw sewage per day, according to one estimate. Heavy rains in many communities lead to large volumes of pollutants from storm sewers and sanitary sewers flowing into rivers and lakes.[20] Pollution of groundwater is particularly difficult to correct after it has taken place.[21] Additional water problems include heavy consumption of water, which contributes to falling groundwater and surface water levels in many parts of the country, and dams that interfere with fish migrations and gradually accumulate great volumes of sediment.[22]

Air Pollution Control

At the Federal Level: Setting National Policies The first federal air pollution law was enacted in 1955. Like the first water pollution efforts, it limited the federal government to providing support to state and local governments for research. The federal role was increased by the 1963 Clean Air Act, which established a $95 million grant-in-aid program to help states establish and enforce air pollution standards. In 1965, Congress authorized emission standards for motor vehicles. The 1967 Air Quality Act divided the nation into 247 air-quality-control regions so that levels of air pollution could be monitored and cities could issue air pollution alerts when their air quality declined to dangerous levels. But it was not until the passage of the **Clean Air Act of 1970** that the federal government became a major partner in the battle to manage air pollution. This act set air-quality standards and obliged the states to draft **state implementation plans (SIPs)** for meeting the standards. The states could set higher standards than those set by the EPA, but they could not set lower standards.

Most states were unable to meet a 1977 deadline that Congress had imposed for meeting the air-quality standards, and Congress reacted by passing the **Clean Air Act Amendments of 1977.** These amendments tightened the air-quality standards, extended the deadlines for meeting them, and authorized the EPA to withhold federal highway and sewage-treatment funds from states failing to meet the law's requirements.[23]

The 1977 amendments also provided that the act be renewed and upgraded every few years, but the Reagan administration (1981–1989) adamantly opposed efforts to strengthen the law.[24] In the meantime, serious acid rain problems were damaging forests and fish populations, a huge hole was growing in the ozone layer, and the amount of toxic pollutants being emitted into the air continued to grow. It was not until the **Clean Air Act Amendments of 1990** that Congress and the White House addressed these issues.[25] As the Highlight feature shows, this act took giant steps toward coping with these and other air pollution problems.

With the major air cleanup goals enacted into law by the 1990 Clean Air Act Amendments, the focus since then has primarily been on the implementation of the law's provisions rather than on the passage of new legislation. To date, the implementation record since 1990 has been mixed. On the positive side, the EPA and its counterpart agencies in most states have made some progress on the implementation process. Air quality has demonstrably improved in some communities, including Denver, Los Angeles, and New York City. Emissions and concentrations of some pollutants, including sulfur dioxide, lead, carbon monoxide, and particulates, have declined noticeably.[26]

The Clean Air Act came under attack from Republicans when they gained control of Congress in 1994. To mollify these critics, the EPA found it expedient to relax several implementation rules of the act. As a result, by 1996, only three of the fifty states were clearly on track to meet enforcement deadlines that had been established by the 1990 act. The states have used their environmental discretion in varying ways. In general, the states that have made the most effort to protect the environment have been relatively prosperous, with growing economies and well-educated populations. Poorer states have often been more lenient, apparently in hopes of attracting new businesses to promote economic growth. Bakersfield, Baltimore, Fresno, Houston, Los Angeles-Long Beach, Philadelphia,

HIGHLIGHT

Main Provisions of the Clean Air Act and Its Amendments

1. The EPA was required by the 1970 act to set primary and secondary air-quality standards. **Primary air-quality standards** aim at protecting public health, whereas **secondary air-quality standards** aim at protecting crops, vegetation, forests, animals, and other materials essential to the public welfare. The states were required to draft state implementation plans (SIPs) for EPA approval, proposing how they would meet the air-quality standards.

2. Emissions from automobiles were required to meet rigorous limits, beginning with the 1975 model year. The EPA was also required to set emission standards for stationary power plants.

3. The 1990 amendments would phase out and eventually halt the production of four major chemicals that lead to the destruction of the ozone layer (chlorofluorocarbons, carbon tetrachloride, methyl chloroform, and hydrochlorofluorocarbon).

4. The 1990 amendments sought further reductions in automobile emissions by requiring auto manufacturers to improve emission-control devices on cars and requiring gasoline companies to manufacture cleaner burning fuels.

5. The 1990 amendments attacked acid rain by reducing the emissions of two critical chemicals (sulfur dioxide and nitrogen oxide) from power plants and factories.

6. The 1990 amendments attacked urban smog by classifying cities into five nonattainment categories of ozone reduction and setting periodic timetables for meeting the reduction standards.

7. The 1990 amendments attacked toxic air pollutants. They listed 250 categories of hazardous pollutants and required companies to establish pollution-control equipment that would reduce emission of these pollutants by up to 90 percent by the year 2003.

8. The 1990 act empowered citizen groups to sue the EPA or polluters for enforcement of the act.

Sources: Congressional Quarterly Almanac: 1975 (Washington, DC: Congressional Quarterly Press, 1975), p. 246; *Congressional Quarterly Almanac, 1991*, pp. 229–249. ∎

Washington, DC, and a number of other metropolitan areas averaged 30 or more days of unhealthy air pollution levels from 1993 through 2002.[27] A 2004 study found that 224 counties, some of them heavily populated, did not comply with clean air standards.[28] However, a number of cities have made significant progress since then.[29]

In sum, the 1970 Clean Air Act created a complicated system of regulation that reflects the complexities of the federal system of government and the complexity of pollution problems. Legislation at the national level provides an overall framework for air pollution control, but state and local of governments conduct most of the air pollution control activities. States and localities have more than five times the number of personnel working in air pollution management than does the EPA, and they also take five times as many enforcement actions. Since 1993, delegation of enforcement responsibilities to the states has increased dramatically, and so has state enforcement activity. In addition, the states collect the vast majority of the pollution data for a number of important areas of environmental protection.[30] How the intergovernmental politics of this system work in practice is shown by Charles O. Jones's excellent study of cleaning up the air in Pittsburgh.

At the State and Local Level: Cleaning Up Pittsburgh   As America's preeminent steel-producing city, Pittsburgh was historically known for its dirty air. Pittsburgh began passing smoke abatement ordinances as early as the 1860s, but these were seldom enforced. Either the corporations simply ignored them or the courts ruled the ordinances invalid (as in the attempts to get emission standards for steel mills in 1895 and 1906). The first effective smoke abatement ordinance was not passed until 1941; because of the need to increase steel production during World War II, enforcement was delayed.

The first effective leadership in cleaning up Pittsburgh's air came after World War II from Richard King Mellon of Pittsburgh's influential Mellon family. He helped found the Allegheny Conference on Community Development (ACCD), which took the lead in redeveloping the city's central business district and in seeking industrial compliance with the smoke abatement ordinance. Mellon also used his personal influence to reduce pollution from coal-burning locomotives. In 1947, the Pennsylvania Railroad opposed legislation that would prohibit bituminous-coal-burning locomotives. Legislative leaders found it impossible to round up the necessary votes for passage, so they appealed to Mellon. He was one of the Pennsylvania's major stock-holders. He informed the railroad that if it kept fighting the new law, his companies might shift their business to other railroads. Other companies made similar threats to the railroad. Soon afterwards, the state legislature acted. Coal-burning locomotives gradually gave way to diesel equipment.[31]

The key political leader for renewal and clean air was Pittsburgh mayor David Lawrence. One of Lawrence's first acts as mayor was to set immediate deadlines for compliance with the 1941 smoke abatement ordinance. Lawrence worked hard during his long tenure as mayor (1941–1959) to establish a cooperative business and political alliance in the smoke-control struggle.

Because smoke crossed municipal boundaries, it was necessary to combat it on the county as well as the city level. Allegheny County appointed a Smoke Control Advisory Committee that was dominated by representatives of the major polluting industries and their labor unions. Thus, the pollution-control system was, for all practical purposes, a system of self-regulation by the industries.

By the end of the 1950s, this cooperation between government and the polluting industries had achieved mixed results. Considerable progress had been made in clearing the air of dense smoke, but little had been done to eliminate less visible emissions such as particulates and gases.[32]

In the late 1960s, public concern over the environment rose sharply, and environmental groups formed and grew around the nation. Given Pittsburgh's air pollution problems, environmentalists there cleverly named their organization GASP (Group Against Smog and Pollution). GASP had an extraordinary knack for getting favorable publicity and pulling off highly imaginative public relations stunts: awarding "Dirtie Gertie" prizes to polluting companies, selling cans of clean air, lobbying for improvements in regulations, and rounding up support for stronger air pollution regulations.

Environmentalists also succeeded in expanding the scope of the conflict beyond the closed doors of Allegheny County's industry-dominated advisory committee. In addition to attracting attention with their imaginative tactics, environmentalists looked to the federal government for stronger curbs on air pollution. These pressures led both the county and the state to draft stiffer regulations than had originally been anticipated.

The new regulations, adopted in the fall of 1969, replaced the industry-dominated advisory committee with a new Allegheny County Variance Board, whose members had few ties with the steel industry. For the first time, the regulatory body had the authority to enforce its rules and regulations. The burden of proof was put on the companies. If a company could not meet the air-quality standards, then it had to either get a permit of noncompliance from the variance board or shut down.

The new regulatory system was tested almost immediately by the U.S. Steel Corporation's Clairton coke-producing plant. Coke is a processed form of coal that burns hotter than coal, but produces less smoke. The final step in producing coke is to cool it by quenching it with water. As the water is poured over the coke, it releases several lethal chemicals—phenols, ammonia, cyanide, hydrogen sulfide, and chlorides. Under the regulations of Allegheny County, the state of Pennsylvania, and the federal Clean Air Act of 1970, U.S. Steel would have to remove 99 percent of these dangerous chemicals from the steam. The company asked for a variance on the grounds that it did not have the technology to remove 99 percent of the dangerous chemicals. The technology did exist for eliminating 90 percent of the pollutants, but U.S. Steel felt it could not justify expenditures to achieve an emission level that would still be illegal and would leave the company open to lawsuits.

Faced with this uncompromising attitude, the variance board denied the variance and recommended that the issue be transferred to courts that could deal directly with the legal ramifications of the case. The courts attempted to force the board and the corporation to work out a compromise. U.S. Steel was reluctant to accept the compromise devised at the local level because it might be rejected at the federal level. Under the 1970 Clean Air Act, the EPA had authority to veto any implementation plans that did not meet its own emission standards, and it refused to commit itself to any compromise.

In the fall of 1972, the court issued three consent decrees that would achieve a 90 percent reduction in sulfur emissions and would also set standards for other emissions. In exchange for U.S. Steel's agreement to these terms, local officials granted the company a ten-year immunity from being sued and being forced to install new equipment that might become available during the ten-year period.

Hazardous-Waste Management

A third major area of environmental concern lies in the disposal of millions of pounds of hazardous and toxic wastes that are produced each year. These range from low-level radioactive waste from medical testing and treatment facilities to the extremely toxic chemical wastes dumped into Love Canal over the years. The EPA has identified hundreds of dangerous toxic-waste sites around the nation. According to the EPA, 70 million people live within four miles of a toxic-waste site, and approximately two-thirds of all Americans have a higher risk of cancer because of toxic pollutants.[33] Cleaning them up and finding suitable locations for disposing of other hazardous wastes is a major environmental problem.

Federal and State Roles As in other aspects of environmental protection, hazardous-waste management requires the cooperation of federal, state, and local levels of government. At the federal level, hazardous-waste management has followed a three-pronged approach. First, to reduce the amount of new toxic substances reaching the environment, the **Toxic Substances Control Act of 1976** required the EPA to set up regulations for testing new chemical substances before they are marketed, authorized the EPA to ban any chemical it deemed unsafe, and prohibited the sale of extremely toxic PCBs (polychlorinated biphenyls) not contained in enclosed systems. The second prong focused on cleaning up existing unsafe hazardous-waste sites and relied on a so-called **Superfund** created in 1980 to finance this task. The third prong stemmed from the **Resource Conservation and Recovery Act of 1976 (RCRA)**, which set up a so-called cradle-to-grave process for controlling and disposing of hazardous wastes.

Superfund Cleanups   To clean up existing unsafe hazardous-waste sites, the Superfund was created by the Comprehensive Environmental Response Compensation and Liability Act in 1980 and reauthorized with a larger budget in 1986. The Superfund operates on a "polluters pay" principle under which seven-eighths of the Superfund's budget comes from a special tax on chemicals and oils that are believed to cause much hazardous waste. Additional cleanup costs are billed to specific companies and organizations that contributed to a waste site.[34]

Although the Superfund began rather slowly, it has made gradual progress in cleaning up a considerable number of hazardous waste sites around the country. Progress has been limited somewhat by modest funding compared to the size of the problem, national political tides (Republican presidents have tended to be less supportive of cleanup efforts than have Democrats), and continuing discoveries of additional hazardous waste sites. Under the "polluters pay" principle, potential violators have a powerful incentive to delay cleanup as long as possible through legal battles. In some instances, major polluters use these legal battles to pass off the cleanup costs to third parties. In addition, some of the companies responsible for hazardous-waste sites have gone out of business or gone bankrupt.[35]

The Superfund program has also encountered difficulties because some of the sites are more difficult to clean up than was originally thought, in part because officials do not always know what wastes or how much of various wastes are contained in a site until cleanup efforts are underway. In addition, some sites present technical problems because experts disagree about what would be the best method for making the sites safer. Cleanup efforts are also awkward at sites where toxic wastes were originally placed by governmental entities, such as the U.S. Department of Defense.[36]

The polluters pay principle has become a major issue in the struggle to reauthorize the Comprehensive Environmental Response Compensation and Liability Act that established the Superfund in 1980. The act's scheduled reauthorization in 1993 fell between the cracks when congressional Republicans wanted to end the polluters pay principle and the Clinton White House wanted to retain it. In the absence of reauthorization, Superfund appropriations have not grown and, in 1996, the EPA announced that lack of money was forcing it to postpone cleanups at 55 sites.[37] Financial problems are not limited to the newer environmental programs, either; see the Where Do I Fit In? feature on page 446.

LULUs and NIMBY   If the cleanup of existing waste sites has been slow and plagued by difficulties, it is even more difficult to find *new* and safe waste sites for the tons of potentially dangerous wastes that are still generated and discarded each year. These range from mercury flashlight batteries (that should *not* be thrown into your garbage can) to low-level radioactive wastes generated in hospitals to chemical by-products generated in petrochemical factories. Disposal sites for these wastes are called LULUs (locally unwanted land uses), and the common approach to LULUs is the NIMBY syndrome (not in my back yard). These conflicts have multiplied as landfills near many large cities have reached capacity and those cities have sought new landfills in other areas.[38] Other, larger scale controversies have erupted from how to deal with low-level radioactive waste, toxic waste, and energy production and transportation.

WHERE DO I FIT IN?

Although state park programs are not usually as controversial as pollution control efforts, that does not mean that all is well in state park systems. State park attendance has been quite high in recent years, with about 748 million individual visits in 2007. California's state parks led the nation with 80 million visits, and New York's parks had 62 million. However, funding for state parks has often not kept pace with the rising workload. In years when revenues are tight, park budgets are often trimmed. When revenues are more abundant, other programs often have stronger political support. As a result, many older park facilities, including some historic landmarks, are seriously in need of repair or renovation, and some parks have gone without new facilities that are needed to cope with heavy public demand.

States have responded to this problem in a variety of ways.

Some states have closed some parks and/or reduced the hours in which some parks are open. Those strategies risk the loss of charges paid by park users and may reduce tourism in the communities near those parks. A number of states are also trying to attract corporate sponsors to help fund parks in exchange for placing advertising for those sponsors in various places.

Some parks have made growing use of unpaid volunteers to perform tasks when there are not enough paid employees to cope with all the work. Volunteers have built hiking trails, conducted interpretive programs for visitors, counted wildlife, picked up trash, and constructed bridges. More dramatically, volunteers have participated in numerous search parties and rescues, some of them on difficult and dangerous terrain, over the years.

State park programs are vulnerable to financial problems because they are not usually protected by powerful interest groups and because other issues often attract more media coverage and public attention. Maintenance budgets are often subject to cuts when revenues are tight; if the situation persists for very long, a large backlog of maintenance needs will accumulate and will be quite expensive to correct. Park officials at all levels of government are likely to face continuing difficulties in meeting the financial needs of parks for the foreseeable future, particularly when the economy is not performing very well, as has been the case in recent years.

If you would like to help care for public lands by volunteering to serve in a park, forest, or other facility, contact one or more of the following:

Earthwatch: **www.earthwatch.org** or 800-776-0188
Sierra Club: **www.sierraclub.org** or 415-977-5500
Wilderness Volunteers: **www.wildernessvolunteers. org** or 9288-56-0038
Local park authorities (they may be part of a city government, county government, or a special district government or authority)
State Park Departments
People in charge of internship programs at your college or university

Sources: Elizabeth Daigneau, "Parks and Re-Cessation," *Governing* (May 2010): 17; William Yardley, "In State Parks, the Sharpest Ax Is the Budget's," *New York Times,* June 6, 2011 (electronic edition); Chris Blank, "State Parks Delay Maintenance," *Moscow, ID/Pullman, WA Daily News,* December 31, 2010, p. 5A; Laura Bruno, "Tourist Stops, Parks Falling on Hard Times," *USA Today,* December 14, 2008 (electronic edition); Melissa Maynard, "This State Park Brought to You By...," *Stateline,* August 17, 2010 (electronic edition); Vanita Gowda, "Too Many Visitors, Too Little Money," *Governing* 13 (March 2000): 40–41; Jeff Rennicke, "Keepers of the Light," *National Parks,* 81, no. 2 (Spring, 2007): 40–45; *Statistical Abstract, 2011–2012* (Washington, DC: U.S. Government Printing Office, 2011), p. 771. ∎

Local opposition to LULUs is sometimes highly emotional and occasionally unruly, but that is not necessarily typical. One study of more than 66,000 statements in public hearings over the siting of radioactive waste sites in four states found that the persons giving testimony typically were fairly knowledgeable about the risk issues involved, phrased their testimony in unemotional terms, and had broader concerns than simply keeping the facility out of their backyards. Nevertheless, 88 percent of the testimony opposed the siting that was being proposed.[39]

Leaders of movements against LULUs deny, of course, that their activities are against the public good. Some are opposed not only to siting such facilities in their own backyard, but to siting them in anybody's backyard. From their viewpoint, there is something one-sided about an approach to hazardous waste that focuses more on disposal sites than it does on decreasing the amount of such waste in the first place. They believe that more should be done to break down toxic material chemically before it is shipped to disposal sites[40] and to develop manufacturing processes that produce fewer toxic materials in the first place. Some hazardous materials can be recycled and many people feel this is an approach that deserves more attention.

Although statistics are not fully comparable over time, toxic chemical releases have declined significantly over the years. A considerable amount of production-related waste is being recycled now, but the amount being recycled does not seem to be increasing very much. In addition, some states have much greater toxic chemical problems than do others; much of the variation is related to the states' economies.[41]

Although some progress has been made, the states are still faced with major waste-disposal problems. The U.S. Supreme Court has prohibited interstate bans on toxic waste shipments. Nevertheless, some political creativity is needed to get beyond the NIMBY syndrome in dealing with this problem. One example may be several states' bans on the disposal of computer monitors, televisions, and other glass picture tubes in landfills and incinerators; those products contain a number of chemicals that can pollute the environment. Although program details vary, they generally emphasize incentives so that the monitors and televisions will be collected and refurbished or recycled.[42]

Despite these difficulties with hazardous-waste regulation, it should not be concluded that the states are sitting on their hands. In fact, considerable policy has been established in the states to deal with the toxic materials. Not surprisingly, the most far-reaching policy has been set in states where the problem is most severe.[43] Californians, for example, passed an initiative measure in 1986 that requires businesses to warn consumers and the public of chemicals the companies use that pose significant risk of cancer or birth defects. After the bill's passage, the state compiled a list of 29 such chemicals, and companies are barred from discharging any significant amount of them into potential drinking water sources.[44]

Regulating and Operating Public Utilities   Many states and localities have been involved in regulation and/or operation of public utilities for many years. Much of their regulatory emphasis has traditionally been focused on the rates that utilities charge rather than environmental issues in an explicit sense.[45] However, pricing policies can be used to encourage or discourage energy use, and regulation of utilities can go well beyond prices. State regulators may have a voice in whether and where new utilities can be built. Regulators may press utilities to encourage conservation in a variety of ways, from having them distribute water-saving shower heads for free or at a discount, to pressing utilities to include conservation messages in their advertising or with their utility bills.

When a state or locality owns and operates utilities of its own, it has somewhat more leeway in shaping operations to promote environmental protection, at least at first glance, because the state or locality has more control over operations. However, that control comes with a price: If people are unhappy with the results, government officials are at greater risk of being blamed. If officials regulate a private utility company, that company may attract a share of the blame if people are unhappy with the results.

In recent years, utility regulation and ownership came under direct attack. Opponents of regulation claimed that it produced too few benefits to justify its costs and that it produced all manner of economic inefficiencies. Opponents of public ownership and operation declared that private companies would do a better job at a lower cost. Many regulations were trimmed back, and some public utilities were either sold to private firms or at least turned over to private managers while remaining publicly owned.

Deregulation ran into criticisms of its own. Some critics charged that deregulation seemed to benefit large business customers of utilities but not homeowners or small businesses. In part, this resulted because the expectation of increased competition among utility companies often failed to materialize. With considerable encouragement from homeowners and small businesses, local government officials in a number of communities began to discuss moving back into the utility field in some form or other, and some local officials have become more involved. Deregulation also provoked a storm of criticism in California, after a wave of energy shortages and rapid increases in utility bills struck the state. Some of the problems may not have been due to regulation, but the events there, coupled with difficulties in other parts of the country, have raised doubts regarding the wisdom of deregulation.[46]

DOES THE POLLUTION CONTROL SYSTEM WORK?

Is the pollution control system actually cleaning up the nation's environment? The answer seems to be yes, but....There is no doubt that the nation's air and water are cleaner than they were three decades ago when the environmental protection goals were first articulated. But some of the problems have turned out to be much more intractable than first thought, and new issues have arisen. Moreover, progress has been unevenly distributed across the country and from one type of pollution to another.

Much of the improvement in water quality can be attributed to the construction of sewage-treatment plants and the NPDES's effluent-discharge control system. One serious water pollution problem that is more difficult to cure, however, has been the presence of lead in drinking water in older cities served by lead pipes that were installed decades ago. In 1992, the EPA found excess lead levels in about 20 percent of the cities it examined. This does not mean that the average resident has unsafe drinking water, but it does mean that steps still need to be taken to keep the lead from leaching into the tap water.[47] Another persistent water pollution problem is contamination of the groundwater. As discussed earlier, the Section 208 planning process for dealing with groundwater has been much less successful than the pollution discharge elimination system that has worked for surface water, in part because groundwater pollution can come from a wide variety of sources and in part because less is known about how to remove pollutants from groundwater.

Measurable improvements have also been made in air quality since the late 1960s.[48] In the mid-1980s, the CEQ reported a significant decline in the concentrations of five major air pollutants in cities (carbon monoxide, sulfur dioxide, lead, larger airborne particles, and ozone).[49] A decade later, the EPA reported that significant progress had been made in reducing concentrations of four out of the five major pollutants. The exception was ozone, which is the main ingredient of urban smog. Improvements continued in some localities through the 1990s, but other areas saw little change.[50] Of particular concern were the facts that a number of the communities with the worst ozone levels were having a difficult time meeting standards set more than 25 years ago, and that over half of America's population lived in areas with serious air pollution or that produced considerable pollution of adjacent communities. A recent analysis also found that 224 counties, including a number of heavily populated communities, do not meet new air-quality standards regarding fine particles, such as those produced by diesel engines.[51]

The most intractable problems seem to be those arising from the production of toxic materials that are necessary for a highly technological society to function. We know, for example, that farmers with prolonged exposure to pesticides have abnormally high rates of cancer, but few people would be willing to ban the use of pesticides and bring about the major devastation to food production that would follow. Some medical procedures use radioactive materials that eventually create serious disposal problems, but those procedures also save lives.

We have also had difficulties in dealing with environmental problems that grow from people's lifestyle choices. If large numbers of people want to drive, and they do, we can reduce lead emissions by switching to unleaded fuel, but other emissions are more difficult to reduce unless people are willing to drive less or drive more fuel-efficient or alternative-fuel vehicles. Meanwhile, the production of greenhouse gases actually increased until they reached a plateau around 2004.[52]

The convenience of some disposable products seems difficult for many people to relinquish. The average American generates about the same amount of solid waste per day as he or she did in 1990. Although recycling has increased since 1980, it has grown very little since 2008 and has not kept pace with the increased total production of solid wastes.[53]

How we deal with these complicated problems is a very important issue in state and local politics. Some environmentalists demand that we turn our backs on high technology and return to a simpler lifestyle or at least be more selective in our use of technologies. The terms *sustainable agriculture* and *sustainable development* are sometimes associated with this idea, although sustainability also has a much broader definition: the development of social and economic systems to minimize excessive resource production, particularly nonrenewable resources. In addition, sustainability includes considering whether a community or state (or nation) is preparing for the future, from giving young people an adequate education to providing employment for people in the future. The broader views of sustainability acknowledge that some technologies may actually help foster sustainability, as in the case of energy from renewable sources.[54]

Others insist that there is a technological fix to our problems and we can achieve a clean environment without reducing our standards of living or altering our modes of living. Still others think that we should acknowledge that trade offs exist between our lifestyle and environmental quality. Inevitably, they think, we need to incorporate life-quality measures (such as cancer rates and birth defect rates) in our understanding of living standards. From this viewpoint, each state needs not only a measure of its state economic product, but a measure of its quality of life as well. Complicating this view is the fact that different people have different views regarding quality of life standards.

In the meanwhile, annual state environmental spending in recent years has fallen approximately one billion dollars short of the cost of implementing the federal programs that have been delegated to the states. Some of the funding shortfalls are caused by federal and state restrictions on various funds, such as grants that require matching funds that a state or locality cannot afford to provide. Even without those restrictions, there is not enough funding to cover the costs of the mandated programs.[55] A similar, less visible problem affects state parks (see the Highlight feature on p. 442).

SOCIAL CONFLICT AND THE ENVIRONMENT: ENVIRONMENTAL JUSTICE

These concerns over quality of life have put environmental protection in the middle of the social conflicts we have been discussing in this book. This happens in at least three ways: (1) charges of environmental racism, (2) land use policy, and (3) the interplay of environmental protection and the political economy.

Charges of Environmental Racism

It turns out that many of the nation's LULUs are found in very poor or minority neighborhoods and communities. It might be that these groups are less effective than middle-class residents at using the NIMBY tactic to keep LULUs out of their neighborhoods. It might be that these neighborhoods are more amenable to LULUs because of lower property values and the lure of jobs.[56] Certainly some poorer communities have actively sought facilities, such as a smoky factory, a solid waste landfill, or a prison, that more prosperous communities have fought against having. Or it might be that the broader society simply has less regard for the safety of its poor and minorities. Another contributing factor may be the tendency for factories, which may produce pollution, and lower-cost housing to be in older parts of communities (some of the housing is inexpensive because it is old and may be somewhat deteriorated). Whatever the reason, the disproportionate siting of LULUs in poor and minority neighborhoods gave birth to the charge of environmental racism, a charge that is underscored by pollution levels that tend to be more severe in these areas.[57]

Environmental Racism at Prairie Island?   A fascinating example of the intertwining of LULUs, NIMBY, and race took place in Minnesota in the early 1990s. About a fifth of the Minneapolis–St. Paul metropolitan area's electricity is generated from a nuclear power plant operated by the Northern States Power Company (NSP) located immediately adjacent to the Prairie Island Indian Reservation, which includes a popular gambling casino. By the mid-1990s, the plant was running out of underground storage space for its highly radioactive nuclear wastes and sought permission from the state legislature to store them in steel casks above ground until a disposal site could be agreed upon.

In the ensuing debate, supporters of the request were called "environmental racists" for wanting to store the fuel rods next to Indian reservation land. The tribal president charged that the above-ground storage might endanger the reservation's residents and suggested instead that the rods be stored in one of the area's richest suburbs, populated almost exclusively by whites. The tribe eventually agreed to a compromise providing them with payments for use of the land as well as compensatory land nearby.

Wrangling over the appropriate course of action pitted the power company against environmentalists and affected local party politics. Democrats were torn between organized labor and local utility customers, on one hand, that sided with the utility and, on the other, environmentalists and liberal Democratic activists who supported a stricter environmental policy. Democrats did not want to appear insensitive to the tribe's concerns, because Democratic officials and candidates had sometimes criticized Republicans for ignoring the problems of the poor and minorities. Many Democrats now found themselves vulnerable to the same charge.

The chief senate sponsor of the bill was subjected to death threats, and by the time the final vote was taken in the senate, tempers were so enflamed that spectators were screened by metal detectors to ensure that nobody brought weapons into the capitol building. The legislature finally agreed to allow NSP to store 17 casks of the spent fuel above ground until the year 2004. If an alternative disposal site was not found by that time, the nuclear reactor would have to close down. In the meantime, NSP was obliged to provide financial support for windmills, biomass power, and other alternative forms of generating electricity.[58]

Transformational Politics   Also at issue in the Prairie Island dispute was what political scientist Betty H. Zisk calls **transformational politics**.[59] Had the debate over the storage casks been confined to the state's Public Utilities Commission where it started, it probably would have been handled through the traditional political process that tends to use pragmatic tactics and seek incremental goals. The two sides would have bargained quietly; but the continued existence of the nuclear power plant would not have been called into question. Environmentalists, however, followed a transformational politics approach that sought a major change in the lifestyles of their fellow citizens. It sought to ban the storage of casks next to the Indian reservation but also to shut down the nuclear plant, reduce energy consumption by Minnesotans, and force the power company to convert to "green" methods of generating electricity. Because the goals of transformational politics are about society's ultimate values, transformational activists may claim to hold the moral high ground and brand their opponents as immoral (or environmentally racist as in the Prairie Island case). Because the transformational activists often did not hold elective offices, they did not have to worry about whether they would be voted out of office in the next election or what would happen if the metropolitan area lost a quarter of its electricity supply. Hence, they could reject the pragmatic and incremental goals associated with traditional politics as betrayals of moral principle.

Environmentalism and Civic Activism   It is impossible to know how extensive transformational politics are in the overall politics of environmentalism. But there can be no doubt that protecting the environment has broad public support throughout the country, at least in the abstract, and millions of people back up their support with at least modest changes in their lifestyle. When asked about environmentalism in 1997, over two-thirds of Americans considered themselves to be environmentalists.[60] Almost 60 percent of people said they always or often make a special effort to sort their waste for recycling. About three-fourths of people said they now use less heat or air conditioning in order to conserve energy. About a fourth of the people belonged to at least one environmental group, and more than a fourth had signed an environmental petition over the previous five years.

At the same time, many Americans oppose environmental regulations that threaten their jobs, and many people make lifestyle choices that, collectively, cause significant environmental harm. Our fondness for the freedom that automobiles afford us (especially sport utility vehicles, most of which get poor gas mileage), the speed of air travel, the convenience products that are used once (or only a few times) and then thrown away, our lush green lawns in dry climates, and a host of other amenities are often stronger than our abstract concern for the environment.

Social Conflict and Land Use Regulation

Next to the siting of LULUs, the most volatile issue in environmental politics probably involves land use regulation. Especially in rapidly growing metropolitan areas, environmentalists argue that continued urban sprawl needs to be brought under control. As metropolitan areas sprawl outward and house increasingly large numbers of people in low-density settlements, they pave over countless acres of land—including farmland, create a community that is heavily dependent on automobiles, increase the nation's vulnerability to petroleum shortages, make public transit so expensive as to be inefficient, drive up the cost of public infrastructure needed to serve low-density populations, and lead to social arrangements such as social and economic segregation, that one school of thought (the New Urbanists)[61] criticizes as sterile and dysfunctional.

To rein in uncontrolled sprawl, a number of interesting experiments have been tried. Portland, Oregon, and Minneapolis–St. Paul, Minnesota, drew growth boundary lines around their built-up areas and tried to contain most future growth within those boundaries.[62] California created a Coastal Zone Plan to gain some control over the sprawl of developments along the Pacific Coast.[63] Vermont's landmark Act 250 legislation gave the state authority to override local development initiatives if they challenged the state's development regulations.[64] Seattle has recently changed its zoning guidelines to allow homeowners with large yards to build cottages in their back yards to permit greater concentration of the population and reduce the amount of driving people must do.[65]

The National Trust for Historic Preservation, which traditionally emphasized protecting historic buildings, has recently added an emphasis on preserving farmland and relatively undeveloped land that may have historical significance because of events that occurred there.[66] A group of private builders have taken a creative tack by building very small homes (some as small as 100 square feet, in contrast to the average home of 2,500 square feet today) that require fewer materials and permit denser development.[67]

These attempts to protect the environment from sprawl have come under bitter attack in recent years by property rights advocates who challenge land use regulations as a violation of the U.S. Constitution's Fifth Amendment protections against the taking of property without just compensation. Legally, this is called **the taking issue**. If a city requires a business to install a public bike path through the business property as a precondition for being allowed to expand the size of the business facility, has the company's property been "taken" without just compensation? Yes, ruled the U.S. Supreme Court in the case of Tigard City, Oregon.[68] This decision and a number of others in recent years[69] have sent shivers down the spines of land use regulators. These decisions have also encouraged a "property rights movement" that seems to oppose almost any land use regulation for the purpose of attaining environmental goals.[70]

Environment and the Political Economy

Finally, environmentalism engenders social conflict when it seems to be incompatible with economic growth and prosperity. Growth advocates complain that environmental regulations hinder growth either because of their excessive restrictions or because they impose expenses that could otherwise be invested in job-creating enterprises. Critics charge that in some cases, environmental protection efforts may damage local economies by driving some firms out of business. Environmentalists deny this and charge in return that unbridled development has "damage costs" that might well be greater than the costs of reducing environmental deterioration.

To take one example: Dramatic population growth in relatively dry areas and in areas subject to periodic droughts, coupled with a frequent tendency to use water generously, has led to expensive efforts to bring water from remote locations and competition between growing cities and agricultural users for the use of that water.[71] A serious drought in Alabama, Florida, and Georgia from 2007 through 2009 led to a serious water shortage there, and another drought may begin soon. Some local officials have tried to encourage water conservation without imposing major costs on property owners, but population growth in the region is likely to place additional pressure on the water supply.[72]

Another current controversy involving the environment and the political economy involves a proposed oil pipeline from the huge Oil Sands Project in northern Canada to the Gulf of Mexico. A number of state and local officials and numerous environmental groups have expressed opposition to the pipeline, in large measure due to fears of possible oil spills. Those fears have been stoked, in part, by recent major oil spills, especially the huge spill in the Gulf of Mexico, which released an estimated five million barrels of oil into the Gulf, and smaller spills on Montana and Michigan.[73] The proposed Canada–Gulf pipeline has even roused opposition in politically conservative states such as Nebraska.[74]

Sorting out these charges is not easy. There is no doubt about the assertion that the environmental gains of the past three decades have cost a significant amount of money. Some of these costs are quite visible. For example, the next new automobile you purchase would be somewhat cheaper if it were not required to have a catalytic converter, a PCV valve, and other pollution control equipment. The costs of other environmental protection regulations are not so easy to identify, however.

Two big issues have grown out of the question of costs. First, do the benefits of environmental legislation exceed the costs? Second, who pays for the costs?

The Cost–Benefit Approach to Environmental Protection Just as we can quantify some of the costs of environmental protection, we can also quantify some of the benefits. For example, if air quality were to revert to the level of 1970, it is estimated that the health bill for increased illnesses would total $40–$100 billion per year.[75] By contrast, the cost of implementing the Clean Air Act amendments of 1990 has been put at $20 billion per year.[76] If these figures are anywhere close to being accurate, the Clean Air Act seems to be worth the costs.

With some other environmental programs, however, the benefits of regulation are not so clear-cut. During the George H. W. Bush administration, the Office of Management and Budget (OMB) estimated cost–benefit figures for various regulatory rules involving health, safety, and environmental protection. The OMB released its results in the context of a grisly trade-off. How much money are we willing to spend to prevent one premature death? The ban on asbestos cost $110.7 million for each premature death averted. And the cost for banning the disposal of hazardous wastes in garbage landfills amounted to $4.19 billion for each premature death averted.[77]

One must take the accuracy of these figures with a large grain of salt. They were compiled under political pressure to make the costs of regulation look inordinately expensive, and even under the best of circumstances, it would be difficult to be very precise about the costs of dying from asbestos exposure since the deaths do not occur until many years after the exposure first took place. Nevertheless, the idea of "costs per premature death averted" does illustrate for us the inevitable trade-off that exists between the costs and benefits of environmental regulation.

Note, too, that some of the costs and benefits of environmental protection are not easy to measure. What is the value of scenic beauty or the cost of its loss? What is the loss of no longer being able to fish in a stream that has become polluted? What is the value of having more flexibility in my personal schedule because I drive alone rather than carpooling or using public transportation? Costs and benefits are partly a function of personal values, which vary from one person to another and vary over time as well. That variation helps to produce disputes regarding whether specific efforts are worth the cost.

Paying the Costs of Regulation The second big political economy issue is who pays for the costs? One way to approach this question is to determine whether the costs and benefits are disseminated throughout society or are concentrated on particular groups of people. On this basis, James Q. Wilson identifies four patterns of regulatory politics.[78] First, *majoritarian politics* take place when both the costs and benefits are widely distributed. The benefits of safe drinking water, for example, are shared by the entire population, as are the costs.

A second pattern, *client politics,* emerges when the benefits of the policy are concentrated in a small group of people, but the costs are spread widely. The regulation of utility rates for electricity, telephones, and natural gas serves as a good example. These rates are usually approved by public service commissions or public utility commissions. Utility companies regularly request rate increases that will concentrate profits in the company and its shareholders. Because the costs are so broadly spread among the general population, each person's share of the cost is so small that he or she will hesitate to invest time or energy opposing the rate increases. The regulatory commissions were created to protect consumer interests, but regulated industries spend large sums of money in pressing their cases and lobbying before the commissions. Public utilities commissioners are often appointed by the governor, which means that the companies themselves have ample opportunity to influence the governor's appointment choices.

A third type of regulatory politics, *entrepreneurial politics,* is best exemplified by the regulation of hazardous-waste disposal. Here the benefits are broadly diffused because the policies aim to protect everyone from the ravages of toxic and hazardous wastes, but the costs are largely born by a small group. Under Superfund legislation, for example, the costs of regulation are narrowly concentrated on those companies that have to contribute fees to the federal Superfund and various state Superfunds that have been established for hazardous-waste-site cleanups. With entrepreneurial politics, a policy cycle sometimes occurs in which issues eventually move out of the public limelight. When this happens, the entrepreneurial groups may weaken or dissolve, and the regulations become routinized and sometimes weakened.

A final type of regulation, *interest group politics,* occurs when both the costs and benefits are concentrated on small groups—and sometimes the costs go primarily to one set of groups while the benefits largely go to another. A group of people interested in preserving a specific historic site may clash with property owners in the area, who might make more money if the historic site was bulldozed and converted to other uses. A factory polluting the air may produce profits for its owners and jobs for its workers, but dirty air for people who live nearby. The people who bear the costs will dislike that state of affairs, and the people who reap the benefits do not want to lose them.

In sum, it is very difficult to determine precisely the costs and benefits of environmental policies. Not only is the obvious question of whether the costs outweigh the benefits involved, but so is the question of who pays which costs and who gets what benefits. As we have seen, there are four patterns in the states—the majoritarian-politics pattern, the client-politics pattern, the entrepreneurial-politics pattern, and the interest-group-politics pattern. Business groups are most likely to dominate the client-politics pattern. Consumers and environmentalists are most likely to dominate the entrepreneurial-politics pattern. But they find it difficult achieving permanent, effective regulation, because the entrepreneurial interest groups tend to weaken and dissolve, and the regulatory apparatus that was established tends to degenerate into the client-politics pattern. As a result, state officials are often hesitant to impose major costs on industries that cause environmental harm, a hesitancy that is reinforced by the fear that industries may circumvent those costs by leaving the state and taking jobs and investment with them. Instead, costs are often spread among all taxpayers, and environmental programs must compete for funds with all other state programs.[79]

In spite of those political complications, the states are major players in environmental policy making today. State funding for environmental programs has risen dramatically since the mid-1980s, and a great many state laws establish environmental standards. Moreover, the states provide most of the enforcement of environmental laws and collect much of the information used to assess the condition of the environment and the impact of environmental policies. The George W. Bush administration's reluctance to tackle some environmental problems, and partisan conflict in Congress, reinforced the leadership role that some states and localities are taking. That pattern has been further strengthened by the Obama administration's focus on other issues, such as the economy. The states are virtually certain to continue playing a major role in environmental programs, although some states are clearly more inclined to protect the environment than are others.[80]

SUMMARY

1. The Environmental Protection Act of 1970 declared "a broad national policy for environmental protection." It established the Environmental Protection Agency (EPA) and the Council on Environmental Quality (CEQ), and established the environmental impact statement.

2. Water pollution management requires joint federal, state, and local action. The key federal legislation is the Water Pollution Control Act of 1972 and its later amendments, which set goals of making all the nation's water fishable and swimmable by 1983, and of eliminating all polluting discharges into the nation's waterways by 1985. To deal with point-source pollution, the act established the National Pollution Discharge Elimination System (NPDES). To deal with nonpoint-source pollution, the act established so-called Section 208 agencies, which were environmental planning agencies in 176 different regions of the country. The Section 208 agencies work through a complicated interaction of federal, state, and local interests.

3. The key air pollution legislation at the federal level were the Clean Air Act amendments of 1970 and 1977. These directed the EPA to set primary and secondary air-quality standards. The states draft state implementation plans (SIPs) to indicate how they will meet the EPA standards. A very controversial aspect of air pollution in recent years involves greenhouse gases that are believed to contribute to global warming, a development that could cause enormous problems for many millions of people.

4. A noteworthy example of air pollution cleanup took place in Pittsburgh. As examined in Charles O. Jones's study, Pittsburgh started with a system of voluntary partnership between government and business, but ended with a system of mandatory compliance.

5. The federal role in hazardous-waste management stems primarily from three acts: the Toxic Substances Control Act of 1976 that requires the EPA to provide for the testing of new chemicals and the banning of unsafe ones; the Resource Conservation and Recovery Act that established a cradle-to-grave process for hazardous wastes; and the Comprehensive Environmental Response Compensation and Liability Act of 1980, which established the so-called Superfund to finance the cleanup of abandoned dump sites with toxic materials. Most of the responsibility for finding new disposal sites rests with the states.

6. The extent to which these environmental regulation measures work is hard to determine. The least progress has probably been made in managing hazardous wastes, and the most progress has probably been made in reducing some types of air pollution, but not greenhouse gases. In water pollution

control, substantial progress has occurred in reducing the discharge of pollutants into the lakes and streams. But much doubt remains about whether all cities can comply with requirements for sewage-treatment plants, and little has been done to date to improve the quality of groundwater.

7. Environmental and social conflicts converge in at least three ways: charges of environmental racism, land use regulation versus property rights revolution, and trade-offs between environmental regulation and the political economy.

8. Regulatory policies at the state level fall into four categories: majoritarian-politics regulation, entrepreneurial-politics regulation, client-politics regulation, and interest-group-politics regulation.

STUDY QUESTIONS

1. Why did the national government become more involved in environmental policy making beginning in the 1970s? What forms did that increased involvement take? How has the role of state governments shifted?

2. How effective have national, state, and local efforts to combat pollution been?

3. Why have pollution control and other environmental programs often been controversial? How have the local effects of environmental decisions provoked disagreement and criticism?

4. What types of regulatory politics are often found in environmental policy making? How have those political dynamics affected who pays for environmental programs?

KEY TERMS

Clean Air Act Amendments of 1977 Amendments that extended several deadlines for meeting the standards established in the 1970 Clean Air Act, stiffened the standards, and gave the EPA increased authority to enforce them.

Clean Air Act Amendments of 1990 The first major attempt to combat acid rain and the depletion of the ozone layer. The amendments also stiffened emissions-control requirements for new automobiles and obliged oil companies to produce cleaner burning fuels.

Clean Air Act of 1970 The act that established the fundamental authority for the federal regulation of air quality.

Clean Water Act See *Water Pollution Control Act of 1972*.

Environmental Impact Statement (EIS) An assessment of the environmental impacts of a proposed development project. Required before the project can be approved. Applies to federal, state, and local government agencies.

Environmental Protection Act of 1970 The keystone of federal authority to regulate the environment. It established the Environmental Protection Agency and the Council on Environmental Quality, and established a broad national policy for environmental protection.

Externalities Costs that are not borne directly by the buyers or sellers of a particular product. For example, the costs of cleaning up greenhouse gases produced by automobiles are not included in the price of cars.

Merit goods Goods that society judges all citizens should have as a matter of right.

Nonpoint-source pollution Pollution whose specific point of entry into the water cannot be traced. Acid rain, which starts from smokestacks of coal-burning facilities and then falls in the form of rain over a wide region, is an example.

Point-source pollution Pollution that is introduced into the water supply at a specific, identifiable point of entry, such as a storm sewer draining into a river.

Primary air-quality standards Established by the 1970 Clean Air Act, these focus on protecting public health.

Resource Conservation and Recovery Act of 1976 (RCRA) This act set up a cradle-to-grave process for controlling and disposing of hazardous wastes.

Secondary air-quality standards Set by the 1970 Clean Air Act, these focus on protecting crops, vegetation, forests, animals, and other materials essential to the public welfare.

Social goods Goods whose benefits are nondivisible and nonexclusive. Their enjoyment by one person does not prevent their enjoyment by others.

State implementation plan (SIP) A plan that states are required to draft to show how they will meet the primary and secondary air-quality standards established by the EPA.

Superfund A federal fund set up to finance the cleanup of hazardous-waste sites.

Sustainability Narrowly conceived sustainable community or state has a relationship with the environment that can continue well into the future. In a broader view, a sustainable community has public and private mechanisms and policies to enable it to provide suitable lives for its residents. That community will be able to offer people clean air and water,

jobs, public safety, educational opportunities, and other services over the long term.

The taking issue The issue of whether land use regulations "take" people's property under the meaning of the Fifth Amendment's clause, "nor shall private property be taken for public use, without just compensation."

Toxic Substances Control Act of 1976 The act that gave the EPA authority to test new chemicals, to ban any chemical it considered unsafe, and to prohibit sale of PCBs except in enclosed systems.

Transformational politics A form of politics that seeks to change the focus of politics from pragmatic give and take over specific issues to the uncompromising pursuit of ultimate social values.

Water Pollution Control Act of 1972 (Clean Water Act) The keystone of federal environmental policy for water quality. Established the pollution discharge-elimination system and required municipalities to install secondary sewage treatment facilities.

THE INTERNET CONNECTION

The Environmental Council of the States compiles and distributes information on state environmental activities and needs. You can contact the Council at **www.sso.org/ecos**. You can also find information compiled by the U.S. Environmental Protection Agency at **www.epa.gov**. The Sierra Club, the National Parks Conservation Association, the National Arbor Day Foundation, and other environmental groups also have considerable information available on their Web sites.

NOTES

1. Dina Cappiello, "Regulation of Greenhouse Gases Rejected," *Moscow, ID-Pullman, WA Daily News*, July 12–13, 2008, pp. 5C, 8C; Juliet Eilperin and William Booth, "As Climate-Change Talks Continue, Lack of Consensus Spurs Smaller-Scale Actions," *Washington Post*, December 10, 2010 (online edition); Peter Harkness, "Greener at the Grassroots," *Governing* (January 2010): 12–13; Stephanie Simon, "Global Warming, Local Initiatives," *Los Angeles Times*, December 10, 2006 (online edition).

2. See American Council for an Energy-Efficient Economy, "Automobiles Cause Air Pollution," in James Haley, ed. *Pollution* (San Diego: Greenhaven, 2003), pp. 50–52.

3. See Seth Borenstein, "The Heat Is on," *Moscow, ID-Pullman Daily News*, April 7–8, 2007: 7C; Seth Borenstein, "Panel Blunt about Rising Temperatures, Bleak Future," *Daily News*, February 2, 2007; John Heilprin, "Former Republican EPA Chiefs Accuse Bush of Neglecting Global Warming," *Daily News*, January 19, 2006, p. 11A; Seth Borenstein, "Skeptic Finds He Agrees Global Warming Is Real," *Daily News*, October 31, 2011, p. 2A.

4. See John Buntin, "Cap and Fade," *Governing* (December 2010): 28–30.

5. Peter Harkness, "Greener at the Grassroots," *Governing* (January 2010): 12–13; John Heilprin, "Energy Study: Greenhouse Gas Limits Are Affordable," *Daily News*, April 16–17, 2005, p. 12A; Stephanie Simon, "Global Warming, Local Initiatives," *Los Angeles Times* Web document, December 11, 2006 (**www.latimes.com/neews/nationworld/nation/la-na-climate10dec10,0,5837570.story**); Katherine Barrett and Richard Greene, "Energy Boost," *Governing* (September 2011): 58–60; Caroline Cournoyer, "Students' Green

Solutions Save Governments Money," *Governing* (October 2011) (online edition).

6. Susan Montoya Bryan, "Court: Governor Can't Delay Anti-Pollution Measures," *Santa Fe New Mexican*, January 26, 2011 (online edition); Traci Watson, "States Not Meeting Renewable Energy Goals," *USA Today*, October 9, 2009 (online edition); Jim Malewitz, "Energy Efficiency Push Survives State Budget Crunch," *Stateline*, October 21, 2011 (online edition).

7. See Charles Duhigg, "Health Ills Abound as Farm Runoff Fouls Wells," *New York Times*, September 18, 2009 (online edition).

8. Andrew Danzo, "The Big Sleazy: Love Canal Ten Years Later," *The Washington Monthly* 28, no. 8 (September 1988): 11–18; *The New York Times*, September 28, 1988, p. 28A; July 26, 1990, p. 1C.

9. *The New York Times*, July 26, 1990, p. 1C.

10. Dianah Bewar, "The National Environmental Policy Act," *Intergovernmental Perspective* 18, no. 3 (Summer 1992): 17–19; Charles Jones, "Regulating the Environment," in Herbert Jacob and Kenneth Vines, eds. *Politics in the American States,* 3rd ed. (Boston: Little, Brown, 1976), pp. 395–403; Bruce Williams, "Economic Regulation and Environmental Protection," in Virginia Gray, Russell Hanson, and Herbert Jacob, eds. *Politics in the American States,* 7th ed. (Washington, DC: CQ Press, 1999), pp. 450–455.

11. Bewar, "The National Environmental Policy Act," pp. 17–19.

12. See Thaddeus C. Trzyna, *Environmental Impact Requirements in the States: NEPA's Offspring* (Washington, DC: U.S. Environmental Protection Agency, Office of Research and Development, 1974), p. 19.

13. Ora Huth, "Managing the Bay Area's Environment: An Experiment in Collaborative Planning," *Public Affairs Report* 18, no. 2 (April 1977): 4 (Bulletin of the Institute of Governmental Studies; University of California, Berkeley).

14. John Heilprin, "EPA Cites Lack of Progress on Smog," *Moscow-Pullman Daily News*, October 2–3, 2004, p. 9A; *Statistical Abstract of the United States, 2003* (Washington, DC: U.S. Government Printing Office, 2003), p. 233.

15. Evan J. Ringquist, *Environmental Protection at the State Level: Politics and Progress in Controlling Pollution* (New York: M. E. Sharpe, 1993) pp. 57–58.

16. R. Steven Brown, "Trends in State Government Programs in Environmental Protection," in *The Book of the States* (Lexington, KY: Council of State Governments, 2002), pp. 452–460.

17. R. Steven Brown, "Trends in State Environmental Spending," in *The Book of the States* (Lexington, KY: Council of State Governments, 2004), pp. 540–543.

18. Matthew Eshbaugh-Soha and Kenneth Meier, "Economic and Social Regulation," in Virginia Gray and Russell Hanson, eds. *Politics in the American States*, 9th ed. (Washington, DC: CQ Press, 2008), pp. 391–393; Charles Duhigg, "Clean Water Laws Are Neglected at a Cost in Suffering," *New York Times*, September 13, 2009 (electronic edition).

19. Duhigg, "Clean Water Laws; Tom Arrandale, "Working on Watersheds," *Governing* 15, no. 3 (December 2001): 50–57; Tom Arrandale, "Stirring up the Headwaters," *Governing* 15, no. 12 (September 2002): 76.

20. Linda Baker, "Pipe Dreams," *Governing* (February 2011): 36–38.

21. Zachary Smith, *The Environmental Policy Paradox*, 2nd ed. (Englewood Cliffs, NJ: Prentice-Hall, 1995), p. 108; Tom Arrandale, "The Hazard of Ooze," *Governing* 14, no. 11 (August 2001): 73–77; *New York Times Almanac* (New York: New York Times, 2002), pp. 778–779.

22. William Dooth, "A Dam-Demolishing Movement Is Building," *Washington Post National Weekly Edition*, December 18, 2000, p. 30; Matthew Daley, "'Extravagant' Water Use Blamed for Endangering Rivers," *Moscow-Pullman Daily News*, April 12–13, 2003, p. 13A.

23. See *Congressional Quarterly Almanac, 1977*, p. 627.

24. See *Congressional Quarterly Almanac, 1989*, p. 665.

25. For background on the passage of this law, see Gary C. Bryner, *Blue Skies, Green Politics: The Clean Air Act of 1990* (Washington, DC: CQ Press, 1993).

26. *Statistical Abstract, 2011–2012,* (Washington, DC: U.S. Government Printing Office, 2011), p. 227; *World Almanac* (New York: Infobase Learning, 2011), p. 303; *New York Times Almanac* (2002), p. 775; *Statistical Abstract, 2003* (Washington, DC: U.S. Government Printing Office, 2003), p. 233.

27. Garr Lee, "The Clean Air Act Evaporates, One Program at a Time," *Washington Post National Weekly*, May 11–17, 1996, p. 11; Williams,

"Economic Regulation," pp. 451, 453; *Governing Source Book* (a supplement to *Governing,* 2004), p. 23.

28. John Heilprin, "EPA Says 224 Counties Fail to Meet Clean Air Standards," *Daily News,* December 18–19, 2004, p. 10A.

29. *World Almanac* (2011), p. 302.

30. B. Dan Wood, "Federalism and Policy Responsiveness: The Clean Air Case," *Journal of Politics* 53, no. 3 (August 1991): 852; R. Steven Brown, "Trends in State Government Progress in Environmental Protection," in *The Book of the States* (Lexington, KY: Council of State Governments, 2002), pp. 452–460; *Statistical Abstract, 2011–2012,* p. 300.

31. Jeanne Lowe, *Cities in a Race with Time: Progress and Poverty in America's Renewing Cities* (New York: Random House, 1968), p. 138.

32. Charles Jones, *Clean Air* (Pittsburgh, PA: University of Pittsburgh, 1976), pp. 97–98.

33. H. Joseph Hebert, "Two-thirds of Americans at Elevated Risk of Cancer Due to Toxic Chemicals," *Moscow-Pullman Daily News* (June 1–2, 2002), p. 7A; *New York Times Almanac* (2009), pp. 789–791; *World Almanac* (2011), p. 304.

34. Marc K. Landy and Mary Hague, "Private Interests and Superfund," *Public Interest,* no. 108 (Summer 1992): 98–101.

35. B. Guy Peters, *American Public Policy,* 7th ed. (Washington, DC: CQ Press, 2007), pp. 374–376; *New York Times Almanac* (2002), p. 780.

36. Peters, *American Public,* p. 376; Tom Arrandale, "Dredging Up Old Problems," *Governing* 13, no. 12 (September 2000): 100.

37. Gary Lee, "A Cleanup Operation Falls by the Wayside," *Washington Post National Weekly,* June 3–9, 1996, p. 33.

38. David Caruso, "As Landfills Close in Big Cities, Garbage Travels Farther for Disposal," *Daily News,* July 14, 2005, p. 10A.

39. Michael E. Kraft and Bruce B. Clary, "Citizen Participation and the NIMBY Syndrome: Public Response to Radioactive Waste Disposal," *Western Political Quarterly* 44, no. 2 (June 1992): 299–327.

40. Michael Heiman, "From 'Not in My Backyard!' to 'Not in Anybody's Backyard!'" *APA Journal* 56, no. 3 (Summer 1990): 359–362.

41. See *Statistical Abstract, 2010–2011,* pp. 231–233.

42. Herbert Inhaber, "Of LULUs, NIMBYs, and NIMTOOs," *Public Interest,* no. 107 (Spring 1992): 52–64 (NIMTOO is "Not in My Term

of Office"); "State Bans Computer Dumping," *Moscow-Pullman Daily News,* April 1–2, 2000; Tom Arrandale, "The Pit and the Pentium," *Governing* 17, no. 12 (September 2004): 44–45.

43. James P. Lester, James L. Franke, Ann O'M. Bowman, and Kenneth W. Kramer, "Hazardous Wastes, Politics, and Public Policy: A Comparative State Analysis," *Western Political Quarterly* 36, no. 2 (June 1983): 257–283; Williams, "Economic Regulation," p. 454.

44. Robert K. Landers, "Living with Hazardous Wastes," *Editorial Research Reports* (July 19, 1988): 385.

45. *The Book of the States* (Lexington, KY: Council of State Governments, 1998), p. 377.

46. Christopher Swope, "Power to the People?," *Governing* 14, no. 4 (January 2001): 36–39; Christopher Swope, "Taking Out Enron's Trash," *Governing* 15, no. 8 (May 2002): 56.

47. Reported in *The New York Times,* October 21, 1992, p. A-15.

48. *Statistical Abstract, 2011–2012,* p. 227.

49. U.S. Council on Environmental Quality, *Environmental Quality Annual Report: 1983* (Washington, DC: U.S. Government Printing Office, 1984), pp. 18–19.

50. Reported in *The New York Times,* October 20, 1992, p. 17A; *New York Times Almanac* (New York: *New York Times,* 2002), p. 775–778.

51. John Heilprin, "EPA Cites Lack of Progress on Smog," *Moscow-Pullman Daily News,* October 2–3, 2004, p. 9A; John Heilprin, "EPA Says 224 Counties Fail to Meet Clean Air Standards," *Moscow-Pullman Daily News,* December 18–19, 2004, p. 10A.

52. *Statistical Abstract, 2003,* p. 374; *Statistical Abstract, 2011–2012,* 228.

53. *Statistical Abstract, 2011–2012,* p. 229.

54. The literature on sustainability is growing rapidly. See *Governing in a Sustainable World* (Washington, DC: e.Republic, Inc., 2011); James Svara, Anna Read, and Evelina Moulder, *Breaking New Ground: Promoting Environmental and Energy Programs in Local Government* (Washington, DC: IBM Center for the Business of Government, 2011); *Future Visions of a Sustainable Palouse,* Gundars Rudzitis, ed. (Moscow, ID: Sustainable Idaho, University of Idaho, 2010).

55. R. Steven Brown, "Trends in State Environmental Spending," in *The Book of the States* (Lexington, KY: Council of State Governments, 2004), pp. 540–543.

56. Robert D. Bullard, ed., *Confronting Environmental Racism: Voices from the Grassroots* (Boston: South End Press, 1993).

57. Manuel Pastor, James Sadd, and Rachel Morello-Frosch, "Waiting to Inhale: The Demographics of Toxic Air Release Facilities in 21st-Century California," *Social Science Quarterly* 85 (2004), pp. 420–440; Michael Ash and T. Robert Fetter, "Who Lives on the Wrong Side of the Environmental Tracks? Evidence from the EPA's Risk-Screening Environmental Indicators Model," *Social Science Quarterly* 85 (2004), pp. 441–462; Diane Sicotte and Samantha Swanson, "Whose Risk in Philadelphia? Proximity to Unequally Hazardous Industrial Facilities," *Social Science Quarterly* 88 (2007), pp. 515–534; Sara Grineski, Bob Bolin, and Christopher Boone, "Criteria Air Pollution and Marginalized Populations: Environmental Inequity in Metropolitan Phoenix, Arizona," *Social Science Quarterly* 88 (2007), pp. 535–554.

58. *St. Paul Pioneer Press*, February 6, 1994, p. 1A; March 20, 1994, p. D-1; *Minneapolis Star Tribune*, March 31, 1994, p. 1–A; April 7, 1994, p. 16–A.

59. Betty H. Zisk, *The Politics of Transformation: Local Activism in the Peace and Environmental Movements* (Westport, CT: Praeger, 1992).

60. The sources for these data and other data cited in this paragraph are a summary of public opinion polling on the issue and are summarized in *The Public Perspective* (June–July 1996): 29, and in B. Guy Peters, *American Public Policy*, 5th ed. (New York: Chatham House, 1999), p. 367.

61. See especially, James Howard Kunstler, "Home from Nowhere," *The Atlantic Monthly*, September 1996, pp. 43–66.

62. John J. Harrigan, "Minneapolis–St. Paul: Structuring Metropolitan Government," in H.V. Savitch and Ronald K. Vogel, eds. *Regional Politics in a Post-City Age*, vol. 45, (Thousand Oaks, CA: Sage Publications, 1996) and Carl Abbot, *Portland* (Lincoln: University of Nebraska Press, 1983).

63. Melvin B. Mogulof, *Saving the Coast: California's Experiment in Inter-Government Land Use Regulation* (Lexington, MA: Lexington Books, 1975).

64. Elizabeth H. Haskell and Victoria S. Price, *State Environmental Management* (New York: Praeger, 1973), pp. 173–194.

65. Zach Patton, "Thinking Small," *Governing* (May 2011): 36–41.

66. Christopher Swope, "The Politics of Preservation," *Governing* 15, no. 6 (March 2002): 22–29.

67. J. Poet, "Living Small," *American Profile* (March 4–10, 2007): 8–11.

68. *Dolan v. City of Tigard*, 512 U.S. 374 (1994).

69. *First English Evangelical Lutheran Church of Glendale v. County of Los Angeles*, 107 S.Ct. 2378 (1987); *Nollan v. California Coastal Commission*, 107 S.Ct. 3141 (1987).

70. See, for example, Bruce Yandle, "The Property Rights Revolution," *Madison Review* 1, no. 1 (Fall 1995): 26–32.

71. Christopher Conte, "Dry Spell," *Governing* 16, no. 6 (March 2003): 20–25.

72. Josh Goodman, "Water Wars," *Governing* (February 2010): 28–31.

73. Joel Achenbach and David Fahrenthold, "Oil Spill Dumped 4.9 Million Barrels into Gulf of Mexico, Latest Measure Shows," *Washington Post*, August 3, 2010, p. A1; Kari Lydersen and David Fahrenthold, "Oil Spill in Michigan's Kalamazoo River Has Echoes of Gulf of Mexico Disaster," *Washington Post*, August 6, 2010, p. A3.

74. Monica Davey, "Nebraska Seeks a Say on the Route of a Pipeline," *New York Times*, October 30, 2011 (electronic edition).

75. Jackie Cummins and Larry Morandi, "Now You See It, Now You Don't," *State Legislatures* 19, no. 10 (October 1993): 30–34.

76. Ibid.

77. Reported in *The New York Times*, March 24, 1993, p. C-19.

78. James Q. Wilson, ed., *The Politics of Regulation* (New York: Basic Books, 1980), pp. 367–372.

79. Williams, "Economic Regulation," pp. 454–455.

80. R. Steven Brown, "The States Protect the Environment," Environmental Council of the States Web site, 2000. Originally published in *ECOStates* (Summer 1999); Tom Arrandale, "The Pollution Puzzle," *Governing* 15, no. 11 (August 2002): 22–26; Carl Pope, "States Abhor a Vacuum," *Sierra* 89, no. 4 (July–August 2004): 6–7; Bob Fick, "Environmentalists Blast Bush Plan to Open More Forests to Logging," *Moscow-Pullman Daily News*, July 13, 2004, p. 3A; *Statistical Abstract, 2011–2012*, pp. 280–281.

State and Community Economic Development Policies

CHAPTER PREVIEW

This chapter examines the politics of promoting economic development at the state and community levels. We will explore:

1 How changes in the national economy and foreign competition have affected states and communities.

2 The economic development strategies that states and communities follow to improve their economic situation.

3 The political strategies that states and communities follow to influence economic development.

4 Important issues that are raised for state and community politics by the quest for economic development.

Introduction

For a number of years, Kinko's corporate headquarters was one of the largest employers in Ventura, California. In the fall of 2001, the company announced that it was moving its headquarters to Dallas. The Ventura city government offered the company a package of financial incentives in hopes of preventing the departure, but the company turned it down. The relocation meant that most of the people working for Kinko's in Ventura would lose their jobs. The company's departure triggered a wave of anxiety in the city, a feeling that is familiar to many people in communities where major employers have closed or relocated.[1]

If a company is a major player in the local economy, the state and community involved get doubly hit if the company moves or shuts down. First, the loss of a major employer can bring economic and social havoc. As the town's income declines, mortgages fall into arrears, savings are depleted, local businesses close, alcohol abuse and family violence mount, and the town's physical appearance grows seedier as people become afraid to invest their scarce savings in maintenance and repair. For people seeking to move on to more prosperous areas of the country, houses become impossible to sell except at a fraction of their former worth. A second adverse impact involves the state and community governments. Because of the economic decline, states and communities face a greater demand for welfare and social services to help the people who are unemployed. But the state and community governments are less able to provide such services because their own revenue base declines with the economy.

Memphis, Tennessee, had a happier experience. The local airport authority once loaned several million dollars to a company in order to attract it to the city's airport. The city also spent a considerable amount on a new runway to enable the airport to handle larger planes. Today, Memphis is a world leader in air cargo activity. The employer: Federal Express.[2]

What, if anything, should governments do to cope with the dramatically changing economic conditions exemplified by Ventura and Memphis? To answer these questions and gain a broader insight into the dynamics of state and local political economies, we will examine four broad issues in this chapter. First, how do the changing American and world economies affect state and community politics? Second, what economic development strategies can states and communities pursue to protect themselves? Third, what political strategies can they follow? And fourth, what issues surface in the quest for economic development?

THE CHANGING CLIMATE FOR STATE AND COMMUNITY ECONOMIES

To appreciate the causes of Ventura's problems and Memphis's good fortune, we must first examine three broad trends taking place in the American economy. First is the transformation from an industrial to a postindustrial economy. Second is the intensification of foreign competition. Third is the changing distribution of income in American society.

From Industrial to Postindustrial Economy

Economists distinguish among three sectors of the economy. The *primary sector* refers to extractive activities such as oil production, mining, timber production, and farming. The *secondary (industrial) sector* refers to manufacturing activities. And the *tertiary sector* refers to a broad range of service activities, from retail trade to banking to hospital management. As Table 17.1 shows, while the total number of jobs in the overall economy grew by 20 percent between 1990 and 2009, employment in manufacturing actually declined, while employment in the service sector rose substantially. The growing importance of service businesses has led some social scientists to conclude that America has shifted from an industrial base to a *postindustrial economy*.[3] In part that shift reflects the closing of manufacturing plants in the United States and their replacement by manufacturing plants in other countries. In part, however, the shift also reflects increased use of automation in the manufacturing process.

Within the manufacturing sector of the economy, dramatic changes are also occurring that have devastating impacts on communities based on older manufacturing firms. The most dynamic growth in the manufacturing sector has involved high-technology products such as computers, lasers, and sophisticated medical equipment. Those industries have been more competitive against foreign industries than have manufacturers of traditional products such as steel, automobiles, and clothing, which have been badly damaged by foreign competition and have lost heavily in their share of the market. In 2007, Texas and California were the two largest sources of U.S. exports, and computers and electronic products were major components of

TABLE 17.1		
Changes in the American Economy		
Selected Aspects	Year	Percentage
International Interdependence		
1. Exports as a percentage of GDP	1970	4
	2009	11
2. Imports as a percentage of GDP	1970	4
	2009	14
Postindustrialization		
Growth of civilian labor force in manufacturing and services and total growth, 1990–2009		
Services		29
Manufacturing		−33
Total economy		20

Source: Derived from *Statistical Abstract of the United States, 2011–2012* (New York: Skyhorse, 2011), pp. 406, 408, 792.

both states' exports (although both relied on machinery manufacturing as well.)[4] The decline in U.S. manufacturing leveled off in the late 1980s, and manufacturers enjoyed a brief comeback. During the 1990s, however, the decline resumed.[5] Service employment now far exceeds manufacturing employment.

Intensification of Foreign Competition

Part of the reason for the relative decline of the manufacturing sector can be traced to the intensification of foreign competition in the last quarter-century.

Table 17.1 shows that exports nearly tripled their share of the gross domestic product (GDP) between 1970 and 2009 and that imports more than tripled their share. These percentages are likely to continue to grow in the future. A major step toward international interdependence came in 1992 when the United States, Mexico, and Canada signed the North American Free Trade Agreement (NAFTA). Through this pact, these three nations opened their borders more widely to increased trade and mobility of capital, thus increasing their exposure to economic interdependence. Not surprisingly, Canada and Mexico are two of America's top trading partners, both in terms of imports and exports.[6]

On the positive side, this interdependence enriches the quality of American life by making a greater variety of imported goods and services available and, in some cases, provides them at a lower cost. Moreover, aggressive expansion of American exports opens up larger world markets to American companies, thus creating more jobs and income. In theory, the increased need to compete in both the import and export markets leads to better products at more reasonable prices.

On the negative side, many corporations and communities are poorly prepared to compete in international markets. Foreign nations have become increasingly successful in their abilities to manufacture and market high-quality consumer products such as automobiles and clothing. For years, much American manufacturing was done in outmoded plants, using old-fashioned production methods as compared with the highly automated plants in eastern Asia, with their extensive use of robots and other innovations (although a number of U.S. firms have modernized their production operations in recent years). A number of industrializing countries such as Brazil, the Republic of Korea, Taiwan, and the People's Republic of China have constructed manufacturing plants that are able to hire workers at a tiny fraction of the wages paid in developed countries such as the United States and Japan. Apple Computer Corporation, for example, now does most of its manufacturing in relatively poor countries.

Further complicating the problem for American communities is the fact that much of the foreign competition comes from countries with authoritarian governments that curb free labor unions, hold down wages for multinational corporations, and do not enforce environmental and safety standards that are prevalent in the United States. Additionally, the host governments sometimes subsidize the export of their products to the United States in various ways (what American-based manufacturers call "dumping"). Finally, some countries restrict imports from other countries, including from the United States. Despite the huge transportation distances and costs involved, these and other factors combined to give many imported products a distinct price advantage over comparable American goods.

Additionally, the relative advantage of American goods versus foreign goods varies directly with international exchange rates. When the value of the dollar rose in comparison to the Japanese yen and other foreign currencies in the early 1980s, imports became cheaper, American goods became more expensive abroad, and this was precisely the period of greatest devastation for American manufacturers. When the dollar began declining relative to foreign currencies in the mid-1980s, that decline propelled the comeback of American manufacturers by making it easier for them to export their products and by raising the prices of products imported to the United States. To complicate matters, although a strong dollar tends to be bad for American manufacturers, it helps other parts of the American economy (major banks, for example).

The net result is that the economic fortunes of communities across America are influenced by the actions of foreign bankers, foreign investors, foreign manufacturers, and foreign politics to a very considerable degree. That was forcefully brought to our attention by the oil embargoes that took place in the 1970s and the dramatic rise in fuel prices beginning in 2004. The 1970s oil shocks increased unemployment and inflation and, for a time, made Americans serious about energy independence. Interest in energy independence plummeted in the early 1980s, but has recently increased, in part because of the second war in Iraq and the dramatic increase of world oil prices.

Bear in mind that some of those decisions made overseas can be beneficial for states and communities in the United States. In recent years, a number of foreign automobile companies have built manufacturing plants in the United States, primarily in the South. The results have been large numbers of new jobs and, in some cases, a changed image for the states and communities involved.[7]

The Changing Distribution of Income

As the American economy adapts to these technological and foreign challenges, that adaptation is provoking profound consequences in the social and political structures of individual states and communities. Some economists flatly assert that the American middle class is shrinking, that the percentage of people earning middle-level incomes (defined as 75–125 percent of the median income) has decreased since 1970, while the number of lower- and upper-income families has increased. Certainly the 20 percent of American families with the highest incomes increased their share of family income between 1970 and 2006, although their share declined slightly from 2006 to 2009. The top 5 percent of families increased their share of total family income by 34 percent from 1970 to 2006. In the same period, the four-fifths of families with lower incomes saw their share decline by 13 percent. The families in the bottom 20 percent saw their share of income fall by 17 percent.[8]

Other economists deny that the middle class is shrinking.[9] The most detailed examination of the question is found in Frank Levy's *Dreams and Dollars,* which denies that there has been a significant shrinking of the middle class, but presents considerable data to show that the living standards of most Americans have declined since 1973, with the lower- and middle-income classes suffering the worst declines.[10] Following the period covered by Levy's analysis, median family incomes, adjusted for inflation, rose between 1990 and 2000 but declined from 2000 to 2008, with the decline striking families in all major racial groups and combinations of labor force involvement.[11] A long period of corporate downsizing has helped produce what former secretary of labor Robert Reich called an "anxious class."[12] This refers to the millions of middle-level corporate workers threatened with losing their jobs in a corporate downsizing.

STRATEGIES FOR ECONOMIC DEVELOPMENT

In the quest to promote jobs and attract industries, as well as retaining existing firms, states and communities follow a number of strategies. Among the most important of these are public relations, promoting a positive business climate, creating incentives for business growth, and facilitating community development. In fact, the techniques used are limited only by the imaginations of state and local officials and, in some cases, business leaders seeking benefits.[13]

Public Relations

The most visible and inexpensive approach to economic development is public relations. Some states spend lavishly to promote themselves as a good place for business. States and localities with significant tourist advantages (such as Colorado and Florida) use public relations to attract tourist dollars and convention business. Because tourists and other travelers spend more than $12 billion dollars annually, on average, per state, and many times that much in some states,[14] a great deal is at stake in competing for vacation visitors. And states with extensive retirement communities, such as Arizona, use public relations to enhance their image as an attractive place to resettle. Retirees with their pension checks and tourists with their recreational dollars are just as effective a means of pumping money into a state and creating jobs as is a new manufacturing plant or a high-technology venture.

Some of the public relations efforts are targeted to people or businesses with a special interest and/or special needs of one sort or other. One community may present itself as a fine base for a skiing vacation; another may emphasize its excellent golf courses. One town will call attention to its lovely beaches while another town notes that it is a great spot for train watching. A state or locality may promote ecotourism by calling attention to opportunities for observing wildlife, hiking, camping, visiting the natural wonders of national or state parks, fishing, and/or hunting. A partly related strategy promotes agritourism, which gives visitors opportunities to visit, live on, and even work at farms and ranches in the state or locality. A community including or near a major historic site may try to attract history enthusiasts who are interested in the Civil War, Native American history, or the life of a famous entertainer, such as Elvis Presley.[15]

A major development in public relations efforts in recent years involves using the newer information and communications technologies in order to help an area attract tourists, conventioneers, and new employers. All of the states and many, many communities have Web sites to help people learn about the area's attractions, assess available services and resources, make reservations, and contact officials who may be of assistance. Some of these technologies involve joint efforts by one or more governments and private firms in the area. More traditional techniques can also be used, even if they involve some stretching of the truth. Communities with little or no international air traffic have, nonetheless, added the term "international" to the names of their airports in hopes of making the airport and the community seem more substantial and cosmopolitan than they actually are.[16] Photographic effects and creative camera angles may improve an area's perceived appearance.

Promoting a Favorable Business Climate

Of key interest in many states is the **business climate** that will (or might) make the state attractive to the business community. What makes a positive business climate is not absolutely clear, however, because different types of businesses have different needs. The features that make a climate attractive to one type of business might be irrelevant to a different type. Traditional manufacturing firms, for example, tend to be very sensitive to labor costs and seek a business climate that discourages labor unions and holds down costs for workers' compensation and unemployment compensation. Those firms may also need rail freight service.

These concerns are less important to fast-growing companies in fields such as computer software or medical technology, and these companies need a business climate that facilitates venture capital and a highly educated workforce. They may also be more interested in the availability of air freight service than rail service. Property taxes are a very important part of the business climate for companies with sprawling real estate holdings, but they are less crucial to firms that depend mostly on renting office space for their operations.

Taxing and Spending   Of the issues most involved in creating a favorable business climate, taxes and the level of government expenditures on public services are the most politically controversial. Many business organizations argue that the low-tax, low-spending states of the South and Southwest are more attractive to industry than are states with high taxes and high levels of public expenditures. According to this viewpoint, when firms decide to relocate or to expand, they often go to the South or West in order to avoid the punitive tax structures of the Northeast and Midwest. But how true is this assumption?

Roy Bahl surveyed numerous studies of the impact of taxes on decisions to relocate from one state to another and concluded that although taxes do affect relocation within a metropolis, "the consensus of a great deal of such research would seem to be that taxes are not a major factor in interregional location."[17] State taxes represent a relatively small percentage of a firm's income, and most firms can save relatively little on taxes by moving from one state to the next.

The limited impact of taxes on locational decisions was also discovered by Roger W. Schmenner's study of location decisions by 410 of the *Fortune* 500 companies. Schmenner found that "tax and financial incentives have little influence on almost all plant location decisions." At best they are "tie breakers" when competing sites are otherwise equally desirable.[18] Another study concluded that tax incentives for existing businesses were generally unsuccessful in creating jobs.[19]

Labor Costs   For some companies, the costs of labor are more important to the business climate than taxes. At issue is whether or not a state's labor force is extensively unionized and whether unemployment compensation and workers' compensation benefits are high. Bear in mind that only a small fraction of the nation's private sector workers belong to or are represented by unions (in 2009, 7.2 percent belonged and another 8 percent were represented by unions).[20] However, labor union representation varies a great deal from state to state and from one industry to another. A business leader may not care whether workers in other industries are unionized but care more about whether workers in the leader's industry are unionized.

Unemployment compensation is paid to laid-off workers for up to six months after they have been laid off. Workers' compensation awards payments to workers who suffer injuries on the job. Another growing labor cost is health care coverage (for those companies that offer it). Not surprisingly, workers' compensation, unemployment compensation, wages, and benefits tend to be higher in states with strong unions. Most southern and southwestern states have passed so-called **right-to-work laws** that prohibit the union shop. Most northeastern and midwestern states do permit the union or closed shop.

Offsetting this factor, however, is the fact that many firms also want a labor force that is relatively well educated and has a reputation for reliable, hard work. For this reason, a state that reduced taxes by cutting back on public schools and higher education, which help produce quality workforces, may in the long run worsen its business climate rather than improve it. Mississippi, for example, scores high on the business climate criteria of low taxes, low spending, and antiunion legislation. But it also scores among the nation's lowest in educational levels, and for that reason Mississippi is not a very desirable location for corporations that require a well-educated workforce. However, it scored a major economic development success when it attracted a major new Toyota plant in 2007.[21]

Business–labor relations involve more than just salaries and unionization. If a state has a history of bitter labor–management disputes, potential new businesses may be reluctant to locate there. Governor Bob Wise attacked this problem in West Virginia by actively promoting more cooperation between businesses and workers and, not coincidentally, between Republicans and Democrats. His hope was that businesses in other states may be attracted by an environment that emphasizes having everyone work together.[22]

Bear in mind that state and local officials have only limited influence over private labor–management relations. If business leaders or workers provoke one another, tensions are sure to follow. A case in point: After a major U.S. airline's workers agreed to pay cuts to help the company survive, they discovered that the company's leaders had arranged to give themselves additional compensation, but declined to disclose that fact.

Uncontrollable Factors   Finally, many locational criteria are not very directly under a state's or community's control. Other things being equal, a mild climate would be more attractive than extended bouts of extreme heat or cold. A region with a variety of first-class cultural, sports, and entertainment amenities would be more attractive to many people than a state or city without such amenities. And perhaps most important, a region close to a firm's markets or sources of supplies would be more attractive than a region far from a firm's markets or suppliers.

Does Business Climate Make Any Difference?   In sum, a state's business climate depends on many factors, and each state has its own peculiar combination of strengths and weaknesses. For example, South Dakota has little in the way of metropolitan cultural or entertainment amenities. Yet it has enjoyed a fair amount of success attracting the credit-card billing operations of major banks by relaxing limits on interest rates and by having no personal or corporate income tax.

Seldom discussed, however, is the question of how much difference the business climate actually makes in promoting a state's economy. If business climate were the single most important factor in economic development, then states like South Dakota and Mississippi would be among the wealthiest in the country, and states like New York and California would be among the poorest. In fact, the high-spending, high-taxing states of the Northeast enjoyed higher incomes per person over the years than did most of the allegedly good business climate states.[23] A number of studies have found that business climates and business incentives are not major influences on economic performance, although they may matter somewhat if two or more locations are equally attractive in other respects.[24] Moreover, a recent overview of economic development efforts concluded that their costs often exceed their benefits, in part because companies may fail to keep their part of economic development agreements.[25]

If theory says that corporations will move to states with the lowest taxes, then why is there not a stronger relationship between tax levels and economic development? In part it is because corporations are limited in their ability to relocate their facilities. Corporations continuously monitor their branch operations (deciding to open some new plants, expand some existing ones, and shut down others), but they do not commonly relocate entire facilities from one state or region to another. One of the most widely respected studies of the impact of corporate in- and out-migrations on jobs was David Birch's study of over two million firms in the early and middle 1970s. He found that such migrations had a negligible impact on the number of jobs a state gains or loses.[26]

Creating Incentives for Business Growth

Whatever the facts may be about the importance of company migrations from state to state, governors, mayors, and legislators find themselves pressured by political forces to provide an extensive array of incentives for business growth. The focus today in many places is less on recruiting businesses to move in from elsewhere than it is to help local businesses prosper,[27] although poorer states and communities may try for more dramatic results by recruiting outside firms. Many states and localities in recent years have set up venture capital funds, sometimes in partnership with private companies or organizations, to help new businesses get started and to help very small firms expand.[28]

Other states have offered tax credits to help corporations spin off new companies and help them get started. Tax credits and deductions are often granted for a set period of time, although that time period may be revised in later months or years. Moreover, if a business fails to deliver on its promises (jobs created, advertising to help boost the area's public image, and so forth), the government involved may seek to recapture some of the tax dollars covered by the credit or deduction.[29]

Another important economic development strategy is creating infrastructure that will make a state or community more appealing to various businesses. A number of recent efforts have focused on improving high-speed and/or wireless access to the Internet. These efforts have provoked mixed results, in part because private companies providing Internet access have opposed public involvement that might cost them customers or money. Their lobbying has helped to pass laws restricting local government involvement in providing Internet service, although governmental provision that is primarily for public agencies or in poorer areas where services may be unprofitable appear to be more acceptable. Some projects have been plagued by higher-than-expected costs and/or declining private sector interest.[30]

The most imaginative states and communities have adopted an entrepreneurial attitude that helps "develop and create markets for private producers to exploit."[31] These jurisdictions try to use existing resources to assist in technology transfers, to help small businesses, and to finance research and development for new products.[32] A good example of that entrepreneurial spirit is found in the Mississippi Delta, an area with chronic poverty and low job skills. Leaders of the Emerging Markets Partnership there are pursuing a joint, public–private partnership that will improve infrastructure and make loans to help boost the prosperity of the area. Much of the money to launch the project came from the W. K. Kellogg Foundation.[33]

Mayor R. T. Rybak of Minneapolis has also taken the entrepreneurial path. He has pulled together nonprofit groups, small businesses, and some large companies to revitalize areas in economic difficulty. He has employed a complex mix of tax breaks, private funding, transportation improvements, and reorganization of the city's planning and economic development resources into a single department. He has also targeted poorer areas of the city for economic development. Some observers have complained that Mayor Rybak has been too hesitant to commit major financial support to economic development efforts, but he hopes that creative thinking can be an alternative to large masses of city revenue.[34]

Urban Enterprise Zones and Empowerment Zones

As part of their incentives for business, most states and many localities have established **urban enterprise zones** or their equivalent to entice firms to set up operations and employ local residents in blighted or economically depressed areas.[35] Los Angeles, for example, established an enterprise zone covering Watts and the South Central areas of the city that have been torn by riots, high crime, extreme poverty, and an outward migration of jobs. Employers who create jobs in the zone can receive wage credits on their state income taxes, lower property taxes, credit assistance, and reduced prices for public utilities such as electricity and gas. Other states and localities, in addition to tax incentives, offer relaxed enforcement of environmental, health, and safety regulations for firms that expand in their urban enterprise zones.[36]

Despite more than 3,000 urban enterprise zones across the nation, the results have been disappointing. In Watts, as in most of the other zones, it is hard to find a concrete example of a declining neighborhood being turned around because of an enterprise zone.[37] Advocates of the enterprise zone concept argue that this is because the federal government has failed to provide adequate support for the program. According to this argument, the costs of federal taxes and federal regulations far outweigh those imposed by the states, and without relief from federal taxes and regulations, enterprise zones cannot reach their full potential. In addition, a general decline in regulatory efforts of many types and multiple, unclear goals for many enterprise zone programs have undercut their effectiveness.[38]

In 1994, the Clinton administration introduced a plan for *empowerment zones* that differed from the traditional enterprise zones in some key respects. In addition to tax breaks and regulatory relief, empowerment zones were eligible for a concentration of federal social service programs to promote community development, reduce crime, and "empower" residents with the skills, attitudes, and social resources needed to prosper as employees. Further, instead of the 3,000 urban enterprise zones scattered throughout the nation, there were to be only nine empowerment zones (six urban and three rural) in an attempt to target federal resources where they could do the most good. It was the targeting of resources and the inclusion of social services that distinguished empowerment zones from their enterprise zone cousins.[39]

Facilitating Community Development

Perhaps the most visible thing that states do to promote business growth is to facilitate strategies for economic development in local communities. Communities rely on their states for legal authority and financial or tax authority to offer development packages. Working together, states and communities can offer a variety of specific incentives to companies to expand in place rather than move somewhere else.

Tax Abatement Perhaps the most widespread state and/or local inducement to economic development is the **tax abatement**.[40] This is the tactic of forgiving or reducing a firm's property or other taxes for a number of years if it locates or expands in that jurisdiction.[41] One of the most generous tax abatement programs exists in Missouri, which permits local governments to forgive real estate taxes on property improvements for up to 25 years.[42] Tax abatement sometimes triggers complaints from other businesses and from citizens who do not receive similar tax breaks. In addition, critics sometimes complain that the tax abatements may cost a government more than the new or expanded firm gives back.[43]

Providing a Good Location Suppose a firm wishes to expand in Bigtown, USA, but is hampered by lack of developable land. Using its powers of eminent domain, the city of Bigtown can force the owners of a desirable piece of land to sell the land to the local government, usually to a local development agency or a port authority. Purchasing and clearing such land may be expensive, but cities have many sources of financial aid for this purpose. From the federal government, there are Community Development Block Grant (CDBG) funds and Economic Development Administration funds to purchase and clear the land and lay the groundwork for road and sewer installations. These actions create incentives for private developers and corporations to build on the new sites, other things being equal.

However, these efforts have been called into question by recent court cases and their political aftermath. The Michigan Supreme Court ruled that the state and its local governments could not force landowners to sell their land if the land would ultimately be turned over to a private firm. A critic of the ruling charged that the court went too far in its decision.[44] A subsequent U.S. Supreme Court case concluded that, as far as federal law is concerned, a state or locality could use the power of eminent domain to force land sales to enhance private development projects. However, the political backlash against the ruling led a number of states to pass new laws prohibiting that use of eminent domain; a number of other states already had similar laws. The overall result is that a number of states and many localities have lost a mechanism for assisting economic development.[45]

Industrial Development Revenue Bonds A city or county can issue **Industrial Development Revenue Bonds (IDRBs)** to raise money for a development project. The local government in effect acts as an intermediary to help a company raise development money at a lower cost than if the company had to go directly to the market and sell its own bonds. Because the interest earned by municipal bonds is exempt from federal income tax (and usually state income tax in the issuing state), such bonds carry lower interest rates than corporate bonds. A city will entice a corporation to expand by issuing IDRBs, and the bonds will be paid off with revenues from the company's development project. Thus, for most corporations interest costs are reduced, and at no expense to the city, for the federal and state governments bear the entire cost in the form of lower income tax revenues. Until 1987, IDRBs were the single most popular method of funding urban economic development. But in 1986 Congress put a cap on the total amount of IDRBs that each state is allowed.[46] However, states and localities can still provide other forms of discount credit assistance to attract new businesses or help existing businesses expand.[47]

Tax-Increment Financing   Under **tax-increment financing (TIF)**, a city declares a tax-increment financing district in the neighborhood it wants to develop. The city issues bonds to clear the land and entice a developer to build a commercial structure on the site. Because the new structure is usually more valuable than the former use of the land, it generates more property taxes. This increment, or increase, in generated property taxes is used to pay off the tax-increment financing bonds. Thus, the new development does not bring new property tax revenues into the city's general revenue until *after* the TIF bonds are paid off, which will usually be 15 or 20 years. But it is hoped that the development itself will create many new jobs for city residents and ultimately improve the city's fiscal picture.

Venture Capital   Many states today have **venture capital** programs to invest start-up capital in new companies that have excellent prospects for growth.[48] The Sky Computer Company of Lowell, Massachusetts, for example, urgently needed capital in 1982 to market plug-in computer boards for scientific and engineering applications. The Massachusetts Technology Development Corporation (MTDC) then invested public funds in the company to help it get off the ground. Within three years, the company's workforce expanded from 15 to 85, and annual sales shot up to $10 million. By using its governmentally supplied venture capital for projects like this, MTDC was able to increase the number of jobs in the state. Between 1979, when it was created, and 1984, the MTDC invested about $5.7 million of venture capital in 27 companies, which added more than 1,000 jobs and $2 million a year in state income tax collections. By 1990, the MTDC had produced so many successful investments that it no longer depended on public funds.[49] In addition to public venture capital corporations like MTDC, three states (New York, New Jersey, and Michigan) allow public employee pension funds to invest in venture capital projects.[50] Louisville, Kentucky, has established a forum where venture capitalists, economic development officials, and other people meet with entrepreneurs to assess their ideas and, when appropriate, help arrange financing for their business enterprises.[51] Although venture capital is extremely risky, the Massachusetts example shows that under the proper circumstances it can produce benefits far exceeding the costs.

Seeking Foreign Investment   Increasingly popular among governors is the tactic of enticing foreign corporations to build plants in their states. Japanese companies have been especially receptive to these initiatives because they view it as a means of avoiding trade wars with the United States. Nissan automobiles manufactured in Tennessee, for example, would not likely be subject to any trade restrictions imposed on Japanese imports. And the estimated 3,400 jobs created at Nissan's Tennessee plants[52] help defuse American complaints about foreign competition stealing jobs from American workers.

The Commerce Department estimated in the early 1980s that 2.3 million jobs in the United States were a direct result of foreign investment, almost 20 percent of them in California and New York alone. Overall, approximately 5.5 million jobs were in companies that were largely foreign-owned, although some of those jobs were in preexisting U.S. firms that later attracted foreign investment.[53] To make themselves look attractive to foreign investors, state governments compete vigorously with each other in offering most of the incentives described earlier plus paying for some direct costs such as land purchase, site improvements, and road construction. State and local governments in Alabama provided a variety of incentives worth more than $250 million to induce Mercedes-Benz to locate a manufacturing plant in Alabama. South Carolina committed $150 million to win a BMW factory with 3,000 jobs. Mississippi pledged almost $300 million dollars to attract the Toyota plant mentioned earlier in this chapter.[54]

Expanding Exports

State governments also exploit international interdependency by seeking to expand the export of products or services based in their states. During the 1980s, 26 states increased the number of state offices overseas, 30 states increased their budgets for export promotion, and 31 states increased the number of state employees working on export promotion. Although state exports did not appear to be boosted by setting up state offices overseas, there was an increase in exports in those states that added agency staff for export promotion. Staff workers can perform very useful services for businesses that want to expand by lending a personal hand "to guide businesses on a one-to-one basis through the maze of problems they are likely to encounter" as they enter the export markets.[55]

Convention Centers and Sports Facilities

Perhaps the most visible symbols of government action that promotes development are the numerous public subsidies for convention centers and major league sports facilities to capture the tourist and entertainment dollar. During the 1980s, more than 200 convention centers were built or expanded around the country, leading to a 60 percent increase in convention center floor space.[56] St. Louis, for example, opened a $123 million expansion of its convention center in 1993 that it hoped would reverse decades of decline in the city.[57] With its central geographic location and its distinctive cultural history, St. Louis officials believed that a contemporary convention center would catapult the city onto the top rung of cities attracting conventions and trade shows.

These activities can bring enormous money into a city, bolster its image, and create few environmental costs. In recent years, local governments have been spending roughly $2 billion per year on convention centers. Unfortunately, demand for conference facilities has not been very strong in recent years, so some conference centers have produced disappointing results.[58]

Attracting conventions and trade shows requires a community to have large, attractive hotels and motels that are located near the convention center. Some communities find that they must subsidize those hotels; in extreme cases, local government officials have chosen to build a major hotel and retain it under local government ownership.[59]

State-of-the-art sports facilities have a similar appeal to cities, and they become a tourist attraction. If tourists come in to see a major league baseball game, they not only spend money at the ball park, but also they might eat in a local restaurant, spend the night at a local hotel, and shop at a local mall. Baltimore, for example, built the highly praised Camden Yards baseball stadium to keep the Orioles from moving to another location. Local boosters argue that the park has been well worth the $214 million in public funds that it cost because the number of out-of-towners who came to see the Orioles play doubled the year after Camden Yards park opened, and city businesses raked in more than $200 million in retail sales.[60]

Even if these estimates are grossly inflated, local stadium boosters (including team owners) in many other cities want to follow Baltimore's lead and construct their own state-of-the-art facilities. This puts enormous pressure on local elected officials to provide the facilities that will attract or retain a major league sports team. The chances are small that a central-city mayor will be voted out of office if he or she loses a team,[61] but few mayors would want to take that chance, and no politician would want to be remembered in local history as the mayor who cost the city big league status. Critics, however, complain that ordinary taxpayers should not be asked to subsidize a major league sports facility when team owners and players are generally very wealthy people. Those concerns are likely to be heightened when state and/or local revenues are scarce. In the autumn of 2011, the Minnesota Vikings proposed construction of a new stadium costing $1.1 billion dollars, with two-thirds of the funds provided by the state of Minnesota and Ramsey County, where the stadium would be located. State and local opponents complained that they did not favor a tax increase and that many state programs had already been cut due to the recession. Stadium advocates, however, argued that it would create new jobs and add to the tax base. Looming in the background is a proposal for a new stadium in Los Angeles, which might provide a new home for a football team wanting a new stadium.[62]

Assessing Economic Development Strategies

Cities and states are under so much economic and fiscal pressure that they have little choice but to take any reasonable action that seems likely to improve the local economy. However, before a city or state enters a public–private venture, a number of questions should be asked.

First, does the development project result in a *net* increase in jobs? Although development projects often generate new jobs, they may also destroy jobs that existed on the site prior to the project. A newly opened business may also drive older businesses in town out of business, especially if the new firm is part of a large national chain and the older firms are small, local establishments. The community should also ask whether the people who lose jobs will find new ones in the area.

Second, does the project bring a *net* fiscal benefit to the area? Wellston, Ohio, for example, suddenly gained 980 new jobs when Jeno's, Incorporated, decided to consolidate its $200-million-per-year pizza-making facilities in that city. To help Jeno's relocate to Wellston, the local county and the state of Ohio lent the firm more than $5 million at a very generous 1 7/8 percent interest rate. But once the new facility began operations, its waste products clogged the city sewage system with a mass of cheese, meat, and other ingredients with the consistency of toothpaste and the color of tomato soup. When the EPA threatened to close down the plant as an environmental danger, Ohio had to give the firm $500,000 to find a way to clean up the wastes.[63] In the long run, Jeno's may be a net fiscal contributor to Wellston, the county, and the state. But in the short run, the location inducements appear to have been fairly costly.

Third, does a public–private redevelopment project actually generate new economic activity? Or does it just relocate activity that would have occurred anyway? Much of the redevelopment of the 1980s focused on central-city downtown areas. It is a fair guess that if the city governments had not acted, most of the investments would have been made anyway. They might not have been made downtown, but in the suburbs of the same metropolitan areas. Larger suburbs have learned that they, too, must compete for new development; so now they also are engaged in the game of offering a variety of tax or bond inducements to promote development. Many older regions probably had good reasons to redevelop their old, run-down central business districts. But from a broader perspective, one has to ask whether it makes sense to have different communities in the same area competing with one another by offering financial incentives for development projects that in all likelihood would occur somewhere in the same area even without government inducement.

The same observation could be made about giving incentives to attract foreign investment. Japanese automobile companies had already decided by the early 1980s to build manufacturing plants in the United States; no incentives were needed to get that investment. But the keen economic competition among the states led to a number of bidding wars to see which state could offer the most advantages to the Japanese. Kentucky, for example, spent $150 million on land purchase, site improvements, road construction, and worker training in order to attract a Toyota plant that would employ about 3,000 workers, a cost of about $50,000 per worker.[64] Alabama spent $253 million to attract a Mercedes Benz sport-utility-vehicle assembly plant that would employ 1,500 people. Critics objected to the price tag of $170,000 per job created, but enthusiasts argued that the deal would put Alabama on the map as an industrial player and that the long-term benefits of the deal would outweigh the costs.[65]

A number of researchers have tried to assess the impact of economic development policies. Making those assessments is difficult for a number of reasons. One of the major problems is that some components of an economic development agreement may be concealed from the public, the press, and policy analysts. Although more information is available today than several years ago, some states still conceal significant information about some economic development deals.[66]

Trying to determine what might have happened without the policies is a difficult task, especially if, as some observers suspect, business executives sometimes choose a location and then approach state and local officials to request assistance—possibly giving the impression that other sites are also being considered. When that occurs, adoption of various incentives will be followed by the arrival of a new business, but the incentives did not actually influence the business decision.[67]

In addition, development programs that appear to work are often copied by other jurisdictions. Any advantage they may have had initially is then diluted because many other jurisdictions have the same program. Although some researchers conclude that economic development policies do help to encourage economic growth, other researchers find no impact or inconsistent results.[68]

It was partially concern over the effectiveness of federally subsidized development policies that prompted Congress in 1986 to restrict the amount of IDRBs that a city or state could issue in order to promote its own growth. With the federal government the target of great criticism for its own huge budget deficits, Congress became less willing to let the federal treasury underwrite a huge volume of development projects that might well have occurred without federal subsidies. The Reagan administration eliminated the Urban Development Action Grant program and pushed unsuccessfully to kill two other development subsidy programs, the Community Development Block Grant program and the Economic Development Administration development grants.

Finally, in addition to their economic feasibility, economic development projects must also be judged for their political feasibility. Generally, public opinion supports state and local economic development efforts—but not always. Substantial tax incentives to lure new industries can sometimes draw the ire of existing businesses that may feel they are not getting their share of tax breaks. Small business owners may complain that they do not have the political clout to gain the benefits awarded to large firms and may especially resent helping to pay for programs to attract large, outside companies that may draw customers away from the small firms. A recent analysis of state business taxation shows that larger corporations tend to pay a below-average share of their incomes in state corporate income taxes, with some profitable firms paying nothing at all.[69] Local residents may also be concerned that a new firm could adversely affect the quality of life in a community.

Those concerns have erupted again with expanded exploration for petroleum and natural gas in some parts of the United States. Increasing energy production requires more workers, who need housing and other amenities. That can put upward pressure on prices. Increased traffic and wear and tear on roads and highways can upset people, as may environmental damage. Many landowners have also discovered that, because they do not own the mineral rights under their land, they may have little or no control over energy development on their farms and ranches. That lack of control worries some farmers and ranchers, who fear that energy development may pollute groundwater that is vital to their crops and livestock. That worry seems to be particularly acute with **hydrofracking**, which injects a mixture of water, sand, and several chemicals into rock formations that contains natural gas. The process can yield great volumes of natural gas but may also threaten the water supply with contamination from the huge volumes of water and chemicals injected into the rock.[70]

A dramatic example of the political conflict that may erupt over economic development plans occurred in Iowa's program to attract movie production to the state. Like a number of other states, Iowa offered tax credits to filmmakers who would make movies there. However, charges of mismanagement in the program eventually led to the ouster of six officials working in the program, and one was charged with several felonies. Five filmmakers and a tax credit broker were also charged. Iowa's governor suspended the program, and a number of other states have trimmed back their film subsidies.[71]

Conflicts have also erupted over efforts to change laws regulating or prohibiting a type of business activity, such as electronic bingo. A number of Alabama officials and two lobbyists were recently charged with corruption for allegedly offering campaign contributions and good-paying jobs in exchange for votes for legalizing electronic bingo machines in existing casinos and in new ones as well.[72] Whenever large sums of money are at stake, there is always the risk of misconduct.

MORE ACTIVE STRATEGIES

The economic development strategies just discussed seek to use public resources to promote private economic development, usually with the idea that governmental help will be limited in scope and temporary. Sometimes the strategies do not work, however, and communities are obliged to follow more active and possibly longer term strategies to protect themselves from the fallout of broken economic dreams.

Plant-Closing Legislation

States usually cannot prevent plants from closing, and a majority of economists would probably maintain that in most instances they should not do so. From a national economic perspective, it makes little sense to force a corporation to keep open an inefficient plant that can be replaced by a new, more automated and efficient one. Protecting such inefficiencies, so the argument goes, will in the long run only make American manufacturers less competitive in the world economy. Instead, we should encourage disinvestment from failing facilities or industries so that those resources can be reinvested in more viable economic activities.[73]

Although states cannot prevent plant closings, they can pass legislation that softens the blow to local communities.[74] Some states, in fact, have done so (Connecticut, Maine, Massachusetts, and Wisconsin). The most extensive legislation was in Massachusetts, which encouraged companies to give 90 days' notice of a plant closing so that the workers would have more time to plan and make the necessary adaptations. The legislation also provided for an extra three months of health insurance, unemployment compensation, and job retraining.[75] At a minimum, each state seemed to want to require the closing companies to provide severance pay and funds for retraining and job counseling. Many companies do provide severance benefits. But the results are not always as good as the promises. U.S. Steel Corporation (now called USX Corp.) established a job counseling program for laid-off workers when it closed its Clairton mills outside Pittsburgh. Despite the counseling and the motivational sessions, few workers were able to find full-time jobs in the area. Heavily dependent on the now-closed mills, the local economy simply was not strong enough to absorb all the laid-off workers.[76]

In 1988, the federal government passed a worker notification law less stringent than the one in Massachusetts. Called WARN (Worker Adjustment and Retraining Notification Act), the federal law required companies to give 60 days advance notice of mass layoffs and plant closings for companies with at least 100 workers. Although WARN did not provide any federal funds for health insurance and retraining, earlier federal legislation required each state to set up a displaced workers unit (DWU), and the DWUs were responsible for providing key services to dislocated workers.[77]

In practice, how much workers got in the form of outplacement services seemed to depend less on state or federal plant closing laws than it did on how hard their unions fought against plant closings. A study of four plant closings in northern Indiana found that the unions were not able to prevent any of the closings, but when they allied with community groups and political leaders they were able to get more severance assistance for the laid-off workers.[78]

Outsourcing Policies

State and local governments buy a wide variety of goods and services from private companies. Traditionally, state and local officials paid little or no attention to whether the private companies hired American workers to do the work. However, increasing concerns regarding job losses have led some observers to press for more attention to where (and by whom) the work is done. This was part of the controversy over the Iowa film subsidy program; some of the films receiving state assistance shifted large sums out of the state instead of spending in Iowa.

State legislators in most states have introduced bills to limit or block outsourcing of work done under contract with the state, but a recent assessment found that none of the bills have yet passed. Several governors have pushed state agencies to pay more attention to whether the goods and services they buy are produced by American workers. Whether those efforts are helpful is not yet known, but the issue is not likely to go away.[79]

Buy the Business to Keep It Running

A more drastic approach to keeping a firm in operation is for one or more governments to purchase it. One example of this strategy is found in the railroad industry. As private railroads have abandoned rail lines, state and local governments have acquired a number of those lines in order to prevent them from being dismantled. State and local governments now own more than 100 railroads, which range from quite small operations to a few rather large systems. Most are operated by private companies, but just under one-fourth of the lines are publicly operated. Most of the lines were acquired because of concerns that a loss of rail service would cause the decline of other local industries and harm the area's ability to attract new businesses that would need rail transportation.[80]

Sometimes a business is assisted by a mix of public and private assistance. In a number of small towns across America, people have mobilized to maintain or restore their local movie theaters as a community resource. Some individuals donate their skills or modest amounts of money to help keep the theater operating. Some communities assign juvenile offenders sentenced to community service to work at the local theater to help keep it running.[81]

Take the Plant to Court (or Threaten To)

When a state or locality provides incentives for a business to locate there, expand current operations, or at least maintain current operations, the business may not always deliver on what it has promised. In some cases, state or local officials may grudgingly accept the situation, but some governments have responded more forcefully. If the business and the state or local government have made a fairly clear contract, with certain incentives being granted if the company creates or preserves a certain number of jobs, officials may threaten or initiate legal action if the company fails to keep its commitments. Particularly with the revenue shortages in recent years, a number of states and localities have "clawed back" funds given to a business if it reneges on its part of the agreement. Sometimes this is done informally, and sometimes only part of the funding is cut off. If, for example, a company is able to create only half as many jobs as it promised, state or local officials may demand the return of half the financial help given to the company.[82]

This is what Wisconsin governor Tommy Thompson did when Chrysler Corporation announced in January 1988 that it planned to close its Kenosha plant at the end of the year. Before 1988, on the understanding that Chrysler would keep the plant open until 1992, the state of Wisconsin and the city of Kenosha gave Chrysler tens of millions of dollars in assistance plus air pollution credits that would absolve the plant from further pollution-control expenditures. Arguing that the company had broken a contract with the state, Governor Thompson threatened to sue Chrysler for $100 million if the company proceeded with its plans to close the plant.

The idea of suing a major corporation did not sit well with Wisconsin business leaders, however. They argued that such a suit would be bad for the state's business climate, and in the end the governor dropped the idea.

Although the threat of the suit did not prevent the plant closing, it may have increased the pressure on Chrysler to negotiate a settlement with the unions. This settlement provided for two years of health benefits and severance payments of $100 per week for two years. When put to a vote, the settlement was approved by 80 percent of the union members.[83]

Continuing Subsidies

Sometimes community leaders may feel that a facility is so vitally necessary that they are willing to give it financial assistance on an ongoing basis, especially if much of the financial assistance is paid for by someone else. One of the most important examples of that phenomenon is America's smaller airports. Many of those airports lose money, but they receive financial help from the federal government's Airport Improvement Program. Local officials often feel that having an airport, even a relatively small one, may help the community attract future business activity, particularly if the runways are long enough to handle business aircraft.[84]

Making the Most of What You Have   Communities that appear to have very few options in promoting economic development have sometimes tried creative strategies to make the most of what is available. A number of communities with few assets other than vacant land have revived the old idea of homesteading. They make vacant lots available for free or very low cost in exchange for the owner building a house on it and staying there for at least a certain length of time, such as three years. The local government no longer needs to pay to take care of the vacant property, and a new neighborhood will result. The developed properties will add to the property tax base.[85]

A number of communities in the Midwest have found an unexpected source of economic growth: Hispanic immigrants. Many of the communities went through a period of general decline, with businesses closing and people moving away. The arrival of Hispanic immigrants has meant that vacant homes are being repaired and occupied, businesses are reopening, and local schools have more students. Although there have been racial and cultural frictions at times, people in a number of communities have come to realize that the arrival of Hispanic residents has saved a number of communities from becoming virtual ghost towns.[86]

ISSUES IN THE SEARCH FOR ECONOMIC DEVELOPMENT

High Technology and the Quest for Its Holy Grail

In contrast to the decline of heavy industries (such as automobiles and steel) in the Midwest during the 1970s and early 1980s, there was a boom in high-technology industries, such as computer hardware, peripheral computer equipment, computer software applications, medical technology, and biotechnology. California's Silicon Valley and Boston's Route 128 symbolized this new boom as an unprecedented number of high-technology companies were created and expanded in those two areas. Certain other areas, such as Austin, Texas, and Research Triangle, North Carolina, did almost as well. These places became the models that other communities tried to emulate. Why not use economic development packages such as those just discussed to create high-technology industrial parks?

The logic of the argument seemed compelling. The economic development tools existed, and high-technology industry seemed to be much more insulated from foreign competition than were more traditional industries. The Japanese, Brazilians, and Koreans might be able to manufacture better automobiles more cheaply than could Detroit, but they were years behind the United States in high-technology research. So compelling was the argument for high tech that most states began to try to stimulate as much of it as they could. Just as the computer age has spawned a new generation of computer wizards seeking to design this year's most advanced computer, it has also created a new generation of community leaders seeking to turn their communities into next year's version of Silicon Valley.

But the quest for high technology is no more likely to produce economic salvation today than the quest for the Holy Grail produced spiritual salvation during the Middle Ages. There are two reasons for this. First, high technology in fact is no more immune to foreign competition and recession than is more traditional industry. Silicon Valley and Boston's Route 128, for example, suffered badly in the economic environment of the early 1990s, due in no small measure to a slowdown in global demand for computers as well as growing foreign competition in microchips and other computer products. If anything, the situation grew worse by the late 1990s and early 2000, and the industry is still struggling. The United States lost approximately 540,000 high-tech jobs in 2002 and roughly 230,000 more in 2003.[87]

The second reason is that few communities have the combination of characteristics that facilitated the concentration of high-technology companies in places such as Silicon Valley, Boston, and Austin, Texas. Competitive industries are often located in small geographic clusters,[88] and the concentration of computer technology in these locations was no accident. These places all were located near major research universities. There already existed numerous high-technology industries that could supply the materials needed by the new and expanding high-tech firms. And the areas had sophisticated workforces capable of making high-technology research productive and profitable. In short, some communities are more blessed than others.

If there is no future in basic industrial manufacturing, and if high technology is not in the future for most communities, then what activities can provide the growth that community leaders desire? The answer to this question, according to John Mollenkopf, is government jobs, third-sector institutions (for example, hospitals, universities, foundation headquarters), and advanced corporate services (such as legal work, accounting, computing, advertising, insurance, and investment banking).[89] The expansion of advanced corporate services has been especially important because cities with many such services become very attractive sites for corporate headquarters.

Mollenkopf argues that three types of cities exist today. First are the old, industrial cities, like Gary, Indiana, and Youngstown, Ohio. Despite dramatic changes in the national economy that have seen the industrial manufacturing sector decline relative to the service sector, these old cities have clung to their industrial economic bases. Gary and Youngstown are especially good examples because their basic industry (steel manufacturing) is heavily dependent on the fortunes of the automobile industry. As that industry suffered major setbacks in the 1970s and early 1980s, Gary, Youngstown, and many other old, industrial cities were economically shattered, although some industrial cities prospered during the late 1980s' resurgence of manufacturing.

Some recent research, however, presents a more positive picture of some of the older, northeastern and midwestern cities. Although a number of the older cities continue to lose population, some of them have recently seen increases in average incomes. This somewhat surprising development results, in part, from childless couples who do not need large homes with spacious yards. Concern over high gasoline prices and traffic have increased the appeal of living closer to workplaces. Some cities have also encouraged projects to provide middle and upper-income housing in buildings that previously housed stores or factories.[90]

In an entirely different situation are the newer service and administrative centers of the Southwest. Cities such as Phoenix and San Diego have attracted administrative and service corporations and high-technology industries, along with health care and higher education, that weathered the economic swings since the 1970s better than did the old, basic industries of the Midwest. However, the rapid population growth of a number of southwestern cities has yielded increasing traffic congestion and growing concern that the region's need for water will soon exceed available supplies. Las Vegas officials are currently assessing proposals to provide additional water sources for the city, but a proposal to draw water from rural areas of eastern Nevada has triggered major protests from people in those areas, who fear for the future of their farms and ranches.[91]

Finally, contends Mollenkopf, a third type of city has transformed its economy from old industry to banking and other advanced corporate services and third-sector institutions, such as universities and hospitals. Typical cities in this category are New York, Chicago, Philadelphia, Boston, and San Francisco. Although all have suffered significant population declines, they have maintained themselves as important locales for corporate headquarters and service-sector activities.

Although economic development issues are often discussed regarding cities, small towns and rural areas face economic strains as well; some of them appear to be suffering more than most cities. Between 2000 and 2005, half of all nonmetropolitan area counties lost population. Between 2000 and 2009, the combined populations of incorporated communities with 10,000 or fewer people declined slightly, while the combined populations of larger incorporated areas grew, though sometimes not by very much in some categories of community size. America's rural areas have higher rates of poverty and unemployment than do urban areas. Unemployment in nonmetropolitan areas is particularly high among young people: 17 percent in 2005.[92] Where the economy is poor, the best educated and youngest people are likely to move elsewhere in search of greater opportunities, and attracting new employers becomes even more difficult.[93]

As noted earlier in the chapter, some small towns have experimented with giving free land to attract new residents. For communities with a healthy economy or within commuting distance of other communities with employment opportunities, the strategy may have some value, but one analyst doubts that the effort will work in communities with little else to offer.[94] Another new strategy combines the resources of a local college or university with local officials and real estate developers to create a more attractive environment for attracting students and new residents with a combination of improved university amenities, some of which (such as exercise facilities) are open to the public for a fee, new housing, and upgraded community services.[95]

Counterproductive Competition

Although states have been trying to move away from the traditional competitive tactic of recruiting businesses away from each other, they still hold expensive bidding wars to attract large installations. In 1992, Minnesota pledged a package of $838 million to Northwest Airlines to get that company's maintenance facility. The state of Florida and one of its counties offered in 2003 a package worth roughly one billion dollars to attract a biomedical research facility. In the following year, North Carolina gave a package worth at least $240 million to attract a Dell Computer Corporation plant. The state of Washington offered a package worth approximately $3.2 billion to convince Boeing to build the 7E7 "Dreamliner" in Washington instead of elsewhere. At some point, these packages become counterproductive, for a state or community may spend more to attract a new facility than that facility contributes to the economy. In addition, generous inducements to attract one firm may trigger complaints from other firms or may foster expectations of similar concessions from other businesses. As a result, some states have tended to move away from costly incentive strategies in recent years and have placed increasing reliance on less expensive approaches that emphasize public–private partnerships, small businesses, and greater administrative flexibility to accommodate the changing needs of businesses. However, costly incentive packages have not disappeared entirely, as critics have noted.[96]

SOCIAL CONFLICT AND THE COMPETITION FOR ECONOMIC DEVELOPMENT

Without doubt, economic growth is essential for the nation to resolve its social conflicts, provide people with higher living standards, and finance public services. If growth rates are too slow or if economic growth turns negative, the competition intensifies between social groups to get their share of a diminishing economic pie. If growth rates are dynamic, however, and inflation is held in check, there are more jobs for most people, and there is greater potential for the nation's many social groups to prosper together. To use the old rising tide metaphor, a rising tide lifts all (or many of) the boats, and a growing economy helps everybody, or at least many people. Rapid growth can create headaches of its own—traffic jams, crowded schools, overloads on public utilities—but most people are likely to prefer those headaches to the specter of an economic slump.

The problem for some observers, however, is that the use of government resources to promote economic development is not a neutral process. Because it helps some sets of interests and harms others, it is integral to the issues of social conflict that have concerned us throughout this book. This occurs in at least three ways.

First, despite the infusion of new money into community redevelopment projects, the economic benefits for the poor and minorities have been disappointing. As indicated earlier, a number of central cities and many nonmetroplitan counties have experienced serious losses in the number of jobs over the past two decades. Even in the sunbelt, where cities are still growing, population increases may have outpaced job increases, and most of the growth occurs on the expanding edge of a metropolis, not in its inner, low-income residential neighborhoods.

Second, part of the reason for the lack of improvement in many areas' economies must be attributed to the biases inherent in the redevelopment process itself. One of the most commonly used redevelopment tools, the IDRB, for example, does not appear to be utilized to stimulate economically depressed regions, even though the rationale offered in the legislation establishing it named that as a prime objective. To examine how extensively IDRBs were aimed at depressed locations, Thomas A. Pascarella and Richard D. Raymond sought to determine if high-unemployment areas in Ohio used IDRBs more than low-unemployment areas. They found no relationship.[97] By the early 1980s, IDRBs were used in 47 states, and they were so popular they composed 70 percent of all municipal bond issues, whereas in 1970 they composed only 33 percent.[98] In short, the IDRB historically did little to generate permanent, well-paying jobs in poverty-stricken neighborhoods.

In part because of these disappointments, Congress in 1986 limited the further issuance of IDRBs. In a similar manner, urban enterprise zones were originally created to help promote economic development in low-income areas, but their use has spread to areas at all income levels and, consequently, blunted whatever effect the zones might have otherwise had.[99]

Paul Peterson has argued that there are limits to what local governments can raise money for.[100] In Peterson's view, a community that tries to raise too much money for redistributive services for needy residents will drive out its middle-income residents to the less redistributive-oriented jurisdictions. Cities that focus on raising money for economic development are on a much sounder footing, according to Peterson.

Whether Peterson's view is accurate or not is difficult to prove. But most communities engaged in the redevelopment game today act as though it is accurate. That is, the most praised and successful redevelopments focused on economic activities in the mainstream of the nation's economy—primarily providing support and office space for service industries and retail commerce. Significant redevelopment endeavors also went into retaining or attracting manufacturing facilities and were especially helpful in efforts to industrialize the South and Southwest over the past decades. But urban redevelopment activities also seem to be reinforcing the polarization of cities between the upper-middle class and the low-income classes while driving out the middle-income groups.

Much public money has been spent supporting downtown development and gentrification projects. With the aid of public funds, many cities greatly overbuilt their hotel-room and office-space capacity and were left with high vacancy rates when the commercial real estate market unraveled in the 1990s. Some cities responded to the problem rather ingeniously, however. San Francisco and New York City, faced with large number of empty offices, are converting a number of them into homes—more than 10,000 just in New York City's financial district. A number of other communities have also tried that strategy with unwanted buildings. If the offices can be remodeled into attractive and safe homes in good locations, the local economy may benefit.[101]

People find it very difficult to evaluate much of the urban redevelopment and gentrification activities of recent decades. Remembering the seedy and run-down appearance of many big-city downtown areas two decades ago, and then comparing them to the elaborate redevelopments in many of these same cities today, it is hard to say that the cities should not have initiated most of these projects. At the same time, however, many central-city residential neighborhoods have had trouble holding their own as their former middle-class occupants moved to the suburbs, and today they are increasingly occupied by people subsisting on marginal incomes. Many cities are moving toward a bipolar status, as George Sternlieb and James Hughes expressed it,[102] and urban redevelopment activities have not slowed that trend down—they may even have hastened it. Many smaller communities in rural areas have lost both wealthy and middle-income residents.

Accompanying these biases in the economic development process has been an abrogation of what Bennett Harrison and Barry Bluestone called the basic "social contract" that existed in America from about 1945 to the early 1970s.[103] Under this social contract, American business was assured of government policies enacted to maintain national economic conditions conducive to corporate profitability. Business, in turn, agreed to cooperate with labor unions and support general overall improvements in living standards. By the late 1970s, however, inflation was squeezing corporate profits, foreign competition was intensifying, and American business bailed out of the tacit social contract it had agreed to for a generation. Between 1967 and 2002, the average income of households in the top 20 percent of the income distribution rose by 75 percent (adjusting for inflation). The average income of households in the bottom 20 percent of the income distribution rose by only 35 percent. The 20 percent of households with the highest incomes took home an average income that was 14 times the size of the typical families income in the bottom 20 percent of the distribution. The jobs created since 2000 generally offer lower pay and fewer benefits than the jobs they replaced.[104] Many state and local officials are reluctant to challenge this behavior for fear that doing so might encourage businesses to move elsewhere entirely.

Critics, therefore, complain that the emphasis on economic development often benefits larger businesses at the expense of small businesses and ordinary citizens. Some efforts appear to generate few, if any, new jobs, and companies sometimes fail to deliver what they have promised. Moreover, some state and local officials are reluctant to punish companies that fail to deliver on their commitments.[105]

SUMMARY

1. Today, states and communities are buffeted by dramatic changes in the national economy. Among the most important of these are: (1) the transformation from an industrial to a postindustrial economy, (2) the intensification of foreign economic competition, and (3) the increasingly unequal distribution of income in America. States and localities are also struggling with the recession which began in 2007–2008.

2. To cope with these changes, states and communities have turned increasingly to economic development strategies. These strategies include: (1) public relations campaigns to attract tourists and industry, (2) promotion of a favorable business climate, (3) creation of business-growth incentives, and (4) the facilitation of community development. The most common community development approaches are tax abatements, the use of federal seed-money programs, industrial development revenue bonds, tax-increment financing, venture capital, and seeking foreign investment.

3. In assessing economic development strategies, it is important to consider the negative consequences of these approaches as well as the positive ones. A number of studies have raised doubts about the effectiveness of some of the strategies, and critics complain that larger businesses receive better treatment than do smaller firms.

4. To combat the out-migration of businesses, state and local governments have used plant-closing legislation, the purchase of businesses by the state government or local communities, and the threat of legal action against firms that move out after receiving local subsidies.

5. Major issues in the search for economic development include questions over the quest for high-technology industries as a solution to local economic problems, what to do about the competition that arises from variations among regional economies, and biases in the fight for economic development.

6. Although economic growth is essential to the task of alleviating the nation's social divisions, it is difficult to show that state economic development policies of the last two decades have contributed significantly to this goal.

STUDY QUESTIONS

1. How have national and international economic trends affected state and local economies?

2. What strategies have state and local governments tried to encourage economic growth in recent decades? How have they tried to preserve existing business activity?

3. How effective are state and local economic development policies? Why is assessing their impact difficult?

4. Why have economic development programs sometimes been controversial? What criticisms have been directed at economic development programs?

KEY TERMS

Business climate A term used by the business community to refer to the receptivity of a state to the business community. Although different ways of assessing the business climate exist, the business community usually prefers a business climate characterized by low taxes, low public expenditures, and limited state regulation.

Hydrofracking A technique for producing natural gas by injecting gas-bearing rock with a mixture of water, sand, and various chemicals in order to release the gas. Once that is done, the gas can be pumped up to the surface.

Industrial Development Revenue Bond (IDRB) A tax-exempt municipal bond that a city sells to enable a local business or development project to obtain financing at below-market interest rates.

Right-to-work law Legislation that prohibits the union shop.

Tax abatement The forgiving of local property taxes or other taxes for a firm that dramatically expands a facility. The abatement may forgive the entire tax or may reduce the tax by a certain amount (such as 50 percent).

Tax-increment financing (TIF) A local development financing process under which the increases in property-tax revenue from a development project are reserved for a number of years to pay off the local government's subsidies or bonds issued for the project.

Urban enterprise zone A blighted urban neighborhood that is designated as an enterprise zone where safety, health, and environmental restrictions are eased and where companies are offered generous incentives for locating facilities there.

Venture capital Investment capital targeted for small start-up firms that have trouble raising investment funds through more conventional means.

THE INTERNET CONNECTION

All 50 states and many localities now have Web sites designed to provide information for potential tourists and to attract more tourist traffic. Can you find the tourism Web site for your state? What kinds of information does it offer? Does it make your state appear to be an attractive vacation destination? Try contacting the National Association of Development Organizations at **www.nado.org** and see how easily you can move from it to local development Web sites in your area. How well do localities in your area present themselves?

NOTES

1. William Fulton, "Growing Pangs," *Governing* 15, no. 3 (December 2001): 62.
2. William Fulton, "The FedEx Story," *Governing* 13, no. 7 (April 2000): 68.
3. See John Kenneth Galbraith, *The New Industrial State* (Boston: Houghton Mifflin, 1967); and Daniel Bell, *The Coming of Post-industrial Society* (New York: Basic Books, 1973).
4. See Sujit CanagaRetna, "State Economic Development Efforts During Extreme Fiscal Stress," in *Book of the States*, vol. 41 (Lexington, KY: Council of State Governments, 2009), p. 489.
5. See Robert J. Samuelson, "Manufacturing Renaissance?" *Newsweek*, November 17, 1986, p. 72; *Statistical Abstract, 2001* (Washington, DC: U.S. Government Printing Office, 2001), p. 384.
6. *Statistical Abstract, 2011–2012* (New York: Skyhorse Publishing, 2011).
7. CanagaRetna, "State Economic Development," pp. 492–493.
8. See especially Lester C. Thurow, "The Disappearance of the Middle Class," *The New York Times*, February 5, 1984, p. F-3. Thurow asserts that the percentage of people earning between 75 and 125 percent of the median income dropped from 28.2 percent in 1967 to 23.7 percent in 1982. At the same time, there was an increase in both the percentage of people earning more than that level and the percentage earning less than that. For related discussions, see David Gordon, *Fat and Mean* (New York: Free Press, 1996); Andrew Hacker, *Money* (New York: Scribner, 1997); *Statistical Abstract, 2011–2012*, p. 454.
9. The argument against a shrinking middle class is well articulated by Marvin H. Kosters and Murray N. Ross, "A Shrinking Middle Class," *Public Interest*, no. 90 (Winter 1988): 3–27.
10. Frank Levy, *Dollars and Dreams: The Changing American Income Distribution* (New York: Norton, 1988).
11. *Statistical Abstract, 2011–2012*, pp. 455–457.
12. Robert B. Reich, "Toward a New Social Compact: The Role of Business," A speech to the National Alliance of Business, Dallas, Texas, September 27, 1994.
13. For a good general overview, see Steven Koven and Thomas Lyons, *Economic Development: Strategies for State and Local Practices* (Washington, DC: International City/County Manager Association, 2003).
14. *Statistical Abstract, 2011–2012*, p. 775.
15. See Koven and Lyons, *Economic Development Strategies*, pp. 69–70. On appealing to railfans,

see Robert Collins, *Kansas Railroad Attractions* (David City, NE: South Platte Press, 2004); *Trains* 67, no. 1 (January 2007): 101–102.

16. Alan Greenblatt, "Meet Marketing," *Governing* 15, no. 6 (March 2002): 34–37.

17. Roy Bahl, *The Impact of Local Tax Policy on Urban Economic Development* (Washington, DC: U.S. Department of Commerce; Economic Development Administration; Urban Consortium Information Bulletin, September 1980), p. 15; see also Koven and Lyons, *Economic Development*, pp. 34–35.

18. Robert W. Schmenner, *Making Business Location Decisions* (Englewood Cliffs, NJ: Prentice-Hall, 1982), pp. 50–51; see also Koven and Lyons, *Economic Development*, p. 62.

19. See William Fulton, "Making Work," *Governing* 16, no. 9 (June 2003): 56.

20. *Statistical Abstract of the United States, 2011–2012* (New York: Skyhorse, 2011), p. 429.

21. Micheline Maynard, "Toyota to Build $1.3 Billion Plant in the Land of Elvis and Honey," *New York Times*, February 28, 2007 (electronic edition).

22. Alan Ehrenhalt, "Moving Mountains," *Governing* 16, no. 3 (December 2002): 36–39.

23. See Koven and Lyons, *Economic Development*, pp. 61–62, and the studies they cite; and Bernard L. Weinstein and Harold T. Gross, "What Counts in the Race for Development," *State Legislatures* 14, no. 5 (May–June 1988): 22–24. For information on median family income in each state, see *Statistical Abstract, 2011–2012*, p. 461.

24. See Fulton, "Making Work"; DeLysa Burnier, "State Economic Development Policy: A Decade of Activity," *Public Administration Review* 51, no. 2 (1991), pp. 171–175.

25. Greg LeRoy, *The Great American Jobs Scam* (San Francisco, CA: Berrett-Koehler, 2005).

26. David L. Birch, *The Job Generation Process* (Cambridge, MA: M.I.T. Program on Neighborhoods and Regional Change, 1979), p. 21; see also Koven and Lyons, *Economic Development*, p. 62.

27. Dan Pilcher, "The Third Wave of Economic Development," *State Legislatures* 17, no. 11 (November 1991): 34–37. Pilcher describes recruiting businesses from other states as the first wave of development policy from the 1930s to the 1970s. The second wave, during the 1970s and 1980s, focused on developing local business incentives. A third wave in the 1990s focused on long-term investments in education, workforce training, and public–private cooperation. Also see *The New York Times*, November 25, 1992, p. 1B.

28. Russell Nichols, "Nothing Ventured," *Governing*, (March 2011): 24–30.

29. "Cities, Counties Take Back Corporate Tax Breaks," *New York Times*, January 3, 2010 (electronic edition).

30. Melissa Maynard, "In North Carolina, a Reversal on Municipal Broadband," *Stateline*, August 24, 2011 (electronic edition); Ellen Perlman, "Wi-Fi and Social Justice," *Governing* (June 2009): 52; Ellen Perlman, *Governing* (August 2009): 42-43; Ian Urbina, "Hopes for Wireless Cities Fade as Internet Providers Pull Out," *New York Times*, March 22, 2008 (electronic edition); Becky Bohrer, "Rural Wyoming Community Moves Toward Municipal High-Speed Network," *Moscow, ID-Pullman Daily News*, August 9, 2006, 6A.

31. Peter Eisinger, *The Rise of the Entrepreneurial State* (Madison: University of Wisconsin Press, 1988), p. 9.

32. Delysa Burnier, "State Economic Development Policy: A Decade of Activity," *Public Administration Review* 51, no. 2 (March–April 1991): 171.

33. Mark Trumbull, "States Step up Push to Lure Innovators and Investors," *Christian Science Monitor*, February 26, 2007 (electronic edition); "Developing the Delta," *Governing* 15, no. 4 (January 2002): 46.

34. Josh Goodman, "Radical Renewal," *Governing* (February 2009): 20–26.

35. *Book of the States*, vol. 38 (Lexington, KY: Council of State Governments, 2006), pp. 519–520.

36. Robert Mier and Scott E. Gelzer, "State Enterprise Zones: The New Frontier?" *Urban Affairs Quarterly* 18, no. 1 (September 1982): 39–52; *The Book of the States* (Lexington, KY: Council of State Governments, 2004), pp. 528–529.

37. William Fulton and Morris Newman, "The Strange Career of Enterprise Zones," *Governing* 7, no. 6 (March 1994): 32–34.

38. William Fulton, "In the Zone," *Governing* 17, no. 3 (December 2003): 66.

39. Ibid.

40. Bahl, *The Impact of Local Tax Policy*, pp. 8–9.

41. For a recent tabulation of provisions, see *Book of the States*, vol. 38 (Lexington, KY: Council of State Governments, 2006), pp. 521–522.

42. Ibid.

43. Rick Brooks, "How Big Incentives Won Alabama a Piece of the Auto Industry," *Wall Street Journal*, April 3, 2002, p. 1.

44. Jonathan Walters, "To Take or Not to Take," *Governing* 18, no. 1 (October 2004): 51.

45. Jeffrey Finkle, "State Economic Development Strategies: Trends and Issues," in *Book of the States*, vol. 38 (Lexington, KY: Council of State Governments, 2006), pp. 516–517; *Statistical Abstract 2006* (Washington, DC: U.S. Government Printing Office), p. 464.

46. *Congressional Quarterly Weekly Report* (Washington, DC: Congressional Quarterly), October 4, 1986, p. 2354.

47. *Book of the States*, vol. 38, pp. 519–520.

48. Marianne C. Clarke, *Revitalizing State Economies* (Washington, DC: National Governors Association, 1986), pp. 5, 7, 19, 81–82.

49. Jane Carroll, "Economic Development Through Venture Capital," *State Legislatures* 11, no. 3 (March 1985): 24–25; Margery Marzahn Ambrosius, "The Changing Nature of State Economic Development Policymaking," A paper presented to the Midwest Political Science Association. Chicago, IL, April 1992.

50. *The New York Times*, June 23, 1986, pp. 1A, 9A.

51. Koven and Lyons, *Economic Development*, pp. 102–103.

52. See *The New York Times*, March 25, 1985, p. D-4.

53. Carol Steinbach and Neal R. Peirce, "Cities Are Setting Their Sights on International Trade and Investment," *National Journal*, April 28, 1984, pp. 818–822; *Statistical Abstract, 2011–2012*, p. 798.

54. Bobbi Murray, "Money for Nothing," in Bruce Stinebrickner, ed. *State and Local Government*, 12th ed. (Dubuque, IA: McGraw-Hill/Dushkin, 2005), p. 187; Koven and Lyons, *Economic Development*, pp. 60–61; Maynard, "Toyota to Build."

55. Richard Thomas Cupitt and Margaret Reid, "State Government International Business Promotion Programs and State Export of Manufacturers," *State and Local Government Review* 23, no. 3 (Fall 1991): 131.

56. David Laslo, "Convention Centers and the Urban Political Economy: The Case of St. Louis' Convention Center Expansion," A paper presented to the Midwest Political Science Association. Chicago, IL, April 1996, p. 2.

57. Ibid., p. 14. The St. Louis population dropped by more than half from 856,000 in 1950 to 397,000 in 1990. During the same period, the number of jobs in the city dropped by 40 percent.

58. LeRoy, *Great American Jobs Scam*, pp. 166–167.

59. William Fulton, "Paying the Hotel Bill," *Governing* 15, no. 11 (August 2002): 60.

60. Carla Nielson, "Government at Bat," *State Government News* (June 1994): 6–10.

61. Timothy Krebs and Michael H. Walsh, "Mayors and Sports Franchises: The Electoral Consequences of Losing a Team," A paper presented to the Midwest Political Science Association. Chicago, IL, April 1994. The authors identified 26 instances of cities losing a major league franchise from 1950 to 1990. In only seven of those cases did an incumbent mayor lose a reelection bid after the loss. In eight cases, the mayor's percent of the vote actually *increased* in the election following the loss of a team.

62. Josh Goodman, "Minnesota Vikings Stadium Subsidy Debate Heats Up," *Stateline*, October 24, 2011 (electronic edition).

63. *St. Paul Pioneer Press*, March 13, 1983, p. A-11.

64. H. Brinton Milward and Heidi Hosbach Newman, "State Incentive Packages and the Industrial Location Decision," in Ernest J. Yanarella and William C. Green, eds. *The Politics of Industrial Recruitment* (New York: Greenwood Press, 1989), Tables 4-5.

65. Charles Mahtesian, "Romancing the Smokestack," *Governing* 8, no. 2 (November 1994): 36–40; Peter Behr, "Strategic Job Creation—or a Handout?" *Washington Post National Weekly*, August 28–September 3, 1995, p. 32.

66. Philip Mattera, et al., *Show Us the Subsidies* (Washington, DC: Good Jobs First, 2010).

67. Adam Bruns, "State Business Incentives: Some Companies 'More Equal' than Others," in *Book of the States*, vol. 38, p. 518.

68. Koven and Lyons, *Economic Development*, p. 62; Thomas Dye, *American Federalism* (Lexington, MA: Lexington, 1990), pp. 169–171; David Lowery and Virginia Gray, "The Compensatory Impact of State Industrial Policy: An Empirical Assessment of Mid-Term Effects," *Social Science Quarterly* 76 (1995): 438–446; Martin Saiz and Susan Clarke, "Economic Development and

Infrastructure Policy," in Virginia Gray, Russell Hanson, and Herbert Jacob, eds. *Politics in the American States*, 7th ed. (Washington, DC: CQ Press, 1999), pp. 497–498, and the studies they cite.

69. Michael Cooper, "Big Firms Limit Paying State Taxes, Study Finds," *New York Times*, December 11, 2011 (Web edition).

70. Ryan Holeywell, "Crude Awakening," *Governing* (August 2012): 24–31; Kirk Johnson, "Drilling in Fast-Growing Areas Ushers in New Era of Tension," *New York Times*, October 24, 2011 (Web edition); Sabrina Tavernise, "Rush for Gas Rights Plunges Towns into Battle for Control," *New York Times*, December 15, 2011 (Web edition); Jonathan Walters, "The Shale Bonanza," *Governing* (October 2009): 35–38.

71. Richard Verrier, "Iowa Film Tax Credit Program Racked by Scandal," *Los Angeles Times*, January 19, 2011 (Web edition).

72. Kim Chandler, "Big Names in Alabama Politics Set for Bingo Trial Opening on Monday," *Birmingham News*, June 5, 2011 (Web edition).

73. Lester Thurow, *The Zero Sum Society: Distribution and Possibilities for Economic Change* (New York: Penguin Books, 1980).

74. See especially Barry Bluestone and Bennett Harrison, *The Deindustrialization of America* (New York: Basic Books, 1982), pp. 8, 35, 63–66, 86–92.

75. Thomas J. Leary, "Deindustrialization, Plant Closing Laws, and the States," *State Government* 58, no. 3 (Fall 1985): 113–118; *The New York Times*, July 12, 1984, p. 7A.

76. David Corn, "Dreams Gone to Rust: The Monongahela Valley Mourns for Steel," *Harper's* 273, no. 1636 (September 1986): 56–64.

77. John Portz, "WARN and the States: Implementation of the Federal Plant Closing Law," A paper presented at the 1992 meeting of the Midwest Political Science Association, Chicago, IL, April 1992.

78. Bruce Nissen, "Union Battles Against Plant Closings: Case Study Evidence and Policy Implications," *Policy Studies Journal* 18, no. 2 (Winter 1989–1990): 382–395.

79. Alan Greenblatt, "Offshoring Hits Home," *Governing* 17, no. 8 (May 2004): 54.

80. David Nice, "Public Ownership of Railroads in the U.S.," *Transportation Quarterly* 51 (1997): 23–30.

81. Patricia Leigh Brown, "Old Movie Houses Find Audience in the Plains," *New York Times*, July 4, 2010 (Web edition).

82. "Cities, Counties Take Back Corporate Tax Breaks," *New York Times*, January 3, 2010 (Web edition).

83. Thomas S. Moore and Gregory D. Squires, "Two Tales of a City: Economic Restructuring and Uneven Economic Development in a Former Company Town," *Journal of Urban Affairs* 13, no. 2 (1991): 159–173.

84. Jeff Bailey, "Subsidies Keep Airlines Flying to Small Towns," *New York Times*, October 6, 2006 (Web edition); Curt Woodward, "Millions Spent on Money-Losing Wash. Airports," *Moscow, ID-Pullman Daily News*, April 16, 2007, p. 5A.

85. Monica Davey, "Cities View Homesteads as a Source of Income," *New York Times*, July 25, 2010 (Web edition).

86. A. G. Sulzberger, "Hispanics Reviving Faded Towns on the Plains," *New York Times*, November 13, 2011 (Web edition).

87. Mark Arend, "Trends in Job Creation Strategies in the States," in *The Book of the States* (Lexington, KY: Council of State Governments, 2004), p. 522.

88. See Michael Porter, *The Competitive Advantage of Nations* (New York: The Free Press, 1990).

89. John H. Mollenkopf, *The Contested City* (Princeton, NJ: Princeton University Press, 1983), pp. 31–36.

90. Haya El Nasser, "Aging Industrial Cities Get Boost," *USA Today*, April 21, 2006, p. 3A.

91. Jim Malewitz, "More Water for Las Vegas Means More Resentment in Rural Areas," *Stateline*, January 4, 2012 (Web edition).

92. *Rural America at a Glance* (Washington, DC: U.S. Department of Agriculture, August, 2006); *Statistical Abstract, 2011–2012* (New York: Skyhorse, 2011), p. 36.

93. Sharon Cohen, "Census Shows Remote, Rural Midwest Towns Face 'Death Spiral,'" *Moscow-Pullman Daily News*, March 24–25, 2001, p. 7-A; Joel Kotkin, "The Withering of Rural America," *Washington Post National Weekly Edition*, July 29–August 4, 2002, p. 22.

94. Carl Manning, "Modern Homesteading," *Moscow-Pullman Daily News*, March 27–28, 2004, p. 12-A.

95. Alan Finder, "Rural Colleges Seek New Edge and Urbanize," *New York Times*, February 7, 2007

(Web document **www.nytimes.com/2007/02/07/ education/07campus.html?th=&emc**).

96. *Newsweek*, February 17, 1992, pp. 40–41. Financial problems forced the company to cancel the facility, so Minnesota's actual costs turned out to be substantially less than the $838 million pledged. On the subject of shifting economic development strategies, see Saiz and Clarke, "Economic Development and Infrastructure Policy," pp. 489–492. For a discussion of recent, costly incentive deals, see Greg LeRoy, "The Terrible Ten: Corporate Candy Store Deals of 1998," *The Progressive* (May 1999) pp. 27–30; Greg LeRoy, *Great American Jobs Scam*, pp. 34–35, 87–88.

97. Thomas A. Pascarella and Richard D. Raymond, "Buying Bonds for Business: An Evaluation of the Industrial Revenue Bond Program," *Urban Affairs Quarterly* 18, no. 1 (September 1982): 73–89.

98. John E. Peterson, "The Municipal Bond Market: Recent Changes and Future Prospects," in Norman Walzer and David L. Chicoine, eds. *Financing State and Local Governments in the 1980s: Issues and Trends*, (Cambridge, MA: Oelgeschlager, Gunn & Hain, Publ., 1981), ch. 7.

99. LeRoy, *Great American Jobs Scam*, pp. 133–134.

100. Paul E. Peterson, *City Limits* (Chicago: University of Chicago Press, 1981).

101. "Turning Empty Offices into Home Sweet Home," *Governing* 15, no. 10 (July 2002): 64.

102. George Sternlieb and James W. Hughes, "The Uncertain Future of the Central City," *Urban Affairs Quarterly* 18, no. 4 (June 1983): 455–572.

103. Bennett Harrison and Barry Bluestone, *The Great U-Turn: Corporate Restructuring and the Polarizing of America* (New York Basic Books, 1988).

104. Leigh Strope, "Gap Between Haves, Have-Nots Expands Over Two Decades," *Moscow-Pullman Daily News*, August 17, 2004, p. 5A.

105. Michael Cooper, "With States Desperate to Keep Jobs, Companies Have Upper Hand, Report Shows," *New York Times*, December 14, 2011 (Web edition); A. G. Sulzberger, "Businesses Stand to Gain Most in Rivalry of States," *New York Times*, April 7, 2011 (Web edition).

GLOSSARY

Absolute deprivation   A definition of poverty that says that one is deprived of the necessities of life if one falls below a specific income line.

Affirmative action   The principle that special efforts should be made to encourage the hiring of minorities and women for public jobs. The objective of affirmative action is to make up for past discrimination against minorities and women.

Aid for Families with Dependent Children (AFDC)   A federal program from 1935 to 1997 that provided cash assistance primarily for single parents without income, but with dependent children.

Amendatory veto   Power of the governor in some states to return a bill to the legislature with proposed revisions. If the legislature accepts the revisions, the bill becomes law. If not, the bill is vetoed.

Amicus curiae   Friend of the court. Refers to a third party permitted to file a brief arguing on behalf of one of the two parties involved in a legal dispute.

Antidiversion legislation   State laws that prohibit gasoline taxes and highway-use funds from being used for purposes not related to highways and automobiles or trucks.

Apportionment   The allocation of legislative seats among the population. *Malapportionment* refers to a very unequal division of legislative seats. *Reapportionment* refers to the act of apportioning the seats once again to make their division more equal.

At-large election   A city council or county commission election in which a candidate runs in the city or county as a whole rather than from a specific district.

Attentive constituent   The citizen who pays attention to political news and is, therefore, likely to learn about the actions of public officials.

Attorney general   The chief law enforcement officer of a state.

Auditor   The state officer responsible for ascertaining that funds are spent properly and legally.

Balloon mortgage   A mortgage plan in which one makes interest payments over the life of the mortgage, but does not make any repayment of principal until the end of the mortgage, when the entire principal is due in a single, so-called balloon payment.

Bill of Rights   The first ten amendments to the Constitution of the United States.

Blanket primary   A primary election in which the ballot lists all the parties. Voters are allowed to vote in the primary of one party for some offices and the primary of another party for other offices. Voters cannot vote in more than one party's primary for the same office. Recently declared unconstitutional by the federal courts.

Block grant   A grant that can be used for almost anything in a broad functional area, such as education or transportation. A block grant may be created by consolidating several categorical grants into a single grant.

Board of education   The governing board of a local school district.

Bracket creep   The phenomenon of a person being boosted into a higher income tax bracket by inflation.

Building code   A municipal ordinance that establishes minimum requirements for space, electricity, plumbing, and health issues for residential buildings.

Business climate   A term used by the business community to refer to the receptivity of a state to the business community. Although different ways of assessing the business climate exist, the business community usually prefers a business climate characterized by low taxes, low public expenditures, and limited state regulation.

Calendar   A list of bills that have been acted on by committee and are waiting for debate or final vote. There are specific types of calendars with a wide variety of names for the specific stages of floor consideration of bills.

Capital expenditure   Expenditure for buildings and other durable equipment.

Caretaker   A gubernatorial style in which the governor maintains the operations of the office, but rarely pushes for new legislation, new programs, or new authority.

Caretaker mayor   A mayor who has a primary focus on providing current services and keeping the community intact, but who fails to set a broad agenda of new goals to be accomplished.

Casework   The practice of helping constituents handle their problems with government agencies (and sometimes with other organizations as well). So called because each constituent's problem becomes a "case" to be solved or processed.

Categorical aid   A grant-in-aid for a specific purpose. Also called *categorical grant*.

Categorical grant   A grant-in-aid given for a specific purpose, such as building airports or improving foreign language instruction in high schools. Also called *categorical aid*.

Caucus   A group of legislative members who meet jointly to push a legislative program. Usually refers to a party caucus such as the House Republican caucus or the Senate Democratic caucus.

Cease-and-desist order   A court order to a person to stop carrying out a particular act.

Ceremonial mayor   A mayor who tackles problems individually and devotes much time and effort to ceremonial and symbolic acts.

Challenge primary   A primary election held only if more than one candidate receives a significant show of support in their party's nominating convention.

Circuit breaker   A device that limits the amount of a person's income that can be taken in property taxes.

City-county consolidation   A reform strategy in which the city and its surrounding county are merged into a single government.

City manager   A city chief executive who is a professionally trained administrator picked by the city council and serves at the pleasure of the council. City managers oversee city agencies and develop policy proposals to submit to the council.

Civil law   That portion of law that deals with conflicts between individuals and groups rather than with crimes (though some cases involve both civil and criminal aspects).

Civil service   A form of recruitment for government jobs in which people are hired on the basis of merit, as measured by their training, work experience, and performance on competitive examinations.

Clean Air Act Amendments of 1977   Amendments that extended several deadlines for meeting the standards established in the 1970 Clean Air Act, stiffened

the standards, and gave the EPA increased authority to enforce them.

Clean Air Act Amendments of 1990   The first major attempt to combat acid rain and the depletion of the ozone layer. The amendments also stiffened emissions-control requirements for new automobiles and obliged oil companies to produce cleaner burning fuels.

Clean Air Act of 1970   The act that established the fundamental authority for the federal regulation of air quality.

Clean Water Act   See *Water Pollution Control Act of 1972*.

Closed primary   A primary election in which only identifiable party supporters may vote. Only Republicans may vote in the Republican primary and only Democrats may vote in the Democratic primary.

Collective bargaining   The process of workers banding together and bargaining as a unit with their employer over wages and job conditions.

Commerce Clause   The provision in Article II, Section 8, of the Constitution that grants Congress the authority to regulate interstate and international commerce.

Commissioner of education   See *Superintendent of schools*.

Commission government   A form of city government in which the council members (commissioners) also serve as the city's executives, with individual council members in charge of individual departments.

Compact theory   The theory of John C. Calhoun that the U.S. Constitution was a compact between the state governments rather than a charter from the people. This theory could be used to justify the states defying the national government.

Compensatory education   The tenet that disadvantaged children suffer from poor preparation for school and must be given special educational help to compensate for their backgrounds. See *Elementary and Secondary Education Act of 1965*.

Conference committee   A temporary joint legislative committee created to work out a compromise when the house-passed version of a bill differs from the senate-passed version.

Constitutional convention   A convention that drafts a new constitution and proposes it to voters for ratification.

Constitutional revision commission   A commission appointed by the legislature to study the constitution and make recommendations for change. The revision commission may be either a study commission (which presents its results to the legislature) or a preparatory commission (which presents its results to the constitutional convention).

Cooperative federalism   The theory of federalism in which federal, state, and local levels of government cooperate in domestic policy making. This theory largely replaced *dual federalism*.

Cost–benefit analysis   A budgeting procedure that weighs the costs of different programs against the benefits to be derived from them so that officials can select the programs that achieve agency goals at the lowest cost–benefit ratio.

Council of governments (COG)   An agency composed of representatives from counties and larger municipalities, usually in a metropolitan area. The council meets to discuss issues facing the various local governments in the area.

County   The general-purpose local government that is the basic geographic subdivision of the state and which usually plays a major role in administering many state programs. Used throughout the country.

County board of commissioners   See *County board of supervisors*.

County board of supervisors   The legislative body for the county in states where towns and governmental units have representatives on the board. Called *board of commissioners* in counties where the representatives come from districts or are elected at-large instead of coming from existing governmental units.

Court stripping   Passing legislation that prevents the courts from hearing cases involving certain issues.

Criminal law   Law that deals with the violation of legislative statutes that prohibit various behavior, such as murder, kidnapping, and robbery.

Crusader mayor   An active and aggressive mayor, but one who lacks many of the preconditions for strong mayoral leadership and whose job is, therefore, frustrating.

Cultural pluralism   An educational emphasis on including instruction about many cultural groups in American society. Does not reject the ideal of a mainstream, overall American culture.

Culture of poverty   A term used to describe a combination of psychological traits among many people who are permanently poor. These traits include cynicism toward the social system, lack of hope for escape from their plight, inability to defer gratification, and inability to plan for the future.

Decision-making approach   The approach to analyzing community power that relies on identifying the people who participate in and influence local governmental decisions as the preferred method for determining who has power in the community.

Declaratory judgment   A legally binding court order.

Dedicated funds   A portion of a budget set aside for a specific purpose, such as education. Those funds cannot be spent for anything else.

De *facto* segregation   Segregation that arises because of residential practices rather than because of laws requiring segregation. See *De jure segregation*.

Deinstitutionalization   A process of weakening legislatures as institutions. The adoption of term limits, the increasing use of initiatives and referenda to make policy outside of the legislature, and reductions in staff and salaries may be elements of that process.

De *jure* segregation   Segregation that is imposed by law rather than by informal residential practices. See *De facto segregation*.

Delegate   The representational role in which legislators vote as their constituents wish rather than voting their own consciences.

Delegated powers   See *Enumerated powers*.

Demagogue   A political leader who builds his or her political support partly by enflaming people's passions over emotional political issues.

Determinate sentencing   The practice of sentencing inmates to very specific prison terms rather than giving a sentence with a wide range of possible time in prison, and adjusted to the inmate's behavior in prison.

Dillon's Rule   The principle that city government powers must be interpreted very narrowly. This rule gives the states considerable authority over localities and sometimes has left local governments unable to deal with local problems on their own.

Direct action   Such political tactics as group protests, civil disobedience, strikes, sit-ins, and political violence. These activities may be directed at public officials or at other people with whom the group disagrees.

Direct democracy   The initiative, the referendum, and the recall as political devices.

Direct-production strategy   The housing production strategy that focuses on providing housing assistance directly to low-income people.

Displacement   The phenomenon whereby low-income people are forced to move out of their homes by urban renewal agencies, the gentrification process, or freeway construction.

Distributive policy   A policy that allocates benefits to citizens, but does not upset the prevailing distributions of wealth and influence. Also called *distributive services*.

District election   See *Ward election*.

Dual federalism   The concept of federalism in which the state and national levels of government have separate areas of authority. Local governments were largely ignored. Popular until the 1930s. Distinct from *cooperative federalism*.

Direct primary   A means of nominating candidates for office. The nominees are chosen directly by the voters at the ballot box. Primaries may or may not be conducted with candidates identified by party.

Due Process Clause   The provision of the Fifth and Fourteenth Amendments that protects a person from deprivation of life, liberty, or property without due process of law.

Education Consolidation and Improvement Act of 1981   A law that consolidated several educational categorical grant programs into a block grant, reduced the total funding for the programs involved, and increased state discretion in dispensing the funds.

Earmarked revenues   Revenues raised from specific sources (such as gasoline taxes) that can be spent only for related purposes (such as transportation).

Economic Opportunity Act of 1965   The fundamental legislation of President Johnson's War on Poverty. It created the Office of Economic Opportunity to conduct experiments in social services and to coordinate all the poverty-related efforts of the agencies of the federal government.

Electioneering   The interest group tactic of trying to get favorable or sympathetic people elected to public office.

Elementary and Secondary Education Act of 1965   The first extensive form of federal aid to public schools. Famous for its Title I compensatory-education provisions. See also *Compensatory education*.

Elitist theory   The theory of community power that sees communities as being dominated by a top elite composed principally of major business leaders.

Energy crisis   A situation in the 1970s when petroleum and natural gas sources were scarce and prices for them increased precipitously.

Enumerated powers   The powers specifically granted to Congress and/or the national government more generally by the Constitution. Also called *delegated powers*.

Environmental Impact Statement (EIS)   An assessment of the environmental impacts of a proposed development project. Required before the project can be approved. Applies to federal, state, and local government agencies.

Environmental Protection Act of 1970   The keystone of federal authority to regulate the environment. It established the Environmental Protection Agency and the Council on Environmental Quality, and established a broad national policy for environmental protection.

Equal employment opportunity   The practice of giving equal opportunity to all job applicants, regardless of race or religion.

Equal Protection Clause   The provision of the Constitution's Fourteenth Amendment that forbids any state to deny any person in its jurisdiction the equal protection of the laws. Sometimes used to stop states from discriminating against nonresidents, although a number of exceptions have been allowed.

Ethnic particularism   A form of cultural pluralism that rejects the idea of a mainstream American culture as oppressively Eurocentric.

Exclusionary rule   The rule that prohibits illegally obtained evidence from being used in a trial.

Exclusionary zoning   The practice by a municipality of putting expensive construction requirements in the local zoning plan and building code. This drives up the cost of new housing and thus excludes low-income people.

Executive leadership   The belief that the chief executives in governmental jurisdictions (principally governors and mayors) should exercise considerable authority over other executives.

Executive representation   The belief that people can be represented in the executive branch by elected executives just as they are represented in the legislative branch by elected legislators.

Exit option   The option of exiting the community's problems by moving to another community or using the private marketplace to purchase services that are normally public services.

Externalities   Costs that are not borne directly by the buyers or sellers of a particular product. For example, the costs of cleaning up greenhouse gases produced by automobiles are not included in the price of cars.

Family Assistance Plan (FAP) An income maintenance proposal of the Nixon administration that did not pass Congress.

Federal Aid Highway Act of 1956 The act that established the federal gasoline tax and provided revenue earmarked for construction of the interstate highway system.

Federalism A formal or informal allocation of authority between a national government and one or more levels of subnational governments. Responsibilities may be clearly divided or may be shared among levels of government.

Felony A major crime.

Filter-down strategy A housing production strategy that focuses on constructing new housing for upper-middle-income people on the assumption that their old housing will "filter down" to poor- and moderate-income people.

Fiscal disparities The situation in which neighboring governmental jurisdictions vary widely in their ability to raise revenue. One jurisdiction may have a substantial tax base, while a neighboring one has a meager tax base.

Food stamps program A program that provides vouchers to low-income people to help them buy food.

Formula grant A grant-in-aid in which the funds are dispensed according to a formula specified by law. When the formula is adopted, officials at the receiving level of government know how much funding they will receive.

Foundation aid program A program of state aid for public schools in which the state provides a specific amount of money to each school district for each full-time pupil enrolled in that district.

Frostbelt The Northeast and Midwest.

Fundamental law The law of a constitution, with particular emphasis on the structure of government, what officials it will have, and how they will be chosen. Fundamental law also usually includes an outline of the most important rights that people have.

Fungibility The tendency for grant money given to one program being used to replace money the recipient planned to spend on the program. The freed-up money may then be spent on a different program. This phenomenon limits the influence of grants-in-aid over the policies of the lower level of government.

Gated communities Exclusive upper-income housing developments surrounded by walls. Entrances are limited to a small number of security gates which can be used to keep out unauthorized people.

Gateway amendment A constitutional amendment that makes it easier to pass future constitutional amendments.

General-obligation bond A government bond that is backed by the taxing authority of the issuing government.

General revenue sharing A program in which the federal government turned funds over to state and local governments to use as they saw fit with very few federal guidelines on how the money was to be spent. Many states have similar programs.

Gentrification The process whereby upper-middle-income people move into innercity neighborhoods and rehabilitate the homes there (or move into homes rehabilitated by developers).

Gerrymander The practice of drawing legislative district boundaries with the intent of reducing the political influence of a certain group of people.

Gladiator A person active in the more demanding types of political activities, including campaigning for a candidate, contributing to a political party, and serving as an officer in an interest group.

Grand jury A group of citizens impaneled to examine a particular situation and determine whether enough evidence exists to indict somebody for a crime.

Grant-in-aid A federal payment to a state or local government, or a state payment to a local government to carry out an activity or to run a program.

Great Society See *War on Poverty*.

Gross national product (GNP) A nation's total output of goods and services.

Horatio Alger An author who grew rich writing stories about boys who climbed to the top of the social ladder. The "Horatio Alger myth" is synonymous with upward social mobility.

Housing and Community Development Act of 1974 The federal legislation that established the Section 8 housing program and the Community Development Block Grant program.

Housing voucher plan A proposal of the Reagan administration to replace existing housing programs with a voucher plan in which poor people could receive government vouchers that would be redeemable for rent payments much in the same way that food stamps are redeemable for groceries.

Hypothesis A scientific term that refers to an educated guess or tentative assessment about the factors that explain some phenomenon.

Hydrofracking A technique for producing natural gas by injecting gas-bearing rock with a mixture of water, sand, and various chemicals in order to release the gas. Once that is done, the gas can be pumped up to the surface.

Ideological spectrum The traditional left–right spectrum, in which liberal (or left-leaning) ideological positions are on the left side of the spectrum and conservative (or right-leaning) ideological positions are on the right side. Liberals often favor a greater governmental role and greater efforts to aid disadvantaged people. Conservatives often favor a smaller governmental role and letting private charities do more to care for the needy.

Inclusionary zoning The practice, as adopted in New Jersey, of requiring municipalities to include in their housing plans provisions for low-income people.

Income maintenance An approach to social welfare that seeks to provide cash assistance that will maintain people's income above the poverty line.

Incrementalism A budgeting process in which budgets change in proportionally small amounts from one year to the next.

Independent school district The basic governing unit for public schools.

Indexation The practice of adjusting income tax brackets to rise with the cost of living. Also refers to the practice of making benefit levels in certain programs adjustable for inflation.

Index crime The seven types of crime listed annually in the FBI's Uniform Crime Reports.

Individualistic political culture A viewpoint that believes government exists to distribute favors to individual people and believes politics should be dominated by professional politicians. Citizens have only a limited role in the political process.

Industrial Development Revenue Bond (IDRB) A revenue bond issued by a government to enable a particular company or a collection of companies to raise funds to develop a site by selling bonds with the tax and interest rate advantages of government bonds.

Infrastructure The roads, buildings, sewers, water supply systems, and similar structures essential for an economy to operate.

Initiative A political device that lets voters draft legislative proposals and, if they gather enough petition signatures, put their proposals on a ballot, where they can be decided directly by the people. Some states refer the proposal (if it gains enough signatures) to the state legislature. If it fails to act, the proposal is then referred to the voters.

Injunction A court order prohibiting a person from carrying out a particular act.

In-kind assistance Social programs, such as medical aid, that provide help that has a cash value, even though the help is not received in the form of cash.

Intensity problem Officials' difficulty in deciding whether they should support the preferences of a smaller group that feels very intensely about an issue or the larger group that feels much less intensely about it.

Interest group Any organization of people who try to influence government decisions. This includes many organizations that primarily exist to serve some other purpose—manufacturing automobiles, saving souls, or helping the sick get well.

Intergovernmental relations (IGR) A term used for contemporary federalism in which many different layers of government interact with each other in a complex system. May also include private organizations.

Interstate highway system The system of more than 40,000 miles of divided, limited-access highways that crisscross the United States.

Iron law of oligarchy The tendency of groups to become less democratic over time and to fall under the dominance of a small number of leaders.

Item veto Power of the governor in some states to veto specific provisions of appropriations bills without vetoing the entire bill.

Jacksonian democracy A governing concept, attributed to the terms of President Andrew Jackson (1829–1837), that government should rule for the benefit of the common people and that the public should select many state and local officials.

Joint committee A committee composed of members of the house and senate.

Judicial activism Judges' practice of using judicial review to impose their own beliefs on the law and to overrule policies set by legislators and executives; the term is typically used by people who disagree with a particular court decision.

Judicial restraint Judges' practice of making limited use of judicial review and generally restraining from overruling the policies set by legislators and/or executives.

Judicial review The power of courts to evaluate the constitutionality of acts of other members of government, including the governor, state legislators, local officials, state administrators, and lower courts.

Laissez-faire The concept that government should leave the economy to the forces of the marketplace and should not seek to regulate the economy.

Legislative oversight The legislature's responsibility to see that the executive branch implements laws as the legislature intended and to monitor the effectiveness of agency actions.

Legislative veto A device whereby the legislature can reverse an action of the governor or executive agencies by passing a resolution (the legislative veto) opposing the action within a short period after its announcement (usually 30 to 90 days).

Lieutenant governor A statewide officer who succeeds the governor if the governor leaves the governorship; lieutenant governors often have other responsibilities as well.

Light rail transit (LRT) A modern-day version of the streetcar. A large vehicle that's powered by overhead electric cables, runs on tracks in city streets, and is capable of carrying up to 200 passengers.

Line-item budgeting A form of budgeting in which budgets are organized by specific items that agencies buy or expend money for, such as motor vehicles, office supplies, and employee salaries.

Little Hoover Commission A type of commission appointed in the 1950s to study the organization of state government and make recommendations for improvement. About 35 states formed such commissions.

Lobbying The interest group tactic of trying to influence a decision of the legislature or some other governmental body.

Long ballot An election ballot containing many offices to be filled by election.

Loyalty option The option of remaining in a community in spite of its problems, but doing relatively little in the political arena to solve those problems.

Majority leader The majority-party leader responsible for managing legislation on the floor of the legislature and helping majority-party members accomplish their work.

Majority-minority district A legislative district deliberately created so that a majority of the people in it belong to a minority group. This may be done to encourage election of a minority representative or for other reasons.

Management by objectives (MBO) A procedure in which managers and supervisors set annual objectives that are consistent with agency goals. Managers' performance is then measured by their ability to attain their objectives.

Means test A test that makes eligibility for benefits dependent on a person's ability to show need, usually by showing an income that falls under a specified level.

Medicaid A program that provides medical assistance for people who cannot afford their own health care.

Medicare A government-run health insurance program for elderly people of all income levels.

Merit goods Goods that society judges all citizens should have as a matter of right.

Merit plan A plan for judicial selection on the basis of qualification for office. A common version begins with a nominating committee that selects a list of qualified judicial candidates; the governor then appoints one of those candidates to office; after a set period of time, the voters have the chance to decide whether to keep or remove the judge from office. See *Missouri Plan.*

Merit system (employment) A recruitment method for government that hires and promotes people on the basis of their training and competence to perform specific jobs. See *Civil service system.*

Metropolitan planning The attempt to develop long-range plans for land use and the extension of local government services throughout the metropolis.

Metropolitan statistical area (MSA) The official U.S. government definition of a metropolitan area. Prior to 1983, the term used was *standard metropolitan statistical area (SMSA).*

Minority leader The minority-party leader responsible for managing legislation on the floor of the legislature and leading the minority party.

Miranda rule The rule that police officers must warn suspects of their constitutional rights to remain silent and to be represented by an attorney before they are questioned.

Misdemeanor A lesser crime, which usually brings a limited fine or short jail sentence.

Missouri Plan A merit plan for judicial selection under which a nominating commission suggests a list of three nominees to the governor, who makes the appointment from that list. See *Merit plan.*

Model state constitution A proposal for constitutions advanced by the National Municipal League that would concentrate authority in the governor and legislature and would reduce the number of elected executives. It would also contain relatively few public policy provisions.

Moralistic political culture   A viewpoint that believes government should seek to achieve moral goals in the public interest. Places a high value on citizen participation and government taking an active role in society.

Municipality   A city government.

National Commission on Excellence in Education   A commission that reported in 1983 that the nation's school systems were failing to provide children with the quality of education they need in the contemporary world.

National Supremacy Clause   The provision in Article VI of the Constitution that makes the Constitution and all legislation passed under its authority the supreme law of the land.

Necessary and Proper Clause   The clause in Article I, Section 8, of the Constitution that gives Congress power to pass all laws necessary and proper for carrying into execution the enumerated powers.

Neutral competence   The belief that public services should be provided competently and in a politically neutral fashion. Elected officials should make policy decisions, but the administrators responsible for carrying out those policies should be insulated from political influence.

New Federalism   Attempts by the Nixon and Reagan administrations, and congressional Republicans since that time, to turn federal responsibilities over to the states, in part by giving the states more flexibility in spending federal grants. The Reagan administration added the concept of "devolution" and made sharp cutbacks in federal aid to states and communities.

No Child Left Behind Act   A federal law adapted in 2001. It requires creation of statewide school performance measures, improvement of failing schools, and allowance for low-income children in persistently failing schools to use some federal aid funds to transfer to other schools.

Nondecision   The exercise of power by keeping an issue off the decision-making agenda of a governmental body, out of the news, and out of public discussion generally.

Nonpartisan election   An election in which the party affiliation of the candidates is not printed on the ballot.

Nonpartisan primary   A primary election in which the ballot does not list the nominees by party affiliation, and the nomination goes to the two candidates who get the most votes.

Nonpoint-source pollution   Pollution whose specific point of entry into the water cannot be traced. Acid rain, which starts from smokestacks of coal-burning facilities and then falls in the form of rain over a wide region, is an example.

Old Age, Survivors, Disability, and Health Insurance (OASDHI)   The fundamental social insurance programs for retirement, disability, and Medicare set up under the Social Security Act.

Ombudsman   An office established to follow up on citizen complaints about government services and to get the complaints resolved.

Open-ended reimbursement   A grant-in-aid in which the federal government automatically reimburses state or local governments for a share of whatever program funds are spent. Primarily used for entitlement programs, such as unemployment compensation, in which the funds spent will vary greatly with economic conditions.

Open primary   A primary election in which anyone can vote, regardless of party affiliation, but each voter can vote in only one party's primary for that election.

Patronage   A recruitment method for government jobs in which people are hired as a reward for their political support of the winning candidates.

Personal Responsibility and Assistance Act   The 1996 welfare reform law that replaced AFDC with a block grant.

Pigeonholing   The act of filing a bill for the record, but never taking it up for consideration or giving it only perfunctory consideration before discarding it.

Planning program budgeting   A form of budgeting organized around programs rather than line items and planned out two or three years into the future. Budgeters try to compare different activities devoted to a common goal, such as environmental protection, and target money to the activities that seem most efficient.

Plea bargaining   A bargaining process between a prosecutor and defense attorney; the prosecutor offers a reduction in charges or a milder penalty in exchange for a guilty plea from the defendant.

Pluralist theory   The theory of community power that sees communities as being run through the competition of a variety of power centers.

Pocket veto   The governor's act of killing a bill he or she has received after the close of a legislative session simply by not signing it within the required number of days (usually five to fifteen).

Point-source pollution   Pollution that is introduced into the water supply at a specific, identifiable point of entry, such as a storm sewer draining into a river.

Political action committee (PAC)   A group that collects money from various sources and uses it to make campaign contributions and to try to influence election outcomes.

Political culture   People's attitudes, beliefs, and expectations about what governments should do, who should participate, and what rules should govern the political game.

Political economy   The interaction between public policy and the economy. The condition of a state or local economy will affect revenue raising and, consequently, many public services. Public officials may also select policies in the hope that they may improve the area's economy.

Policy entrepreneur   A dynamic governor or mayor who sets an agenda of goals to be accomplished and builds alliances with the interests needed to reach the goals.

Political machine   A tightly knit party organization that controls the party's nominations for public office and controls many patronage jobs. The people in those jobs are expected to work for the party during campaigns.

Political participation   Individual or group activity that seeks to influence the selection of government officials or the actions of government.

Politico   The representational role in which legislators sometimes vote their consciences and other times vote as their constituents wish, depending on circumstances.

Poverty line   The federal government's official definition of poverty, based on the assumption that having less than three times the income needed to buy food on a modest food plan constitutes poverty.

Primary air-quality standards   Established by the 1970 Clean Air Act, these focus on protecting public health.

Primary election   An election held to choose nominees to compete for public office in the general election.

Privatization   The practice of governmental contracting with private firms to provide public services.

Proactive accountability   The idea that elections give winners a mandate to establish a specific line of policy. Voters assess the candidates' positions on issues and vote for the candidate who most shares their political values.

Program entrepreneur   A dynamic mayor (or other official) who sets an agenda of goals to be accomplished, has a reasonable amount of governmental authority, and builds alliances with the interests needed to reach the goals.

Program evaluation   A procedure for determining if programs meet their objectives. Program evaluations seek to determine how much a program is accomplishing relative to its costs.

Progressive Movement   An early twentieth-century political movement that sought to replace boss-dominated machine-style politics with a less corrupt and less partisan form of politics.

Progressive tax   A tax that takes a higher percentage of the income of upper-income people than it does of lower-income people.

Project grant   A grant-in-aid in which the recipient government has to make an application to the granting agency, and the granting agency has considerable discretion in deciding which applicants will receive the grant.

Property tax   A tax levied on real estate.

Proportional tax   A tax that takes the same percentage of each person's income, regardless of whether the income is high, medium, or low.

Public interest group   An interest group that claims to represent a widely held interest. Members of the group do not expect their efforts to produce benefits just for the membership.

Public opinion   The general population's views on politically relevant issues.

Public relations   The use of the media to create a favorable public opinion. This includes generating agreement with the group's political values as well as drawing attention to an issue.

Quorum   The number of members needed to be present for the legislature to conduct its business. A usual quorum is a majority of the members.

Rapid transit   The traditional big-city subway or elevated train systems that run large, electrically driven trains along fixed guideways that may be at ground level, elevated, or underground.

Recall   A political device that allows voters to remove from office, before his or her term ends, an official who has invoked popular displeasure. The first phase of the process is gathering signatures on petitions calling for a recall election affecting the official; if enough signatures are gathered, a special election is called on the question of whether the official should be retained in office.

Recidivism   Describes the problem of convicts who, after serving their terms, commit new crimes when they are released.

Redistributive policy   A policy that takes wealth or income from one class of citizens and gives it to another class.

Redlining   The practice of mortgage lenders and insurance firms not providing mortgages or home insurance in risky areas of cities. So called because the lending associations have supposedly drawn a red line around the affected areas.

Referendum   The practice of allowing voters to vote directly on public policy proposals. Proposals may come from initiatives, from the legislature, or because a law (possibly a constitutional law) requires voter approval for certain decisions. Almost all states require voter approval of state constitutional amendments.

Reformed election system   An election system characterized by nonpartisan, at-large elections, preferably held on a different day than other elections.

Regressive tax   A tax that takes a higher percentage of the income of lower-income people than it does of upper-income people.

Representative bureaucracy   The concept that different ethnic and categorical groups should be represented in the public bureaucracy in proportion to their percentage of the overall population.

Relative deprivation   A definition of poverty that says that a person can be considered poor only in relation to the rest of the people in a society.

Reputational approach   The approach to analyzing community power that relies on asking a panel of judges to indicate the most powerful people and institutions.

Reserved powers   The powers reserved to the states or to the people of the United States by the Tenth Amendment to the Constitution.

Resource Conservation and Recovery Act of 1976 (RCRA)   This act set up a cradle-to-grave process for controlling and disposing of hazardous wastes.

Responsible-party model   A model of politics similar to that in Britain in which voters elect a party with a fairly clear program to power and the individual legislators are accountable to the party, which in turn is accountable to the voters. When voters become displeased with the party's performance, they can vote it out of power.

Retroactive accountability   The idea of holding someone accountable after the fact. When an incumbent official runs for reelection, voters assess whether he or she has done a reasonably good job thus far. If the answer is yes, the person is kept in office. If the answer is no, he or she is voted out. This type of accountability is less demanding for voters than proactive accountability.

Revenue-anticipation note   A short-term note a government uses to borrow money to make payments that will come due before a next revenue payment comes in. The note is paid off from the proceeds of the next revenue payment.

Revenue bond   A public bond that is paid off from revenue earned by the facility that was built with the bond's proceeds.

Right-to-work law   Legislation that prohibits the union shop.

Runoff   A type of primary in which, if no candidate wins a majority of his/her party's votes, or if no candidate wins a majority overall in a nonpartisan primary, then the top two candidates must go through a second round of campaigning and a second round of voting.

Sagebrush Rebellion   The rebellion of many states in the West against federal ownership and management of significant amounts of western land. Partly a reaction to federal environmental protection policies.

Sales tax   A tax levied on retail sales.

School district   A special-purpose government that runs a school system.

Scope of conflict   The size and location of a political conflict—where it is addressed, and who gets involved. It may be private, local, state, or federal. It may involve one or more chief executives, legislatures, courts, and/or agencies, as well as various interest groups and parties. The scope of conflict dictates what sorts of policies are chosen. People who are unhappy with a decision often try to change the scope of conflict to another arena where they hope to get a different decision.

Secondary air-quality standards   Set by the 1970 Clean Air Act, these focus on protecting crops, vegetation, forests, animals, and other materials essential to the public welfare.

Secretary of state   A statewide office responsible for administering the state election system, publishing a legislative manual, caring for state records, and conducting various clerical duties.

Section 8   A housing program initiated by the Housing and Community Development Act of 1974. It provides for leased public housing by authorizing a local housing authority to pay a portion of poor people's rent directly to the landlord.

Select committee   A temporary legislative committee that is responsible for an issue that has surfaced in a particular legislative session, but that is not expected to recur permanently.

Sense of civic duty   The belief that one has a moral obligation to vote and take part in political activities.

Sense of political efficacy   The belief that an individual's participation in politics can have some effect. This typically includes the belief that the person can understand what is happening, knows how to become involved, and that the political system will respond to his or her efforts.

Separate-but-equal doctrine   The principle established in *Plessy v. Ferguson* (1896) that segregated facilities do not violate the Equal Protection Clause as long as the separate facilities are equal.

Severance tax   A tax levied on natural resources extracted from the earth. Much of the cost of the tax can be passed on to customers in other states or even other countries.

Short ballot   An election in which only a few local officials are chosen by the voters.

Social Darwinism   A reference to the social sphere of Darwin's theory of natural selection and survival of the fittest. Accordingly, Social Darwinists oppose social welfare policies.

Social goods   Goods whose benefits are nondivisible and nonexclusive. Their enjoyment by one person does not prevent their enjoyment by others.

Social insurance   A societal program in which one pays money into a government-sponsored trust fund and draws benefits from that fund later, when one becomes eligible.

Social mobility   Movement upward or downward in society's class structure.

Social Security Act of 1935   The original legislative authority for much of the social welfare programs existing today.

Soft money   The channeling of campaign contributions from one party organization or campaign to another party organization or campaign, sometimes to circumvent legal regulations of campaign finance, but sometimes to help tie different party or campaign organizations together.

Speaker of the house   The key party leader, who presides over the lower house of the state legislatures.

Special district   A government that performs only a single function, such as a waste-control commission or, less commonly, a small number of related functions.

Spectator   A person whose main political activities are voting and observing politics. The spectator rarely engages in more demanding activities, such as joining an interest group, making a campaign contribution, or writing to a public official.

Spoils system   A patronage theory of public hiring in which the winning candidates in elections should be able to find jobs for their supporters in the public bureaucracies. "To the victors go the spoils" was the slogan of this theory.

Standing committee   A permanent legislative committee that is responsible for legislation in each subject area that recurs in every legislative session, such as education or transportation.

State education agency (SEA)   State educational policy maker, composed of the state board of education, the chief state school officer, and the department of education.

State implementation plan (SIP)   A plan that states are required to draft to show how they will meet the primary and secondary air-quality standards established by the EPA.

Statutory law   A law enacted by a legislature (in contrast to constitutional law).

Stratarchy   An organization, such as a political party, in which each level of the organization has considerable freedom to act as people in that level prefer. Different parts of the party, then, will not always work together harmoniously.

Stratificationist theory   See *Elitist theory*.

Strong mayor   A mayor who has power to appoint the city department heads, oversee the operations of city agencies, and the authority to develop proposals to submit to the city council. The strong mayor often has authority to veto bills passed by the city council.

Sunbelt   The South and Southwest.

Sunset law   A law requiring programs to terminate in a given number of years unless they are reauthorized by the legislature. This forces the legislature to reevaluate the purposes and operations of the sunset agencies and programs.

Sunshine law   Legislation requiring that all government business, including legislative business, be open to the public.

Superfund   A federal fund set up to finance the cleanup of hazardous-waste sites.

Superintendent of schools   The chief executive officer for public schools. May be either a local or state superintendent. The state superintendent is sometimes called the *commissioner of education.*

Super legislation   Detailed public policy provisions of a constitution that should, according to the higher law tradition, more properly be a part of ordinary statutory law.

Surface Transit Assistance Act of 1982   A federal law that earmarked, through 1988, 1 cent of federal gasoline tax revenues for public transit.

Tax abatement   The forgiving of local property taxes for a firm that dramatically expands a facility.

Tax-anticipation note   A short-term note a government uses to borrow money to make payments that will come due before a next tax payment comes in. The note is paid off from the proceeds of the next tax payment.

Tax-base breadth   The broadness or narrowness of the base on which a tax is levied.

Tax burden   The total amount of taxes paid as a percentage of a person's income.

Tax-increment financing (TIF)   A local development financing process under which the increases in property-tax revenue from a development project are reserved for a number of years to pay off the local government's subsidies or bonds issued for the project.

Tax or expenditure limitation (TEL) movement   The movement, especially strong in the late 1970s and early 1980s, to put legal or constitutional limits on the amount of money a government can raise or the amount of money it can spend.

The taking issue   The issue of whether land use regulations "take" people's property under the meaning of the Fifth Amendment's clause, "nor shall private property be taken for public use, without just compensation."

Total Quality Management   A management reform that involves continually gathering information on the quality of public services (including the public's views of the services), using modern information technologies to gather and analyze evidence about agency performance, and involving agency employees and the public in developing plans of action.

Town   A general-purpose form of local government especially prominent in New England.

Township   A form of local government in rural areas, prominent in the Midwest. Traditionally, townships had responsibility for a number of programs, including transportation, but many states have shifted township responsibilities to county governments over the years.

Toxic Substances Control Act of 1976   The act that gave the EPA authority to test new chemicals, to ban any chemical it considered unsafe, and to prohibit sale of PCBs except in enclosed systems.

Traditionalistic political culture   A viewpoint that believes government's purpose is to preserve the existing social order. Political power is best exercised by the limited number of people that have traditionally been influential, and government will play a fairly limited role in society.

Transfer payment   A direct payment of government money to individuals.

Transformational politics   A form of politics that seeks to change the focus of politics from pragmatic give-and-take over specific issues to the uncompromising pursuit of ultimate social values.

Treasurer   The state officer responsible for custody of state funds and for writing the checks that pay state obligations.

Trial jury   A group of citizens selected to determine the innocence or guilt of a person being tried.

Tripartite organization   The view of the political party as composed of three components: the party organization, the party in the electorate, and the party in government.

Trustee   The representational role in which the legislators vote their consciences rather than as their constituents wish.

Two-tier government   A metropolitan reform strategy that divides public services into those to be performed by a metropolitan-wide central government and those to be performed by local governments.

Unitary government   A system of government in which all governmental authority resides in the national government. If lower levels of government exist, they have no independent authority.

Unreformed election system   An election system characterized by partisan, ward elections, often held on the same day as elections for other offices.

Urban enterprise zone   A blighted urban neighborhood that is designated as an enterprise zone where safety, health, and environmental restrictions are eased and where companies are offered generous incentives for locating facilities there.

Urban Mass Transit Act of 1974   The act that authorized the first extensive federal funding of mass transportation, including operating expenses as well as capital expenses.

Urban renewal   This program has traditionally relied on local governments to acquire and clear parcels of land in run-down areas. The land is sold to developers to use for new buildings.

Venture capital   Investment capital targeted for small start-up firms that have trouble raising investment funds through more conventional means.

Veto   Power of a governor to prevent a bill's passage by the legislature and block it from becoming law. Vetoes may be overridden by the state legislature, usually by a two-thirds majority in each house, but successful overrides are relatively rare.

Voice option   The option of staying in the community and fighting to improve the quality of life there.

Volunteerism   Refers to elected officials who look on themselves as community volunteers doing a civic duty rather than as professional politicians attempting to build a career. Many of these elected officials are originally appointed to the office, often face only weak opposition when running for reelection, and do not much care whether they are reelected. Common among local officials in smaller jurisdictions but also found in many other offices.

Voting Rights Act of 1965   This law was very effective in striking down the legal barriers that had prevented the majority of racial minorities in the South from registering and voting.

Voucher plan   A proposal that gives parents vouchers to pay the cost of sending their children to the public or private school of their choice.

Ward election   An election in which city council members are elected from neighborhood units called wards or districts.

War on Poverty   President Lyndon Johnson's Great Society approach to poverty. Johnson vastly expanded social service programs in the hopes of eliminating poverty.

Water Pollution Control Act of 1972 (Clean Water Act)   The keystone of federal environmental policy for water quality. Established the pollution discharge-elimination system and required municipalities to install secondary sewage treatment facilities.

Weak mayor   A mayor who cannot appoint the city department heads and who has little authority over the city council.

White-collar crime   Crimes such as embezzlement, fraud, and commercial theft, usually committed by professionals (people in "white collar" jobs).

White flight   The theory that middle-class whites have, in large numbers, withdrawn their children from the central-city public schools in order to avoid school desegregation.

Zoning code   A municipal ordinance that divides the city into different zones, with each zone being limited to specific kinds of structures. Some zones permit only single-family residences, others permit retail commercial buildings, and others permit heavy industry.

NAME INDEX

SUBJECT INDEX

Note: The italicized locators refer to boxes, figures and tables cited in the text.